INTERCULTURAL
COMMUNICATION
IN CONTEXTS

INTERCULTURAL COMMUNICATION IN CONTEXTS

FIFTH EDITION

Judith N. Martin
Arizona State University

Thomas K. Nakayama
Northeastern University

McGraw Hill **Higher Education**

Boston   Burr Ridge, IL   Dubuque, IA   New York   San Francisco   St. Louis
Bangkok   Bogotá   Caracas   Kuala Lumpur   Lisbon   London   Madrid   Mexico City
Milan   Montreal   New Delhi   Santiago   Seoul   Singapore   Sydney   Taipei   Toronto

Higher Education

INTERCULTURAL COMMUNICATION IN CONTEXTS
Published by McGraw-Hill, a business unit of The McGraw-Hill Companies, Inc., 1221 Avenue of the Americas, New York, NY 10020. Copyright © 2010 by The McGraw-Hill Companies, Inc. All rights reserved. No part of this publication may be reproduced or distributed in any form or by any means, or stored in a database or retrieval system, without the prior written consent of The McGraw-Hill Companies, Inc., including, but not limited to, any network or other electronic storage or transmission, or broadcast for distance learning.

Some ancillaries, including electronic and print components, may not be available to customers outside the United States.

2 3 4 5 6 7 8 9 0 DOC/DOC 0 9

ISBN: 978-0-07-338512-9
MHID: 0-07-338512-3

Vice president and editor-in-chief: *Michael Ryan*
Publisher: *Frank Mortimer*
Sponsoring editor: *Katie Stevens*
Director of development: *Dawn Groundwater*
Development editor: *Craig Leonard*
Editorial coordinator: *Erika Lake*
Marketing manager: *Leslie Oberhuber*
Marketing Specialist: *Rebecca Saidlower*
Senior production editor: *Mel Valentín*
Production assistant: *Rachel J. Castillo*
Production service: *Matrix Productions Inc.*

Design manager: *Preston Thomas*
Designer: *Allister Fein*
Cover designer: *Allister Fein*
Photo researcher: *Poyee Oster*
Media project manager: *Thomas Brierly*
Production supervisor: *Louis Swaim*

The text was set in 10.5/12 Janson by Laserwords, and printed on acid-free 45# New Era Matte Plus by R.R. Donnelly & Sons.

Cover image: © William Whitehurst/Corbis

Library of Congress Cataloging-in-Publication Data
Martin, Judith N.
   Intercultural communication in contexts / Judith Martin, Thomas Nakayama. — 5th ed.
      p. cm.
      Includes bibliographical references.
      ISBN-13: 978-0-07-338512-9 (alk. paper)
      ISBN-10: 0-07-338512-3 (alk. paper)
      1. Intercultural communication. I. Nakayama, Thomas K. II. Title.

HM1211.M373 2010
303.48'2—dc22   2008051898

The two authors of this book come to intercultural communication from very different backgrounds and very different research traditions. Yet we believe that these differences offer a unique approach to thinking about intercultural communication. We briefly introduce ourselves here, but we hope that by the end of the book you will have a much more complete understanding of who we are.

Judith Martin grew up in Mennonite communities, primarily in Delaware and Pennsylvania. She has studied at the Université de Grenoble in France and has taught in Algeria. She received her doctorate at the Pennsylvania State University. By background and training, she is a social scientist who has focused on intercultural communication on an interpersonal level and has studied how people's communication is affected as they move or sojourn between international locations. She has taught at the State University of New York at Oswego, the University of Minnesota, the University of New Mexico, and Arizona State University. She enjoys gardening, going to Mexico, and hosting annual Academy Awards parties, and she does not miss the harsh Midwestern winters.

Tom Nakayama grew up mainly in Georgia, at a time when the Asian American presence was much less than it is now. He has studied at the Université de Paris and various universities in the United States. He received his doctorate from the University of Iowa. By background and training, he is a critical rhetorician who views intercultural communication in a social context. He has taught at the California State University at San Bernardino and Arizona State University. He is now professor and chair of communication studies at Northeastern University in Boston. He lives near the Back Bay station and loves walking to work. He loves the change of seasons, especially autumn.

The authors' very different life stories and research programs came together at Arizona State University. We have each learned much about intercultural communication through our own experiences, as well as through our intellectual pursuits. Judith has a well-established record of social science approaches to intercultural communication. Tom, in contrast, has taken a nontraditional approach to understanding intercultural communication by emphasizing critical perspectives. We believe that these differences in our lives and in our research offer complementary ways of understanding intercultural communication.

Since the early 1990s, we have engaged in many different dialogues about intercultural communication—focusing on our experiences, thoughts, ideas, and analyses—which led us to think about writing this textbook. But our interest was not primarily sparked by these dialogues; rather, it was our overall interest in improving intercultural relations that motivated us. We believe that communication is an important arena for improving those relations. By helping people become more aware as intercultural communicators, we hope to make this a better world for all of us.

Brief Contents

Contents

THE INCREASING IMPORTANCE OF INTERCULTURAL COMMUNICATION IN A RAPIDLY CHANGING WORLD

The falling value of the U.S. dollar against many other world currencies, the rising price of fuel, and the impact these changes have had on travel and business costs point to new international relationships. How will the expansion of globalization be affected? What kind of impact will there be on the exchange of products and movement of people around the world? How will economic changes influence where tourists come from and where they visit? Changes such as these are likely to influence the shape of intercultural communication.

When we look back upon the international and intercultural situation at the time we first began writing this book, we recognize how rapidly the world has changed and how, as a result, these changes have raised even more pressing issues for intercultural communication scholars and practitioners. As the U.S. dollar remains weak, foreign businesses may find buying opportunities in the United States, such as the recent acquisition of Anheuser-Busch by a Belgian company. U.S. tourists may find it expensive to travel to many locations overseas, but tourists from those places may find it much cheaper to come to the United States. Natural disasters such as the typhoon in Myanmar and earthquakes in China, as well as the ongoing conflict in Darfur, have summoned a variety of positive responses, including tremendous caring and compassion across intercultural and international divides, but these tragedies also exacerbated enduring social group inequities. Regional identities continue to challenge national identities, such as is the case in Belgium, which appears closer than ever to dissolution along the lines of linguistic identities. In addition, the Internet and cell phones have made intercultural interactions that once may have seemed distant or peripheral to our lives now far more immediate.

In this climate, the study of intercultural communication takes on special significance, because it offers tools to help us as we grapple with questions about religious and ethnic differences, hate crimes, and many other related issues. Those who study, teach, and conduct research in intercultural communication face an increasing number of challenges and difficult questions: Is it enough to identify differences among people? Are we actually reinforcing stereotypes in emphasizing differences? Is there a way to understand the dynamics of intercultural communication without resorting to lists of instructions? Don't we have to talk about the broader social, political, and historical contexts when we teach intercultural communication? How can we use our intercultural communication skills to help enrich our lives and the lives of those around us? Can intercultural communication scholars promote a better world for all?

Such questions are driven by rapidly changing cultural dynamics—both within the United States and abroad. On the one hand, attempts to establish peace between Israel and Palestine by withdrawing Israeli settlements from Gaza, as well as the continued expansion of the European Union, CAFTA (Central American Free Trade Agreement), and the African Union (formerly the Organization of African States), reflect some global movement toward unity. On the other hand, the increase in nuclear armaments, continuing clashes between India and Pakistan over Kashmir, and the tribal and religious struggles within Iraq exemplify continuing intergroup conflict. These extremes demonstrate the dynamic nature of culture and communication.

We initially wrote this book in part to address questions and issues such as these. Although the foundation of intercultural communication theory and research has always been interdisciplinary, the field is now informed by three identifiable and competing *paradigms*, or "ways of thinking." In this book, we attempt to integrate three different research approaches: (1) the traditional social-psychological approach that emphasizes cultural differences and how these differences influence communication, (2) the interpretive approach that emphasizes understanding communication in context, and (3) the more recent critical approach that underscores the importance of power and historical context to understanding intercultural communication, including postcolonial approaches.

We believe that each of these approaches has important contributions to make to the understanding of intercultural communication and that they operate in interconnected and sometimes contradictory ways. In this fifth edition, we have further strengthened our *dialectical* approach, which encourages students to think critically about intercultural phenomena as seen from these various perspectives.

Throughout this book, we acknowledge that there are no easy solutions to the difficult challenges of intercultural communication. Sometimes our discussions raise more questions than they answer. We believe that this is perfectly reasonable. The field of intercultural communication is changing, but the relationship between culture and communication is as well—because that relationship is, and probably always will be, complex and dynamic. We live in a rapidly changing world where intercultural contact will continue to increase, creating an increased potential for both conflict and cooperation. We hope that this book provides the tools needed to think about intercultural communication, as a way of understanding the challenges and recognizing the advantages of living in a multicultural world.

SIGNATURE FEATURES OF THE BOOK

Students usually come to the field of intercultural communication with some knowledge about many different cultural groups, including their own. Their understanding often is based on observations drawn from television, movies, the Internet, books, personal experiences, news media, and other sources. But many students have a difficult time assimilating information that does not readily fit into their preexisting knowledge base. In this book, we hope to move students gradually to the notion of a *dialectical framework* for thinking about cultural issues. That is, we show that knowledge can be acquired in many different ways—through social scientific studies, experience, media reports, and so on—but these differing forms of knowledge need to be seen dynamically and in relation to each other. We offer students a number of ways to begin thinking critically about intercultural communication in a dialectical manner. These include:

- An explicit discussion of differing research approaches to intercultural communication, focusing on both the strengths and limitations of each
- Ongoing attention to history, popular culture, and identity as important factors in understanding intercultural communication
- Student Voices boxes in which students relate their own experiences and share their thoughts about various intercultural communication issues
- Point of View boxes in which diverse viewpoints from news media, research studies, and other public forums are presented
- Incorporation of the authors' own personal experiences to highlight particular aspects of intercultural communication

NEW TO THE FIFTH EDITION

- In each chapter we have added a section on Internet Resources to enable students to find additional relevant information, examples, and illustrations on the chapter topic.
- To reflect the increasing influence of globalization, we continue to emphasize its importance to intercultural communication. For example, in Chapter 1, we discuss how globalization and related economic disparities influence intercultural communication. In Chapter 8, we expanded our discussion of the impact of globalization on the continuing worldwide migration and the resulting intercultural encounters.
- The continuing and expanding influence of communication technology in our daily lives is addressed by new material in Chapter 10 acknowledging the increasing role of social networking sites (SNS) in intercultural relationships and by new material in Chapter 12 addressing developing intercultural competence in online interaction.
- Our expanded discussion of the implications of religious identity in Chapters 5 and 11 is prompted by continued awareness of the important role religion plays in intercultural communication.
- We have also enhanced discussion of the important roles that institutions play in intercultural contact. In Chapter 10, we continue to address the role of institutions in supporting or discouraging intercultural relationships.

SUPPLEMENTAL RESOURCES

The Online Learning Center at www.mhhe.com/martinnakayama5 provides interactive resources to fit the needs of a variety of teaching and learning styles. For every chapter, students and instructors can access chapter outlines, sample quizzes with feedback, crossword puzzles using key terms, and Internet activities. For instructors specifically, the OLC offers an online *Instructor's Resource Manual* with sample syllabi, discussion questions, and general pedagogical tips for teaching the course and to help meet the special challenges arising from the controversial nature of much of the material. In addition, a computerized test bank that allows instructors to edit and add their own questions is available in both Windows and Macintosh formats.

CHAPTER-BY-CHAPTER OVERVIEW

Intercultural Communication in Contexts is organized into three parts: Part I, "Foundations of Intercultural Communication"; Part II, "Intercultural Communication Processes"; and Part III, "Intercultural Communication Applications."

Part I, "Foundations of Intercultural Communication," explores the history of the field and presents various approaches to this area of study, including our own.

We begin Chapter 1 with a focus on the dynamics of social life and global conditions as a rationale for the study of intercultural communication. We introduce ethics in this chapter to illustrate its centrality to any discussion of intercultural interaction. In this edition, we have emphasized the importance of the self-awareness imperative as a starting point for enhanced intercultural effectiveness and have also expanded our discussion of the impact of globalization and immigration on intercultural encounters.

In Chapter 2, we introduce the history of intercultural communication as an area of study as well as the three paradigms that inform our knowledge about intercultural interactions. We establish the notion of a dialectical approach so that students can begin to make connections and form relationships among the paradigms and use the example of Hurricane Katrina to help explicate the three paradigms. In this edition, we have included new examples of recent postcolonial approaches, focusing on Africa, to help students learn how past colonization impacts contemporary intercultural relations.

In Chapter 3, we focus on four basic intercultural communication components— culture, communication, context, and power. In this edition we have strengthened the discussion of culture to include its emotional dimension and have also strengthened the definition of communication to more clearly reflect our multiparadigmatic approach.

Chapter 4 focuses on the importance of historical forces in shaping contemporary intercultural interaction. We have reorganized the discussion of history into mainstream and nonmainstream histories, provided additional information on sexual histories, and added a section on religious histories.

Part II, "Intercultural Communication Processes," establishes the factors that contribute to the dynamics of intercultural communication: identity, language, and nonverbal codes.

Chapter 5 on identity has extended coverage of religious identity, multicultural identity, and sexual identity (in addition to gender identity). We have also included a new summary table on identity development (majority, minority, biracial).

Chapter 6 addresses language issues, including a new section on metaphor, and enhanced discussions of code switching, multiple language competencies, and contextual language practices.

Chapter 7 focuses on nonverbal codes and cultural spaces and includes new examples of nonverbal issues at military checkpoints during wartime, integration of expectancy violation theory as one organizing framework, a new section on cultural variations on paralinguistics, and enhanced discussion of nonverbal elements of prejudice and discrimination in intercultural encounters.

Part III, "Intercultural Communication Applications," helps students apply the knowledge of intercultural communication presented in the first two parts.

Chapter 8 addresses intercultural transitions. We have strengthened the discussion of immigration, including the dialectic nature (push-pull) of immigration and the important role of social support during adaptation, the role of racism and discrimination in migrants' lives, and have incorporated examples of military sojourners—an increasingly important sojourner group. Finally, we have included a new summary table on the four types of migrants.

In Chapter 9, we focus on popular and folk culture and their impact on intercultural communication. We have refined the definition of popular culture and have added new, recent international examples of popular culture.

Chapter 10 explores intercultural relationships. We have reorganized the chapter so that benefits/challenges of intercultural relationships precedes the discussion of dialectics, updated information on the status of same-sex relationships in the United States, and strengthened the discussion of the effect of contemporary institutions on intercultural relationships.

In Chapter 11, we focus more clearly on intercultural conflicts. We have strengthened the discussion on the roles of forgiveness and revenge in intercultural conflict and added an example of generational conflict.

Finally, in Chapter 12, as reflected by the new title for this chapter, we address the topic of striving for effective and engaged intercultural communication. Here we more explicitly incorporate the three research perspectives in a discussion of competence and have strengthened the discussion problematizing competence. We have added a new discussion on competence in mediated communication and have extended the discussion of social justice in intercultural relations in the workplace.

ACKNOWLEDGMENTS

The random convergence of the two authors in time and place led to the creation of this textbook. We both found ourselves at Arizona State University in the early 1990s. Over the course of several years, we discussed and analyzed the multiple approaches to intercultural communication. Much of this discussion was facilitated by the ASU Department of Communication's "culture and communication" theme. Department faculty met to discuss research and pedagogical issues relevant to the study of communication and culture; we also reflected on our own notions of what constituted intercultural communication. This often meant reliving many of our intercultural experiences and sharing them with our colleagues.

Above all, we must recognize the fine work of the staff at McGraw-Hill: sponsoring editor Katie Stevens, media project manager Thomas Brierly, marketing manager Leslie Oberhuber, and project manager Aaron Downey, and especially developmental editor Craig Leonard, who so effectively guided us through yet another project.

In addition, we want to thank all the reviewers of this and previous editions of *Intercultural Communication in Contexts*, whose comments and careful readings were enormously helpful. They are:

First Edition Reviewers

Rosita D. Albert, *University of Minnesota*

Carlos G. Aleman, *University of Illinois, Chicago*

Deborah Cai, *University of Maryland*

Gail Campbell, *University of Colorado, Denver*

Ling Chen, *University of Oklahoma*

Alberto Gonzalez, *Bowling Green State University*

Bradford "J" Hall, *University of New Mexico*

Mark Lawrence McPhail, *University of Utah*

Richard Morris, *Northern Illinois University*

Catherine T. Motoyama, *College of San Mateo*

Gordon Nakagawa, *California State University, Northridge*

Joyce M. Ngoh, *Marist College*

Nancy L. Street, *Bridgewater State College*

Erika Vora, *St. Cloud State University*

Lee B. Winet, *State University of New York, Oswego*

Gust A. Yep, *San Francisco State University*

Second Edition Reviewers

Eric Akoi, *Colorado State University*

Jeanne Barone, *Indiana/Purdue University at Fort Wayne*

Wendy Chung, *Rider University*

Ellen Shide Crannell, *West Valley College*

Patricia Holmes, *University of Missouri*

Madeline Keaveney, *California State University, Chico*

Mark Neumann, *University of South Florida*

Margaret Pryately, *St. Cloud State University*

Kara Shultz, *Bloomsburg University*

Third Edition Reviewers

Marguerite Arai, *University of Colorado at Colorado Springs*

Rona Halualani, *San José State University*

Piper McNulty, *De Anza College*

Karla Scott, *St. Louis University*

Candace Thomas-Maddox, *Ohio University, Lancaster*

Susan Walsh, *Southern Oregon University*

Jennifer Willis-Rivera, *Southern Illinois State University*

Fourth Edition Reviewers

Sara DeTurk, *University of Texas, San Antonio*

Christopher Hajek, *University of Texas, San Antonio*

Mary M. Meares, *Washington State University*

Kimberly Moffitt, *DePaul University*

James Sauceda, *California State University, Long Beach*

Kathryn Sorrells, *California State University, Northridge*

David Zuckerman, *Sacramento State University*

Fifth Edition Reviewers

Shirene Bell, *Salt Lake Community College*

Lisa Bradford, *University of Milwaukee-Wisconsin*

John Chiang, *State University of New York-Oneonta*

Susan DeTurk, *University of Texas at San Antonio*

Charles Elliott, *Cedarville University*

Gayle Houser, *Northern Arizona University*

Tema Oliveira Milstein, *University of New Mexico*

Marc Rich, *California State University-Long Beach*

Our colleagues and students have provided invaluable assistance. Thanks to our colleagues for their ongoing moral support and intellectual challenges to our thinking. Thanks to graduate students Elizabeth Cantu and Zachary Justus for their productive library research, for searching for interesting examples to make our writing come alive, and for being so cooperative and helpful even when they had their own competing study and projects to complete. And as always, we owe thanks to our undergraduate students, who continue to challenge us to think about intercultural communication in ways that make sense to their lives.

We thank our families and friends for once again allowing us absences and silences as we directed our energies toward the completion of this revision. We want to acknowledge both Ronald Chaldu and David L. Karbonski, who continue to be supportive of our academic writing projects.

Our international experiences have enriched our understanding of intercultural communication theories and concepts. We thank all of the following people for helping us with these experiences: Tommy and Kazuko Nakayama; Michel Dion and Eliana Sampaïo of Strasbourg, France; Jean-Louis Sauvage and Pol Thiry of the Université de Mons-Hainaut, Belgium; Christina Kalinowska and the Café "Le Ropieur" in Mons, Belgium; Scott and the others at Le BXL in Brussels, Belgium; Emilio, Vince, Jimmy, Gene and the others at the Westbury Bar in Philadelphia; Jerzy, Alicja, Marek, and Jolanta Drzewieccy of Bedzin, Poland; as well as Margaret Nicholson of the Commission for Educational Exchange between Belgium, Luxembourg, and the United States; and Liudmila Markina from Minsk, Belarus. Some research in this book was made possible by a scholarship from the Fulbright Commission and the Fonds National de la Recherche Scientifique in Brussels. In addition, we thank the countless others we have met in cafés, train stations, bars, and conferences, if only for a moment of international intercultural interaction.

Other people helped us understand intercultural communication closer to home, especially the staff and students at the Guadalupe Center at South Mountain Community College, and also Dr. Amalia Villegas, Laura Laguna, Cruzita Mori, and Lucia Madril and family.

In spirit and conceptualization, our book spans the centuries and crosses many continents. It has been shaped by the many people we have read about and encountered. It is to these guiding and inspiring individuals—some of whom we had the good fortune to meet and some of whom we will never encounter—that we dedicate this book. It is our hope that their spirit of curiosity, openness, and understanding will be reflected in the pages that follow.

Many textbooks emphasize in their introductions how you should use the text. In contrast, we begin this book by introducing ourselves and our interests in intercultural communication. There are many ways to think about intercultural interactions. One way to learn more about intercultural experiences is to engage in dialogue with others on this topic. Ideally, we would like to begin a dialogue with you about some of the ways to think about intercultural communication. Learning about intercultural communication is not about learning a finite set of skills, terms, and theories. It is about learning to think about cultural realities in multiple ways. Unfortunately, it is not possible for us to engage in dialogues with our readers.

Instead, we strive to lay out a number of issues to think about regarding intercultural communication. In reflecting on these issues in your own interactions and talking about them with others, you will be well on your way to becoming both a better intercultural communicator and a better analyst of intercultural interactions. There is no endpoint from which we can say that we have learned all there is to know. Learning about communication is a lifelong process that involves experiences and analysis. We hope this book will generate many dialogues that will help you come to a greater understanding of different cultures and peoples and a greater appreciation for the complexity of intercultural communication.

COMMUNICATING IN A DYNAMIC, MULTICULTURAL WORLD

We live in rapidly changing times. Although no one can foresee the future, we believe that changes are increasing the imperative for intercultural learning. In Chapter 1, you will learn more about some of these changes and their influence on intercultural communication.

You stand at the beginning of a textbook journey into intercultural communication. At this point, you might take stock of who you are, what your intercultural communication experiences have been, how you responded in those situations, and how you tend to think about those experiences. Some people respond to intercultural situations with amusement, curiosity, or interest; others may respond with hostility, anger, or fear. It is important to reflect on your experiences and to identify how you respond and what those reactions mean.

We also think it is helpful to recognize that in many instances people do not want to communicate interculturally. Sometimes people see those who are culturally different as threatening, as forcing them to change. They may believe that such people require more assistance and patience, or they may simply think of them as "different." People bring to intercultural interactions a variety of emotional states and attitudes; further, not everyone wants to communicate interculturally. Because of this dynamic, many people have had negative intercultural experiences that influence subsequent intercultural interactions. Negative experiences can range from simple misunderstandings to physical violence. Although it may be unpleasant to discuss such situations, we believe that it is necessary to do so if we are to understand and improve intercultural interaction.

Intercultural conflict can occur even when the participants do not intentionally provoke it. When we use our own cultural frames in intercultural settings, those hidden assumptions can cause trouble. For example, when renting a small apartment in a private home in Grenoble, France, coauthor Judith Martin invited a number of her U.S. friends who were traveling in Europe to stop by and stay with her. The angry and frustrated response that this drew from her landlady came as a surprise. She told Judith that she would have to pay extra for all of the water they were using, that the apartment was not a motel, and that Judith would have to move out if the practice of having overnight guests continued. Differing notions of privacy and appropriate renter behavior contributed to the conflict. Intercultural experiences are not always fun. Sometimes they are frustrating, confusing, and distressing.

On a more serious level, we might look at "Operation Iraqi Freedom" in the spring of 2003 as yet another example of intercultural communication. The subsequent interpretations of and reactions to that televised event by different communities of people reflect important differences in our society and in the world at large. Although some people in the United States and abroad saw this effort as an attempt to liberate an oppressed people, others viewed it as imperialist aggression on the part of the United States. These differing views highlight the complexity of intercultural communication. We do not come to intercultural interactions as blank slates; instead, we bring our identities and our cultures.

IMPROVING YOUR INTERCULTURAL COMMUNICATION

Although the journey to developing awareness in intercultural communication is an individual one, it is important to recognize the connections we all have to many different aspects of social life. You are, of course, an individual. But you have been influenced by culture. The ways that others regard you and communicate with you are influenced largely by whom they perceive you to be. By enacting cultural characteristics of masculinity or femininity, for example, you may elicit particular reactions from others. Reflect on your social and individual characteristics; consider how these characteristics communicate something about you.

Finally, there is no list of things to do in an intercultural setting. Although prescribed reactions might help you avoid serious faux pas in one setting or culture, such lists are generally too simplistic to get you very far in any culture and may cause serious problems in other cultures. The study of communication is both a science and an art. In this book, we attempt to pull the best of both kinds of knowledge together for you. Because communication does not happen in a vacuum but is integral to the many dynamics that make it possible—economics, politics, technology—the ever-changing character of our world means that it is essential to develop sensitivity and flexibility to change. It also means that you can never stop learning about intercultural communication.

PART I

Foundations of Intercultural Communication

WHY STUDY INTERCULTURAL COMMUNICATION?

CHAPTER OBJECTIVES

After reading this chapter, you should be able to:

1. Identify six imperatives for studying intercultural communication.
2. Describe how technology can impact intercultural interaction.
3. Describe how global and domestic economic conditions influence intercultural relations.
4. Explain how understanding intercultural communication can facilitate resolution of intercultural conflict.
5. Explain how studying intercultural communication can lead to increased self-understanding.
6. Understand the difference among a universalistic, a relativist, and a dialogic approach to the study of ethics and intercultural communication.
7. Identify and describe three characteristics of an ethical student of culture.

When I was back home [Kuwait], before I came to the United States to go to college, I knew all about my culture and about my religion. However, I did not really know what other people from the other world [United States] think of Middle Eastern people or Muslims in general. So, what I have witnessed is a lot of discrimination in this country, not only against my race but against other groups. . . . Yet I understand that not all Americans hate us, I met a lot of Americans who are cooperative with me and show me love and are interested to know about my country and culture.

—Mohamad

Our world is run by money. The only way to be able to gain power in the world is through your economic status. A major part of gaining economic status is to be able to negotiate and do business with people of different cultures. The technology available in this age simplifies the task.

—Alex

Both Mohamad's and Alex's experiences point to the benefits and challenges of intercultural communication. Through intercultural relationships, we can learn a tremendous amount about other people and their cultures, and about ourselves and our own cultural background. At the same time, there are many challenges. Intercultural communication can also involve barriers like stereotyping and discrimination. And these relationships take place in complex historical and political contexts. Mohamad's experience in the United States is probably more challenging today than it would have been several years ago because of recent political events. An important goal in this book is how to increase your understanding of the dynamics at work in intercultural interaction.

This book will expose you to the variety of approaches we use to study intercultural communication. We also weave into the text our personal stories to make theory come alive. By linking theory and practice, we hope to give a fuller picture of intercultural communication than either one alone could offer.

We bring many intercultural communication experiences to the text. As you read, you will learn not only about both of us as individuals but also about our views of intercultural communication. Don't be overwhelmed by the seeming complexity of intercultural communication. Not knowing everything that you would like to know is very much a part of this process.

Why is it important to focus on intercultural communication and to strive to become better at this complex pattern of interaction? We can think of at least six reasons; perhaps you can add more.

THE SELF-AWARENESS IMPERATIVE

One of the most important reasons for studying intercultural communication is the awareness it raises of our own cultural identity and background. This is also one of the least obvious reasons. Peter Adler (1975), a noted social psychologist, observes that the study of intercultural communication begins as a journey into another culture and reality and ends as a journey into one's own culture.

We gain insights in intercultural experiences overseas. When Judith was teaching high school in Algeria, a Muslim country in North Africa, she realized something about her religious identity as a Protestant. December 25 came and went, and she taught classes with no mention of Christmas. Judith had never thought about how special the celebration of Christmas was or how important the holiday was to her. She then recognized on a personal level the uniqueness of this particular cultural practice. Erla, a graduate student from Iceland, notes the increased knowledge and appreciation she's gained concerning her home country:

> *Living in another country widens your horizon. It makes you appreciate the things you have, and it strengthens the family unit. You look at your country from a different point of view. We have learned not to expect everything to be the same as "at home," but if we happen to find something that reminds us of home, we really appreciate it and it makes us very happy. Ultimately we are all very thankful that we had the opportunity to live in another country.*

However, it is important to recognize that intercultural learning is not always easy or comfortable. Sometimes intercultural encounters makes us aware of our own **ethnocentrism**—a tendency to think that our own culture is superior to other cultures. This means that we assume, subconsciously, that the way we do things is the only way. For example, when Tom first visited France he was surprised to discover that shoppers are expected to greet shopkeepers when entering a small store. Or that French people sometimes ate horsemeat, snails, and very fragrant cheeses. Sometimes Americans think that these foods shouldn't be eaten. This attitude that foods we eat are somehow normal and that people shouldn't eat these other foods is a kind of ethnocentrism. To be surprised or even taken aback by unfamiliar customs is not unexpected; however, a refusal to expand your cultural horizons or to acknowledge the legitimacy of cultural practices different from your own can lead to intergroup misunderstandings and conflict.

ethnocentrism A tendency to think that our own culture is superior to other cultures.

What you learn depends on your social and economic position in society. Self-awareness through intercultural contact for someone from a racial or minority group may mean learning to be wary and not surprised at subtle slights by members of the dominant majority—and reminders of their place in society. For example, a Chinese American colleague is sometimes approached at professional meetings by white communication professors who ask her to take their drink order.

If you are white and middle class, intercultural learning may mean an enhanced awareness of your privilege. A white colleague tells of feeling uncomfortable staying in a Jamaican resort, being served by blacks whose ancestors were brought there as slaves by European colonizers. On the one hand, it is privilege that allows travelers like our colleague to experience new cultures and places. On the other hand, one might wonder if we, through this type of travel, are reproducing those same historical postcolonial economic patterns.

Self-awareness, then, that comes through intercultural learning may involve an increased awareness of being caught up in political, economic, and historical systems—not of our own making.

THE DEMOGRAPHIC IMPERATIVE

You have probably observed that your world is increasingly diverse. You may have classes with students who differ from you in ethnicity, race, religion, and/or nationality. College and university student bodies are becoming increasingly diverse. According to a recent report, minority student enrollment will rise both in absolute number of students—up about 2 million—and in percentage terms, growing from 29.4% of overall undergraduate enrollment in 1995 to 37.2% in 2015. The share of white students on campuses nationwide will decline to 62.8% in 2015, a drop of 7.8% over 1995 levels (Carnevale & Fry, 2000).

Sports are a very visible part of this increasing diversity. In professional men's basketball, for example, "As of April 16, 2008, official rosters for the 2007–08 NBA season featured 76 international players from 31 countries and territories" (NBA, 2008). This increasing diversity extends to women's sports as well, including the LPGA where "Sixteen of the top-20 current money earners were born outside of the United States. Eight of those women are South Korean followed by two Swedes, two Australians, a Mexican, a Norwegian, a Brazilian and a Taiwanese" (The Canadian Press, 2008). This increasing diversity comes from changing U.S. demographics and more global interaction of people. (See Figure 1-1.)

Changing U.S. Demographics

demographics The characteristics of a population, especially as classified by race, ethnicity, age, sex, and income.

U.S. **demographics** are projected to change dramatically during your lifetime—the next 50 years. Another source of increased opportunity for intercultural contact exists because of the increasing cultural diversity in the United States. The 2000 census revealed a dramatic increase in ethnic/racial diversity, and this trend is expected to continue, as shown in Figure 1-2 (Passel & Cohn, 2008). The Hispanic population will triple in size and constitute approximately 30% of the population by 2050; in the same time period, the Asian American population will double in size and will constitute about 10% of the total population. African Americans will remain approximately the same in numbers and comprise 13% of the population; whites will continue to be a smaller majority as minority populations increase in number.

The nation's elderly population will more than double in size from 2005 through 2050, as the baby boom generation enters the traditional retirement years. The number of working-age Americans and children will grow more slowly than the elderly population and will shrink as a share of the total population (Passel & Cohn, 2008).

What is also interesting is the racial distribution in the various geographical regions. The Population Reference Bureau (PRB) computed a "diversity index" showing that the highest ethnic diversity is concentrated in the southeastern and southwestern regions of the United States. Minority concentrations are projected to increase especially in the South, Southwest, and West. The PRB estimates that, by 2025, minority groups will account for over 50% of the population in four states (Hawaii, California, New Mexico, Texas) (www.prb.org/AmeristatTemplate.cfm?Section=Estimates).

FIGURE 1-1   Rapid changes in technology, demographics, and economic forces mean that you are likely to come into contact with many people with diverse backgrounds and experiences. Although many of these communication experiences will be in professional and work situations, many other interactions will be in public and social settings. (© *Esbin-Anderson/The Image Works*)

There is increasing diversity in the U.S. workforce as well. The workforce is expected to continue to get older, and there will also be proportionately more women working. What accounts for these changes? The workforce will be older because the baby boomers are aging. More women are in the workforce for several reasons. First, economic pressures have come to bear; more women are single parents, and even in two-parent families, it often takes two incomes to meet family expenses. Second, the women's movement of the 1960s and 1970s resulted in more women seeking careers and jobs outside the home. In addition, the workforce is more ethnically and racially diverse—in part, simply because there are more minorities now than before, but also because of civil rights efforts, which led to more opportunities for minorities in business and industry.

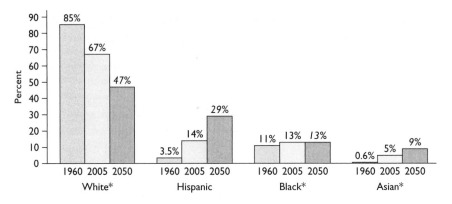

FIGURE 1-2   Population by race and ethnicity, actual and projected: 1960, 2005 and 2050 (% of total)
Source: From Jeffrey S. Passel and D'Vera Cohn, U.S. Population Projections: 2005–2050, Pew Research Center, 2008, p. 9.
Note: All races modified and not Hispanic (*); American Indian/Alaska Native not shown. See "Methodology." Projections for 2050 indicated by light gray bars.

Changing Immigration Patterns

The second source of demographic change is different immigration patterns. Although the United States has often been thought of as a nation of immigrants, it is also a nation that established itself by subjugating the original inhabitants and that prospered to some extent as a result of slave labor. These aspects of national identity are important in understanding contemporary society.

Today, immigration has changed the social landscape significantly. Prior to the 1970s, most of the immigrants to the United States came from Europe, but this changed in the 1980s and 1990s. As of 2006, almost one-third (30.8%) of the foreign-born population came from Mexico. South America, Central America, and the Caribbean combined to account for one in four immigrants (24.8%). Similarly, Asian immigrants accounted for 23.6% of the population increase (http://pewhispanic.org/files/factsheets/foreignborn2006/Table-3.pdf). European immigration continues to decline; as of 2002, only 14% of immigrants to the United States were from Europe (www.cis.org/articles/2002/back1302.pdf). These shifts in patterns of immigration have resulted in a much more racially and ethnically diverse population. It's not hard to see that the United States is becoming more heterogeneous. We address the issue of whites losing majority status in Chapter 5.

Sometimes more **heterogeneous** cultures are contrasted to more **homogeneous** cultures. Instead of thinking of cultures as either heterogeneous or homogeneous, it is more useful to think about cultures as more or less heterogeneous (or more or less homogeneous). Cultures can change over time and become more or less homogeneous. They can also be more heterogeneous than another culture.

heterogeneous Difference(s) in a group, culture, or population.

homogeneous Similarity in a group, culture, or population.

This heterogeneity presents many opportunities and challenges for students of intercultural communication. The tensions among heterogeneous groups, as well as fears on the part of the politically dominant groups, must be acknowledged. California's Proposition 187, which passed in the November 1994 election, excludes nondocumented immigrants from receiving public health and social services. This proposition has remained highly controversial and has led to protests and court challenges. The subsequent California Civil Rights Initiative (Proposition 209), which passed in November 1996, further extended the challenges to diversity by eliminating many affirmative action programs. And in 1997, Californians passed Proposition 227, which will eliminate bilingual education in schools, pending court rulings. Yet in October 2003, Californians voted to defeat Proposition 54, the Racial Privacy Initiative, that would have prohibited much of the racial information collected and used by the state and local governments in California. Fearful that the loss of this information would further erode protections against racial discrimination, as well as other concerns, led to the defeat of this proposition, but its proponent, Ward Connerly, had indicated his interest in bringing it forward again (Flores, Moon, & Nakayama, 2006).

We should also note the potential opportunities in a culturally diverse society. **Diversity** can expand our conceptions of what is possible—linguistically, politically, socially—as various lifestyles and ways of thinking converge. However, increased opportunity does not always lead to increased interaction. A recent "freshman survey" conducted by a research institute at UCLA reported that "a growing number of students appeared unlikely to have a diverse set of friends in college" (Farrell, 2005). This may be because these students are graduating from high schools that are becoming increasingly more segregated (see Point of View).

diversity The quality of being different.

To get a better sense of the situation in the United States today, let's take a look at our history. As mentioned previously, the United States has often been referred to as a nation of **immigrants**, but this is only partly true. When Europeans began arriving on the shores of the New World, an estimated 8 to 10 million Native Americans were already living here. Their ancestors probably began to arrive via the Bering Strait at least 40,000 years earlier. The outcome of the encounters between these groups—the colonizing Europeans and the native peoples—is well known. By 1940, the Native American population of the United States had been reduced to an estimated 250,000. Today, about 1.9 million Native Americans (from 542 recognized tribes) live in the United States (Brewer & Suchan, 2001).

immigrants People who come to a new country, region, or environment to settle more or less permanently. (Compare with **sojourners.**)

African American Immigrants   African Americans represent a special case in the history of U.S. immigration. African Americans did not choose to emigrate but were brought here involuntarily, mainly as slave labor. Many Europeans also emigrated as indentured servants. However, the system of contract servitude was gradually replaced by perpetual servitude, or slavery, almost wholly of Africans. Many landowners wanted captive workers who could not escape and who could not become competitors. They turned to slave labor.

The slave trade, developed by European and African merchants, lasted about 350 years, although slavery was outlawed in Europe long before it was

In this article Harinder Bahra tackles some problems relating to race in university education in the United Kingdom. Do you think this article could apply to the United States as well?

Far from celebrating the growing diversity of UK university staff and students, the higher education sector is almost doing the opposite. There has been a collective failure of employers in the university sector to tackle race discrimination and racism, or even accept it exists.

Like football clubs, universities are descending on developing countries, picking up cheaper black and minority ethnic (BME) researchers and lecturers in response to the transatlantic brain drain and continued pressure on operating costs. BME staff are often on part-time or fixed-term contracts with lower salaries and have difficulty in progressing through to senior positions. Meanwhile, BME students are increasingly being stereotyped as "extremists" in addition to being seen as academically less able.

As the University and College Union today launches a race equality campaign it is high time to ask what is being done.

Some universities, like the trade union sector, have appointed BME chancellors or presidents in voluntary, unpaid roles, but without corresponding changes in senior paid positions. This window dressing presents a diverse public profile, but still preserves the status quo.

Source: From H. Bahra, "Time to kick racism out of university." *The Guardian*, November 16, 2008. Retrieved May 13, 2008, from http://education.guardian.co.uk/racism/comment/0,,1949487,00.html.

outlawed in the United States. Roughly 10 million Africans reached the Americas, although most died in the brutal overseas passage (Curtin, 1969). Slavery is an important aspect of U.S. immigration history. As James Baldwin (1955) suggested, the legacy of slavery makes contemporary interracial relations in the United States very different from interracial relations in Europe and other regions of the world.

Slavery presents a moral dilemma for many whites even today. A common response is simply to ignore history. Many people assert that because not all whites owned slaves we should forget the past and move on. For others, forgetting the past is not acceptable. In fact, some historians, like James Loewen, maintain that acknowledging and understanding the past is the only viable alternative in moving forward. In his book *Lies My Teacher Told Me*, Loewen (1995) analyzes the content in contemporary high school history books and acknowledges that they do present the horrors of slavery. What is missing, however, is the connection of slavery to the current racial tensions in the United States:

Perhaps telling realistically what slavery was like for slaves is the easy part. After all, slavery as an institution is dead. We have progressed beyond it, so we

*can acknowledge its evils. . . . Without explaining its relevance to the present,
however, extensive coverage of slavery is like extensive coverage of the
Hawley-Smoot Tariff—just more facts for hapless eleventh graders to memorize. Slavery's twin legacies to the present are the social and economic inferiority
it conferred upon blacks and the cultural racism it instilled in whites. Both
continue to haunt our society. Therefore, treating slavery's enduring legacy is
necessarily controversial. Unlike slavery, racism is not over yet. To function
adequately in civic life in our troubled times, students must learn what causes
racism. (p. 143)*

Scholar and theologian Cornel West (1993) agrees that we should begin
by acknowledging the historical flaws of U.S. society and recognizing the historical consequences of slavery. For instance, the United States has several
Holocaust museums but no organized, official recognition of the horrors of
slavery. Perhaps it is easier for us to focus on the negative events of another
nation's history than on those of our own. On the other hand, many U.S.
Americans feel that the election of Barack Obama, the first African-American
president, shows some progress in U.S. race relations. In Chapter 4, we
explore the importance of history in understanding the dynamics of intercultural communication.

Relationships with New Immigrants   Relationships between residents and
immigrants—between oldtimers and newcomers—have often been filled
with tension and conflict. In the 19th century, Native Americans sometimes
were caught in the middle of European rivalries. During the War of 1812,
for example, Indian allies of the British were severely punished by the United
States when the war ended. In 1832, the U.S. Congress recognized the Indian
nations' right to self-government, but in 1871, a congressional act prohibited
treaties between the U.S. government and Indian tribes. In 1887, Congress
passed the Dawes Severalty Act, terminating Native Americans' special relationship with the U.S. government and paving the way for their removal from
their homelands.

As waves of immigrants continued to roll in from Europe, the more firmly
established European—mainly British—immigrants tried to protect their way of
life, language, and culture. As one citizen lamented in 1856,

*Four-fifths of the beggary and three-fifths of the crime spring from our foreign
population; more than half the public charities, more than half the prisons and
almshouses, more than half the police and the cost of administering criminal justice
are for foreigners. (quoted in Cole, 1998, p. 126)*

The foreigners to which this citizen was referring were mostly from Ireland,
devastated by the potato famines, and from Germany, which had fallen on hard
economic and political times. Historian James Banks (1991) identifies other anti-
immigrant events throughout the nation's history. As early as 1729, an English
mob prevented a group of Irish immigrants from landing in Boston. A few years
later, another mob destroyed a new Scots-Irish Presbyterian church in Worcester,

Anglocentrism Using Anglo or white cultural standards as the criteria for interpretations and judgments of behaviors and attitudes.

melting pot A metaphor that assumes that immigrants and cultural minorities will be assimilated into the U.S. majority culture, losing their original cultures.

nativistic Extremely patriotic to the point of being anti-immigrant.

Massachusetts. In these acts, we can see the **Anglocentrism** that characterized early U.S. history. Later, northern and western European (e.g., German and Dutch) characteristics were added to this model of American culture. Immigrants from southern, central, and eastern Europe (e.g., Italy and Poland) were expected to assimilate into the so-called mainstream culture—to jump into the **"melting pot"** and come out "American."

In the late 19th and early 20th centuries, a **nativistic** (anti-immigrant) movement propagated violence against newer immigrants. In 1885, 28 Chinese were killed in an anti-Chinese riot in Wyoming; in 1891, a white mob attacked a Chinese community in Los Angeles and killed 19 people; also in 1891, 11 Italian Americans were lynched in New Orleans.

Nativistic sentiment was well supported at the government level. In 1882, Congress passed the Chinese Exclusion Act, officially prohibiting anyone who lived in China from immigrating to this country. In 1924, the Johnson-Read Act and the Oriental Exclusion Act established extreme quotas on immigration, virtually precluding the legal immigration of Asians. According to Ronald Takaki (1989), these two laws "provided for immigration based on nationality quotas: the number of immigrants to be admitted annually was limited to 2% of the foreign-born individuals of each nationality residing in the United States in 1890" (p. 209). The nativistic sentiment increasingly was manifested in arguments that economic and political opportunities should be reserved solely for whites, and not just for native-born Americans.

By the 1930s, southern and eastern European groups were considered "assimilatable," and the concept of race assumed new meaning. All of the so-called white races were now considered one, so racial hostilities could focus on ethnic (nonwhite) groups, such as Asian Americans, Native Americans, and Mexican Americans (Banks, 1991). Sociologist David Roediger (1991) traces how devastating this racialization was, particularly for African Americans. In the growing, but sometimes fragile, economy of the first half of the 20th century, white workers had an advantage. Although white immigrants received low wages, they had access to better schools and to public facilities, and they were accorded greater public acceptance. People of color often were considered less fit to receive economic benefits and, to some extent, to be not truly American (Foner, 1998).

The notion of the melting pot began to break down as immigrants came in larger numbers from outside of Europe. Although European immigrants were able to melt into white society, other immigrants were barred from doing so. In order to melt into white society, European immigrants were encouraged to assimilate by speaking English only and dropping their culturally specific customs. As part of this melting pot experience, many Americans of European ancestry today do not speak their forebearers' languages, such as German, Dutch, Norwegian, Polish, or Hungarian.

Although the notion of the melting pot could explain European immigrant experiences, the metaphor did not explain other immigrant experiences. Immigrants from Asia, Latin America, and Africa did not simply blend into white

The politics of immigration are always a topic of interest in America. An especially divisive year for immigration policy, 2008, highlighted the remarkably different approaches of various regions of the United States.

	Arizona's Employer Sanctions Law	Bay Area Day Laborer Policies
Policy	A statewide effort to punish employers who knowingly hire illegal immigrants	A San Francisco area effort to benefit the working conditions of day laborers, many of whom are undocumented immigrants
Specifics	Employers who violate the law will potentially have their business licenses revoked	Laborers in specific areas are eligible for English classes, a variety of free health clinics, and other services
Results	Many illegal immigrants are leaving Arizona for other areas or for their home countries (CNN, 2007)	Workers show up at the day labor centers even when the economy is slow to commune and learn. (Nieves, 2008)

Sources: From Evelyn Nieves, "Housing Slowdown Puts Day Laborers in Limbo," *USA Today*, February 17, 2008. Retrieved from http://www.usatoday.com/money/economy/housing/2008-02-17-day-laborers_N.htm; CNN, "Illegal immigrants packing up and leaving Arizona," December 22, 2007. Retrieved from http://www.cnn.com/2007/US/12/22/immigrants.leave.ap/.

society. As we will see in Chapter 4, there are many legal and historical reasons why this did not happen. Some people are critical of the melting pot metaphor, not only because it does not explain the experiences of non-European immigrants but also because it implies that immigrants should give up their unique cultural backgrounds to become white and American.

Economic conditions make a big difference in attitudes toward foreign workers and immigration policies. During the Depression of the 1930s, Mexicans and Mexican Americans were forced to return to Mexico to free up jobs for white Americans. When prosperity returned in the 1940s, Mexicans were welcomed back as a source of cheap labor. This type of situation is not limited to the United States, but occurs all over the world. For example, Algerian workers are alternately welcomed and rejected in France, depending on the state of the French economy and the demand for imported labor. Guest workers from Turkey have been subjected to similar uncertainties in Germany. Indian workers in Kenya, Chinese immigrants in Malaysia, and many other workers toiling outside their native lands have suffered the vagaries of fluctuating economies and immigration policies. In Chapter 8, we discuss the implications of these migration patterns for intercultural communication.

The tradition of tension and conflict among cultures continues to this day. The conflicts that arise in Southern California exemplify many aspects of the demographic changes in the United States. We can examine on a variety of levels the tensions in Los Angeles among Latinos/as, African Americans, Korean Americans, and European Americans. Some of the conflict is related to different languages, values, and lifestyles. Some African Americans resent the economic success of recent Korean immigrants—a reaction that reflects a typical historical pattern. The conflict may also be due to the pattern of settlement that results in cultural **enclaves.**

enclaves (1) The territories that are surrounded by another country's territory; (2) cultural minority groups that live within a larger cultural group's territory.

Immigration and Economic Classes   Some of the conflict may be related to the economic disparity that exists among these different groups. To understand this disparity, we need to look at issues of economic class. Most Americans are reluctant to admit that a class structure exists and even more reluctant to admit how difficult it is to move up in this structure. Indeed, most people live their lives in the same economic class into which they were born. And there are distinct class differences in clothing, housing, recreation, conversation, and other aspects of everyday life (Fussell, 1992). For example, the driveways to the homes of the very rich are usually obscured, whereas those of upper-class homes usually are long and curved and quite visible. Driveways leading to middle-class homes, in contrast, tend to go straight into garages.

The myth of a classless society is hardly benign. It not only reinforces middle- and upper-class beliefs in their own superior abilities but also promotes a false hope among the working class and the poor that they can get ahead. Whereas real-life success stories of upward mobility are rare, fictitious ones abound in literature, film, and television. But all such accounts perpetuate the myth. The reality is that the income gap between rich and poor in the United States is more extreme than in most industrialized countries. The ratio between rich and poor (measured as the percentage of total income held by the wealthiest 20% versus the poorest 20%) is approximately 11:1, one of the highest ratios in the industrialized world. The ratio in Germany and Japan, in contrast, is 4:1 (Mantsios, 2001). "According to recent data from the Internal Revenue Service, the richest 1% of Americans earned 21.2% of all U.S. income earned in 2005. That is a significant increase from 2004 when the top 1% earned 19% of the nation's income" (Wutkowski, 2007). And while the very rich U.S. Americans increased their wealth, the "average incomes for those in the bottom 90% dipped slightly compared with the year before, dropping $172, or 0.6%" (Johnston, 2007). These trends point to an increasing income gap.

It may be common knowledge that the gap between the wealthy and everyone else is growing wider, but the extent of the current gap is staggering. In a series investigating class in the United States, *New York Times* writer David Caty Johnston (2005) reported that between 1950 and 1970, for every additional dollar earned by the bottom 90% of the population, the top 0.01% earned an additional $162. Since then, that gap has skyrocketed. In revisiting this issue with more recent data, Johnston (2007) noted that "Per person, the top group received 440 times as much as the average person in the bottom half earned, nearly doubling the gap from 1980." The widening gap is due partly to the loss of stable industrial jobs as companies move to cheaper labor markets within the United States and abroad. Class and demographic issues also play a role, with racial and ethnic minorities typically hardest hit by economic downturns.

Religious Diversity   Immigration also contributes to religious diversity, bringing increasing numbers of Muslims, Buddhists, Confucians, Catholics, and others to the United States. The religious composition of the United States is rapidly changing due to a number of factors. According to the U.S. Religious Landscape Survey (2008) done by the Pew Forum on Religion and Public Life, 28% of adults have left the religion they were raised in (some choosing another religion, some choosing no religion). Catholics have lost the greatest number of members, but they also gained the most from immigration. The greatest growth has been among adults who are unaffiliated with any religion. What do these changes mean to the role of religion in a diverse society? What is the future of religion in the United States? Religious beliefs and practices often play an important role in everyday cultural life. One example is the very different views on abortion, described by our student Tanya:

> *Pro-choice and pro-lifers have incredibly different worldview lenses. These different lenses they see through are most of the time influenced by religion and social upbringing. The values are different, yet no side is wrong and cannot see through the same worldview lens as their opponents.*

These different worldviews can sometimes lead to prejudices and stereotypes. For example, stereotypes about Islam are widespread in U.S. popular culture. Political scientist Ali Muzrui (2001) describes Islam as the "ultimate negative 'Other' to the Christian tradition" and laments the rising tide of "Islamophobia" (fear of Islam and the hostility toward it). He lists the contrasting stereotypes:

> *Whereas Christianity is supposed to be peace loving, Islam is portrayed as fostering holy war (Jihad). Whereas Christianity liberates women, Islam enslaves them. Whereas Christianity is modern, Islam is medieval. Whereas Christianity is forward looking, Islam is backward looking. Whereas Christians prefer nonviolence, Muslims easily resort to terrorism. (p. 110)*

Muzrui goes on to present evidence to debunk each of these stereotypes. Religious diversity is part of the demographic imperative that challenges us to learn more about intercultural communication.

These increasingly diverse ethnic, racial, economic, and religious groups come into contact mostly during the day in schools, businesses, and other settings, bringing to the encounters different languages, histories, and economic statuses. This presents great challenges for us as a society and as individuals. The main challenge is to look beyond the stereotypes and biases, to recognize the disparities and differences, and to try to apply what we know about intercultural communication. Perhaps the first step is to realize that the melting pot metaphor probably was never viable, that it was not realistic to expect everyone to assimilate into the United States in the same way. Today we need a different metaphor, one that

The U.S. Religious Landscape Survey points to some interesting religious demographic information. Note how religion intersects with other social categories. Here are some interesting findings:

- Among people who are married, nearly four in ten (37%) are married to a spouse with a different religious affiliation. (This figure includes Protestants who are married to another Protestant from a different denominational family, such as a Baptist who is married to a Methodist.) Hindus and Mormons are the most likely to be married (78% and 71%, respectively) and to be married to someone of the same religion (90% and 83%, respectively).

- The Midwest most closely resembles the religious makeup of the overall population. The South, by a wide margin, has the heaviest concentration of members of evangelical Protestant churches. The Northeast has the greatest concentration of Catholics, and the West has the largest proportion of unaffiliated people, including the largest proportion of atheists and agnostics.

- Of all the major racial and ethnic groups in the United States, black Americans are the most likely to report a formal religious affiliation. Even among those blacks who are unaffiliated, three in four belong to the "religious unaffiliated" category (that is, they say that religion is either somewhat or very important in their lives), compared with slightly more than one-third of the unaffiliated population overall.

- Nearly half of Hindus in the United States, one-third of Jews, and a quarter of Buddhists have obtained postgraduate education, compared with only about one in ten of the adult population overall. Hindus and Jews are also much more likely than other groups to report high income levels.

- People not affiliated with any particular religion stand out for their relative youth compared with other religious traditions. Among the unaffiliated, 31% are under age 30 and 71% are under age 50. Comparable numbers for the overall adult population are 20% and 59%, respectively.

- By contrast, members of mainline Protestant churches and Jews are older, on average, than members of other groups. Roughly half of Jews and members of mainline churches are age 50 and older, compared with approximately four in ten American adults overall.

- Members of Baptist churches account for one-third of all Protestants and close to one-fifth of the total U.S. adult population. Baptists also account for nearly two-thirds of members of historically black Protestant churches.

Source: From U.S. Religious Landscape Survey (2008), *Pew Forum on Religion and Public Life*, http://religions.pewforum.org/reports.

One of my friends is in a relationship with someone from another race who happens to believe an entirely different religion than she does. She is Hispanic and Catholic and he is Caucasian and Christian. When I was talking to her boyfriend he told me that one of the things he has learned about my friend's culture is that in a Hispanic family everything is traditional. When you greet everyone you greet with a kiss on the cheek instead of a handshake which was very different from his culture. My friend states that everything has been pretty much easier except for the fact that her family has told her that they would prefer to see her with someone from her own culture. This makes it very hard to feel comfortable around her family when she brings her boyfriend around. The advice she gave me about entering an intercultural relationship is to not take other people's opinions seriously. Everyone has their views on things and you can't stop that. You have to live your life they way you want to and don't let people's words and thoughts bring you down.
— Brenna

reflects the racial, ethnic, and cultural diversity that truly exists in our country. Perhaps we should think of the United States as a "salad," in which each group retains its own flavor and yet contributes to the whole. Or we might think of it as a "tapestry," with many different strands contributing to a unified pattern.

In any case, the United States is hardly a model of diversity; many countries are far more diverse ethnically. For example, Nigeria has some 200 ethnic groups, and Indonesia has a similar number. Nigeria was colonized by the British, and artificially drawn boundaries forced many different groups into one nation-state, which caused many conflicts. The diverse groups in Indonesia, in contrast, have largely coexisted amiably for many years. Diversity, therefore, does not necessarily lead to intercultural conflicts.

Fortunately, most individuals are able to negotiate day-to-day activities in spite of cultural differences. Diversity can even be a positive force. Demographic diversity in the United States has given us tremendous linguistic richness and culinary variety, varied resources to meet new social challenges, as well as domestic and international business opportunities.

THE ECONOMIC IMPERATIVE

The recent trend toward globalization—the creation of a world market in goods, services, labor, capital, and technology—is shown dramatically in the account of a journalist who asks a Dell computer manager where his laptop is made. The answer? It was codesigned by engineers in Texas and Taiwan; the microprocessor was made in one of Intel's factories in the Philippines, Costa Rica, Malaysia, or China; the memory came from factories in Korea, Germany, Taiwan, or Japan. Other components (keyboard, hard drive, batteries, etc.)

were made by Japanese, Taiwanese, Irish, Israeli, or British firms with factories mainly in Asia, and finally, the laptop was assembled in Taiwan (Friedman, 2005).

What is the ultimate impact of globalization on the average person? Some economists defend it, saying the losses are always offset by the gains in cheaper consumer prices. However, many working people, seeing their jobs outsourced to cheap labor in India, China, and Malaysia, feel threatened. An increasing number of economists agree. As one of the world's leading economists, Paul Samuelson (2005), argues, consumer gains are offset by income losses—if globalization causes enough Americans to suffer lower wages, America as a whole loses. The answer is not to resign from the world trading system, but rather to understand how and why the big winners from globalization, the Asian nations, are gaining and to learn from them, just as in the past, they learned from us (Maital, 2005).

The point is that, to compete effectively in this new global market, Americans must understand how business is conducted in other countries. American businesspeople should be able to negotiate deals that are advantageous to the U.S. economy. However, they are not always willing to take the time and effort to do this. For example, most U.S. automobile manufacturers do not produce automobiles that have right-hand drive, which prevents them from penetrating markets in nations like Japan. Stories abound of U.S. marketing slogans that were inaccurately translated, like Pepsi's "Come alive with the Pepsi Generation," which was translated into Chinese as "Pepsi brings your ancestors back from the grave" ("Ten Great Global Marketing Mistakes," 1998).

Cross-cultural trainers in the United States report that Japanese and other business personnel often spend years in the United States studying English and learning about the country before they decide to establish operations here or invest money. In contrast, many American companies provide little or no training before sending their workers overseas and expect to close business deals quickly, with little regard for cultural idiosyncrasies.

Many management experts have examined other countries' practices for ways to increase U.S. productivity. One such idea was "quality circles," borrowed from the Japanese and now popular in the United States. Another Japanese strength is the belief in effort for its own sake. Japanese employees work longer hours and sometimes produce better products simply as a result of persistence. This trait also pays off in schools: Japanese students score higher on standardized exams than do American students (Fallows, 1989).

It will also behoove Americans to research how to do business in the huge emerging market that is 21st-century China. As shown in the Point of View box (see page 30), a recent gaffe by Nike reflects the general lack of cultural understanding about the Chinese.

Why do so many businesspeople have difficulty succeeding in Chinese and other Asian markets? The reasons involve both differences in business practices and cultural differences between East and West. Ambler and Witzel (2000) explain that business dealings in China, as in many Eastern countries,

Americans, including myself, sometimes have this belief that what we do here in the United States is the best and only way to do things. We put these "cultural blinders" on and are oblivious to any other cultures and/or values. Although American tradition has been and can be a big influence on other markets and business sectors, we are failing to realize that the way we do business is not the basis for all businesses. Most of our international business ventures are failing due to our stubbornness. In the past we felt that we could send someone to Mexico or Japan without any intercultural training and still show them how to do business. How wrong were we?

Today we realize it takes an understanding of others and their beliefs and values to truly gain respect and further our business and personal relationships. Businesses are taking the time and money to train their employees about the new culture that they will be submerged in. People in the past failed because we did not take into account that companies' attitudes and beliefs differed from ours. Good relations with other international businesses can produce a lifelong bond that can create great economic wealth for each country. The companies are not only training their employees for this culture shock but are training their families as well, because they know that without family support, this venture will surely fail. The United States has taken strides to correct their errors of the past and are continuing their efforts to produce intercultural employees, and I hope this trend continues.

—Luis

are relationship oriented, that businesses cannot succeed without respect and harmony. Specifically, in China, three concepts are crucial:

- *Qingmian* (human feelings), which involves respect for the feelings of others
- *He* (harmony), which emphasizes the smooth functioning of a group or society
- *Guanxi* (relationship or connection), which underscores the importance of relationships in Chinese business. (In Taiwan, it is known as "Kuan-hsi.")

The high value placed on these concepts highlights other differences as well. For example, contract law is practiced very differently in China. Whereas in the West the law is the essential set of rules of conduct, the "rules of conduct" in China are the ethics and standards of behavior required in a Confucian society. This means that social pressures rather than legal instruments are used to ensure compliance. Thus, what we might conceptualize as a legal issue may be seen in China as a relationship issue.

Sometimes there are cultural differences in work ethics. One of our students, Vincent, describes a difference he observed while working as an intern in a manufacturing company:

When looking back at this internship I can easily see that Mexican workers were more loyal to the company. I constantly noticed that American workers at this

In the corporate world in Bangkok, the new year beginning on January 1 (as opposed to the Thai New Year or the Chinese New Year) is a time of giving gifts to valued customers. The company I worked for was real big on ethics, which was nice; they wanted to treat everyone equally and be fair in their business dealings, which was good, but they took it too far. During New Year's, companies usually give gifts to their customers as a way of saying thanks for their patronage. The gift you give depends on the customers' place in society and the amount of business they do with your company. What I hated is that this company (an American company) viewed that as unethical, as some form of a bribe. We could only go out and buy one item in bulk, and we'd have to give the same gift to all of the customers. I was so embarrassed to give those gifts. I hope the customers knew that I worked for an American company that just didn't understand the way things were done in Thailand.
—Chris

company would be walking around talking or smoking while they were supposed to be at their work stations, but the Mexican workers would never leave their stations until it was time for break. This sometimes created problems between Mexicans and other employees because of the differences in work ethics.

We discuss the implications of these types of cultural differences for relationships (Chapter 10) and conflicts (Chapter 11).

Cultural differences in business practices have implications not only when people from different companies do business with each other but also when people from different cultures work on the same team. One effect of globalization is increasing numbers of international teams—sometimes working as virtual teams and rarely meeting face-to-face. These teams present large challenges in intercultural communication. A recent Hewlett-Packard project involved a 16-country multilingual virtual team that operated on both sides of the international dateline. The leaders describe the challenges: "Relatively routine tasks, such as scheduling a meeting, become complex and fraught with interpersonal friction when one person's work day begins as another is sitting down to dinner or sound asleep. A simple e-mail exchange frazzles nerves because of cultural misunderstandings" (Snyder, 2003).

Even when employees have good language skills, they naturally interpret written and verbal communication through the filter of their own culture. For example, Israeli workers in the project just described wondered why their U.S. counterparts would sometimes seem upset by e-mail exchanges. It turned out that Israelis, who tend to be rather direct and sometimes blunt, were sending e-mails that seemed rude to their American counterparts. And Americans' e-mails seemed "wishy-washy" to the Israelis. The Americans' requests, with phrases like "Thanks in advance for sending me . . . ," mystified the Israelis who would say, "Thanks for what? I haven't done anything yet." After some cultural training, both sides adapted to the other (Snyder, 2003). In later chapters, we explore the implications of these and other cultural differences in communication practices.

Globalization presents many new issues. Increasingly, **multinational corporations** are moving operations to new locations, often overseas, because of lower labor costs. These business moves have far-reaching implications, including the loss of jobs at closed facilities. Many U.S.-owned companies have established production facilities, known as *maquiladoras,* along the U.S.–Mexican border, where workers produce goods bound mainly for U.S. markets. These companies benefit from lower labor costs, tax breaks, and relaxed environmental regulations. Although Mexican laborers profit from the jobs, there is a cost in terms of environmental hazards. *Maquiladoras* thus present intercultural challenges for Mexicans and U.S. Americans.

Domestic diversity also requires businesses to be attentive to cultural differences. As the workforce becomes more diverse, many businesses are interested in capitalizing on these differences for economic gain. As trainers Bernardo M. Ferdman and Sara Einy Brody (1996) suggest, "Once organizations learn to adopt an inclusive orientation in dealing with their members, this will also have a positive impact on how they look at their customer base, how they develop products and assess business opportunities, and how they relate to their communities" (p. 289).

Understanding cultural differences involves not only working with diverse employees but also recognizing new business markets, developing new products, and so on. From this perspective, diversity is a potentially powerful economic resource if organizations view the challenge as an opportunity. In this sense, then, business can capitalize on diversity.

multinational corporations Companies that have operations in two or more nations.

maquiladoras Assembly plants or factories (mainly of U.S. companies) established on the U.S.–Mexican border and using mainly Mexican labor.

THE TECHNOLOGICAL IMPERATIVE

Today, with the explosion of computers and other communication technologies, we truly live in the **global village** envisioned by media expert Marshall McLuhan (1967). Communication technology links us to events from the most remote parts of the world and connects us to persons we may never meet face-to-face from around the world. Perhaps the most revolutionary advancement has been the Internet.

global village A term coined by Marshall McLuhan in the 1960s that refers to a world in which communication technology unites people in remote parts of the world.

Technology and Human Communication

The impact of technology on our everyday communication is staggering. Think of how often you use technology to communicate in any given day: You may text-message friends about evening plans, e-mail your family to tell them the latest news, participate in a discussion board for one of your courses, and check your cell phone Web site to see how many more minutes you can use this month without getting charged. And you are not alone. The number of hours U.S. Americans spent online continues to increase, and young people are the most frequent users of the Internet (Pew Internet and American Life Project, 2005) and cell phones (Progue, 2004; http://www.clickz.com/stats/sectors/wireless/print.php/3530886).

More and more people around the world are using technology to communicate with each other. Consider these statistics:

- The rate of Internet usage in Latin America/Caribbean went up 660% between 2000 and 2008 (www.internetworldstats.com/stats.htm).
- The rate of Internet usage in the Middle East went up 1,176% between 2000 and 2008 (www.internetworldstats.com/stats.htm).
- By the end of 2009, half of the world's population will be using cell phones. Africa alone will add 265 million subscribers by 2012 (www.mobiledia. com/news/43104.html).
- Over 77% of Sweden's population spends time online. This is the highest usage rate in the world (www.internetworldstats.com/europa.htm#se).

The advent of the Internet and other communication technologies has tremendous implications for intercultural communication. We will focus on five aspects of culture and technology: (1) increased information about peoples and cultures; (2) increased contact with people who are different from us; (3) increased contact with people who are similar to us who can provide communities of support; (4) identity, culture, and technology; and (5) differential access to communication technology.

Increase in Information   You may have found that the Internet provides access to information about other cultures and other peoples. We can now instantaneously find out almost anything about any group in the world simply by searching the Internet. This *should* give us a better understanding of our global neighbors and perhaps some motivation to coexist peacefully in our global village; however, the evidence seems to be to the contrary. According to the Center for Systemic Peace, of the approximately 75 armed conflicts in the world between 1990 and 2004, only 10 have been traditional international conflicts. The rest have arisen between ethnic or political groups within a country—for example, in Cyprus, Russia, Turkey, Kashmir, Ethiopia, Bosnia, and Sudan (http://members.aol.com/cspmgm/warlist.htm). Apparently, knowledge about others does not necessarily lead to better communication or heightened understanding. We will tackle issues like this in later chapters.

Through communication technologies like the World Wide Web, people also have access to increasing amounts of information about what is happening in their own and other countries. This is especially important in countries where media are government controlled. For example, people in Pakistan and Afghanistan learn more about military actions in their countries by accessing CNN.com than through their local newspapers. In some ways, the Internet has democratized information, in that more people control and disseminate information than ever before. For example, there are some 32,000 Internet police in China, who frequently find and arrest people for criticizing the government online. They block search engine sites, close Internet cafés, and block e-mails; they can even can reroute Web site traffic to alternate sites maintained by routers in Shanghai and Beijing (http://ezinearticles.com/?Chinese-Ministry-of-Information-Internet-Registration-Laws&id=41850).

In spite of this and other governments' attempts to limit their citizens' access to computer-mediated communication (CMC), the Internet is providing information, world news, and possibilities for interpersonal communication that were not available previously (Scanlon, 2003; Wheeler, 2001).

Increased Contact with People Who Differ   Communication technology brings us in contact with people we might never have the opportunity to know otherwise. And many of these people are from different cultural backgrounds. The Internet/e-mail allows us to have "pen pals" from different cultures and to carry on discussions with these people in virtual chat rooms and on discussion boards.

However, such mediated communication across cultures does present unique challenges. Unlike face-to-face communication, mediated communication filters out important nonverbal cues. One of our students, Val, described the challenges of intercultural e-mails:

> *I met a girl from Korea my junior year of college, and we became good friends. When it came time for her to go back to Korea we decided we would stay friends and become pen pals via e-mail. I found it much more difficult to communicate with her because she didn't always understand what I was writing and I couldn't repeat my sentences like I could if I were speaking to her, and the same applied to her. It definitely puts a strain on our relationship.*

When we are talking to individuals face-to-face, we use nonverbal information to help us interpret what they are *really* saying—tone of voice, facial expressions, gestures, and so on. The absence of these cues in mediated contexts (e.g., e-mail, chat rooms) makes communication more difficult and can lead to misunderstandings. And these misunderstandings can be compounded when communicating across cultures. For example, a U.S. colleague reports that she was offended when the e-mails she received from colleagues overseas seemed too brief and to the point. She has since discovered that her colleagues overseas are charged computer time by the minute and so have learned to be very concise in their e-mail messages. What she interpreted as rudeness had more to do with the economic context in which the interaction took place than with the communicators themselves. If she had been able to observe their nonverbal cues while communicating, she probably would have known that they were not being rude.

Also, language may be a factor. The people we talk to on e-mail networks may speak languages different from our own. An interesting situation arose recently for one of the authors of this book. Tom was using an electronic bulletin board when someone posted a message in Dutch. It was met with a flurry of hostile responses from people protesting the use of an exclusionary language, one most people couldn't read. A discussion ensued about which languages might be acceptable on the network.

The decision reached was that subscribers could post messages in any language as long as there was an English translation. In a subsequent posting, someone from a university in South Africa recommended a book "for those of you who can read Dutch (heh-heh, all four of us)"—an apparent reaction to the exclusionary sentiments of other subscribers. Machine and other translation techniques are new ways to facilitate online intercultural communication, as seen in the "Point of View" box. The use of some languages is given even more privilege in the high-tech communication world, where we are likely to encounter many more people. Although many experts think that the Internet is dominated by English, there are indications that Chinese is becoming a formidable linguistic player in the Internet world. According to one source, the first day that registration opened for Chinese language domain names, 360,000 applications were filed (english1.e21times.com/asp/sacd.asp?r=880&p=0). Surprisingly, the most recent research suggests that the move is actually toward more multilingualism on the Net—rather than toward a global English Internet (Dor, 2004). Some speculate that this is because global businesses need to adapt to local languages to sell their products and also that learning a language is an awesome task and it is not feasible to think of the entire world learning a second language to accommodate.

Increased Contact with People Who Are Similar   Communication technology also allows us to have more contact with people who are very similar to ourselves. Perhaps you participate in chat rooms or discussion boards with people who share your interests and opinions. Perhaps you turn to Internet groups for support and community. For example, international students can stay in touch with their local communities, keep up with what's going on at home, and receive emotional support during difficult times of cultural adaptation.

The Internet can also be used to strengthen a sense of identity, as is the case for some **diasporic groups**—ethnic and/or national groups that are geographically dispersed throughout the world, sometimes as refugees fleeing from war, sometimes as voluntary emigrants. A recent study of children of South Asian immigrants found that the Internet plays a major role in creating a sense of community and ethnic identity for these young people. Whereas earlier generations of immigrants were expected to assimilate as quickly as possible into the host culture, the Internet now allows these children of immigrants to connect with other Indian adolescents, discussing religion and issues concerning Indian and immigrant identity. Similar diasporic discussions are held in the *Kava Bowl* and the *Kamehameha Roundtable*, online meeting places for the Polynesian diaspora and other people from the Pacific Islands who live in the United States, Australia, and New Zealand (Franklin, 2003). Similarly, discussion boards can provide virtual communities of support for cultural minorities (e.g., Planetout.com, a discussion board for gays and lesbians). However, the Internet can also provide a venue for like-minded people to promote prejudice and hatred. According to a recent report from a British e-mail filtering company, the number of hate and violence Web sites has grown by nearly 300% since 2000. In 2000, this company was monitoring about 2,756 Web sites that were categorized as hate and violence

diasporic groups Ethnic and/or national groups that are geographically dispersed throughout the world.

New techniques and technologies of translation have helped to bring different bodies of literature to English audiences. Remember from earlier that the Middle East has seen a sharp increase in Internet usage since 2008. In this article, the topic of Arabic literature is explored.

Saudi author Raja Alsanea spoke on topic [of Arabic literature in the English language], talking interestingly about her successful novel Girls of Riyadh *and receiving the lion's share of questions from the audience.*

Translated into 23 languages and started when the author was only 18, this novel, Alsanea explained, could be seen as having captured the experience of a generation of young Saudi women who have used the Internet—blogs, forums and chat sites—to create a "virtual liberating space" allowing freedom of expression. A new language, "Arabish," had been invented for use in this space, consisting of a mix of English and colloquial Arabic written in the Latin alphabet.

Asked whether the success of Girls of Riyadh *in translation had surprised her, Alsanea said that she had collaborated on the English translation and was aware that "western readers are more interested in Saudi Arabia than they are in Saudi literature." She was not "a feminist or an activist," though the novel did show up the "confused boundary" between "freedom in virtual space and the traditions that dominate the non-virtual space of family and society."*

Source: From David Tresilian, "The fun of the fair." Retrieved May 13, 2008, from http://weekly.ahram.org.eg/2008/894/cu21.htm.

sites. By April 2004, that figure had risen to 10,926. Even more worrying, however, is that since January 2004, the number of sites that promote hatred against Americans, Muslims, Jews, homosexuals, and people of non-European ancestry, as well as graphic violence, has risen by more than 25% (http://www.theregister.co.uk/2004/05/10/hate_websites_flourish/).

Identity, Culture, and Technology Advances in communication technology lead us to think differently about ourselves and our **identity management.** In *The Saturated Self,* psychologist Kenneth Gergen describes the changes that occur as technology alters our patterns of communication. Gergen suggests that with the removal of traditional barriers to forming relationships—time and space—these technological advancements lead to **multiphrenia,** a splitting of the individual into many different selves. We are available for communication, via answering machine, fax, and e-mail, even when we're not physically present. Gergen (1991) writes:

The relatively coherent and unified sense of self inherent in a traditional culture gives way to manifold and competing potentials. A multiphrenic condition emerges in which one swims in ever-shifting, concatenating, and contentious currents of

identity management The way individuals make sense of their multiple images concerning the sense of self in different social contexts.

multiphrenia The splitting of the individual psychologically into multiple selves.

being. One bears the burden of an increasing array of oughts, of self-doubts and irrationalities. (p. 80)

Identity on the Internet not only is potentially fragmented but also involves more choice and management issues than in face-to-face interaction. As noted previously, many of the identity cues individuals use to figure out how to communicate with others—such as age, gender, and ethnicity—are filtered out on the Internet. For instance, when you send an e-mail, you can choose whether to reveal certain aspects of your identity. The recipients won't know if you are male or female, young or old, and so on—unless you tell them. The same is true for chat room participation. You can choose which aspects, if any, of your identity you want to reveal. In fact, you can even give false information about your identity.

identity tourism A concept that refers to people taking on the identities of other races, genders, classes, or sexual orientations for recreational purposes.

This capability has resulted in the opportunity for **identity tourism**—taking on the identities of other races, gender, classes, or sexual orientations for recreational purposes. And some online contexts (e.g., virtual games like *Dungeons and Dragons*) *require* users to take on new identities. How is this related to intercultural communication? One of the oft-touted skills of intercultural communication is empathy, the ability to understand what it's like to "walk in someone's shoes." Communication technology now affords an opportunity to do this—virtually. Thus, for instance, by taking on the virtual identity of a male, by participating in male-only online discussions, females might come to understand better what it feels like to be a male (Danet, 1999). The same might be true for other identities as well.

Although identity tourism provides intriguing possibilities for improving intercultural understanding, it also raises some important ethical questions. In one celebrated example, a male psychiatrist participated in online discussions as a disabled female. Ostensibly, he did so because he wanted to understand something of what it felt like to be a woman and to be disabled. The project backfired, however, as other chat room participants responded to him as a woman and, over time, even fell in love with him. Ultimately, many of the women suffered severe psychological problems as a result of their experiences with him (Turkle, 1995).

The idea of identity tourism may seem somewhat scary, but the same lack of nonverbal cues can result in less prejudice and stereotyping in mediated intercultural interaction. Some of these same nonverbal cues that are filtered out (indicators of age, gender, ethnicity, race) are often the basis for stereotyping and prejudice in initial interactions. When these cues are absent, communication may be more open because people cannot use the information to form impressions that often negatively impact communication (Carter, 2004).

Access to Communication Technology

As we've seen, technology plays a huge role in our everyday lives and often has a lot to do with our success as students and professionals. What would you do if you had no access to communication technology? If you were not able to text-message your friends or could not use your cell phone? Could not e-mail your family? How might you feel in our technology-dominated world? Although communication technologies are a fact of life for millions of people around the world, lack of access to these technologies is a reality for many people. Consider that

- As of 2007 only 47% of Americans have a broadband Internet connection at home. Only 15% of people with a household income of under $30,000 per year have broadband at home.
- The rates of broadband adoption in rural areas trail those in urban areas by about two years, meaning that the 2005 rate of broadband use in rural areas equates to the 2003 rate of use in cities.
- Even when education and income are the same, blacks and Latinos are less likely to have broadband access than whites.

Even larger inequalities exist outside the United States:

- Africa contains over 14% of the world's population, but just 3% of the world's Internet users, while North America contains only 5% of the world's population, but accounts for 17.5% of the world's Internet users.
- There are more Internet users in Germany than there are in the entire continent of Africa.
- The United States, Canada, France, Germany, Italy, Japan, Russia, and the United Kingdom account for less than 20% of the world's population but "own" 80% of Internet hosts and most traffic.

Source: From http://www.pewinternet.org/pdfs/PIP_Broadband%202007.pdf and http://www.allaboutmarketresearch.com/articles/art006.htm.

These inequities are called the "digital divide" and have enormous implications for intercultural communication. In the global information society, information is an important commodity. Everybody needs it to function. This ability is especially important in an increasingly "networked" society. It is easy to see how without these skills and knowledge one can feel marginalized and disconnected from the center of society (Rojas, Straubhaar, Roychowdhury, & Okur, 2004; van Dijk, 2004).

The implications for intercultural communication are enormous. How do people relate to each other when one is information technology rich and the other is not? When there is increasing use of English on the Internet, what happens to those who don't speak English? Can this lead to resentment? Will the increase in communication technology lead to increasing gaps between haves and have-nots? To more misunderstandings?

Recent communication technology has impacted our lives in ways our grandparents could not have imagined and requires that we reexamine even our most basic conceptions of self, others, and culture. As Sherry Turkle (1995) observes, once we take virtuality seriously as a way of life, we need a new language for talking about the simplest things. Each individual must ask: What is the nature of my relationships? What are the limits of my responsibilities? And even more importantly: Who and what am I? What is the connection between my physical and virtual bodies? And is it different in different cyberspaces? . . . What kind of society or societies are we creating, "both on and off the screen"

(p. 231)? We might also examine our own technological use: Who are we in contact with? People who are like ourselves? People who are different? Do we use technology to increase our contact with and understanding of other cultures or merely to hang out with people who are like us? What does this say about us and our identities?

THE PEACE IMPERATIVE

The bottom line seems to be this: Can individuals of different genders, ages, ethnicities, races, languages, socioeconomic statuses, and cultural backgrounds coexist on this planet? (See Figure 1-3.) Both the history of humankind and recent world events lead us not to be very optimistic on this point. And this imperative is even more evident after the events of September 11, 2001. Contact among different cultural groups—from the earliest civilizations until today—often has led to disharmony. For example, consider the ethnic/religious strife between Muslims and the Western world; the ethnic struggles in Bosnia and the former Soviet Union; the war between Hutus and Tutsis in Rwanda (Africa); the continued unrest in the Middle East; and the racial and ethnic struggles and tensions in neighborhoods in Boston, Los Angeles, and other U.S. cities.

colonialism (1) The system by which groups with diverse languages, cultures, religions, and identities were united to form one state, usually by a European power; (2) the system by which a country maintains power over other countries or groups of people to exploit them economically, politically, and culturally.

Some of these conflicts are tied to histories of **colonialism** around the world, whereby European powers lumped diverse groups—differing in language, culture, religion, or identity—together as one state. For example, the division of Pakistan and India was imposed by the British; eventually, East Pakistan declared its independence to become Bangladesh. Nevertheless, ethnic and religious differences in some areas of India and Pakistan continue to cause unrest. And the acquisition of nuclear weapons by both India and Pakistan makes these antagonisms of increasing concern. The tremendous diversity—and accompanying antagonisms—within many former colonies must be understood in the context of histories of colonialism.

Some of the conflicts are also tied to economic disparities and influenced by U.S. technology and media. Many people in the United States see these influences as beneficial, but they also stimulate resistance. Communication scholar Fernando Delgado (2002) explains:

> *Such cultural dominance, though celebrated at home, can spark intercultural conflicts because it inhibits the development of other nations' indigenous popular culture products, stunts their economic development and foists U.S. values and perspectives on other cultures. These effects, in turn, often lead to resentment and conflict. (p. 353)*

For example, according to many Canadians, a Canadian cultural identity is almost impossible because of the dominance of U.S. media. This type of cultural domination is very complex. Delgado recalls that he noticed anti-American sentiments in graffiti, newspapers, and TV programs during a recent

FIGURE 1-3   This Iraqi boy looks at shoes and clothes of victims of a car bomb explosion in Baghdad on March 1, 2006. The causes of this violence stem from long histories of intercultural conflict and are likely to influence intercultural relations in the future. (© *Akram Saleh/Getty*)

trip to Europe, but that he also saw U.S. influence everywhere—in music, television, film, cars, fast food, and fashion. He notes that "resentment, frustration, and disdain among the locals coexisted with an amazement at the penetration of U.S. popular culture" (p. 355).

Some of the conflicts have roots in past foreign policies. For example, the attacks in September 2001 were partly related to the confusing and shifting alliances among the United States, Afghanistan, and Arab and Muslim countries. In Afghanistan in the early 1990s, the Taliban seized power in response to the destructive rule of the Northern Alliance, a loose coalition of warlords. The United States had supported the Taliban in the fight against Soviet aggression in the late 1980s and had promised aid in rebuilding their country after the hostilities were over. However, with the withdrawal of Soviet forces and the fall of the Soviet Union, the United States wasn't as concerned about fulfilling its promises to the Afghan nation, leaving the Afghan people at the mercy of the Taliban. In addition, U.S. foreign policies toward many Arab countries in the last half century, coupled with open support for Israel, have caused widespread resentment (Friedman, 2002). Although there is no simple explanation for why terrorists attacked the United States, the attacks clearly did not happen

CHINA CHOPS NIKE AD

The U.S. sportswear firm Nike has apologized for running a commercial in China which has been banned by popular demand for offending the country's national dignity.

The 90-second advertisement was meant to combine Kill Bill–*style martial arts with sassy basketball bravado. U.S. National Basketball Association star LeBron James is shown running rings around the animated figure of a wizened and bearded kung fu master, who resembles the martial arts teacher from Quentin Tarantino's latest movie.*

In the commercial, the American athlete also gets the better of two women in traditional Chinese attire, and a pair of dragons—considered to be a symbol of China.

In a sign of the growing influence of internet opinion, the government has pulled the "Chamber of Fear" advertisement off the airwaves, after protests in online chat rooms overturned the initial approval by state censors.

According to the U.S. company, the commercial was designed by its advertising agent, Wieden and Kennedy, to encourage teenagers to overcome temptation, envy, complacency and self-doubt. But it has only managed to stir up irritation in China.

The state administration for radio, television and film posted a statement saying that Nike had violated the condition that all advertisements in China should uphold national dignity.

"This ad shows Chinese characters losing again and again. It makes our country look helpless against America," said one chat room contributor.

Faced with the loss of business from a market in which its sales have nearly doubled in the past year, Nike meekly accepted the government's decision.

"We had no intention of hurting the emotions of Chinese consumers," the company said in a statement.

"We place much attention on the Chinese market and there was a lot of careful consideration before launching the advertisement," they said.

Source: From J. Watts, "China Chops Nike Ad; Multinational Apologizes After Outcry," *The Guardian* (London), December 8, 2004, p. 15.

in a vacuum. They need to be understood in historical, political, religious, and economic contexts.

It would be naive to assume that simply understanding the issues of intercultural communication would end war and intercultural conflict, but these problems do underscore the need for individuals to learn more about social groups other than their own. (See Figure 1-4.) Ultimately, people, and not countries,

This Peace Corps volunteer, Ian Derk, shares a meal with his host family in Morocco. Experiencing different cuisines and customs can also help you learn a lot about yourself and the complex world you live in. (© *Chor Sokunthea/Reuters/Corbis*)

negotiate and sign peace treaties. An example of how individual communication styles may influence political outcomes can be seen in the negotiations between Iraqi president Saddam Hussein and representatives of the United States and the United Nations just prior to the Gulf War, in 1990. Many Middle East experts assumed that Hussein was not ready to fight, that he was merely bluffing, using an Arabic style of communication. This style emphasizes the importance of animation, exaggeration, and conversational form over content (Feghali, 1997). Communication specialists note that in conflict situations Arab speakers may threaten the life and property of their opponents but have no intention of actually carrying out the threats. Rather, Arab speakers use threats to buy time and intimidate their opponents. Thus, declaratory statements by U.S. leaders, such as "We will find the cancer and cut it out," seemed mundane and unintimidating to Arab listeners. Verbal exchanges, regardless of the different speech styles, often take the place of physical violence (Griefat & Katriel, 1989).

However, we always need to consider the relationship between individual and societal forces in studying intercultural communication. Although communication on the interpersonal level is important, we must remember that individuals often are born into and are caught up in conflicts that they neither started nor chose.

This writer decries a certain kind of intercultural learning—the learning that some study-abroad students pursue—whereby people in other countries are objectified and viewed as exotic and strange. The real problem arises when these students are hired to write television commercials and to present ideas about other cultures.

One type of commercial model shows us exotic humans in all their tribal finery, but, in a multicultural twist, they—Masai warriors, Sicilian matrons, Tibetan monks, Irish fishermen—are revealed as strangely prescient consumers with a quirky knowledge of luxury cars or Internet stock trading. In one commercial, we witness an Inuit elder teaching his grandson about tracking by identifying marks in the snow. "That," he says, "is a caribou." Then, after a pause, during which the wise man stares at the snow, he reverentially intones the single word "Audi." From ads like those, astute students learn that foreigners are obsessed with us—our commodities and displays. What we may learn from them pales in comparison with the glories that they see in our consumer lifestyle.

Other commercials reduce distant lands to images of animals or nature and imply that nature can be thoroughly dominated by SUVs or swaggering, extreme-sports youths. Athletes and Nissan Pathfinders fight bulls in a ring, giant outdoorsmen tap the miniaturized Rockies, a hiker butts heads with a bighorn sheep. And, of course, sophisticated viewers know that all those animals are the creation of technology.

In one commercial, a driver—insulated in his fully self-sufficient cocoon—is able to program both the road and the various beautiful and exotic settings it passes through. Not only is the technologically empowered American greater than nature, we create nature to suit our whims. There is no outside world anymore, no dark places of mystery, yet to be seen. Our SUVs do not travel to an unknown world so much as create different options from a well-known list. Television's emphasis is on how the actor—whether a contestant on a reality-TV show or the driver in a car ad—is seen and manipulates how she is seen. Even when outsiders exist, everyone is looking at us.

When a promotional piece for the reality-TV show The Amazing Race *shows an American woman in a clearly foreign space—perhaps India—she*

THE ETHICAL IMPERATIVE

ethics Principles of conduct that help govern behaviors of individuals and groups.

Living in an intercultural world presents ethical challenges as well. **Ethics** may be thought of as principles of conduct that help govern the behavior of individuals and groups. These principles often arise from communities' consensus on what is good and bad behavior. Cultural values tell us what is "good" and what "ought" to be good. Ethical judgments focus more on the degrees of rightness *is not troubled, confused or interested in her environment. Instead she strips down to a bikini emblazoned with a U.S. flag to get directions to the next challenge from a bug-eyed and eager native. "Will I wear this if it helps me get home?" she says. "Hell, yeah!" The young woman clearly did not travel to broaden her horizons. For her, India becomes, as much as Salt Lake City or Kandahar, a place for aggressive performance of her American identity— unwrapping herself in the flag, so to speak.*

We now are the world, to be looked at, admired, or despised; what is important about the activity of others is their response to our display. . . . [Study-abroad students] talk about interactions with outsiders only in vague abstractions, while expostulating brilliantly about the nuances of American students' interactions with one another. The few individuals who left their peers to engage the outside world explained that move as an individual rejection of the group and still found it easier to discuss their fellow students than the generically defined "friends" they met at bars.

One young American who traveled to Guatemala bragged that "I have a surprising ability to relate to almost everyone," but "everyone" turned out to mean members of preconceived categories of human-rights workers, Indians, and children, whom she described as objects of more first-person sentences. She specifically excluded less exotic, fast-talking city folk who were "just different" and not worth mentioning.

Students return from study-abroad programs having seen the world, but the world they return to tell tales about is more often than not the world they already knew, the imaginary world of globalized, postmodern capitalism where everything is already known, everyone speaks the same language, and the outside world keeps its eyes on those of us who come from the center.

. . . we should avoid pre- and post-travel orientation sessions that focus on group dynamics and individual growth. Instead, those sessions could be used as opportunities for students to learn how to question the way that we tell stories about our travels, and to discover for themselves how those stories share features with commercials about men who play football with lions and reality shows where contestants dare each other to swallow centipedes.

Source: From B. Feinberg, "What Students Don't Learn Abroad," *The Chronicle Review,* May 2, 2000, p. B20.

and wrongness in human behavior than do cultural values (Johannesen, 1990).

Some judgments are stated very explicitly. For example, the Ten Commandments teach that it is wrong to steal, tell a lie, commit murder, and so on. Many other identifiable principles of conduct that arise from our cultural experience may be less explicit—for instance, that people should be treated equally and should work hard. Several issues come to mind in a discussion of ethics in intercultural communication. For example, what happens when two ethical systems collide?

Although an individual may want to "do the right thing" to contribute to a better society, it is not always easy to know what is "right" in specific situations. Ethical principles are often culture bound, and intercultural conflicts arise from various notions of what is ethical behavior.

One common cross-cultural ethical dilemma involves standards of conducting business in multinational corporations. The U.S. Congress and the Securities and Exchange Commission consider it unethical to make payments to government officials of other countries to promote trade. (Essentially, such payments smack of bribery.) However, in many countries, like China, government officials are paid in this informal way instead of being supported by taxes (Ambler & Witzel, 2000). What, then, is ethical behavior for personnel in multinational subsidiaries?

Relativity Versus Universality

In this book, we stress the relativity of cultural behavior—that no cultural pattern is inherently right or wrong. So, is there any universality in ethics? Are any cultural behaviors always right or always wrong? The answers depend on one's perspective. A universalist might try, for example, to identify acts and conditions that most societies think of as wrong, such as murder, theft, or treason. Someone who takes an extreme universalist position would insist that cultural differences are only superficial, that fundamental notions of right and wrong are universal. Some religions take universal positions—for example, that the Ten Commandments are a universal code of behavior. But Christian groups often disagree about the universality of the Bible. For example, are the teachings of the New Testament mainly guidelines for the Christians of Jesus's time, or can they be applied to Christians in the 21st century? These are difficult issues for many people searching for ethical guidelines (Johannesen, 1990). The philosopher Immanuel Kant (1949) believed in the universality of moral laws. His well-known "categorical imperative" states that people should act only on maxims that apply universally, to *all* individuals.

The extreme relativist position holds that any cultural behavior can be judged only within the cultural context in which it occurs. This means that only those members of a community can truly judge the ethics of their own members. According to communication scholar William S. Howell (1982),

> *The environment, the situation, the timing of an interaction, human relationships, all affect the way ethical standards are applied. . . . The concept of universal ethics, standards of goodness that apply to everyone, everywhere, and at all times, is the sort of myth people struggle to hold onto. (pp. 182, 187)*

And yet, to accept a completely relativistic position seems to tacitly accept the horrors of Nazi Germany, South African apartheid, or U.S. slavery. In each case, the larger community developed cultural beliefs that supported persecution and discrimination in such extreme forms that worldwide condemnation ultimately resulted (Hall, 1997, p. 23).

Philosophers and anthropologists have struggled to develop ethical guidelines that seem universally applicable but that also recognize the tremendous cultural variability in the world. And many ethical relativists appeal to more natural, humanitarian principles. This more moderate position assumes that people can evaluate cultures without succumbing to ethnocentrism, that all individuals and cultural groups share a fundamental humanistic belief in the sanctity of the human spirit and the goodness of peace, and that people should respect the well-being of others (Kale, 1994).

Communication scholar Bradford J. Hall (1997) reminds us that relativistic and universalistic approaches to ethics should be viewed not as a dichotomy, but rather as a compound of universalism and relativism. All ethics systems involve a tension between the universal and the relative. So, although we recognize some universal will toward ethical principles, we may have to live with the tension of not being able to impose our "universal" ethic on others.

A recent suggestion for meeting the ethical imperative is to employ a **dialogical approach** (Evanoff, 2004). The dialogical approach emphasizes the importance of relationships and dialogues between individuals and communities in wrestling with ethical dilemmas. Communication scholars Stanley Deetz, Deborah Cohen, and Paige P. Edley (1997) suggest that even in international business contexts, a dialogical approach can work. As an example, they cite the ethical challenges that arise when a corporation relocates its operations overseas. Although this relocation may make good business sense, the move often has difficult personal and social (and therefore ethical) ramifications. The move may cause a wave of unemployment in the old location and raise issues of exploitation of the workforce and harm to the environment in the new location (especially where poverty is a problem).

> **dialogical approach** Focuses on the importance of dialogue in developing and maintaining relationships between individuals and communities.

Deetz and colleagues (1997) suggest that moving from an owner/manager model to a dialogical stakeholder model can help clarify some of the ethical issues. The dialogical approach emphasizes the importance of the relationship and dialogue between the company and the various communities and stakeholders. They propose forums for discussion even while acknowledging that sometimes discussions and forums are used by management to suppress or diffuse conflict rather than to promote genuine debate for the sake of company improvement. In this case, a dialogical approach

> *does not rest in agreement or consensus but in the avoidance of the suppression of alternative conceptions and possibilities . . . the heterogeneity of the international community and the creative possibilities residing in intercultural communication provide possibilities that may have been overlooked in national cultures. (Deetz, et al., 1997, pp. 222–223)*

The study of intercultural communication not only provides insights into cultural patterns but also helps us address the ethical issues involved in intercultural interaction. Specifically we should be able to (1) judge what is ethical and unethical behavior given variations in cultural priorities, and (2) identify guidelines for ethical behavior in intercultural contexts in which ethics clash.

Being Ethical Students of Culture

Related to the issue of judging cultural patterns as ethical or unethical are the issues surrounding the study of culture. Part of learning about intercultural communication is learning about cultural patterns and cultural identities—our own and others. There are three issues to address here: developing self-reflexivity, learning about others, and acquiring a sense of social justice.

Developing Self-Reflexivity   In studying intercultural communication, it is vital to develop **self-reflexivity**—to understand ourselves and our position in society. In learning about other cultures and cultural practices, we often learn much about ourselves. Immigrants often comment that they never felt so much like someone of their own nationality until they left their homeland.

self-reflexivity A process of learning to understand oneself and one's position in society.

Think about it: Many cultural attitudes and ideas are instilled in you, but these can be difficult to unravel and identify. Knowing who you are is never simple; rather, it is an ongoing process that can never fully capture the ever-emerging person. Not only will you grow older but your intercultural experiences will change who you are and who you think you are. It is also important to reflect on your place in society. By recognizing the social categories to which you belong, and the implications of those categories, you will be in a better position to understand how to communicate. For example, being an undergraduate student positions you to communicate your ideas on specific subjects and in particular ways to various members of the faculty or staff at your school. You might want to communicate to the registrar your desire to change majors—this would be an appropriate topic to address to that person. But you would not be well positioned during an exam to communicate to your chemistry professor your problems with your girl- or boyfriend.

Learning About Others   It is important to remember that the study of cultures is actually the study of other people. Never lose sight of the humanity at the core of the topic. Try not to observe people as if they are zoo animals. Communication scholar Bradford Hall (1997) cautions against using the "zoo approach" to studying culture:

> *When using such an approach we view the study of culture as if we were walking through a zoo admiring, gasping and chuckling at the various exotic animals we observe. One may discover amazing, interesting and valuable information by using such a perspective and even develop a real fondness for these exotic people, but miss the point that we are as culturally "caged" as others and that they are culturally as "free" as we are. (p. 14)*

Remember that you are studying real people who have real lives, and your conclusions about them may have very real consequences for them and for you. Cultural studies scholar Linda Alcoff (1991/1992) acknowledges the ethical issues involved when students of culture try to describe the cultural patterns of others; she recognizes the difficulty of speaking "for" and "about" others who have different lives. Instead, she suggests, students of culture should try to speak "with" and "to" others. Rather than merely describe others from a distance, it's better to engage others in a dialogue about their cultural realities.

Learn to listen to the voices of others, to cultivate experiential knowledge. Hearing about the experiences of people who are different from you can broaden

I have spent three years in the United States seeking an education. I am from Singapore, and I believe that in many ways both countries are similar. They are both multicultural. They both have a dominant culture. In the United States the dominant culture is white, and in Singapore it is Chinese.

Coming to the United States has taught me to be more aware of diversity. Even though in Singapore we are diverse, because I was part of the majority there, I didn't feel the need to increase my level of intercultural awareness. In the United States I became a minority, and that has made me feel the need to become more culturally competent.

—Jacqueline

your ways of viewing the world. Many differences—based on race, gender, sexual orientation, nationality, ethnicity, age, and so on—deeply affect people's everyday lives. Listening carefully as people relate their experiences and their ways of knowing will help you learn about the many aspects of intercultural communication.

Developing a Sense of Social Justice A final ethical issue involves the responsibility that comes with the acquisition of intercultural knowledge and insights— that this educational experience is not just transformative for the individual but should also benefit the larger society and other cultural groups in the increasingly interdependent world.

Everett Kleinjans (1975), an international educator, stresses that intercultural education differs from some other kinds of education: Although all education may be potentially transformative, learning as a result of intercultural contact is particularly so in that it deals with fundamental aspects of human behavior. Learning about intercultural communication sometimes calls into question the core of our basic assumptions about ourselves, our culture, and our worldviews and challenges existing and preferred beliefs, values, and patterns of behavior. Liliana, a Colombian student, describes such a transformation:

When I first came to the States to study and live I was surprised with all the diversity and different cultures I encountered. I realized I came from a country, society, school and group of friends with little diversity. During all the years I lived in Colombia I did not meet more than five people from other countries. Even at my school, there was little diversity—only two students of color among three thousand students. I realized that big difference when I was suddenly sharing a college classroom with students from all over the world, people of all colors and cultures. At the beginning it was difficult getting used to it because of the wide diversity, but I like and enjoy it now and I wish my family and friends could experience and learn as much as I have.

As you learn about yourself and others as cultural beings, as you come to understand the larger economic, political, and historical contexts in which interaction occurs, is there an ethical obligation to continue learning? We believe that as members of an increasingly interdependent global community, intercultural communication students have a responsibility to educate themselves, not just about interesting cultural differences but also about intercultural conflicts, the impacts of stereotyping and prejudice, and the larger systems that can oppress and deny basic human rights—and to apply this knowledge to the communities in which they live and interact.

What constitutes ethical and unethical applications of intercultural communication knowledge? One questionable practice involves people who study intercultural communication in order to proselytize others without their consent. (Some religious organizations conduct Bible study on college campuses for international students under the guise of English language lessons.) Another questionable practice is the behavior of cross-cultural consultants who misrepresent or exaggerate their ability to deal with complex issues of prejudice and racism in brief, one-shot training sessions (Paige & Martin, 1996).

A final questionable practice concerns research on the intercultural communication of U.S. minority groups. A common approach in the United States is for a white tenured faculty member to conduct such research employing graduate and undergraduate students from the minority groups being studied:

> *Minority students are sometimes used as a way to gain immediate access to the community of interest. These students go into communities and the (usually white) professors are spared the intense, time-consuming work of establishing relationships in the community. (Martin & Butler, 2001, p. 291)*

These students are then asked to report their findings to and interpret their community for the faculty member. Unfortunately, doing so can jeopardize their relationship to their community, which may be suspicious of the academic community. The faculty member publishes articles and reaps the tangible rewards of others' hard work—promotions, pay raises, and professional visibility. Meanwhile, the community and the students may receive little for their valuable contributions to this academic work.

We feel there is a concomitant responsibility that goes along with this intercultural knowledge: to work toward a more equitable and fair society and world. We want you to keep in mind this ethical issue as you study the various topics covered in this book. In the final chapter, we'll address this issue again with practical suggestions for meeting this ethical challenge.

INTERNET RESOURCES

www.intercultural.org/
This is the Web site of a nonprofit organization dedicated to improving intercultural communication. It contains a lot of valuable information aimed

at a broad audience, including businesses. The most interesting aspect of the Web site is that it is full of actual training materials used by intercultural practitioners in helping their clients develop a greater intercultural proficiency.

www.refintl.org/
This Web site explores the topic of refugees. Many people consider intercultural communication in the business setting, but intercultural communication due to refugee migrations is actually rather common. This site estimates that there are over 34 million refugees around the world. What special intercultural issues are present when considering refugees?

www.kwintessential.co.uk/cultural-services/articles/intercultural-communication-tips.html
This is a "quick-tip" guide to intercultural communication. There are some good tips on this page, like encouragement to reflect on the practices you engage in while communicating in an intercultural context. It is worth considering that this is the type of information many people use when engaging in intercultural business, etc. What types of information or analysis are missing from its list of tips?

SUMMARY

There are six reasons or imperatives for studying intercultural communication:

- The self-awareness imperative involves increasing understanding of our own location in larger social, political, and historical contexts.
- The demographic imperative includes the changing domestic and international migration—raising questions of class and religious diversity.
- The economic imperative highlights issues of globalization and the challenges for increased cultural understanding needed to reach the global market.
- The technological imperative gives us increasing information and increased contact with people who are similar and different from us. Increased use of communication technology also raises questions about identity and access to these technologies.
- The peace imperative involves working through issues of colonialism, economic disparities, and racial, ethnic, and religious differences.
- The ethical imperative calls for an understanding of the universalist, relativist, and dialogic approach to ethical issues.

Being an ethical student of culture involves developing self-reflexivity, learning about others, and developing a sense of social justice and responsibility.

DISCUSSION QUESTIONS

1. How do electronic means of communication (e-mail, the Internet, fax, and so on) differ from face-to-face interactions?
2. How do these communication technologies change intercultural communication interaction?
3. What are some of the potential challenges organizations face as they become more diverse?
4. Why is it important to think beyond ourselves as individuals in intercultural interaction?
5. How do economic situations affect intergroup relations?

 Go to the self-quizzes on the Online Learning Center at www.mhhe.com/martinnakayama5 to further test your knowledge.

ACTIVITIES

1. *Family Tree.* Interview the oldest member of your family you can contact. Then answer the following questions:
   a. When did your ancestors come to the United States?
   b. Where did they come from?
   c. What were the reasons for their move? Did they come voluntarily?
   d. What language(s) did they speak?
   e. What difficulties did they encounter?
   f. Did they change their names? For what reasons?
   g. What were their occupations before they came, and what jobs did they take on their arrival?
   h. How has your family status changed through the generations?

   Compare your family experience with those of your classmates. Did most immigrants come for the same reasons? What are the differences in the various stories?

2. *Intercultural Encounter.* Describe and analyze a recent intercultural encounter. This may mean talking with someone of a different age, ethnicity, race, religion, and so on.
   a. Describe the encounter. What made it "intercultural"?
   b. Explain how you initially felt about the communication.
   c. Describe how you felt after the encounter, and explain why you think you felt as you did.
   d. Describe any challenges in trying to communicate. If there were no challenges, explain why you think it was so easy.
   e. Based on this experience, identify some characteristics that may be important for successful intercultural communication.

KEY WORDS

Anglocentrism (12)
colonialism (28)
demographics (6)
dialogical approach (35)
diasporic groups (24)
diversity (9)
enclaves (14)
ethics (32)

ethnocentrism (5)
global village (21)
heterogeneous (8)
homogeneous (8)
identity
   management (25)
identity tourism (26)
immigrants (9)

maquiladoras (21)
melting pot (12)
multinational
   corporations (21)
multiphrenia (25)
nativistic (12)
self-reflexivity (36)

 The Online Learning Center at www.mhhe.com/martinnakayama5 features flashcards and crossword puzzles based on these terms and concepts.

REFERENCES

Adler, P. S. (1975). The transition experience: An alternative view of culture shock. *Journal of Humanistic Psychology, 15,* 13–23.

Alcoff, L. (1991/1992). The problem of speaking for others. *Cultural Critique, 20,* 5–32.

Ambler, T., & Witzel, M. (2000). *Doing business in China.* New York: Routledge.

Baldwin, J. (1955). *Notes of a native son.* Boston: Beacon Press.

Banks, J. (1991). *Teaching strategies for ethnic studies.* Needham, MA: Allyn & Bacon.

Brewer, C. A., & Suchan, T. A. (2001). *Mapping Census 2000: The geography of U.S. diversity.* (U.S. Census Bureau, Census Special Reports, Series CENSR/01–1.) Washington, DC: U.S. Government Printing Office.

Canadian Press. (2008, August 27). Tour requires foreign golfers to speak English by next year. *Toronto Star.* Retrieved August 28, 2008 from http://www.thestar.com/Sports/Golf/article/486172.

Carnevale, A. P., & Fry, R. A. (2000). *Crossing the great divide: Can we achieve equity when generation Y goes to college?* Princeton, NJ: Educational Testing Service. (ERIC Document Reproduction Service No. ED443907)

Carter, D. M. (2004). Living in virtual communities: Making friends online. *Journal of Urban Technology, 11,* 109–136.

Cole, D. (1998). Five myths about immigration. In P. S. Rothenberg (Ed.), *Race, class, and gender in the United States: An integrated study* (4th ed., pp. 125–129). New York: St. Martin's Press.

Curtin, P. D. (1969). *The Atlantic slave trade: A census.* Madison: University of Wisconsin Press.

Danet, B. (1999). Text as mask: Gender, play and performance on the Internet. In S. G. Jones (Ed.), *Cybersociety 2.0: Revisiting computer-mediated communication and community* (pp. 129–159). Thousand Oaks, CA: Sage.

Deetz, S., Cohen, D., & Edley, P. P. (1997). Toward a dialogic ethic in the context of international business organization. In F. L. Casmir (Ed.), *Ethics in intercultural and international communication* (pp. 183–226). Mahwah, NJ: Lawrence Erlbaum.

Delgado, F. (2002). Mass-mediated communication and intercultural conflict. In J. N. Martin, T. K. Nakayama, & L. A. Flores (Eds.), *Readings in intercultural communication* (pp. 351–359). Boston: McGraw-Hill.

Dor, D. (2004). From Englishization to imposed multilingualism: Globalization, the Internet, and the political economy of the linguistic code. *Public Culture, 16,* 97–118.

Evanoff, R. J. (2004). Universalist, relativist, and constructivist approaches to intercultural ethics. *International Journal of Intercultural Relations, 28,* 439–458.

Fallows, J. (1989). *More like us: Putting America's native strengths and traditional values to work to overcome the Asian challenge.* Boston: Houghton Mifflin.

Farrell, E. (2005, February 4). More students plan to work to help pay for college. *The Chronicle of Higher Education,* pp. A1, A34.

Feghali, E. (1997). Arab cultural communication patterns. *International Journal of Intercultural Relations, 21,* 345–379.

Ferdman, B. M., & Brody, S. E. (1996). Models of diversity training. In D. Landis & R. Bhagat (Eds.), *Handbook of intercultural training* (2nd ed., pp. 282–303). Thousand Oaks, CA: Sage.

Flores, L. A., Moon, D. G., & Nakayama, T. K. (2006). Dynamic rhetorics of race: California's Racial Privacy Initiative and the shifting grounds of racial politics. *Communication and Critical/Cultural Studies.*

Foner, E. (1998). Who is an American? In P. S. Rothenberg (Ed.), *Race, class, and gender in the United States: An integrated study* (4th ed., pp. 84–92). New York: St. Martin's Press.

Franklin, M. I. (2003). I define my own identity: Pacific articulations of 'race' and 'culture' on the Internet. *Ethnicities, 3,* 465–490.

Friedman, T. L. (2002, March 6). The core of Muslim rage. *The New York Times,* www.nytimes.com/2002/03/06/opinion/06FRIE.html?ei=1&en=%20bd6293bb96564

Friedman, T. L. (2005). *The world is flat: A brief history of the twenty-first century.* New York: Farrar, Straus & Giroux.

Fussell, P. (1992). *Class: A guide through the American status system.* New York: Touchstone Books.

Gergen, K. (1991). *The saturated self: Dilemmas of identity in contemporary life.* New York: HarperCollins/Basic Books.

Griefat, Y., & Katriel, T. (1989). Life demands *musayara:* Communication and culture among Arabs in Israel. In S. Ting-Toomey & F. Korzenny (Eds.), *Language, communication and culture: International and intercultural communication annual* (Vol. 13, pp. 121–138). Newbury Park, CA: Sage.

Hacker, K. L., & Steiner, R. (2002). The digital divide for Hispanic Americans. *Howard Journal of Communications, 13,* 267–283.

Hall, B. J. (1997). Culture, ethics and communication. In F. L. Casmir (Ed.), *Ethics in intercultural and international communication* (pp. 11–41). Mahwah, NJ: Lawrence Erlbaum.

Hochman, (2004, June 21). NBA teams continue to look outside U.S. *Times-Picayune* (New Orleans), p. 2.

Howell, W. S. (1982). *The empathic communicator.* Belmont, CA: Wadsworth.

Jackson, L. A., Barbatsis, G., Biocca, F. A., von Eye, A., Zhao, Y., & Fitzgerald, H. E. (2004). Home Internet use in low-income families: Is access enough to eliminate the digital divide? In E. P. Bucy & J. E. Newhagen (Eds.), *Media access: Social and psychological dimensions of new technology use* (pp. 155–186). Mahwah, NJ: Lawrence Erlbaum.

Johannesen, R. L. (1990). *Ethics in human communication* (3rd ed.). Prospect Heights, IL: Waveland Press.

Johnston, D. C. (2005, June 5). Richest are leaving even the rich far behind. *New York Times,* p. 1.

Johnston, D. C. (2007, March 29). Income gap is widening, data shows. *New York Times.* Retrieved August 29, 2008 from http://www.nytimes.com/2007/03/29/business/29tax.html?ex=1332820800&en=fb472e72466c34c8&ei=5088&partner=rssnyt&emc=rss

Kale, D. W. (1994). Peace as an ethic for intercultural communication. In L. Samovar & R. E. Porter (Eds.), *Intercultural communication: A reader* (7th ed., pp. 435–441). Belmont, CA: Wadsworth.

Kant, I. (1949). *Fundamental principles of the metaphysics of morals* (T. Abbott, Trans.). Indianapolis, IN: Library of Liberal Arts/Bobbs-Merrill.

Kleinjans, E. (1975). A question of ethics. *International Education and Cultural Exchange, 10,* 20–25.

Lenhart, A., Horrigan, J., Rainie, L., Allen, K., Boyce, A., Madden, M., & O'Grady, E. (2003, April 16). *The ever-shifting Internet population: A new look at Internet access and the digital divide.* Washington, DC: Pew Internet & American Life Project (http://www.pewinternet.org).

Loewen, J. W. (1995). *Lies my teacher told me.* New York: Simon & Schuster.

Maital, S. (2005, May 26). Globalization is a two-way street: It's time we started taking ideas from China and India. Global Newswire.

Mantsios, G. (2001). Class in America: Myths and realities. In P. S. Rothenberg (Ed.), *Race, class, and gender in the United States: An integrated study* (5th ed., pp. 168–182). New York: Worth.

Martin, J. N., & Butler, R. L. W. (2001). Toward an ethic of intercultural communication research. In V. H. Milhouse, M. K. Asante, & P. O. Nwosu (Eds.), *Transcultural realities: Interdisciplinary perspectives on cross-cultural relations* (pp. 283–298). Thousand Oaks, CA: Sage.

McLuhan, M. (1967). *The medium is the message.* New York: Bantam Books.

Muzrui, A. (2001). Historical struggles between Islamic and Christian worldviews: An interpretation. In V. H. Milhouse, M. K. Asante, & P. O. Nwosu (Eds.), *Transcultural realities: Interdisciplinary perspectives on cross-cultural relations* (pp. 109–120). Thousand Oaks, CA: Sage.

NBA. (2008, August 7). NBA players from around the world: 2007–08 Season. NBA.com. Retrieved August 28, 2008 from http://www.nba.com/players/int_players_0708.html

Now a nation of more immigrants than ever. (2002, February 7). *Christian Science Monitor,* p. 1.

Paige, R. M., & Martin, J. N. (1996). Ethics in intercultural training. In D. Landis & R. Bhagat (Eds.), *Handbook of intercultural training* (pp. 35–60). Newbury Park, CA: Sage.

Passel, J. S., & Cohn, D. V. (2008, February 11). *U.S. populations projections: 2005–2050.* Washington, DC: Pew Research Center.

Pew Internet and American Life Project. (May–June 2005). Tracking. http://www.pewinternet.org/trends/User_Demo_08.09.05.htm

Progue, D. (2004, August 19). RUOK? A tutorial for parents. *New York Times*, p. E1.

Roediger, D. (1991). *The wages of whiteness: Race and the making of the American working class.* New York: Verso.

Rojas, V., Straubhaar, J., Roychowdhury, D., & Okur, O. (2004). Communities, cultural capital, and the digital divide. In E. P. Bucy & J. E. Newhagen (Eds.), *Media access: Social and psychological dimensions of new technology use* (pp. 107–130). Mahwah, NJ: Lawrence Erlbaum.

Samuelson, P. J. (2005). Think locally, act globally [Editorial and opinion]. *New York Sun*, p. 9.

Scanlon, J. (2003, August). 7 ways to squelch the Net. *Wired*, p. 31.

Scheer, R. (2005, September 6). The real costs of a culture of greed. *Los Angeles Times*, p. B11.

Schmitt, E. (2001, April 3). Analysis of census finds segregation along with diversity, www.nytimes.com/2001/04/04/national/04CENS.html?ex=987410510&ei=1&en=a2cf77e31f7952.

Scommegna, P. (2003). U.S. growing bigger, older and more diverse. Population Reference Bureau Web site. http://www.prb.org/Template.cfm?Section=PRB&template=/ContentManagement/ContentDisplay.cfm&ContentID=10201.

Shepard, B. (2005, April 7). International numbers grow. *Chattanooga Times Free Press*, p. D6.

Snyder, B. (2003, May). Teams that span time zones face new work rules. Stanford Graduate School of Business Web site: http://www.gsb.stanford.edu/news/bmag/sbsm0305/feature_virtual_teams.shtml

Takaki, R. (1989). *Strangers from a different shore.* New York: Penguin Books.

Ten great global marketing mistakes. (1998, January 19). *Sarasota Herald-Tribune.*

Turkle, S. (1995). *Life on the screen: Identity in the age of the Internet.* New York: Simon & Schuster.

U.S. Religious Landscape Survey. (2008). *Pew Forum on Religion and Public Life.* Retrieved May 13, 2008 from http://religions.pewforum.org/pdf/report-religious-landscape-study-full.pdf

van Dijk, J. (2004). Divides in succession: Possession, skills, and use of new media for societal participation. In E. P. Bucy & J. E. Newhagen (Eds.), *Media access: Social and psychological dimensions of new technology use* (pp. 233–254). Mahwah, NJ: Lawrence Erlbaum.

West, C. (1993). *Race matters.* Boston: Beacon Press.

Wheeler, D. (2001). New technologies, old culture: A look at women, gender and the Internet in Kuwait. In C. Ess (Ed.), *Culture, technology, communication: Towards an intercultural global village* (pp. 187–212). Albany: State University of New York Press.

Wutkowski, K. (2007, October 12). U.S. income gap widens, richest share hits record. *Reuters.* Retrieved August 29, 2008 from http://www.reuters.com/article/idUSN1241503820071012?pageNumber=1&virtualBrandChannel=0

CHAPTER

2

THE HISTORY OF
THE STUDY OF
INTERCULTURAL
COMMUNICATION

CHAPTER OBJECTIVES

After reading this chapter, you should be able to:

1. Identify four early foci in the development of intercultural communication.
2. Describe three approaches to the study of intercultural communication.
3. Identify the methods used within each of the three approaches.
4. Explain the strengths and weaknesses of each approach.
5. Identify three characteristics of the dialectical approach.
6. Explain the strengths of a dialectical approach.
7. Identify six intercultural communication dialectics.

Now that we've described a rationale for studying intercultural communication, we turn to ways in which the study of intercultural communication is conducted. To understand the contemporary approaches to this discipline, it's important to examine its historical and philosophical foundations. Why should you study how the field of intercultural communication got started? Before answering this question, let us pose a few others: Whom do you think should be regarded as an expert in intercultural communication? Someone who has actually lived in a variety of cultures? Or someone who has conducted scientific studies on how cultural groups differ in values and attitudes? Or someone who analyzes what popular culture (movies, television, magazines, and so on) has to say about a particular group of people?

Consider a related question: What is the best way to study intercultural communication behavior? By observing how people communicate in various cultures? By asking people to describe their own communication patterns? By distributing questionnaires to various cultural groups? Or by analyzing books, videos, movies, and other cultural performances of various groups?

The answers to these questions help determine what kind of material goes into a textbook on intercultural communication. And intercultural communication scholars do not agree on what are the "right" answers to these questions. Thus, these questions and answers have implications for what you will be exposed to in this book and this course. By choosing some types of research (questionnaire, observation data), we may neglect other types (interviews, travel journal, media analysis).

To help you understand why we chose to include the material we did, we describe the origins of the discipline in the United States and the philosophical worldviews that inform the current study and practices of intercultural communication. We then outline three contemporary perspectives that recognize contributions from other disciplines. Finally, we outline our dialectical approach, which integrates the strengths from all three contemporary perspectives.

THE EARLY DEVELOPMENT OF THE DISCIPLINE

The current study of intercultural communication is influenced in part by how it developed in the United States and in part by the **worldviews,** or research philosophies, of the scholars who pursue it. The roots of the study of intercultural communication can be traced to the post–World War II era, when the United States increasingly came to dominate the world stage. However, government and business personnel working overseas often found that they were ill equipped to work among people from different cultures. The language training they received, for example, did little to prepare them for the complex challenges of working abroad.

In response, the U.S. government in 1946 passed the Foreign Service Act and established the Foreign Service Institute (FSI). The FSI, in turn, hired Edward T. Hall and other prominent anthropologists and linguists (including Ray Birdwhistell and George Trager) to develop "predeparture" courses for overseas

worldview Underlying assumptions about the nature of reality and human behavior.

workers. Because intercultural training materials were scarce, they developed their own. In so doing, FSI theorists formed new ways of looking at culture and communication. Thus, the field of intercultural communication was born.

Nonverbal Communication

The FSI emphasized the importance of nonverbal communication and applied linguistic frameworks to investigate nonverbal aspects of communication. These researchers concluded that, just like language, nonverbal communication varies from culture to culture. E. T. Hall pioneered this systematic study of culture and communication with *The Silent Language* (1959) and *The Hidden Dimension* (1966), which influenced the new discipline. In *The Silent Language*, for example, Hall introduced the notion of **proxemics,** the study of how people use personal space to communicate. In *The Hidden Dimension*, in elaborating on the concept of proxemics, he identified four **distance zones**—intimate, personal, social, and public—at which people interact and suggested that people know which distance to use depending on the situation. He noted that each cultural group has its own set of rules for personal space and that respecting these cultural differences is critical to smooth communication.

Application of Theory

The staff at the FSI found that government workers were not interested in theories of culture and communication; rather, they wanted specific guidelines for getting along in the countries they were visiting. Hall's initial strategy in developing materials for these predeparture training sessions was to observe variations in cultural behavior. At the FSI, he was surrounded by people who spoke many languages and who were from many cultures, so it was a great place to observe and test his theories about cultural differences. For example, he might have observed that Italians tend to stand close to each other when conversing, or that Greeks use lots of hand gestures when interacting, or that Chinese use few hand gestures in conversations. He could then have confirmed his observations by consulting members of different cultural groups. Today, most textbooks in the discipline retain this focus on practical guidelines and barriers to communication.

This emphasis on the application of theory spawned a parallel "discipline" of **cross-cultural training,** which began with the FSI staff and was expanded in the 1960s to include training for students and business personnel. More recently, it has come to include **diversity training,** which facilitates intercultural communication among members of various gender, ethnic, and racial groups, mostly in the corporate or government workplace (Landis & Bhagat, 1996).

An Emphasis on International Settings

Early scholars and trainers in intercultural communication defined *culture* narrowly, primarily in terms of "nationality." Usually, scholars mistakenly compared middle-class U.S. citizens with all residents of other nations, and trainers tended to focus on helping middle-class professionals become successful overseas.

proxemics The study of how people use personal space.

distance zones The area, defined by physical space, within which people interact, according to Edward Hall's theory of proxemics. The four distance zones for individuals are intimate, personal, social, and public. (See also **proxemics.**)

cross-cultural training Training people to become familiar with other cultural norms and to improve their interactions with people of different domestic and international cultures.

diversity training The training meant to facilitate intercultural communication among various gender, ethnic, and racial groups in the United States.

One might ask why so few scholars focused on domestic contexts, particularly in the 1960s and 1970s when the United States was fraught with civil unrest. One reason may be the early emphasis of the FSI on helping overseas personnel. Another reason may be that most scholars who studied intercultural communication gained their intercultural experience in international contexts such as the Peace Corps, the military, or the transnational corporation.

An Interdisciplinary Focus

The scholars at the FSI came from various disciplines, including linguistics, anthropology, and psychology. Not surprisingly, in their work related to communication, they drew from theories pertinent to their specific disciplines. Contributions from these fields of study blended to form an integrated approach that remains useful to this day.

Linguists help us understand the importance of language and its role in intercultural interaction. They describe how languages vary in "surface" structure and are similar in "deep" structure. They also shed light on the relationship between language and reality. For example, the **Sapir-Whorf hypothesis,** developed by linguists Edward Sapir and Benjamin Whorf, explores phenomena such as the use of formal and informal pronouns. French and Spanish, for instance, have both formal and informal forms of the pronoun *you*. (In French, the formal is *vous* and the informal is *tu;* in Spanish, the formal is *usted* and the informal is *tu*.) In contrast, English makes no distinction between formal and informal usage; one word, *you*, suffices in both situations. Such language distinctions affect our culture's notion of formality. In Chapter 6, we'll look at some more recent studies that problematize this hypothesis. Linguists also point out that learning a second or third language can enhance our **intercultural competence** by providing insights into other cultures and expanding our communication repertoire.

Anthropologists help us understand the role that culture plays in our lives and the importance of nonverbal communication. Anthropologist Renate Rosaldo (1989) encouraged scholars to consider the appropriateness of cultural study methods, and other anthropologists have followed Rosaldo's lead. They point out that many U.S. and European studies reveal more about the researchers than about their subjects. Further, many anthropological studies of the past, particularly of non-Europeans, concluded that the people studied were inferior. To understand this phenomenon, science writer Stephen Jay Gould (1993) argues that "we must first recognize the cultural milieu of a society whose leaders and intellectuals did not doubt the propriety of racial thinking, with Indians below whites, and blacks below everyone else" (p. 85).

The so-called scientific study of other peoples is never entirely separate from the culture in which the researchers are immersed. In his study of the Victorian era, for example, Patrick Brantlinger (1986) notes that "evolutionary anthropology often suggested that Africans, if not nonhuman or a different species, were such an inferior 'breed' that they might be impervious to 'higher

Sapir-Whorf hypothesis The assumption that language shapes our ideas and guides our view of social reality. This hypothesis was proposed by Edward Sapir, a linguist, and his student, Benjamin Whorf, and represents the relativist view of language and perception.

intercultural competence The ability to behave effectively and appropriately in interacting across cultures.

influences" (p. 201). Consider this famous case, which dates back to the early 19th century:

> *The young African woman was lured to Europe with false promises of fame and fortune. She was paraded naked before jeering mobs. She was exhibited in a metal cage and sold to an animal trainer. When she died in Paris in 1816, she was penniless and friendless among people who derided her as a circus freak.*
>
> *White scientists intent on proving the inferiority of blacks dissected her body, bottled her brain and genitals, wired her skeleton and displayed them in a French museum. That might have been the end of Saartjie Baartman, the young African woman derisively labeled the "Hottentot Venus."*
>
> *[However,] 192 years after she last looked on these rugged cliffs and roaring sea [of South Africa], her remains returned to the land of her birth. In an agreement negotiated after years of wrangling between South Africa and France, her remains were finally removed from the Musée de l'Homme in Paris and flown back home. (Swarns, 2002, p. A28)*

This return of Baartman's remains is part of a larger movement away from a scientific "era when indigenous people were deemed worthy of scientific study, but unworthy of the consideration commonly accorded to whites" (Swarns, 2002, p. A28). Indeed, the conclusions from such studies reveal more about the cultural attitudes of the researchers (e.g., ethnocentrism, racism, sexism) than they do about the people studied. An **interdisciplinary** focus can help us acquire and interpret information in a more comprehensive manner—in ways relevant to bettering the intercultural communication process, as well as producing knowledge.

interdisciplinary Integrating knowledge from different disciplines in conducting research and constructing theory.

Psychologists such as Gordon Allport help us understand notions of stereotyping and the ways in which prejudice functions in our lives and in intercultural interaction. In his classic study *The Nature of Prejudice* (1979), he describes how prejudice can develop from "normal" human cognitive activities such as categorization and generalization. Other psychologists, such as Richard Brislin (1999) and Dan Landis (Landis & Wasilewski, 1999), reveal how variables like nationality, ethnicity, personality, and gender influence our communication.

Whereas the early study of intercultural communication was characterized as interdisciplinary, over time, it became increasingly centered in the discipline of communication. Nevertheless, the field continues to be influenced by interdisciplinary contributions, including ideas from cultural studies, critical theory, and the more traditional disciplines of psychology and anthropology (Hart, 1999).

In her historical overview of the ways that "culture" has been viewed in intercultural communication, communication scholar Dreama Moon (1996) noted that how culture is defined determines how it is studied. She also argues for expanding the notion of culture to include the idea of a struggle over power. So while intercultural communication is more firmly rooted in the communication field, the definition of "culture" has expanded to make intercultural communication more interdisciplinary.

As a child, I did not consciously think of myself as a German or as a Norwegian. Since I never viewed myself in terms of my culture, cultural heritage was something with which I never used to identify others. When I communicated with others, the cultural background of the person I was talking with never crossed my mind. To someone who constantly sees racism and prejudice, this situation may seem ideal, but ignoring a person's culture can cause as much harm as judging someone based upon that culture. Knowledge of someone's historical background is necessary when communicating on anything other than a superficial level.

    —Andrew

I grew up in northern Minnesota and we were very aware that we were Norwegian and not Swedish. We ate lutefisk and lefse, but we also ate American food. I really don't like lutefisk. My dad belonged to the Sons of Norway, but I think he was more interested in socializing with his friends than insisting that we learned about Norwegian culture. I don't speak Norwegian, but we always knew we were Norwegian. I guess that I mostly feel like an American, and most of the time people probably see me as white.

    —Juliann

PERCEPTION AND WORLDVIEW OF THE RESEARCHER

A second influence on the current study of intercultural communication is the research **paradigm,** or worldview, of the scholars involved. People understand and learn about the world through filtering lenses; they select, evaluate, and organize information (stimuli) from the external environment through **perception.** As Marshal Singer (1987) explains:

> *We experience everything in the world not "as it is"—because there is no way that we can know the world "as it is"—but only as the world comes to us through our sensory receptors. From there, these stimuli go instantly into the "data-storage banks" of our brains, where they have to pass through the filters of our censor screen, our decoding mechanism, and the collectivity of everything we have learned from the day we were born. (p. 9)*

In this sense, all of the information we have already stored in our brains (learning) affects how we interpret new information. Some of our learning and perception is group related. That is, we see the world in particular ways because of the cultural groups (based on ethnicity, age, gender, and so on) to which we belong. These group-related perceptions (worldviews or value orientations) are so fundamental that we rarely question them (Singer, 1998). They involve our assumptions about human nature, the physical and spiritual world, and the ways in which humans should relate to one another. For example, most U.S. Americans perceive human beings as separate from nature and believe that

paradigm A framework that serves as the worldview of researchers. Different paradigms assume different interpretations of reality, human behavior, culture, and communication.

perception The process by which individuals select, organize, and interpret external and internal stimuli to create their view of the world.

there is a fundamental difference between, say, a human and a rock. However, other cultural groups (Japanese, Chinese, traditional Native Americans) see humans and human reality as part of a larger physical reality. For them, the difference between a human and a rock is not so pronounced.

The key point here is that academic research is also cultural behavior because research traditions require particular worldviews about the nature of reality and knowledge and particular beliefs about how research should be conducted. For example, researchers studying communication often reflect their own cultural assumptions in their research projects. Asian scholars say that U.S. communication scholars often emphasize individuality and rationality—two strong cultural beliefs held by many U.S. Americans—and ignore human interdependence and feeling in human encounters, important beliefs for many people around the world (Miike, 2007a, 2007b; Gordon, 2007; Satoshi, 2007). And these research paradigms are often held as strongly as cultural or spiritual beliefs (Burrell & Morgan, 1988; Kuhn, 1970). There are even examples of intercultural conflicts in which scholars strongly disagree. For example, Galileo was excommunicated from the Catholic Church in the 17th century because he took issue with theologians' belief that the earth was the center of the universe.

More recent examples of the relation between academic research and cultural behavior can be seen in the social sciences. Some communication scholars believe there is an external reality that can be measured and studied, whereas others believe that reality can be understood only as lived and experienced by individuals (Casmir, 1994). In short, beliefs and assumptions about reality influence research methods and findings, and so also influence what we currently know about intercultural communication.

At present, we can identify three broad approaches, or worldviews, that characterize the study of culture and communication (Gudykunst, 2002a, 2002b; Gudykunst & Nishida, 1989; Hall, 1992). All three approaches involve a blend of disciplines and reflect different worldviews and assumptions about reality, human behavior, and ways to study culture and communication. As you read about each of these approaches, think about what kinds of assumptions concerning "culture" are used in each approach. How we think about "culture" influences how it is studied.

THREE APPROACHES TO STUDYING INTERCULTURAL COMMUNICATION

Three contemporary approaches to studying intercultural communication are (1) the social science (or functionalist) approach, (2) the interpretive approach, and (3) the critical approach. (See Table 2-1 and 2-2.) These approaches are based on different fundamental assumptions about human nature, human behavior, and the nature of knowledge (Burrell & Morgan, 1988). Each one contributes in a unique way to our understanding of the relationship between

TABLE 2-1   THREE APPROACHES TO INTERCULTURAL COMMUNICATION

	Social Science (or Functionalist)	Interpretive	Critical
Discipline on which approach is founded	Psychology	Anthropology, sociolinguistics	Various
Research goal	Describe and predict behavior	Describe behavior	Change behavior
Assumption of reality	External and describable	Subjective	Subjective and material
Assumptions of human behavior	Predictable	Creative and voluntary	Changeable
Method of study	Survey, observation	Participant observation, field study	Textual analysis of media
Relationship of culture and communication	Communication influenced by culture	Culture created and maintained through communication	Culture a site of power struggles
Contribution of the approach	Identifies cultural variations; recognizes cultural differences in many aspects of communication but often does not consider context	Emphasizes that communication and culture and cultural differences should be studied in context	Recognizes the economic and political forces in culture and communication; asserts that all intercultural interactions are characterized by power

culture and communication, but each also has limitations. These approaches vary in their assumptions about human behavior, their research goals, their conceptualization of culture and communication, and their preferred methodologies. As a student of intercultural communication, you may not see yourself doing research on intercultural communication issues; however, it is important to understand the assumptions behind the scholarship that is being undertaken. Think about the strengths and weaknesses of each assumption and what each approach reveals (and also hides) about other cultures and their communication patterns.

To examine these three approaches, let us start with a situation that illustrates a communication dilemma. You may remember when you first heard about Hurricane Katrina (see Figure 2-1). Perhaps it was when it was in the Atlantic, maybe when it hit Florida, maybe when it strengthened over the Gulf of Mexico or when it hit Louisiana, Mississippi, and Alabama. A second hurricane, Rita,

TABLE 2-2 THE SIGNIFICANCE OF RESEARCH APPROACHES	
Social scientific	This research style emphasizes statistical measures. Understanding quantitative approaches is critical to analyzing data and statistics. These are skills important in any walk of life.
Interpretive	Interpretive approaches emphasize using language to describe human behavior. Understanding interpretive approaches is important to understanding how news is reported, how information is transferred, and how most people make decisions.
Critical	Critical methodologies analyze the large power structures that guide everyday life. Understanding this approach helps students to grasp the invisible forces that alter our lives.

shortly followed, bringing more devastation to the Gulf Coast. Four years after September 11, 2001, the *Los Angeles Times* noted,

> *If 9/11 showed how much the world had changed, then 8/29 showed how much it hadn't. Four years ago, when terrorists crashed jets into the World Trade Center and the Pentagon, history was cleaved in half—the era before 9/11 and after. Will 8/29, the day Hurricane Katrina made landfall along the Gulf Coast, prove to be a similar demarcation line? The answer is complicated by the slow realization, with each anniversary, that 9/11 did not change the world (or America) as much as we thought. The response to Katrina, from both the government and the public, is the best illustration. ("9/11 and 8/29," 2005)*

The federal, state, and local government response to the needs of those affected by the hurricanes was highlighted by communication about these events on television, the Internet, and blogs. Communication played a key role in shaping our understanding of these events. Howard Kurtz of the *Washington Post* noted, "Journalism seems to have recovered its reason for being. As in the weeks after 9/11, news organizations have plunged into the calamity in New Orleans, with reporters chronicling heartbreaking stories under harrowing conditions in a submerged city" (2005, p. C1). Similarly, the British Broadcasting Corporation reported that "good reporting lies at the heart of what is changing. But unlike Watergate, 'Katrinagate' was public service journalism ruthlessly exposing the truth on a live and continuous basis. [. . .] Amidst the horror, American broadcast journalism just might have grown its spine back, thanks to Katrina" (Wells, 2005). The kind of journalism that emerged in the wake of Katrina recentered the importance of communication in our national discussions, along with "bloggers who have organized aid drives for Katrina's victims" (Kurtz, 2005, p. C1). Many people watched television news; read magazines and newspapers, as well as Internet blogs and e-mails; listened to the radio; and talked with family and friends to get a better understanding of what was going on. We read e-mails from colleagues at universities in the New Orleans area and read their reports.

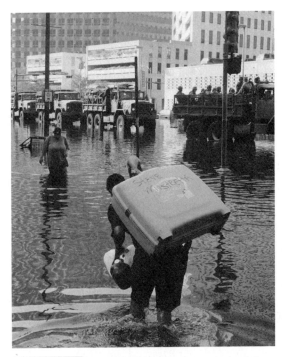

FIGURE 2-1   It may be difficult to understand the various meanings of the aftermath of Hurricane Katrina. In this photo, people are trying to make their way to safety while the National Guard comes into New Orleans. How would you study the meanings of Katrina? What kinds of questions can you ask from each paradigm? What kinds of questions can't be asked from each paradigm? (© *Bill Haber/Associated Press, AP*)

Many of those in New Orleans turned to WWL-AM as it turned to serving New Orleans with reports of lost people, trapped people who called into the radio station, and generally people who "needed to communicate with one another: to seek or offer help, to criticize this agency or praise that one, to vent, cry, reassure or just find comfort in the soothing radio voice of someone who has shared their loss" (Barry, 2005).

The events surrounding the hurricanes are another example of intercultural communication interaction that offers useful insights into how we might think about intercultural communication and the ways that different cultural groups understood what happened and why. In analyzing Hurricane Katrina, we will also outline the characteristics of the three approaches to studying intercultural communication—both contributions and limitations.

The Social Science Approach

social science
approach See **func-
tionalist approach.**

functionalist
approach A study of
intercultural communica-
tion, also called the *social
science approach,* based
on the assumptions that
(1) there is a describable,
external reality, (2) human
behaviors are predict-
able, and (3) culture is a
variable that can be mea-
sured. This approach aims
to identify and explain
cultural variations in communication and to predict
future communication.
(Compare with **critical
approach** and **interpretive approach.**)

quantitative
methods Research
methods that use
numerical indicators to
capture and ascertain
the relationships
among variables. These
methods use survey and
observation.

variable A concept
that varies by existing in
different types or different
amounts and that can
be operationalized and
measured.

The **social science approach** (also called the **functionalist approach**), popular in the 1980s, is based on research in psychology and sociology. This approach assumes a describable external reality. It also assumes that human behavior is predictable and that the researcher's goal is to describe and predict behavior. Researchers who take this approach often use **quantitative methods,** gathering data by administering questionnaires or observing subjects firsthand.

Social science researchers assume that culture is a **variable** that can be measured. This suggests that culture influences communication in much the same way that personality traits do. The goal of this research, then, is to predict specifically how culture influences communication.

Applications   Other social scientists might investigate some of the perceived reasons for the response of local, state, and federal officials to the hurricane and then try to frame appropriate action based on these findings. For instance, they might measure differences in perception among various cultural groups to try to understand how different cultures experienced Katrina and what they view as appropriate and inappropriate responses by the government. In this type of study, social scientists would be using culture as a variable to measure these differences while focusing on the perceptions that are widely held in a particular culture. To understand the aftermath of Hurricane Katrina, social scientists might try to measure how African Americans and whites viewed the government response. One study done on September 6–7, 2005, about a week after the hurricane, found that 70% of African Americans felt angry, whereas only 46% of whites felt angry (Kohut et al., 2005). In this same study, 66% of African Americans felt the government response would have been faster if the victims had been white, whereas only 17% of whites shared this view. Based on these differences, social scientists might then try to predict how these different views may influence future differences in political views and conflicts between these groups.

Or social scientists might study what kinds of communication media people used after the hurricane and how they used them. In this same study, the researchers found that "television, and cable news channels in particular, are the main sources of news for most Americans during a crisis, and that was again the case for Hurricane Katrina" (Kohut et al., 2005, p. 7). CNN was most cited as the main source of their news at 31%, whereas newspapers, radio, and the Internet all fell in the ratings compared to their use in more normal circumstances. Two-thirds gave favorable ratings of the media coverage that "is considerably more favorable than the public's ratings a year ago for press coverage of the presidential election campaign" (p. 7). This kind of study tries to see trends in communication usage and can then predict that people will again turn to cable television, particularly CNN, for news when a similar crisis situation emerges.

Other contemporary research programs illustrate the social science approach. One such program was headed by William Gudykunst, a leading communication researcher. Gudykunst was interested in whether people from different cultures varied in their strategies for reducing uncertainty on first encounter. He found that strategies varied depending on whether people were from **individualistic** or **collectivistic** cultures (Gudykunst, 1985, 1988). For example, many people in the United States, which has an individualistic orientation, ask direct questions when interacting with acquaintances. In cultures with a more collectivistic orientation, such as Japan and China, people are more likely to use an indirect approach.

Social scientists are interested in predicting human behavior, and each of these theories tries to predict intercultural communication interaction by emphasizing different aspects of the process, as well as different points in the process. In focusing on initial encounters with others, Gudykunst (1998, 2005) later extended his theory to include the element of anxiety and mindfulness in the **anxiety uncertainty management** (AUM) **theory,** which explains the role of anxiety and uncertainty in individuals' communicating with host culture members when they enter a new culture. The theory suggests certain optimal levels of uncertainty and anxiety motivate individuals to engage in successful interaction. This theory is explained further in Chapter 8.

A related social science program is Stella Ting-Toomey's (1985, 2005) **face negotiation theory.** *Face* is the sense of favorable self-worth, and in all cultures people are concerned about saving face. Ting-Toomey suggests that conflict is a face negotiation process in which people often have their face threatened or questioned. She and her colleagues have conducted a number of studies in which they try to identify how cultures differ in conflict style and face concerns. For example, they found that members of individualistic societies like the United States are concerned with saving their own face in conflict situations and so use more dominating conflict resolution styles. In contrast, members of collectivistic cultures, like China, South Korea, and Taiwan, are more concerned with saving the other person's face in conflict situations and use more avoiding, obliging, or integrating conflict resolution styles (Ting-Toomey et al., 1991; Ting-Toomey, 2005). More recent research shows that Latino and Asian Americans in the United States use more avoiding and third-party conflict styles than African Americans and more than do European Americans (Ting-Toomey, Yee-Jung, Shapiro, Garcia, Wright, & Oetzel, 2000).

Another social science research program focuses on cultural differences conversational strategies. In contrast to AUM, **conversational constraints theory,** developed by Min-Sun Kim (2005), attempts to explain how and why people make particular conversational choices. It suggests five universal conversational constraints, or concerns: (1) clarity, (2) minimizing imposition, (3) consideration for the other's feelings, (4) risking negative evaluation by the hearer, and (5) effectiveness. Kim and her colleagues have discovered that people from individualistic and collectivistic cultures place varying importance on these various conversational concerns. Individualists seem to be most concerned with clarity; collectivists, with concerns about hurting the other's feelings and minimizing imposition. Concerns for effectiveness and avoidance of negative evaluation by others seem to be universally important (Kim, 1994, 2005).

individualistic The tendency to emphasize individual identities, beliefs, needs, goals, and views rather than those of the group. (Compare with **collectivistic.**)

collectivistic The tendency to focus on the goals, needs, and views of the ingroup rather than individuals' own goals, needs, and views. (Compare with **individualistic.**)

anxiety uncertainty management theory The view that the reduction of anxiety and uncertainty plays an important role in successful intercultural communication, particularly when experiencing new cultures.

face negotiation theory The view that cultural groups vary in preferences for conflict styles and face-saving strategies.

conversational constraints theory The view that cultural groups vary in their fundamental concerns regarding how conversational messages should be constructed.

Especially in times of tragedy, people use humor to cope with overwhelming events. Communication of this kind helps to create bounds and coping strategies among people.

washingtonpost.com
HUMOR HELPS HURRICANE KATRINA VICTIMS COPE

By MATT SEDENSKY
The Associated Press
Saturday, October 22, 2005; 2:43 PM

ARABI, La. — The grimy residue of receded floodwater covered the blue Chevrolet pickup parked outside a shattered two-story house, but the offer spray-painted on the vehicle in white overflowed with enthusiasm: "For Sale. Like New. Runs Great."

The tongue-in-cheek sale pitch in this New Orleans suburb is evidence that Hurricanes Katrina and Rita didn't necessarily destroy victims' sense of humor, which is surfacing in signs painted on wrecked homes and on bumper stickers and inevitable T-shirts.

It jumps out from an Arabi auto glass shop: "Katrina was bad. The old lady and the dogs were more trouble."

And from a refrigerator left on a French Quarter street: "Loot this!!!!"

The drink offerings at popular eatery Bacco's now include "Katrina Rita," "Cat 5 Hurricane," and "Curfew & Coke."

communication accommodation theory The view that individuals adjust their verbal communication to facilitate understanding.

The **communication accommodation theory** is the result of another social science program in which researchers attempted to identify how and when individuals accommodate their speech and nonverbal behavior to others during an interaction. Unlike AUM and conversational constraints theory, communication accommodation theory focuses on adaptation during intercultural interaction. The researchers posited that in some situations individuals change their communication patterns to accommodate others (Gallois, Giles, Jones, Cargile, & Ota, 1995). Specifically, individuals are likely to adapt during low-threat interactions or situations in which they see little difference between themselves and others. The underlying assumption is that we accommodate when we feel positive toward the other person. For example, when we talk to international students, we may speak more slowly, enunciate more clearly, use less jargon, and mirror their communication. We also may adapt to regional speech. For example, when Tom talks with someone from the South, he sometimes starts to drawl and use words like "y'all." Of course, it is possible to overaccommodate. For example, if a white

Elsewhere, bumper stickers and T-shirts are available with the saying "Make levees not war."

Another T-shirt picks on a popular target: "Where is FEMA? Federal Employees Missing Again."

"It's been known for a long time one of the best coping mechanisms we have is humor," said Kathryn Kirkhart, a clinical psychologist who has been working with evacuees in New Orleans. "It's best used in situations where we have no control."

Some anonymous jokesters have chosen subtlety: "Garage Sale. Shoes. Games. Toys," says a sign posted along a driveway that leads to a foundation where only the barest traces of the garage are still attached.

A house that floated off its foundation came to rest at the side of 38-year-old Philip Troxclair's house. Another house is at the end of the driveway, decorated with the phrase "Wicked witch of the East was here."

"Thank you Katrina," deadpans a sign painted in blue on a hard-hit, one-level brick house.

Friday night in the French Quarter, a musician taking a break between songs at a restaurant blurted out: "We're all trying here in New Orleans to get back to abnormal."

Note: Associated Press Writers Ross Sneyd and John Christoffersen contributed to this report. © 2005 The Associated Press

Source: From http://www.washingtonpost.com/wpdyn/content/article/2005/10/22/AR2005102200690_pf.html.

American speaks black English to an African American, this may be perceived as overaccommodation.

The **diffusion of innovations theory,** developed by communication scholar Everett Rogers (2003), explains how cultural practices can be changed—largely due to communication. This theory explains why some innovations, like computer technology of the Internet, or certain behaviors, like "safe sex," are accepted by some people and rejected by others. The theory posits that in order for people to accept a new technology, they have to see the usefulness of it and it has to be compatible with their values and lifestyle. Communication also plays a key role; usually people first learn of innovations through impersonal channels—like mass media—but only decide to adopt an innovation later, after asking the opinion or observing the behavior of someone who is known, trusted, or considered an expert—an "opinion leader." If people important to the individual (e.g., peers for adolescents) adopt the innovation first, then the individual is more likely to adopt it. Opinion leaders can also be responsible for innovations *not* diffusing, if they ignore or speak out against an

diffusion of innovations theory The view that communication and relationships play important roles in how new ideas are adopted (or not) by individuals and groups.

innovation. There seems to be a predictable, over-time pattern for the spread of an innovation, first to early adopters and then to many more individuals (Singhal & Dearing, 2006).

Many social science studies explain how communication styles vary from culture to culture. Dean Barnlund (Barnlund & Yoshioka, 1990), a well-known intercultural communication scholar, compared Japanese and U.S. communication styles. He identified many differences, including how members of the two groups give compliments and offer apologies. Although people in both countries seem to prefer a simple apology, U.S. Americans tend to apologize (and compliment) more often; further, Japanese prefer to *do* something, whereas Americans tend to *explain* as a way to apologize.

Another group of social science studies investigated how travelers adapted overseas. In trying to predict which travelers would be the most successful, the researchers found that a variety of factors—including age, gender, language, preparation level, and personality characteristics—played a role (Kim, 2001).

Strengths and Limitations   Many of these social science studies have been useful in identifying variations in communication from group to group and specifying psychological and sociological variables in the communication process. However, this approach is limited. Many scholars now realize that human communication is often more creative than predictable and that reality is not just external but also internally constructed. We cannot identify all of the variables that affect our communication. Nor can we predict exactly why one intercultural interaction seems to succeed and another does not.

Scholars also recognize that some methods in this approach are not culturally sensitive and that researchers may be too distant from the phenomena or people they are researching. In other words, researchers may not really understand the cultural groups they are studying. For example, suppose we conducted a study that compared self-disclosure in the United States and Algeria using the social science perspective. We might distribute Jourard's self-disclosure measure (a common instrument used in U.S. research) to students in both countries. However, we might not realize that the concept of self-disclosure does not translate exactly between the United States and Algeria, and that Algerians and U.S. Americans have different notions of this concept.

translation equivalence The linguistic sameness that is gained after translating and back-translating research materials several times using different translators. (See also **conceptual equivalence.**)

To overcome these kinds of problems, social scientists have developed strategies for achieving equivalence of measures. A leading cross-cultural psychologist, Richard Brislin (1999), has written extensively on guidelines for cross-cultural researchers. He has identified several types of equivalencies that researchers should establish, including **translation equivalence** and **conceptual equivalence.** For example, in cross-cultural studies, literal translations are inadequate. To establish translation equivalence, research materials should be translated several times, using different translators. Materials that proceed smoothly through these multiple steps are considered translation equivalent.

conceptual equivalence The similarity of linguistic terms and meanings across cultures. (See also **translation equivalence.**)

In Chapter 6, we explore issues of translation in more detail; however, the advances in machine translation have been impressive. While computer translation cannot yet match human translators, machine translation has vastly improved. The European Union has been a major force behind these improvements, as well as in the goals of machine translation:

> *Machine translation has been an elusive goal since the earliest days of computer science. The Pentagon poured millions of dollars into efforts to get computers to translate Russian sentences into English. But disillusionment set in the 1960s when it became clear that producing results indistinguishable from a human translator wasn't going to happen soon, if ever. The major obstacles were not computational but linguistic. The missing ingredient was a fuller understanding of language itself.*
>
> *That is still true. But computational linguists are nowadays making greater strides by being less ambitious (Mark my words, 2007).*

Machine translation can be enormously helpful for common phrases and rough drafts, but these translations cannot yet do away with humans. Advances are being made rapidly and, as the databases increase, the computer-generated translations will improve.

Researchers can establish conceptual equivalence by ensuring that the notions they are investigating are similar at various levels. For example, problem solving is one aspect of intelligence that may be conceptually equivalent in many cultures. Once this equivalence is established, researchers can identify culture-specific ways in which problem solving is achieved. In the United States and western Europe, good problem solving might mean quick cognitive reasoning; in other cultures, it might involve slow and careful thought (Serpell, 1982). Establishing these equivalencies allows researchers to isolate and describe what distinguishes one culture from another.

The Interpretive Approach

The **interpretive approach** gained prominence in the late 1980s among communication scholars. One interpretive approach, rooted in sociolinguistics, is the **ethnography** of communication (Hymes, 1974). Ethnographers of communication are devoted to descriptive studies of communication patterns within specific cultural groups. Interpretive researchers assume not only that reality is external to humans but also that humans construct reality. They believe that human experience, including communication, is subjective and human behavior is neither predetermined nor easily predicted.

The goal of interpretive research is to understand and describe human behavior. (Predicting behavior is not a goal.) Whereas the social scientist tends to see communication as influenced by culture, the interpretivist sees culture as created and maintained through communication (Carbaugh, 1996). This type of research uses **qualitative methods** derived from anthropology and linguistics such as field studies, observations, and participant observations. An example is shown in Figure 2-2. (A researcher engaging in **participant observation** contributes actively to the communication processes being observed and studied. The researcher thus is intimately involved in the research and may become good friends with members of the communities he or she is studying.)

interpretive approach An approach to intercultural communication that aims to understand and describe human behavior within specific cultural groups based on the assumptions that (1) human experience is subjective, (2) human behavior is creative rather than determined or easily predicted, and (3) culture is created and maintained through communication. (Compare with **critical approach** and **functionalist approach**.)

ethnography A discipline that examines the patterned interactions and significant symbols of specific cultural groups to identify the cultural norms that guide their behaviors, usually based on field studies.

qualitative methods Research methods that attempt to capture people's own meanings for their everyday behavior in specific contexts. These methods use participant observation and field studies.

participant observation A research method where investigators interact extensively with the cultural group being studied.

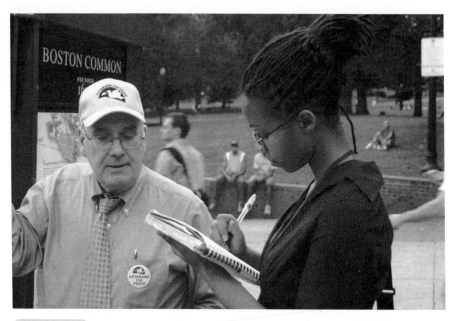

One way to study and learn about cultural patterns is to interview other people, which is this woman's approach. What are the strengths and weaknesses of interviewing as a research strategy? (© *Digital Vision/Alamy*)

rhetorical approach A research method, dating back to ancient Greece, in which scholars try to interpret the meanings or persuasion used in texts or oral discourses in the contexts in which they occur.

etic A term stemming from *phonetic*. The etic inquiry searches for universal generalizations across cultures from a distance. (Compare with **emic**.)

emic A term stemming from *phonemic*. The emic way of inquiry focuses on understanding communication patterns from inside a particular cultural community or context. (Compare with **etic**.)

Another example of interpretive research is the **rhetorical approach,** perhaps the oldest communication scholarship, dating back to the ancient Greeks. Rhetoricians typically examine and analyze texts or public speeches in the contexts in which they occur.

Cross-cultural psychologists use the terms **etic** and **emic** to distinguish the social science and interpretive approaches (Berry, 1997). These terms were borrowed from linguistics—*etic* from *phonetic* and *emic* from *phonemic*. Social science research usually searches for universal generalizations and studies cultures objectively, with an "outsider's" view; in this way, it is "etic." In contrast, interpretive research usually focuses on understanding phenomena subjectively, from within a particular cultural community or context; in this way, it is "emic." These researchers try to describe patterns or rules that individuals follow in specific contexts. They tend to be more interested in describing cultural behavior in one community than in making cross-cultural comparisons.

Applications   How might an interpretive researcher investigate the various meanings given to the hurricane events? One possible approach would be to interview people who were in the Gulf Coast and experienced the hurricane, as well as those people who watched the media coverage but did not live in the affected areas. From these interviews, as well as conversations with others, the researcher might gain insight into a variety of potential responses. For

I was shocked to see so much poverty after Hurricane Katrina. I knew about racism and poverty in America, but I didn't really see it until I saw the people needing help. I didn't see many white people in the crowds. They must have left earlier.
   —Didier

I was surprised that more people didn't leave New Orleans before the hurricane. After all, they know that their city is below sea level. I know that some of them are poor, but I don't think it's fair to blame FEMA for the hurricane. If you choose to live in a city like that, you have to be prepared for Mother Nature.
   —Debra

Hurricane Katrina shows how much poverty still exists in the richest country in the world. While we see rich people on television all the time, we can overlook the poverty and the racism in this country. I hope that we do not forget that there are many poor African Americans in the United States and our responsibilities to all of our citizens.
   —Brent

example, in the weeks after Katrina, many of the people from the Gulf Coast were evacuated across the nation. An interpretive researcher might interview them about their experiences and their adaptation to their new environment. One reporter noted, " 'The people are so nice, but this place is really strange to me,' said Desiree Thompson, who arrived in Albuquerque last Sunday with six of her children and two grandchildren, along with about 100 other evacuees. 'The air is different. My nose feels all dry. The only thing I've seen that looks familiar is the McDonald's' " (Egan, 2005, pp. A1, A32). Many will have to decide if they wish to stay or move on, but the adaptation issues they face can be explored by an interpretive researcher to see how they make sense of their new environments, environmental differences as well as demographic differences.

Other interpretive researchers may want to focus on the rich oral culture of Louisiana and interview many who experienced Hurricane Katrina and/or Rita. One reporter after talking to survivors writes, "The disaster was incremental rather than cataclysmic. Instead of a crystalline moment of memory, there are infinite numbers, each with its own marker: a long journey, a recurring noise, the last words of a dear relative. Depending on where people were, what decisions they made in the blur of the crisis and how the authorities responded, every portrait of the storm is different, like a jigsaw puzzle in which no two pieces are alike" (Johnson, 2005, p. A25).

Some interpretive studies investigate the language patterns in many different groups—from the Burundi in Africa, to the Athabascan in northern Canada, to various groups within the United States, such as urban blacks or Cajuns. Other interpretive studies investigate the different communication patterns of one cultural group. For example, communication scholar Gerry Philipsen

Michael Brown, former director of the Federal Emergency Management Agency (FEMA), came under tremendous fire for the response of his agency to the aftermath of Hurricane Katrina. Later, a series of e-mails sent to Brown from his FEMA agent in New Orleans and Brown's responses were posted on the Web site of Louisiana representative Charles Melancon at http:// www.melancon.house.gov/SupportingFiles/documents/Brown_Emails.pdf.

These e-mails point to the importance of communication, especially e-mail and the Internet, in helping better understand how communication shaped the federal response. Think about how a social scientist, an interpretivist, and a critical scholar might study these e-mails.

For example, on August 31, 2005, Marty Bahamonde, the FEMA agent in New Orleans, wrote this e-mail:

```
From:           Brown, Michael D
Sent:           Wednesday, August 31, 2005 12:24 PM
To:             'Marty.Bahamonde@dhs.gov'
Subject:        Re: New orleans


Thanks for update. Anything specific I need to do or tweak?


-----Original Message-----
From: Bahamonde, Marty <Marty.Bahamonde@dhs.gov>
To: 'michael.d.brown@dhs.gov' <Michael.D.Brown@dhs.gov>
Sent: Wed Aug 31 12:20:20 2005
Subject: New orleans

Sir, I know that you know the situation is past critical. Here some things you might not know.
Hotels are kicking people out, thousands gathering in the streets with no food or water.
Hundreds still being rescued from homes.

The dying patients at the DMAT tent being medivac. Estimates are many will die within hours. Evacuation in process. Plans developing for dome evacuation but hotel situation adding to problem. We are out of food and running out of water at the dome, plans in works to address the critical need.

FEMA staff is OK and holding own. DMAT staff working in deplorable conditions. The sooner we can get the medical patients out, the sooner wecan get them out.

Phone connectivity impossible

More later
--------------------------
Sent from my BlackBerry Wireless Handheld
```

(1990) studied communication patterns in a white working-class neighborhood of Chicago called Teamsterville. Philipsen discovered that men in this community consider speaking to be important only in some situations. For example, Teamsterville men speak when expressing male solidarity but not when asserting power and influence in interpersonal situations. That is, they are more likely to talk when they are with their equals—their buddies—than when they are with their children or with authority figures. With superiors or subordinates, other forms of communication are appropriate. With children, for example, they are more likely to use gestures or disciplinary action than speech. When they are with someone of higher status, such as a school principal, they may seek out a mediator (e.g., the neighborhood priest) rather than speak directly to the principal.

In more recent ethnography of communication studies, Donal Carbaugh (1999) describes the important role of silence and listening in Blackfeet (American Indian) communication; Carbaugh and Berry (2001) describe the tendency of Finns to be rather reserved in communication. More importantly, they show how these communication patterns are inextricably tied to cultural identities in these communities (Carbaugh, 1996).

A number of interpretive scholars have emphasized that descriptions of the communication rules of a given people must be grounded in their beliefs and values. Most scholarly studies of communication are rooted in a European American perspective, and this frame of references is not necessarily applicable to communication of all cultural groups. For example, Molefi Asante (1987, 2001) developed the framework of **Afrocentricity** to apply to studies about African or African American communication. He identifies five cultural themes shared by peoples of African descent:

Afrocentricity An orientation toward African or African American cultural standards, including beliefs and values, as the criteria for interpreting behaviors and attitudes.

- A common origin and experience of struggle
- An element of resistance to European legal procedures, medical practices, and political processes
- Traditional values of humaneness and harmony with nature
- A fundamentally African way of knowing and interpreting the world
- An orientation toward communalism

Communication scholars have used this framework to understand various aspects of contemporary African American communication. For example, Thurmon Garner (1994) stresses the strong oral tradition of African Americans and identifies rhetorical patterns such as indirection, improvisation and inventiveness, and playfully toned behavior. These patterns underlay communication in many African American contexts, including rapping, playing the dozens (an aggressive verbal contest, often involving obscene language), and signifying (the verbal art of insult, in which a speaker jokingly talks about, needles, and puts down the listener).

Similarly, Asian scholars have developed Asiacentric frameworks to study communication of people from Asian cultures. Communication scholar Yoshitaka Miike (2003, 2004) has identified five Asiacentric themes (circularity, harmony, other-directedness, reciprocity, and relationality). Based on these themes, he developed five propositions on human communication. Communication is a process in which

- We remind ourselves of the interdependence and interrelatedness of the universe.
- We reduce our selfishness and egocentrism.

- We feel the joy and suffering of all beings.
- We receive and return our debts to all beings.
- We moralize and harmonize the universe.

From this Asiacentric framework, other scholars are developing specific communication theories, for example, a Chinese model of human relationship development (Chen, 1998) and a Buddhist consciousness-only model of intrapersonal communication (Ishii, 2004).

It is important to remember that scholars like Asante and Miike are not suggesting that these culture-specific frameworks are superior or should replace the traditional Eurocentric models, only that that they are not inferior.

Another important interpretive theory, a communication theory of identity, was developed by Michael Hecht (1993). He argues that communication is a communicative process and our identities emerge in relationships with others and are expressed in core symbols, meaning, and labels. He also contends there are four identity frames: personal, enacted, relational, and communal. These frames help us interpret reality and understand the social world. We discuss this theory further in Chapter 5.

Several scholars have used this framework to understand the identities of various cultural groups. For example, Mark Orbe (2004) conducted a recent study investigating how first-generation college students negotiated this identity—using the four frames in Hecht's identity theory. Through interviewing the students, he discovered that their identities as first-generation college students clearly emerged as personal (in the pressure to succeed and in the economic hardships they experienced), enacted, and relational (in their experiences with friends and families, who often give them special attention). However, they did not seem to develop a communal identity—they did not really know or interact with other groups of first-generation college students.

In a related study, Saskia Witteborn (2004) used this theory to understand how some Arab women changed the expression of their identity after 9/11. Through extensive interviews, she found that before September 11, the women referred to themselves mainly with their communal identities as Arab, Palestinian, or Arab American. And one of the core symbols related to this communal label was family. After September 11, the women emphasized their national identities, and the core symbol of family was expanded to include social relationships in a community organization.

Strengths and Limitations   The utility of the interpretivist approach is that it provides an in-depth understanding of communication patterns in particular communities because it emphasizes investigating communication in context. Thus, for example, we learn more about African American communication in religious contexts and more about popular U.S. communication in talk show contexts than we would by distributing questionnaires with general questions on African American or European American communication.

The main limitation of this approach is that there are few interpretivist studies of *intercultural* communication. Interpretive scholars typically have not studied what happens when two groups come in contact with each other. However, there are some comparative studies, including Charles Braithwaite's (1990), which compares rules for silence in 15 different communities, and Hammer and Rogan's (2002) study comparing how Latino and Indochinese view and negotiate conflict with law enforcement officers.

A second limitation is that the researchers often are outsiders to the communities under investigation, which means they may not represent accurately the communication patterns of members of that community. For example, Fred Jandt and Dolores Tanno (2001) recount the dilemma of many marginalized cultural groups who have been studied by outsiders who characterize the group rather erroneously and negatively. A number of scholars, members of these groups, are now trying to rewrite these cultural descriptions. One of these is Tuhiwai Smith (1999), a Maori scholar, who lists the words used to describe her people in anthropological accounts: not civilized, not literate, incapable of inventing, creating, or imagining, and not fully human. After analyzing the impact of these negative labels, she makes arguments for insider research and develops an indigenous research agenda and process—part of a movement by peoples throughout the world who have too long been explained by outsiders and have been offered no opportunity to explain themselves. One of her contributions is a Maori-based code of conduct for ethnographic researchers:

- A respect for people
- Presenting yourself face-to-face
- Look, listen . . . speak
- Share and host people, be generous
- Do not flaunt your knowledge

Jandt and Tanno conclude that this ethical code should apply to all those who study groups of people who traditionally have been the object of study rather than participants in research.

The Critical Approach

A third approach to the study of intercultural communication includes many assumptions of the interpretive approach. For instance, researchers who use the **critical approach** believe in subjective (as opposed to objective) and material reality. They also emphasize the importance of studying the context in which communication occurs—that is, the situation, background, or environment. However, critical researchers usually focus on **macrocontexts,** such as the political and social structures that influence communication. Critical scholars, unlike most social scientists and interpretivists, are interested in the historical context of communication (Delgado, 2002; Putnam & Pacanowsky, 1983). (See Figure 2-3.)

Critical scholars are interested in the power relations in communication. For them, identifying cultural differences in communication is important only in relation to power differentials. In this perspective, culture is, in essence, a

critical approach A metatheoretical approach that includes many assumptions of the interpretive approach but that focuses more on macrocontexts, such as the political and social structures that influence communication. (Compare with **interpretive approach** and **functionalist approach.**)

macrocontexts The political, social, and historical situations, backgrounds, and environments that influence communication.

FIGURE 2-3   This photo of Louisiana Governor Kathleen Blanco (left) and FEMA director Michael Brown (right) highlights the importance of communication in helping to shape our understanding of the response to Hurricane Katrina. How might each of the paradigms study these communication messages and their influence in shaping the response to Hurricane Katrina? (© *Jocelyn Augustino/Corbis*)

battleground—a plan where multiple interpretations come together but a dominant force always prevails. The goal of critical researchers is not only to understand human behavior but also to change the lives of everyday communicators. Researchers assume that by examining and reporting how power functions in cultural situations, they can help the average person learn how to resist forces of power and oppression.

textual analysis Examination of cultural texts such as media—television, movies, journalistic essays, and so on.

The methods preferred by critical scholars are usually **textual analyses,** which sometimes occur within the economic contexts of the culture industries that produce these texts. That is, the scholars generally analyze cultural "products," such as media (television, movies, journals, and so on), as powerful voices in shaping contemporary culture, rather than observing or participating in face-to-face interactions or conducting surveys.

Applications   In analyzing the aftermath of the hurricanes that swept the Gulf Coast, a critical scholar might try to situate the attacks within a larger cultural struggle that has much longer history than simply the hurricanes that roared through the Gulf. *Newsweek* noted that Katrina put the image of the United States on the world stage again: "It takes a hurricane, it takes a catastrophe like Katrina to strip away the old evasions, hypocrisies and not-so-benign neglect. It takes the sight of the United States with a big black eye—visible around the world—to help the rest of us begin to see again [see Figure 2-3]. For the moment, at least,

Americans are ready to fix their restless gaze on enduring problems of poverty, race and class that have escaped their attention" (Alter, 2005, p. 42).

Communication scholar Marita Sturken (2005) looked at the Department of Homeland Security (DHS) public service ad campaign and concludes,

> *Government campaigns that sell the idea of individual preparedness operate to reassure citizens that the government is doing everything it can to keep the country safe. Thus, the emphasis in the DHS campaigns on how individuals should respond to a crisis elides the fact that individuals and families can do little to affect the most important security decisions of the country. [. . .] The disaster of Katrina has dramatically exposed the way that resources have been drained away from the "homeland" by the war in Iraq. The homeland, we learned from Katrina, is primarily at risk not from the weather or from foreign terrorists, but from its own failed infrastructure and its callous disregard for the rights of all citizens to the most basic of human needs.*

Thrust on to the world stage, the international image of the United States was up for discussion. The British Broadcasting Corporation wondered why, in this time of need, did the food donations from Britain, France, Germany, Russia, and Spain get turned down because of U.S. legalities ("Why Was UK's Katrina Aid Rejected by the US?," 2005). One French magazine, *L'Express,* played off the Steinbeck novel *The Grapes of Wrath* and pointed to the "grapes of poverty" and underscored the tremendous poverty and neglect in New Orleans before the hurricanes (Coste, 2005). Similarly, the French newspaper *Le Monde* reported on "The Third World in Louisiana," noting that "After Katrina, America interrogates the weaknesses of its model" (Dhombres, 2005). Another commentator for *Le Monde* asks, "Four years after the attacks of September 11, 2001 which disrupted American foreign policy, has Hurricane Katrina also had such a profound effect, but in the opposite sense?" (Vernet, 2005).

At the same time, however, the *New York Times* offered a different view from Paris: "The French news media were captivated by Hurricane Katrina, pointing out how the American government's faltering response brought into plain view the sad lot of black Americans. But this time the French, who have long criticized America's racism, could not overlook the parallels at home" (Tagliabue, 2005, p. A4). In light of the riots that broke out in the fall of 2005, a *New York Times* writer noted: "Just two months ago, the French watched in horrified fascination at the anarchy of New Orleans, where members of America's underclass were seen looting stores and defying the police in the wake of Hurricane Katrina. Last week, as rioters torched cars and trashed businesses in the immigrant-concentrated suburbs of Paris, the images of wild gangs of young men silhouetted against the yellow flames of burning cars came as an unwelcome reminder for France that it has its own growing underclass" (C. S. Smith, 2005, sec. 4, p. 3). Thus, the struggle over the image of each nation is, in part, fought out in the press.

A critical scholar might also look at the struggle over the maintenance of Creole culture that has lost its geographical base: "The Creoles have been more distinctly connected to a place—New Orleans—than perhaps any other American ethnic group but their rural Louisiana neighbors, the Cajuns. But unlike the Cajuns, who settled in Louisiana after being expelled from Canada by the British, the Creoles lived in the birthplace of their culture" (Saulny, 2005). Some people fear the loss of this cultural identity after the hurricane dispersed them across the nation. Others predict that this dispersal will make them stronger. By watching how they rebuild their cultural community, what communication media they use, and what resources and barriers they encounter, a critical scholar can situate the rebirth of this cultural community within the larger social structure of the United States. A critical scholar might ask if the pressure from other U.S. Americans and institutions to assimilate will overwhelm their attempts to hang on to their unique culture.

Similarly, a critical scholar might focus on how different cultural groups are responding to Hurricanes Katrina and Rita by looking at the ways that different media are covering Katrina. The anger in the African American news is very clear in the editorial pages. For example, *Amsterdam News*, an African American newspaper in New York City, wrote, "We will be told again that this has nothing to do with race or economic circumstance, but by an accident of history. Black Americans, white Americans who have a vision about what America is to become, should not allow this big lie to sit there like a 'Raisin in the Sun.' Black people know that there is little regard for them and for their lives here in America" (Tatum, 2005). Another African American newspaper, the *Chicago Defender*, in a guest editorial, noted, "Bush's poll free-fall or dip is chalked up to his comatose response to Katrina disaster relief, the horrific scenes of poor Blacks fleeing for their lives in New Orleans, and his walk on eggshell reaction to William Bennett's foot-in-the mouth racial slur. Whether Bush actually skidded to rock bottom, or simply skidded in the ratings, it mattered little" (Hutchinson, 2005).

Asian Week, an Asian American newspaper, focused on the "tens of thousands [of Vietnamese Americans who] lived along the Louisiana and Mississippi coasts. Most of them worked in shrimping, shipbuilding and operating convenience stores" (Tang, 2005). This newspaper focused on the stories of these Asian Americans: "Kim Vu was a member of the Queen Mary of Vietnam church in Versailles, Louisiana. About 300 members of the church were stranded in the church for days in neck-deep floodwater. For days, rescue helicopters flew missions around New Orleans, but did not rescue the church-full of Vietnamese Americans" (Tang, 2005), which may not have been covered by the mainstream media. Yet the newspaper notes their plans to rebuild: "Their community is now scattered across the American South due to Hurricane Katrina. Those who have returned are laying a foundation for the rest to rejoin them. The church and the nonprofit Vietnamese American Community in Louisiana are calling on community members to join work crews to rehabilitate and reconstruct homes and businesses" (Joe, 2005).

Likewise, *The Advocate*, a gay and lesbian newsmagazine, noted, "Thousands of other gay men and lesbians say they owe it to the city to return. It's not an easy choice. Many New Orleans residents, especially those in lower income brackets, will likely never come back. [. . .] For more than a century this has been their town. Since the early 1800s New Orleans welcomes those with same-sex attractions into a sea of fabulous architecture, boozy decadent affairs, outrageous

I think 9/11 is an intercultural issue because what happens in Jerusalem (Palestine) is actually the real definition of terrorism. But people from the West (i.e., the U.S., Canada) don't admit that, and the citizens of those countries don't know what's going on in the outside world. They claim that all Arabs are terrorists, but they don't take a minute to discover the truth. Also, in the news, you don't see what actually is going on in the Middle East, and this is just not fair to the Arab communities around the world.
    —Mohammad

parades, fabulous costumes, and gender-bending" (Hernandez, 2005, p. 43). The emphasis on returning and rebuilding is emphasized in this report because of the importance of New Orleans' gay history, its community, and the commitment of the people.

Taken together, these various viewpoints emphasize how different cultural groups are dealing with Hurricane Katrina, what different experiences they had, and how they look to the future. A critical perspective would emphasize the economic, political, and cultural differences among these groups, in understanding what happens to these cultural groups in the rebuilding phase, and how they do or do not recover.

An important recent critical perspective is **postcolonialism,** an intellectual, political, and cultural movement that calls for the independence of colonized states and liberation from colonialist *mentalité*, or ways of thinking. The legacy of this cultural invasion often lasts much longer than the political relationship. "It theorizes not just colonial conditions but why those conditions are what they are, and how they can be undone and redone" (Shome & Hegde, 2002, p. 250).

Postcolonialism is not simply the study of colonialism but the study of how we might deal with that past and its aftermath, which may include the ongoing use of the colonial language, culture, and religion. For example, a study by Marwan Kraidy (2005) explores how youth in Lebanon negotiate their postcolonial identity though their media consumption. Lebanon was colonized at various times by Arabs, Ottomans, and the French, and partly because of this colonial past, Lebanese have access to a wide range of television channels (all Arab satellite channels, some Indian, and the major U.S. and European cable and satellite channels). Kraidy shows how the young people pick and choose specific shows to watch, and then he analyzes how they interpret those shows. He concludes that, because of their colonialist legacy, they gravitate toward Western shows in addition to the Arabic shows, and this media consumption ultimately contributes to their having a **hybrid identity**—an identity comprised of both Western and Arabic elements.

Hybrid identities form around the world where people mix and meld aspects of their cultural life from more than one culture. While Kraidy looked at the case in Lebanon, hybrid identities are emerging around the world. In his study

postcolonialism An intellectual, political, and cultural movement that calls for the independence of colonialized states and also liberation from colonialist ways of thinking.

hybrid identity An identity that is consciously a mixture of different cultural identities and cultural traditions.

of the use of Kiswahili as a regional language in East Africa, lingusitics professor Benson Oduor Ojwang' (in press) points to the colonial past of this part of Africa as a foundation for unification. Formerly British colonies, Kenya, Uganda, and Tanzania are looking for greater cooperation, as they were earlier closer under British colonial rule. Known as East African Cooperation, the former colonies have a colonial past that they are using to forge a new postcolonial entity. Kiswahili is emerging as the language on which this new integration might occur, rather than English.

Another example of a critical study is Davin Grindstaff and Kevin DeLuca's (2004) analysis of the media coverage of the kidnapping and execution of Daniel Pearl, a journalist for the *Wall Street Journal* who was pursuing terrorism leads in Pakistan and was later captured and decapitated, which was videotaped. This videotape becomes a contested site where it "takes on starkly different meanings in the construction of both claims to 'terrorism' and to national identities in both Pakistan and the United States" (p. 306). The struggle between these readings must be contextualized within the larger power relations between Pakistan and the United States.

Grindstaff and DeLuca note that the same week Daniel Pearl was murdered, two Pakistani children were murdered in the United States. The outcry over Pearl and the deafening silence over these children's murders underscores the way that bodies represent national identities and "exacerbates Pakistani anti-Americanism and complicates Pakistani national identity" (2004, p. 316). In contrast, U.S. American discourses about Pearl's murder focus on Pearl as both a hero in the "war on terrorism" *and* an innocent victim. This paradox points to the way that multiple ideological needs are serviced and empowered by this video and its meanings.

A final example of a critical study is Dreama Moon's (1997) investigation of gender and social class communication. In her study, Moon analyzed interviews of white women from working-class backgrounds. She discovered that social class is a "marked feature" in the communication practices in academia that restricts upward mobility. Subtle communication practices that reinforce social class differences are not so invisible to women from working-class backgrounds. Moon shows how culture, social class, and communication work together to reproduce the contemporary social structure. She also identifies some strategies used by these women to resist this process of **social reproduction.**

social reproduction The process of perpetuating cultural patterns.

Strengths and Limitations   The critical approach emphasizes the power relations in intercultural interactions and the importance of social and historical contexts. However, one limitation is that most critical studies do not focus on face-to-face intercultural interaction. Rather, they focus on popular media forms of communication—TV shows, music videos, magazine advertisements, and so on. Such studies, with their lack of attention to face-to-face interactions, may yield less practical results. Thus, for example, although understanding different discourses about racism may give us insights into U.S. race relations, it may not provide individuals with specific guidelines on how to communicate better ere are three different student perspectives on the various approaches to studying intercultural communication.

I am an engineer, so I think that hypotheses and research are very important in order to describe and predict a subject. On the other hand, it is important to understand the individual more like a person and not like a number.

—Liliana

I like the interpretive approach. I think that it is important to understand and to actually get involved hands-on to understand something so important and complicated as intercultural communication. Even though outsiders may never fully be considered an insider, they are better off than neither an insider nor an outsider.

—Matt

Having three different paradigms allows me to view intercultural communication from three different perspectives. I can then incorporate all three into how I interpret other cultures. I personally like the critical view the most because I agree that often cultural groups are in a power struggle against one another, and that's just human nature.

—Andrew

across racial lines. However, one exception is co-cultural theory, presented in Chapter 6, which is used to understand how people's location in a social hierarchy influences their perceptions of reality regarding, among other things, relational issues or problems (Orbe, 1998).

Also, this approach does not allow for much empirical data. For example, Davin Grindstaff and Kevin DeLuca did not measure Pakistani or U.S. American reactions to the decapitation of Daniel Pearl; instead, their essay analyzed the media discourses. Grindstaff and DeLuca's argument rests on the discussions about the videotape of the murder, how it was used, and its influence on these international audiences.

A DIALECTICAL APPROACH TO UNDERSTANDING CULTURE AND COMMUNICATION

Combining the Three Traditional Paradigms: The Dialectical Approach

The social science, interpretive, and critical approaches operate in interconnected and sometimes contradictory ways. Rather than advocating any one approach, we propose a **dialectical approach** to intercultural communication

dialectical approach An approach to intercultural communication that integrates three approaches—functionalist (or social science), interpretive, and critical—in understanding culture and communication. It recognizes and accepts that the three approaches are interconnected and sometimes contradictory.

research and practice (see also Martin, Nakayama, & Flores, 2002). The dialectical approach emphasizes the processual, relational, and contradictory nature of intercultural communication, which encompasses many different kinds of intercultural knowledge.

processual Refers to how interaction happens rather than to the outcome.

First, with regard to the **processual** nature of intercultural communication, it is important to remember that cultures change, as do individuals. For example, the many cultures that constituted New Orleans and the Gulf Coast included Cajuns, Creoles, African Americans, white Americans, Vietnamese Americans, Chinese Americans, gay and lesbian Americans, and many other cultural groups. Intercultural communication studies provide a static but fleeting picture of these cultural groups. It is important to remember that the adaptation, communication, and other patterns identified are dynamic and ever changing, even if the research studies only provide a snapshot in time.

Second, a dialectical perspective emphasizes the relational aspect of intercultural communication study. It highlights the relationship among various aspects of intercultural communication and the importance of viewing these holistically rather than in isolation. The key question becomes, Can we really understand culture without understanding communication, and vice versa? Specifically, can we understand the ways that different cultural groups responded to the hurricanes and how they survived without looking at the values, beliefs, and histories of the various cultural groups there, the cultural institutions that different groups had in place, the relative wealth available to different cultural groups, and so on?

A third characteristic of the dialectical perspective involves holding contradictory ideas simultaneously. This notion may be difficult to comprehend because it goes against most formal education in the United States, which emphasizes dichotomous thinking. Dichotomies such as "good and evil," "arteries and veins," and "air and water" form the core of our philosophical and scientific beliefs. The fact that dichotomies such as "far and near," "high and low," and "long and short" sound complete, as if the two parts belong together, reveals our tendency to form dichotomies (Stewart & Bennett, 1991). One such dichotomy that emerged after Hurricane Katrina was that government officials were callous and uncaring and many victims of the hurricane were further victimized by the nonresponse of these officials. However, a dialectical approach requires that we transcend dichotomous thinking in studying and practicing intercultural communication.

Certainly, we can learn something from each of the three traditional approaches, and our understanding of intercultural communication has been enriched by all three. One of our students described how the three perspectives can be useful in everyday communication:

> The three paradigms help me understand intercultural communication by giving me insight into how we can work with people. Understanding how to predict communication behavior will make it easier for us to deal with those of other cultures—the social science approach. By changing unfair notions we have [about people from other cultures], we can gain more equality, as in the critical approach. We try to change things. Finally, the interpretive perspective is important so we can see face-to-face how our culture is.

Combining these approaches, as our discussion of the aftermath of Hurricane Katrina shows, provides us with extensive insight into the problems and challenges of this and other intercultural ventures. Clearly, if we limit ourselves to a specific research orientation, we may fail to see the complexities of contemporary intercultural interaction in contexts. Although this kind of paradoxical thinking is rather foreign to Western minds, it is quite accepted in many Asian cultures. For example, people doing business in China are advised to recognize this dialectical thinking: "It is not possible to overstate the importance of 'and' versus 'or' thinking. It recurs, in various forms, throughout business in China and the Orient as a whole" (Ambler & Witzel, 2000, p. 197).

In fact, research findings can make a difference in the everyday world. From the social science perspective, we can see how specific communication and cultural differences might create differing worldviews, which can help us to predict intercultural conflicts. An interpretive investigation gives us an opportunity to confirm what we predicted in a hypothetical social science study. In the case of Hurricane Katrina, a social science study might show large differences in responses among various cultural groups affected by this storm. An interpretive study might show how these different cultural groups interpreted these experiences and why they believe they had different experiences. These interpretations may help explain different responses and why some cultural groups feel differently from others and how some cultural groups adapted to new environments. The critical approach might focus on the different access to financial, political, and material resources among the cultural groups, such as the state of poverty before and after the storm, which groups were and were not relocated, and how these power differentials influenced their intercultural experiences.

Employing these different perspectives is similar to photographing something from different angles. No single angle or snapshot gives us the truth, but taking pictures from various angles gives a more comprehensive view of the subject. The content of the photos, of course, to some extent depends on the interests of the photographer. And the photos may contradict one another, especially if they are taken at different times. But the knowledge we gain from any of these "angles" or approaches is enhanced by the knowledge gained from the others.

However, a dialectical approach requires that we move beyond simply acknowledging the contributions of the three perspectives and accept simultaneously the assumptions of all three. That is, we need to imagine that reality can be at once external *and* internal, that human behavior is predictable *and* creative *and* changeable. These assumptions may seem contradictory, but that's the point. Thinking dialectically forces us to move beyond our familiar categories and opens us up to new possibilities for studying and understanding intercultural communication.

Six Dialectics of Intercultural Communication

We have identified six **dialectics** that characterize intercultural communication and have woven them throughout this book. Perhaps you can think of other dialectics as you learn more about intercultural communication.

dialectic (1) A method of logic based on the principle that an idea generates its opposite, leading to a reconciliation of the opposites; (2) the complex and paradoxical relationship between two opposite qualities or entities, each of which may also be referred to as a *dialectic.*

Cultural–Individual Dialectic   Intercultural communication is both cultural and individual, or idiosyncratic. That communication is *cultural* means we share communication patterns with members of the groups to which we belong. For example, Sandra, a fifth-generation Italian American, tends to be expressive, like other members of her family. However, some of her communication patterns—such as the way she gestures when she talks—are completely idiosyncratic (that is, particular to her and no one else). Consider another example, that of Angela, who tends to be relationally oriented. Although her role as a woman and the relationships she cultivates in that role are important, being a woman does not completely define her behaviors. In this book, we often describe communication patterns that seem to be related to membership in particular cultural groups. However, it is important to remember that communication for all of us is both cultural and individual. We need to keep this dialectic in mind as we try to understand and develop relationships across cultural differences.

Personal–Contextual Dialectic   This dialectic involves the role of context in intercultural relationships and focuses simultaneously on the person and the context. Although we communicate as individuals on a personal level, the context of this communication is important as well. In some contexts, we enact specific social roles that give meaning to our messages. For example, when Tom was teaching at a Belgian university, he often spoke from the social role of professor. But this role did not correspond exactly to the same role in the United States because Belgian students accord their professors far more respect and distance than do U.S. students. In Belgium, this social role was more important than his communication with the students. In contrast, his communication with students in the United States is more informal.

Differences–Similarities Dialectic   Intercultural communication is characterized by both similarities and differences, in that people are simultaneously similar to and different from each other. In this book, we identify and describe real and important differences between groups of people—differences in values, language, nonverbal behavior, conflict resolution, and so on. For example, Japanese and U.S. Americans communicate differently, just as do men and women. However, there also are many similarities in human experiences and ways of communicating. Emphasizing only differences can lead to stereotyping and prejudice (e.g., that women are emotional or that men are rational); emphasizing only similarities can lead us to ignore the important cultural variations that exist. Therefore, we try to emphasize both similarities and differences and ask you to keep this dialectic in mind.

Static–Dynamic Dialectic   This dialectic suggests that intercultural communication tends to be at once static and dynamic. Some cultural and communication patterns remain relatively constant, whereas other aspects of cultures (or personal traits of individuals) shift over time—that is, they are dynamic. For example, as we learned in Chapter 1, anti-immigrant sentiment traditionally has been a cultural constant in the United States, although the groups and conditions

When I was working in the Philippines there was a privilege–disadvantage dialectic with the general population. My trip got extended for an extra week. I had to go out and buy clothes at a department store in Manila. I did not speak any Filipino so this was a very interesting experience. Knowing that the Filipino people can speak English and Spanish somewhat I knew I would be able to get by. While the prices on the clothes were clearly marked the lady at the register had inflated the price by 1000 pesos ($20). Knowing what the price should be I had to try to explain the situation to get the price down to the correct level. Americans are envied in the Philippines for what we have. After spending a good amount of time trying to explain my situation the Filipino lady appeared not to understand anything I was saying. I ended up not getting the clothes from her.

—Bob

In the past African Americans have dealt with a lot of prejudice and discrimination against them. There used to be separate water fountains, bathrooms, seats on a bus, etc. . . . the list could go on. So today when any African Americans come to dine at the restaurant I work at, we try to avoid seating them at the back of the restaurant. Since there has been a complaint, we don't want them to feel as if we are discriminating against them by putting them in a place where they are tucked away. The discrimination that African Americans once felt should not translate over to the present since our society has come so far. Some might say we are giving them special treatment to make African Americans feel equal but I don't see it like that. I see it as a sign of respect and a way of showing the African American culture that the discrimination they once felt should not exist anymore and they are just as equal as anyone else.

—Jodi

of discrimination have changed. Thus, the antagonism against Irish and Italian immigrants that existed at the turn of the 20th century has largely disappeared but may linger in the minds of some people. To understand interethnic communication in the United States today, we must recognize both the static and dynamic aspects of these relations.

History/Past–Present/Future Dialectic   Another dialectic emphasizes the need to focus simultaneously on the past and the present in understanding intercultural communication. On the one hand, we need to be aware of contemporary forces and realities that shape interactions of people from different cultural groups. On the other hand, we need to realize that history has a significant impact on contemporary events. One of our students described how this dialectic was illustrated in a televised panel discussion on race relations:

The panelists frequently referred to and talked about the history of different cultural groups in the United States and the present. They also touched on racial conflicts of the past and future possible improvement for certain groups. They were, therefore, communicating in a history/past–present/future dialectical manner. The discussions of past and present were critical to the overall goal of understanding current cultural identity. Without understanding the history of, for example, the slave trade or the Jim Crow laws, can we truly comprehend the African American experience in the United States today? The history of each cultural group plays a major role in the present role of that group.

Privilege–Disadvantage Dialectic   A dialectical perspective recognizes that people may be simultaneously privileged and disadvantaged, or privileged in some contexts and disadvantaged in others. For example, many tourists are in the position of economic privilege because they can afford to travel, but in their travels, they also may be disadvantaged if they do not speak the local language. We can also be simultaneously privileged and disadvantaged because of gender, age, race, socioeconomic status, and other identities. One of our Asian American colleagues relates how he is simultaneously privileged because he is educated, middle class, and male and disadvantaged because he experiences subtle and overt mistreatment based on his race and accent (Collier, Hegde, Lee, Nakayama, & Yep, 2002, p. 247).

Keeping a Dialectical Perspective

We ask that you keep a dialectical perspective in mind as you read the rest of this book. The dialectics relate in various ways to the topics discussed in the following chapters and are interwoven throughout the text. Keep in mind, though, that the dialectical approach is not a specific theory to apply to all aspects of intercultural communication. Rather, it is a lens through which to view the complexities of the topic. Instead of offering easy answers to dilemmas, we ask you to look at the issues and ideas from various angles, sometimes holding contradictory notions, but always seeing things in processual, relational, and holistic ways.

The dialectical approach that we take in this book combines the three traditional approaches (social science, interpretive, and critical) and suggests four components to consider in understanding intercultural communication: culture, communication, context, and power. Culture and communication are the foreground, and context and power are the backdrop against which we can understand intercultural communication. We discuss these four components in the next chapter.

INTERNET RESOURCES

http://katrina.louisiana.gov/
Even though Hurricane Katrina came through the Gulf Coast in 2005, the effects are still being felt today. This Web site is maintained by the state government of Louisiana in an attempt to keep the storm victims updated

and in contact with appropriate resources. Along with insurance information and government assistance programs, the site also has information about contacting displaced loved ones—highlighting the long-term personal effects of the storm.

www.state.gov/m/fsi/
This is the State Department's Web site for the Foreign Service Institute. The FSI is the primary mechanism the federal government uses for training individuals to go overseas to serve, in some capacity, as representatives of the United States government.

www.peacecorps.gov/
This is the home page for the Peace Corps. Volunteering in the Peace Corps is a way that many young people travel overseas and experience different cultures. It is worth considering how traveling abroad is portrayed differently by the Peace Corps and the State Department.

www.aliveintruth.org
Alive in Truth is a group of New Orleans residents who got together to collect oral histories of those who survived Hurricane Katrina. Go to their Web page and read some of these oral histories. Think about how this might help you better understand their experiences from an interpretivist perspective. Note the interviewing guidelines they suggest, and keep in mind the larger context for these interviews. How is this information different from what a social scientist or critical theorist might find?

SUMMARY

- The field of intercultural communication in the United States began with the establishment of the Foreign Service Institute in 1946.
- This new field was interdisciplinary and pragmatic. It emphasized nonverbal communication in international contexts.
- The perceptions and worldviews of scholars have an impact on the study of intercultural communication and have led to three contemporary approaches: the social science, interpretive, and critical approaches.
- This textbook advocates a dialectical approach that combines these three approaches.
- A dialectical approach emphasizes a processual, relational, and holistic view of intercultural communication, and it requires a balance of contradictory views.
- Intercultural communication is both cultural *and* individual, personal *and* contextual, characterized by differences *and* similarities, static *and* dynamic, oriented to both the present *and* the past, and characterized by both privilege *and* disadvantage.

DISCUSSION QUESTIONS

1. How have the origins of the study of intercultural communication in the United States affected its present focus?
2. How did business and political interests influence what early intercultural communication researchers studied and learned?
3. How have the worldviews of researchers influenced how they studied intercultural communication?
4. How have other fields contributed to the study of intercultural communication?
5. What are the advantages of a dialectical approach to intercultural communication?

 Go to the self-quizzes on the Online Learning Center at www.mhhe.com/ martinnakayama5 to further test your knowledge.

ACTIVITIES

1. *Becoming Culturally Conscious.* One way to understand your cultural position within the United States and your own cultural values, norms, and beliefs is to examine your upbringing. Answer the following questions:

   a. What values did your parents or guardians attempt to instill in you?
   b. Why were these values considered important?
   c. What were you expected to do when you grew up?
   d. How were you expected to contribute to family life?
   e. What do you know about your ethnic background?
   f. What was your neighborhood like?

   Discuss your answers with classmates. Analyze how your own cultural position is unique and how it is similar to that of others.

2. *Analyzing Cultural Patterns.* Find a text or speech that discusses some intercultural or cultural issues, and analyze the cultural patterns present in the text. Consider, for example, the "I Have a Dream" speech by Martin Luther King, Jr. (Andrews & Zarefsky, 1992), or Chief Seattle's 1854 speech (Low, 1995).

3. *Analyzing a Video.* View a feature film or video (e.g., *Crash* or *Brokeback Mountain*) and assume the position of a researcher. Analyze the cultural meanings in the film from each of the three perspectives: social science, interpretive, and critical. What cultural patterns (related to nationality, ethnicity, gender, and class) do you see? What does each perspective reveal? What does each one fail to reveal?

KEY WORDS

Afrocentricity (63)
anxiety uncertainty
    management
    theory (55)
collectivistic (55)
communication
    accommodation
    theory (56)
conceptual
    equivalence (58)
conversational
    contraints theory (55)
critical approach (65)
cross-cultural
    training (46)
dialectic (73)
dialectical approach (71)
diffusion of innovations
    theory (57)

distance zones (46)
diversity training (46)
emic (60)
ethnography (59)
etic (60)
face negotiation
    theory (55)
functionalist
    approach (54)
hyprid identity (69)
individualistic (55)
intercultural
    competence (47)
interdisciplinary (48)
interpretive approach (59)
macrocontexts (65)
paradigm (49)
participant
    observation (59)

perception (49)
postcolonialism (69)
processual (72)
proxemics (46)
qualitative
    methods (59)
quantitative
    methods (54)
rhetorical approach (60)
Sapir-Whorf
    hypothesis (47)
social reproduction (70)
social science
    approach (54)
textual analyses (66)
translation
    equivalence (58)
variable (54)
worldview (45)

The Online Learning Center at www.mhhe.com/martinnakayama5 features
flashcards and crossword puzzles based on these terms and concepts.

REFERENCES

9/11 and 8/29. (2005, September 11). *Los Angeles Times*, p. M4.

Allport, G. W. (1979). *The nature of prejudice*. Reading, MA: Addison-Wesley.

Alter, J. (2005, September 19). The other America. *Newsweek*, pp. 42–48.

Ambler, T., & Witzel, M. (2000). *Doing business in China*. New York: Routledge.

Andrews, J. R., & Zarefsky, D. (1992). *Contemporary American voices: Significant speeches in American history, 1945–present* (pp. 78–81). New York: Longman.

Après Katrina, l'Amérique s'interroge sur les failles de son modèle. (2005, September 7). *Le Monde*. http://www.lemonde.fr/web/imprimer_element/0,40-0@2-3222,50-686407,0.html

Asante, M. K. (1987). *The Afrocentric idea*. Philadelphia: Temple University Press.

Asante, M. K. (2001). Transcultural realities and different ways of knowing. In V. H. Milhouse, M. K. Asante, & P. O. Nwosu (Eds.), *Transcultural realities: Interdisciplinary perspectives on cross cultural relations* (pp. 71–82). Thousand Oaks, CA: Sage.

Barnlund, D. C., & Yoshioka, M. (1990). Apologies: Japanese and American styles. *International Journal of Intercultural Relations, 14*, 193–205.

Barry, D. (2005, September 9). The radio station that could, and did, and still does, help. *New York Times*, p. A15.

Berry, J. W. (1997). Preface. In P. R. Dasen, T. S. Saraswathi, & J. W. Berry (Eds.), *Handbook of cross cultural psychology: Vol. 2. Basic processes and human development* (pp. xi–xvi). Boston: Allyn & Bacon.

Braithwaite, C. (1990). Communicative silence: A cross cultural study of Basso's hypothesis. In D. Carbaugh (Ed.), *Cultural communication and intercultural contact* (pp. 321–328). Hillsdale, NJ: Lawrence Erlbaum.

Brantlinger, P. (1986). Victorians and Africans: The genealogy of the myth of the dark continent. In

H. L. Gates Jr. (Ed.), *"Race," writing and difference* (pp. 185–222). Chicago: University of Chicago Press. (Original work published 1985)

Brislin, R. (1999). *Understanding culture's influence on behavior* (2nd ed.). Belmont, CA: Wadsworth.

Burrell, G., & Morgan, G. (1988). *Sociological paradigms and organizational analysis.* Portsmouth, NH: Heinemann.

Carbaugh, D. (1996). *Situating selves: The communication of social identities in American scenes.* Albany: State University of New York Press.

Carbaugh, D. (1999). "Just listen": "Listening" and landscape among the Blackfeet. *Western Journal of Communication, 63,* 250–270.

Carbaugh, D., & Berry, M. (2001). Communicating history, Finnish and American discourses: An ethnographic contribution to intercultural communication inquiry. *Communication Theory, 11,* 352–366.

Casmir, F. L. (1994). The role of theory and theory building. In F. L. Casmir (Ed.), *Building communication theories* (pp. 7–41). Hillsdale, NJ: Lawrence Erlbaum.

Chen, G.-M. (1998). A Chinese model of human relationship development. In B. L. Hoffer & J. H. Koo (Eds.), *Cross-cultural communication East and West in the 90's* (pp. 45–53). San Antonio, TX: Institute for Cross-Cultural Research, Trinity University.

Chomsky, N. (2001). *9–11.* New York: Seven Stories Press.

Collier, M. J., Hegde, R. S., Lee, W., Nakayama, T. K., & Yep, G. A. (2002). Dialogue on the edges: Ferment in communication and culture. In M. J. Collier (Ed.), *Transforming communication about culture* (*International and Intercultural Communication Annual,* Vol. 24, pp. 219–280). Thousand Oaks, CA: Sage.

Coste, P. (2005, September 15). Les raisons de la misère. *L'Express,* p. 33.

Delgado, F. (2002). Mass-mediated communication and intercultural conflict. In J. N. Martin, T. K. Nakayama, & L. A. Flores (Eds.), *Readings in intercultural communication: Experiences and contexts* (2nd ed., pp. 351–359). Boston: McGraw-Hill.

Dhombres, D. (2005, September 6). Le tiers-monde en Louisiane. *Le Monde.* http://www.lemonde.fr/web/imprimer_element/0,40-0@2-3232,50-686223,0.html

Egan, T. (2005, September 11). Uprooted and scattered far from the familiar. *New York Times,* pp. A1, A32.

Gallois, C., Giles, H., Jones, E., Cargile, A. C., & Ota, H. (1995). Accommodating intercultural encounters: Elaborations and extensions. In R. L. Wiseman (Ed.), *Intercultural communication theory* (pp. 115–147). Newbury Park, CA: Sage.

Garner, T. (1994). Oral rhetorical practice in African American culture. In A. González, M. Houston, & V. Chen (Eds.), *Our voices: Essays in culture, ethnicity and communication* (pp. 81–91). Los Angeles: Roxbury.

Gordon, R. D. Beyond the failures of Western communication theory. *Journal of Multicultural Discourses, 2*(2), 89–107.

Gould, S. J. (1993). American polygeny and craniometry before Darwin: Blacks and Indians as separate, inferior species. In S. Harding (Ed.), *The "racial" economy of science: Toward a democratic future* (pp. 84–115). Bloomington: Indiana University Press. (Original work published 1981)

Grindstaff, D. A., & DeLuca, K. M. (2004). The corpus of Daniel Pearl. *Critical Studies in Media Communication, 21,* 305–324.

Gudykunst, W. B. (1985). A model of uncertainty reduction in intergroup encounters. *Journal of Language and Social Psychology, 4,* 79–98.

Gudykunst, W. B. (1998). Individualistic and collectivistic perspectives on communication: An introduction. *International Journal of Intercultural Relations, 22,* 107–134.

Gudykunst, W. B. (2002a). Intercultural communication theories. In W. B. Gudykunst & B. Mody (Eds.), *Handbook of international and intercultural communication* (2nd ed., pp. 183–205). Thousand Oaks, CA: Sage.

Gudykunst, W. B. (2002b). Cross-cultural communication theories. In W. B. Gudykunst & B. Mody (Eds.), *Handbook of international and intercultural communication* (2nd ed., pp. 25–50). Thousand Oaks, CA: Sage.

Gudykunst, W. B. (2005). An anxiety/uncertainty management (AUM) theory of effective communication: Making the mesh of the net finer. In W. B. Gudykunst (Ed.), *Theorizing about intercultural communication* (pp. 281–323). Thousand Oaks, CA: Sage.

Gudykunst, W. B., & Nishida, T. (1989). Theoretical perspectives for studying intercultural communication. In M. K. Asante & W. B. Gudykunst (Eds.), *Handbook of international and intercultural communication* (pp. 17–46). Newbury Park, CA: Sage.

Hall, B. J. (1992). Theories of culture and communication. *Communication Theory, 1,* 50–70.

Hall, E. T. (1959). *The silent language.* Garden City, NY: Doubleday.

Hall, E. T. (1966). *The hidden dimension.* Garden City, NY: Doubleday.

Hammer, M. R., & Rogan, R. G. (2002). Latino and Indochinese interpretive frames in negotiating conflict with law enforcement: A focus group analysis. *International Journal of Intercultural Relations, 26,* 551–576.

Hart, W. B. (1999). Interdisciplinary influences in the study of intercultural relations: A citation analysis of the *International Journal of Intercultural Relations*. *International Journal of Intercultural Relations, 23,* 575–590.

Hecht, M. L. (1993). A research odyssey: Towards the development of a communication theory of identity. *Communication Monographs, 60,* 76–82.

Hernandez, G. (2005, October 11). Rebuilding our city. *The Advocate,* pp. 42–44, 49–50, 52.

Hutchinson, E. O. (2005, September 19). Guest editorial: How low can Bush go? *Chicago Defender.* http://www.chicagodefender.com/page/ local.cfm?ArticleID=2642

Hymes, D. (1974). *Foundations in sociolinguistics: An ethnographic approach.* Philadelphia: University of Pennsylvania Press.

Ishii, S. (2004). Proposing a Buddhist consciousness-only epistemological model for intrapersonal communication research. *Journal of Intercultural Communication Research, 33,* 63–76.

Jandt, F. E., & Tanno, D. V. (2001). Decoding domination, encoding self-determination: Intercultural communication research processes. *Howard Journal of Communications, 12,* 119–135.

Joe, M. (2005, October 28). Resurrecting the church after Katrina. *Asian Week.* http://news.asianweek .com/news/view_article.html?article_id=387bf08b8 c87729a3144164b9850fb4c

Johnson, K. (2005, September 11). For storm survivors, a mosaic of impressions rather than a crystalline moment. *New York Times,* pp. A25, A32.

Kim, M.-S. (1994). Cross-cultural comparisons of the perceived importance of conversational constraints. *Human Communication Research, 21,* 128–151.

Kim, M.-S. (2005). Culture-based conversational constraints theory: Individual and culture-level analyses. In W. B. Gudykunst (Ed.), *Theorizing about intercultural communication* (pp. 93–117). Thousand Oaks, CA: Sage.

Kim, Y. Y. (2001). *Becoming intercultural: An integrative theory of communication and cross-cultural adaptation.* Thousand Oaks, CA: Sage.

Kohut, A., Allen, J., Keeter, S., Doherty, C., Dimock, M., Funk, C., et al. (2005). *Two-in-three critical of Bush's relief efforts: Huge racial divide over Katrina and its consequences.* The Pew Center for the People & the Press. Available at http://people-press.org/ reports/pdf/255.pdf. Accessed November 1, 2005.

Kraidy, M. M. (2005). *Hybridity, or the cultural logic of globalization.* Philadelphia: Temple University Press.

Kuhn, T. (1970). *The structure of scientific revolutions* (Rev. ed.). Chicago: University of Chicago Press.

Kurtz, H. (2005, September 5). At last, reporters' feelings rise to the surface. *Washington Post,* p. C1.

Landis, D., & Bhagat, R. (1996). *Handbook of intercultural training* (2nd ed.). Thousand Oaks, CA: Sage.

Landis, D., & Wasilewski, J. H. (1999). Reflections on 22 years of the *International Journal of Intercultural Relations* and 23 years in other areas of intercultural practice. *International Journal of Intercultural Relations, 23,* 535–574.

Low, D. (1995). Contemporary reinvention of Chief Seattle's 1854 speech. *American Indian Quarterly, 19*(3), 407.

Mark my words. (2007, February 16). *The Economist.* Retrieved May 13, 2008 from http://www.economist .com/science/displaystory.cfm?story_id= E1_RSNTRJD

Martin, J. N., Nakayama, T. K., & Flores, L. A. (2002). A dialectical approach to intercultural communication. In J. N. Martin, T. K. Nakayama, & L. A. Flores (Eds.), *Readings in intercultural communication: Experiences and contexts* (2nd ed., pp. 3–13). Boston: McGraw-Hill.

Miike, Y. (2004). Rethinking humanity, culture and communication: Asiacentric critiques and contributions. *Human Communication, 7,* 69–82.

Miike, Y. (2003). Beyond Eurocentrism in the intercultural field: Searching for an Asiacentric paradigm. In W. J. Storosta & G. M. Chen (Eds.), *Ferment in the intercultural field (International and Intercultural Communication Annual,* Vol. 26). Thousand Oaks, CA: Sage.

Miike, Y. (2007a). An Asiacentric reflection on Eurocentric bias in Communication theory. *Communication Monographs, 74*(2), 272–278.

Miike, Y. (2007b). Asian contributions to communication theory: An introduction. *China Media Research, 3*(4), 1–6.

Moon, D. (1997). *Deconstructing the 'intra'/'inter' divide: Toward a critical inter/cultural practice.* Unpublished Ph.D. disssertation. Tempe: Arizona State University.

Moon, D. G. (1996). Concepts of "culture": Implications for intercultural communication research. *Communication Quarterly, 44,* 70–84.

Ojwang, B. O. (2008). Prospects of Kishwahili as a regional language in a socioculturally heterogeneous East Africa. *Journal of International and Intercultural Communication, 1* (4), in press.

Orbe, M. (1998). *Constructing co-cultural theory: An explication of culture, power and communication.* Thousand Oaks, CA: Sage.

Orbe, M. P. (2004). Negotiating multiple identities with multiple frames: An analysis of first-generation college students. *Communication Education, 53,* 131–149.

Philipsen, G. (1990). Speaking "like a man" in Teamsterville. In D. Carbaugh (Ed.), *Cultural communication and intercultural contact* (pp. 11–20). Hillsdale, NJ: Lawrence Erlbaum.

Putnam, L., & Pacanowsky, M. (Eds.). (1983). *Communication and organizations: An interpretive approach.* Newbury Park, CA: Sage.

Rogers, E. M. (2003). *Diffusion of innovations* 5th ed. New York: Free Press.

Rosaldo, R. (1989). *Culture and truth: The remaking of social analysis.* Boston: Beacon Press.

Satoshi, I. (2007). A Western contention of Asia-centred communication scholarship paradigms: A commentary on Gordon's paper. *Journal of Multicultural Discourses, 2*(2), 108–114.

Saulny, S. (2005, October 11). Cast from their ancestral home, Creoles worry about culture's future. *New York Times,* p. A13.

Serpell, R. (1982). Measures of perception, skills and intelligence: The growth of a new perspective on children in a third world country. In W. Hartrup (Ed.), *Review of child development research* (Vol. 6). Chicago: University of Chicago Press.

Shome, R., & Hegde, R. (2002). Postcolonial approaches to communication: Charting the terrain, engaging the intersections. *Communication Theory, 12,* 249–270.

Singer, M. R. (1987). *Intercultural communication: A perceptual approach.* Englewood Cliffs, NJ: Prentice-Hall.

Singer, M. R. (1998). Culture: A perceptual approach. In M. J. Bennett (Ed.), *Basic concepts of intercultural communication* (pp. 97–110). Yarmouth, ME: Intercultural Press.

Singhal, A., & Dearing, J. W. (Eds.). (2006). *Communication of innovations: A journey with Ev Rogers.* Thousand Oaks, CA: Sage.

Smith, C. S. (2005, November 6). France has an underclass, but its roots are still shallow. *New York Times,* sec. 4, p. 3.

Smith, L. T. (1999). *Decolonizing methodologies: Research and indigenous peoples.* New York: St. Martin's Press.

Stewart, E. C., & Bennett, M. J. (1991). *American cultural patterns: A cross-cultural perspective* (Rev. ed.). Yarmouth, ME: Intercultural Press.

Sturken, M. (2005, October 5). Weather media and homeland security: Selling preparedness in a volatile world. *Understanding Katrina: Perspectives from the social sciences.* http://understandingkatrina.ssrc.org/Sturken/

Swarns, R. (2002, May 5). France returns old remains to homeland. *The Arizona Republic,* p. A28.

Tagliabue, J. (2005, September 21). A French lesson: Taunts about race can boomerang. *New York Times,* p. A4.

Tang, I. (2005, September 16). Hurricane Katrina victims recover from 'tragic shock.' *Asian Week.* http://news.asianweek.com/news/view_article.html?article_id=736da18dle494642b993e854400c7f30

Tatum, W. A. (2005, September 21). Proof positive of a racist president, misleading a racist America. *Amsterdam News.* http://www.amsterdamnews.org/News/search/Article_Search.asp?NewsID=61723&sID=16

Ting-Toomey, S. (1985). Toward a theory of conflict and culture. In W. Gudykunst, L. Stewart, & S. Ting-Toomey (Eds.), *Communication, culture and organizational processes* (pp. 71–86). Beverly Hills, CA: Sage.

Ting-Toomey, S. (2005). The matrix of face: An updated face-negotiation theory. In W. B. Gudykunst (Ed.), *Theorizing about intercultural communication* (pp. 71–92). Thousand Oaks, CA: Sage.

Ting-Toomey, S., Gao, G., Trubisky, P., Yang, Z., Kim, H. S., Lin, S.-L., et al. (1991). Culture, face maintenance, and styles of handling interpersonal conflict: A study in five cultures. *International Journal of Conflict Management, 2,* 275–296.

Ting-Toomey, S., Yee-Jung, K. K., Shapiro, R. B., Garcia, W., Wright, T. J., & Oetzel, J. G. (2000). Ethnic/cultural identity salience and conflict styles in four US ethnic groups. *International Journal of Intercultural Relations, 24,* 47–81.

Vernet, D. (2005, September 8). Katrina bouscule la diplomatie américaine. *Le Monde.* http://www.lemonde.fr/web/imprimer_element/0,40-0@2-3232,50-686932,0.html

Wells, M. (2005, September 5). Viewpoint: Has Katrina saved US media? *British Broadcasting Corporation News.* http://news.bbc.co.uk/1/hi/world/americas/4214516.stm Accessed November 1, 2005.

Witteborn, S. (2004). Of being an Arab woman before and after September 11: The enactment of communal identities in talk. *Howard Journal of Communications, 15,* 83–98.

Why was UK's Katrina aid rejected by US? (2005, September 18). *British Broadcasting Corporation News.* http://news.bbc.co.uk/1/hi/magazine/4349916.stm

CULTURE, COMMUNICATION, CONTEXT, AND POWER

CHAPTER OBJECTIVES

After you read this chapter, you should be able to:

1. Identify three approaches to culture.
2. Define communication.
3. Identify and describe nine cultural value orientations.
4. Describe how cultural values influence communication.
5. Understand how cultural values influence conflict behavior.
6. Describe how communication can reinforce cultural beliefs and behavior.
7. Explain how culture can function as resistance to dominant value systems.
8. Explain the relationship between communication and context.
9. Describe the characteristics of power.
10. Describe the relationship between communication and power.

In Chapter 2, we touched on the history of intercultural communication studies, examined three theoretical approaches, and outlined an integrated dialectical approach to intercultural communication. In this chapter, we continue our discussion of the dialectical approach and identify four interrelated components or building blocks in understanding intercultural communication: culture, communication, context, and power. As noted previously, culture and communication are the foreground and context and power form the backdrop against which we can understand intercultural communication. First, we define and describe culture and communication. Then we examine how these two components interact with issues of context and power to enhance our understanding of intercultural communication.

WHAT IS CULTURE?

Culture is often considered the core concept in intercultural communication. Intercultural communication studies often focus on how cultural groups differ from one another: Muslims differ from Christians; Japanese differ from U.S. Americans; men differ from women; environmentalists differ from conservationists; pro-lifers differ from pro-choicers; old differ from young, and on and on (Gudykunst, 2002).

Perhaps it is more helpful here to think of the similarities–differences dialectic in trying to understand intercultural communication. That is, we are all similar to *and* different from each other simultaneously. Humans, regardless of cultural backgrounds, engage in many of the same daily activities and have many of the same wants and desires. We all eat, sleep, love, pursue friendships and romantic relationships and want to be respected and loved by those who are important to us.

And yet some real differences exist between cultural groups. How we pursue these activities varies from culture to culture. Men and women often do not see the world in the same way. Old and young have different goals and dreams. Muslims and Christians have different beliefs, and the old adage "When in Rome do as the Romans do" implies that it is easy simply to adapt to different ways of thinking and behaving, yet anyone who has struggled to adapt to a new cultural situation knows that only the Romans are Romans and only they know how to be truly Romans. The challenge is to negotiate these differences and similarities with insight and skill. First, we need to examine what we mean by the term *culture*.

Culture *Learned patterns of behavior and attitudes shared by a group of people.*

Culture has been defined in many ways—from a pattern of perceptions that influence communication to a site of contestation and conflict. Because there are many acceptable definitions of culture, and because it is a complex concept, it is important to reflect on the centrality of culture in our own interactions. The late British writer Raymond Williams (1983) wrote that culture "is one of the two or three most complicated words in the English language" (p. 89). And this very complexity indicates the many ways in which it influences intercultural communication (Williams, 1981). Culture is more than merely one aspect of the practice of intercultural communication. How we think about culture frames our ideas n this essay, communication scholar Wen Shu Lee identifies different common uses of the term *culture* and then describes how each definition serves particular interests. She also defends her preferred choice, the sixth definition.

1. Culture = unique human efforts (as different from nature and biology). For example, "*Culture* is the bulwark against the ravages of nature."

2. Culture = refinement, mannerism (as different from things that are crude, vulgar, and unrefined). For example, "Look at the way in which he chows down his food. He has no *culture* at all."

3. Culture = civilization (as different from backward barbaric people). For example, "In countries where darkness reigns and people are wanting in *culture*, it is our mandate to civilize and Christianize those poor souls."

4. Culture = shared language, beliefs, values (as different from language beliefs and values that are not shared; dissenting voices; and voices of the "other"). For example, "We come from the same *culture*, we speak the same language, and we share the same tradition."

5. Culture = dominant or hegemonic culture (as different from marginal cultures). For example, "It is the *culture* of the ruling class that determines what is moral and what is deviant." [This definition is a more charged version of definitions 2, 3, and 4 through the addition of power consciousness.]

6. Culture = the shifting tensions between the shared and the unshared (as different from shared or unshared things). For example, "American *culture* has changed from master/slave, to white only/black only, to antiwar and black power, to affirmative action/multiculturalism and political correctness, to transnational capital and anti-sweatshop campaigns."

Each of these definitions privileges certain interests. Definition 2 privileges high culture and leaves out popular culture. . . . Definition 3 privileges nations that are/were imperialistic, colonizing. . . . Definition 4 privileges a "universal and representative" view of a society, but such a view often represents only a specific powerful group and silences other groups that do not readily share this view. Definition 5 privileges the interaction of the culture authorized by the dominant group/sector/nation—more politically explicit than definitions 2, 3, and 4. Definition 6 is the one I like the most. It is more of a meta view of cultures. It focuses on the "links" between "the shared" and the "little shared." But the sharedness, *the* unsharedness, *and their* links *remain not only situated but also unstable, shifting, and contested.*

Source: From Collier, Hegde, Lee, Nakayama, and Yep, "Dialogue on the Edges: Ferment in Communication and Culture." In M. J. Collier et al. (Eds.), *Transforming Communication About Culture* (Thousand Oaks, CA: Sage, 2002), pp. 229–230.

TABLE 3-1 THREE PERSPECTIVES ON DEFINING CULTURE		
Social Science	**Interpretive**	**Critical**
Culture is:		
Learned and shared	Learned and shared	Heterogeneous, dynamic
Patterns of perception	Contextual symbolic meanings	Site of contested meanings
	Involves emotion	
The relationship between culture and communication:		
Culture influences communication.	Culture influences communication.	Communication reshapes culture.
	Communication reinforces culture.	

Source: Adapted from J. N. Martin and T. K. Nakayama, "Thinking Dialectically About Culture and Communication," *Communication Theory, 9* (1999): 5.

and perceptions. For example, if we think that culture is defined by nation-states, then communication between a Japanese and an Italian would be intercultural communication because Japan and Italy are different nation-states. However, according to this definition, an encounter between an Asian American from North Carolina and an African American from California would not be intercultural because North Carolina and California are not different nation-states.

We do not advocate a singular definition of culture because any one definition is too restrictive (Baldwin & Lindsley, 1994). A dialectical approach suggests that different definitions offer more flexibility in approaching the topic. We believe that the best approach to understanding the complexities of intercultural communication is to view the concept of culture from different perspectives (see Table 3-1).

By and large, social science researchers focus not on culture per se but on the *influence* of culture on communication. In other words, such researchers concern themselves with communication differences that result from culture. They pay little attention to how we conceptualize culture or how we see its functions. In contrast, interpretive researchers focus more on how cultural contexts influence communication. Critical researchers, for their part, often view communication—and the power to communicate—as instrumental in reshaping culture. They see culture as the way that people participate in or resist society's structure.

Although research studies help us understand different aspects of intercultural communication, it is important to investigate how we think about culture, not simply as researchers but as practitioners as well. We therefore broaden our scope to consider different views of culture, especially in terms of how they influence intercultural communication.

Social Science Definitions: Culture as Learned, Group-Related Perceptions

Communication scholars from the social science paradigm, influenced by research in psychology, view culture as a set of learned, group-related perceptions (B. Hall, 1992). Geert Hofstede (1984), a noted social psychologist, defines culture as "the programming of the mind" and explains his notion of culture in terms of a computer program:

> *Every person carries within him or herself patterns of thinking, feeling, and potential acting which were learned throughout [his or her] lifetime. Much of [these patterns are] acquired in early childhood, because at that time a person is most susceptible to learning and assimilating. (p. 4)*

Hofstede goes on to describe how these patterns are developed through interactions in the social environment and with various groups of individuals—first in the family and neighborhood, then at school and in youth groups, then at college, and so on. Culture becomes a collective experience because it is shared with people who live in and experience the same social environments.

To understand this notion of the collective programming of the mind, Hofstede and other scholars studied organizational behavior at various locations of a multinational corporation; this study is discussed in detail later in the chapter. Social scientists also have emphasized the role of perception in cultural patterns. They contend that cultural patterns of thought and meaning influence our perceptual processes, which, in turn, influence our behavior:

> *Culture is defined as a pattern of learned, group-related perception—including both verbal and nonverbal language attitudes, values, belief system, disbelief systems, and behavior. (Singer, 1987, p. 34)*

Interpretive Definitions: Culture as Contextual Symbolic Patterns of Meaning, Involving Emotions

Interpretive scholars, influenced by anthropological studies, also view culture as shared and learned; however, they tend to focus on contextual patterns of communication behavior, rather than on group-related perceptions. Many interpretive scholars borrow anthropologist Clifford Geertz's definition of culture. According to Geertz (1973), culture denotes

> *an historically transmitted pattern of meaning embodied in symbols, a system of inherited conceptions expressed in symbolic forms by means of which men (sic) communicate, perpetuate and develop their knowledge about and attitudes toward life. (p. 89)*

One of the most common examples of interpretive scholarship is **ethnography of communication;** these scholars look for symbolic meaning of verbal and nonverbal activities in an attempt to understand patterns and rules of communication. This area of study defines cultural groups rather broadly—for example, as talk show participants or Vietnam War veterans.

ethnography of communication A specialized area of study within communication. Taking an interpretive perspective, scholars analyze verbal and nonverbal activities that have symbolic significance for the members of cultural groups to understand the rules and patterns followed by the groups. (See **interpretive approach** on page 59.)

Ethnography of communication scholar Donal Carbaugh (1988) suggests that it is best to reserve the concept of culture for patterns of symbolic action and meaning that are deeply felt, commonly intelligible, and widely accessible. Patterns that are deeply felt are sensed collectively by members of the cultural group. Gathering around the coffee machine at work every morning, for example, could be a cultural pattern, but only if the activity holds **symbolic significance** or evokes feelings that extend beyond itself. Then the activity more completely exemplifies a cultural pattern. Suppose that gathering around the coffee machine each morning symbolizes teamwork or the desire to interact with colleagues. To qualify as a cultural pattern, the activity must have the same symbolic significance for all members of the group; they must all find the activity meaningful in more or less the same way. Further, all participants must have access to the pattern of action. This does not mean that they must all use the pattern; it only means the pattern is available to them.

symbolic significance
The importance or meaning that most members of a cultural group attach to a communication activity.

Communication theorist Gerry Philipsen extends Carbaugh's notion of culture by emphasizing that these patterns must endure over time, passed along from person to person. Philipsen (1992) writes,

> Culture . . . refers to a socially constructed and historically transmitted pattern of symbols, meaning, premises, and rules. . . . A cultural code of speaking, then, consists of a socially constructed and historically transmitted system of symbols and meanings pertaining to communication—for instance, symbols "Lithuanian" or "communication" and their attendant definitions; beliefs about spoken actions (that a man who uses speech to discipline boys is not a real man); and rules for using speech (that a father should not interrupt his daughter at the dinner table). (pp. 7–8)

These definitions of culture suggested by Philipsen are influenced by communication ethnographer Dell Hymes's (1972) framework for studying naturally occurring speech in depth and in context. The framework comprises eight elements: scene, participant, end, act sequence, key, instrumentality, norm, and genre. In this sequence, the terms form the acronym *SPEAKING*. The *Scene* is the setting of the communication event. The *Participants* are the people who perform or enact the event. The *End* is the goal of the participants in conversation. The *Act* sequence is the order of phrases during the enactment. The *Key* is the tone of the conversation. The channel of communication is the *Instrumentality*. The *Norms*, as you know, are the rules that people follow. And *Genre* is the type or category of talk. By analyzing speech using this descriptive framework, we can gain a comprehensive understanding of the rules and patterns followed in any given speech community. Later in this chapter, we'll provide an example of how the framework can be used to explore cultural communication in context.

Culture is not only experienced as perceptions and values, and contextual, but the concept of culture also involves emotions. When we are in our own cultural surroundings we *feel* a sense of familiarity and a certain level of comfort in the space, behavior and actions of others. We might characterize this feeling as a kind of **embodied ethnocentrism**, which is normal (Bennett & Castiglioni, 2004). (Later on we'll discuss the negative side of ethnocentrism.) This aspect of culture has implications for understanding adaptation to other cultural norms

embodied ethnocentrism
Feeling comfortable and familiar in the spaces, behaviors, and actions of others in our own cultural surroundings.

iger Woods' media statement on his race/ethnicity:

The purpose of this statement is to explain my heritage for the benefit of members of the media who may be seeing me play for the first time. It is the final and only comment I will make regarding the issue.

My parents have taught me to always be proud of my ethnic background. Please rest assured that is, and always will be, the case—past, present, and future.

The media has portrayed me as African-American; sometimes, Asian. In fact, I am both. Yes, I am the product of two great cultures, one African-American and the other Asian. On my father's side, I am African-American. On my mother's side, I am Thai. Truthfully, I feel very fortunate, and EQUALLY PROUD, to be both African-American and Asian! The critical and fundamental point is that ethnic background and/or composition should NOT make a difference. It does NOT make a difference to me. The bottom line is that I am an American . . . and proud of it!

That is who I am and what I am. Now, with your cooperation, I hope I can just be a golfer and a human being.
Signed,
TIGER WOODS

http://www.geocities.com/Colosseum/2396/tigerrace.html

and spaces. That is, the stronger your identification with a particular space/cultural situation, the more difficult it might be to change spaces without experiencing a lot of discomfort—actual psychological and physiological changes. For example, students studying in France described their feelings in coping with the French language. Their self-esteem dropped and they became very self-conscious. Their whole bodies were entrenched in this effort of trying to communicate in French; it was a laborious and involved process that was connected to all aspects of themselves—a feeling of being out of their cultural comfort zone (Kristjánsdóttir, 2009). We should not underestimate the importance of culture in providing us a feeling of familiarity and comfort.

Although the notion of culture as shared, learned group patterns of perception or symbolic behavior has long been the standard in a variety of disciplines, more and more people are beginning to question its utility. They question how much of "culture" is truly shared. For example, one colleague reports that in a class discussion about the definition of culture in which most students were giving the usual definitions, "one student almost indignantly jumped into our discussion and said, 'Do we really have a common culture?'" She then followed with the question "Whose version of a shared and common culture are we talking about?" (Collier, Hegde, Lee, Nakayama, & Yep, 2002, p. 269). Indeed, these are important questions, and so the next section describes an alternative approach to defining culture. (For a challenge to common notions of a "shared" U.S. culture, take the "Test of U.S. Cultural Knowledge" on pages 92–93.)

Critical Definitions: Culture as Heterogeneous, Dynamic, and a Contested Zone

A more recent approach to culture, influenced by cultural studies scholarship, emphasizes the heterogeneity of cultural groups and the often conflictual nature of cultural boundaries. For example, what is the "U.S. American culture"? Is there *an* American culture? How many perceptions, attitudes, and beliefs and behaviors are actually shared among the many diverse people living in the United States? Critical scholars suggest that in emphasizing only the shared aspects of culture, we gloss over the many interesting differences among U.S. Americans. Further, they emphasize that cultural boundaries are often contested and not easily agreed upon. For example, increasing numbers of people like Tiger Woods have multicultural identities. He considers himself Cablinasian— Caucasian, black, Indian, and Asian—because of his racially diverse background. He resists the many efforts by some to pigeonhole his race/ethnicity or to focus more on his cultural background than his achievements as a golfer, as shown in the "Point of View" box on page 89.

This notion of culture as heterogeneous and often conflictual originated with British cultural studies scholars in the 1960s. Cultural studies scholars were fiercely interdisciplinary and dedicated to understanding the richness, complexity, and relevance of cultural phenomena in the lives of ordinary people. This desire to make academic work relevant to everyday life resonated in other fields. Most people, in fact, want to find the connections between what they learn in the classroom and what is occurring in contemporary society. In any case, this movement led to the reconfiguration of the role of the university in society. Cultural studies soon spread from Britain to Australia, Latin America, and other parts of the world. Because of differing cultural and political situations, the specific construction of cultural studies differs from place to place. In the United States, for instance, cultural studies developed mainly within departments of communication (Grossberg, 1993).

You may sense that the concept of culture that emerged from this area of inquiry differs markedly from the concept expressed in social science or even interpretive research. However, it is in agreement with concepts found in recent work in anthropology. Many anthropologists have criticized research that categorizes people and characterizes cultural patterns as set, unchanging, and unconnected to issues of gender, class, and history (Keesing, 1994). Recent anthropological research sees cultural processes as dynamic and fluid "organizations of diversity" that extend across national and regional borders within contexts of history and power (Hannerz, 1996). Communication scholars who embrace the critical notions encourage us to

> *move beyond hegemonic definition of culture as "shared and transmitted from generation to generation" that assumes that we all experience a "common culture" and . . . is passed down from one generation to the next in a linear and seemingly static fashion. . . . [T]his is a dangerous myth . . . that works in invisible yet*

FIGURE 3-1 You probably notice many differences among the people in this crowd, despite not having communicated with them. You are likely to encounter people who are culturally different from you in everyday life. What are some assumptions you might hold that would influence your communication with them? (© *Digital Vision/PunchStock*)

extremely powerful ways to suppress and erase marginalized voices and experiences. (Gust Yep, in Collier et al., 2002, p. 231)

Viewing culture as a contested site or zone helps us understand the struggles of various groups—Native Americans, Asian Americans, Pacific Islanders, African Americans, Latinos/as, women, gays and lesbians, working-class people, and so on—as they attempt to negotiate their relationships and promote their well-being within U.S. society. By studying the communication that springs from these ongoing struggles, we can better understand several intercultural concerns. Consider, for example, Proposition 227 in California, passed by voters in 1998, which eliminated public funding for bilingual education. The controversy surrounding the passage of this proposition illustrates the concerns of many different cultural groups. Similar debates surrounded the prior passage of Propositions 187 and 209 in California.

Viewing culture as a contested site opens up new ways of thinking about intercultural communication. After all, the individuals in a given culture are not identical, which suggests that any culture is replete with cultural struggles. Thus, when we use terms like *Chinese culture* and *French culture*, we gloss over the heterogeneity, the diversity, that resides in that culture. Yet the ways in which various cultures are heterogeneous are not the same elsewhere as in the United States, which means it would be a mistake to map our structure of differences onto other cultures. (See Figure 3-1.) How sexuality, ethnicity, gender, and class

TEST OF U.S. CULTURAL KNOWLEDGE

This test examines your knowledge of many of the cultures that comprise the contemporary United States.

1. *Lagniappe* is a term used in southern Louisiana for:
   a. Hurricanes
   b. Something free or sometimes a small gift given by a store owner to a customer after a purchase
   c. Inviting someone over for a meal
   d. Helping a friend with home remodeling or yard work

2. What is the name of the dish that features black-eyed peas and rice (although sometimes collards, ham hocks, stewed tomatoes, or other items) and is served in the South, especially on New Year's Day?
   a. Chitlings
   b. Jowls
   c. Hoppin' John
   d. Red rice

3. A very sweet pie made from molasses that originated with the Pennsylvania Dutch:
   a. Mincemeat pie
   b. Sugar pie
   c. Shoofly pie
   d. Lancaster pie

4. Which of the following is *not* the name of a Native American tribe?
   a. Seminole
   b. Apache
   c. Arapaho
   d. Illini

5. The month of Ramadan, a month of fasting for Muslims, ends with which holiday?
   a. Eid ul-Fitr
   b. Allahu Akbar
   c. Takbir
   d. Abu Bakr

6. On June 12 every year, some U.S. Americans celebrate "Loving Day" to commemorate:
   a. Your legal right to love someone of another race
   b. Your legal right to love someone of the same sex
   c. Your legal right to be a single parent
   d. Your legal right to get a divorce

7. The celebration of Buddha's birthday is not held on Christmas, but instead on:

    a. Fourth of July
    b. July 14
    c. Asian Lunar New Year's Day
    d. Hanamatsuri

8. Sometimes viewed as a Scandinavian tortilla, these potato flatcakes are often sold in areas with high Scandinavian American populations:

    a. Lefse
    b. Lutefisk
    c. Aquavit
    d. Fiskepudding

9. This traditional Mexican soup is made mostly from tripe, hominy, and chili:

    a. Tortilla soup
    b. Tomatillo
    c. Chorizo soup
    d. Menudo

10. Like a coconut pudding, this food comes from Hawaii:

    a. Lomi lomi
    b. Poke
    c. Haupia
    d. Kalua

Answers can be found on page 115.

function in other cultures is not necessarily the same as, or even similar to, their function in the United States. By viewing any culture as a contested zone or site of struggle, we can understand the complexities of that culture; we can become more sensitive to how people in that culture live.

Our dialectical approach, though, enables us to accept and see the interrelatedness of these different views. Culture is at once a shared and a learned pattern of beliefs and perceptions that are mutually intelligible and widely accessible. It is also a site of struggle for contested meanings. A dialectic perspective can help facilitate discussions on conflicting cultural notions (e.g., how to reconcile U.S. patriotism and instances of anti-Americanism). Our task in taking a dialectical approach is not to say whose views are right or wrong, but to recognize "the truth in all sides of the conflict and understanding the ways in which multiple realities constitute the whole of the cultural quandary" (Cargile, 2005, p. 117).

WHAT IS COMMUNICATION?

communication A symbolic process whereby reality is produced, maintained, repaired, and transformed.

The second component, **communication,** is as complex as culture and can be defined in many different ways. The defining characteristic of communication is meaning, and we could say that communication occurs whenever someone attributes meaning to another person's words or actions. Communication may be understood as a "symbolic process whereby reality is produced, maintained, repaired and transformed" (Carey, 1989, p. 23). The three perspectives emphasize different aspects of this communication process.

For example, the social science perspective emphasizes the various components of communication: There is a sender/receiver, message, channel, and context. This perspective also emphasizes that communication tends to be patterned and therefore can be predicted. This tradition also focuses on the variables, or influences on the communication, like gender, or the nature of a relationship. For example, people in long-term relationships will communicate in a different way from individuals who have recently met, or men and women will tend to communicate in different ways.

The interpretive perspective emphasizes the symbolic, processual nature of communication; the symbolic nature of communication means that the words we speak or the gestures we make have no inherent meaning. Rather, they gain their significance from an agreed-upon meaning. When we use symbols to communicate, we assume that the other person shares our symbol system. Also, these symbolic meanings are conveyed both verbally and nonverbally. Thousands of nonverbal behaviors (gestures, postures, eye contact, facial expressions, and so on) involve shared meaning.

To make things more complicated, each message has more than one meaning; often, there are many layers of meaning. For example, the message *I love you* may mean, "I'd like to have a good time with you tonight," "I feel guilty about what I did last night without you," "I need you to do me a favor," "I have a good time when I'm with you," or "I want to spend the rest of my life (or at least the next few hours) with you." When we communicate, we assume that the other person takes the meaning that we intend. It is more likely, when individuals come from different cultural backgrounds and experiences, that this assumption may be faulty.

The interpretive perspective also emphasizes that the *process* by which we negotiate meaning is dynamic. Communication is not a singular event but is ongoing. It relies on other communication events to make sense. When we enter into communication with another person, we simultaneously take in messages through all of our senses. The messages are not discreet and linear but simultaneous, with blurry boundaries of beginning and end. When we negotiate meaning, we are creating, maintaining, repairing, or transforming reality. This implies that people are actively involved in the communication process. One person cannot communicate alone.

The critical perspective emphasizes the importance of societal forces in the communication process. That is, that all voices and symbols are not equal, but are arranged in a social hierarchy in which some individual characteristics are more highly valued than others; for example, people are more likely to listen carefully to a police officer than to a young child. In addition, powerful social symbols—for example, flags, national anthems, and Disney logos—also communicate meaning nonverbally. Many of these symbols are material as well; that is, they have material consequences in the world. For example, when schoolchildren in the United States bring guns to school and kill schoolmates, the symbolism of these acts communicates something, and the acts themselves are material.

THE RELATIONSHIP BETWEEN CULTURE AND COMMUNICATION

The relationship between culture and communication is complex. A dialectical perspective assumes that culture and communication are interrelated and reciprocal. That is, culture influences communication, and vice versa. Thus, cultural groups influence the process by which the perception of reality is created and maintained: "All communities in all places at all times manifest their own view of reality in what they do. The entire culture reflects the contemporary model of reality" (Burke, 1985, p. 11). However, we might also say that communication helps create the cultural reality of a community. Let's see how these reciprocal relationships work.

How Culture Influences Communication

Intercultural communication scholars use broad frameworks from anthropology and psychology to identify and study cultural differences in communication. Two of the most relevant were developed by anthropologists Kluckhohn and Strodtbeck (1961) and by social psychologist Hofstede (1984).

Kluckhohn and Strodtbeck Value Orientations Researchers Florence Kluckhohn and Fred Strodtbeck studied contemporary Diné (Navaho) and descendants of Spanish colonists and European Americans in the Southwest in the 1950s. They emphasized the centrality of **cultural values** in understanding cultural groups. Values are the most deeply felt beliefs shared by a cultural group; they reflect a shared perception of what ought to be, and not what is. Equality, for example, is a value shared by many people in the United States. It refers to the belief that all humans are created equal, even though we must acknowledge that, in reality, there are many disparities, such as in talent, intelligence, or access to material goods.

Intercultural conflicts are often caused by differences in value orientations. For example, some people feel strongly that it is important to consider how

cultural values The worldview of a cultural group and its set of deeply held beliefs.

International students describe the different cultural and communication patterns they encounter in the United States.

A graduate student from India noted the U.S. patterns of greeting. In her native culture people only say hello to those they know. Initially, she was surprised by the frequency with which Americans greet each other; she later became disillusioned:

I thought, they are really interested in how I am. Then . . . "I'm fine and how about you?" Then I realized that people are really not interested in the answer. It is just a way of acknowledging you.

A British student commented on how openly Americans share their religious affiliation.

At first, I felt like a bit separated because I didn't quite fit into any. . . . They didn't know quite how to respond to me. I thought, Oh, am I supposed to be religious? Am I going to fit in here?

A graduate student from Iran noted how Americans are taught to "sell themselves":

The job search is another thing in this country that is culturally quite different. . . . In my society, mostly, they ask the professors in the university about efficient people or good students—there is not, you know, no selling yourself. And for the first couple of months I wasn't very successful because I didn't have the experience in selling myself.

Source: From L. A. Erbert, F. G. Perez, and E. Gareis (2003). Turning points and dialectical interpretations of immigrant experiences in the United States. *Western Journal of Communication, 67,* 113–137.

things were done in the past. For them, history and tradition help provide guidance. Values often conflict among participants in international assistance projects in which future-oriented individuals show a lack of respect for traditional ways of doing things. And conflicts may be exacerbated by power differentials, with some values privileged over others. Organizational communication scholars have pointed out that many U.S. workplaces reward extremely individualistic relationships and "doing" behaviors at the expense of more collaborative (and equally productive) work (Buzzanell, 1994). Kluckhohn and Strodtbeck suggested that members of all cultural groups must answer the following important questions:

- What is human nature?
- What is the relationship between humans and nature?
- What is the relationship between humans?
- What is the preferred personality?
- What is the orientation toward time?

TABLE 3-2 KLUCKHOHN AND STRODTBECK VALUE ORIENTATIONS

	Range of Values		
Human nature	Basically good	Mixture of good and evil	Basically evil
Relationship between humans and nature	Humans dominate	Harmony exists between the two	Nature dominates
Relationships between humans	Individual	Group oriented	Collateral
Preferred personality	"Doing": stress on action	"Growing": stress on spiritual growth	"Being": stress on who you are
Time orientation	Future oriented	Present oriented	Past oriented

Source: Adapted from F. Kluckhohn and F. Strodtbeck, *Variations in Value Orientation* (Chicago: Row, Peterson, 1961).

According to Kluckhohn and Strodtbeck, there are three possible responses to each question as they relate to shared values. (See Table 3-2.) Kluckhohn and Strodtbeck believed that, although all responses are possible in all societies, each society has one, or possibly two, preferred responses to each question that reflect the predominant values of that society. Religious beliefs, for example, may reinforce certain cultural values. The questions and their responses become a framework for understanding broad differences in values among various cultural groups. Although the framework was applied originally to ethnic groups, we can extend it to cultural groups based on gender, class, nationality, and so on.

The Nature of Human Nature   As the table shows, there are three possible responses, or solutions, to basic questions about human nature. One solution is a belief in the fundamental goodness of human nature. Legal practices in a society that holds this orientation would emphasize rehabilitating violators of the law; jails and prisons would be seen as places to train violators to rejoin society as contributing citizens. Religions such as Buddhism and Confucianism tend toward this orientation, focusing on improving the natural goodness of humans.

A second solution reflects a perception of a combination of goodness and evil in human nature. Many groups within the United States hold this value orientation, although there has been a shift in views for many U.S. Americans in the past 50 years. With regard to religious beliefs, there is less emphasis on the fundamental evil of humanity, which many European settlers of the Puritan tradition believed (Kohls, 1996). However, the current emphasis is on incarceration and punishment for violators of the law. For example, consider

alues can take many different forms. In this post, Ahmed explains different cultural value systems as they relate to education professionals.

As we all know, students in the United States do not give as much respect to
their professors as compared to students from other countries. I have had encounters
that can relate to that. When I used to go to school in Pakistan, I remember that we
were taught to show and talk with a lot of respect towards our teachers. We did not call
them by their first names, but we used to call them by madam, sir, or professor. Then
when I moved to Canada and started going to school there, I found it really weird that
I was calling my teachers professor, and the other students were just very casual in get-
ting their attention. That really seemed to surprise me because I had always learned to
respect my professors and call them in a professional way, but the other students around
me were very informal with their teachers. At first it seemed awkward for me, but as
time went on I got used to it, and started to be as informal as the other students.
—Ahmed

the increase in "three strikes" legislation and the lack of interest in rehabilitation and reform. Given this orientation, not surprisingly, the United States
currently has a higher proportion of citizens incarcerated than any other industrialized country.

According to the third orientation, human nature is essentially evil. Societies
that hold this belief would be less interested in rehabilitation of criminals than
in punishment. We often have trouble understanding torture or the practice of
cutting off hands and other limbs—practices prevalent in many societies in the
past—without understanding their orientation to human nature. While he lived
in Belgium, Tom was particularly struck by the display of punishments and tor-
tures in the Counts of Flanders Castle in Ghent. Perhaps the key to understanding these cultural practices is an understanding of the Christian view of humans
as essentially evil and born in sin.

Relationship Between Humans and Nature In most of U.S. society, humans
dominate nature. For instance, scientists seed clouds when we need rain, and
engineers reroute rivers and build dams to meet the needs for water, recreation,
and power. We control births with drugs and medical devices, and we make snow
and ice for the recreational pastimes of skiing and skating. Certainly, not everyone
in the United States agrees that humans should always dominate nature. Conflicts
between environmentalists and land developers often center on disagreements
over this value orientation. And, of course, there are variations in how these values
play out in different societies. For example, a country like Canada, which generally espouses a "humans over nature" orientation, still seems more concerned with
environmental issues than does the United States. As described by a student,

Canada is very concerned about protecting their environment, and this is very
clear even if you are just traveling through. They are concerned about clean water,

ommunication scholars Shim, Kim, and Martin describe how the value of collectivism is expressed through *kibun* in contemporary Korean interpersonal relationships:

For Koreans kibun *is when "an inner, peaceful environment is maintained." For Koreans to develop and maintain harmonious relationships they must be able to accurately "read" the* kibun *of others. Preserving the* kibun *of one or more parties in an interpersonal communicative exchange or relationship takes precedence over all else and a violation of an individual's* kibun *may result in the termination of the communication interaction or even the relationship itself.*

Due to the Confucian emphasis on harmony and hierarchal order in relationships, an individual should always express respect and concern for another's kibun, *as well as express a concern for the* kibun *of the entire group/situation. . . This sense is extremely important in a business context. Within the business world it is socially important not to let your true feelings show through in your facial expressions. This may unconsciously show disrespect to your clients or traders, and can essentially make or break your business relationship or deal. To truly understand someone you must know how to maintain that person's* kibun, *their mood, feelings, or state of mind.*

Source: Adapted from Y-J. Shim, M-S, Kim, and J. N. Martin, *Changing Korea: Understanding Culture and Communication* (New York: Peter Lang, 2008), pp. 77–78.

clean air and not doing too much logging of their trees, keeping streams free of pollution, etc.

In societies that believe mainly in the domination of nature over humans, decisions are made differently. Families may be more accepting of the number of children that are born naturally. There is less intervention in the processes of nature, and there are fewer attempts to control what people see as the natural order.

Many Native Americans and Japanese believe in the value of humans living in harmony with nature, rather than one force dominating the other. In this value orientation, nature is respected and plays an integral part in the spiritual and religious life of the community. Some societies—for example, many Arab groups—emphasize aspects of both harmony with and domination of nature. This reminds us that values are played out in very complex ways in any cultural group.

Relationships Between Humans   Some cultural groups value individualism, whereas others are more group oriented. The cultural differences pertaining to these values distinguish two types of societies. Individualism, often cited as a value held by European Americans, places importance on individuals rather than on families, work teams, or other groups (Bellah, Madsen, Sullivan, Swidler, & Tipton, 1985). This characteristic is often cited as the most important European

American cultural value. In contrast, people from more collectivistic societies, like those in Central and South America, Asia, and many Arab societies, place a great deal of importance on extended families and group loyalty. In the United States, this is the case in Amish communities and in some Latino/a and Native American communities. A visitor to Mexico described one example of collectivism in that culture:

> *I remember that in public that children always seem to be accompanied by someone older, usually a family member. People went around in family groups—children with older siblings, grandparents, aunts—not nearly so age-segregated as it is here in the U.S.*

The collateral orientation emphasizes the collectivist connection to other individuals (mostly family members) even after death. This orientation is found in cultures in which ancestors are seen as a part of the family and are influential in decisions even though they are not alive. Examples of this include the Asian practice of maintaining a table in the house to honor their ancestors or the Mexican "Day of the Dead" practice of having a picnic near the graves of the family members and leaving food for them.

Values may also be related to economic status or rural–urban distinctions. In the United States, for example, working-class people tend to be more collectivistic than middle- or upper-class people. (Working-class people reportedly donate a higher percentage of their time and money to help others.) Historian Roxanne A. Dunbar (1997), who grew up poor in Oklahoma, describes an encounter she had with middle-class individualism while on an extended car trip with her new husband, Jimmy. They passed several stranded motorists, the women sitting in the shade while the men worked on the cars. She was surprised when her husband didn't stop to help:

> *"Why don't we stop?" I asked. No one in my family would ever have passed up a stranded motorist. . . .*
>
> *"They're hustlers, rob you blind, highway bandits," Jimmy said.*
>
> *"How do you know?"*
>
> *"I just know, they use the kids and old people for bait to get you to stop, then rob you, they're transients, fruit pickers, white trash."*
>
> *I stared at the sad faces as we passed by and tried to see the con artists and criminals behind the masks. But they merely looked familiar, like my own relatives. (p. 83)*

These cultural values may influence patterns of communication. For example, people who value individualism *tend* also to favor direct forms of communication and to support overt forms of conflict resolution. People in collectivistic societies *may* employ less direct communication and more avoidance-style conflict resolution. Of course, sometimes people belong to cultural groups that hold contradictory values. For example, most U.S. work contexts require highly individualistic communication, which may conflict with the collectivistic family or ethnic backgrounds of some workers. Workers may find it hard to reconcile and live with these competing values. Consider the experience of Lucia, a Native American college student. When one of her uncles passed away during the first week of

FIGURE 3-2 Holidays are significant ways of enacting and transmitting culture and cultural values across the generations. For example, Kwanzaa is an important holiday for many African Americans. It was established in 1966 by Ron Karenga and lasts seven days—December 26 to January 1—to mark seven important cultural values: unity, self-determination, collective work and responsibility, cooperative economics, purpose, creativity, and faith. What holidays does your family celebrate? What cultural values are being transmitted in those celebrations? (© *Lawrence Migdale/Getty*)

school, she was expected to participate in family activities. She traveled out of state with her family to his home, helped cook and feed other family members, and attended the wake and the funeral. Then her mother became ill, and she had to care for her. Thus, she missed the first two weeks of school. Some of her professors were sympathetic; others were not. As Lucia describes it, she feels almost constantly torn between the demands of her collectivistic family and the demands of the individualistic professors and administration.

Preferred Forms of Activity The most common "activity value" in the United States is the "doing" orientation, which emphasizes productivity. (Remember the expression "Idle hands are the devil's workshop"?) Employment reward systems reflect this value in that workers often must document their progress (e.g., in numbers of sales made or numbers of clients seen). In general, the highest status is conferred on those who "do" (sports figures, physicians, lawyers), rather than on those who "think" (philosophers, professors, priests) (Stewart & Bennett, 1991).

The "growing" orientation emphasizes spiritual aspects of life. This orientation seems to be less prevalent than the other two, perhaps practiced only

In an interview that appears in *Le Nouvel Observateur*, François Mas was asked to explain the popularity of the medication Viagra (a remedy for sexual impotence) in the United States. He relates the popularity to the "can do" value of the U.S. American people.

> *Probably the most revealing is the "can do" attitude. This attitude, inherited from the pioneers, is how American society, in general, deals with existing problems. Centered on the concrete and practical applications, and often seen as naive in the view of older cultures, this approach has the advantage of deploying a kind of energy and rejecting opposition to progress.*
>
> (Le plus révélateur étant le "can do." . . . Cette attitude, héritée de pionniers, est celle de la société américaine en général face aux problèmes de l'existence. Centrée sur le réel et les applications pratiques, souvent naïve dans son expression aux yeux de cultures plus anciennes, cette approach a l'avantage de déployer une certaine énergie et de refuser l'immobilisme.)

Source: From F. Mas, "Vers un Renouveau Sexuel," *Le Nouvel Observateur*, May 1998, pp. 21–27.

in Zen Buddhism and as a cultural motif in the United States in the 1960s (Stewart & Bennett, 1991). Some societies, as in Japan, combine both "doing" and "growing" orientations, emphasizing action and spiritual growth. The third solution is to emphasize "being," a kind of self-actualization in which the individual is fused with the experience. Some societies in Central and South America, as well as in Greece and Spain, exhibit this orientation.

Orientation to Time   Most U.S. cultural communities—particularly European American and middle class—seem to emphasize the future. Consider the practices of depositing money in retirement accounts or keeping appointment books that reach years into the future. Other societies—for example, in Spain or Greece— seem to emphasize the importance of the present, a recognition of the value of living fully in and realizing the potential of the present moment. One of our friends described her impression of this value difference after a visit to Mexico:

> *I had a wonderful experience in Mexico. I liked the energy—there was ALWAYS so much going on in the streets, and in the* zocalo, *all hours of the day and night. And when I returned to the U.S., the streets seemed so dead—everyone individually alone in their own little houses here. I felt suddenly so sensory-deprived!! I guess I also liked it partly because it is so different, culturally, from the way I grew up. The emphasis of expressing and focusing on life in the present. I don't want to imply that life is a constant thoughtless fiesta in Mexico, because it's not. But there was a kind of joie de vivre and enjoyment of life NOW that certainly was not present in my family's very constrained, restrained, serious lifestyle! And so Mexico seemed a great contrast!*

Many European and Asian societies strongly emphasize the past, believing that knowledge and awareness of history has something to contribute to an understanding of contemporary life. For example, the Leaning Tower of Pisa was closed for 10 years while Italian workers repaired structural damage to this historic building.

Hofstede Value Orientations Social psychologist Geert Hofstede (1984) extended the work of Kluckhohn and Strodtbeck, based on extensive cross-cultural study of personnel working in IBM subsidiaries in 53 countries. Whereas Kluckhohn and Strodtbeck (1961) based their framework on cultural patterns of ethnic communities within the United States, Hofstede and colleagues examined value differences among national societies. Hofstede identified five areas of common problems. One problem type, individualism versus collectivism, appeared in the Kluckhohn and Strodtbeck framework. Although the problems were shared by different cultural groups, solutions varied from culture to culture (Hofstede & Hofstede, 2004). As shown in Table 3-3, the problem types are identified as follows:

- Power distance: social inequality, including the relationship with authority
- Femininity versus masculinity: the social implications of having been born male or female
- Ways of dealing with uncertainty, controlling aggression, and expressing emotions
- Long-term versus short-term orientation to life

Hofstede then investigated how these various cultural values influenced corporate behavior in various countries. Let's examine the other problem types more closely. (See Table 3-3.)

Power distance refers to the extent to which less powerful members of institutions and organizations within a country expect and accept the unequal distribution of power. Denmark, Israel, and New Zealand, for example, value small power distance. Most people there believe that less hierarchy is better and that power should be used only for legitimate purposes. Therefore, the best corporate leaders in those countries are those who minimize power differences. In societies that value large power distance—for example, Mexico, the Philippines, and India—the decision-making process and the relationships between managers and subordinates are more formalized. In addition, people may be uncomfortable in settings in which hierarchy is unclear or ambiguous.

The **masculinity–femininity value** is two-dimensional (Hofstede, 1998). It refers to (1) the degree to which gender-specific roles are valued and (2) the degree to which cultural groups value so-called masculine values (achievement, ambition, acquisition of material goods) or so-called feminine values (quality of life, service to others, nurturance, support for the unfortunate). IBM employees in Japan, Austria, and Mexico scored high on the masculine values orientation, expressing a general preference for gender-specific roles, with some roles (e.g., main wage

power distance A cultural variability dimension that concerns the extent to which people accept an unequal distribution of power.

masculinity–femininity value A cultural variability dimension that concerns the degree of being feminine—valuing fluid gender roles, quality of life, service, relationships, and interdependence—and the degree of being masculine—emphasizing distinctive gender roles, ambition, materialism, and independence.

TABLE 3-3 HOFSTEDE VALUE ORIENTATIONS

Power Distance

Low power distance	**High power distance**
Less hierarchy better	More hierarchy better
e.g. Denmark, Israel, New Zealand	e.g. Mexico, India

Femininity/Masculinity

Femininity	**Masculinity**
Fewer gender-specific roles	More gender-specific roles
Value quality of life, support for unfortunate	Achievement, ambition, acquisition of material goods
e.g. Denmark, Norway, Sweden	e.g. Japan, Austria, Mexico

Uncertainty Avoidance

Low uncertainty avoidance	**High uncertainty avoidance**
Dislike rules, accept dissent	More extensive rules, limit dissent
Less formality	More formality
e.g. Great Britain, Sweden, Hong Kong	e.g. Greece, Portugal, Japan

Long-term/Short-term Orientation

Short-term orientation	**Long-term orientation**
Universal guidelines for good and evil	Definition of good and evil depends on circumstances
Prefer quick results	Value perseverance and tenacity
e.g. Western, Religions, Judaism, Christianity, Islam	e.g. Confucianism, Hinduism, Buddhism

Source: Adapted from G. Hofstede and G. J. Hofstede, *Cultures and Organizations: Software of the Mind,* 2nd ed. (Boston: McGraw-Hill, 2004), p. 232.

earner) better filled by men and other roles (e.g., homemaker, teacher) by women. In contrast, employees in northern Europe (Denmark, Norway, Sweden, and the Netherlands) tended to rank higher in feminine values orientation, reflecting more gender equality and a stronger belief in the importance of quality of life for all.

uncertainty avoidance
A cultural variability dimension that concerns the extent to which uncertainty, ambiguity, and deviant ideas and behaviors are avoided.

Uncertainty avoidance concerns the degree to which people who feel threatened by ambiguous situations respond by avoiding them or trying to establish more structure to compensate for the uncertainty. Societies that have a weak uncertainty avoidance orientation (Great Britain, Sweden, Hong Kong, and the United States) prefer to limit rules, accept dissent, and take risks. In contrast, those with a strong uncertainty avoidance orientation (Greece, Portugal, and Japan) usually prefer more extensive rules and regulations in organizational settings and seek consensus about goals.

I recently spent two weeks in Mexico City. It was an amazing experience. The contrast between Phoenix and Mexico City totally blew me away, especially the architecture. I mean, just walking down the street you see buildings all around you that are hundreds of years old. We went to the Basilica of the Virgin of Guadalupe, and our guide showed us the exact hill where Juan Diego supposedly saw the Virgin and brought back roses to prove to the priests that he saw her. The priests then built a church exactly right there because that was what the Virgin told Juan to tell the priests to do. Juan Diego is like a national hero in Mexico, and this place where they built these churches is totally sacred. People come from all over Mexico to this exact place, and it is just so hugely important to them.

We also went to Teotihuacán and Templo Mayor. Both are ancient ruins from the Aztecs. These places were really, really amazing. Our guide pointed out for us places where the Spanish built buildings right on top of the ancient structures. It was their way of winning over the natives, of making the Spanish ways take over the ways of the native people. I realized that this change in architecture conveyed a whole history of different cultures and conquest. I was amazed that as I stood there at Templo Mayor, right in the heart of this huge city, I could literally see hundreds of years of history. And the domination also hit me. The Spanish had to build over the temples and other sacred sites of the Aztecs in order to win the hearts of the people. And they needed to make Juan Diego a national hero and make sacred the spot that he is said to have seen the Virgin of Guadalupe. And in order to make all that real to the people, they had to put it all in the architecture.

—Samantha

Hofstede's original framework contained only four problem types and was criticized for its predominantly western European bias. In response, a group of Chinese researchers developed and administered a similar, but more Asian-oriented, questionnaire to people in 22 countries around the world (Chinese Culture Connection, 1987). Their questionnaire included ideas related to Confucian-based thinking. In comparing their framework to Hofstede's, they concluded that there was, in fact, a great deal of overlap. Indeed, the three dimensions of individualism—collectivism, power distance, and masculinity–femininity—seem to be universal. However, uncertainty avoidance seems to be more relevant to Western societies. A fifth dimension that emerged from the Asian study and that seems to apply to both Eastern and Western societies is the **long-term versus short-term orientation,** which reflects a society's search for virtue or truth.

Those with a short-term orientation are concerned with possessing the truth (reflected in the Western religions of Judaism, Christianity, and Islam), focus on quick results in endeavors, and recognize social pressure to conform. Those with a long-term orientation tend to respect the demands of virtue (reflected in

long-term versus short-term orientation A cultural variability dimension that reflects a cultural-group orientation toward virtue or truth. The long-term orientation emphasizes virtue, whereas the short-term orientation emphasizes truth.

Eastern religions such as Confucianism, Hinduism, Buddhism, and Shintoism); to focus more on thrift, perseverance, and tenacity in whatever they attempt; and to be willing to subordinate themselves to a larger purpose.

Limitations of Value Frameworks   Identifying cultural values helps us understand broad cultural differences, but it is important to remember that not everyone in a given society holds the dominant value (Kirkman, Lone, & Gibson, 2006). We shouldn't reduce individuals to mere stereotypes based on these value orientations. After all, not all Amish or Japanese are group oriented, and not all Americans and Australians are individualistic. Remember that cultures are dynamic and heterogeneous. Although people in small rural communities may be more collectively oriented, or more willing to help their neighbors, we cannot say that people in big cities ignore those around them.

Value heterogeneity may be particularly noticeable in a society that is undergoing rapid change. South Korea, for example has transformed itself in the past 50 years from a poor, agrarian country into a global economic and technological powerhouse; it is now the 10th largest economy, the world's #1 leader in broadband penetration, and has the most techno-savvy young people in the world. Influenced by Western capitalism and individualism, many young Koreans are now embracing more individualistic values, making their own decisions regarding marriage and career, rather than following their family's wishes—a practice unheard of 50 years ago (Shim, Kim, & Martin, 2008).

Another limitation of value frameworks is that they tend to "essentialize" people. In other words, people tend to assume that a particular group characteristic is the essential characteristic of a given member at all times and in all contexts. As early as 1990, researchers found that members of South Korean organizations were pursuing more individualistic values. One study found that the workers saw themselves as both individualistic and collectivistic, valuing competitiveness and self-reliance and a "can do" spirit. The researchers are quite emphatic that the results do not show that Koreans are becoming individualistic, but rather reflect a "discovery of individual in collectivistic frame of society" (Cho, 1994, p. 229); the workers acknowledge that their self-concept is not "I" *or* "we," but "I" *and* "we," both present at the same time (Cho, 1994). Another more recent study found that all Korean women interviewed expressed both a strong family orientation and a "relational" concept of self as well as a concept of the autonomous or independent self (Shim, Kim, & Martin, 2008). Similarly, researchers who have spent many years in China also observe that the contemporary Chinese "are not either individualist or collective but both at the same time" (Ambler & Witzel, 2000). It is useful to keep these tensions in mind when thinking about cultural groups—that they often reflect a set of dynamic contrasts, rather than a static set of specific characteristics or traits.

The cultural–individual dialectic reminds us that these value orientations exist on a continuum and are all present, to a greater or lesser extent, in all societies. For example, we could characterize the debate about health care in the United States as a struggle between "masculine" and "feminine" value orientations. Those with a "masculine" orientation believe that each person should

take care of him- or herself and be free to achieve and to acquire as many material goods as possible. Others, representing a "feminine" position, believe that
everyone should sacrifice a little for the good of the whole and that everyone
should be assured access to health care and hospitalization.

The differences–similarities dialectic reminds us that although people may differ with respect to specific value orientations, they also may hold other value orientations in common. For example, people may have different views on the importance
of individual or group loyalty but share a belief in the essential goodness of human
nature and find similarity in religious faith and practice. Finally, a static–dynamic
dialectic reminds us that although group-related values tend to be relatively consistent, people are dynamic, and their behavior varies contextually. Thus, they may be
more or less individualistic or group oriented depending on the context.

How Communication Reinforces Culture

Culture not only influences communication but also is enacted through, and so
is influenced by, communication. Scholars of cultural communication describe
how various aspects of culture are enacted in speech communities in situ, that is,
in contexts. They seek to understand communication patterns that are situated
socially and give voice to cultural identity. Specifically, they examine how the
cultural forms and frames (terms, rituals, myths, and social dramas) are enacted
through structuring norms of conversation and interaction. The patterns are not
connected in a deterministic way to any cultural group (Philipsen, 2002).

Researcher Tamar Katriel (1990) examines "griping," a **communication
ritual** that takes place among middle-class Israelis. Using the SPEAKING
framework (scene, participant, end, act sequence, key, instrumentality, norm,
and genre), Katriel analyzes the ritual in the following way: The griping topic
must be one related to the domain of public life, and the purpose of the griping
is not to solve the problem but to vent pent-up tensions and to affirm the shared
reality of being Israeli. The ritual is a deeply felt, widely held, accessible behavioral pattern that affirms the cultural identity of Israelis. Although individuals
belonging to other cultural groups may gripe, the activity may not be performed
in this systematic cultural way and may not fill the same function.

The instrumentality (or channel) in griping is face-to-face, and the scene (or
setting) usually is a Friday night gathering in a private home. Participants may
be friends or acquaintances, or even strangers, but not real outsiders. (Katriel
describes an embarrassing incident when a couple of gripers discovered that one
of the group was merely a visiting Jew and not a native Israeli.) The key (or tone)
of this ritual is one of plaintiveness and frustration. The act sequence comprises
an initiation phase, when someone voices a complaint; this is followed by the
acknowledgment phase, when others comment on the opener, and then a pro-
gression of subthemes. Finally, during the termination phase, everyone intellec-
tually sighs and agrees that it is a problem: "It's no joke, things are getting worse
all the time," the participants might say.

It is possible to compare different ways in which cultural norms and forms
such as griping enact aspects of the culture and construct cultural identity. For

**communication
ritual** A set form of systematic interactions that
take place on a regular
basis.

FIGURE 3-3   This photo of tourists watching Aztec dancers in Mexico City reflects an earlier context in which Aztec culture was dominant in Mexico. What role does Aztec culture play in Mexican life today? What does this communicate about the continued vitality of Aztec culture in today's Mexico? (*Courtesy Jackie Martinez, Arizona State University*)

example, although Katriel is not interested in making cross-cultural comparisons, she does allude to the difference between the Israeli griping ritual and a similar communication ritual that many white, middle-class U.S. residents engage in (Katriel & Philipsen, 1990). The communication ritual is a form of close, supportive, and flexible speech aimed at solving personal problems and affirming participants' identities. It is initiated when people sit down together, acknowledge the problem, and negotiate a solution. Katriel identifies similarities in these two rituals: Each fills the function of dramatizing major cultural problems, provides a preferred social context for the venting of problems and frustration, and promotes a sense of community identity (Katriel, 1990).

A related approach from cultural communication studies sees culture as **performative.** If we accept this metaphor, then we are not studying any external (cultural) reality. Rather, we are examining how persons enact and represent their culture's worldviews. (See Figure 3-3.) For example, as Philipsen (1992) reports in his study of Teamsterville, men enact their gender (cultural) roles by remaining silent in many instances, engaging in talk mainly with peers but not with women or children.

These interpretive studies sometimes use cultural values as a way to explain cultural patterns. Kristine Fitch (1994) conducted a cross-cultural study comparing how people in Bogotá, Colombia, and Boulder, Colorado, got others to do what they wanted, a sociolinguistic form known as a *directive*. Fitch found that directives were seen as a problem in both societies, but as different kinds of problems that reflected and reinforced different value orientations.

performative Acting or presenting oneself in a specific way so as to accomplish some goal.

Individuals in Boulder seemed to think that telling someone what to do should be approached carefully so as not to infringe on that person's autonomy—reflecting a value of individualism. In Bogotá, where collectivistic values reign, directives must be negotiated within relationships; there must be enough *confianza* (respect) or authority that one person is required by the social hierarchy to do the other's bidding. As you can see, cultural values can be used to show how culture influences communication or to explain how communication reinforces cultural values.

Communication as Resistance to the Dominant Cultural System

Resistance is the metaphor used in cultural studies to conceptualize the relationship between culture and communication. Borrowing this metaphor, we can try to discover how individuals use their own space to resist the dominant cultural system. For example, in the fall of 2005, nonwhite French youth rioted for days in the suburbs of Paris to communicate their resistance to the ways the French social system works. They felt that their efforts to integrate into mainstream French society were being thwarted by systematic racial discrimination. Similarly, workers often find ways to resist extreme individualism and competition in the workplace. For example, flight attendants may collaborate to protect each other from the critical gaze of supervisors (Murphy, 1998). Or students may sign their advisers' names on course registration forms, thereby circumventing the university bureaucracy. We can interpret these behaviors as resistance to the dominant cultural system.

THE RELATIONSHIP BETWEEN COMMUNICATION AND CONTEXT

Context typically is created by the physical or social aspects of the situation in which communication occurs. For example, communication may occur in a classroom, a bar, or a church; in each case, the physical characteristics of the setting influence the communication. People communicate differently depending on the context. Context is neither static nor objective, and it can be multilayered. Context may consist of the social, political, and historical structures in which the communication occurs.

Not surprisingly, the social context is determined on the societal level. Consider, for example, the controversy over the Calvin Klein underwear ads in the early 1990s that used young adolescents as models: Many critics viewed the ads as equivalent to pedophilia. The controversy took place in a social context in which pedophilia was seen as perverse or immoral. This meant that any communication that encouraged or fed that behavior or perspective, including advertising, was deemed wrong by the majority of observers. However, pedophilia has not been considered wrong in all societies in all periods of history. To interpret the ads adequately, we would have to know something about the current feelings toward and meanings attached to pedophilia wherever the ads were displayed.

The political context in which communication occurs includes those forces that attempt to change or retain existing social structures and relations. For example, to understand the acts of protesters who throw blood or red paint on people who wear fur coats, we must consider the political context. In this case, the political context would be the ongoing informal debates about animal rights and cruelty to animals farmed for their pelts. In other locales or other eras, the protesters' communicative acts would not make sense or would be interpreted in other ways.

We also need to examine the historical context of communication. For example, the meaning of a college degree depends in part on the particular school's reputation. Why does a degree from Harvard communicate a different meaning than a degree from an obscure state university? Harvard's reputation relies on history—the large endowments given over the years, the important persons who have attended and graduated, and so forth.

THE RELATIONSHIP BETWEEN COMMUNICATION AND POWER

Power is pervasive in communication interactions, although it is not always evident or obvious how power influences communication or what kinds of meaning are constructed. We often think of communication between individuals as being between equals, but this is rarely the case (Allen, 2004). As communication scholar Mark Orbe (1998) describes it,

> *In every society a social hierarchy exists that privileges some groups over others. Those groups that function at the top of the social hierarchy determine to a great extent the communication system of the entire society. (p. 8)*

Orbe goes on to describe how those people in power, consciously or unconsciously, create and maintain communication systems that reflect, reinforce, and promote their own ways of thinking and communicating. There are two levels of group-related power: (1) the primary dimensions—age, ethnicity, gender, physical abilities, race, and sexual orientation—which are more permanent in nature, and (2) the secondary dimensions—educational background, geographic location, marital status, and socioeconomic status—which are more changeable (Loden & Rosener, 1991). The point is that the dominant communication systems ultimately impede those who do not share the systems. The communication style most valued in college classrooms, for example, emphasizes public speaking and competition (because the first person who raises his or her hand gets to speak). Not all students are comfortable with this style, but those who take to it naturally are more likely to succeed.

Power also comes from social institutions and the roles individuals occupy in those institutions. For example, in the classroom, there is temporary inequality, with instructors having more power. After all, they set the course requirements, ose Weitz, a communication scholar, describes the importance of hair for women in U.S. society in attracting men. Although some writers say that women who use strategies like the "hair flip" in attracting men do so unconsciously and are just blindly obeying cultural rules, her interviews with women reveal that many are acutely aware of the cultural rules and the power of the "flip." Those who cannot participate feel marginalized.

A young white woman:

I have very long hair and use the hair flip, both consciously and unconsciously. When I do it [consciously], I check the room to see if anyone is looking in my direction but never catch a guy's eye first. I just do it in his line of vision. [I] bend over slightly, pretending to get something from a bag or pick something up) so that some of my hair falls in front of my shoulder. Then I lean back and flip my hair out and then shake my head so my hair sways a little.

A young Latino woman:

In Hispanic culture hair is very important for a woman. It defines our beauty and gives us power over men. Now that I cut my hair short, I miss the feeling of moving my hair around and the power it gave me. . . .

The hair flip is especially aggravating for those black women whose hair will not grow long. As one black graduate student explains,

As an African American woman, I am very aware of non–African American women "flipping" their hair. . . . I will speak only for myself here (but I think it's a pretty global feeling for many African American women), but I often look at women who can flip their hair with envy, wishfulness, perhaps regret?, . . . with my "natural" hair, if I run my fingers through it, it's going to be a mess [and won't] gracefully fall back into place.

Source: R. Weitz, *Rapunzel's Daughters: What Women's Hair Tells Us About Women's Lives.* (New York: Farrar, Straus and Giroux, 2004).

give grades, determine who speaks, and so on. In this case, the power rests not with the individual instructor but with the role that he or she is enacting.

Power is dynamic. It is not a simple one-way proposition. For example, students may leave a classroom at any time during a class period, or they may carry on a conversation while the professor is speaking—thus weakening the professor's power over them. They may also refuse to accept a grade and file a grievance with the university administration to have the grade changed. Further, the typical power relationship between instructor and student often is not perpetuated beyond the classroom. However, some issues of power play out in a broader social context (Johnson, 2001). For example, in contemporary society, cosmetic companies have a vested interest in a particular image of female beauty that involves purchasing and using makeup. Advertisements encourage

Just out of college, I went to Japan and lived with a family for a few months. I vividly remember the sense of shock upon realizing the gap between my Japanese homestay family's perception of my status, power, and role compared to my own view of the situation. I had seen the experience as a chance for them to show and teach me various facets of Japanese home life and, reciprocally, as a time for me to study my language books and appreciate them. And I tried to learn as much as I could from Ken, their son, whom I considered a role model. One day, however, after what I suppose was a lengthy period of frustration on her part, my Japanese mother took me aside and said, "You seem to look for learnings behind each of Ken's actions, Douglas-san, but remember that since you are older it is you who must teach and be the responsible one."
—Douglas

women to feel compelled to participate in this cultural definition. Resistance can be expressed by a refusal to go along with the dominant cultural standards of beauty. Angela, a student from rural Michigan, describes how she resisted the "beauty culture" of her metropolitan university:

I came to school, and when I looked around I felt like I was inadequate. I had one of two choices: to conform to what the girls look like here, or to stay the same. I chose to stay true to my "Michigan" self. I felt more confident this way. I still remember looking at all of the blond girls with their fake boobs and black pants, strutting down campus. Four years later, I have a more mature attitude and realized that this culture wasn't for me.

What happens when someone like Angela decides not to buy into this definition? Regardless of the woman's individual reason for not participating, other people are likely to interpret her behavior in ways that may not match her own reasons. What her unadorned face communicates is understood against a backdrop of society's definitions—that is, the backdrop developed by the cosmetics industry.

Dominant cultural groups attempt to perpetuate their positions of privilege in many ways. However, subordinate groups can resist this domination in many ways too. Cultural groups can use political and legal means to maintain or resist domination, but these are not the only means of invoking power relations. Groups can negotiate their various relations to culture through economic boycotts, strikes, and sit-ins. Individuals can subscribe (or not subscribe) to specific magazines or newspapers, change TV channels, write letters to government officials, or take action in other ways to change the influence of power.

The disempowered can negotiate power in varied and subtle ways. Tracy's (2000) ethnographic study of organizational communication on cruise ships analyzes the complex, subtle power dynamics between the ship's staff and management. The staff found it very stressful to follow management's mandate to "never say no [to the customers]" and "smile, we are on stage"; they demonstrated their

Many of the Thai managers I spoke with while doing research on American companies in Thailand stressed to me that when working with Thais one needed to be very aware of relationships and the hierarchy in which they exist. A Thai woman I spoke with, who was the secretary to the company's American president, provided this example of the need for attention to the details of relationships:

> *I believe in the United States it is common for a boss to ask the secretary to request some materials from another person or to call people and tell them the boss wants to see them. In the United States, you all look at each other as equals. It is not so important what someone's title is, their age, or time with the company. In Thailand, those things are very important. For example, my boss, who is an American, was always asking me to go call so-and-so and request a meeting or go talk to so-and-so and get some reports from them. By having me do this, the Thais were wondering several things: Why should we deal with her; she is just a secretary, and have I done something wrong that the boss does not want to talk with me? Finally, I got my boss to understand that when he had a request for someone—especially someone who was high-ranking in the company, someone who was much older than me or had been with the company longer than me—I would write a short note to that person, he would sign it, then I would pass the note along. That way, everyone's face was saved, their positions were recognized, and the boss came across as show-ing that he cared about his personal relationship with everyone. Mind you, I can run over and ask others of my same rank, age, or time with the company for any information or a meeting, but it is important to show respect toward those in high positions.*
>
> *—Chris*

resistance to management by making fun of the guidelines. Similarly, students might text each other during class or leave the classroom during a lecture as a way of negotiating the power relations between professor and students.

Power is complex, especially in relation to institutions or the social structure. Some inequities, such as in gender, class, or race, are more rigid than those created by temporary roles such as student or teacher. The power relations between student and teacher, for example, are more complex if the teacher is a female challenged by male students. We really can't understand intercultural communication without considering the power dynamics in the interaction.

A dialectical perspective looks at the dynamic and interrelated ways in which culture, communication, context, and power intersect in intercultural communication interactions. Consider this example: When Tom first arrived in Brussels in January 1998, he asked for a national train schedule from the information office at one of the train stations. Because he does not speak Dutch, he talked to the agent behind the counter in French. The agent gave Tom a copy of the national train schedule in Dutch. When Tom asked if it was available in French, the man politely apologized, saying that it was the end of the season and there were no more available in French. It was clear to Tom that, although both parties followed *la forme de la politesse*, the agent did not want to give him the train schedule in French. Indeed, it was not near the end of the season because the 1997–1998 train schedule ran from June 1 to May 23.

From a communication perspective, it might not be at all clear that an intercultural struggle had taken place. None of the traditional signals of conflict were manifested: no raised voices, no harsh words, no curtness. Indeed, the exchange seemed polite and courteous.

From a cultural perspective, however, with various contexts and power differentials in mind, a different view of this intercultural interaction emerges. Belgium is a nation largely divided by two cultures, Flemish and Walloon, although there is a small German-speaking minority in the far eastern part of the country. Belgium is officially trilingual (Dutch, French, German); that is, each language is the official language in its territory. Dutch is the official language in Flanders, and French is the official language in Wallonia, except in the eastern part, where German is the official language. The only part of Belgium that is officially bilingual is the "Brussels-Capital Region."

There are many historical contexts to consider here. For example, Brussels is historically a Flemish city, located in Flanders (but near the border with Wallonia). Also, the French language dominated in Belgium from the time it gained independence from the Netherlands in 1830 until the early 20th century when Flemish gained parity.

There are social and economic contexts to consider as well. Since the 1960s, Flanders has been more economically powerful than Wallonia. The Brussels-Capital Region, despite being in Flanders, has become increasingly French speaking; some estimates place the current percentage of francophones at 85% to 90%. And nearly 30% of Brussels' residents are foreigners, most of whom are francophones. The increasing migration of city dwellers to the suburbs has also caused tensions because a number of communes located in Flanders now have a francophone majority.

So, although the Brussels-Capital Region is officially bilingual, this is the site of a number of struggles between French and Dutch. Indeed, as many Walloons told Tom, one does not get a sense of the conflict in Wallonia, but it is evident in Brussels. In the context of the various tensions that existed at the time of Tom's arrival in Belgium, the intercultural conflict at the train station is merely a playing out of much larger issues in Belgian society. Tom's entry into that society, as another francophone foreigner, situated his communication interactions in largely prefigured ways.

Although he later secured a French train schedule, he continued to use the Dutch one so he could learn the Dutch names of many Belgian cities as well. In any case, Tom's experience involved various dialectical tensions: (1) being a francophone foreigner versus a traditional Flemish resident, (2) being in an officially bilingual region versus an increasingly francophone one, (3) recognizing the

ANSWERS TO THE TEST OF U.S. CULTURAL KNOWLEDGE

1. The correct answer is B. Lagniappe refers to small freebies or sometimes small gifts given by stores when you purchase something. It is used mostly in southern Louisiana and Mississippi but also along the Gulf Coast.

2. The correct answer is C. Hoppin' John is a New Year's tradition across the South. Normally it is simply rice and black-eyed peas, but it can include other items.

3. The correct answer is C. Shoofly pie, traditionally made from molasses, is a very sweet pie.

4. The correct answer is D. The Illini are a nonexistent tribe used as the mascot of the University of Illinois at Urbana-Champaign.

5. The correct answer is A. Also sometimes just called Eid, this is a three-day joyous festival that celebrates family, friendship, community, and the Creator. It is a time of reconciliation.

6. The correct answer is A. It marks the anniversary of the Supreme Court ruling in *Loving v. Virginia* that overturned legal barriers to interracial marriage.

7. The correct answer is D. Hanamatsuri (or flower festival) is in the spring and marks a time of renewal and the birthday of Buddha.

8. The correct answer is A. Lefse is made primarily from potatoes.

9. The correct answer is D. Menudo is traditionally served on New Year's Day.

10. The correct answer is C. Haupia is made from coconut milk.

importance of formality and politeness in French versus the nature of this ancient conflict, (4) having abundant opportunities to learn French versus the lack of opportunities to study Dutch in the United States, and (5) illustrating the economic power of the Flemish in Belgium versus that of the francophones in Brussels. From these dialectical tensions and others, Tom attempted to understand and contextualize his intercultural interaction.

There are no simple lists of behaviors that are key to successful intercultural interaction. Instead, we encourage you to understand the contexts and dialectical tensions that arise in your intercultural communication experiences. In this way, you will better understand the constraints you face in your interactions. You will also come to a better understanding of the culture you are in and the culture you are from. Although the dialectical perspective makes the investigation of culture and communication far more complex, it also makes it far more exciting and interesting and leads to a much richer understanding.

INTERNET RESOURCES

www.geert-hofstede.com/index.shtml
This Geert Hofstede Cultural Dimensions Web site provides a description of Hofstede's cultural values dimensions and the specific value scores for a variety of countries and regions of the world. For those of you who may be studying, working, or traveling abroad, you may find it useful to compare the values scores of your home culture and host culture to better understand how the two cultures are similar and different according to Hofstede's cultural dimensions.

www.powerofculture.nl/en
The Power of Culture Web site provides a review of art and cultural expressions, along with information on human rights, education, the environment, emancipation, and democratization. The Web site provides links to themes, such as cultural exchange and culture, conflict and culture, and ethics, with news stories and articles related to the subject matter.

http://portal.unesco.org/culture/en/ev.php-
URL_ID=34603&URL_DO=DO_TOPIC&URL_SECTION=201.html
This UNESCO Culture Sector Web site provides links to relevant news and events along with general background information about the changing realm of culture, both regionally and globally. The Web site also provides links that describe the culture and people from different regions worldwide, such as the Arab states, Latin America, the Caribbean, Europe, and North America.

www.globalvoicesonline.org/
The Global Voices Online Web site is sponsored by Harvard's Berkman Center for Internet and Society. The site provides blogs, podcasts, photo-sharing sites, and videoblogs from around the world. There is a site search available along with an index of countries and topics. You can select a topic, such as racism or politics, and select the country you wish to read and learn more about in terms of that topic.

SUMMARY

- There are four building blocks to understanding intercultural communication: culture, communication, context, and power.
- Culture can be viewed as
  - Learned patterns of group-related perceptions
  - Contextual symbolic patterns of meaning, involving emotions
  - Heterogeneous, dynamic, and a site of contestation
- Communication is a symbolic process whereby reality is produced, maintained, repaired, and transformed.

- Communication can be viewed as
  - Components of speaker, sender, receiver, message and channel, and variables
  - Symbolic and processual
  - Involving power dynamics
- The relationship between culture and communication is complex:
  - Culture influences communication and is enacted and reinforced through communication.
  - Communication also may be a way of contesting and resisting the dominant culture.
- The context also influences communication: It is the physical and social setting in which communication occurs or the larger political, social, and historical environment.
- Power is pervasive and plays an enormous, although often hidden, role in intercultural interactions.

DISCUSSION QUESTIONS

1. How do definitions of culture influence people's perspectives on intercultural communication?
2. How do the values of a cultural group influence communication with members of other cultural groups?
3. What techniques do people use to assert power in communication interactions?
4. How is culture a contested site?

Go to the self-quizzes on the Online Learning Center at www.mhhe.com/martinnakayama5 to further test your knowledge.

ACTIVITIES

1. *Cultural Values.* Look for advertisements in newspapers and popular magazines. Analyze the ads to see if you can identify the social values to which they appeal.
2. *Culture: Deeply Felt or Contested Zone?* Analyze the lyrics of songs you listen to and try to identify patterns in the songs. Then think about your own cultural position and discuss which framework—the one proposed by cultural ethnographies (culture as deeply felt) or the one proposed by cultural studies (culture as a contested zone)—more adequately articulates the connection between culture and communication.

REFERENCES

Allen, B. (2004). *Difference matters: Communicating social identity.* Long Grove, IL: Waveland Press.

Ambler, T., & Witzel, M. (2000). *Doing business in China.* New York: Routledge.

Baldwin, J. R., & Lindsley, S. L. (1994). *Conceptualizations of culture.* Tempe: Arizona State University Urban Studies Center.

Bellah, R. N., Madsen, R., Sullivan, W. M., Swidler, A., & Tipton, S. M. (1985). *Habits of the heart: Individualism and commitment in American life.* New York: Harper & Row.

Bennett, M. J., & Castiglioni, I. (2004). Embodied ethnocentrism and the feeling of culture. In D. Landis, J. M. Bennett, & M. J. Bennett (Eds.), *Handbook of intercultural training* (3rd ed., pp. 249–265). Thousand Oaks, CA: Sage.

Berger, Y. (1998, January 7). A bout portant. *Le Soir,* p. 2.

Burke, J. (1985). *The day the universe changed.* Boston: Little, Brown.

Buzzanell, P. M. (1994). Gaining a voice: Feminist organizational communication theorizing. *Management Communication Quarterly, 7,* 339–383.

Carbaugh, D. (1988). Comments on "culture" in communication inquiry. *Communication Reports, 1,* 38–41.

Carey, J. W. (1989). *Communication as culture: Essays on media and society.* Boston: Unwin Hyman.

Cargile, A. (2005). Describing culture dialectically. In W. J. Starosta & G.-M. Chen (Eds.), *Taking stock in intercultural communication: Where to now?* (pp. 99–123). Washington, DC: National Communication Association.

Chinese Culture Connection. (1987). Chinese values and the search for culture-free dimensions of culture. *Journal of Cross-Cultural Psychology, 18,* 143–164.

Cho, N.-G. (1994). The emergence of individualism in Korean organizations. In G. Yoon & S.-C. Choi (Eds.), *Psychology of the Korean people: Collectivism and individualism* (pp. 209–232). Seoul, Korea: Dong-A Publishing.

Collier, M. J., Hegde, R. S., Lee, W., Nakayama, T. K., & Yep, G. A. (2002). Dialogue on the edges: Ferment in communication and culture. In M. J. Collier (Ed.), *Transforming communication about culture* (*International and Intercultural Communication Annual* (Vol. 24, pp. 219–280). Thousand Oaks, CA: Sage.

Dunbar, R. A. (1997). Bloody footprints: Reflections on growing up poor white. In M. Wray & A. Newitz (Eds.), *White trash: Race and class in America* (pp. 73–86). New York: Routledge.

Fitch, K. L. (1994). A cross-cultural study of directive sequences and some implications for compliance-gaining research. *Communication Monographs, 61,* 185–209.

Geertz, C. (1973). *The interpretation of culture.* New York: Basic Books.

Grossberg, L. (1993). Can cultural studies find true happiness in communication? *Journal of Communication, 43*(4), 89–97.

Gudykunst, W. B. (2002). Issues in cross-cultural communication research. In W. B. Gudykunst & B. Mody (Eds.). *Handbook of international and intercultural communication* (2nd ed., pp. 165–177). Thousand Oaks, CA: Sage.

Hall, B. (1992). Theories of culture and communication. *Communication Theory, 1,* 50–70.

Hall, S. (1992). Cultural studies and its theoretical legacies. In L. Grossberg, C. Nelson, & P. Treichler (Eds.), *Cultural studies* (pp. 277–294). New York: Routledge.

Hannerz, U. (1996). *Transnational connections.* London: Routledge.

Hofstede, G. (1984). *Culture's consequences.* Beverly Hills, CA: Sage.

Hofstede, G. (1998). *Masculinity and femininity: The taboo dimension of national cultures.* Thousand Oaks, CA: Sage.

Hofstede, G., & Hofstede, G. J. (2004). *Cultures and organizations: Software of the mind* (2nd ed.). Boston: McGraw-Hill.

Hymes, D. (1972). Models of the interaction of language and social life. In J. Gumperz & D. Hymes (Eds.), *Directions in sociolinguistics: The ethnography of speaking* (pp. 35–71). New York: Holt, Rinehart & Winston.

Johnson, A. G. (2001). *Privilege, power, and difference.* Boston: McGraw-Hill.

Katriel, T. (1990). "Griping" as a verbal ritual in some Israeli discourse. In D. Carbaugh (Ed.), *Cultural communication and intercultural contact* (pp. 99–112). Hillsdale, NJ: Lawrence Erlbaum.

Katriel, T., & Philipsen, G. (1990). What we need is communication: "Communication" as a cultural category in some American speech. In D. Carbaugh (Ed.), *Cultural communication and intercultural contact* (pp. 77–94). Hillsdale, NJ: Lawrence Erlbaum.

Keesing, R. M. (1994). Theories of culture revisited. In R. Brofsky (Ed.), *Assessing cultural anthropology.* New York: McGraw-Hill.

Kirkman, B. L., Lowe, K. B., & Gibson, C. B. (2006). A quarter century of Culture's Consequences: A review of empirical research incorporating Hofstede's cultural values framework. *Journal of International Business Studies, 37,* 285–320.

Kluckhohn, F., & Strodtbeck, F. (1961). *Variations in value orientations.* Chicago: Row, Peterson.

Kohls, L. R. (1996). *Survival kit for overseas living.* Yarmouth, ME: Intercultural Press.

Kristjánsdóttir, E. S. (in press). Invisibility dreaded and desired: Phenomenological inquiry of sojourners' cross-cultural adaptation. *Howard Journal of Communications, 20*(22).

Loden, M., & Rosener, J. B. (1991). *Workforce American! Managing employee diversity as a vital resource.* Homewood, IL: Business One Irwin.

Martin, J. N., & Nakayama, T. K. (1999). Thinking dialectically about culture and communication. *Communication Theory, 9,* 1–25.

Murphy, A. G. (1998). Hidden transcripts of flight attendant resistance. *Management Communication Quarterly, 11,* 499–512.

Orbe, M. O. (1998). *Constructing co-cultural theory: An explication of culture, power, and communication.* Thousand Oaks, CA: Sage.

Philipsen, G. (1992). *Speaking culturally: Explorations in social communication.* Albany: State University of New York Press.

Philipsen, G. (2002). Cultural communication. In W. B. Gudykunst & B. Mody (Eds.), *Handbook of international and intercultural communication* (2nd ed., pp. 51–67). Thousand Oaks, CA: Sage.

Shim, Y-j., Kim, M-S., & Martin, J. N. (2008). *Changing Korea: Understanding culture and communication.* New York: Peter Lang.

Singer, M. R. (1987). *Intercultural communication: A perceptual approach.* Englewood Cliffs, NJ: Prentice-Hall.

Stewart, E. C., & Bennett, M. J. (1991). *American cultural patterns: A cross-cultural perspective.* Yarmouth, ME: Intercultural Press.

Tracy, S. J. (2000). Becoming a character for commerce: Emotion labor, self-subordination, and discursive construction of identity in a total institution. *Management Communication Quarterly, 14*(1), 90–128.

Williams, R. (1981). The analysis of culture. In T. Bennett, G. Martin, C. Mercer, & J. Woollacott (Eds.), *Culture, ideology and social process: A reader* (pp. 43–52). London: Open University Press.

Williams, R. (1983). *Keywords: A vocabulary of culture and society* (Rev. ed.). New York: Oxford University Press.

HISTORY AND INTERCULTURAL COMMUNICATION

Frances Fitzgerald (1972), a journalist who has written about the U.S. involvement in the Vietnam War, analyzes the U.S. cultural orientation to the future rather than the past:

> *Americans ignore history, for to them everything has always seemed new under the sun. The national myth is that of creativity and progress, of a steady climbing upward into power and prosperity, both for the individual and for the country as a whole. Americans see history as a straight line and themselves standing at the cutting edge of it as representatives for all mankind. They believe in the future as if it were a religion; they believe that there is nothing they cannot accomplish, that solutions wait somewhere for all problems.*

This difference in orientation to the past framed the Vietnam conflict in a very narrow way for the United States. This contrasts greatly with the Vietnamese view of history, especially in the context of their struggles against outside aggression over thousands of years.

You may think it odd to find a chapter about history in a book on intercultural communication. After all, what does the past have to do with intercultural interaction? In this chapter, we discuss how the past is a very important facet of intercultural communication.

The history that we know and our views of that history are very much influenced by our culture. When people of different cultural backgrounds encounter one another, the differences among them can become hidden barriers to communication. However, people often overlook such dynamics in intercultural communication. We typically think of "history" as something contained in history books. We may view history as those events and people, mostly military and political, that played significant roles in shaping the world of today. This chapter examines some of the ways in which history is important in understanding intercultural interaction. Many intercultural interactions involve a dialectical interplay between past and present.

We have found, in the classes we teach, that European American students often want to deemphasize history. "Why do we have to dwell on the past? Can't we all move on?" they ask. In contrast, some other students argue that without history it is impossible to understand who they are. How do these different viewpoints affect the communication among such students? What is the possibility for meaningful communication interactions among them?

On a larger scale, we can see how history influences intercultural interaction in many different contexts. For example, the ongoing conflict between the Israelis and the Palestinians makes little sense without an understanding of the historical relations among the different groups that reside in the area. Historical antagonisms help explain the present-day animosity felt by many Pakistanis toward Indians. Disputes over the Kashmir region, Indian participation in the struggle for independence of Bangladesh, and conflicts over the Himalayas underscore deep-rooted bases for strife. More recently, protests arose as the Olympic torch for the 2008 summer games in Beijing passed through many countries. These protests were highlighting the role of China in Tibet, which is quite controversial; however, the relationship between China and Tibet has a very long history that influences how people view this situation.

How we think about the past very much influences how we think about ourselves and others even here in the United States. Judith went to college in southern Virginia after growing up in Delaware and Pennsylvania. She was shocked to encounter the antipathy that her dormitory suitemates expressed toward northerners. The suitemates stated emphatically that they had no desire to visit the North; they felt certain that "Yankees" were unfriendly and unpleasant people.

For Judith, the Civil War was a paragraph in a history book; for her suitemates, that historical event held a more important meaning. It took a while for friendships to develop between Judith and her suitemates. In this way, their interactions demonstrated the present–past dialectic. Indeed, this exemplifies the central focus of this chapter: that various histories contextualize intercultural communication. Taking a dialectical perspective enables us to understand how history positions people in different places from which they can communicate and understand other people's messages.

Early in this book, we set forth six dialectical tensions that we believe drive much intercultural interaction. In this chapter, we focus on the history/past–present/future dialectic. As you will see, culture and cultural identities are intimately tied to history because they have no meaning without history. Yet there is no single version of history; the past has been written in many different ways. For example, your own family has its version of family history that must be placed in dialectical tension with all of the other narratives about the past. Is it important to you to feel positive about who your forebears were and where they came from? We often feel a strong need to identify in positive ways with our past even if we are not interested in history. The stories of the past, whether accurate or not, help us understand why our families live where they do, why they own or lost land there, and so on. We experience this dialectical tension between the past, the present, and the future every day. It helps us understand who we are and why we live and communicate in the ways we do.

In this chapter, we first discuss the various histories that provide the contexts in which we communicate: political, intellectual, social, family, national, and cultural-group histories. We then describe how these histories are intertwined with our various identities, based on gender, sexual orientation, ethnicity, race, and so on. We introduce two identities that have strong historical bases: diasporic and colonial. We pay particular attention to the role of narrating our personal histories. As you read this chapter, think about the importance of history in constructing your own identity and the ways in which the past–present dialectic helps us understand different identities for others in various cultural groups. Finally, we explore how history influences intercultural communication.

FROM HISTORY TO HISTORIES

Many different kinds of history influence our understanding of who we are—as individuals, as family members, as members of cultural groups, and as citizens of a nation. To understand the dialectics in everyday interaction, we need to think

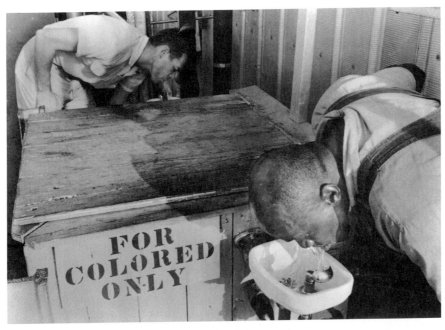

FIGURE 4-1 In the United States, the history of racially segregated facilities extends well beyond drinking fountains. Drinking fountains were not segregated by sexual orientation, gender, or some other cultural difference but by race alone. What are some other facilities that were once racially segregated? How does that history help us understand race relations today? Do you know how your family experienced racial privilege and discrimination in the United States? (© *Corbis/Bettmann*)

about the many histories that help form our different identities. These histories necessarily overlap and influence each other. For example, when Fidel Castro came to power over half a century ago, many Cubans fled to the United States. The families that departed have histories about that experience which help them understand their cultural identity. Political histories tell the story of that exodus but not necessarily the story of every family, even though many families' histories were very much influenced by that event. Identifying the various forms of historical contexts is the first step in understanding how history affects communication. (See Figure 4-1.)

Political, Intellectual, and Social Histories

Some people restrict their notion of history to documented events. Although we cannot read every book written, we do have greater access to written history. When these types of history focus on political events, we call them **political histories.** Written histories that focus on the development of ideas are often called **intellectual histories.** Some writers seek to understand the everyday life experiences of various groups in the past; what they document are called **social histories.**

political histories Written histories that focus on political events.

intellectual histories Written histories that focus on the development of ideas.

social histories Written histories that focus on everyday life experiences of various groups in the past.

Although these types of history seem more manageable than the broad notion of history as "everything that has happened before now," we must also remember that many historical events never make it into books. For example, the strict laws that forbade teaching slaves in the United States to read kept many of their stories from being documented. **Absent history,** of course, does not mean the people did not exist, their experiences do not matter, or their history has no bearing on us today. To consider such absent histories requires that we think in more complex ways about the past and the ways it influences the present and the future.

absent history Any part of history that was not recorded or that is missing. Not everything that happened in the past is accessible to us today because only some voices were documented and only some perspectives were recorded.

Absent history is also the result of concealing the past. One important way that this happens is when governments forbid access to documents that would give us better insight into the past. Recently, the U.S. government has been reclassifying documents so that they are not publicly available. Historian Matthew Aid (2006) of the National Security Archive at George Washington University notes:

> *Beginning in the fall of 1999, and continuing unabated for the past seven years, at least six government agencies, including the Central Intelligence Agency (CIA), the Defense Intelligence Agency (DIA), the Defense Department, the military services, and the Department of Justice, have been secretly engaged in a wide-ranging historical document reclassification program at the principal National Archives and Records Administration (NARA) research facility at College Park, Maryland, as well as at the Presidential Libraries run by NARA.[. . .]*
>
> *The results of the multi-agency reclassification effort since it began have been dramatic and disturbing. According to figures released by NARA, since 2001 security personnel from the agencies involved have "surveyed" 43.4 million pages of documents held by NARA (i.e., NARA records boxes were sampled to determine if a page-by-page security review of these records was required); 6.1 million pages of NARA documents have been reviewed on a page-by-page basis (the NARA term of art for this process is "audited"); and that as a result of these reviews, since 2001 9,500 documents totaling 55,500 pages have been reclassified and withdrawn from public circulation (see* Document 1*). Most of the documents removed to date contained either military or intelligence-related information, in some cases dating back to World War II.*

If documents are not available, then we cannot know this history—even if others have experienced that history, remember that history, and have written about it. Absent history, then, is not always caused by distant historical decisions; it can result from ongoing and contemporary decisions to deliberately withhold material from the public.

Family Histories

family histories Histories of individual families that are typically passed down through oral stories.

Family histories occur at the same time as other histories but on a more personal level. They often are not written down but are passed along orally from one generation to the next. Some people do not know which countries or cities their families emigrated from or what tribes they belonged to or where they lived in the United States. Other people place great emphasis on knowing that their ancestors fought in the Revolutionary War, survived the Holocaust, or traveled the Trail of Tears when the Cherokees were forcibly relocated from the Southeast to present-day Oklahoma. Many of these family histories are deeply intertwined with ethnic-group histories, but the family histories identify each family's participation in these events.

You might talk to members of your own family to discover how they feel about your family's history. Find out, for example, how family history influences their perceptions of who they are. Do they wish they knew more about their family? What things has your family continued to do that your forebears probably also did? Do you eat some of the same foods? Practice the same religion? Celebrate birthdays or weddings in the same way? The continuity between past and present often is taken for granted.

National Histories

The history of any nation is important to the people of that nation. We typically learn **national history** in school. In the United States, we learn about the founding fathers—George Washington, Benjamin Franklin, John Jay, Alexander Hamilton, and so on—and our national history typically begins with the arrival of Europeans in North America in the 16th century.

national history A body of knowledge based on past events that influenced a country's development.

U.S. citizens are expected to recognize the great events and the so-called great people (mostly men of European ancestry) who were influential in the development of the nation. In history classes, students learn about the Revolutionary War, Thomas Paine, the War of 1812, the Civil War, Abraham Lincoln, the Great Depression, Franklin D. Roosevelt, and so on. They are told stories, verging on myths, that give life to these events and figures. For example, students learn about Patrick Henry's "give me liberty or give me death" speech even though the text of the speech was collected by a biographer who "pieced together twelve hundred words from scattered fragments that ear witnesses remembered from twenty years before" (Thonssen, Baird, & Braden, 1970, p. 335). Students also learn about George Washington having chopped down a cherry tree and confessing his guilt ("I cannot tell a lie"), although there's no evidence of this story's truth.

National history gives us a shared notion of who we are and solidifies our sense of nationhood. Although we may not fit into the national narrative, we are expected to be familiar with this particular telling of U.S. history so we can understand the many references used in communication. It is one way of constructing cultural discourses. Yet U.S. students seldom learn much about the histories of other nations and cultures unless they study the languages of those countries. As any student of another language knows, it is part of the curriculum to study not only the grammar and vocabulary of the language but also the culture and history of the people who speak that language.

Judith and Tom both studied French. Because we learned a great deal about French history, we understand references to the *ancien régime* (the political system prior to the French Revolution in 1789), *les Pieds-noirs* (colonial French who returned to France during the struggle for Algerian independence in the mid-20th century), *la Bastille* (the notorious prison), and other commonly used terms. The French have their own national history, centering on the development of

My history is somewhat vague, but I will write what I know.

Father's side: My great-grandfather came to the United States in the late 1800s. He and my great-grandmother came from Yugoslavia. My great-grandfather worked as a coal miner in Hazleton, P.A. He died of "black lung." I don't know much about my great-grandmother. My grandfather and grandmother moved to Philadelphia in the 1940s.

Mother's side: My great-grandfather on my mom's side came to the United States in 1908 from Ireland. My great-grandmother is Scottish. As I write this I realize I don't know much about the maternal side of the family. I will definitely find out. I strongly believe it is important to know the history of my family in the United States. It is something to pass on to children and keep the spirit of this country alive!
—Jennifer

My distant ancestors came to the new world in the 1600s from England and settled in the Northeast. It is assumed they came over, like many others, to escape different political and religious persecutions. Family history is extremely important to my family. We have gone to great lengths to preserve and document where and who we are descendants from. I really did not know the full extent of how much trouble and time my family has gone to prove certain relationships. All the females in my family are part of an organization called Daughters of the American Revolution. In order to be in this organization you have to prove blood lineage to ancestors that have helped in achieving the independence of the United States of America. My grandmother's family is of blood relation to an original signer of the Declaration of Independence and a Union general, whom I am named after.
—Daniel

France as a nation. For example, French people know that they live in the *Vème République* (or Fifth Republic), and they know what that means within the grand narrative of French history.

When Judith lived in Algeria, her French friends spoke of *les Événements* (the events), but her Algerian friends spoke of *la Libération*—both referring to the war between France and Algeria that led to Algerian independence. When Tom lived in France, he also heard the expression *la Libération*, but here it referred to the end of the German occupation in France during World War II. Historical contexts shape language, which means we must search for salient historical features in communicating across cultural differences.

Cultural-Group Histories

Although people may share a single national history, each cultural group within the nation may have its own history. The history may be obscure (hidden), but it is still related to the national history. **Cultural-group histories** help us understand the identities of various groups.

cultural-group histories The history of each cultural group within a nation that includes, for example, the history of where the group originated, why the people migrated, and how they came to develop and maintain their cultural traits.

I am the fourth generation of females raised in Philadelphia. My great-grandmother raised me until she died, when I was 13. Her mother was a slave who had 19 children. Charlotte, North Carolina, was the place my great-grandmother said she was born. I care because my grandmother had personal information about why blacks should be glad slavery is over. She encouraged my family to make use of all of the benefits of freedom. She always said, "Get an education so you can own something, because we couldn't own anything. We couldn't even go to school." So that is why she moved to the city of Philadelphia. She made getting an education a reward instead of a joke.

—Marlene

I was born and raised in Pakistan, and lived there until I was 7 years old. I remember growing up there very well, but I also remember very well when we moved out of Pakistan. I am basically the first generation in my family to grow up outside of Pakistan. Today most of the immigrants that live in the United States moved here a very long time ago. They have ancestors that came to the United States a long time ago. That is not the case with my family. In addition the immigration to the United States for my family was different in the fact that at first we moved to Canada and then we moved to the United States.

—Waleed

My family immigrated to the United States for a better life. I didn't realize that my family history had so much involvement with the history I learned in class. For instance, my great-grandfather was an orphan who rode the orphan train west from New York until a family chose him and his brother to work on their farm. I also had a member of my family die during WWII, some lived in Chicago during the Chicago Fire, and my great grandpa was a rural mail carrier who used a horse and buggy to deliver the mail. Something I didn't know before was my grandpa, who now works for Burlington Northern, started out as an apprentice telegraph operator. . . . He has come quite far from that!

—William

Consider, for example, the expulsion of many Acadians from eastern Canada and their migration to and settlement in Louisiana. These historical events are central to understanding the cultural traits of the Cajuns. Their neighbors, the Creoles, have been displaced by a more recent historical event, Hurricane Katrina. It remains unclear how the hurricane will shape Creole culture. "With their geographic underpinnings swept away, many New Orleanians of Creole descent are trying to figure out how best to preserve a community separated from both its birthplace and home base" (Saulny, 2005, p. A13). The forced removal in 1838 of the Cherokees from Georgia to settlements in what eventually became the state of Oklahoma resulted in a 22% loss of the Cherokee population. This event, known as the Trail of Tears, explains much about the Cherokee Nation. The migration in 1846 of 12,000 Latter Day Saints from Nauvoo, Illinois, to the

Great Basin region in the western United States was prompted by anti-Mormon attacks. These events explain much about the character of Utah. The northward migration of African Americans in the early part of the 20th century helps us understand the settlement patterns and working conditions in northern cities such as Cleveland, Detroit, Chicago, and New York. These cultural histories are not typically included in our national history, but they are important in the development of group identity, family histories, and contemporary lives of individual members of these co-cultures.

We prefer to view history as the many stories we tell about the past, rather than one story on a single time continuum. Certainly, the events of families, cultural groups, and nations are related. Even world events are related. Ignorance of the histories of other groups makes intercultural communication more difficult and more susceptible to misunderstandings.

HISTORY, POWER, AND INTERCULTURAL COMMUNICATION

Power is a central dynamic in the writing of history. It influences the content of the history we know and the way it is delivered. Power dictates what is taught and what is silenced, what is available and what is erased. Let's look at what this means.

The Power of Texts

History is extremely important in understanding identity. Think about all of the stories about the past that you have been taught. Yet, as literature professor Fredric Jameson (1981) notes, although history is not a narrative at all, it is accessible to us only in textual, narrative form. However, people do not have equal access to the writing and production of these texts.

Political texts reflect the disparities of access to political participation in various countries at various times in history. Some languages have been forbidden, making the writing of texts difficult if not impossible. For example, U.S. government Indian schools did not permit Native American children to speak their native languages, which makes it more difficult for people today to understand what this experience was about.

With regard to the language we use to understand history, think about the difference between the terms *internment camp* and *concentration camp*. In 1942, at the height of World War II, after President Franklin Roosevelt signed Executive Order 9066, anyone of Japanese ancestry—whether they were U.S. citizens or not—was rounded up from a restricted zone, including parts of Arizona, Oregon, and Washington and all of California, and placed mostly into 10 camps. (See Figure 4-2.) The U.S. federal government used both terms in the 1940s, but the historical weight of the German concentration camps of the same era, in which millions of Jews perished, often casts a shadow over our understanding of the U.S. concentration camps. Denotatively, the use of the term *concentration*

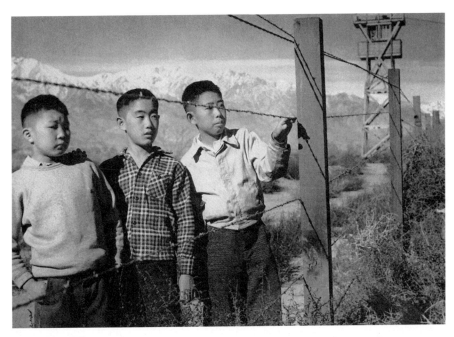

FIGURE 4-2   These young boys are looking through the barbed wire fence at Manzanar, a U.S. internment camp for those of Japanese ancestry, which operated during World War II on the West Coast. Note the guard tower in the back. (© *Associated Press/National Park Service*)

camp is correct, but connotatively, it invokes quite different responses. You may wish to keep this in mind as you read Chapter 6, which discusses the importance of language and discourse in intercultural communication.

When U.S. Americans are taught history, they also learn a particular way of looking at the world from their history textbooks. This worldview, as James Loewen (1995) tells us, reinforces a very positive white American identity. In his analysis of history textbooks, he notes, "History is furious debate informed by evidence and reason. Textbooks encourage students to believe that history is facts to be learned" (p. 16). Yet these "facts" are often wrong or portray the past in ways that serve the white American identity. For example, he analyzes the way in which Native Americans are depicted in history texts:

> *Even if no Natives remained among us, however, it would still be important for us to understand the alternatives forgone, to remember the wars, and to learn the unvarnished truths about white–Indian relations. Indian history is the antidote to the pious ethnocentrism of American exceptionalism, the notion that European Americans are God's chosen people. Indian history reveals that the United States and its predecessor British colonies have wrought great harm in the world. We must not forget this—not to wallow in our wrongdoing, but to understand and to learn, that we might not wreak harm again. (p. 136)*

The internment, or mass imprisonment, of Japanese Americans by the U.S. government in the 1940s has led to much discussion about the right term for these camps. What difference does it make if we call them "concentration camps" or "relocation centers"? This entry from the *Encyclopedia of Japanese American History* provides food for thought.

> **Concentration camps.** *Euphemistically called "relocation centers" by the War Relocation Authority (WRA), the concentration camps were hastily constructed facilities for housing Japanese Americans forcibly removed from their homes and businesses on the West Coast during World War II. Located in isolated areas of the United States on either desert or swampland, the camps were usually surrounded by barbed wire and guarded by armed sentries. Although these sentries were presumably in place to protect the inmates from hostile outsiders, their guns usually pointed into the camps instead of away from them. Most inmates were transported to their camp by train from an assembly center between April and September 1942. In all, over 120,000 Japanese Americans served time in these camps.*

Source: From B. Niiya (Ed.), *Encyclopedia of Japanese American History: An A-to-Z Reference from 1868 to the Present* (New York: Checkmark Books, 2001), p. 142.

But the prevailing value of teaching history lies not in serving the future but in reinforcing a positive cultural identity for white Americans. How does power function in determining which stories are told and how they are told?

The relative availability of political texts and the ways that they reflect powerful inequities are reinscribed in the process of writing history. History writing requires documentation and texts and, of course, is limited by what is available. In writing history, we often ask ourselves, "What was important?" without asking, "Important to whom? For what purposes?" Once texts are written, they are available for teaching and learning about the past. But the seeming unity of the past, the linear nature of history, is merely the reflection of a **modernist identity**, grounded in the Western tradition.

modernist identity The identity that is grounded in the Western tradition of scientific and political beliefs and assumptions—for example, the belief in external reality, democratic representation, liberation, and independent subjects.

The Power of Other Histories

We live in an era of rapid change, which causes us to rethink cultural struggles and identities. It may be difficult for you to envision, but at one time a unified story of humankind—the **"grand narrative"**—dominated how people thought of the past, present, and future. The grand narrative refers to the overarching, all-encompassing story of a nation or humankind in general. Because of the way it is built, this grand narrative organizes history into an understandable story that leads to some "truths" over other possible conclusions. In the story of humankind, the grand narrative was one of progress and an underlying assumption that developments in science, medicine, and education would lead to progress

grand narrative A unified history and view of humankind.

and better lives. This is no longer the case. French philosopher Jean-François Lyotard (1984) writes:

> *In contemporary society and culture—postindustrial society, postmodern culture— the grand narrative has lost its credibility, regardless of what mode of unification it uses, regardless of whether it is a speculative narrative or a narrative of emancipation. (p. 37)*

More recently, communication scholar Dave Tell (2008) has analyzed how a grand narrative about the murder of Emmett Till arose. Tell argues that an article in *Look* magazine about the murder is key to establishing the narrative of Till's murder, which played an important role in the rise of the civil rights movement.

The difficulty in maintaining the grand narrative is evident in a study done by Teresa Housel (2007). In her study, she examined the coverage of the Sydney Olympic games and the ways that the grand narrative of Australia was reinforced at the opening ceremony but also fragmented by the newspaper coverage of the games. Embedded in this flourish of communication messages about the games are Australian "anxieties about what defines its borders [which] are rooted in colonial notions of nation and race" (p. 457). In a global world with much migration, it may be more difficult to know who is and is not "Australian," as older notions may not encompass the diversity of contemporary Australia.

In the wake of continuous wars and global conflicts, global warming, failed promises of liberation, new diseases such as human immunodeficiency virus (HIV) and bird flu, and other events that challenge what we know and what has changed, the master narrative no longer seems as believable to many. In its place are many other narratives that tell different stories. In the context of intercultural communication, the master narratives of many cultures and nations are also undergoing reconsideration, and many new narratives are emerging.

In her work on the constructions of white identity in South Africa, communication scholar Melissa Steyn (2001) notes how the grand narrative in South Africa served white interests and led to the establishment of **apartheid.** Although racially restrictive laws existed in South Africa for many years, the South African government instituted a rigid framework for regulating race in 1948. This system, apartheid, lasted until it was dismantled from 1990 to 1994, but only after a long struggle against it. Under this apartheid system, everyone was required to register their race in one of four categories: black, white, Indian, and coloured. These categories were used to restrict where people could live (e.g., blacks were permitted to live on only 13% of the land, although they constituted 60% of the population), employment, access to public facilities (e.g., hospitals, ambulances, educational institutions), and other aspects of public life. Although they were numerically a minority, whites dominated this social system and accrued most of the benefits of it. To do so, they needed to tell a master narrative in which this system seemed to make sense. It was only under tremendous domestic and international pressure that the system was dismantled (Bureau of African Affairs, 2005; Guelke, 2005; Thompson, 2001). The popular film *Cry Freedom* (Attenborough, 1987), starring Denzel Washington as

apartheid A policy that segregated people racially in South Africa.

Since the ending of apartheid in South Africa, there has been a rewriting of the nation's history textbooks in an attempt to forge a new national identity and a different understanding of the past. However, there are strongly contested and very different views about the South African past. Compare, for example, the apartheid view and the postapartheid view of the establishment of separate areas for whites and blacks during the 1950s and 1960s. Think about how any understanding of history is important in creating cultural identity.

Apartheid View: The Group Areas Act is passed, dividing the country by race. Apartheid is an absolute necessity, because all nationalisms are mutually exclusive, and it is in the best interest of both races to live separately from one another. Hence black people must be relocated to "some of the best parts of the country."

Post-Apartheid View: Tens of thousands of black people are violently removed from their homes, entire neighborhoods are bulldozed, and dispossessed residents are forced to move to some of the least fertile and most remote regions of the country, where employment opportunities are scarce, if not non-existent. Meanwhile, the white minority secures control of the best land and its mineral wealth.

Source: From Sasha Polakow-Suransky, "Reviving South African History," *The Chronicle of Higher Education*, June 14, 2002, p. A37.

Steven Biko, a black leader, highlights the struggle and consequences of apartheid. Steyn writes:

In drawing on the master narrative, interpreting it and adapting it to the particular circumstances in which they found themselves in the country, whites were able to maintain their advantage as the dominating group that controlled the political, material, and symbolic resources of the country for three centuries. (p. 43)

By telling and retelling one view of the past, white South Africans were able to create a society in which a white minority dominated.

In place of the grand narrative are revised and restored histories that previously were suppressed, hidden, or erased. The cultural movements making this shift possible are empowering to the cultural identities involved. Recovering various histories is necessary to rethinking what some cultural identities mean. It also helps us rethink the dominant cultural identity.

For example, on June 30, 1960, at the signing of the treaty granting independence to the former Belgian colony of the Congo (as Zaire), the king of the Belgians, Baudouin, constructed one way of thinking about the past:

All of our thoughts should be turned toward those who founded the African emancipation and after them, those who made the Congo into what it is today. They merit at the same time our admiration and your recognition since it was they who consecrated all of their efforts and even their lives for a grand ideal, bringing you peace and enriching your homeland materially and morally. They must never be forgotten, not by Belgium, not by the Congo. (Quoted in Gérard-Libois & Heinen, 1989, p. 143)

In response, Patrice Lumumba, who would become prime minister, offered a different view of Belgian colonialism:

After eighty years of colonial rule, our wounds are still too fresh and too deep to be chased from our memory. . . . We have known the ironies, the insults, the beatings to which we had to submit morning, noon, and night because we were negroes. Who will forget that they spoke to Blacks with "tu" certainly not because of friendship, but because the honorary "vous" was reserved only for speaking to whites. (p. 147)

Lumumba's words created a different sense of history. These differences were clear to the people of the time and remain clear today. In this way, the grand narrative of Belgian colonialism has been reconfigured and no longer stands as the only story of the Belgian Congo.

Power in Intercultural Interactions

Power is also the legacy, the remnants of the history that leaves cultural groups in particular positions. We are not equal in our intercultural encounters, nor can we ever be equal. Long histories of imperialism, colonialism, exploitation, wars, genocide, and more leave cultural groups out of balance when they communicate. Regardless of whether we choose to recognize the foundations for many of our differences, these inequalities influence how we think about others and how we interact with them. They also influence how we think about ourselves—our identities. These are important aspects of intercultural communication. It may seem daunting to confront the history of power struggles. Nevertheless, the more you know, the better you will be positioned to engage in successful intercultural interactions.

HISTORY AND IDENTITY

The development of cultural identity is influenced largely by history. In this next section, we look at some of the ways that cultural identities are constructed through understanding the past. Note how different cultural-group identities are tied to history.

Histories as Stories

Faced with these many levels or types of history, you might wonder how we make sense of them in our everyday lives. Although it might be tempting to ignore them all and merely pretend to be "ourselves," this belies the substantial influence that history has on our own identities.

According to communication scholar Walter Fisher (1984, 1985), storytelling is fundamental to the human experience. Instead of referring to humans as

We must always recognize how the past can be used for contemporary purposes. China and Japan have a very long history that includes the occupation of large parts of China during World War II. While many Chinese remain bitter over the brutal and humiliating occupation by Japan, "a growing number of Japanese had come to feel that their country had apologised enough for its wartime brutality" ("Blossoming," 2008). How should China and Japan deal with this past, in order to build more positive political and economic relationships?

> *China has overtaken America as Japan's biggest trading partner. China is hungry for know-how, and Japan thinks it can be of particular help in providing environmental technology—after all, Chinese pollution reaches Japan.*
>
> *Not long ago comments by China's leaders, thundering editorials and crude films about the second world war did much to stoke anti-Japanese nationalism—violent street protests broke out in 2005, and in 2004 Chinese football fans went on the rampage after their team was beaten by Japan. Now, China wants to tamp such nationalism down. Anti-Japan behaviour at the Olympics would be a disaster.*
>
> *[T]he attitudes of urban Chinese are turning more positive towards Japan. A growing number think historical differences should be set aside. But it will take a lot more ping-pong to erase the impression of many Japanese that they are loathed in China more than they are admired.*

Source: "Blossoming," *The Economist*, May 8, 2008, http://www.economist.com/world/asia/displaystory.cfm?story_id=11332789.

Homo sapiens, Fisher prefers to call them *Homo narrans* because it underscores the importance of narratives in our lives. Histories are stories that we use to make sense of who we are and who we think others are.

It is important to recognize that a strong element in our cultural attitudes encourages us to forget history at times. French writer Jean Baudrillard (1988) observes:

> *America was created in the hope of escaping from history, of building a utopia sheltered from history. . . . [It] has in part succeeded in that project, a project it is still pursuing today. The concept of history as the transcending of a social and political rationality, as a dialectical, conflictual vision of societies, is not theirs, just as modernity, conceived precisely as an original break with certain history, will never be ours [France's]. (p. 80)*

The desire to escape history is significant in what it tells us about how our culture negotiates its relation to the past, as well as how we view the relations of other nations and cultures to their pasts. By ignoring history, we sometimes come to wrongheaded conclusions about others that only perpetuate and reinforce stereotypes. For example, the notion that Jewish people are obsessed with money and are disproportionately represented in the world of finance belies the history of anti-Semitism, whereby Jews were excluded from many professions. The paradox is that we cannot escape history even if we fail to recognize it or try to suppress it.

Nonmainstream Histories

People from nonmainstream cultural groups often struggle to retain their histories. Theirs are not the histories that everyone learns about in school, yet these histories are vital to understanding how others perceive them and why. These nonmainstream histories are important to the people in these cultural groups, as they may play a significant role in their cultural identities.

Nonmainstream histories sometimes stand alongside the grand narrative, but sometimes they challenge the grand narrative. As we saw earlier, some nonmainstream histories are absent histories, as these histories have been lost or are not recoverable. Sometimes these nonmainstream histories are **hidden histories,** as they offer different views on the grand narrative and, therefore, have been suppressed or marginalized in our understanding of the past. Let's look at some of these nonmainstream histories and how these views of the past help us better understand different cultural groups.

hidden histories The histories that are hidden from or forgotten by the mainstream representations of past events.

Racial and Ethnic Histories Mainstream history has neither the time nor the space nor the inclination to include all **ethnic histories** and **racial histories.** This is especially true given that the histories of cultural groups sometimes seem to question, and even undermine, the celebratory nature of the mainstream national history.

ethnic histories The histories of ethnic groups.

racial histories The histories of nonmainstream racial groups.

When Tom's parents meet other Japanese Americans of their generation, they are often asked, "What camp were you in?" This question makes little sense outside of its historical context. Indeed, this question is embedded in understanding a particular moment in history, a moment that is not widely understood. Most Japanese Americans were interned in concentration camps during World War II. In the aftermath of the experience, the use of that history as a marker has been important in maintaining cultural identity.

The injustices done by any nation are often swept under the carpet. In an attempt to bring attention to and promote renewed understanding of the internment of Japanese Americans during World War II, academician John Tateishi (1984) collected the stories of some of the internees. He notes at the outset that

> *this book makes no attempt to be a definitive academic history of Japanese American internment. Rather it tries to present for the first time in human and personal terms the experience of the only group of American citizens ever to be confined in concentration camps in the United States. (p. vii)*

Although not an academic history, this collection of oral histories provides insight into the experiences of many Japanese Americans. Because this historical event demonstrates the fragility of our constitutional system and its guarantees in the face of prejudice and ignorance, it is not often discussed as significant in U.S. history. For Japanese Americans, however, it represents a defining moment in the development of their community.

his letter from the president of the United States was sent to all of the surviving Japanese American internees who were in U.S. concentration camps during World War II. In recognizing that there is no way to change mistakes made in the past, what does this letter do? If you were to compose this letter, what would you write? How should we deal with the past to construct better intercultural relations in the future?

THE WHITE HOUSE
WASHINGTON

A monetary sum and words alone cannot restore lost years or erase painful memories; neither can they fully convey our Nation's resolve to rectify injustice and to uphold the rights of individuals. We can never fully right the wrongs of the past. But we can take a clear stand for justice and recognize that serious injustices were done to Japanese Americans during World War II.

In enacting a law calling for restitution and offering a sincere apology, your fellow Americans have, in a very real sense, renewed their traditional commitment to the ideals of freedom, equality, and justice. You and your family have our best wishes for the future.

Sincerely,

GEORGE BUSH
PRESIDENT OF THE UNITED STATES

OCTOBER 1990

While Pearl Harbor may feel like a distant historical event, the internment of Japanese Americans has drawn important parallels to the treatment of Muslims after 9/11. Because of the fears that arose after these events, "In recent years, many scholars have drawn parallels and contrasts between the internment of Japanese-Americans after the attack on Pearl Harbor, and the treatment of hundreds of Muslim noncitizens who were swept up in the weeks after the 2001 terror attacks, then held for months before they were cleared of links to terrorism and deported" (Bernstein, 2007). "When a federal judge in Brooklyn ruled last June that the government had wide latitude to detain noncitizens indefinitely on the basis of race, religion or national origin" (Bernstein, 2007), a number of Japanese Americans spoke out against the broad ruling and the parallels it had to their cultural group's historical experience.

Similarly, for Jewish people, remembering the Holocaust is crucial to their identity. A Jewish colleague recalls growing up in New York City in the 1950s and 1960s and hearing stories of Nazi atrocities. Survivors warned that such atrocities could happen again, that being victimized was always a possibility. Recent attempts by revisionists to deny that the Holocaust even happened have met with fierce opposition and a renewed effort to document that tragedy in unmistakable detail. The Holocaust Museum in Washington, D.C., is a memorial to that history for all of us.

Ethnic and racial histories are never isolated; rather, they crisscross other cultural trajectories. We may feel as if we have been placed in the position of victim or victimizer by distant historical events, and we may even seem to occupy both of these positions simultaneously. Consider, for example, the position of German American Mennonites during World War II. They were punished as pacifists and yet also were seen as aggressors by U.S. Jews. To further complicate matters, U.S. citizens of German ancestry were not interned in concentration camps, as were U.S. citizens of Japanese ancestry. How we think about being victims and victimizers is quite complex.

French writer Maurice Blanchot, in confronting the horrors of the Holocaust, the devastation of the atom bomb, and other human disasters, redefines the notion of responsibility, separating it from fault. In *The Writing of the Disaster*, Blanchot (1986) asserts,

> *My responsibility is anterior to my birth just as it is exterior to my consent, to my liberty. I am born thanks to a favor which turns out to be a predestination—born unto the grief of the other, which is the grief of all. (p. 22)*

This perspective can help us face and deal with the different positions that history finds for us.

The displacement of various populations is embedded in the history of every migrating or colonizing people. Whether caused by natural disasters such as the drought in the Midwest during the Great Depression of the 1930s or determined by choice, migrations influence how we live today. Native peoples throughout most of the United States were exterminated or removed to settlements in other regions. The state of Iowa, for example, has few Native Americans and only one reservation. The current residents of Iowa had nothing to do with the events in their state's history, but they are the beneficiaries through the ownership of farms and other land. So, although contemporary Iowans are not in a position of fault or blame, they are, through these benefits, in a position of responsibility. Like all of us, their lives are entangled in the web of history from which there is no escape, only denial and silence.

The history of my race will never be forgotten. I am German and fit the typical blond hair, blue-eyed description. My mother and grandmother both were German so I do have German influences such as the food I eat and some German customs that have been passed down to me. I was always mistaken as a "skinhead," which was quite embarrassing for me. Kids would walk by me and throw up their arm doing the Heil Hitler salute, which was quite offensive to me. "I did not live in that time period, so don't affiliate me with the ignorance of thousands of Germans," is the way I used to handle the people that would insult me.
    —Steve

I was in Germany for a few hours in April. My boyfriend is Jewish, so lately I have been thinking about how the Holocaust has affected his family. I found myself angry at every German in the airport. I knew that I was placing a ridiculous stereotype on the German people.
    —Angela

Gender Histories   Feminist scholars have long insisted that much of the history of women has been obliterated, marginalized, or erased. Historian Mei Nakano (1990) notes:

> *The history of women, told by women, is a recent phenomenon. It has called for a fundamental reevaluation of assumptions and principles that govern traditional history. It challenges us to have a more inclusive view of history, not merely the chronicling of events of the past, not dominated by the record of men marching forward through time, their paths strewn with the detritus of war and politics and industry and labor.. (p. xiii)*

gender histories The histories of how cultural conventions of men and women are created, maintained, and/or altered.

Although there is much interest in women's history among contemporary scholars, documenting such **gender histories** is difficult because of the traditional restrictions on women's access to public forums, public documents, and public records. Even so, the return to the past to unearth and recover identities that can be adapted for survival is a key theme of writer Gloria Anzaldúa (1987). She presents *la Llorana* (the crying woman) as a cultural and historical image that gives her the power to resist cultural and gender domination. *La Llorana* is well known in northern Mexico and the U.S. Southwest. This legend tells the story of a woman who killed her children and who now wanders around looking for them and weeping for them. Her story has been retold in various ways, and Anzaldúa rewrites the tale to highlight the power that resides in her relentless crying. This mythical image gives her the power to resist cultural and gender domination:

> *My Chicana identity is grounded in the Indian woman's history of resistance. The Aztec female rites of mourning were rites of defiance protesting the cultural changes which disrupted the equality and balance between female and male, and protesting their demotion to a lesser status, their denigration. Like* la Llorana, *the Indian woman's only means of protest was wailing. (p. 21)*

NA testing has helped uncover the hidden histories of families. For Hispanics in the Southwest, DNA testing has helped many realize that they are likely descendants of Marranos (Sephardic Jews) who fled the Inquisition over 400 years ago. Some of these descendants reclaim their Jewish heritage; others do not.

When she was growing up in a small town in southern Colorado, an area where her ancestors settled centuries ago, when it was on the fringes of the northern frontier of New Spain, Bernadette Gonzalez always thought some of the stories about her family were unusual, if not bizarre.

Her grandmother, for instance, refused to travel on Saturday and would use a specific porcelain basin to drain blood out of meat before she cooked it. [. . .]

Ms. Gonzalez started researching her family history and concluded that her ancestors were Marranos, or Sephardic Jews, who had fled the Inquisition in Spain and in Mexico more than four centuries ago. Though raised in the Roman Catholic faith, Ms. Gonzalez felt a need to reconnect to her Jewish roots, so she converted to Judaism three years ago. [. . .]

Modern science may now be shedding new light on the history of the crypto-Jews after molecular anthropologists recently developed a DNA test of the male or Y chromosome that can indicate an ancestral connection to the Cohanim, a priestly class of Jews that traces its origin back more then 3,000 years to Aaron, the older brother of Moses. [. . .]

Not everyone who discovers Jewish ancestry, either through genealogical research or DNA testing, has decided to convert to Judaism, but some Hispanics who have found links still feel drawn to incorporate Jewish customs into their life.

Source: Simon Romero, "Hispanics Uncovering Roots as Inquisition's 'Hidden' Jews," *New York Times*, October 29, 2005, p. A17.

Anzaldúa's history may seem distant to us, but it is intimately tied to what her Chicana identity means to her.

Sexual Orientation Histories   In recounting his experiences as a young man whom the police registered as "homosexual," Pierre Seel (1994) recounts how police lists were used by the Nazis to round up homosexuals for internment. The incarceration and extermination of gays, as members of one of the groups deemed "undesirable" by Nazi Germany, is often overlooked by World War II historians. Seel recalls one event in his **sexual orientation history:**

> *One day at a meeting in the SOS Racisme [an antiracism organization] room, I finished by getting up and recounting my experience of Nazism, my deportation for homosexuality. I remarked as well the ingratitude of history which erases that which is not officially convenient for it. (p. 162)*

sexual orientation histories The historical experiences of gays and lesbians.

TABLE 4-1 HISTORICAL CONTROVERSY: ABRAHAM LINCOLN'S SEXUALITY

Year	Event	Reaction	Outcome
1924	Carl Sandburg alludes to Lincoln's homosexual tendencies using euphemisms of the day like "streak of lavender."	This claim was not central to Sandburg's work and was widely dismissed.	Lingering questions over Lincoln's sexual history (Nobile, 2005).
1999	Prominent gay activist Larry Kramer claims to have acquired a journal of one of Lincoln's lovers.	Many historians and commentators rail against Kramer and his claim to have found the journal.	Kramer has kept the journal private, but the controversy has lived on (Lloyd, 1999).
2004	C. A. Tripp makes the definitive claim that Lincoln was gay in his 2004 biography.	Controversy erupts over Tripp's objectivity, his research, and the topic.	Most historians continue to claim that Lincoln was heterosexual, while some question this claim (Brookhiser, 2005).
2008	Charles E. Morris publishes an account of Lincoln's sexual history and an analysis of reactions to the topic (Morris, 2008).		

Sources: Philip Nobile, "Broken Promises, Plagiarism, Misused Evidence and the New Gay Lincoln Book Published by the Free Press," *The History News Network,* January 10, 2005. Retrieved from http://hnn.us/articles/9514.html; Carol Lloyd, "Was Lincoln Gay?" *Salon.com,* May 3, 1999. Retrieved from http://www.salon.com/books/it/1999/04/30/lincoln/index.html; Richard Brookhiser, "Was Lincoln Gay?" *The New York Times,* January 9, 2005. Retrieved from http://query.nytimes.com/gst/fullpage.html?res=9F05E5D61439F93AA35752C0A9639C8B63; Charles E. Morris III, "Profile," 2008. Retrieved from http://www.bc.edu/schools/cas/communication/faculty/fulltime/morris.html.

(Un jour de réunion, dans la salle de SOS Racisme, je finis par me lever et par raconter mon expérience du nazisme, ma déportation pour homosexualité. Je fis également remarquer l'ingratitude de l'histoire qui gomme ce qui ne lui convient pas officiellement.)

This suppression of history reflects attempts to construct specific understandings of the past. If we do not or cannot listen to the voices of others, we miss the significance of historical lessons. For example, a legislative attempt to force gays and lesbians to register with the police in the state of Montana ultimately was vetoed by the governor after he learned of the law's similarities to laws in Nazi Germany.

The late Guy Hocquenghem (Hocquenghem & Blasius, 1980), a gay French philosopher, lamented the letting go of the past because doing so left little to sustain and nurture his community:

> *I am struck by the ignorance among gay people about the past—no, more even than ignorance: the "will to forget" the German gay holocaust. . . . But we aren't even the only ones who remember, we don't remember! So we find ourselves beginning at zero in each generation. (p. 40)*

How we think about the past and what we know about it help us to build and maintain communities and cultural identities. And our relationships with the past are intimately tied to issues of power. To illustrate, the book *The Pink Swastika: Homosexuality in the Nazi Party* attempts to blame the Holocaust on German gays and lesbians ("Under Surveillance," 1995). This book, in depicting gays and lesbians as perpetrators, rather than victims, of Nazi atrocities, presents the gay identity in a markedly negative light. However, stories of the horrendous treatment of gays and lesbians during World War II serve to promote a common history and influence intercultural communication among gays and lesbians in France, Germany, the Netherlands, and other nations. Today, a monument in Amsterdam serves to mark that history, to help ensure that we remember that gays and lesbians were victims of the Nazi Holocaust as well.

In the U.S., Bayard Rustin is often forgotten, despite his enormous contributions to the civil rights movement. "His obscurity stemmed not only from amnesia but also from conscious suppression" (Kennedy, 2003), despite his major role in U.S. history. *The Nation* (2003) observed: "Rustin helped found the Congress of Racial Equality (CORE) and the Southern Christian Leadership Conference (SCLC). He advised Martin Luther King Jr., organized the 1963 March on Washington and wrote several essays that continue to repay close study. Throughout these pursuits, Rustin expressed a gay sexuality for which he was stigmatized as a sexual criminal, a smear that crippled his ability to lead the movements to which he passionately contributed ideas and inspiration."

Abraham Lincoln's sexual history has also been a major point of contention over a number of years (see Table 4.1 in the "Point of View" box). Psychologist C. A. Tripp's book *The Intimate World of Abraham Lincoln* once again raised the possibility that the former president's sexual history included men. While we may never know whatever really happened, the concern over this history underscores the way it may influence our national history. The Lincoln case points to the difficulty in understanding this type of history. The words, *homosexual, heterosexual,* and *bisexual* did not exist during Lincoln's era; therefore, those words would not be used to describe his private life. Among other examples, Tripp points to a member of Lincoln's bodyguard, Captain David V. Derickson, who would come over to the White House and sleep in the same bed with Lincoln. Is this evidence for how we might understand this sexual history? On the one hand, it seems odd for Captain Derickson to come to the White House and sleep in the same bed with Lincoln; however, "as many historians have noted, same-sex bed sharing was common at the time and hardly proof of homosexual activities or feelings" (Greenberg, 2005). There is no general agreement about Lincoln's sexual history, but more importantly, the debate over how we should think about Lincoln points to the power of these histories in understanding our national identity.

This concern about national identity is reflected in the way that the president of Iran insisted that there are no gay people in Iran. At a speech at Columbia University in 2007, President Mahmoud Ahmadinejad was booed for saying, "In Iran, we don't have homosexuals, like in your country. We don't have that in our country. In Iran, we do not have this phenomenon. I don't know who's told you that we have it" (quoted in Goldman, 2007). This claim was met with a lot of laughing and jeering from the audience. Interestingly, these comments were "cut out of official Farsi transcripts" (Ahmadinejad's comments, 2007), which influences the writing of history, although a different version is today evident on YouTube.com and other Web sites. It may seem unclear how these sexual histories influence national identity and cultural identity, but the controversies that arise over them highlight the need to view the past in particular ways.

Diasporic Histories   The international relationships that many racial and ethnic groups have with others who share their heritage and history are often overlooked in intercultural communication. These international ties may have been created by transnational migrations, slavery, religious crusades, or other historical forces. Because most people do not think about the diverse connections people have to other nations and cultures, we consider these histories to be hidden. In his book *The Black Atlantic*, scholar Paul Gilroy (1993) emphasizes that to understand the identities, cultures, and experiences of African descendants living in Britain and the United States, we must examine the connections between Africa, Europe, and North America.

diaspora A massive migration often caused by war, famine, or persecution that results in the dispersal of a unified group.

diasporic histories The histories of the ways in which international cultural groups were created through transnational migrations, slavery, religious crusades, or other historical forces.

A massive migration, often caused by war or famine or persecution, that results in the dispersal of a unified group is called a **diaspora.** The chronicles of these events are **diasporic histories.** A cultural group (or even an individual) that flees its homeland is likely to bring some customs and practices to the new homeland. In fact, diasporic migrations often cause people to cling more strongly to symbols and practices that reflect their group's identity. Over the years, though, people become acculturated to some degree in their new homelands. Consider, for example, the dispersal of eastern European Jews who migrated during or after World War II to the United States, Australia, South America, Israel, and other parts of the world. They brought their Jewish culture and eastern European culture with them, but they also adopted new cultural patterns as they became New Yorkers, Australians, Argentinians, Israelis, and so on. Imagine the communication differences among these people over time. Imagine the differences between these groups and members of the dominant culture of their new homelands.

History helps us understand the cultural connections among people affected by diasporas and other transnational migrations. Indeed, it is important that we any U.S. Americans may not be aware that the United States sent troops into Iraq during World War II. This history has prefigured the contemporary involvement in Iraq. In a 1942 guide for soldiers being sent to Iraq, the U.S. government made a number of intercultural communication suggestions:

You will enter Iraq (i-RAHK) both as a soldier and as an individual, because on our side a man can be both. That is our strength—if we are smart enough to use it. It can be our weakness if we aren't. As a soldier your duties are laid out for you. As an individual, it is what you do on your own that counts—and it may count for a lot more than you think.

American success or failure in Iraq may well depend on whether the Iraqis (as the people are called) like American soldiers or not. It may not be quite that simple. But then again it could. . . .

Most Americans and Europeans who have gone to Iraq didn't like it at first. Might as well be frank about it. But nearly all of these same people changed their minds, largely on account of the Iraqi people they began to meet. So will you. . . .

But you will find out that the Iraqi is one of the most cheerful and friendly people in the world. If you are willing to go just a little out of your way to understand him, everything will be okay.

Differences? Sure, there are differences. Differences galore! But what of it? You aren't going to Iraq to change the Iraqis. Just the opposite. We are fighting this war to preserve the principle of "live and let live."

Source: From U.S. government, "A Short Guide to Iraq," 1942. Reprinted in *Harper's Magazine*, October 2004. Also reprinted in *L'actualité*, trans. M. Desjardins, November 1, 2005, pp. 94–96. Available at http://www.harpers.org/BluebirdsOverBaghdad.html. Posted October 27, 2005.

recognize these relationships. But we must also be careful to distinguish between the ways in which these connections are helpful or hurtful to intercultural communication. For example, some cultures tend to regard negatively those who left their homeland. Thus, many Japanese tend to look down on Japanese Canadians, Japanese Americans, Japanese Brazilians, Japanese Mexicans, and Japanese Peruvians. In contrast, the Irish tend not to look down on Irish Americans or Irish Canadians. Of course, we must remember, too, that many other intervening factors can influence diasporic relationships on an interpersonal level.

Colonial Histories   As you probably know, throughout history, societies and nations have ventured beyond their borders. Because of overpopulation, limited resources, notions of grandeur, or other factors, people have left their homelands to colonize other territories. It is important to recognize these **colonial histories** so we can better understand the dynamics of intercultural communication today.

colonial histories The histories that legitimate international invasions and annexations.

Let's look at the significance of colonialism in determining language. Historically, three of the most important colonizers were Britain, France, and Spain. As a result of colonialism, English is spoken in Canada, Australia, New Zealand, Belize, Nigeria, South Africa, India, Pakistan, Bangladesh, Zimbabwe, Hong Kong, Singapore, and the United States, among many places in the world. French is spoken in Canada, Senegal, Tahiti, Haiti, Benin, Côte d'Ivoire, Niger, Rwanda, Mali, Chad, and the Central African Republic, among other places. And Spanish is spoken in most of the Western Hemisphere, from Mexico to Chile and Argentina, and including Cuba, Venezuela, Colombia, and Panama.

Many foreign language textbooks proudly display maps that show the many places around the world where that language is commonly spoken. Certainly, it's nice to know that one can speak Spanish or French in so many places. But the maps don't reveal *why* those languages are widely spoken in those regions, and they don't reveal the legacies of colonialism in those regions. For example, the United Kingdom maintains close relations with many of its former colonies, and the queen of England is also the queen of Canada, Australia, New Zealand, and the Bahamas.

Other languages have been spread through colonialism as well, including Portuguese in Brazil, Macao, and Angola; Dutch in Angola, Suriname, and Mozambique; and a related Dutch language, Afrikaans, in South Africa. Russian is spoken in the former Soviet republics of Kazakhstan, Azerbaijan, and Tajikistan. In addition, many nations have reclaimed their own languages in an effort to resist the influences of colonialism. For example, today Arabic is spoken in Algeria and Vietnamese is spoken in Vietnam; at one time, French was widely spoken in both countries. And in the recently independent Latvia, the ability to speak Latvian is a requirement for citizenship.

The primary languages that we speak are not freely chosen by us. Rather, we must learn the languages of the societies into which we are born. Judith and Tom, for example, both speak English, although their ancestors came to the United States from non-English-speaking countries. We did not choose to learn English among all of the languages of the world. Although we don't resent our native language, we recognize why many individuals might resent a language imposed on them. Think about the historical forces that led you to speak some language(s) and not others. Understanding history is crucial to understanding the linguistic worlds we inhabit, and vestiges of colonialism are often part of these histories.

Postcolonialism is useful in helping us understand the relationship between history and the present. In struggling with a colonial past, people have devised many ways of confronting that past. As explained in Chapter 2, postcolonialism is not simply the study of colonialism, but the study of how we might deal with that past and its aftermath, which may include the *ongoing* use of the colonial language, culture, and religion. For example, many companies are locating parts of their businesses in India because of the widespread use of English in this former British colony. How should people in India deal with the ongoing dominance of English, the colonizer's language, but also the language of business?

For example, Hispanics or Latinos/as share a common history of colonization by Spain, whether their families trace their origins to Mexico, Puerto Rico, Cuba, and so on. Although Spain is no longer in political control of these lands, how do those who live in the legacy of this history deal with that history? In what ways does it remain important, as a part of this cultural identity, to embrace the colonizer's language (Spanish)? The colonizer's religion (Catholicism)? And are there other aspects of Spanish culture that continue to be reproduced over and over again? Postcolonialism is not simply a call to make a clean break from that colonial past, but "to examine the violent actions and erasures of colonialism" (Shome & Hegde, 2002, p. 250). In this case, that interrogation might even mean reconsidering the category "Hispanic" that incorporates a wide range of groups that share a Spanish colonial history but do not share other histories that constitute their cultures. The legacy of this cultural invasion often lasts much longer than the political relationship.

Socioeconomic Class Histories   Although we often overlook the importance of socioeconomic class as a factor in history, the fact is that economic and class issues prompted many people to emigrate to the United States. The poverty in Ireland in the 19th century, for example, did much to fuel the flight to the United States; in fact, today, there are more Irish Americans than Irish.

Yet it is not always the socioeconomically disadvantaged who emigrate. After the Russian Revolution in 1917, many affluent Russians moved to Paris. Likewise, many affluent Cubans left the country after Castro seized power in 1959. Today, Canada offers business immigration status to investors who own their own businesses and "who have a net worth, accumulated by their own endeavors, of at least CAD [Canadian dollars] $500,000" ("Immigrant Investor Program Redesign," 1998). Although the program varies somewhat from province to province, the policy ensures that socioeconomic class continues to influence some migrations.

The key point here is that socioeconomic class distinctions are often overlooked in examining the migrations and acculturation of groups around the world. Historically, the kinds of employment that immigrants supplied and the regions they settled were often marked by the kinds of capital—cultural and financial—that they were or were not able to bring with them. These factors also influence the interactions and politics of different groups; for example, Mexican Americans and Cuban Americans, as groups, frequently are at odds with the political mainstream.

Religious Histories   In the past, as well as today, religion is an important historical force that has shaped our planet. Religious conflicts have led to wars, such as the Christian Crusades nearly a thousand years ago. Religious persecution has also led to migration of various religious groups to new places. In the United States, one example of this movement are the Mormons, who left New York, settled in Illinois, and then left to go to Utah. Many French Huguenots (Protestants), persecuted by French Catholics, left France to settle primarily in North America, South Africa, and elsewhere in Europe.

Because many of these religious histories remain controversial, they are viewed differently, depending on with which side one identifies. In 2001, President Bush used the term "Crusades" to describe the war on terror, which provoked strong reactions among many Muslims around the world. In explaining the president's use of this historical reference, White House press secretary, Ari Fleischer (2001), answered in a press briefing:

Q: The other question was, the President used the word crusade last Sunday, which has caused some consternation in a lot of Muslim countries. Can you explain his usage of that word, given the connotation to Muslims?

Mr. Fleischer: I think what the President was saying was—had no intended consequences for anybody, Muslim or otherwise, other than to say that this is a broad cause that he is calling on America and the nations around the world to join. That was the point—purpose of what he said.

Q: Does he regret having used that word, Ari, and will he not use it again in the context of talking about this effort?

Mr. Fleischer: I think to the degree that that word has any connotations that would upset any of our partners, or anybody else in the world, the President would regret if anything like that was conveyed. But the purpose of his conveying it is in the traditional English sense of the word. It's a broad cause.

In this example, we can see that the use of historical references in communication can create cultural conflicts. Although the Crusades may seem like a distant historical event, to some that event is much more immediate and its consequences far more pressing.

INTERCULTURAL COMMUNICATION AND HISTORY

One way to understand specific relationships between communication and history is to examine the attitudes and notions that individuals bring to an interaction; these are the antecedents of contact. A second way is to look at the specific conditions of the interaction and the role that history plays in these contexts. Finally, we can examine how various histories are negotiated in intercultural interaction, applying a dialectical perspective to these different histories.

Antecedents of Contact

We may be able to negotiate some aspects of history in interaction, but it is important to recognize that we bring our personal histories to each intercultural interaction. These personal histories involve our prior experience and our attitudes. Social psychologist Richard Brislin (1981) has identified four elements of personal histories that influence interaction.

First, people bring childhood experiences to interactions. For example, both Judith and Tom grew up hearing negative comments about Catholics. As a result, our first interactions with adherents to this faith were tinged with some he complexities of dealing with racial history is reflected in the many actions taken in Florida. History, although it is past, continues to shape contemporary cultural experiences.

Mar. 30—It's not just sound bites that stir the melting pot.

Last week in Florida's Legislature, lawmakers approved a resolution expressing "profound regret" for slavery. At the same time, they are considering a bill that establishes a Confederate license plate. There's also a bill that would retire the state song — a tune known as "Swanee River" that is loved by some and considered a racist throwback by others.

Another bill prohibits hanging nooses to intimidate.

All of this is going on in a state Capitol that flew the Confederate flag until seven years ago, when former Gov. Jeb Bush quietly removed it and put it in a history museum a few blocks away.

And in Hillsborough County, the county commission declared 2007 the year of Robert E. Lee — on the same day it honored local civil rights activist James A. Hammond. In another twist, the same body last year refused to acknowledge Confederate Memorial Day, a Florida holiday since 1895.

Whether Floridians see any of these measures as race-biased, their existence at the same time in the same place illustrates how complex the issue of race still is today.

"If people think race relations are solved, they're not living in our world," said Tony Morejon, Hillsborough County's liaison with Hispanic residents.

It's not just lawmakers who are dealing with the conflicts.

Twenty thousand people went to tiny Jena, La., last year to protest charges against six black teenagers arrested in the beating of a white classmate. Race was at the center of the Duke lacrosse rape case fiasco, which made national news when white players were accused of raping a black woman.

Here, a Seminole Heights resident found a noose hanging in her neighborhood last month, prompting questions about who would hang it and why.

Five months ago, 700 protesters marched in Tallahassee after boot camp guards were acquitted in the death of a black teen. They wore T-shirts and carried signs that recalled the killing of Emmett Till, a 14-year-old black boy who was killed in 1955 in Mississippi for whistling at a white woman.

They sang "We Shall Overcome."

Source: Gretchen Parker. "Dealing With Issues Of Race In America," *Tampa Tribune*, March 30, 2008, http://www2.tbo.com/content/2008/mar/30/dealing-issues-race-america/.

suspicion. This personal history did not affect initial interactions with people of other religions.

Second, people may bring historical myths to interactions. These are myths with which many people are familiar. The Jewish conspiracy myth—that Jewish people are secretly in control of U.S. government and business—is one example.

How we commemorate the past can create intercultural conflicts, in that many historical events are entangled in contemporary cultural identities (See Figure 4-3.) Note the powerful language used in this condemnation of Columbus Day.

Columbus Day as a national, and international, phenomenon reflects a much larger dynamic that promotes myriad myths and historical lies that have been used through the ages to dehumanize Indians, justifying the theft of our lands, the attempted destruction of our nations, and the genocide against our peoples. From the 15th century to the present, the myth of Columbus' discovery has been used in the development of laws and policies that offend the most basic human rights principles: theft equals the righteous spread of civilization, genocide is God's deliverance of the wilderness from the savages, and the destruction of Indian societies proves the spiritual and moral superiority of European values and institutions over indigenous ones.

Columbus Day is a perpetuation of racist assumptions that the Western Hemisphere was a wasteland cluttered with savages awaiting the blessings of Western "civilization." Throughout the hemisphere, educational systems perpetuate these myths—suggesting that indigenous peoples have contributed nothing to the world, and, consequently, should be grateful for their colonization and their microwave ovens.

Source: From "Why the American Indian Movement of Colorado Opposes Columbus Day and Columbus Day Parades," *Transform Columbus Day,* 2004, http://www .transformcolumbusday.org/.

Third, the languages that people speak influence their interactions. Language can be an attraction or a repellent in intercultural interactions. For example, many people from the United States enjoy traveling in Britain because English is spoken there. However, these same people may have little desire, or even be afraid, to visit Russia, simply because it is not an English-speaking country.

Finally, people tend to be affected by recent, vivid events. For example, after the bombing of the World Trade Center in New York, interactions between Arab Americans and other U.S. residents were strained, characterized by suspicion, fear, and distrust. The media's treatment of such catastrophic events often creates barriers and reinforces stereotypes by blurring distinctions between Arabs, Persians, Muslims, and Palestinians. Perhaps recent histories, such as the racially motivated riots in Los Angeles in the mid-1990s, are more influential in our interactions than the hidden or past histories, such as the massacre in 1890 of some 260 Sioux Indians at Wounded Knee in South Dakota or the women's suffrage movement around the turn of the 20th century.

FIGURE 4-3   The controversy surrounding Columbus Day celebrations reflects the various ways that historical events are entangled with contemporary identities. (© *Spencer Platt/Getty Images*)

The Contact Hypothesis

The **contact hypothesis** is the notion that better communication between groups of people is facilitated simply by bringing them together and allowing them to interact. Although history does not seem to support this notion, many public policies and programs in the United States and abroad are based on this hypothesis. Examples include desegregation rulings; the prevalence of master-planned communities like Reston, Virginia; and many international student exchange programs. All of these programs are based on the assumption that simply giving people from different groups opportunities to interact will result in more positive intergroup attitudes and reduced prejudice.

Gordon Allport (1979) and Yehudi Amir (1969), two noted psychologists, have tried to identify the conditions under which the contact hypothesis does and does not hold true. The histories of various groups figure prominently in their studies. Based on these and subsequent studies, psychologists have outlined at least eight conditions that must be met (more or less) to improve attitudes and facilitate intergroup communication (Schwarzwald & Amir, 1996; Stephan & Stephan, 1996). These are particularly relevant in light of increasing diversity in U.S. society in general and the workforce in particular. The eight conditions are as follows:

1. Group members should be of equal status, both within and outside the contact situation. Communication will occur more easily if there is no disparity

contact hypothesis The notion that better communication between groups is facilitated simply by putting people together in the same place and allowing them to interact.

between individuals in status characteristics (education, socioeconomic status, and so on). This condition does not include temporary inequality, such as in student–teacher or patient–doctor roles. Consider the implications of this condition for relations among various ethnic groups in the United States. How are we likely to think of individuals from specific ethnic groups if our interactions are characterized by inequality? A good example is the interaction between longtime residents and recent immigrants in the Southwest, where Mexican Americans often provide housecleaning, gardening, and similar services for whites. It is easy to see how the history of these two groups in the United States contributes to the lack of equality in interaction, leads to stereotyping, and inhibits effective intercultural communication. But the history of relations between Mexican Americans and whites varies within this region. For example, families of Spanish descent have lived in New Mexico longer than other European-descent families, whereas Arizona has a higher concentration of recent immigrants from Mexico. Intergroup interactions in New Mexico are characterized less by inequality (Stephan & Stephan, 1989).

2. Strong normative and institutional support for the contact should be provided. This suggests that when individuals from different groups come together, positive outcomes do not happen by accident. Rather, institutional encouragement is necessary. Examples include university support for contact between U.S. and international students, or for contact among different cultural groups within the university, and local community support for integrating elementary and high schools. Numerous studies have shown the importance of commitment by top management to policies that facilitate intercultural interaction in the workplace (Brinkman, 1997). Finally, institutional support may also mean government and legal support, expressed through court action.

3. Contact between the groups should be voluntary. This may seem to contradict the previous condition, but it doesn't. Although support must exist beyond the individual, individuals need to feel that they have a choice in making contact. If they believe that they are being forced to interact, as with some diversity programs or affirmative action programs, the intercultural interaction is unlikely to have positive outcomes. For example, an air traffic controller was so incensed by a required diversity program exercise on gender differences that he sued the Department of Transportation for $300,000 (Erbe & Hart, 1994). A better program design would be to involve all participants from the beginning. This can be done by showing the benefits of an inclusive diversity policy—one that values all kinds of diversity, and not merely that based on gender, for example. Equally important is the mounting evidence of bottom-line benefits of diverse personnel who work well together (Harris, 1997).

4. The contact should have the potential to extend beyond the immediate situation and occur in a variety of contexts with a variety of individuals from all groups. This suggests that superficial contact between members of

different groups is not likely to have much impact on attitudes (stereotypes, prejudice) or result in productive communication. For instance, simply sitting beside someone from another culture in a class or sampling food from different countries is not likely to result in genuine understanding of that person or appreciation for his or her cultural background (Stephan & Stephan, 1992). Thus, international students who live with host families are much more likely to have positive impressions of the host country and to develop better intercultural communication skills than those who go on "island programs," in which students interact mostly with other foreigners in the host country.

5. Programs should maximize cooperation within groups and minimize competition. For example, bringing a diverse group of students together should not involve pitting the African Americans against the European Americans on separate sports teams. Instead, it might involve creating diversity within teams to emphasize cooperation. Especially important is having a superordinate goal, a goal that everyone can agree on. This helps diverse groups develop a common identity (Gaertner, Dovidio, & Bachman, 1996). For instance, there is a successful summer camp in Maine for Arab and Jewish youths; the camp brings together members of these historically conflicting groups for a summer of cooperation, discussion, and relationship building.

6. Programs should equalize numbers of group members. Positive outcomes and successful communication will be more likely if members are represented in numerical equality. Research studies have shown that being in the numerical minority can cause stress and that the "solo" minority, particularly in beginning a new job, is subject to exaggerated expectations (either very high or very low) and extreme evaluations (either very good or very bad) (Pettigrew & Martin, 1989).

7. Group members should have similar beliefs and values. A large body of research supports the idea that people are attracted to those whom they perceive to be similar to themselves. This means that, in bringing diverse groups of people together, we should look for common ground—similarities based on religion, interests, competencies, and so on. For example, an international group of mothers is working for peace in the Middle East. Although members represent different ethnic groups, they come together with a shared goal—to protect their children from military action between the warring factions in the region.

8. Programs should promote individuation of group members. This means that they should downplay the characteristics that mark the different groups (such as language, physical abilities, or racial characteristics). Instead, group members might focus on the characteristics that express individual personalities.

This list of conditions can help us understand how domestic and international contexts vary (Gudykunst, 1979). It is easy to see how the history within a nation-state may lead to conditions and attitudes that are more difficult to facilitate. For example, historical conditions between African Americans and white Americans may make it impossible to meet these conditions; interracial interactions in the United States cannot be characterized by equality.

Note that this list of conditions is incomplete. Moreover, meeting all of the conditions does not guarantee positive outcomes when diverse groups of people interact. However, the list is a starting place, and it is important to be able to identify which conditions are affected by historical factors that may be difficult to change and which can be more easily facilitated by communication professionals.

Negotiating Histories Dialectically in Interaction

How can a dialectical perspective help us negotiate interactions, given individual attitudes and personal and cultural histories? How can we balance past and present in our everyday intercultural interactions?

First, it is important to recognize that we all bring our own histories (some known, some hidden) to interactions. We can try to evaluate the role that history plays for those with whom we interact.

Second, we should understand the role that histories play in our identities, in what we bring to the interaction. Communication scholar Marsha Houston (1997) says there are three things that white people who want to be her friends should never say: "I don't notice you're black," "You're not like the others," and "I know how you feel." In her opinion, each of these denies or rejects a part of her identity that is deeply rooted in history.

Sometimes it is unwise to ask people where they are "really from." Such questions assume that they cannot be from where they said they were from, due to racial characteristics or other apparent features. Recognizing a person's history and its link to her or his identity in communication is a first step in establishing intercultural relationships. It is also important to be aware of your own historical blinders and assumptions.

Sometimes the past–present dialectic operates along with the disadvantage–privilege dialectic. The Hungarian philosopher György Lukács wrote a book titled *History and Class Consciousness* (1971), in which he argues that we need to think dialectically about history and social class. Our own recognition of how class differences have influenced our families is very much affected by the past and by the conditions members experienced that might explain whom they married, why they lived where they did, what languages they do and do not speak, and what culture they identify with.

Two dialectical tensions emerge here: (1) between privilege and disadvantage, and (2) between the personal and the social. Both of these dialectics affect our view of the past, present, and future. As we attempt to understand ourselves and our situations (as well as those of others), we must recognize that we arrived at universities for a variety of reasons. Embedded in our backgrounds are dialectical tensions between privilege and disadvantage and the ways in which those factors were established in the past and the present. Then there is the eetha Kothari, a native New Yorker, explains her anger at being asked where she is from. How does this question communicate to her that she is not a U.S. American?

"Where are you from?"

The bartender asks this as I get up from my table. It's quiet at the Bloom-field Bridge Tavern, home of the best pirogies in Pittsburgh. I have just finished eating, just finished telling my boyfriend how much I love this place because it's cheap and simple, not crowded in the early evening, and has good food.

"New York."

He stares at me, but before he can ask another question, I'm down the stairs in the ladies' room, washing my hot face. When I come up again, I glare at him.

"I hate this place," I say to my boyfriend. "That man asked me where I'm from."

The man has no reason to ask me that question. We are not having a conversation. I am not his friend. Out of the blue, having said no other words to me, he feels that it is ok for him, a white man, to ask me where I am from. The only context for this question is my skin color and his need to classify me. I am sure he doesn't expect me to say New York. I look different, therefore it's assumed that I must be from somewhere, somewhere that isn't here, America. It would never occur to him to ask my boyfriend, who is white—and Cana-dian—where he's from.

Source: From "Where Are You From?" by Geetha Kothari, 1995, *Under Western Eyes: Per-sonal Essays From Asian America*, edited by G. Hongo (New York: Anchor Books, 1995), pp. 151–173.

dialectical tension between seeing ourselves as unique persons and as members of particular social classes. These factors affect both the present and the future. In each case, we must also negotiate the dialectical tensions between the past and the present, and between the present and the future. Who we think we are today is very much influenced by how we view the past, how we live, and what culture we believe to be our own.

INTERNET RESOURCES

http://americanradioworks.publicradio.org/features/remembering/
The American Radio Works has compiled information and documents relating to segregation in the United States and posted them online. Students can listen to accounts of segregation and retrospective analyses as well as read many detailed accounts. There is also a section that outlines key laws of the Jim Crow era.

www.santacruzpl.org/history/ww2/9066/contents.shtml
This is a local and national resource for those interested in Japanese internment during World War II. The Web site provides information on national laws and local implementation in Santa Cruz, CA. In addition to legal documents, the Web site archives local newspaper articles on the topic.

www.discovernikkei.org/wiki/index.php/Japanese-American_and_Arab-American_Parallels
This site is part of a larger resource on Japanese migrants. The entire Web site is worth exploring; however, this specific page is of special interest. It hosts a number of articles and essays linking the experiences of Japanese Americans with the experiences of Arab Americans, which provides insight into the ways that America has changed and the ways it has stayed the same regarding race relations and national security.

www.monticello.org/plantation/hemingscontro/hemings-jefferson_contro.html
This Web site provides an accounting of the relationship between Thomas Jefferson and his slave Sally Hemmings. This controversial issue is explored through original documentation, narrative accounts, and links to other resources.

www.rumormillnews.com/jefferson.htm
This article is a response to the type of allegations put forth in the link listed above. A direct descendent of Thomas Jefferson responds to the proposed relationship between Hemmings and Jefferson. This site also contains links to primary documents and other accounts. Together, these Web sites are indicative of the controversies that can stem from contested intercultural history.

www.ushmm.org/museum/

www.ushmm.org/research/center/

www.ushmm.org/wlc/article.php?lang=en&ModuleId=10007058
The first Web address is for the United States Holocaust Museum. The museum Web site offers many exhibits related to the Holocaust that are viewable online. The second Web address is specifically designed for university students. This section includes a searchable database for tracing Holocaust survivors and archiving information. The third Web address is an article/exhibit hosted by the museum on a forged document used to justify the persecution of Jews. This article is an especially powerful example of how rewriting intercultural history can have profound effects.

SUMMARY

- Multiple histories are important for empowering different cultural identities.
- Multiple histories include:
  - Political histories
  - Intellectual histories

- Social histories
- Family histories
- National histories
- Culture-group histories

■ Histories are constructed through narrative.

■ Hidden histories are those typically not conveyed in a widespread manner and are based on gender, sexual orientation, race, and ethnicity.

■ People bring four elements of personal history to intercultural interactions:
- Childhood experience
- Historical myths
- Language competence
- Memories of recent political events

■ Contact hypothesis suggests that simply bringing people from diverse groups together will only work if certain conditions are met:
- Group members must be of equal status and relatively equal numbers.
- Contact must be voluntary, extend beyond the superficial, have institutional support, and promote similarity and individuation of group members.
- There should be maximum cooperation among participants.

■ A dialectical perspective helps negotiate histories in intercultural interaction.

DISCUSSION QUESTIONS

1. What are some examples of hidden histories, and why are they hidden?

2. How do the various histories of the United States influence our communication with people from other countries?

3. What kinds of histories are likely to influence your interactions with an international student of the same gender and age?

4. What factors in your experience have led to the development of positive feelings about your own cultural heritage and background? What factors have led to negative feelings, if any?

5. When can contact between members of two cultures improve their attitudes toward each other and facilitate communication between them?

6. How do histories influence the process of identity formation?

7. What is the significance of the shift from history to histories? How does this shift help us understand intercultural communication?

8. Why do some people in the United States prefer not to talk about history? What views of social reality and intercultural communication does this attitude encourage?

 Go to the self-quizzes on the Online Learning Center at www.mhhe.com/ martinnakayama5 to further test your knowledge.

Cultural-Group History. This exercise can be done by individual students or in groups. Choose a cultural group in the United States that is unfamiliar to you. Study the history of this group, and identify and describe significant events in its history. Answer the following questions:

a. What is the historical relationship between this group and other groups (particularly the dominant cultural groups)?

b. Are there any historical incidents of discrimination? If so, describe them.

c. What are common stereotypes about the group? How did these stereotypes originate?

d. Who are important leaders and heroes of the group?

e. What are notable achievements of the group?

f. How has the history of this group influenced the identity of group members today?

KEY WORDS

absent history (124)
apartheid (131)
colonial histories (143)
concentration camps (130)
contact hypothesis (149)
cultural-group
   histories (126)
diaspora (142)

diasporic histories (142)
ethnic histories (135)
family histories (124)
gender histories (138)
grand narrative (130)
hidden histories (135)
intellectual histories
   (123)

modernist identity
   (130)
national history (125)
political histories (123)
racial histories (135)
sexual orientation
   histories (139)
social histories (123)

The Online Learning Center at www.mhhe.com/martinnakayama5 features flashcards and crossword puzzles based on these terms and concepts.

REFERENCES

Ahmadinejad's comments on homosexuality cut out of transcripts on state-run Farsi Web sites. (2007, September 26). *San Diego Union-Tribune.* http://www.signonsandiego.com/news/world/20070926-1422-iran-ahmadinejad.htmlv. Retrieved May 8, 2008.

Aid, M. M. (2006, February 21). Declassification in reverse. The National Security Archive. http://www.gwu.edu/~nsarchiv/NSAEBB/NSAEBB179/#doc1. Retrieved May 9, 2008.

Allport, G. (1979). *The nature of prejudice.* New York: Addison-Wesley.

Amir, Y. (1969). Contact hypothesis in ethnic relations. *Psychological Bulletin, 71,* 319–343.

Anzaldúa, G. (1987). *Borderlands/La frontera: The new mestiza.* San Francisco: Spinsters/Aunt Lute.

Attenborough, R. (Director). (1987). *Cry Freedom* [Motion picture]. United States: Universal Studios.

Baudrillard, J. (1988). *America* (C. Turner, Trans.). New York: Verso.

Bernstein, N. (2007, April 3). Relatives of interned Japanese-Americans side with Muslims. *The New York Times.* http://www.nytimes.com/2007/04/03/nyregion/03detain.html?pagewanted=1&sq=muslim&scp=153. Retrieved May 8, 2008.

Blanchot, M. (1986). *The writing of the disaster* (A. Smock, Trans.). Lincoln: University of Nebraska Press.

Brinkman, H. (1997). Managing diversity: A review of recommendations for success. In C. D. Brown, C. Snedeker, & B. Sykes (Eds.), *Conflict and diversity* (pp. 35–50). Cresskill, NJ: Hampton Press.

Brislin, R. W. (1981). *Cross cultural encounters: Face to face interaction.* New York: Pergamon.

Bureau of African Affairs. (2005, September). Background note: South Africa. United States Department of State. http://www.state.gov/r/pa/ei/bgn/2898.htm#history. Accessed October 30, 2005.

Erbe, B., & Hart, B. (1994, September 16). Employer goes overboard on "gender sensitivity" issue. *The Evansville Courier*, p. A13.

Fisher, W. (1984). Narration as a human communication paradigm: The case of public moral argument. *Communication Monographs, 51*, 1–22.

Fisher, W. (1985). The narrative paradigm: An elaboration. *Communication Monographs, 52*, 347–367.

Fitzgerald, F. (1972). *Fire in the lake: Vietnamese and Americans in Vietnam.* New York: Vintage Books.

Fleischer, A. (2001, September 18). Press briefing by Ari Fleischer. *The White House.* http://www.whitehouse.gov/news/releases/2001/09/20010918-5.html. Retrieved May 8, 2008.

Gaertner, S. L., Dovidio, J. F., & Bachman, B. A. (1996). Revisiting the contact hypothesis: The induction of a common ingroup identity. *International Journal of Intercultural Relations, 20*, 271–290.

Gérard-Libois, J., & Heinen, J. (1989). *Belgique-Congo, 1960.* Brussels: Politique et Histoire.

Gilroy, P. (1993). *The Black Atlantic: Modernity and double consciousness.* New York: Verso.

Goldman, R. (2007, September 24). Ahmadinejad: No gays, No oppression of women in Iran. *ABC News.* http://a.abcnews.com/US/story?id=3642673&page=1. Retrieved May 8, 2008.

Greenberg, D. (2005, January 14). The gay emancipator? Slate. http://www.slate.com/id/2112313/. Retrieved May 8, 2008.

Gudykunst, W. B. (1979). Intercultural contact and attitude change: A review of literature and suggestions for future research. *International and Intercultural Communication Annual, 4*, 1–16.

Guelke, A. (2005). *Rethinking the rise and fall of apartheid: South Africa and world politics.* New York: Palgrave Macmillan.

Harris, T. E. (1997). Diversity: Importance, ironies, and pathways. In C. D. Brown, C. Snedeker, & B. Sykes (Eds.), *Conflict and diversity* (pp. 17–34). Cresskill, NJ: Hampton Press.

Hocquenghem, G., & Blasius, M. (1980, April). Interview. *Christopher Street, 8*(4), 36–45.

Housel, T. H. (2007). Australian nationalism and globalization: Narratives of the nation in the 2000 Sydney Olympics' opening ceremony. *Critical Studies in Media Communication, 24*, 446–461.

Houston, M. (1997). When Black women talk with White women: Why dialogues are difficult. In A. González, M. Houston, & V. Chen (Eds.), *Our voices: Essays in ethnicity, culture, and communication* (2nd ed., pp. 187–194). Los Angeles: Roxbury.

Immigrant Investor Program Redesign. (1998, December). Guide for applying for permanent residence in Canada: Business applicants. cicnet.ci.gc.ca/press/98/9865-pre.html

Jameson, F. (1981). *The political unconscious: Narrative as a socially symbolic act.* Ithaca, NY: Cornell University Press.

Kennedy, R. (2003, September 11). From protest to patronage. *The Nation.* http://www.thenation.com/doc/20030929/kennedy. Retrieved May 8, 2008.

Kothari, G. (1995). Where are you from? In G. Hongo (Ed.), *Under Western eyes: Personal essays from Asian America* (pp. 151–173). New York: Anchor Books/Doubleday.

Loewen, J. W. (1995). *Lies my teacher told me: Everything your American history textbook got wrong.* New York: Touchstone.

Lukács, György. (1971). *History and class consciousness: Studies in Marxist dialectics* (R. Livingstone, Trans.). Cambridge, MA: MIT Press.

Lyotard, J.-F. (1984). *The postmodern condition: A report on knowledge* (G. Bennington & B. Massumi, Trans.). Minneapolis: University of Minnesota Press.

Nakano, M. (1990). *Japanese American women: Three generations, 1890–1990.* Berkeley and San Francisco: Mina Press/National Japanese American Historical Society.

Pettigrew, T. F., & Martin, J. (1989). Organizational inclusion of minority groups: A social psychological analysis. In J. P. VanOudenhoven & T. M. Willemsen (Eds.), *Ethnic minorities: Social psychological perspectives* (pp. 169–200). Amsterdam/Lisse: Swets & Zeitlinger.

Saulny, S. (2005, October 11). Cast from their ancestral home, Creoles worry about culture's future. *The New York Times*, p. A13.

Schwarzwald, J., & Amir, Y. (1996). Guest editor's introduction: Special issue on prejudice, discrimination and conflict. *International Journal of Intercultural Relations, 20*, 265–270.

Seel, P., with Bitoux, J. (1994). *Moi, Pierre Seel, déporté homosexuel.* Paris: Calmann-Lévy.

Shaffer, M. (2002, June 9). Navajos protest national status for Old Spanish Trail. *The Arizona Republic*, pp. B1, B8.

Shome, R., & Hegde, R. (2002). Postcolonial approaches to communication: Charting the terrain, engaging the intersections. *Communication Theory, 12,* 249–270.

Stephan, C. W., & Stephan, W. G. (1989). Antecedents of intergroup anxiety in Asian Americans and Hispanic Americans. *International Journal of Intercultural Relations, 13,* 203–216.

Stephan, C. W., & Stephan, W. G. (1992). Reducing intercultural anxiety through intercultural contact. *International Journal of Intercultural Relations, 16,* 89–106.

Stephan, W. G., & Stephan, C. W. (1996). *Intergroup relations.* Boulder, CO: Westview Press.

Steyn, M. (2001). *"Whiteness just isn't what it used to be": White identity in a changing South Africa.* Albany: State University of New York Press.

Tateishi, J. (1984). *And justice for all: An oral history of the Japanese American detention camps.* New York: Random House.

Tell, D. (2008). The "shocking story" of Emmett Till and the politics of public confession. *Quarterly Journal of Speech, 94,* 156–178.

Thompson, L. (2001). *A history of South Africa* (3rd ed.). New Haven: Yale University Press.

Thonssen, L., Baird, A. C., & Braden, W. W. (1970). *Speech criticism* (2nd ed.). New York: Ronald Press.

Tripp, C. A. (2004). *The intimate world of Abraham Lincoln.* New York: Free Press.

Under surveillance. (1995, December 26). *The Advocate,* p. 14.

PART II

Intercultural Communication Processes

IDENTITY AND INTERCULTURAL COMMUNICATION

CHAPTER OBJECTIVES

After reading this chapter, you should be able to:

1. Identify three communication approaches to identity.
2. Define identity.
3. Explain the relationship between identity and language.
4. Describe phases of minority identity development.
5. Describe phases of majority identity development.
6. Identify and describe nine social and cultural identities.
7. Identify characteristics of whiteness.
8. Explain the relationship among identity, stereotyping, and prejudice.
9. Describe phases of multicultural identity development.
10. Explain the relationship between identity and communication.

Now that we have examined some sociohistorical contexts that shape culture and communication, let us turn to a discussion of identity and its role in intercultural communication. Identity serves as a bridge between culture and communication. It is important because we communicate our identity to others, and we learn who we are through communication. It is through communication—with our family, friends, and others—that we come to understand ourselves and form our identity. Issues of identity are particularly important in intercultural interactions.

Conflicts can arise, however, when there are sharp differences between who we think we are and who others think we are. For example, a female college student living with a family in Mexico on a homestay may be treated protectively and chaperoned when she socializes, which may conflict with her view of herself as an independent person. In this case, the person's identity is not confirmed but is questioned or challenged in the interaction.

In this chapter, we describe a dialectical approach to understanding identity, one that encompasses three communication approaches: social science, interpretive, and critical. We then explore the important role language plays in understanding identity and how minority and majority identities develop. We then turn to the development of specific aspects of our social and cultural identity including those related to gender, race or ethnicity, class, religion, and nationality. We describe how these identities are often related to problematic communication—stereotypes, prejudice, and discrimination. We also examine an increasingly important identity—that of multicultural individuals. Finally, we discuss the relationship between identity and communication.

THINKING DIALECTICALLY ABOUT IDENTITY

identity The concept of who we are. Characteristics of identity may be understood differently depending on the perspectives that people take—for example, social science, interpretive, or critical perspectives.

impression management theory The ways by which individuals attempt to control the impressions others have of them.

Identity is a core issue for most people. It is about who we are and who others think we are. How do we come to understand who we are? And how do we communicate our identity to others? A useful theory is that of **impression management**—how people present themselves and how they guide the impression others form of them (Goffman, 1959). Some scholars suggest that individuals are constantly performing "spin control" campaigns to highlight their strengths and virtues while also attempting "damage control" by minimizing deficiencies (Tedeschi, Lindskold, & Rosenfeld, 1985; Rosenfeld and Giaclone, 1991). As we will see, individuals cannot control others' impressions completely, as those we interact with also play an important role in how our identities develop and are expressed.

What are the characteristics of identity? In this section we use both the static–dynamic and the personal–contextual dialectics in answering this question.

There are three contemporary communication perspectives on identity (see Table 5-1). The social science perspective, based largely on research in psychology, views the self in a relatively static fashion in relation to the various cultural communities to which a person belongs: nationality, race, ethnicity, religion,

TABLE 5-1 THREE PERSPECTIVES ON IDENTITY AND COMMUNICATION

Social Science	Interpretive	Critical
Identity created by self (by relating to groups)	Identity formed through communication with others	Identity shaped through social, historical forces
Emphasizes individualized, familial, and spiritual self (cross-cultural perspective)	Emphasizes avowal and ascribed dimensions	Emphasizes contexts and resisting ascribed identity

gender, and so on. The interpretive perspective is more dynamic and recognizes the important role of interaction with others as a factor in the development of the self. Finally, the critical perspective views identity even more dynamically—as a result of contexts quite distant from the individual. As you read this chapter, keep in mind that the relationship between identity and intercultural interaction involves both static and dynamic elements and both personal and contextual elements.

The Social Science Perspective

The social science perspective emphasizes that identity is created in part by the self and in part in relation to group membership. According to this perspective, the self is composed of multiple identities, and these notions of identity are culture bound. How, then, do we come to understand who we are? That depends very much on our cultural background. According to Western psychologists like Erik Erikson, our identities are self-created, formed through identity conflicts and crises, through identity diffusion and confusion (Erikson, 1950, 1968). Occasionally, we may need a moratorium, a time-out, in the process. Our identities are created not in one smooth, orderly process but in spurts, with some events providing insights into who we are and long periods intervening during which we may not think much about ourselves or our identities.

Cross-Cultural Perspectives In the United States, young people are often encouraged to develop a strong sense of identity, to "know who they are," to be independent and self-reliant, which reflects an emphasis on the cultural value of individualism. However, this was not always the case, and even today in many countries there is a very different, more collectivist notion of self. Min-Sun Kim (2002), a communication scholar, traces the evolution of the individualistic self. Before 1500, people in Europe as well as in most other civilizations lived in small cohesive communities, with a worldview characterized by the interdependence of spiritual and material phenomena. With the beginning of the industrial revolution in the 1600s came the notion of the world as a machine; this mechanistic view extended to living organisms and has had a profound effect on Western ommunication scholar Ge Gao contrasts the Western idea of the independent self with the Chinese notion of the interdependent self.

In the Western world, an "individual" signifies an independent entity with free will, emotions and personality. An individual, however, is not conceptualized in this way in the Chinese culture. . . . The incomplete nature of the self is supported by both Taoism and Confucianism even though they differ in many fundamental ways. Taoism defines self as part of nature. Self and nature together complete a harmonious relationship. Self in the Confucian sense is defined by a person's surrounding relations, which often are derived from kinship networks and supported by cultural values such as filial piety, loyalty, dignity, and integrity. . . .

The other-orientation thus is key to an interdependent self. Congruous with the notion of an interdependent self, the Chinese self also needs to be recognized, defined, and completed by others. The self's orientation to others' needs, wishes, and expectations is essential to the development of the Chinese self.

Source: From Ge Gao, "Self and Other: A Chinese Perspective on Interpersonal Relationships." In W. G. Gudykunst et al. (Eds.), *Communication in Personal Relationships Across Cultures.* (Thousand Oaks, CA: Sage, 1996), pp. 83–84.

thought. It taught people to think of themselves as isolated egos—unconnected to the natural world and society in general. Thus, according to Kim, a person in the West came to be understood as "an individual entity with a separate existence independent of place in society" (Kim, 2002, p. 12). In contrast, people in many other regions of the world have retained the more interdependent notion of the self.

Cross-cultural psychologist Alan Roland (1988) has identified three universal aspects of identity present in all individuals: (1) an individualized identity, (2) a familial identity, and (3) a spiritual identity. Cultural groups usually emphasize one or two of these dimensions and downplay the other(s). Let's see how this works. The **individualized identity** is the sense of an independent "I," with sharp distinctions between the self and others. This identity is emphasized by most groups in the United States, where young people are encouraged to be independent and self-reliant at a fairly early age—by adolescence.

In contrast, the **familial identity,** evident in many collectivistic cultures, stresses the importance of emotional connectedness to and interdependence with others. For example, in many African and Asian societies, and in some cultural groups in the United States, children are encouraged and expected to form strong, interdependent bonds, first with the family and later with other groups. As one of our students explains,

to be Mexican American is to unconditionally love one's family and all it stands for. Mexican-Americans are an incredibly close-knit group of people, especially when it comes to family. We are probably the only culture that can actually recite

individualized identity The sense of self as independent and self-reliant.

familial identity The sense of self as always connected to family and others.

the names of our fourth cousins by heart. In this respect our families are like clans, they go much further than the immediate family and very deep into extended families. We even have a celebration, Dia de los Muertos *(Day of the Dead), that honors our ancestors.*

In these societies, educational, occupational, and even marital choices are made by individuals with extensive family guidance. The goal of the developed identity is not to become independent from others but rather to gain an understanding of and cultivate one's place in the complex web of interdependence with others. Communication scholar Ge Gao (1996) describes the Chinese sense of self:

> *The other-orientation thus is key to an interdependent self. Congruous with the notion of an interdependent self, the Chinese self also needs to be recognized, defined, and completed by others. The self's orientation to others' needs, wishes, and expectations is essential to the development of the Chinese self. (p. 84)*

In addition, the understanding of the familial self may be more connected to others and situation bound. According to studies comparing North Americans' and East Asians' senses of identity, when asked to describe themselves, the North Americans give more abstract, situation-free descriptions ("I am kind," "I am outgoing," "I am quiet in the morning"), whereas East Asians tend to describe their memberships and relationships to others rather than themselves ("I am a mother," "I am the youngest child in my family," "I am a member of a tennis club") (Cross, 2000).

The third dimension is the **spiritual identity,** the inner spiritual reality that is realized and experienced to varying extents by people through a number of outlets. For example, the spiritual self in India is expressed through a structure of gods and goddesses and through rituals and meditation. In Japan, the realization of the spiritual self tends more toward aesthetic modes, such as the tea ceremony and flower arranging (Roland, 1988).

spiritual identity Identification with feelings of connectedness to others and higher meanings in life.

Clearly, identity development does not occur in the same way in every society. The notion of identity in India, Japan, and some Latino/a and Asian American groups emphasizes the integration of the familial and the spiritual self but very little of the more individualized self.

This is not to say there is not considerable individuality among people in these groups. However, the general identity contrasts dramatically with the predominant mode in most U.S. cultural groups, in which the individualized self is emphasized and there is little attention to the familial self. However, there may be some development of the spiritual self among devout Catholic, Protestant, Jewish, or Muslim individuals.

Groups play an important part in the development of all these dimensions of self. As we are growing up, we identify with many groups, based on gender, race, ethnicity, class, sexual orientation, religion, and nationality (Tajfel, 1981, 1982). And depending on our cultural background, we may develop tight or looser bonds with these groups (Kim, 2002). By comparing ourselves and others with members of these groups, we come to understand who we are. Because we belong to various groups, we develop multiple identities that come into play at different times, depending on the context. For example, in going to church or temple, we may highlight our religious identity. In going to clubs or bars, we may highlight our sexual orientation identity. Women who join social groups exclusive to women (or men who attend social functions just for men) are highlighting their gender identity.

identity negotiation theory A theory that emphasizes the process of communicating one's own desired identities while reinforcing or resisting others' identities as the core of intercultural communication.

Communication scholar Ting-Toomey (1993, 2005) argues in her **identity negotiation theory** that cultural variability influences our sense of self and ultimately influences how successful we are in intercultural interactions. Her argument goes like this: Individuals define themselves in relation to groups they belong to due to the basic human need for security and inclusion. At the same time, humans also need differentiation from these same groups. Managing relationships to these various groups involves boundary regulation and working through the tension between inclusion and differentiation and can make us feel secure or vulnerable. How we manage this tension influences the coherent sense of self (identity)—individuals who are more secure are more open to interacting with members of other cultures. When people feel good about themselves and the groups to which they belong, they are more successful in intercultural interactions. However, as we will see in the next section, identities are formed not just by the individual but also through interactions with others.

The Interpretive Perspective

The interpretive perspective builds on the notions of identity formation discussed previously but takes a more dynamic turn. That is, it emphasizes that identities are negotiated, co-created, reinforced, and challenged though communication with others; they emerge when messages are exchanged between persons (Hecht, Warren, Jung, & Krieger, 2005; Ting-Toomey, 2005). This means that presenting our identities is not a simple process. Does everyone see you as you see yourself? Probably not. To understand how these images may conflict, the concepts of avowal and ascription are useful.

avowal The process by which an individual portrays himself or herself.

ascription The process by which others attribute identities to an individual.

Avowal is the process by which individuals portray themselves, whereas **ascription** is the process by which others attribute identities to them. Sometimes these processes are congruent. For example, we (Judith and Tom) see ourselves as professors and hope that students also see us as professors. We also see ourselves as young, but many students do not concur, ascribing an "old person" identity to us. This ascribed identity challenges our avowed identity. And these conflicting views influence the communication between us and our students.

Different identities are emphasized depending on the individuals we are communicating with and the topics of conversation. For example, in a social conversation with someone we are attracted to, our gender or sexual orientation identity is probably more important to us than other identities (ethnicity, nationality). And our communication is probably most successful when the person we are talking with confirms the identity we think is most important at the moment. In this sense, competent intercultural communication affirms the identity that is most salient in any conversation (Collier & Thomas, 1988). For example, if you are talking with a professor about a research project, the conversation will be most competent if the interaction confirms the salient identities (professor and student) rather than other identities (e.g., those based on gender, religion, or ethnicity).

How do you feel when someone does not recognize the identity you believe is most salient? For example, suppose your parents treat you as a child (their ascription) and not as an independent adult (your avowal). How might this affect communication? One of our students describes how he reacts when people ascribe a different identity than the one he avows:

> Pretty much my entire life I was seen not as American but as half Mexican. In reality I am 50% Mexican and 50% Dutch. So technically I am half Mexican and half Dutch American. I always say it like that but it was obvious that not everybody saw it like that. I was asked if I was Hawaiian, Persian, and even Italian, but I was able to politely tell them about myself.

Central to the interpretive perspective is the idea that our identities are expressed communicatively—in core symbols, labels, and norms. **Core symbols** (or cultural values) tell us about the fundamental beliefs and the central concepts that define a particular identity. Communication scholar Michael Hecht and his colleagues (Hecht, 1998; Hecht, Jackson, & Ribeau, 2003) have identified the contrasting core symbols associated with various ethnic identities. For example, core symbols of African American identity may be positivity, sharing, uniqueness, realism, and assertiveness. Individualism is often cited as a core symbol of European American identity. Core symbols are not only expressed but also created and shaped through communication. Labels are a category of core symbols; they are the terms we use to refer to particular aspects of our own and others' identities—for example, *African American*, *Latino*, *white*, or *European American*.

Finally, some norms of behavior are associated with particular identities. For example, women may express their gender identity by being more concerned about safety than men. They may take more precautions when they go out at night, such as walking in groups. People might express their religious identity by participating in activities such as going to church or Bible study meetings.

core symbols The fundamental beliefs that are shared by the members of a cultural group. *Labels,* a category of core symbols, are names or markers used to classify individual, social, or cultural groups.

The Critical Perspective

Like the interpretive perspective, the critical perspective emphasizes the dynamic nature of identities, but in addition, it emphasizes the contextual and often conflictual elements of identity development. This perspective pays particular attention to the societal structures and institutions that constrain identities and are often the root of injustice and oppression (Collier, 2005).

Contextual Identity Formation   The driving force behind a critical approach is the attempt to understand identity formation within the contexts of history, economics, politics, and discourse. To grasp this notion, ask yourself, How and why do people identify with particular groups and not others? What choices are available to them?

FIGURE 5-1   We have many different identities—including gender, ethnicity, age, religion, and sexuality—that we express in different ways at different times. Celebrations are one way to highlight identity. Here, Sikhs in the northern Indian city of Chandigarh light candles in a temple to celebrate Diwali. Diwali marks the age-old culture of India and celebrates knowledge and the vanquishing of ignorance. (© *Ajay Verma/Reuters/Getty Images*)

We are all subject to being pigeonholed into identity categories, or contexts, even before we are born. (See Figure 5-1.) Many parents ponder a name for their unborn child, who is already part of society through his or her relationship to the parents. Some children have a good start at being, say, Jewish or Chicana before they are even born. We cannot ignore the ethnic, socioeconomic, or racial positions from which we start our identity journeys.

To illustrate, French psychoanalyst Jacques Lacan (1977) offers the example of two children on a train that stops at a station. Each child looks out a window and identifies the location: One says that they are in front of the door for the ladies' bathroom; the other says they are in front of the gentlemen's. Both children see and use labels from their seating position to describe where they are; they are on the same train, but they describe their locations differently. Just as we are never "out" of position, we are never "outside" of language and its system that helps define us. And, like the two children, where we are positioned—by language and by society—influences how and what we see and, most importantly, what it means.

The identities that others may ascribe to us are socially and politically determined. They are not constructed by the self alone. We must ask ourselves what drives the construction of particular kinds of identities. For example, the label "heterosexual" is a relatively recent one, created less than a hundred years ago (Katz, 1995). Today, people do not hesitate to identify themselves as "heterosexuals." A critical perspective insists on the constructive nature of this process and attempts to identify the social forces and needs that give rise to these identities.

These contextual constraints on identity are also reflected in the experience of a Palestinian woman who describes her feelings of not having a national "identity" as represented by a passport—because of political circumstances far beyond her control:

> *I am Palestinian but I don't have either a Palestinian passport or an Israeli passport. . . . If I take the Palestinian passport, the Israeli government would prevent me from entering Jerusalem and Jerusalem is a part of my soul. I just can't NOT enter it. And of course I'm not taking an Israeli passport, so . . . I get frustrated when I talk to people WITH identity, especially Palestinians with Israeli identity. I just get like kind of offended because I think they're more comfortable than me. (Collier, 2005, p. 243)*

Resisting Ascribed Identities   When we invoke such discourses about identity, we are pulled into the social forces that feed the discourse. We might resist the position they put us in, and we might try to ascribe other identities to ourselves. Nevertheless, we must begin from that position in carving out a new identity.

French philosopher Louis Althusser (1971) uses the term **interpellation** to refer to this process. He notes that we are pushed into this system of social forces

> *by that very precise operation which I have called interpellation or hailing, and which can be imagined along the lines of the most commonplace everyday police (or other) hailing: "Hey you there!" . . . Experience shows that the practical tele-communication of hailings is such that they hardly ever miss their man: verbal call or whistle, the one hailed always recognizes that it is really him who is being hailed. And yet it is a strange phenomenon, and one which cannot be explained solely by "guilt feelings." (p. 163)*

interpellation The communication process by which one is pulled into the social forces that place people into a specific identity.

This hailing process that Althusser describes operates in intercultural communication interactions. It establishes the foundation from which the interaction occurs. For example, occasionally someone will ask Tom if he is Japanese, a question that puts him in an awkward position. He does not hold Japanese citizenship, nor has he ever lived in Japan. Yet the question probably doesn't mean to address these issues. Rather, the person is asking what it means to be "Japanese." How can Tom reconfigure his position in relation to this question?

The Dynamic Nature of Identities   The social forces that give rise to particular identities are never stable but are always changing. Therefore, the critical perspective insists on the dynamic nature of identities. For example, the emergence of the European Union has given new meaning to the notion of being "European" as an identity. Similarly, the terrorist attacks of September 11, 2001, have caused many Americans to reconsider what it means to be "American." And the various riter Philippe Wamba describes how his multicultural identity developed across several continents and languages. His father (from the Republic of the Congo, formerly Zaire) and mother (an African American midwesterner) met and married while attending college in Michigan. His father's career took the family first to Boston (where Philippe was one of only a few blacks in his school), then to Dar es Salaam, Tanzania, where he learned flawless Swahili and added a third heritage to his cultural background: "half American, half Zairean, and half Tanzanian." Now an adult, he describes his answer to the question "Where are you from?"

> *I used to try to find succinct ways of responding to the question "Where are you from"—simple one-word answers that would satisfy the curious. I envied my friends their ability to state one place confidently and simply say "New York" or "Kenya." . . . For a period, I even referred to myself as a "a citizen of the world," a high-minded moniker, bred of my own boredom and frustration, that used to annoy people. . . . Now I have decided that the succinct answer is always inadequate and that the story of origin is always a complex saga. . . . I have come to reject the idea of a simple, dualized family heritage and the simple bicultural understanding of self I internalized as a child. . . . For a time I lived as a sophisticated cultural chameleon, attempting to blend with my shifting surroundings by assuming the appearance and habits of those around me. . . . In the end I am both African and African American and therefore neither. I envy others their hometowns and unconflicted patriotism, but no longer would I exchange them for my freedom to seek multiple homes and nations and to forge my own.*

Source: From P. Wamba, "A Middle Passage." In C. C. O'Hearn (Ed.), *Half and Half: Writers on Growing up Biracial + Bicultural* (New York: Pantheon Books, 1998), pp. 168–169.

and sometimes contradictory notions of what it means to be an American highlights the fluidity and dynamic nature of identities. For some, being "American" now means having a renewed patriotism, as described by one of our students:

> *To be an American is to be proud. After September 11, a sense of patriotism swept through this country that I have never felt before. Growing up I heard about how patriotic the United States was during WW I and WW II, but I had never experienced it personally. After that day, it was as if racial, religious, and democratic differences had stopped. Even if that tension only stopped temporarily, the point is that it did stop. Our country came together to help, pray, and donate. The feeling of being an American is a sense of feeling and strength and pride.*

For others, the events of 9/11 led to more ambivalence about being "American":

> *The media showed negative responses that other countries displayed toward Americans. This makes me ponder what I've done, as a white mutt American*

to make people feel this way. I know it is not necessarily my fault but actually American beliefs as a whole. . . . The "cop in the head" feeling occurs in me whenever I see a group of people gathered around speaking a foreign language and staring at me. Maybe it is an insecurity issue within me, aided by rumors I've heard, that initiates this uneasy feeling. I really hope Americans, as a whole, become more accepting of each other so that other countries will see that we can work together with such diversity.

For another example, look at the way that identity labels have changed from "colored" to "Negro" to "black" to "Afro-American" to "African American." Although the labels seem to refer to the same group of people, the political and cultural identities of those so labeled are different. The term "Negro" was replaced by "Black" during the civil rights movement in the 1960s because it stood for racial pride, power, and rejection of the status quo. "Black is beautiful" and "Black power" became slogans during this time. In the late 1980s, Black leaders proposed that "Black" be replaced with "African American," saying that this label would provide African Americans a cultural identification with their heritage and ancestral homeland. The changes in these labels have worked to strengthen group identity and facilitate the struggle for racial equality (Smith, 1992). Currently, both terms are used—depending on people's preference—and "Black" is preferred by some because it shows commonality with people of African descent who are not U.S. American (e.g., Caribbean Islanders) (Sigelman, Tuch, & Martin, 2005; Why Black . . . , 2008).

IDENTITY AND LANGUAGE

The labels that refer to particular identities are an important part of intercultural communication. These labels do not, of course, exist outside of their relational meanings. It is the relationships—not only interpersonal but social—that help us understand the importance of the labels.

Communication scholar Dolores Tanno (2000) describes her own multiple identities reflected in the various labels applied to her. For instance, the label "Spanish" was applied by her family and designates an ancestral origin in Spain. The label "Mexican American" reflects two important cultures that contribute to her identity. "Latina" reflects cultural and historical connectedness with others of Spanish descent (e.g., Puerto Ricans and South Americans), and "Chicana" promotes political and cultural assertiveness in representing her identity. She stresses that she is all of these, that each one reveals a different facet of her identity: symbolic, historical, cultural, and political.

In emphasizing the fluidity and relational nature of labels, communication scholar Stuart Hall (1985) notes that

at different times in my thirty years in England, I have been "hailed" or interpellated as "coloured," "West-Indian," "Negro," "black," "immigrant." Sometimes in the street; sometimes at street corners; sometimes abusively; sometimes in a friendly manner; sometimes ambiguously. (p. 108)

Hall underscores the dynamic and dialectic nature of identity and the self as he continues:

> *In fact I "am" not one or another of these ways of representing me, though I have been all of them at different times and still am some of them to some degree. But, there is no essential, unitary "I"—only the fragmentary, contradictory subject I become. (pp. 108–109)*

These and other labels construct relational meanings in communication situations. The interpersonal relationships between Hall and the other speakers are important, but equally important are such labels' social meanings.

Like culture, labels also change over time. At one time, it was acceptable to use the label *oriental* to refer to people, but today the social meaning of that term is considered negative. There are many terms that you may not know are considered offensive, but as you interact with others around the world, you should be aware that you need to learn what terms to use and what terms to avoid. For example, referring to Quebeckers, especially French-speaking Quebeckers, as *pepsi's* may get you in trouble. Pepsi is considered a derogatory term for Quebeckers. Québec is reputedly one of the few places around the world where Pepsi outsells Coca-Cola, which may be because of the bottle size, but the term may also come from the Pepsi's glass bottles that were empty from the neck up. Other terms are still contested. For example, some gays and lesbians do not like the term *queer;* others have embraced it. Cultures change over time, as do languages. It is important that you stay aware of these changes as much as possible so you do not unintentionally offend others.

IDENTITY DEVELOPMENT ISSUES

People can identify with a multitude of groups: gender, age, religion, nationality, to name only a few. How do we come to develop a sense of identities? As we noted earlier, our identities develop over a period of time and always through interaction with others. How an individual's identity develops depends partly on the relative position or location of the identity within the societal hierarchy. Some identities have a higher position on the social hierarchy. For example, a heterosexual identity has a more privileged position than a homosexual identity; a Christian religious identity is generally more privileged than a Jewish or Muslim religious identity in the United States. To distinguish among the various positions, we label the more privileged identities "majority identities" and label the less privileged "minority identities." This terminology refers to the relative dominance or power of the identity position, not the numerical quantity.

Social science researchers have identified various models that describe how minority and majority identities develop. (See Table 5-2) Although the models center on racial and ethnic identities, they may also apply to other identities, such as class, gender, or sexual orientation (Ponterotto & Pedersen, 1993). It is also important to remember that, as with any model, these represent the experience of many people, but the stages are not set in stone. Identity development is a complex process; not everyone experiences these phases in exactly the same way. Some people spend more time in one phase than do others; individuals may experience the phases in different ways, and not everyone reaches the final phase.

Minority Identity Development

In general, minority identities tend to develop earlier than majority identities. For example, straight people tend to not think about their sexual orientation identity often, whereas gay people are often acutely aware of their sexual orientation identity being different from the majority and develop a sense of sexual orientation identity earlier than people who are straight. Similarly, while whites may develop a strong ethnic identity, they often do not think about their racial identity, whereas members of racial minority groups are aware of their racial identities at an early age (Ferguson, 1990).

Minority identity often develops in the following stages (as shown in Table 5-2):

minority identity A sense of belonging to a nondominant group.

Stage 1: Unexamined Identity   This stage is characterized by the lack of exploration of identity, be it racial, ethnic, sexual orientation, gender, or whatever. At this stage, individuals may simply lack interest in the identity issue. As one African American woman put it, "Why do I need to learn about who was the first black woman to do this or that? I'm just not too interested." Or minority group members may initially accept the values and attitudes of the majority culture, expressing positive attitudes toward the dominant group and negative views of their own group. Young girls may idolize their successful professional fathers and disparage their stay-at-home mothers. Gay young people may try very hard to act "straight" and may even participate in "gay bashing."

Stage 2: Conformity   This stage is characterized by the internalization of the values and norms of the dominant group and a strong desire to assimilate into the dominant culture. Individuals in this phase may have negative, self-deprecating attitudes toward both themselves and their group. As one young Jewish woman said, "I tried very hard in high school to not let anyone know I was Jewish. I'd talk about Christmas shopping and Christmas parties with my friends even though my parents didn't allow me to participate at all in any Christmas celebration."

Individuals who criticize members of their own ethnic or racial group may be given negative labels such as "Uncle Tom" or "oreo" for African Americans, "banana" for Asian Americans, "apple" for Native Americans, and "Tio Taco" for Chicanos. Such labels condemn attitudes and behaviors that support the dominant white culture. This stage often continues until they encounter a situation that causes them to question prodominant culture attitudes, which initiates the movement to the next stage.

TABLE 5-2   MAJORITY, MINORITY, AND BIRACIAL IDENTITY DEVELOPMENT STAGES

Minority	Majority	Biracial
1. Unexamined Identity • Lack of exploration of ethnicity • Acceptance of majority group values • Positive attitudes toward the majority group • Lack of interest in issues of ethnicity	1. Unexamined Identity • Lack of exploration of ethnicity • Acceptance of majority group values • Positive attitudes toward the majority group • Lack of interest in issues of ethnicity	1. May cycle through 3 stages of identity development • Awareness of differences and resulting dissonance • Awareness that they are different from other children • Sense that they don't fit in anywhere
2. Conformity • Internalization of dominant group norms; desire for assimilation into this group • Negative attitudes toward themselves and their groups until an experience causes them to question the dominant culture attitudes	2. Acceptance • Internalization of a racist ideology (passive or active acceptance) • The key point is that individuals are not aware that they have been programmed to accept this worldview.	2. Struggle for acceptance • May feel that they need to choose one race or another
3. Resistance and Separatism • Growing awareness that not all dominant values are beneficial to minorities • Often triggered by negative events • Blanket endorsement of one's group's values and attitudes • Rejection of dominant group values and norms	3. Resistance • Moving from blaming minority members for their situations and beginning to blame their own dominant group	3. Self-acceptance and self–assertion
4. Integration • Ideal outcome of identity development—achieved identity • Strong sense of their own group identity and an appreciation for other cultural groups	4. Redefinition • Nonacceptance of society's definition of white • Able to see positive aspects of being white • Becoming comfortable with being in dominant group	
	5. Integration • Ideal outcome of identity development—achieved identity • Strong sense of their own group identity and an appreciation for other cultural groups	

I believe that one of the most important identities to me is the minority identity, especially now. Ever since my arrival at college, I have felt more and more like a real minority. My hometown was over 90% Hispanic, and I really wasn't a minority. Here, there really aren't that many Hispanics. Every day, I feel a bit uncomfortable because I hear so many stereotypes about Hispanics, specifically Mexican-American. I feel as though I really can't speak up simply because this university is dominated by Anglo-Americans and it would be overwhelming. In one of my classes, we were talking about Mexican illegal immigration and a lot of people were cracking jokes. It made me feel quite uncomfortable, so I left. The only thing that I guess can improve this misunderstanding is to better communicate with one another and not base our judgments on stereotypes.
—Adrian

Stage 3: Resistance and Separatism   Many kinds of events can trigger the move to the third stage, including negative ones such as encountering discrimination or name-calling. A period of dissonance, or a growing awareness that not all dominant group values are beneficial to minorities, may also precede this stage. For example, Tomiko, a young professional woman, never thought much about her gender identity. However, she became more self-reflective and was propelled into this stage of identity development after discovering that she could not join the country club that many of her male colleagues belonged to—where they often discussed important job-related issues—because of her gender. And she then learned that the leave policies at her firm were such that if she decided to have a child she would likely be penalized professionally. Her gender identity then became very important to her, and she moved to the resistance and separation stage. For a time she decided only to patronize businesses where women were treated equally. She selected a female doctor as her primary care physician, shopped at a hardware store owned by a group of women, and when she tackled a home remodeling project she solicited bids only from female construction firms.

International students sometimes develop their national identity as a minority identity when they study overseas. Dewi, an Indonesian student, reported that when she first arrived in the United States, she thought little of her national identity (because this was a majority identity in *her* country). She told everyone she thought the United States was the greatest place and really tried hard to use American slang, dress American, and fit in. After several experiences with discrimination, she moved to a more separate stage where she only socialized with other Indonesian or other international students for a time. For writer Ruben Martinez (1998), a defining moment was when he was rather cruelly rejected by a white girl whom he had asked to dance at a high school prom:

I looked around me at the dance floor with new eyes: Mexicans danced with Mexicans, blacks with blacks, whites with whites. Who the hell did I think I was?

Still, it would take a while for the gringo-hater in me to bust out. It was only a matter of time before I turned away from my whiteness and became the ethnic rebel. It seemed like it happened overnight, but it was the result of years of pent-up rage in me. (p. 256)

Sometimes the move to this phase happens because individuals who have been denying their identity meet someone from that group who exhibits a strong identity. This encounter may result in a concern to clarify their own identity. So the young woman who was ashamed of being Jewish and tried hard to act "Christian" met a dynamic young man who was active in his synagogue and had a strong Jewish faith. Through their relationship she gained an appreciation of her own religious background, including the Jewish struggle for survival throughout the centuries. As often happens in this stage, she wholeheartedly endorsed the values and attitude attributed to the minority (Jewish) group and rejected the values and norms associated with the dominant group—she dropped most of her Christian friends and socialized primarily with her Jewish friends.

This stage may be characterized by a blanket endorsement of one's group and all the values and attitudes attributed to the group. At the same time, the person may reject the values and norms associated with the dominant group.

Stage 4: Integration According to this model, the ideal outcome of the identity development process is the final stage—an achieved identity. Individuals who have reached this stage have a strong sense of their own group identity (based on gender, race, ethnicity, sexual orientation, and so on) and an appreciation of other cultural groups. In this stage, they come to realize that racism and other forms of oppression occur, but they try to redirect any anger from the previous stage in more positive ways. The end result is individuals with a confident and secure identity characterized by a desire to eliminate all forms of injustice, and not merely oppression aimed at their own group.

Brenda: I had a hard time accepting my "old age identity." And for a while, I didn't even want to be around younger people. However, now I realize there will always be some discrimination against older women. We're really just invisible. I walk into a store and if there is anyone younger and more attractive, salespeople will often look right though me. However, I accept that this is the way our society is. And I can enjoy being around younger people now—I love their energy and their optimism. And I know that there are positive things about being older. Like, many things I just don't worry about anymore.

Ryan: Because my name is Irish, people generally assume I'm Catholic, but my family has always been Protestant. I knew from an early age that we were different from other Irish. I didn't really understand anything about the history of Ireland, and I always thought of myself as just an American. Now that I know more about this history and my family's history, I feel comfortable being a Protestant and Irish American. I'm happy to be both and different from other Irish Americans.

Sam(antha): I never liked to wear dresses and play with makeup. I knew I was different from a very young age, but I never understood what any of that meant. I used to deny who I was—loudly. Today, I still avoid wearing dresses, hose, heels, and makeup, but I no longer worry if people will think I'm a lesbian. I *am* a lesbian and I prefer that others know, so that men, in particular, don't approach me assuming that I might be interested.

Majority Identity Development

Rita Hardiman (1994, 2003), educator and pioneer in antiracism training, presents a model of **majority identity** development that has similarities to the model for minority group members. Although she intended the model to represent how white people develop a sense of healthy racial identity, it can also be helpful in describing how other majority identities develop—straight sexual orientation, Christian religious identity, male gender identity, middle-class identity, and so on. Again, remember that majority identity, like minority identity, develops through a complex process. And this model—unlike some other identity development models—is prescriptive. In other words, it outlines the way some scholars think a majority identity *should* develop, from accepting societal hierarchies that favor some identities and diminish others to resisting these inequities.

majority identity A sense of belonging to a dominant group.

Hardiman (1993, 2004) outlines five stages:

Stage 1: Unexamined Identity   This first stage is the same as for minority identities. In this case, individuals may be aware of some physical and cultural differences, but they do not fear the other or think much about their own identity. There is no understanding of the social meaning and value of gender, sexual orientation, religion, and so on. Although young boys may develop a sense of what it means to be a male by watching their fathers or other males, they are not aware of the social consequences of being born male over female. Those with majority identities, unlike those with minority identities, may stay in this stage for a long time.

Stage 2: Acceptance   The second stage represents the internalization, conscious or unconscious, of a racist (or otherwise biased) ideology. This may involve passive or active acceptance. The key point is that individuals are not aware that they have been programmed to accept this worldview.

In the passive acceptance stage, individuals have no conscious identification with being white, straight, male, etc. However, they may hold some assumptions based on an acceptance of inequities in the larger society. In general, the social hierarchy is experienced as "normal" for the dominant group, and they may view minority groups as being unduly sensitive and assume that if the minority members really wanted to change their lot in life they could. Here are some possible assumptions.

Being male in this stage may involve the following (sometime unconscious) assumptions:

- Men and women may be different, but they are basically equal. Kyle, a student, tells us, "I never heard so much whining from 'feminists' until

I came to college. Frankly, it is a little much. Although women may have faced barriers in the past, that's in the past. Women can pretty much do whatever they want in society today. If they want to be doctors, lawyers, police officers, firefighters, or anything else, they just need to set their minds to it and do it."

- If women really want to make it professionally, they can work as hard as men work and they will succeed.

Being straight may involve these assumptions:

- Gay people choose to be gay.
- Gay people whine a lot, unfairly, about discrimination. There is no recognition of the many privileges given to those who are straight.
- Gay people put their gayness in straight people's faces. At this stage there is no recognition of the vast societal emphasis on heterosexuality.

Being white may involve these assumptions:

- Minority groups are culturally deprived and need help to assimilate.
- Affirmative action is reverse discrimination because people of color are being given opportunities that whites don't have.
- White culture—music, art, and literature—is "classical"; works of art by people of color are folk art or "crafts."
- People of color are culturally different, whereas whites have no group identity or culture or shared experience of racial privilege.

Individuals in this stage usually take one of two positions with respect to interactions with minorities: (1) They avoid contact somewhat with minority group members, or (2) they adopt a patronizing stance toward them. Both positions are possible at the same time.

In contrast, those in the active acceptance stage are conscious of their privileged position and may express their feelings of superiority collectively (e.g., join male-only clubs). Some people never move beyond this phase—whether it is characterized by passive or active acceptance. And if they do, it is usually a result of a number of cumulative events. For example, Judith gradually came to realize that her two nieces, who are sisters—one of whom is African American and one of whom is white—had very different experiences growing up. Both girls lived in middle-class neighborhoods, both were honor students in high school, and both went to Ivy League colleges. However, they often had very different experiences. On more than one occasion, the African American girl was followed by security while shopping; she also was stopped several times by police while driving her mother's sports car. Her white sister never had these experiences. Eventually, awareness of this reality prodded Judith to the next stage. As was true with Judith, the move to the next stage often comes because of personal relationships.

I realized how difficult it is for gay people when I became good friends with a gay colleague. I had never realized how many cheap jokes about gays there are in movies, how many financial benefits I had because I was straight. Since I'm married, my spouse and I can have joint health benefits, death benefits, hospital visitation rights when my spouse is in ICU, to say nothing of the fact that I can always refer to my husband in any conversation without anyone lifting an eyebrow or looking at me weird.

This model recognizes that it is very difficult to escape the societal hierarchy that influences both minority and majority identity development because of its pervasive, systemic, and interlocking nature. The hierarch is a by-product of living within and being impacted by the institutional and cultural systems that surround us.

Stage 3: Resistance The next stage represents a major paradigm shift. It involves a move from blaming minority members for their condition to naming and blaming their own dominant group as a source of problems. This resistance may take the form of passive resistance, with little behavioral change, or active resistance—trying to reduce, eliminate, or challenge the institutional hierarchies that oppress. In reference to one's own identity, this stage is often characterized by embarrassment about one's own privileged position, guilt, shame, and a need to distance oneself from the dominant group.

> *Our student, Kayla, says: I was raised as a Christian, so I was never taught to question our beliefs. Since I've left home, I have met gay and lesbian students and I no longer understand why my church has such a problem with homosexuality. I get angry and sometimes I speak out when I'm at home and my parents get upset, but I don't want to stand around and let bigots take over my church. I have begun to question my Christian values, as I no longer know if they are compatible with my sense of right and wrong.*

Kevin says that:

> *For a while, I couldn't stand to be around white people, even though I'm white. After I learned more about how we tried to exterminate Indians, put Japanese Americans (but not German Americans) in internment camps during World War II and how many people of color are still subjected to incidents of racism and discrimination even today, I felt so awful and depressed. I started just hanging around with people who weren't white, listening to their music and going to their parties.*

Stage 4: Redefinition In the fourth stage, people begin to refocus or redirect their energy toward redefining their identity in a way that recognizes their privilege and works to eliminate oppression and inequities. They realize that they don't have to accept uncritically the definitions of being white, straight, male, Christian, U.S. American that society has instilled in them. For example, Nick tells us, "As a straight white guy, I often find myself in social situations in which people feel free to make offhand remarks or jokes that are somewhat racist, heterosexist, or sexist. They assume that I would agree with them, since I'm not a minority, gay, or a woman, but I don't. I am happy to be who I am, but this doesn't mean that being a straight white man means I need to be racist, sexist, or homophobic. I am proud to be who I am, but I don't think that means I have to put down others."

Stage 5: Integration As in the final stage of minority identity development, majority group individuals now are able to internalize their increased consciousness and integrate their majority identities into all other facets of their identity. They not only recognize their identity as white but also appreciate other groups. This integration affects other aspects of social and personal identity, including religion and gender.

Hardiman (2003) acknowledges that this model is rather simplistic in explaining the diverse experiences of people. It does not acknowledge the impact of diverse environments and socialization processes that influence how people experience their dominant identities or the realities of interlocking identities.

Systems of privilege are complicated; this is one reason why people can belong to a privileged category and not feel privileged. You may have several identities that are more privileged and several that are less privileged. So, for example, a middle-class white lesbian, benefiting from and yet unaware of the privileges of race or class, may think that her experience of sexual orientation and gender inequality enables her to understand what she needs to know about other forms of privilege and oppression. Or a straight working-class white man may be annoyed at the idea that his sexual orientation, whiteness, and maleness somehow gives him access to privilege. As a member of the working class, he may feel insecure in his job, afraid of being outsourced, downsized, and not at all privileged (Johnson, 2001).

To make it more complicated, our multiple identities exist all at once in relation to one another. People never see us solely in terms of race or gender or nationality—they see us as a complex of identities. So it makes no sense to talk about the experience of one identity—being white, for example—without looking at other identities. A dialectical perspective helps here in avoiding falling into the trap of thinking we are or are not privileged. Most of us are both.

SOCIAL AND CULTURAL IDENTITIES

People can identify with a multitude of groups. This section describes some of the major types of groups.

Gender Identity

gender identity The identification with the cultural notions of masculinity and femininity and what it means to be a man or a woman.

We often begin life with gender identities. When newborns arrive in our culture, they may be greeted with clothes and blankets in either blue for boys or pink for girls. To establish a **gender identity** for the newborn, visitors may ask if the baby is a boy or a girl. But gender is not the same as biological sex or sexual identity. This distinction is important in understanding how our views on biological sex influence gender identities.

What it means to be a man or a woman in our society is heavily influenced by cultural notions. For example, some activities are considered more masculine or more feminine. Thus, whether people hunt or sew or fight or read poetry can transform the ways that others view them. Similarly, the programs that people watch on television—soap operas, football games, and so on—affect how they socialize with others, contributing to gendered contexts.

As culture changes, so does the notion of what we idealize as masculine or feminine. Cultural historian Gail Bederman (1995) observes,

> *Even the popular imagery of a perfect male body changed. In the 1860s, the middle class had seen the ideal male body as lean and wiry. By the 1890s, however, an ideal male body required physical bulk and well-defined muscles. (p. 15)*

In this sense, the male body, as well as the female body, can be understood not in its "natural" state but in relation to idealized notions of masculinity and femininity. To know that this man or that woman is particularly good-looking requires an understanding of the gendered notions of attractiveness in a culture.

Our notions of masculinity and femininity change continually, driven by commercial interests and other cultural forces. For example, there is a major push now to market cosmetics to men. However, advertisers acknowledge that this requires sensitivity to men's ideas about makeup:

> *Unlike women, most men don't want to talk about makeup, don't want to go out in public to shop for makeup and don't know how to use makeup. The first barrier is getting men to department stores or specialty shops to buy products. (Yamanouchi, 2002, p. D1)*

Our expression of gender not only communicates who we think we are but also constructs a sense of who we want to be. Initially, we learn what masculinity and femininity mean in our culture. Communication scholar Julia T. Wood (2005) has identified feminine and masculine themes in U.S. society. These are the femininity themes: appearance still counts; be sensitive and caring; accept negative treatment by others; and be a superwoman. The masculinity themes are don't be female; be successful; be aggressive; be sexual; and be self-reliant. Masculinity themes are often the opposite of what it means to be a woman or a gay man. According to Wood, U.S. American men are socialized first and foremost that, being a man is about *not* being a woman. Then, through various media, we monitor how these notions shift and negotiate to communicate our gendered selves to others.

Consider, for example, the contemporary trend in the United States for women to have very full lips. If one's lips are not naturally full, there is always the option of getting collagen injections or having other body fat surgically inserted into the lips. In contrast, our Japanese students tell us that full lips are not considered at all attractive in Japan. The dynamic character of gender reflects its close connection to culture. Society has many images of masculinity and femininity; we do not all seek to look and act according to a single ideal.

At the same time, we *do* seek to communicate our gendered identities as part of who we are.

Gender identity is also demonstrated by communication style. For example, women's communication style is often described as supportive, egalitarian, personal, and disclosive, whereas men's is characterized as competitive and assertive (Wood, 2005). However, these differences may be more perception than fact. Results of recent research suggest that women's and men's communication styles are more similar than they are different (Canary & Hause, 1993; Pennebaker, Mehl, & Niederhoffer, 2003). And yet these stereotypes of gender differences persist, maybe partly because of the stereotypical depictions of men and women in magazines, on television, and in movies.

However, what it means to be feminine and masculine are not stable, clear-cut identity categories. Rather, these notions are created, reinforced, and reconstructed by society through communication and overlap with our other identities.

Sexual Identity

sexual identity One's identification with various categories of sexuality.

Sexual identity refers to one's identification with various categories of sexuality. You are probably most familiar with heterosexual, gay or lesbian, and perhaps bisexual categories; however, sexual identity categories vary from culture to culture and have been variously viewed throughout history (Foucault, 1988). These sexual identities are connected to notions of what was and was not permissible or desirable, e.g., Iranian President Mahmoud Ahmadinejad sparked controversy when he denied there were gay people in Iran when he said in a public speech at Columbia University, "In Iran, we don't have homosexuals, like in your country." (Ahmadinejad speaks, 2007). Also, views on sexual identities differ in various historical contexts. Same-sex activities were not always looked down upon, pedophilia was accepted in some eras and cultures, and on the occasions when children were born with both male and female sexual organs, they were not necessarily operated on or forced to be male or female (Foucault, 1988).

Our sexual identities influence our consumption, which television shows we watch, which magazines we read, which Internet sites we visit. Some assume a certain level of public knowledge about sexual identities or stereotypes; for example, *Queer Eye for the Straight Guy* and *Will & Grace* assumed viewers were familiar with stereotypes of gays. What are some cultural products that assume knowledge of heterosexual culture?

Age Identity

age identity The identification with the cultural conventions of how we should act, look, and behave according to our age.

As we age, we also play into cultural notions of how individuals our age should act, look, and behave; that is, we develop an **age identity.** As we grow older, we sometimes look at the clothes displayed in store windows or advertised in newspapers and magazines and feel that we are either too old or too young for that "look." These feelings stem from an understanding of what age means and how we identify with people that age.

I think that my being in college with kids just a little older than my son has helped me "learn the language" of the younger generation. So my college classmates have helped me acculturate into the younger generation at a more rapid speed than others my age. When I sit in class with these young people who have graduated from high school and are going to college, it is very easy to focus on these kids as being representative of the younger generation. Then there are the stereotypical "bad" teenagers—the gang members, the druggies, and so on. It isn't fair to generalize the younger generation with these stereotypes, either.

Are the cultural differences of our two age groups just as approachable as in any other intercultural exchange? I believe that they are. By using the skills that I am learning in bridging cultural differences, I am getting better at bridging the generation gap between "old mom" and "18-year-old teenager." Interpersonal skills, flexibility, motivation, attitudes, knowledge, skills, and love are all applicable when communicating interculturally with teenagers.

—Marcia

Some people feel old at 30; others feel young at 40 or 50. Nothing inherent in age tells us we are young or old. Rather, our notions of age and youth are all based on cultural conventions. The United States is an age-conscious society. One of the first things we teach children is to tell their age. And children will proudly tell their age, until about the mid 20s on, when people rarely mention their age. In contrast, people older than 70 often brag about their age. Certain ages have special significance in some cultures. Latino families sometimes celebrate a daughter's 15th birthday with a *quinceañera* party—marking the girl's entry into womanhood. Some Jewish families celebrate with a bat mitzvah ceremony for daughters and a bar mitzvah for sons on their 13th birthday (Allen, 2004). These same cultural conventions also suggest that it is inappropriate to engage in a romantic relationship with someone who is too old or too young.

Our notions of age often change as we grow older ourselves. When we are quite young, someone in college seems old; when we are in college, we do not feel so old. Yet the relative nature of age is only one part of the identity process. Social constructions of age also play a role. Different generations often have different philosophies, values, and ways of speaking. For example, recent data show that today's college freshmen are more liberal politically and more interested in volunteer work and civic responsibility than were Gen Xers. Scholars who view generations as "cultural groups" say that these characteristics make them similar to the World War I generation—politically curious and assertive and devoted to a sense of personal responsibility (Sax, Lindholm, Astin, Korn, & Mahoney, 2001).

Different generations often have different philosophies, values, and ways of speaking (Strauss & Howe, 1997). For example, recent data show that the millennium generation (or Gen Y, those born between 1982–2001) are more diverse and globally oriented and more knowledgeable about computers and technology than any preceding generation. They are also more optimistic, more committed to contributing to society and more interested in life balance between work and play than the previous, Gen X, group (those born between 1961–1981) (Strauss & Howe, 2006). This also is reflected in the way they learn and work (e.g., multitasking, use of multimedia, etc.).

Sometimes these generational differences can lead to conflict in the workplace. For example, young people who entered the job market during the "dot .com" years have little corporate loyalty and think nothing of changing jobs when a better opportunity comes along. This can irritate baby boomer workers, who emphasize the importance of demonstrating corporate loyalty, of "paying one's dues" to the establishment while gradually working one's way "up the corporate ladder" (Howe & Strauss, 2007). Although not all people in any generation are alike, the attempt to find trends across generations reflects our interest in understanding age identity.

Racial and Ethnic Identities

racial identity Identifying with a particular racial group. Although in the past racial groups were classified on the basis of biological characteristics, most scientists now recognize that race is constructed in fluid social and historical contexts.

Racial Identity   Race consciousness, or **racial identity,** is largely a modern phenomenon. In the United States today, the issue of race is both controversial and pervasive. It is the topic of many public discussions, from television talk shows to talk radio. Yet many people feel uncomfortable talking about it or think it should not be an issue in daily life. Perhaps we can better understand the contemporary issues if we look at how the notion of race developed historically in the United States.

Current debates about race have their roots in the 15th and 16th centuries, when European explorers encountered people who looked different from themselves. The debates centered on religious questions of whether there was "one family of man." If so, what rights were to be accorded to those who were different? Debates about which groups were "human" and which were "animal" pervaded popular and legal discourse and provided a rationale for slavery. Later, in the 18th and 19th centuries, the scientific community tried to establish a classification system of race, based on genetics and cranial capacity. However, these efforts were largely unsuccessful.

Most scientists have abandoned a strict biological basis for classifying racial groups, especially in light of the recent genetic research. To date, researchers have found only 55 genes out of almost 3 million that differentiate various groups. Their conclusions about the implications of their research: "All in all, the school of thought which holds that humans, for all their outward variety, are a pretty homogenous species received a boost" ("Human races or human race," 2008, p. 86). Rather than adhere to the rather outdated notion of a biological basis for racial categorization, most scholars hold a social science viewpoint—agreeing that racial categories like white and black are constructed in social and historical contexts.

Several arguments refute the physiological basis for race. First, racial categories vary widely throughout the world. In general, distinctions between white and black are fairly rigid in the United States, and many people become uneasy when they are unable to categorize individuals. In contrast, Brazil recognizes a wide variety of intermediate racial categories in addition to white and black. These variations indicate a cultural, rather than a biological, basis for racial classification (Omi & Winant, 2001). Terms like *mulatto* and *Black Irish* demonstrate cultural classifications; terms like *Caucasoid* and *Australoid* are examples of biological classification.

Second, U.S. law uses a variety of definitions to determine racial categories. A 1982 case in Louisiana reopened debates about race as socially created rather than biologically determined. Susie Phipps applied for a passport and discovered that under Louisiana law she was black because she was $^1/_{32}$ African (her great-grandmother had been a slave). She then sued to be reclassified as white. Not only did she consider herself white, inasmuch as she grew up among whites, but she also was married to a white man. And because her children were only $^1/_{64}$ African, they were legally white. Although she lost her lawsuit, the ensuing political and popular discussions persuaded Louisiana lawmakers to change the way the state classified people racially. It is important that the law was changed, but this legal situation does not obscure the fact that social definitions of race continue to exist (Hasian & Nakayama, 1999).

A third example of how racial categories are socially constructed is illustrated by their fluid nature. As more and more southern Europeans immigrated to the United States in the 19th century, the established Anglo and German society tried to classify these newcomers (Irish and Jewish, as well as southern European) as nonwhite. However, this attempt was not successful because, based on the narrower definition, whites might have become demographically disempowered. Instead, the racial line was drawn to include all Europeans, and people from outside of Europe (e.g., immigrants from China) were designated as nonwhite (Roediger, 2005). We intentionally use the term *nonwhite* here to highlight the central role of *whiteness* in defining racial identity in the United States.

Racial categories, then, are based to some extent on physical characteristics, but they are also constructed in fluid social contexts. It probably makes more sense to talk about racial *formation* than racial *categories*, thereby casting race as a complex of social meanings rather than as a fixed and objective concept. How people construct these meanings and think about race influences the ways in which they communicate.

Ethnic Identity   In contrast to racial identity, **ethnic identity** may be seen as a set of ideas about one's own ethnic group membership. It typically includes several dimensions: (1) self-identification, (2) knowledge about the ethnic culture (traditions, customs, values, and behaviors), and (3) feelings about belonging to a particular ethnic group. Ethnic identity often involves a shared sense of origin and history, which may link ethnic groups to distant cultures in Asia, Europe, Latin America, or other locations.

Having an ethnic identity means experiencing a sense of belonging to a particular group and knowing something about the shared experience of group members. For instance, Judith grew up in an ethnic community. She heard her

ethnic identity (1) A set of ideas about one's own ethnic group membership; (2) a sense of belonging to a particular group and knowing something about the shared experience of the group.

parents and relatives speak German, and her grandparents made several trips back to Germany and talked about their German roots. This experience contributed to her ethnic identity.

For some U.S. residents, ethnicity is a specific and relevant concept. They see themselves as connected to an origin outside the United States—as Mexican American, Japanese American, Welsh American, and so on—or to some region prior to its being absorbed into the United States—Navajo, Hopi, and so on. As one African American student told us, "I have always known my history and the history of my people in this country. I will always be first African American and then American. Who I am is based on my heritage." For others, ethnicity is a vague concept. They see themselves as "American" and reject the notion of **hyphenated Americans.** One of our students explains:

> *I am American. I am not German American or Irish American or Native American. I have never set foot on German or Irish land. I went to Scotland a couple years ago and found a Scottish plaid that was my family crest. I still didn't even feel a real connection to it and bought it as more of a joke, to say, "Look! I'm Scottish!" even though in my heart I know I'm not.*

We discuss the issues of ethnicity for white people later.

What, then, does *American* mean? Who defines it? Is there only one meaning, or are there many different meanings? It is important to determine what definition is being used by those who insist that we should all simply be "Americans." If one's identity is "just American," how is this identity formed, and how does it influence communication with others who see themselves as hyphenated Americans (Alba, 1985, 1990; Carbaugh, 1989)?

Racial Versus Ethnic Identity Scholars dispute whether racial and ethnic identity are similar or different. Some suggest that ethnic identity is constructed by both selves and others but that racial identity is constructed solely by others. They stress as well that race overrides ethnicity in the way people classify others (Cornell & Hartmann, 1998). The American Anthropological Association has suggested that the U.S. government phase out use of the term *race* in the collection of federal data because the concept has no scientific validity or utility.

On the one hand, discussions about ethnicity tend to assume a "melting pot" perspective on U.S. society. On the other hand, discussions about race as shaped by U.S. history allow us to talk about racism. If we never talk about race, but only about ethnicity, can we consider the effects and influences of racism?

Bounded Versus Dominant Identities One way to sort out the relationship between ethnicity and race is to differentiate between bounded and dominant (or normative) identities (Frankenburg, 1993; Trinh, 1986/1987). Bounded cultures are characterized by groups that are specific but not dominant. For most white people, it is easy to comprehend the sense of belonging in a bounded group (e.g., an ethnic group). Clearly, for example, being Amish means following the *ordnung* (community rules). Growing up in a German American home, Judith's identity included a clear emphasis on seriousness and very little on

hyphenated Americans U.S. Americans who identify not only with being U.S. citizens but also as being members of ethnic groups.

communicative expressiveness. This identity differed from that of her Italian American friends at college, who seemed much more expressive.

However, what it means to belong to the dominant, or normative, culture is more elusive. *Normative* means "setting the norm for a society." In the United States, whites clearly are the normative group in that they set the standards for appropriate and effective behavior. Although it can be difficult for white people to define what a normative white identity is, this does not deny its existence or importance. It is often not easy to see what the cultural practices are that link white people together. For example, we seldom think of Thanksgiving or Valentine's Day as white holidays.

Our sense of racial or ethnic identity develops over time, in stages, and through communication with others. These stages seem to reflect our growing understanding of who we are and depend to some extent on the groups we belong to. Many ethnic or racial groups share the experience of oppression. In response, they may generate attitudes and behaviors consistent with a natural internal struggle to develop a strong sense of group identity and self-identity. For many cultural groups, these strong identities ensure their survival.

Characteristics of Whiteness

What does it mean to be white in the United States? What are the characteristics of a white identity? Is there a unique set of characteristics that define whiteness, just as other racial identities have been described?

A scene from the 2006 film *Something New* illustrates the lack of awareness of racial identity of many white people. Kenya, a high-profile financial broker is dating Brian, a white landscape designer. One evening while shopping for groceries together, Kenya tells Brian about yet another experience of racial prejudice in the all-white firm where she works. Brian asks her to "put the white boys on hold for a while"—saying that he had a rough day and wants to relax and not talk about race, that it makes him feel uncomfortable. Kenya reminds him,

> *you don't have to talk about being white because no one reminds you everyday that you're white. The only time you guys know you're white is when you're in a room full of black people. I'm in a world full of white people, and every day they remind me that I'm black. . . . When I show up at an account meeting they always have to regroup when they find out I'm the one who's responsible for their multimillion dollar acquisition. They'd rather trust it to a file clerk. The guy who gets me my goddamn coffee, because he's white . . . . Do you know how insulting that is?*

It may be difficult for most white people to describe exactly what cultural patterns are uniquely white, but scholars have tried to do so. For example, scholar Ruth Frankenburg (1993) says that whiteness may be defined not only in terms of race or ethnicity but also as a set of linked dimensions. These dimensions include (1) normative race privilege; (2) a standpoint from which white people look at themselves, others, and society; and (3) a set of cultural practices (often unnoticed and unnamed).

THE INVISIBLE KNAPSACK

Scholar Peggy McIntosh compares the everyday privileges of being white in the United States to an invisible, weightless "knapsack" she carries, full of unearned assets, like road maps, codes, and blank checks that she is not supposed to notice, but that she can count on every day nevertheless. She compiled a list of these privilege that "as far as I can tell, my African American coworkers, friends, and acquaintances with whom I come into daily or frequent contact in this particular time, place and time of work cannot count on most of the [time]." Although she initially compiled this list about 20 years ago, which do you think are still applicable today?

As a White person

- *I can if I wish arrange to be in the company of people of my race most of the time.*
- *When I am told about our national heritage or about "civilization," I am shown that people of my color made it what it is.*
- *Whether I use checks, credit cards or cash, I can count on my skin color not to work against the appearance of financial reliability.*
- *I can swear, or dress in second hand clothes, or not answer letters, without having people attribute these choices to the bad morals, the poverty or the illiteracy of my race.*
- *I can do well in a challenging situation without being called a credit to my race.*
- *I am never asked to speak for all the people of my racial group.*
- *I can be pretty sure that if I ask to talk to the "person in charge," I will be facing a person of my race.*
- *I can go home from most meetings of organizations I belong to feeling somewhat tied in, rather than isolated, out-of-place, outnumbered, unheard, held at a distance or feared.*
- *I can be late to a meeting without having the lateness reflect on my race.*
- *I can easily find academic courses and institutions which give attention only to people of my race.*
- *I will feel welcomed and "normal" in the usual walks of public life, institutional and social.*

Source: Adapted from Working Paper 189, "White Privilege and Male Privilege: A Personal Account of Coming To See Correspondences through Work in Women's Studies" (1988), The Wellesley College Center for Research on Women, Wellesley, MA 02181.

Normative Race Privilege Historically, whites have been the normative (dominant) group in the United States and, as such, have benefited from privileges that go along with belonging to the dominant group (see "Point of View" with list of "white" privileges). However, not all whites have power, and not all have equal access to power. In fact, at times during U.S. history, some white communities were not privileged and were viewed as separate, or different, if not inferior. Examples include the Irish and Italians in the early 20th century and German Americans during World War II. And as scholars point out, the memory of marginality outlasts the marginality. For example, memories of discrimination may persist in the minds of some Italian Americans although little discrimination exists today. There also are many white people in the United States who are poor and so lack economic power.

There is an emerging perception that being white no longer means automatic privilege, particularly as demographics change in the United States and as some whites perceive themselves to be in the minority. This has led some whites to feel threatened and "out of place." A Chicago college professor tells the story of how her white students thought that 65% of the population near their university was African American; they perceived themselves to be in the minority and based their estimate on their observations and anecdotes. When she corrected them, they were stunned. In fact, according to the 2000 U.S. Census, the percentage of blacks in Chicago is only 37% (Myers, 2003, p. 130). Students' perceptions affected their sense of identity, which, in turn, can affect intercultural communication.

Some white young people today are very aware of their whiteness (Frankenburg, 2001). Further, they believe that being white is a liability, that they are sometimes prejudged as racist and blamed for social conditions they personally did not cause, and that they are denied opportunities that are unfairly given to minority students. One of our white students describes this feeling:

> *When I was trying to get into college I had to fight for every inch. I didn't have a lot of money to go to school with, so to get a scholarship was of great importance to me. So I went out and bought a book titled* The Big Book of Scholarships. *Ninety percent of the scholarships that this book contained didn't apply to me. They applied to the so-called minorities. . . . I think this country has gone on so long with the notion that white equals wealth or with things like affirmative action, that it has lost sight of the fact that this country is not that way any longer.*

In addition, because of corporate downsizing and the movement of jobs overseas in recent decades, increasing numbers of middle-aged white men have not achieved the degree of economic or professional success they had anticipated. They sometimes blame their lack of success on immigrants who will work for less or on the increasing numbers of women and minorities in the workplace. In these cases, whiteness is not invisible; it is a salient feature of the white individuals' identities. A study by communication scholars Bahk and Jandt (2004) revealed significant differences in perceptions of white privilege by whites and nonwhites. They surveyed 700 students, asking them to indicate how strongly they agreed or disagreed with various statements regarding the meaning of whiteness. Nonwhites indicated high agreement with the following statements, whereas whites agreed significantly less:

- "White people have privilege in the United States."
- "When people refer to 'Americans,' it is usually whites they have in mind."
- "White people are regarded as superior to people of other racial groups."

The study shows that although whites may not perceive their racial privilege, it is quite clearly seen by those who are not white.

There were also interesting differences in perceptions regarding whites' communication behavior. This same study revealed that nonwhites perceive that whites tend to distance themselves from other racial groups, that they choose to interact with other whites rather than nonwhites in social situations, and that they tend to mingle much better with whites than other groups (Bahk & Jandt, 2004).

The point is not whether these perceptions are accurate. Rather, the point is that identities are negotiated and challenged through communication. People act on their perceptions, not on some external reality. As the nation becomes increasingly diverse and whites no longer form a majority in some regions, there will be increasing challenges for all of us as we negotiate our cultural identities.

How can whites in the United States incorporate the reality of not belonging to a majority group? Will whites find inclusive and productive ways to manage this identity change? Or will they react in defensive and exclusionary ways?

One reaction to feeling outnumbered and being a "new member" of an ethnic minority group is to strengthen one's own ethnic identity. For example, white people may tend to have stronger white identities in those U.S. states that have a higher percentage of nonwhites (e.g., Mississippi, South Carolina, Alabama). In these states, the white population traditionally has struggled to protect its racial privilege in various ways. As other states become increasingly less white, we are beginning to see various moves to protect whiteness, as in California with a series of propositions (187, prohibiting undocumented workers from receiving public services; 209, making affirmative action programs illegal in public universities; and 227, banning bilingual education in public schools) and increasing concerns about immigration. Historically, California has enacted measures to ensure that whites retained dominance in population, as well as in politics, economics, and so on. It is unclear what will happen in California and other states if, as predicted, whites become a demographic minority group. How do you think that whites will respond?

A Standpoint from Which to View Society   Opinion polls reveal significant differences in how whites and blacks view many issues. For example, according to a survey conducted by the Pew Research Center (2005), the aftermath of Hurricane Katrina in the fall of 2005 revealed continuing significant differences in black and white perception. In this Pew Research survey, blacks and whites drew very different lessons from the Katrina tragedy. Seven in ten blacks (71%) said the disaster showed that racial inequality remains a major problem in the country, compared to only 32% of whites. More striking was the disagreement over whether the government's response to the crisis would have been faster if most of the storm's victims had been white; 66% of African Americans expressed that view, compared to 17% of whites (http://people-press .org/reports/pdf/255.pdf).

A 2007 survey showed large gaps in perception between blacks and whites on other topics. For example, blacks believe that antiblack discrimination is still

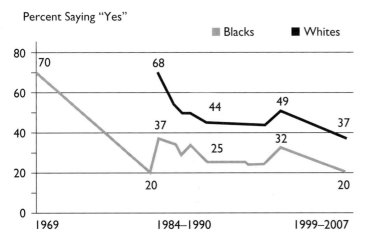

Are Blacks Better Off Now Than Five Years Ago?
(Source: From Pew Research Center, http://pewsocialtrends.org/assets/pdf/
Race.pdf).

pervasive in everyday life; whites disagree. Only one in five blacks say things are better for blacks now than they were five years ago (Figure 5-2). Whites have a different perspective; they are nearly twice as likely as blacks to see black gains in the past five years. Looking ahead, fewer than half of all blacks (44%) say they think life for blacks will get better in the future, down from the 57% who said so in a 1986 survey ("Optimism about Black Progress Declines," 2007).

A Set of Cultural Practices   Is there a specific, unique "white" way of viewing the world? As noted previously, some views held consistently by whites are not necessarily shared by other groups. And some cultural practices and core symbols (e.g., individualism) are expressed primarily by whites and significantly less by members of minority groups. We need to note here that not everyone who is white shares all cultural practices. (See Figure 5-3.) For example, recent immigrants who are white, but not born in the United States, may share in the privilege accorded all white people in the United States; however, they might not necessarily share in the viewpoints or the set of cultural practices of whites whose families have been in the United States for many generations. It is important to remember that some whites may identify fairly strongly with their European roots, especially if their families are more recent immigrants and they still have family members in Europe; other whites may not feel any connection to Europe and feel completely "American." These cultural practices are most clearly visible to those who are not white, to those groups who are excluded (Bahk & Jandt, 2004). For example, in the fairy tale of Snow White, the celebration of her beauty—emphasizing her beautiful, pure white skin—is often seen as problematic by people who are not white.

FIGURE 5-3   White culture is difficult to define. White people do not often
think of some of their activities as white cultural practices, such as sunbathing, a
common leisure activity among many white people. Not all cultural groups place a high
value on suntans. In this photo, a Chinese man holds an umbrella to shield his wife
from the sun as she takes a photo of her parents at Tiananmen Square. In this culture,
darker skin, particularly on a woman, is seen as more negative than light skin. Gender
and racial identities function together to place a low cultural value on suntanning.
(© Andrew Wong/Reuters/Corbis)

Religious Identity

religious identity A
sense of belonging to a
religious group.

Religious identity can be an important dimension of many people's identities,
as well as an important site of intercultural conflict. Religious identity often is
conflated with racial or ethnic identity, which makes it difficult to view religious
identity simply in terms of belonging to a particular religion. For example, when
someone says, "I am Jewish," does it mean that he practices Judaism? That he views
Jewish identity as an ethnic identity? Or when someone says, "She has a Jewish last
name," is it a statement that recognizes religious identity? With a historical view,
we can see Jews as a racial group, an ethnic group, and a religious group.

Drawing distinctions among various identities—racial, ethnic, class, national,
and regional—can be problematic. For example, Italians and Irish are often viewed
as Catholics, and Episcopalians are frequently seen as belonging to the upper
classes. Issues of religion and ethnicity have come to the forefront in the war
against Al-Qaeda and other militant groups. Although those who carried out the
attacks against the Pentagon and the World Trade Center were Muslims and
Arabs, it is hardly true that all Muslims are Arabs or that all Arabs are Muslims
(Feghali, 1997).

FIGURE 5-4   You might not know someone's religious identity, except for certain religious observances, like Ash Wednesday for some Christians. (© *Sean Gardner/Getty Images*)

Religious differences have been at the root of contemporary conflicts from the Middle East to Northern Ireland, and from India and Pakistan to Bosnia-Herzegovina. In the United States, religious conflicts caused the Mormons to flee the Midwest for Utah in the mid-19th century. More recently, religious conflicts have become very real for some Arab Americans as the U.S. government presses the war against terrorism, with many of those people subject to suspicion if not persecution. And militant Muslims in the Middle East and elsewhere see their struggle against the United States as a very serious endeavor and are willing to die for their religious beliefs.

In the United States, we often believe that people should be free to practice whatever religion they wish. Conflicts arise, however, when the religious beliefs of some individuals are imposed on others who may not share those beliefs. For example, some Jews see the predominance of Christmas trees and Christian crosses as an affront to their religious beliefs. The influence of religious identities on Americans' attitudes was evidenced in 2007 during Mitt Romney's (a Mormon politician) presidential campaign. A research study found that bias against Mormons was significantly more intense than bias against either African Americans or women and that bias against Mormons was even more pronounced among conservative Evangelicals (Luo, 2007; "New Vanderbuilt . . .," 2007).

People in some religions communicate and mark their religious differences by their clothing. For example, Hassidic Jews wear traditional, somber clothing, and Muslim women are often veiled according to the Muslim guideline of female modesty. Of course, most religions are not identified by clothing. For example, you may not know if someone is Buddhist, Catholic, Lutheran, or atheist based upon the way he or she dresses. (See Figure 5-4.) Because religious identities are less salient, everyday interactions may not invoke religious identity.

Class Identity

We don't often think about socioeconomic class as an important part of our identity. Yet scholars have shown that class often plays an important role in shaping our reactions to and interpretations of culture. For example, French sociologist Pierre Bourdieu (1987) studied the various responses to art, sports, and other cultural activities of people in different French social classes. According to Bourdieu, working-class people prefer to watch soccer, whereas upper-class individuals like tennis, and middle-class people prefer photographic art, whereas upper-class individuals favor less representational art. As these findings reveal, class distinctions are real and can be linked to actual behavioral practices and preferences.

class identity A sense of belonging to a group that shares similar economic, occupational, or social status.

English professor Paul Fussell (1992) shows how similar signs of **class identity** operate in U.S. society. According to Fussell, the magazines we read, the foods we eat, and the words we use often reflect our social class position. At some level, we recognize these class distinctions, but we consider it impolite to ask directly about a person's class background. Therefore, we may use communication strategies to place others in a class hierarchy. Unfortunately, these strategies don't always yield accurate information. For example, people may try to guess your class background by the foods you eat. Some foods are seen as "rich folk's food"—for instance, lamb, white asparagus, brie, artichokes, goose, and caviar. Do you feel as if you are revealing your class background if you admit that these foods are unfamiliar to you? Perhaps not admitting your unfamiliarity is a form of "passing," of representing yourself as belonging to a group you really don't belong to. Another strategy that people may use to guess a person's class background is to ask where that person did her or his undergraduate work.

It may be that class identity can even be seen in the particular social network sites young people join (Hargittai, 2007). For example, some scholars find that Facebook tends to be accessed by youth from more educated, affluent families while MySpace is used by "kids whose parents didn't go to college, who are expected to get a job when they finish high school. These are the teens who plan to go into the military immediately after school" (Boyd, 2007). The military sparked a controversy in Spring 2007 when it banned MySpace but not Facebook; officers, more likely to be on Facebook, could continue accessing their social network site while many soldiers, on MySpace, were prohibited (DeRusha, 2007).

Most people in the United States recognize class associations even as they may deny that such class divisions exist. What does this apparent contradiction indicate? Most importantly, it reveals the complexities of class issues, particularly in the United States. We often don't really know the criteria for inclusion in a given social class. Is membership determined by financial assets? By educational level? By profession? By family background? These factors may or may not be indicators of class.

Another reason for this apparent contradiction is that people in the majority or normative class (the middle class) tend not to think about class, whereas those in the working class are often reminded that their communication styles and lifestyle choices are not the norm. David Engen (2004), a communication scholar, describes his own experience of entering college from a working-class background and feeling like he had entered a new culture. For one thing, the working-class communication style he was accustomed to was very different from the proper English required in his classes. "I vividly recall coming to college saying things such as 'I seen that,' 'I ain't worried about that' and 'that don't mean nothing to me.' I am glad my professors and friends helped me acquire a language that allowed me to succeed in mainstream American society" (p. 253). And the philosophical conversations expected in class were a challenge. As he describes it, working-class communication is about getting things done, very different from the abstract conversations he was expected to participate in—designed to broaden perspective rather than to accomplish any particular task. In this respect, class is like race. For example, terms like *trailer trash* and *white trash* show the negative connotations associated with people who are not middle class (Moon & Rolison, 1998).

A central assumption of the American dream is that, with hard work and persistence, individuals can improve their class standing, even in the face of overwhelming evidence to the contrary. And the American dream seems alive and well. An estimated 94% of Americans still think that "people who work full time should be able to earn enough to keep their families out of poverty" (Allen, 2004, p. 105). Yet the reality is shown dramatically by Barbara Ehrenreich's (2001) study. Ehrenreich, a journalist, wanted to see how people can survive on minimum wage. She left her home, accepted whatever jobs she could get, staying in the cheapest lodging and working around the country as a waitress, hotel maid, cleaning woman, and nursing home aide. In her book, she describes how much of the "unskilled" work was mentally and physically exhausting, and concludes that one minimum-wage job is not enough; you need two if you want a roof over your head. In a more recent book, Ehrenreich (2007) shows how even middle-class people have little job security and have trouble achieving the American dream. She poses as a professional "in transition" applying for relevant jobs and is rejected again and again, concluding that her (and many others') problems are not simply due to the vagaries of the business cycle but the results of today's ultra-lean corporations, who shed their "surplus" employees—causing them to spend months or even years in the twilight zone of white-collar unemployment—with few social or financial "safety nets."

The mobility myth, like the American dream, is just that, a myth. The United States has the most unequally distributed wealth and income in the world. A recent report by the Economic Policy Institute concludes that there remains a highly unequal distribution of wealth by class, and no reason to believe these wealth disparities will lessen anytime soon. A significant share of

Communication scholar Kathleen Wong (Lau) describes how she gradually became aware of the intersections of race, class, and ethnicity through her own life experiences. Her parents were Chinese immigrant factory workers. She entered an elite college where the students were mostly white and children of teachers, attorneys, doctors, and other professionals.

> *It took me many years to understand the many dimensions of alienation I felt as a young Asian American woman coming of age. I didn't understand the complexity and muddiness of my own internalized oppression that had rendered me silent about my Chinese American parents, their occupations and about my working-class neighborhood. . . . didn't understand how the dimensions of one's marginalized identities are interwoven so tightly that at times, one doesn't recognize the different threads.*
>
> *I spent most of my undergraduate career in total culture shock entering an institution and community that was considerably whiter than the one in which I had grown up. . . . I remember the familiar awkwardness of silence when asked about my parents' occupations . . . I found I had little in common with my Chinese American friends in terms of ethnic culture. Some of the distinctly Chinese practices in which my family engaged were seen by their parents as very "village," quaint and cute. Somehow I had grown up thinking our practices were universally Chinese immigrant. I had grown up paradoxically aware of class and at the same time totally unaware of how my own ethnic culture was shaped by class. . . . In trying to erase class, I was erasing my own ethnic and racial identity . . . with each new [experience] I understand [more about] the connectedness of the many parts of my identities and how these parts cannot be separate from one another.*

Source: From K. Wong (Lau), "Working Through Identity: Understanding Class in the Context of Race, Ethnicity and Gender." In A. Gonzalez et al. (Eds.), *Our voices: Essays in culture, ethnicity and communication* (Los Angeles: Roxbury, 2004), pp. 256–263.

the population has little or no net worth, while, over the last 40 years at least, the wealthiest 20% has consistently held over 80% of all wealth and the top 1% has controlled at least a third. More specifically, the incomes of the poorest (bottom fifth) of U.S. families grew by an average of 19% ($2,660) over the past 20 years. Meanwhile, the incomes of the richest fifth of families grew by almost 60% ($45,100) (Mishel, Bernstein, & Allegretto, 2006). An even more recent report shows that most workers have not benefited from the economic good times. The real wage of the typical male worker, for example, is up only 1% since 2000 and not at all since 2003. As of 2006, the median income of working-age families was actually down −4.2% in real terms, a loss of −$2,375 (2006 dollars). Poverty, at 12.3%, remains 1.0 percentage point above its 2000 trough (Bernstein & Mishel 2007).

However, holding on to the mobility myth has consequences. According to Allen (2004), the ideology underlying the myth persuades us that poor people are the ones to blame for being poor, that "poor people collectively exhibit traits that keep them down. . . . [It] blames the poor for their plight and ignores the fact that many wealthy people have inherited their wealth and resources or that they were better positioned to attain the American dream. This does not acknowledge that economic, cultural and social capital can tilt the playing field in favor of those who have accumulated wealth, knowledge, and/or connections" (p. 105). And the media often reinforce these notions. As Leonardo DiCaprio's character in the movie *Titanic* shows us, upward mobility is easy enough—merely a matter of being opportunistic, charming, and a little bit lucky.

Working-class individuals who aren't upwardly mobile are often portrayed in TV sitcoms and movies as unintelligent, criminal, or unwilling to do what they have to do to better their lot in life. (Consider, for example, the TV show *Married With Children*.) Members of the real working class, as frequent guests on television talk shows like *Rikki Lake* and *Jerry Springer* and on court shows like *Judge Judy* and *Judge Joe Brown*, are urged to be verbally contentious and even physically aggressive with each other.

The point is that although class identity is not as readily apparent as, say, gender identity, it still influences our perceptions of and communication with others. Race, class, and sometimes gender identity are interrelated. For example, statistically speaking, being born African American, poor, and female increases one's chances of remaining in poverty (Mishel, Bernstein, & Allegretto, 2006). But, of course, race and class are not synonymous. There are many poor whites, and there are increasing numbers of wealthy African Americans. In this sense, these multiple identities are interrelated but not identical.

National Identity

Among many identities, we also have a **national identity,** which should not be confused with racial or ethnic identity. Nationality, unlike racial or ethnic identity, refers to one's legal status in relation to a nation. Many U.S. citizens can trace their ethnicity to Latin America, Asia, Europe, or Africa, but their nationality, or citizenship, is with the United States.

national identity
National citizenship.

Although national identity may seem to be a clear-cut issue, this is not the case when the nation's status is unclear. For example, bloody conflicts erupted over the attempted secession in the mid-1800s of the Confederate States of America from the United States. Similar conflicts erupted in more recent times when Eritrea tried to separate from Ethiopia, and Chechnya from Russia. Less bloody conflicts that involved nationhood led, in the former Czechoslovakia, to the separation of Slovakia and the Czech Republic.

Contemporary nationhood struggles are being played out as Quebec attempts to separate from Canada and as Corsica and Tahiti attempt to separate from France. Sometimes nations disappear from the political map but persist in the social imagination and eventually reemerge, such as Poland, Ukraine,

What is Japanese national identity? I have to say that many things are in the very psyche, the Japanese psyche. They are more than feelings—the way you feel when the spring is around and see cherry blossoms everywhere. You become grateful to the cycle of nature and the promise that spring always comes. Such a feeling that you believe that you share with others, as people talk about it, is a big part of national identity, I think. It is also in big sport events, where you can feel one with others by sharing emotions. It is in the fixation to the food, the meticulous attention and kodawari *(fixation) about food. And it is felt in many folk songs* (douyou), *which sing a lot about nature, living creatures, etc. In sum, there are so many things about Japanese national identity. But, to me, they are never about the national flag or pledging allegiance to your country.*
    —Tamie

Latvia, Lithuania, and Estonia. Other times, national identity may shift in significant ways, as in the United States after the attacks of September 11, 2001, when ideas about national identity seemed to incorporate increased expressions of patriotism. One of our Japanese graduate students explains how her feeling of national identity is much different from what she sees in the United States:

> *I have seen so many "God bless America," "Proud to be American" messages EVERYWHERE as I have lived here as a Japanese sojourner. . . . Coming from Japan, I don't think I have the same notion of "I am proud about my country." I love my culture, the beauty, the meanings, the spirituality that surround it. But I feel that I have been consciously or subconsciously taught that being proud of your country can be* dangerous, misleading, blinding. *Look at what happened before 1945—how many people in my country thought about their country and framed the "cause" which led to a disaster (WW II). In fact, I have talked to my Japanese friends about this sentiment and mixed emotion I feel about the concept of "patriotism," and almost all of them agreed with me—we were not taught to be proud of our country in the post–WW II era. Of course, each country has a different history, political situation, so what I am saying here doesn't necessarily translate to other people in other cultures.*
>
> *It may sound funny, but one thing I would say I am proud of about my country is that I don't have to say I am proud of my country. I am proud that I can see both beautiful and ugly sides of my country's history. I feel free there, for not being pressured by anyone to say that I am proud of my country.*

In sum, people have various ways of thinking about nationality, and they sometimes confuse nationality and ethnicity. Thus, we have overheard students asking minority students, "What is your nationality?" when they actually meant, "What is your ethnicity?" This confusion can lead to—and perhaps reflects—a lack of understanding about differences between, say, Asian Americans (ethnic group) and Asians (nationality groups). It can also tend to alienate Asian Americans and others who have been in the United States for several generations but are still perceived as foreigners.

Regional Identity

Closely related to nationality is the notion of **regional identity.** Many regions of the world have separate, but vital and important, cultural identities. The Scottish Highlands is a region of northern Scotland that is distinctly different from the Lowlands, and regional identity remains strong in the Highlands.

Here in the United States, regional identities remain important, but perhaps less so as the nation moves toward homogeneity. Southerners, for example, often view themselves, and are viewed by others, as a distinct cultural group. Similarly, Texas advertises itself as "A Whole Other Country," promoting its regional identity. Although some regional identities can fuel national independence movements, they more often reflect cultural identities that affirm distinctive cuisines, dress, manners, and language. These identities may become important in intercultural communication situations. For example, suppose you meet someone who is Chinese. Whether the person is from Beijing, Hong Kong, or elsewhere in China may raise important communication issues. After all, Mandarin is not understood by Cantonese speakers, although both are dialects of the Chinese language. Indeed, there are many dialects in China, and they certainly are not understood by all other Chinese speakers.

One fairly recent variation in regional identities has to do with the degree of diversity within certain parts of the United States. Data from the 2000 census reveal that the South and the West are the most diverse, along with the coastal Northeast. The Midwest, in contrast, with a few exceptions, remains relatively homogenous (Brewer & Suchan, 2001, pp. 22–23). In addition, the overwhelming majority of multiracial individuals (67%) live in the South and the West (pp. 87–89). What are the implications for identity and intercultural communication? It could mean that people in these areas have more opportunities for understanding and practicing intercultural communication and so benefit from the diversity. Or they may withdraw into their own groups and protect their racial and ethnic "borders."

regional identity Identification with a specific geographic region of a nation.

PERSONAL IDENTITY

Many issues of identity are closely tied to our notions of self. Each of us has a **personal identity,** which is the sum of all our identities, but it may not be unified or coherent. A dialectical perspective allow us to see identity in a more complex way. We are who we think we are; at the same time, however, contextual and external forces constrain and influence our self-perceptions. We have many identities, and these can conflict. For example, according to communication scholar Victoria Chen (1992), some Chinese American women feel caught between the traditional values of their parents' culture and their own desire to be Americanized. From the parents' point of view, the daughters are never Chinese enough. From the perspective of many people within the dominant culture, though, it is difficult to relate to these Chinese American women simply as "American women, born

personal identity Who we think we are and who others think we are.

and reared in this society" (p. 231). The dialectical tension related to issues of identity for these women reveals the strain between feeling obligated to behave in traditional ways at home and yet holding a Western notion of gender equality. A dialectical perspective sees these contradictions as real and presenting challenges in communication and everyday life.

Our personal identities are important to us, and we try to communicate them to others. We are more or less successful depending on how others respond to us. We use the various ways that identity is constructed to portray ourselves as we want others to see us.

MULTICULTURAL PEOPLE

Multicultural people, a group currently dramatically increasing in number, are those who live "on the borders" of two or more cultures. They often struggle to reconcile two very different sets of values, norms, worldviews, and lifestyles. Some are multicultural as a result of being born to parents from different racial, ethnic, religious, or national cultures or they were adopted into families that are racially different from their own family of origin. Others are multicultural because their parents lived overseas and they grew up in cultures different from their own, or because they spent extended time in another culture as an adult, or married someone from another cultural background. Let's start with those who are born into biracial or multiracial families.

According to the most recent census, the United States has almost 7 million multiracial people—that is, people whose ancestry includes two or more races (Brewer & Suchan, 2001). The 2000 census was the first one in which people were given the option of selecting several categories to indicate their racial identities. This rapidly growing segment of our population must be understood in its historical context. The United States has a long history of forbidding miscegenation (the mixing of two races). The law sought not to prevent *any* interracial marriage but to protect "whiteness"; interracial marriage between people of color was rarely prohibited or regulated (Root, 2001). Thus, in 1957, the state of Virginia ruled the marriage of Mildred Jeter (African American and Native American heritage) and Peter Loving (white) illegal. The couple fought to have their marriage legalized for almost 10 years. Finally, in 1967, the Supreme Court ruled in their favor, in *Loving v. Virginia*, overturning 200 years of antimiscegenation legislation.

As shown in Table 5-2, the development of racial identity for the children of parents like the Lovings is a fluid process of complex transactions between the child and the broader social environment (Nance & Foeman, 2002). Whereas majority and minority identities seem to develop in a fairly linear fashion, biracial children may cycle through three stages: (1) awareness of differentness and resulting dissonance, (2) struggle for acceptance, and (3) self-acceptance and self-assertion. And as they mature, they may experience the same three phases with greater intensity and awareness.

In the first stage, multiracial children realize that they are different from other children—they may feel that they don't fit in anywhere. Tiffany, whose mother is white and father is black, describes her experience:

Growing up I had kids make fun of me because they said I did not know what color I was. That really hurt me as a kid because even at a young age, I started questioning my own race.

At the next stage, struggle for acceptance, multiracial adolescents may feel that they have to choose one race or the other—and indeed this was Tiffany's experience:

During my teenage years I still was a little confused about my race because I would only choose one side. When people asked me what color I was I would tell them I was black because I was embarrassed about being mixed. I was afraid of not being accepted by the black community if I said I was mixed. . . . I would go around telling people that I am black and would get mad if someone said I was white. I never thought about being mixed with both black and white.

After being torn between the two (or more) races, multiracial individuals may reach the third stage, of self-acceptance and self-assertion. Tiffany describes how this happened for her:

I can recall a time when I had to spend Christmas with my mother's side of the family. This was the first time I met her side of the family and I felt myself being scared. Honestly, I have never been around a lot of white people, and when I was there I realized that I am mixed and this is who I am and I cannot hide it anymore. . . . From then on I claimed both sides.

And she goes on to demonstrate her self-acceptance and self-assertion:

Being mixed is wonderful, and most importantly, being mixed taught me many things especially growing up. It taught me how to be strong, not to worry about what other people think and to just be myself. It also taught me not to like only one color and that all colors are beautiful. My race made me who I am today. I am strong and I know my race. I no longer have to deny what my race is or who I am.

As you might imagine, many positive aspects are associated with having a biracial identity. In one recent study, the majority of biracial respondents "did not express feelings of marginality as suggested by traditional theories of bicultural identity. Instead, these youth exhibited a clear understanding and affiliation with both groups' cultures and values" (Miller, Watling, Staggs, & Rotheram-Borus, 2003, p. 139). Later in the chapter we discuss further the important role that multicultural people can play in intercultural relations.

In addition to multicultural identities based on race and ethnicity, there are multicultural identities based on religion, sexual orientation, or other identities. For example, children growing up with a Jewish and a Christian parent may feel torn between the two and follow some of the same identity development phases as biracial children—where they feel different, forced to choose between one or the other. Teresa says, "My father is Mexican American and my mother is white, so I have a Latino last name. When I was younger, some kids would tease me with racial slurs about Mexicans. My mother totally didn't understand and just said that I should ignore them, but my father understood much better. He faced the same taunting as a child in Indiana." A straight child of gay parents may have similar feelings of needing to negotiate between straight and gay worldviews.

Individuals develop multicultural identities for other reasons. For example, **global nomads** (or **third-culture kids**—TCKs) grow up in many different cultural contexts because their parents move around a lot (e.g., missionaries, international business employees, and military families). According to a recent study, these children have unique challenges and unique opportunities. They move an average of about eight times, experience cultural rules that may be constraining (e.g., in cultures where children have less freedom), and endure periods of family separation. At the same time, they have opportunities not provided to most people—extensive travel, living in new and different places around the world. As adults they settle down and often feel the need to reconnect with other global nomads (easier now through technologies such as the Internet) (Ender, 2002). President Barack Obama is a good example of a global nomad—his father was an African exchange student and his mother a U.S. American college student. He spent his childhood first in Hawaii and then in Indonesia when his mother and his Indonesian stepfather moved there. Like many TCKs, he was separated from his family during high school when he returned to Hawaii to live with his grandparents. His stepsister credits his ability to understand people from many different backgrounds to his many intercultural experiences as a child and adolescent—like many global nomads, these experiences "gave him the ability to . . . understand people from a wide array of backgrounds. People see themselves in him . . . because he himself contains multitudes" ("Obama's sister talks about his childhood," 2008).

Children of foreign-born immigrants may also develop multicultural identities. Foreign-born immigrants in the United States represent one of the fastest-growing segments—almost a third of the current foreign-born population arrived in the United States since 1990. These include refugees from war zones like Kosovo and the Balkans and migrants who come to the United States to escape dire economic conditions. They often struggle to negotiate their identities, torn between family expectations and their new American culture. Khoa, a first-generation Vietnamese American, describes how important his family's values are:

> *What does it mean to be "Asian" then? Being Asian is being proud of my heritage, my family, and the values that they have passed down to you. I am proud of my parents' discipline upon me. . . . I learned very early in life the differences between right and wrong. . . . I am proud that my parents taught me to respect my elders. I value the time I spend with my grandparents. I love the time I spend with my uncles and aunts, and my cousins. Having a deep love and honest respect for my family, both immediate and extended, is what being "Asian" means to me.*

global nomads
third-culture kids
People who grow up in many different cultural contexts because their parents relocated.

Then he recounts the struggle to reconcile being both Vietnamese and American:

> *There are a few things, though, that my parents believe in that I do not agree with. I think it is important that you know where you came from and to have pride in your nationality. However, I do not think that just because I am Vietnamese I am obligated to marry a Vietnamese girl. A Vietnamese girl is not any better or worse than any other girl of another nationality.*

Like Khoa, multicultural adolescents often feel pulled in different directions as they develop their own identities.

A final category of multicultural people includes those who have intense intercultural experiences as adults—for example, people who maintain long-term romantic relationships with members of another ethnic or racial group or who spend extensive time living in other cultures. Miguel tells us, "My father is an American, but my mother is from Chile. Because they divorced when I was young and my father returned to the United States, I spent a lot of time traveling back and forth and learning to adapt to two different cultures and languages. I don't feel completely Chilean or American, but I feel like I am both. I have family and friends in both places and I feel connected in different ways."

We discuss these multicultural identities more in Chapter 8, "Understanding Intercultural Transitions." All multicultural people may feel as if they live in cultural margins, struggling with two sets of cultural realities: not completely part of the dominant culture but not an outsider, either.

Social psychologist Peter Adler (1974) describes the multicultural person as someone who comes to grips with a multiplicity of realities. This individual's identity is not defined by a sense of belonging; rather, it is a new psychocultural form of consciousness. Milton Bennett (1993) describes how individuals can develop an "ethnorelative" perspective based on their attitudes toward cultural difference. The first, and most ethnocentric, stage involves the denial or ignoring of difference. The next stage occurs when people recognize difference but attach negative meaning to it. A third stage occurs when people minimize the effects of difference—for example, with statements like "We're really all the same under the skin" and "After all, we're all God's children." Bennett recognizes that minority and majority individuals may experience these phases differently. In addition, minority individuals usually skip the first phase. They don't have the option to deny difference; they are often reminded by others that they are different.

The remainder of the stages represent a major shift in thinking—a paradigm shift—because positive meanings are associated with difference. In the fourth phase (acceptance), people accept the notion of cultural difference; in the fifth phase (adaptation), they may change their own behavior to adapt to others. The final phase (integration) is similar to Peter Adler's (1974) notion of a "multicultural person."

culture brokers
Individuals who act as bridges between cultures, facilitating cross-cultural interaction and conflict.

According to Adler, multicultural individuals may become **culture brokers**—people who facilitate cross-cultural interaction and reduce conflict, which we'll discuss in more detail in Chapter 12. For example, third-culture kids/global nomads often develop resilience, tolerance, and worldliness, characteristics essential for successful living in an increasingly diverse and global social and economic world (Ender, 1996). And, indeed, there are many challenges and opportunities today for multicultural people, who can reach a level of insight and cultural functioning not experienced by others. One of our students, who is Dutch (ethnicity) and Mexican (nationality), describes this:

Being the makeup I am to me means I come from two extremely proud cultures. The Dutch in me gives me a sense of tradition and loyalty. The Mexican side gives me a rich sense of family as well as closeness with not only my immediate family, with my aunts, uncles, and cousins as well. My unique mix makes me very proud of my identity. To me it means that I am proof that two parts of the world can unite in a world that still believes otherwise.

However, Adler (1974) also identifies potential stresses and tensions associated with multicultural individuals:

They may confuse the profound with the insignificant, not sure what is really important.

They may feel multiphrenic, fragmented.

They may suffer a loss of their own authenticity and feel reduced to a variety of roles.

They may retreat into existential absurdity. (p. 35)

Communication scholar Janet Bennett (1993) provides insight into how being multicultural can be at once rewarding *and* challenging. She describes two types of multicultural individuals: (1) *encapsulated marginals*, who become trapped by their own marginality, and (2) *constructive marginals*, who thrive in their marginality.

Encapsulated marginals have difficulty making decisions, are troubled by ambiguity, and feel pressure from both groups. They try to assimilate but never feel comfortable, never feel "at home." In contrast, constructive marginal people thrive in their marginal existence and, *at the same time*, they recognize the tremendous challenges. They see themselves (rather than others) as choice makers. They recognize the significance of being "in between," and they are able to make commitments within the relativistic framework. Even so, this identity is constantly being negotiated and explored; it is never easy, given society's penchant for superficial categories. Writer Ruben Martinez (1998) describes the experience of a constructive marginal:

And so I can celebrate what I feel to be my cultural success. I've taken the far-flung pieces of myself and fashioned an identity beyond that ridiculous, fraying old border between the United States and Mexico. But my "success" is still marked by anxiety, a white noise that disturbs whatever raceless utopia I might imagine. I feel an uneasy tension between all the colors, hating and loving them all, perceiving and speaking from one and many perspectives simultaneously. The key word here is "tension": nothing, as yet, has been resolved. My body is both real and unreal, its color both confining and liberating. (p. 260)

IDENTITY, STEREOTYPES, AND PREJUDICE

The identity characteristics described previously sometimes form the basis for stereotypes, prejudice, and racism. We will see in the next chapter that these can be communicated verbally, nonverbally, or both. The origins of these have both individual and contextual elements. To make sense out of the overwhelming amount of information we receive, we necessarily categorize and generalize, sometimes relying on **stereotypes**—widely held beliefs about some group. Stereotypes help us know what to expect from others. They may be positive or negative. For example, Asian Americans have often been subjected to the positive **"model minority"** stereotype, which characterizes all Asians and Asian Americans as hardworking and serious. This stereotype became particularly prevalent in the United States during the civil rights movement of the 1960s and 1970s. At that time, Asian Americans were seen as the "good" minority—in contrast to African Americans, who were often confrontative and even militant in their fight for equality.

Even positive stereotypes can be damaging in that they create unrealistic expectations for individuals. Simply because someone is Asian American (or pretty, or smart) does not mean that he or she will excel in school or be outgoing and charming. Stereotypes become particularly detrimental when they are negative and are held rigidly. Research has shown that, once adopted, stereotypes are difficult to discard. In fact, people tend to remember information that supports a stereotype but may not retain information that contradicts it (Hamilton, Sherman, & Ruvolo, 1990).

We pick up stereotypes in many ways, including from the media. In TV shows and movies, older people often are portrayed as needing help, and Asian Americans, African Americans, or Latinos/as rarely play leading, assertive roles. Current research also shows that although obvious negative stereotypes of Native American Indians are less common in the media, they are still commonly represented in print media as degraded outsiders, often "corrupt, alcoholic and doomed objects of pity" (Miller & Ross, 2004, p. 255) or as either the "good" or "bad" Indians. Communication scholar Bishetta D. Merritt (2000) analyzes portrayals of African American women on television shows and decries the lack of multidimensional roles. She identifies the kinds of roles that perpetuate stereotypes:

> *Portrayals that receive little or no attention today are the background characters that merely serve as scenery on television programs. These characters include the homeless person on the street, the hotel lobby prostitute, or the drug user making a buy from her dealer. They may not be named in the credits or have recurring roles, but their mere appearance can have an impact on the consciousness of the viewer and, as a result, an impact on the imagery of the African American women. (p. 52)*

stereotypes Widely held beliefs about a group of people.

model minority A stereotype that characterizes all Asians and Asian Americans as hardworking and serious and so a "good" minority.

I fell in love with a first-generation Mexican American. It took many arguments and lots of time before he was accepted into my family. Once everyone saw what an incredible person Gabe is, I think they favored him more than me. . . . He and I had been together for a year and a half and the time had come for me to meet his family. I was extremely nervous because his parents spoke only Spanish and I only spoke English. How was I going to communicate with my boyfriend's family? To my surprise, this was the least of my worries. When we were introduced, I thought his parents were going to faint. I am "white." I am not the same race as this family, and they resented my having a relationship with their son. I must be very naive, but I never thought prejudices would be directed toward me. This was quite an eye-opener for me. . . .

Unfortunately, Gabriel's sisters spoke English. They made quite a point to be rude and neglect me in every conversation they had. I felt terrible. Before I knew it, Gabe's sister, Amelia, pulled me into her room. She began explaining to me how I would never be part of their family. Because I was not of Hispanic descent, I was not worthy to be with her brother. She went on to tell me that her parents hated me. . . . This was really difficult for me to swallow. This family hated me because of something I have absolutely no control over, my race.

I sat there, not sure of what to say or do. I was so hurt and upset, I stood up and yelled. I told her that this is the problem with society. Why, when we have a chance to change what we hate, do we resist? How can we consciously continue doing these things? Basically, the same countless arguments I had with my parents, I had with Gabe's sister. Whatever happened in that room was the most rewarding experience. We continued discussing the problem. By the end of the conversation, we were such good friends. Shortly after that, Gabe's family felt like my family.

The slight taste of prejudice I felt has to be minimal compared to other people's experiences. I am thankful I was fortunate enough to have such an experience early in my life. I honestly have to admit, Amelia changed me for the better.

—Jennifer

We may learn stereotypes from our families and peers. One student described how she learned stereotyping and prejudice from her classmates:

One of my earliest experiences with a person ethnically diverse from me was when I was in kindergarten. A little girl in my class named Adelia was from Pakistan. I noticed that Adelia was a different color from me, but I didn't think it was a bad thing. I got along with her very well. We played the same games, watched the same cartoons, and enjoyed each other's company. Soon I discovered that my other friends didn't like Adelia as much as I did. They didn't want to hold hands with her, and they claimed that she was different from us. When I told them that

Adelia was my friend, they didn't want to hold hands with me either. They started to poke fun at me and excluded me from their games. This hurt me so much that I stopped playing with Adelia, and I joined my friends in avoiding her. As a result, Adelia began to resent me and labeled me prejudiced.

Stereotypes can also develop out of negative experiences. If we have unpleasant encounters with people, we may generalize that unpleasantness to include all members of that group, whatever group characteristic we focus on (e.g., race, gender, or sexual orientation). This was demonstrated repeatedly after the attacks of September 11, 2001. Many people of Middle Eastern descent became victims of stereotyping, particularly when traveling. For example, one Arab American software developer from Dallas who was waiting for his flight home from Seattle to leave the gate was told by a flight attendant to take his belongings and get off the plane. Apparently, the pilot had been suspicious of his looks. He was questioned for more than an hour by authorities before being allowed to proceed.

Because stereotypes often operate at an unconscious level and so are persistent, people have to work consciously to reject them. First, they must recognize the stereotype, and then they must obtain information to counteract it. This is not easy because, as noted previously, we tend to "see" behavior that fits our stereotypes and to ignore that which doesn't. For example, if you think that most women are bad drivers, you will tend to notice when a female motorist makes a mistake but to ignore bad male driving. To undo this stereotype, you have to be very vigilant and do something that isn't "natural"—to be very conscious of how you "see" and categorize bad driving and to note bad driving by both males and females.

Prejudice is a negative attitude toward a cultural group based on little or no experience. It is a prejudgment of sorts. Whereas stereotypes tell us what a group is like, prejudice tells us how we are likely to feel about that group (Newberg, 1994). Scholars disgree somewhat on the origins of prejudice and its relationship to stereotyping. Prejudice may arise from personal needs to feel positive about our own groups and negative about others, or it may arise from perceived or real threats (Hecht, 1998). Researchers Walter Stephan and Cookie Stephan (1996) have shown that tension between cultural groups and negative previous contact, along with status inequalities and perceived threats, can lead to prejudice.

prejudice An attitude (usually negative) toward a cultural group based on little or no evidence.

Why do people hold prejudices? Psychologist Richard Brislin (1999) suggests that just as stereotyping arises from normal cognitive functioning, holding prejudices may serve understandable functions. These functions may not excuse prejudice, but they do help us understand why prejudice is so widespread. He identifies four such functions:

1. The utilitarian function. People hold certain prejudices because they can lead to rewards. For example, if your friends or family hold prejudices toward certain groups, it will be easier for you simply to share those attitudes, rather than risk rejection by contradicting their attitudes.

2. The ego-defensive function. People hold certain prejudices because they don't want to believe unpleasant things about themselves. For example, if either of us (Judith or Tom) is not a very good teacher, it will be useful

for us to hold negative stereotypes about students, such as that they are lazy and don't work hard. In this way, we can avoid confronting the real problem—our lack of teaching skills. The same kind of thing happens in the workplace: It is easier for people to stereotype women and minorities as unfit for jobs than to confront their own lack of skill or qualifications for a job.

3. The value-expressive function. People hold certain prejudices because they serve to reinforce aspects of life that are highly valued. Religious attitudes often function in this way. Some people are prejudiced against certain religious groups because they see themselves as holding beliefs in the one true God, and part of their doctrine is the belief that others are wrong. For instance, Judith's Mennonite family held prejudices against Catholics, who were viewed as misguided and wrong. This may also be operating today as some U.S. Americans search for validation of prejudices again Muslims. A more extreme example involves the atrocities committed against groups of people by others who want to retain the supposed values of a pure racial stock (e.g., "ethnic cleansing" by Serbs against Muslims in the former Yugoslavia).

4. The knowledge function. People hold certain prejudices because such attitudes allow them to organize and structure their world in a way that makes sense to them—in the same way that stereotypes help us organize our world. For example, if you believe that members of a certain group are flaky and irresponsible, then you don't have to think very much when meeting someone from that group in a work situation. You already know what they're like and so can react to them more automatically.

Prejudices can serve several of these functions over the life span. Thus, children may develop a certain prejudice to please their parents (utilitarian) and continue to hold the prejudice because it helps define who they are (value-expressive). Brislin (1999) points out that many remedial programs addressing the problem of prejudice fail because of a lack of recognition of the important functions that prejudice fulfills in our lives. Presenting people with factual information about groups addresses only one function (knowledge) and ignores the more complex reasons that we hold prejudices. Prejudice and stereotypes can also lead to *acts* of discrimination, which will be discussed in Chapter 7.

IDENTITY AND COMMUNICATION

Identity has a profound influence on intercultural communication processes. We can employ some of the dialectics identified in earlier chapters to illuminate this relationship. First, we can use the individual–cultural dynamic to examine the issues that arise when we encounter people whose identities we don't know. In intercultural communication interactions, mistaken identities are often exacerbated and can create communication problems.

Sometimes we assume knowledge about another person's identity based on his or her membership in a particular cultural group. When we do so, we are ignoring the individual aspect. Taking a dialectical perspective can help us recognize and balance both the individual and the cultural aspects of another's identity. This perspective can guide the ways that we communicate with that person (and conceivably with others). "The question here is one of identity: Who am I perceived to be when I communicate with others? . . . My identity is very much tied to the ways in which others speak to me and the ways in which society represents my interests" (Nakayama, 2000, p. 14).

Think about the assumptions you might make about others based on their physical appearance. What do you "know" about people if you know only that they are from, say, the South, or Australia, or Pakistan? Perhaps it is easier to think about the times that people have made erroneous assumptions about you based on limited information—assumptions that you became aware of in the process of communication. Focusing solely on someone's nationality, place of origin, education, religion, and the like, can lead to mistaken conclusions about the person's identity.

Another way to understand how we communicate our identities comes from the study of performance. Although we can look at someone's individual performance of identity to better understand how they understand who they think they are, we can also look at cultural performance to understand cultural identities. For example, in her essay on martyrdom in Islam, Lindsay Calhoun (2004) explains the importance of this performance as a part of national identity and religious identity. Noting that martyrdom is "found in nearly all the world's major religious traditions" (p. 328), Calhoun observes that in the West, we see martyrs "as fanatics and terrorists" (p. 328). She explores this performance more closely to see that it is "a strategic performance of resistance and/or reification meant to exact both a cost and a reward upon the martyr, his or her supporters, and oppressors" (p. 344). It is a kind of performance that helps the martyr communicate an Islamic identity, but also a national identity. Through this performance of identity, the martyr is reconfigured in a new way.

Sometimes a focus on the performance of identity can help us better understand parts of our cultural past that we would have difficulty understanding today. One part of U.S. history often hidden is the horrific practice of lynching. Yet we must acknowledge that lynching was a widespread and common practice in U.S. culture, and we can often be confused when we see many of the perpetrators smiling in these photos because it seems incomprehensible that they were not horrified by this event.

Performance studies scholar Kirk Fuoss (1999) suggests that a performance perspective can help us better understand how people can participate in these atrocities and the purpose of these lynchings for the perpetrators. For example,

I would have to say that the most important identity to me is being Pakistani and being a Muslim. My religion and culture are both very important to me. I have not really had too many experiences in which I thought that my identity was not being affirmed. However, there have been some minor experiences that I have faced. We all know that after that incident, Muslims really got a bad name. People used to associate all Muslims with being terrorists. During that time, that seemed to be the subject of discussion in every single class.

I remember in one of my classes, a guy said that all Muslims are terrorists. That really hurt me and I took offense to that. I spoke up and said that if you are not a Muslim then you have no right to say that. I said that if you are not a Muslim, then you really do not know what it means to be one, and you do not know the true values and beliefs of the religion. I am a practicing Muslim, and I know my religion very well, and I know that the religion of Islam does not teach anything but to love one another. I did not care if someone did not believe me because everyone is entitled to their own opinion, but my main purpose was to say that it was wrong for the guy to say something that big about a whole group of people. It would be best if people could keep comments like that to themselves. If the guy just kept that comment to himself, it would not have hurt him and it would have not hurt me for sure. That was one time, that I thought that my identity was not being affirmed. But other than that, most people that I have come across and most people who I tell that I am a Muslim do not react with any sort of hostility. That makes me feel really good and accepted in a society in which most people are not Muslims.

—Shazim

Fuoss argues that lynching in the United States functioned as a cultural performance that served to reinforce a particular kind of racial order for those who participated in or heard about the lynching. Lynchings took place outside of the legal system, and therefore a belief in the evilness of the victim substituted for a proof or evidence of guilt. This inversion of right and wrong served to relieve the group identity of the lynchers from their own evil behavior. These murders reflect aspects of our culture that have deep historical roots. By examining these performative acts, we can begin to see what they communicate to others and the kinds of social order they encourage. Thus, lynchings are a public act that serve to communicate the positions of various cultural groups in society. It is important to remember that performances not only are artistic and interesting but can also be horrific. In both cases, performances of identity can offer insights into our culture.

Now let's turn to the static–dynamic dialectic. The problem of erroneous assumptions has increased during the information age, due to the torrent of information about the world and the dynamic nature of the world in which we live. We are bombarded daily with information from around the globe about places and people. This glut of information and intercultural contacts has heightened the importance of developing a more complex view of identity.

Given the many identities that we all negotiate for ourselves in our everyday interactions, it becomes clear how our identities and those of others make intercultural communication problematic. We need to think of these identities as both static and dynamic. We live in an era of information overload, and the wide array of communication media only serves to increase the identities we must negotiate. Consider the relationships that develop via e-mail, for example. Some people even create new identities as a result of online interactions. We change who we are depending on the people we communicate with and the manner of our communication. Yet we also expect some static characteristics from the people with whom we communicate. We expect others to express certain fixed qualities; these help account for why we tend to like or dislike them and how we can establish particular communication patterns with them. The tensions that we feel as we change identities from e-mail to telephone to mail to fax and other communication media demonstrate the dynamic and static characters of identities.

Finally, we can focus on the personal–contextual dialectic of identity and communication. Although some dimensions of our identities are personal and remain fairly consistent, we cannot overlook the contextual constraints on our identity.

INTERNET RESOURCES

www.racialicious.com
This blog was developed to provide perspectives on race and racism in popular culture. It comments on news stories of celebrities dealing with race and media representations of race. Links to other podcasts and blogs, such as "Race in the Workplace," are also available. An archive of former postings is also provided.

http://pewforum.org/
The Pew Forum on Religion and Public Life Web site provides research, news, and discussions regarding topics related to religious identity, e.g., college students' beliefs about religion, the role of religion in debates on gay marriage, science education, politics, etc. The site also provides religious demographic profiles for different countries.

www.pbs.org/race/001_WhatIsRace/001_00-home.htm
This Web site provided by PBS is a comprehensive exploration of myths and constructions of race. It has some interesting interactive links, such as "Sorting People," which allows a person to categorize pictures of people based on contemporary U.S. racial categories and then see how the government would classify the pictures. It also provides a "race timeline"—how the notion of race developed through history.

www.intermix.org.uk/word_up/index.asp
This British Web page was developed to benefit mixed-race families and multiracial individuals. It contains news stories about Mariah Carey, Halle Berry, Craig David, and other multiracial celebrities.

SUMMARY

There are three approaches to identity: social science, interpretive, and critical.

- A dialectical view of identity emphasizes that identities are both static (as described by the social science perspective) and dynamic (described by the interpretive and critical perspectives), as well as personal and contextual.

- Identity is expressed through language and labels.

- Identities also develop in relation to minority and majority group membership.

- Identities are multiple and reflect gender, sexuality, age, race, ethnicity, religion, class, nationality, regionality, and other aspects of our lives.

- Increasing numbers of multicultural people live "on the borders" between two or more cultures—based on race, ethnicity, religion, and nationality.

- Identity characteristics sometimes form the basis for stereotypes and prejudice.

- Communication plays an important role in identity—identities are formed and expressed through communication.

DISCUSSION QUESTIONS

1. How do our perceptions of our own cultural identity influence our communication with others?

2. What are some ways in which we express our identities?

3. How does being white affect one's experience in the United States?

4. What are the roles of avowal and ascription in the process of identity formation?

5. What are some of the ways in which members of minority cultures and members of majority cultures develop their cultural identities?

Go to the self-quizzes on the Online Learning Center at www.mhhe.com/ martinnakayama5 to further test your knowledge.

1. *Stereotypes in Your Life.* List some of the stereotypes you have heard about U.S. Americans. Then answer the following questions:

   a. How do you think these stereotypes developed?

   b. How do they influence communication between U.S. Americans and people from other countries?

2. *Stereotypes in Prime-Time TV.* Watch four hours of television during the next week, preferably during evening hours when there are more commercials. Record the number of representatives of different identity groups (ethnic, racial, gender, age, class, and so on) that appear in the commercials; also record the role that each person plays. Answer the following questions:

   a. How many different groups were represented?

   b. What groups were most represented? Why do you think this is so?

   c. What groups were least represented? Why do you think this is so?

   d. What differences (if any) were there in the roles that members of the various groups played? Did one group play more sophisticated or more glamorous roles than others?

   e. In how many cases were people depicted in stereotypical roles—for example, African Americans as athletes, or women as homemakers?

   f. What stereotypes were reinforced in the commercials?

   g. What do your findings suggest about the power of the media and their effect on identity formation and intercultural communication? (Think about avowal, ascription, and interpellation.)

KEY WORDS

age identity (182)
ascription (166)
avowal (166)
class identity (194)
core symbols (167)
culture brokers (204)
ethnic identity (185)
familial identity (164)
gender identity (180)
global nomads (202)

hyphenated Americans (186)
identity (162)
identity negotiation theory (166)
impression management theory (162)
individualized identity (164)
interpellation (169)
majority identity (177)
minority identity (173)

model minority (205)
national identity (197)
personal identity (199)
prejudice (207)
racial identity (184)
regional identity (199)
religious identity (192)
sexual identity (182)
spiritual identity (165)
stereotypes (205)
third-culture kids (202)

REFERENCES

Adler, P. (1974). Beyond cultural identity: Reflections on cultural and multicultural man. *Topics in culture learning* (Vol. 2, pp. 23–40). Honolulu: East-West Center.

Ahmadinejad speaks; outrage and controversy follow. (24 September, 2007) CNN.com. Retrieved February 7, 2008, from http://www.cnn.com/2007/US/09/24/us.iran/index.html.

Alba, R. D. (1985). The twilight of ethnicity among Americans of European ancestry: The case of Italians. *Ethnic and Racial Studies, 8*, 134–158.

Alba, R. D. (1990). *Ethnic identity: The transformation of white America.* New Haven, CT: Yale University Press.

Allen, B. (2004). *Difference matters: Communicating social identity.* Waveland Press.

Althusser, L. (1971). Ideology and ideological state apparatuses (notes towards an investigation). In B. Brewster (Trans.), *Lenin and philosophy and other essays* (pp. 134–165). London: NLB.

Bahk, C. M., & Jandt, F. E. (2004). Being white in America: Development of a scale. *The Howard Journal of Communications, 15*, 57–68.

Bederman, G. (1995). *Manliness and civilization: A cultural history of gender and race in the United States, 1880–1917.* Chicago: University of Chicago Press.

Bennett, J. M. (1993). Cultural marginality: Identity issues in intercultural training. In R. M. Paige (Ed.), *Education for the intercultural experience* (pp. 109–136). Yarmouth, ME: Intercultural Press.

Bennett, M. J. (1993). Towards ethnorelativism: A developmental model of intercultural sensitivity. In R. M. Paige (Ed.), *Education for the intercultural experience* (pp. 21–72). Yarmouth, ME: Intercultural Press.

Bernstein, J., & Mishel, L. (2007, September 3). *Economy's gains fail to reach most workers' paychecks.* Economic Policy Institute Briefing Paper #195. Retrieved February 18, 2008, from http://www.epi.org/content.cfm/bp195.

Bourdieu, P. (1987). *Distinction: A social critique of the judgment of taste* (R. Nice, Trans.). Cambridge, MA: Harvard University Press.

Boyd, D. (2007, June 24). Viewing American class divisions through Facebook and MySpace. *Apophenia Blog Essay.* Retrieved February 18, 2008 from http://www.danah.org/papers/essays/ClassDivisions.html.

Brewer, C. A., & Suchan, T. A. (2001). *Mapping Census 2000: The geography of U.S. diversity* (U.S. Census Bureau, Census Special Reports, Series CENSR/01-1). Washington, DC: U.S. Government Printing Office.

Brislin, R. (1999). *Understanding culture's influence on behavior* (2nd ed.). Belmont, CA: Wadsworth.

Calhoun, L. R. (2004). Islamic martyrdom in the postcolonial condition. *Text and Performance Quarterly, 24*, 327–347.

Canary, D. J., & Hause, K. S. (1993). Is there any reason to research sex difference in communication? *Communication Quarterly, 41*, 129–144.

Carbaugh, D. (1989). *Talking American: Cultural discourse on* Donahue. Norwood, NJ: Ablex.

Chen, V. (1992). The construction of Chinese American women's identity. In L. F. Rakow (Ed.), *Women making meaning* (pp. 225–243). New York: Routledge.

Collier, M. J. (2005). Theorizing cultural identification: Critical updates and continuing evolution. In W. B. Gudykunst (Ed.), *Theorizing about intercultural communication* (pp. 235–256). Thousand Oaks, CA: Sage.

Collier, M. J., & Thomas, M. (1988). Cultural identity: An interpretive perspective. In Y. Y. Kim & W. B. Gudykunst (Eds.), *Theories in intercultural communication* (pp. 99–122). Newbury Park, CA: Sage.

Cornell, S., & Hartmann, D. (1998). *Ethnicity and race: Making identities in a changing world.* Thousand Oaks, CA: Pine Forge Press.

Cross, S. E. (2000). What does it mean to "know thyself" in the United States and Japan?: The cultural construction of the self. In T. J. Owens (Ed.), *Self and identity through the life course in cross-cultural perspective* (pp. 159–180). Stamford, CT: JAI Press.

DeRusha, J. (2007, May 14). Military Bans MySpace, other web sites to soldiers. Retrieved February 18, 2008, from http://wcco.com/local/MySpace.Internet.Web.2.367379.html.

Ehrenreich, B. (2001). *Nickel and dimed: On (not) getting by in America.* New York: Metropolitan Books.

Ehrenreich, B. (2005). *Bait and switch: The (futile) pursuit of the American Dream.* New York: Metropolitan Books.

Ender, M.D. (1996). Recognizing healthy conflict: The postmodern self. *Global Nomad Perspectives Newletter, 4*(1), 12–14.

Ender, M. G. (2002). Beyond adolescence: The experiences of adult children of military parents. In M. G. Ender (Ed.) *Military brats and other global nomads* (pp. 83–100). Westport, CT: Praeger.

Engen, D. (2004). Invisible identities: Notes on class and race. In A. Gonzalez, M. Houston, & V. Chen (Eds.), *Our voices: Essays in culture, ethnicity and communication* (pp. 250–255). Los Angeles: Roxbury.

Erikson, E. (1950). *Childhood and society.* New York: Norton.

Erikson, E. (1968). *Identity: Youth and crisis.* New York: Norton.

Feghali, E. (1997). Arab cultural communication patterns. *International Journal of Intercultural Relations, 21,* 345–378.

Ferguson, R. (1990). Introduction: Invisible center. In R. Ferguson, M. Gever, T. M. Trinh, & C. West (Eds.), *Out there: Marginalization and contemporary cultures* (pp. 9–14). New York and Cambridge: New Museum of Contemporary Art/MIT Press.

Foucault, M. (1988). *History of sexuality* (R. Hurley, Trans.). New York: Vintage Books.

Frankenburg, R. (1993). *White women, race matters: The social construction of whiteness.* Minneapolis: University of Minnesota Press.

Frankenberg, R. (2001). The mirage of an unmarked whiteness. In B. B. Rasmussen, E. Klineberg, I. J. Nexica, & M. Wray (Eds.), *The making and unmaking of whiteness* (pp. 72–96). Durham, NC: Duke University Press.

Fuoss, K. W. (1999). Lynching performances, theaters of violence. *Text and Performance Quarterly, 19,* 1–37.

Fussell, P. (1992). *Class: A guide through the American status system.* New York: Touchstone Books. (Original work published 1979)

Gallager, C. A. (1994). White construction in the university. *Socialist Review, 1/2,* 167–187.

Gao, G. (1996). Self and other: A Chinese perspective on interpersonal relationships. In W. G. Gudykunst, S. Ting-Toomey, & T. Nishida (Eds.), *Communication in personal relationships across cultures* (pp. 81–101). Thousand Oaks, CA: Sage.

Goffman, E. (1959). *The presentation of self in everyday life.* Garden City, New York: Doubleday.

Hall, S. (1985). Signification, representation, ideology: Althusser and the poststructuralist debates. *Critical Studies in Mass Communication, 2,* 91–114.

Hamilton, D. L., Sherman, S. J., & Ruvolo, C. M. (1990). Stereotype-based expectancies: Effects on information processing and social behavior. *Journal of Social Issues, 46,* 35–60.

Hardiman, R. (1994). White racial identity development in the United States. In E. P. Salett & D. R. Koslow (Eds.), *Race, ethnicity and self: Identity in multicultural perspective* (pp. 117–142). Washington, DC: National MultiCultural Institute.

Hardiman, R. (2003). White racial identity development in the United States. In E. P. Salett & D. R. Koslow (Eds.), *Race, ethnicity and self* (2nd ed., pp. 117–136). Washington, DC: National MultiCultural Institute.

Hargittai, E. (2007). Whose space? Differences among users and non-users of social network sites. *Journal of Computer-Mediated Communication, 13*(1), article 14.

Retrieved February 18, 2008, from http://jcmc.indiana.edu/vol13/issue1/hargittai.html.

Hasian, M., Jr., & Nakayama, T. K. (1999). Racial fictions and cultural identity. In J. Sloop & J. McDaniels (Eds.), *Treading judgment.* Boulder, CO: Westview Press.

Hecht, M. L. (1998). Introduction. In M. L. Hecht (Ed.), *Communicating prejudice* (pp. 3–23). Thousand Oaks, CA: Sage.

Hecht, M. L., Jackson, R. L. III, & Ribeau, S. A. (2003). *African American communication: Exploring identity and culture* (2nd ed.). Mahwah, NJ: Lawrence Erlbaum.

Hecht, M. L., Warren, J. R., Jung, E., & Krieger, J. L. (2005). A communication theory of identity: Development, theoretical perspective and future directions. In W. B. Gudykunst (Ed.), *Theorizing about intercultural communication* (pp. 257–278). Thousand Oaks, CA: Sage.

Howe, N., & Strauss, W. (2007). The next 20 years: How customer and workforce attitudes will evolve. (Managing for the Long Term)(Big Picture) *Harvard Business Review, 85*(7–8), 41.

Human races or human race? *The Economist, 386*(8566), 86.

Katz, J. (1995). *The invention of heterosexuality.* New York: Dutton.

Kim, M.-S. (2002). *Non-western perspectives on human communication.* Thousand Oaks, CA: Sage.

Lacan, J. (1977). The agency of the letter in the unconscious or reason since Freud. In A. Sheridan (Trans.), *Écrits: A selection* (pp. 146–178). New York: Norton. (Original work published 1957)

Leonard, M. F. (2004). Struggling for identity: Multiethnic and biracial individuals in America. In A. Gonzalez, M. Houston, & V. Chen (Eds.), *Our voices* (pp. 228–239). Los Angeles: Roxbury.

Luo, M. (2007, December 6). Crucial test for Romney in speech on his religion. *New York Times.* Retrieved February 4, 2008, from http://www.nytimes.com.

Martinez, R. (1998). Technicolor. In C. C. O'Hearn (Ed.) *Half and half: Writers on growing up biracial + bicultural* (pp. 245–264). New York: Pantheon Books.

Mehl, M. R., & Pennebaker, J. W. (2003). The sounds of social life: A psychometric analysis of students' daily social environments and natural conversations. *Journal of Personality and Social Psychology, 84,* 857–870.

Merritt, B. D. (2000). Illusive reflections: African American women on primetime television. In A. Gonzalez, M. Houston, & V. Chen (Eds.), *Our voices: Essays in culture, ethnicity and communication* (3rd ed., pp. 47–53). Los Angeles: Roxbury.

Miller, A., & Ross, S. D. (2004). They are not us: Framing of American Indians by the *Boston Globe*. *The Howard Journal of Communications, 15*, 245–259.

Miller, R. L., Watling, J. R., Staggs, S. L., & Rotheram-Borus, M. J. (2003). Growing up biracial in the United States. In E. P. Salett & D. R. Koslow (Eds.), *Race, ethnicity and self* (2nd ed., pp. 139–168). Washington, DC: National MultiCultural Institute.

Mishel, L., Bernstein, J., & Allegretto, S. (2006). *The state of working America 2006/2007*. An Economic Policy Institute Book. Ithaca, NY: ILR Press, an imprint of Cornell University Press.

Moon, D. G., & Rolison, G. L. (1998). Communication of classism. In M. L. Hecht (Ed.), *Communicating prejudice* (pp. 122–135). Thousand Oaks, CA: Sage.

Morin, R. (2001, July 11). Misperceptions cloud whites' view of blacks. *The Washington Post*, p. A01.

Myers, K. (2003). White fright: Reproducing white supremacy through casual discourse. In A. W. Doane & E. Bonilla-Silva (Eds.), *White out: The continuing significance of racism* (pp. 129–144). New York: Routledge.

Nakayama, T. K. (2000). Dis/orienting identities: Asian Americans, history, and intercultural communication. In A. González, M. Houston, & V. Chen (Eds.), *Our voices: Essays in ethnicity, culture, and communication* (3rd ed., pp. 13–20). Los Angeles: Roxbury.

Nance, T. A., & Foeman, A. K. (2002). On being biracial in the United States. In J. N. Martin, T. K. Nakayama, & L. A. Flores (Eds.), *Readings in intercultural communication: Experiences and contexts* (pp. 53–62). Boston: McGraw-Hill.

Newberg, S. L. (1994). Expectancy-confirmation processes in stereotype-tinged social encounters: The moderation of social goals. In M. P. Zanna & J. M. Olson (Eds.), *Ontario symposium on personality and social psychology: Vol 7. The psychology of prejudice* (pp. 103–130). Hillsdale, NJ: Lawrence Erlbaum.

New Vanderbilt scientific poll reveals intense bias against Mormons (2007, December 4). Retrieved February 18, 2008 from http://www.vanderbilt.edu/news/releases?.

Obama's sister talks about his childhood. (2008, February 14). CBSNews.com. Retrieved May 1, 2008 from http://www.cbsnews.com/stories/2008/02/14/politics/main3831108.shtml.

Omi, M., & Winant, H. (1998). Racial formation. In P. S. Rothenberg (Ed.), *Race, class and gender in the United States* (pp. 26–35). New York: St. Martin's Press.

Omi, M., & Winant, H. (2001). Racial formation. In P. S. Rothenberg (Ed.), *Race, class and gender in the United States* (pp. 11–21). New York: Worth.

Optimism about Black progress declines. (2007 November). Pew Research Center for the People and the Press. Report available at http://pewsocialtrends.org/assets/pdf/Race.pdf.

Pennebaker, J. W., Mehl, M. R., & Niederhoffer, K. G. (2003). Psychological aspects of natural language use: Our words, our selves. *Annual Review of Psychology, 54*, 547–577.

Pew Research Center for the People & the Press. (2005, September 8). Huge racial divide over Katrina and its consequences. News release. Available from http://people-press.org/reports/pdf/255.pdf.

Pew Research Center for the People & the Press (2007 May). Muslim Americans: Middleclass and mostly mainstream. Report available at http://pewresearch.org/assets/pdf/muslim-americans.pdf.

Phinney, J. S. (1993). A three-stage model of ethnic identity development in adolescence. In M. E. Bernal & G. Knight (Eds.), *Ethnic identity* (pp. 61–79). Albany: State University of New York Press.

Ponterotto, J. G., & Pedersen, P. B. (1993). *Preventing prejudice* (Chaps. 4 & 5). Newbury Park, CA: Sage.

Roediger, D. R. (2005). *Working toward whiteness: How America's immigrants became white*. New York: Basic Books.

Roland, A. (1988). *In search of self in India and Japan: Towards a cross-cultural psychology*. Princeton, NJ: Princeton University Press.

Root, M. P. P. (2001). *Love's revolution: Interracial marriage*. Philadelphia: Temple University Press.

Rosefeld, P., & Giaclone, R. A. (1991). From extreme to the mainstream: Applied impression management in organization. In R. A. Giaclone & P. Rosenfeld (Eds.) *Applied impression management: How image making affects managerial decision making*. Newbury Park, CA: Sage.

Sigelman, L., Tuch, S. A., & Martin, J. K. (2005). What's in a name? Preference for "Black" versus "African-American" among Americans of African descent. *Public Opinion Quarterly, 69*, 429–438.

Smith, T.W. (1992). Changing racial labels: From "Colored" to "Negro" to "Black" to "African American." *The Public Opinion Quarterly, 56*(4), 496–514.

Stephan, W., & Stephan, C. (1996). Predicting prejudice: The role of threat. *International Journal of Intercultural Relations, 20*, 409–426.

Strauss, W., & Howe, N. (1997). *The fourth turning: American Prophecy*. New York: Broadway Books.

Strauss, W., & Howe, N. (2006). *Millennials and the pop culture*. Great Falls, VA: LifeCourse Associates.

Tajfel, H. (1978). Social categorization, social identity and social comparison. In H. Tajfel (Ed.),

Differentiation between social groups (pp. 61–76). London: Academic Press.

Tajfel, H. (1981). *Human categories and social groups.* Cambridge: Cambridge University Press.

Tajfel, H. (1982). *Social identity and intergroup relations.* Cambridge: Cambridge University Press.

Tanno, D. (2000). Names, narratives, and the evolution of ethnic identity. In A. González, M. Houston, & V. Chen (Eds.), *Our voices: Essays in ethnicity, culture, and communication* (3rd ed., pp. 25–28). Los Angeles: Roxbury.

Tedeschi, J. T., Lindskold, S., & Rosenfeld, P. (1985). *Introduction to social psychology.* St. Paul, MN: West.

Ting-Toomey, S. (1993). Communication resourcefulness: An identity negotiation perspective. In R. Wiseman & J. Koester (Eds.), *Intercultural communication.* Newbury Park, CA: Sage.

Ting-Toomey, S. (2005). Identity negotiation theory: Crossing cultural boundaries. In W. B. Gudykunst (Ed.), *Theorizing about intercultural communication* (pp. 211–233). Thousand Oaks, CA: Sage.

Trinh, T. M. (1986/1987). Difference: A special third world women issue. *Discourse,* 8.

Why Black and not African American? (20 April 2007). Retrieved February 16, 2008 from http://theangryblackwoman.wordpress.com/2007/04/20/why-black-and-not-african-american/.

Witteborn, S. (2004). Of being an Arab woman before and after September 11: The enactment of communal identities in talk. *Howard Journal of Communications, 15,* 83–98.

Wood, J. T. (2005). *Gendered lives: Communication, gender and culture* (6th ed). Belmont, CA: Wadsworth.

Yamanouchi, K. (2002, May 19). Cosmetic companies market products aimed at men, *Arizona Republic,* p. D1.

6

LANGUAGE AND INTERCULTURAL COMMUNICATION

CHAPTER OBJECTIVES

After reading this chapter, you should be able to:

1. Discuss the four components of language.
2. Explain the nominalist, relativist, and qualified relativist positions on language and perception.
3. Describe the role of metaphor in understanding intercultural communication.
4. Identify cultural variations in communication style.
5. Give examples of variations in contextual rules.
6. Explain the power of labels.
7. Understand the challenges of multilingualism.
8. Explain the difference between translation and interpretation.
9. Understand the phenomenon of code switching and interlanguage.
10. Discuss the complexities of language policies.

When I first came to Sor Juana, *I wasn't doing well in biology and . . . my mom talked to my teacher about it. My mother has a very thick [Spanish] accent. When she asked my teacher what was wrong, he replied that . . . my junior high probably didn't prepare me as well as others for this course. When my mom said that I went to a prestigious school and had a 4.0, he was stupefied . . . ." Oh, oh, oh. Laurie's your daughter. I'm so sorry, I thought you were someone else's mother," my teacher replied. It was pitiful. My teacher made an obviously racist assumption that because my mother was Hispanic I went to an inferior junior high and that was the reason for my problems in Biology . . . .*

Mendoza-Denton, p. 50

Language use plays an important role in intercultural communication; it is closely tied with our and others' identities as we saw in the chapter on identity, and it is also related to the groups we belong to and our social place in society. In a world of multiple languages, we sometimes think that successful communication is just a matter of whether people speak the same language or not. However, communication is much more than language. In the story above, Laurie's mother and the teacher could communicate easily in English. However the interaction here is about much more than just the language spoken; in this case, *the way* English was spoken played an enormous role in how the encounter unfolded—resulting in (false) assumptions about Laurie's academic preparation, her social class, her place in society—and these assumptions influenced the whole communication encounter.

As this book shows, intercultural communication involves far more than merely language, but language clearly cannot be overlooked as a central element in the process. This chapter focuses on the verbal aspects of intercultural communication; the next chapter focuses on the nonverbal elements.

The social science approach generally focuses on language and its relation to intercultural communication, the interpretive approach focuses on contextual uses of linguistic codes, and the critical approach emphasizes the relations between discourse and power. This chapter uses a dialectical perspective to explore how language works dynamically in intercultural contexts. With the personal–contextual dialectic, we can consider not only how language use operates on an individual level but also how it is influenced by context. We also use the static–dynamic dialectic to distinguish between language and discourse, to identify the components of language, and to explore the relationship among language, meaning, and perception. Although it may seem that the components of language are static, the *use* of language is a dynamic process.

In this chapter, we also explore cultural variations of language. Then we discuss the relationship between language and power, and between language and identity, and examine issues of multilingualism, translation, and interpretation. Finally, we look at language and identity, language policies and politics, and globalization.

SOCIAL SCIENCE PERSPECTIVE ON LANGUAGE

The social science perspective focuses on the individual aspects of language use: the components of language, language perception and thought, and on the way cultural groups use language in different ways. The study of linguistics is just ost languages have from 15 to 50 meaningful sound units, but the total number of all sound units for all languages is in the hundreds (West, 1975). The **International Phonetic Alphabet (IPA)** was developed in 1889 to help linguists transcribe the pronunciation of words in different languages. It can also be useful when learning a foreign language. As you can see from the example below, it seems like another language, but actually is based primarily on the Latin alphabet.

IPA TRANSCRIPTION:

frʌstˈeɪʃnz ə ˈbɜst hotwotə ˈbɒ
dl ɔ ˈləʊθɪŋ evrɪ ˈməʊmn ʌv ə ˈh
ɒlədɑɪ pə ˈpaɪŋ ə   ˈfɔtʃn fɔ. ɪ
ts ˈjusɪŋ ðə ˈroŋ ˈsaɪd ə ðə ˈsɒlət
eɪp ˈfɒgɛdɪŋ wʌ dʃə wə goɪŋ tə ˈ
seɪ ɔ ˈlɒkn jɔsɛlf ˈaʊt frʌstˈeɪʃn
z ʌðə ˈpipl ˈpɑkn ən ˈfrʌnt əv jə
ˈgæredʒ ɔ rə ˈstreɪndʒə ˈrɪdɪŋ ə
ˈrɪvətn ˈlɛdə ʌn ə ˈbʌs n ˈtɜnɪn ɔ
və bəfɔ jə ˈgɔ tə ðə ˈbɒdm̩ əv
ðə ˈpeɪdʒ

ENGLISH "TRANSLATION":

Frustration is a burst hot-water bottle, or loathing every moment of a holiday you're paying a fortune for. It's using the wrong side of the Sellotape, forgetting what you were going to say, or locking yourself out. Frustration is other people parking in front of your garage, or a stranger reading a riveting letter on the bus and turning over before you get to the bottom of the page.

Source: From "English as a Second Language" (About.com), Retrieved August 16, 2008. http://esl.about.com/library/lessons/blphontranscript.htm.

one of many ways to think about language, and this study provides us with a useful foundation for our exploration of language in intercultural communication. As shown Table 6-1, linguists generally divide the study of language into four parts: semantics, syntactics, phonetics, and pragmatics.

Pragmatics is probably the most useful for students of intercultural communication because it focuses on actual language use—what people do with language—the focus of this chapter. People around the world speak many different languages and some scholars think that the particular language we speak influences how

International Phonetic Alphabet (IPA) A system of phonetic notation devised in 1889 to help linguists transcribe the pronunciation of words in different languages.

TABLE 6-1   THE COMPONENTS OF LANGUAGE

Component	Definition	Example
Semantics	The study of meaning—how individual words communicate the meanings we intend	Think about the word *chair*. Do we define *chair* by its shape? By its function? Does a throne count as a chair? How about a table we sit on? Is this a chair?
Syntactics	The study of the structure, or grammar—the rules for combining words into meaningful sentences. Order of words is important.	"The red car smashed into the blue car" has different meaning than "The blue car smashed into the red car."
Pragmatics	The study of how meaning is constructed in relation to receivers, how language is actually used in particular contexts in language communities.	Saying "that's an awesome outfit" has different meanings depending on the context. It could be mocking, flirting, or just descriptive.
Phonetics	The study of the sound system of language—how words are pronounced, which units of sounds (phonemes) are meaningful for a specific language and which sounds are universal. (See Figure 6-1.)	French has no equivalent sound of English *th*; Japanese has a sound which is between *r* and *l*

we see the world. Do speakers of Japanese, Chinese, Arabic, and other languages actually perceive the world differently, depending on the particular language they speak? Or do we all experience the world in the same way but have different ways of expressing our experiences? We tackle these questions in the next section.

Language and Perception

The question of how much of our perception is shaped by the particular language we speak is at the heart of the "political correctness" debate. We can address these questions from two points of view: the nominalist and the relativist.

The Nominalist Position   According to the **nominalist position,** perception is not shaped by the particular language we speak. Language is simply an arbitrary "outer form of thought." Thus, we all have the same range of thoughts, which we express in different ways with different languages. This means that any thought can be expressed in any language, although some may take more or fewer words. The existence of different languages does not mean that people have different thought processes or inhabit different perceptual worlds. After all, a tree may be an *arbre* in French and an *arbol* in Spanish, but we all perceive the tree in the same way.

nominalist position
The view that perception is not shaped by the particular language one speaks. (Compare with **relativist position** and **qualified relativist position**.)

There have been a few different times when an accent has affected my perception of a person. Usually, when the person with the accent is a male, I find it to be attractive. This may seem funny, but I think a lot of people feel this way. At first, I want to ask a whole bunch of questions: where the person is from, what it's like there, and so on. Then I realize I may be sticking my nose where it doesn't belong. So then I try to back down and not be so forward.

    —Lyssa

relativist position The view that the particular language individuals speak, especially the structure of the language, shapes their perception of reality and cultural patterns. (Compare with **nominalist position** and **qualified relativist position.**)

The Relativist Position   According to the **relativist position,** the particular language we speak, especially the structure of that language, determines our thought patterns, our perceptions of reality, and, ultimately, important cultural components. This position is best represented by the Sapir-Whorf hypothesis. As you may recall from Chapter 2, this hypothesis was proposed by Edward Sapir (1921), a linguist, and his student, Benjamin Whorf (1956), based on linguistic research they conducted in the 1930s and 1940s on Native American languages. They proposed that language is not merely an "instrument for voicing ideas but is itself the shaper of ideas, the guide for the individual's mental activity" (Hoijer, 1994, p. 194). According to the Sapir-Whorf hypothesis, language defines our experience. For example, there are no possessives (*his/her/our/your*) in the Diné (Navajo) language; we might conclude, therefore, that the Diné think in a particular way about the concept of possession. Another example is the variation in verb forms in English, Spanish, and French. In English and Spanish, the present continuous verb form is frequently used; thus, a student might say, "I am studying" or *"Estoy estudiando."* A French speaker, in contrast, would use the simple present form, *"J'étudie."* The Sapir-Whorf hypothesis suggests that, based on this variation in verb form, French, English, and Spanish speakers may think differently about movement or action.

Another frequently cited example involves variation in color vocabulary. The Diné use one word for blue and green, two words for two different colors of black, and one word for red; these four words form the vocabulary for primary colors in Diné culture. The Sapir-Whorf hypothesis suggests that English and Diné speakers perceive colors differently. Other examples of variations in syntax and semantics reflect differences in perception.

Similarly, people often cite the example of the languages of the Inuit or Yupik (incorrectly referred to as Eskimos) being rich in snow words. More recent research shows their snow vocabulary is no more extensive than that found in English (Pullum, 1991). However, scholars still say it is a handy example of the way proponents of the Sapir-Whorf hypothesis think about the relations between language and thought (Li & Geitman, 2002).

The Sapir-Whorf hypothesis has had tremendous influence on scholarly thinking about language and its impact on everyday communication. It questions the basic assumption that we all inhabit the same perceptual world, the same social reality.

Language is an important aspect of intercultural communication. The particular symbols used in any language are arbitrary and have no meaning in and of themselves, as these multilanguage optometrist charts illustrate. Language symbols communicate meaning only when used in particular contexts. (© *Bill Aron/Getty Images*)

However, the Sapir-Whorf hypothesis position has been critiqued by a number of studies that challenge the connection between language and how we think (Kenneally, 2008). The most recent position, the **qualified relativist position,** takes a more moderate view of the relationship between language and perception. Steven Pinker (2007), a renowned cognitive scientist, for example, cautions against assuming a simplistic connection between language and thought and rejects the Sapir-Whorf assumption that the particular language we speak compels us to perceive the world in a particular way or prevents us from thinking in different ways. At the same time, he also rejects the extreme nominalist position. He advocates a middle ground, suggesting that the meaning of our words depends on an underlying framework of basic cognitive concepts. The tenses of verbs, for example, are shaped by our innate sense of time. Nouns are constrained by our intuitive notions about matter. He uses the example of applesauce and pebbles to argue that we naturally categorize (and therefore label) these two substances differently (as "hunk" and "goo"). By looking at language from the perspective of our thoughts, he shows that what may seem like arbitrary aspects of speech (hunk and goo distinction) aren't arbitrary at all: They are by-products of our evolved mental machinery. In sum, all languages have the formal and expressive power to communicate the ideas, beliefs, and desires of their users. From this vast range of possibilities, human communities select what they want to say and how they want to say it (Li & Gleitman, 2002, p. 291). This view allows for more freedom than the Sapir-Whorf hypothesis. As you read the research findings that follow, you may see the wisdom of the qualified relativist position.

Recent Research Findings

language acquisition
The process of learning language.

There are three areas of research that investigate the Sapir-Whorf hypothesis: (1) children's **language acquisition,** (2) cross-cultural differences in language, and (3) cognitive development of children who are deaf. As you will see, most of the research in these areas does not support a strict interpretation of the Sapir-Whorf hypothesis.

Language Acquisition in Children   If language structures thought, then language must precede, and only subsequently influence, thought. This raises the question of whether it is possible to think without language. B. F. Skinner, Jean Piaget, Lev Vygotsky, and other psychologists have long wrestled with this question. As their works indicate, they seem to conclude that language and thought are so closely related that it is difficult to speak of one as initiating influence over the other. Their works thus do not provide evidence for a strong relativist position.

Cross-Cultural Differences in Language   Do groups with different language labels perceive the world in different ways? Consider a familiar example. Many men in the United States might identify someone's shirt as "red," whereas women viewing the same shirt might call it "cranberry" or "cherry" or "scarlet." Both the men and the women recognize the color distinctions, but men tend to use fewer words than women to distinguish colors.

The consensus has been that different ways to label color probably does not affect the perception of color in any systematic way. But very recent research shows that language might affect how quickly perceptions of color are categorized. While English speakers have one word for blue, Russian speakers have two words and distinguish between lighter blues (*goluboy*) and darker blues (*siniy*). In one study, Russian and English speakers were asked to look at three blocks of color and say which two were the same. If the Russians were shown three blue squares with two *goluboy* and one *siniy* or the other way around, they picked the two matching colors faster than if all three squares were shades from one blue group.

Other examples of cross-cultural research involves language and spatial reasoning. Can people who speak a language that has few words to describe spatial relationships (like right angles, parallel lines, triangles, etc.) recognize geometric relationships? The results of many recent studies say yes (Li & Gleitman, 2002). For example, one recent study focused on the Munduruku people, who live in isolated villages in Brazil, with no formal schooling. Their language has few words describing geometrical, or spatial, concepts and they had no rulers, compasses, or maps. Researchers showed the Munduruku subjects a diagram of three containers arranged in a triangle with one container identified as holding a hidden object. They were also shown three actual containers on the ground arranged in the same way. The subjects were then asked to identify which of three containers on the ground hid an object. The results showed that the Munduruku were able to relate the geometrical information on the map to the geometrical relationships on the ground at a rate of 71%, about the same as American subjects. They understood parallelism and right angles and can use distance, angles, and other relationships in maps to locate hidden objects. The finding suggests, contrary to the Sapir-Whorf hypothesis, that language is not required to think about or perceive the world in a particular way (Dehaene, Izard, Pica, & Spelke, 2006).

Another example of cross-cultural research involves variations in verb forms. The Chinese language has no counterfactual verb form (illustrated by "If I had known, I *would have gone*, but I did not"). Researchers constructed stories using the counterfactual form and found that the Chinese respondents understood the concept of counterfactual and could answer questions appropriately even though this structure is not present in Chinese (Au, 1983, 1984, 1985; Bloom, 1981, 1984). No evidence indicates that Chinese speakers are unable to think in terms of counterfactuals; rather, they simply do not normally express thoughts using such constructions. Although these research examples do not support the nominalist position, they do not provide strong evidence for the relativist position either.

Cognition of Children Who Are Deaf   Researchers have also tried to determine if children who are deaf or who have limited language use have diminished ability in perception or logical thinking. In one study, children with disabilities had the same categorizing competence, the same level of cognitive skill, as those children who could hear. The children were deficient in purely linguistic skills and short-term memory storage. The researchers concluded that children who are deaf do not seem to have a different worldview (Rhodda & Grove, 1987).

However, recent research comparing hearing children and home-signers (those who have hearing parents but hadn't learned sign language) found that children who knew spatial terms (e.g., middle, top, bottom) could locate a card in a box more quickly than those who did not. All the children were shown a box with cards; one card had a special star on the back. The children were asked to map the position of the target card in the first box to the same position in the second—similar to the activity in the study of the Munduruku. The researchers in this case found that those hearing children who knew words for spatial relationships had less trouble finding the special card in the second box than those without words for spatial relationship, whether young hearing children or home-signers. This may show that words can help us focus our thoughts . . . helps us carve up the world in specific ways (Kenneally, 2008).

Language and Thought: Metaphor

One way of thinking about the relationship between language and thought is to look at metaphors. A *metaphor* is an expression where a word (or words) is used outside of its normal conventional meaning to express a *similar* concept (Lakoff,

Because we live in a more global world, think about the impact of language differences in hospital emergency rooms, as well as other everyday needs, such as fire departments, police departments, and so on. How can we ensure adequate services for everyone?

When a Spanish-speaking hospital receptionist refused to interpret during her lunch hour, doctors at St. Vincent's Staten Island Hospital turned to a 7-year-old child to tell their patient, an injured construction worker, that he needed an emergency amputation.

With no one to bridge the language gap for another patient, a newly pregnant immigrant from Mexico with life-threatening complications, doctors pressed her to sign a consent form in English for emergency surgery. Understanding that the surgery was needed "to save the baby," the young married woman awoke to learn that the operation had instead left her childless and sterile. [. . .]

In some cases, the monitors themselves witnessed the medical consequences of communication failures. Ana Maria Archila, executive director of the Latin American Integration Center, an immigrant rights and social service agency, said she and two others overheard doctors at St. Vincent's telling a construction worker, through his 7-year-old cousin, that the worker needed an amputation.

"The child said, 'I'm not sure if they said foot or said toe,'" Ms. Archila recalled. "This worker, he was about to cry."

The monitors later learned that it was the man's third trip to the emergency room after a construction accident that had crushed his toe weeks earlier. Unable to explain his symptoms in English, he reported, he had been handled dismissively until he returned with his big toe blackened by gangrene.

Later, after the toe was amputated, Ms. Archila added, he had to rely on a patient in the next bed to translate the doctors' instructions for post-operative care.

Source: From N. Bernstein, "Language Barrier Called Health Hazard in E.R.," *New York Times*, April 21, 2005, p. B1.

1992). For example, "you are my sunshine." Although an individual cannot literally *be* sunshine, comparing someone to sunshine expresses a particular positive meaning. Experts used to think that metaphors are about language, or literary writing, not useful for understanding everyday speech. A famous cognitive scientist and linguist, George Lakoff, disagrees and proposes that metaphors are part of thinking, one way we organize our thoughts, in everyday living; in fact, metaphors are "a major and indispensable part of our ordinary conventional way of conceptualizing the world, and that our everyday behavior reflects our metaphorical understanding of experience" (p. 203).

Understanding a culture's metaphors, then, helps us understand something about the culture itself. Consider the English metaphor of likening love to a journey: *Our relationship has hit a dead-end street. Look how far we've come. It's been a long, bumpy road. We can't turn back now. We're at a crossroads. We may have to go our separate ways. The relationship isn't going anywhere. We're spinning our wheels. Our relationship is off the track.* These are ordinary, everyday English expressions. They are not poetic, nor are they necessarily used for special rhetorical effect, but for *reasoning about* our relationships (Lakoff, p. 205).

Metaphors can also be a useful way to understand other cultures. Some metaphors are universal, like the metaphor of an angry person as a pressurized container, for example (Kövecses, 2005). Consider these English phrases: "His pent-up anger *welled up* inside him. Billy's just *blowing off* steam. He was *bursting* with anger. When I told him *he just exploded.*" Other languages have similar expressions. The universality of the metaphor may rest in the universal human physiology—since physical bodily changes actually occur when we are angry (blood pressure rises, pulse rate increases, temperature rises). Metaphors may focus on different parts of the body; the Japanese, for example, have a number of metaphors that refer to the belly—where emotions are thought to rest. In contrast, U.S. Americans and Chinese tend to refer to the heart as the source of emotions (My heart is breaking; his heart swelled with pride).

In English, metaphors for happiness seem to center on a feeling of being up, light, fluid in a container (She was floating on air, bursting with happiness). However, the Chinese have a metaphor that does not exist in English—that happiness is flowers in the heart. Experts suggest that metaphors reflect cultural beliefs and values; in this case, the metaphor reflects the more restrained Chinese communication style, while the English metaphor of "happiness is being off the ground" reflects the relatively expressive English communication style (Kövecses, p. 71).

Cultural Variations in Communication Style

Language is powerful and can have tremendous implications for people's lives. For example, uttering the words *I do* can influence lives dramatically. Being called names can be hurtful and painful, despite the old adage "Sticks and stones can break my bones, but words will never hurt me."

The particular language we use predisposes us to think in particular ways and not in others. For example, the fact that English speakers do not distinguish between a formal and an informal *you* (as in German, with *du* and *Sie*, or in Spanish, with *tu* and *usted*) may mean that English speakers think about formality and informality differently than do German or Spanish speakers. In Japanese, formality is not simply noted by *you*; it is part of the entire language system. Nouns take the **honorific** "o" before them, and verbs take more formal and polite forms. Thus, "*Doitsu-go ga dekimasen*" [I—or you, he, she, we, they—don't speak German] is more polite and formal than "*Doitsu-go ga dekinai.*"

In other languages, the deliberate use of nonformal ways of speaking in more formal contexts can be insulting to another person. For example, French

honorific A term or expression that shows respect.

speakers may use the *tu* form when speaking to their dog or cat, but it can be insulting to use the *tu* form in a more formal setting when speaking to relative strangers. Yet it may be permissible to use the *tu* form in more social settings with relative strangers, such as at parties or in bars. Here, pragmatics becomes important. That is, we need to think about what else might be communicated by others and whether they shift to more informal ways of speaking.

INTERPRETIVE PERSPECTIVE ON LANGUAGE

communication style The metamessage that contexualizes how listeners are expected to accept and interpret verbal messages.

Communication style combines both language and nonverbal communication. It is the **metamessage** that contextualizes how listeners are expected to receive and interpret verbal messages. A primary way in which cultural groups differ in communication style is in a preference for high- versus low-context communication. A **high-context communication** style is one in which "most of the information is either in the physical context or internalized in the person, while very little is in the coded, explicit, transmitted part of the message" (Hall, 1976, p. 79). This style of communication emphasizes understanding messages without direct verbal communication. People in long-term relationships often communicate in this style. For example, one person may send a meaningful glance across the room at a party, and his or her partner will know from the nonverbal clue that it is time to go home.

metamessage The meaning of a message that tells others how they should respond to the content of our communication based on our relationship to them.

high-context communication A style of communication in which much of the information is contained in the contexts and nonverbal cues rather than expressed explicitly in words. (Compare with **low-context communication**.)

In contrast, in **low-context communication,** the majority of meaning and information is in the verbal code. This style of communication, which emphasizes explicit verbal messages, is highly valued in many settings in the United States. Interpersonal communication textbooks often stress that we should not rely on nonverbal, contextual information. It is better, they say, to be explicit and to the point, and not to leave things ambiguous. However, many cultural groups around the world value high-context communication. They encourage children and adolescents to pay close attention to contextual cues (body language, environmental cues), and not simply the words spoken in a conversation (Gudykunst & Matsumoto, 1996).

low-context communication A style of communication in which much of the information is conveyed in words rather than in nonverbal cues and contexts. (Compare with **high-context communication**.)

William Gudykunst and Stella Ting-Toomey (2003) identify two major dimensions of communication styles: direct versus indirect and elaborate versus understated.

Direct Versus Indirect Styles   This dimension refers to the extent to which speakers reveal their intentions through explicit verbal communication and emphasizes low-context communication. A direct communication style is one in which verbal messages reveal the speaker's true intentions, needs, wants, and desires. An indirect style is one in which the verbal message is often designed to camouflage the speaker's true intentions, needs, wants, and desires. Most of the time, individuals and groups are more or less direct depending on the context.

Many English speakers in the United States favor the direct speech style as the most appropriate in most contexts. This is revealed in statements like "Don't beat around the bush," "Get to the point," and "What exactly are you trying to say?" Although "white lies" may be permitted in some contexts, the direct style emphasizes honesty, openness, forthrightness, and individualism.

However, some cultural groups prefer a more indirect style, with the emphasis on high-context communication. Preserving the harmony of relationships has a higher priority than being totally honest. Thus, a speaker might look for a "soft" way to communicate that there is a problem in the relationship, perhaps by providing contextual cues (Ueda, 1974). Some languages have many words and gestures that convey the idea of "maybe." For example, three Indonesians studying in the United States were invited by their adviser to participate in a cross-cultural training workshop. They did not want to participate, nor did they have the time. But neither did they want to offend their professor, whom they held in high regard. Therefore, rather than tell him they couldn't attend, they simply didn't return his calls and didn't show up at the workshop.

An international student from Tunisia told Judith and Tom that he had been in the United States for several months before he realized that if someone was asked for directions and didn't know the location of the place, that person should tell the truth instead of making up a response. He explained that he had been taught that it was better to engage in conversation, to give *some* response, than to disappoint the person by revealing he didn't know.

Different communication styles are responsible for many problems that arise between men and women and between persons from different ethnic groups. These problems may be caused by different priorities for truth, honesty, harmony, and conflict avoidance in relationships.

Elaborate Versus Understated Styles This dimension of communication styles refers to the degree to which talk is used. The elaborate style involves the use of rich, expressive language in everyday talk. For example, the Arabic language has many metaphorical expressions used in everyday speech. In this style, a simple assertive statement means little; the listener will believe the opposite.

In contrast, the understated style values succinct, simple assertions, and silence. Amish people often use this style of communication. A common refrain is, "If you don't have anything nice to say, don't say anything at all." Free self-expression is not encouraged. Silence is especially appropriate in ambiguous situations; if one is unsure of what is going on, it is better to remain silent.

The exact style falls between the elaborate and the understated, as expressed in the maxim "Verbal contributions should be no more or less information than is required" (Grice, 1975). The exact style emphasizes cooperative communication and sincerity as a basis for interaction.

In international negotiations, visible differences in style can contribute to misperceptions and misunderstandings. For example, if we look at two open letters addressed to the Iraqi people in April 2003, we can see striking differences in the styles used by the British prime minister Tony Blair and the former Iraqi leader Saddam Hussein. Saddam Hussein was not captured by U.S. forces until

December 2003. On April 4, 2003, in a leaflet to be distributed to the Iraqi people, Mr. Blair writes:

From Tony Blair

As soon as Saddam Hussein's regime falls, the work to build a new free and united Iraq will begin. A peaceful, prosperous Iraq which will be run by and for the Iraqi people. Not by America, not by Britain, not by the UN—though all of us will help—but by you the people of Iraq.

For the first time in 25 years you will be free from the shadow of Saddam and can look forward to a new beginning for your families and your country.

That is already starting to happen in those parts of your country that have been liberated. But you want to know that we will stay to get the job done. You want to know that Saddam will be gone.

I assure you: he will be. Then, coalition forces will make the country safe, and will work with the United Nations to help Iraq get back on its feet. We will continue to provide immediate humanitarian aid, and we will help with longer-term projects.

Our troops will leave as soon as they can. They will not stay a day longer than necessary. (http://www.guardian.co.uk/Iraq/Story/0,2763,929934,00.html)

In contrast, Saddam Hussein spoke in a more indirect and elaborate style in his open letter to the Iraqi people on April 30, 2003:

From Saddam Hussein to the great Iraqi people, the sons of the Arab and Islamic nation, and honourable people everywhere.

Peace be upon you, and the mercy and blessings of God.

Just as Hulaku entered Baghdad, the criminal Bush entered it, with Alqami, or rather, more than one Alqami.

They did not conquer you—you who reject the occupation and humiliation, you who have Arabism and Islam in your hearts and minds—except through betrayal.

Indeed, it is not a victory while there is still resistance in your souls.

What we used to say has now become reality, for we do not live in peace and security while the deformed Zionist entity is on our Arab land; therefore there is no rift in the unity of the Arab struggle.

Sons of our great people:

Rise up against the occupier and do not trust anyone who talks of Sunni and Shia, because the only issue that the homeland—your great Iraq—faces now is the occupation.

There are no priorities other than driving out the infidel, criminal, cowardly occupier. No honourable hand is held out to shake his, but, rather, the hand of traitors and collaborators.

I say to you that all the countries surrounding you are against your resistance, but God is with you because you are fighting unbelief and defending your rights. (http://www.guardian.co.uk/Iraq/Story/0,2763,946805,00.html)

These different uses of language communicate different things to their culturally disparate audiences. As they also demonstrate, it is not easy to interpret language use from other people's perspectives.

Taking a dialectical perspective, though, should help us avoid stereotyping specific groups (such as Arabic or English speakers) in terms of communication style. We should not expect any group to use a particular communication style all the time. Instead, we might recognize that style operates dynamically and is related to context, historical forces, and so on. Furthermore, we might consider how tolerant we are when we encounter others who communicate in very different ways and how willing or able we are to alter our own style to communicate better.

Variations in Contextual Rules

Understanding some of the cultural variations in communication style is useful. A dialectical perspective reminds us that the particular style we use may vary from context to context. Think of the many contexts in which you communicate during the day—classroom, family, work, and so on—and about how you alter your communication to suit these contexts. You may be more direct with your family and less direct in classroom settings. Similarly, you may be more instrumental in task situations and more affective when socializing with your friends.

For example, one researcher studied the communication patterns involved in the common practice of "nagging" in U.S. American family contexts (Boxer, 2002). Nagging (repeated requests by one family member to another) usually concerns household chores and is often a source of conflict. More importantly, the communication practice seems to be related to issues of gender, power, and control. To be more specific, men are rarely perceived as the naggers; in this study, only six of the seventy sequences involved men nagging women. The researcher suggests that this is because they are perceived as having more power and, therefore, able to successfully request and gain compliance from another family member without resorting to nagging. This also means that children can have power (if they refuse to comply with a request despite lacking status), and parents can lack power despite having status. If our styles constrain how we request and respond to requests, then by nagging we lose power. Without power we are forced into nagging, and so it seems a vicious cycle.

A related study examines communication patterns in the Australian elementary school classroom, specifically "teacher talk" and how teachers dominate through their questioning of students, which makes up a large part of the student-teacher interaction (Gale & Cosgrove, 2004). These researchers, through analysis of very specific teacher-student exchanges, explore the power dynamics revealed in this questioning, as the teacher maintains her position of power as she gives the student a series of questions to which (she) already knows the answers. In this particular instance, the focus of the questions is concerned with eliciting responses from the student that the teacher then examines for their grammatical and pronunciation accuracy in a rather demeaning way. The researchers find that this particular type of "teacher talk" devalues and disempowers the students because of the focus on the "wrong" words they say, rather than values and empowers because of what they do know—taking away their confidence as speakers. In summary, they show how, in a classroom, many things teachers say—by virtue of nglish is spoken in many different ways around the world by native speakers of English, and there are even more nonnative speakers of English. How important is it to learn to listen to the many different world Englishes to be a better intercultural communicator?

There are now many times more nonnative speakers of English in the world than there are native speakers of English, and the gap is likely to widen. But higher education is heading in that direction much faster than are most Midwestern towns. [. . .]

The question is, do such academic breakdowns happen because universities aren't doing enough to prepare international teaching assistants for the classroom, or because American undergraduates, the beleaguered consumers themselves, simply tune out when faced with someone who is sufficiently different from them? [. . .]

In 1988 Donald L. Rubin, a professor of education and speech communication at the University of Georgia, began toying with an experimental model that would occupy him for the next several years: He gathered American undergraduates inside a classroom and then played a taped lecture for them over high-fidelity speakers. The lecture—an introduction to the Mahabharata, say, or a discourse on the growing scarcity of helium—was delivered in the voice of a man from central Ohio.

While the undergraduates sat and listened, they faced an image projected onto the classroom wall in front of them: Half the time, it was a photograph of an American man ("John Smith from Portland"), standing at a chalkboard and staring back at them. For the other half of the testing groups, the slide projected before them was that of an Asian man ("Li Wenshu from Beijing"), standing at the same chalkboard. The two figures were dressed, posed, and groomed as similarly as possible.

Now for the interesting part: When the students were asked to fill in missing words from a printed transcript of the central Ohioan's taped speech, they made 20 percent more errors when staring at the Asian man's image than they did when staring at a picture of "John Smith."

What did that mean? [. . .]

"All the pronunciation improvement in the world," he says, "will not by itself halt the problem of students' dropping classes or complaining about their instructors' language." [. . .]

Mr. Rubin, however, prefers to think of the issue in terms of prerequisites—worldly listening skills are a requirement for graduation. "I consider the ability to listen to and comprehend world Englishes a prerequisite to success in a wide variety of enterprises."

Source: From J. Gravois, "Teaching Impediment: When the Student Can't Understand the Instructor, Who Is to Blame?" *Chronicle of Higher Education,* April 8, 2005, pp. A10, A11, A12.

their position—would be deemed completely "out of line" if said by students, by virtue of their position. This might never be stated explicitly, but is learned through what is commonly referred to as schooling's "hidden curriculum" (Gale & Cosgrove, 2004). Both these studies show, through in-depth contextual analysis, that what we do with words affects many of our important relationships.

Many research studies have examined the rules for the use of socially situated language in specific contexts. They attempt to identify contexts and then "discover" the rules that apply in these contexts for a given speech community. Researchers Jack Daniel and Geneva Smitherman (1990) studied the communication dynamics in black churches. They first identified the priorities among congregation members: unity between the spiritual and the material, the centrality of religion, the harmony of nature and the universe, and the participatory, interrelatedness of life. They then described a basic communication format, the call-response, in both the traditional religious context and secular life contexts. In church, the speaker and audience interact, with sermons alternating with music. In secular life, call-response takes the form of banter between the rapper (rhetor) and others in the social group.

Daniel and Smitherman (1990) go on to discuss problems that can occur in black–white communication:

> When the Black person is speaking, the white person, because call-response is not in his cultural heritage, obviously does not engage in the response process, remaining relatively passive, perhaps voicing an occasional, subdued, "mmmmmmmmhm." Judging from the white individual's seeming lack of involvement in the communication, the Black communicator gets the feeling that the white isn't listening to him . . . and the white person gets the feeling that the Black person isn't listening because he keeps interrupting. (p. 39)

People communicate differently in different speech communities. Thus, the context in which the communication occurs is a significant part of the meaning. Although we might communicate in one way in one speech community, we might change our communication style in another. Understanding the dynamics of various speech communities helps us see the range of communication styles.

CRITICAL PERSPECTIVE ON LANGUAGE

Recall that discourse refers to language in use. This means that all discourse is social. The language used—the words and the meanings that are communicated—depends not only on the context but also on the social relations that are part of that interaction. For example, bosses and workers may use the same words, but the meanings communicated are not always the same. A boss and a worker may both refer to the company personnel as a "family." To the boss, this may mean "one big happy family," whereas to a disgruntled employee, it may mean a "dysfunctional family." To some extent, the disparity is related to the inequality between boss and worker, to the power differential.

In Chapter 2, we introduced communication accommodation theory. There are different ways that people accommodate or resist accommodating, depending on the situation. One such theory that encompasses various approaches is co-cultural communication, which we examine next.

Co-Cultural Communication

The co-cultural communication theory, proposed by communication scholar Mark Orbe (1998), describes how language works between dominant and non-dominant groups—or **co-cultural groups.** Groups that have the most power (whites, men, heterosexuals) consciously or unconsciously formulate a communication system that supports their perception of the world. This means that co-cultural group members (ethnic minorities, women, gays) must function in communication systems that often do not represent their experiences. Nondominant groups thus find themselves in dialectical struggles: Do they try to adapt to the dominant communication style, or do they maintain their own styles? Women in large male-dominated corporations often struggle with these issues. Do they adapt a male corporate style of speaking, or do they assert their own style?

co-cultural groups Nondominant cultural groups that exist in a national culture, such as African American or Chinese American.

In studying how communication operates with many different dominant and co-cultural groups, Orbe has identified three general orientations: nonassertive, assertive, and aggressive. Within each of these orientations, co-cultural individuals may emphasize assimilation, accommodation, or separation in relation to the dominant group. These two sets of orientations result in nine types of strategies (Table 6-2). The strategy chosen depends on many things, including preferred outcome, perceived costs and rewards, and context. These nine types of strategies vary from nonassertive assimilation, in which co-cultural individuals emphasize commonalities and avert controversy, to nonassertive separation, in which they avoid or maintain interpersonal barriers. Assertive assimilation strategies include manipulating stereotypes; assertive accommodation strategies include educating others, using liaisons, and communicating self. Aggressive assimilation involves strategies like ridiculing self and mirroring; aggressive accommodating involves confronting others; and aggressive separation involves attacking or sabotaging others.

The point here is that there are both costs and benefits for co-cultural members when they choose which of these strategies to use. Because language is structured in ways that do not reflect their experiences, they must adopt some strategy for dealing with the linguistic framework. For example, if Mark wants to refer to his relationship with Kevin, does he use the word *boyfriend, friend, roommate, husband, partner,* or some other word? If Mark and Kevin were married where it is legal, (e.g., Massachusetts, Canada, Belgium), should they refer to their "husband" when they are in places that explicitly say they do not recognize same-sex marriages from elsewhere, (e.g., Arizona, Michigan, Texas, or Colorado)? What about work? Thanksgiving dinner with the family? Let's look at how these strategies might work, the costs and the benefits of them.

TABLE 6-2 CO-CULTURAL COMMUNICATION ORIENTATIONS

	Separation	Accommodation	Assimilation
Nonassertive	Avoiding	Increasing visibility	Emphasizing commonalities
	Maintaining interpersonal barriers	Dispelling stereotypes	Developing positive face
			Censoring self
			Averting controversy
Assertive	Communicating self	Communicating self	Extensive preparation
			Overcompensating
	Intragroup networking	Intragroup networking	Manipulating stereotypes
			Bargaining
	Exemplifying strengths	Using liaisons	
		Educating others	
	Embracing stereotypes		
Aggressive	Attacking	Confronting	Dissociating
	Sabotaging others	Gaining advantage	Mirroring
			Strategic distancing
			Ridiculing self

Source: From M. Orbe, *Constructing Co-Cultural Theory: An Explication of Culture, Power, and Communication* (Thousand Oaks, CA: Sage, 1998), p. 110.

Assimilation Strategies   The three assimilation strategies are nonassertive, assertive, and aggressive. Some co-cultural individuals tend to use nonassertive assimilation strategies. These strategies emphasize trying to fit and be accepted by the dominant group. This strategy might be taken if the individual perceives that it is important not to "make waves" in this context. For example, in some work situations, people may benefit by keeping their jobs and feeling more accepted by co-workers. If these individuals hear the boss using sexist language, being insensitive to other religious holidays, joking about gays/lesbians, and so on, they may keep quiet or pretend not to hear what the boss said. There are potential costs to this approach, because these co-cultural individuals may feel they cannot be honest about themselves and may also feel uncomfortable reinforcing the dominant group's worldview and power.

The second assimilation strategy is assertive assimilation. Co-cultural individuals taking this strategy may downplay co-cultural differences and try to fit into the existing structures. Unlike the nonassertive assimilation strategy, this individual will try to fit in but also let people know how she or he feels from time to time. However, this strategy can promote an us-versus-them mentality, and some people find it difficult to maintain this strategy for very long.

The third assimilation strategy is aggressive assimilation. This strategy emphasizes fitting in, and co-cultural members who take this approach can go to great lengths to prove they are like members of the dominant group. Sometimes this means distancing themselves from other members of their co-culture, mirroring (dressing and behaving like the dominant group), or self-ridiculing. The benefit of this strategy is that the co-cultural member is not seen as "typical" of members of that co-culture. The cost may entail ridicule from members of that co-culture who may accuse this individual of acting white, thinking like a man, or "straight." This may lead to ostracizing of this person from the co-culture.

Accommodation Strategies Like assimilation strategies, there are three accommodation strategies: nonassertive, assertive, and aggressive. Nonassertive accommodation emphasizes blending into the dominant culture but tactfully challenging the dominant structure to recognize co-cultural practices. For example, a Jewish co-worker may want to put up a menorah near the company's Christmas tree as a way of challenging the dominant culture. By gently educating the organization about other religious holidays, the co-cultural member may be able to change their presumptions about everyone celebrating Christmas. Using this strategy, the co-cultural individual may be able to influence group decision making while still showing loyalty to the larger organization's goals. The cost of this strategy may be that others feel that she or he is not pushing hard enough to change larger structural issues in the organization. Also, this strategy does not really promote major changes in organizations to make them more inclusive and reflective of the larger society.

Assertive accommodation tries to strike a balance between the concerns of co-cultural and dominant group members. These strategies involve communicating self, doing intragroup networking, using liaisons, and educating others. For example, Asian American co-workers may share information about themselves with their co-workers, but they also share information about words that are offensive, such as *Oriental* and *slope*.

Aggressive accommodation strategies involve moving into the dominant structures and then working from within to promote significant changes—no matter how high the personal cost. Although it may seem as if co-cultural workers who use these strategies are confrontational or self-promoting, they also reflect a genuine desire to work with and not against dominant group workers. For example, a disabled co-worker may consistently remind others that facilities need to be more accessible, such as door handles, bathrooms that can accommodate wheelchairs, and so on.

Separation Strategies The three types of separation strategies are nonassertive, assertive, and aggressive. Nonassertive separation strategies are often used by those who assume that some segregation is part of everyday life in the United

States. For those in dominant groups, it is easier to live, work, learn, socialize, and pray with those who are like them. For co-cultural group members, it may take more effort to live as much as possible among those like them. So although it may not be possible for gay people to live only in a gay world, they can try to socialize as much as possible with other gays. The benefit of this approach is that co-cultural members do not have to deal with any negative feelings or stereotypes about their group, but the cost is that they cannot network and make connections with those in power positions.

Assertive separation strategies are used when a more conscious decision is made to maintain distance between dominant and co-cultural group members. Typical strategies my include stressing strengths and embracing stereotypes, as well as intragroup networking. One of the benefits of this approach, like the nonassertive separation strategy, is that it promotes co-cultural unity and self-determination. The cost, however, is that co-cultural group members must try to survive without having access to resources controlled by the dominant group.

Aggressive separation strategies are used by those who feel that is a high priority for dominant group or co-cultural group members. These strategies can include criticizing, attacking, and sabotaging others. The benefit of this approach for co-cultural members is that it enables them to confront pervasive, everyday, assumed discriminatory practices and structures. The cost may be that the dominant group retaliates against this open exposure of the presumed way of doing things.

Again, when confronted with various situations, dominant and co-cultural group members need to think carefully about how they wish to respond. There are benefits and costs to all of the decisions made. Although dominant group members are likely to be less harmed than co-cultural group members, everyone may suffer in the end. If Miguel is "cut out of the loop" at work and not told about an important meeting that affects his job, how should he handle this situation? He could pursue an assertive accommodation strategy and remind his co-workers that he needs to be included by pointing out when he is excluded. This could work and produce a more inclusive work environment, or the exclusion may continue because he is ignored. Or he could adopt a more aggressive accommodation strategy and meet with the manager and insist he be included. What are the costs and benefits of this approach? There are no easy answers, but it is important to consider what verbal communication strategy you may want to use when interacting in intercultural communication situations.

Discourse and Social Structure

Just as organizations have particular structures and specific positions within them, societies are structured so that individuals occupy social positions. Differences in **social positions** are central to understanding intercultural communication. For one thing, not all positions within the structure are equivalent; everyone is not the same. When men whistle at an attractive woman walking

social positions The places from which people speak that are socially constructed and thus embedded with assumptions about gender, race, class, age, social roles, sexuality, and so on.

by, it has a different force and meaning than if women were to whistle at a man walking by.

Power is a central element, by extension, of this focus on social position. For instance, when a judge in court says what he or she thinks *freedom of speech* means, it carries much greater force than when a neighbor or a classmate gives an opinion about what the phrase means. When we communicate, we tend to note (however unconsciously) the group membership and positions of communication participants. To illustrate, consider the previous example. We understand how communication functions, based on the group membership of the judge (as a member of the judicial system) and of the neighbors and classmates; we need know nothing about their individual identities.

Groups also hold different positions of power in the social structure. Because intercultural contact occurs between members of different groups, the positions of the groups affect communication. Group differences lend meaning to intercultural communication because, as noted previously, the concept of differences is key to language and the semiotic process.

The "Power" Effects of Labels

We often use labels to refer to other people and to ourselves. Labels, as signifiers, acknowledge particular aspects of our social identity. For example, we might label ourselves or others as "male" or "female," indicating sexual identity. Or we might say we are "Canadian" or a "New Englander," indicating a national or regional identity. The context in which a label is used may determine how strongly we feel about the label. On St. Patrick's Day, for example, someone may feel more strongly about being an Irish American than about being a woman or a student or a Texan.

Sometimes people feel trapped or misrepresented by labels. They might complain, "Why do we have to have labels? Why can't I just be me?" These complaints belie the reality of the function of discourse. It would be nearly impossible to communicate without labels. People rarely have trouble when labeled with terms they agree with—for example, "man," "student," "Minnesotan," or "Australian." Trouble arises, however, from the use of labels that they don't like or that they feel describe them inaccurately. Think about how you feel when someone describes you using terms you do not like.

Labels communicate many levels of meaning and establish particular kinds of relationships between speaker and listener. Sometimes people use labels to communicate closeness and affection for others. Labels like "friend," "lover," and "partner" communicate equality. Sometimes people intentionally invoke labels to establish a hostile relationship. Labels like "white trash" and "redneck" intentionally communicate inequality. Sometimes people use labels that are unintentionally offensive to others.

Many times, these labels are spoken without any knowledge or understanding of their meanings, origin, or even current implications and can demonstrate prejudicial feelings (Cruz-Jansen, 2002). For example, many descendents of Spanish-speaking people living in the United States reject the

I was born in Mexico but immigrated into the U.S. I am extremely proud of my Mexican heritage, and I usually feel offended when my identity is not respected. I have a slight accent and occasionally when I go out and mispronounce something people crack jokes. They think that it is all in good humor but it can be offensive. People connect too many stereotypes to Hispanics; society must learn to stop stereotyping minorities. When this happens then everyone can truly be united and respected, without preconceived notions based off a person's race.
   —Alejandro

My native language is Spanish. Since I was a little kid, I've been learning English so I already knew the language when I moved to the U.S. However, even to this day, I have trouble understanding slang. I feel uncomfortable when situations arise where I don't understand what is being said because of slang. . . . I think that when speaking with someone from another culture, specifically with someone who speaks (American) English as a second language, one must be more considerate toward that person's needs; e.g., speaking slower, repeating oneself if necessary, explaining and/or avoiding slang terms.
   —Sergio

term "Hispanic" since it was a census term created by the U.S. government in 1970 to identify a group of people; it was never used by people to describe themselves. Similarly, "Oriental" is a term rejected by many Asians and Asian Americans, and "homosexual" communicates negative characteristics about the speaker and establishes distance between the speaker and listener. Similarly, many indigenous people reject the term "Native American"—saying that it is only used by white people—preferring their more specific tribal name or the terms "American Indian" or "Indian." Many prefer "First Nations" people—to underscore the fact that tribes are in fact nations, recognized by the U.S. government (Yellow Bird, 1999).

Discourse is tied closely to social structure, so the messages communicated through the use of labels depend greatly on the social position of the speaker. If the speaker and listener are close friends, then the use of particular labels may not lead to distancing in the relationship or be offensive. But if the speaker and listener are strangers, then these same labels might invoke anger or close the lines of communication.

Furthermore, if the speaker is in a position of power, then he or she has potentially an even greater impact. For example, when politicians use discourse that invokes racist, anti-Semitic, or other ideologies of intolerance, many people become concerned because of the influence they may have. These concerns were raised in the 2002 presidential elections in France over candidate Jean-Marie Le Pen, whose comments over the years have raised concerns about anti-immigrant, anti-Semitic discourse. Similar concerns have arisen over the political discourse of Austria's Joerg Haider and Louisiana's David Duke. Of course, political office is not the only powerful position from which to speak. Fundamentalist Christian leaders have caused concern with their antigay discourse.

hris Matthews, host of MSNBC's *Hardball*, explains how he came to realize he had an accent in an interview with Blake Miller of *Philadelphia Magazine*. How do you know if you have an accent?

I don't think I ever realized I had a Philadelphia accent until I was away for a while in college and I began to understand that we really did talk differently than most people. Then I went to work in Washington for my first job in the Senate, and I remember meeting some people from out West, from Utah, and I would say "wooder" and they would say "wah-ter." It was like I was talking to cowboys.

We're the only city on the East Coast that pronounces our R's. They don't do it in Boston, certainly. They don't do it in New York. But we do it in Philly. We are loyal to the R.

We add an extra syllable to words, like Act-a-me. It's the extra, unexplained syllable that I think is the heart of the Philadelphia accent. It separates us from the lesser forms out there.

Source: From "Accent on Chris Matthews," *Philadelphia Magazine*, September 2005, p. 100.

Judith and Tom collaborated on a study about reactions to labeling. We asked white students which of the following they preferred to be called: white, Caucasian, white American, Euro-American, European American, Anglo, or WASP. They did not favor such specific labels as "WASP" or "European American" but seemed to prefer a more general label like "white." We concluded that they probably had never thought about what labels they preferred to be called. As we noted in Chapter 5, the more powerful aspects of identity seem to go unnoticed; for many people, whiteness just "is," and the preferred label is a general one that does not specify origin or history. Individuals from powerful groups generally do the labeling of others; they themselves do not get labeled (Martin, Krizek, Nakayama, & Bradford, 1996). For example, when men are asked to describe their identities, they often forget to specify gender as part of their identity. Women, in contrast, often include gender as a key element in their identity. This may mean that men are the defining norm and that women exist in relation to this norm. We can see this in the labels we use for men and women and for people of color. We rarely refer to a "male physician" or a "white physician," but we do refer to a "female doctor" or a "black doctor."

This "invisibility" of being white may be changing. Apparently, whites are becoming increasingly more conscious of their white identity, which may change the practice of labeling. Perhaps as the white norm is challenged by changing demographics, by increased interaction in a more diverse United States, and by racial politics, more whites may think about the meaning of labels for their own group.

MOVING BETWEEN LANGUAGES

Multilingualism

People who speak two languages are often called **bilingual;** people who speak more than two languages are considered **multilingual.** Rarely do bilinguals speak both languages with the same level of fluency. More commonly, they prefer to use one language over another, depending on the context and the topic. Sometimes entire nations are bilingual or multilingual. Belgium, for example, has three national languages (Dutch, German, and French), and Switzerland has four (French, German, Italian, and Romansh).

On either the individual or the national level, multilinguals must engage in language negotiation. That is, they need to work out, whether explicitly or implicitly, which language to use in a given situation. These decisions are sometimes clearly embedded in power relations. For example, French was the court language during the reign of Catherine the Great in 18th-century Russia. French was considered the language of culture, the language of the elite, whereas Russian was considered a vulgar language, the language of the uneducated and the unwashed. Special-interest groups in many U.S. states, especially Arizona and California, have attempted to pass laws declaring English the official language. These attempts reflect a power bid to determine which language will be privileged.

Sometimes a language is chosen as a courtesy to others. For example, Tom joined a small group going to see the fireworks display at the Eiffel Tower on Bastille Day one year. (Bastille Day is a French national holiday, celebrated on July 14, to commemorate the storming of the Bastille prison in 1789 and the beginning of the French Revolution.) One woman in the group asked, *"Alors, on parle français ou anglais?"* ["Are we speaking French or English?"]. Because one man felt quite weak at English, French was chosen as the language of the evening.

The reasons that people become bilingual reflect trends identified in Chapter 1—changes that drive the need for intercultural communication. Bilingualism results from these imperatives, as people move from one country to another, as businesses expand into international markets, and so on. More personal imperatives also drive people to become bilingual. Alice Kaplan (1993), a French professor at Duke University, notes, "Speaking a foreign language is, for me and my students, a chance for growth, for freedom, a liberation from the ugliness of our received ideas and mentalities" (p. 211). Many people use foreign languages to escape from a legacy of oppression in their own languages.

Perhaps it is easier to think of language as a "prisonhouse," to borrow Fredric Jameson's (1972) metaphor. All of the semantic, syntactic, pragmatic, and phonetic systems are enmeshed in a social system from which there is no escape, except through the learning of another language. Consider the case of Sam Sue (1992), a Chinese American born and raised in Mississippi, who

bilingual The ability to speak two languages fluently or at least competently.

multilingual The ability to speak more than two languages fluently or at least competently.

explains his own need to negotiate these social systems—often riddled by stigmatizing stereotypes—by changing the way he speaks:

> *Northerners see a Southern accent as a signal that you're a racist, you're stupid, or you're a hick. Regardless of what your real situation is. So I reacted to that by adapting the way I speak. If you talked to my brother, you would definitely know he was from the South. But as for myself, I remember customers telling my dad, "Your son sounds like a Yankee." (p. 4)*

Among the variations in U.S. English, the southern accent unwittingly communicates many negative stereotypes. Escaping into another accent is, for some, the only way to escape the stereotypes.

Learning another language is never easy, but the rewards of knowing another language are immense. Language acquisition studies have shown that it is nearly impossible for individuals to learn the language of a group of people they dislike. For instance, Tom was talking to a student about meeting the program's foreign language requirement. The student said, "I can't take Spanish. I'm from California." When Tom said that he did not understand what she meant, she blurted that she hated Mexicans and wouldn't take Spanish under any circumstances. As her well-entrenched racism suggested, she would indeed never learn Spanish.

interlanguage A kind of communication that emerges when speakers of one language are speaking in another language. The native language's semantics, syntactics, pragmatics, phonetics, and language styles often overlap and create a third way of communicating.

An interesting linguistic phenomenon known as **interlanguage** has implications for the teaching and learning of other languages. Interlanguage refers to a kind of communication that emerges when speakers of one language are speaking in another language. The native language's semantics, syntactics, pragmatics, and phonetics often overlap into the second language and create a third way of communicating. For example, many English-speaking female students of German might say, "*Ich bin ein Amerikanerin,*" which is incorrect German but is structured on the English way of saying, "I am an American." The correct form is "*Ich bin Amerikanerin.*" The insertion of "*ein*" reveals the English language overlap.

In his work on moving between languages, Tom has noted that this creation of other ways of communicating can offer ways of resisting dominant cultures. He notes that "the powerful potential of translation for discovering new voices can violate and disrupt the systemic rules of both languages" (Nakayama, 1997, p. 240). He gives the example of "*shiros,*" which is used by some Japanese Americans to refer to whites. *Shiro* is the color white, and adding an *s* at the end is the English grammatical way to pluralize words. Tom explains,

> *Using the color for people highlights the overlay of the ideology of the English language onto Japanese and an odd mixing that probably would not make sense to people who speak only English or Japanese, or those who do not live in the spaces between them. (p. 242n)*

Different people react differently to the dialectical tensions of a multilingual world. Some work hard to learn other languages and other ways of communicating, even if they make numerous errors along the way. Others retreat into their familiar languages and ways of living. The dialectical tensions that arise over different languages and different systems of meaning are played out around the world. But these dialectical tensions never disappear; they are always posing new challenges for intercultural communicators.

Translation and Interpretation

Because no one can learn all of the languages in the world, we must rely on translation and interpretation—two distinct but important means of communicating across language differences. The European Union (EU), for example, has a strict policy of recognizing all of the languages of its constituent members. Hence, many translators and interpreters are hired by the EU to help bridge the linguistic gaps.

Translation generally refers to the process of producing a written text that refers to something said or written in another language. The original language text of a translation is called the **source text;** the text into which it is translated is the **target text.**

Interpretation refers to the process of verbally expressing what is said or written in another language. Interpretation can either be simultaneous, with the interpreter speaking at the same time as the original speaker, or consecutive, with the interpreter speaking only during the breaks provided by the original speaker.

As we know from language theories, languages are entire systems of meaning and consciousness that are not easily rendered into another language in a word-for-word equivalence. The ways in which different languages convey views of the world are not equivalent, as we noted previously. Consider the difficulty involved simply in translating names of colors. The English word *brown* might be translated as any of these French words, depending on how the word is used: *roux, brun, bistre, bis, marron, jaune,* and *gris* (Vinay & Darbelnet, 1977, p. 261).

Issues of Equivalency and Accuracy   Some languages have tremendous flexibility in expression; others have a limited range of words. The reverse may be true, however, for some topics. This slippage between languages is both aggravating and thrilling for translators and interpreters. Translation studies traditionally have tended to emphasize issues of **equivalency** and accuracy. That is, the focus, largely from linguistics, has been on comparing the translated meaning with the original meaning. However, for those interested in the intercultural communication process, the emphasis is not so much on equivalence as on the bridges that people construct to cross from one language to another.

Many U.S. police departments are now hiring officers who are bilingual, because they must work with a multilingual public. In Arizona, like many other states, Spanish is a particularly important language. Let's look at a specific case in which a police detective for the Scottsdale (Arizona) Police Department explained an unusual phrase:

> *Detective Ron Bayne has heard his share of Spanish phrases while on the job. But he recently stumped a roomful of Spanish-speaking police officers with an unusual expression.*

translation The process of producing a written text that refers to something said or written in another language.

source text The original language text of a translation. (See also **target text.**)

target text The new language text into which the original language text is translated. (See also **source text.**)

interpretation The process of verbally expressing what is said or written in another language.

equivalency An issue in translation, the condition of being equal in meaning, value, quantity, and so on.

I would love to travel and experience all there is to experience. I think I would experience some culture shock because that is natural. I would want to learn some of the language that the country I would be going to speaks. I think that is extremely important because I should not expect everyone or anyone to speak my language. Seeing as how I am in their country, I should try to speak their language.
—Nate

I have learned some Spanish. I think that it is difficult to learn a new language when you are so set in your own language. I think it would be best to learn a second language when you are young.
—James

A suspect said, "Me llevaron a tocar el piano" [They took me to play the piano].
"I knew it couldn't mean that," said Bayne, a translator for the Scottsdale Police Department. "But I had no idea what it really meant." (Meléndez, 2002, p. B1)

This slang term, popular with undocumented aliens, highlights the differences between "street" Spanish and classroom Spanish. It also points to the importance of context in understanding meaning. In this context, we know that the police did not take a suspect to play a piano. Instead, this suspect was saying that the police had fingerprinted him. The varieties of expression in Spanish reflect social class and other differences that are not always communicated through translation or interpretation.

Yet the context for interpreters and translators must also be recognized. The need for Spanish speakers in the U.S. Southwest represents only the tip of the "linguistic iceberg." The recent attacks on the World Trade Center have created another need for translators and interpreters:

The CIA is looking for a few good speakers of Pashto. And Farsi, Dari and Arabic, too.

Backed with new funds from the White House in the wake of the Sept. 11 terrorist attacks, the spy agency has embarked on an urgent mission to reinforce its depleted ranks of specialists in the languages and cultures of other central Asia nations.

It is a part of the world the United States virtually ignored for the last decade. (Strobel, 2001)

The changing context for intelligence work has changed the context for translators and interpreters as well, to say nothing of the languages that are highly valued. These issues, although beyond the scope of equivalency and accuracy, are an important part of the dynamic of intercultural communication.

The Role of the Translator or Interpreter   We often assume that translators and interpreters are "invisible," that they simply render into the target language ranslation can create amusing and interesting intercultural barriers. Consider the following translation experiences.

1. A Canadian importer of Turkish shirts destined for Quebec used a dictionary to help him translate into French the label "Made in Turkey." His final translation: "Fabriqué en Dinde." True, "dinde" means "turkey." But it refers to the bird, not the country, which in French is Turquie.

2. An Otis Engineering Corp. display at a Moscow exhibition produced as many snickers among the Russians as it did praise. Company executives were not happy to learn that a translator had rendered in Russian a sign identifying "completion equipment" as "equipment for orgasms."

3. Japan's Olfa Corp. sold knives in the United States with the warning "Caution: Blade extremely sharp. Keep out of children."

4. In one country, the popular Frank Perdue Co. slogan, "It takes a tough man to make a tender chicken," read in local language something akin to "It takes a sexually excited man to make a chicken affectionate."

5. One company in Taiwan, trying to sell diet goods to expatriates living there, urged consumers to buy its product to add "roughage" to their systems. The instructions claimed that a person should consume enough roughage until "your tool floats." Someone dropped the "s" from "stool."

6. How about the Hong Kong dentist who advertised "Teeth extracted by the latest Methodists."

7. Or the hotel in notoriously polluted Mexico City that proclaimed: "The manager has personally passed all the water served here."

8. General Motors Corp.'s promotion in Belgium for its car that had a "body by Fisher" turned out to be, in the Flemish translation, "corpse by Fisher."

Source: From Laurel Delaney, "8 Global Marketing Gaffes," 2002. http://www.marketingprofs.com/2/delany2.asp.

whatever they hear or read. The roles that they play as intermediaries, however, often regulate how they render the original. Tom believes that it is not always appropriate to translate everything that one speaker is saying to another, in exactly the same way, because the potential for misunderstanding due to cultural differences might be too great. Translation is more than merely switching languages; it also involves negotiating cultures. Writer Elisabeth Marx (1999) explains,

> *It is not sufficient to be able to translate—you have to comprehend the subtleties and connotations of the language. Walter Hasselkus, the German chief executive of Rover, gave a good example of this when he remarked: "When the British say*

that they have a 'slight' problem, I know that it has to be taken seriously." There are numerous examples of misunderstandings between American English and British English, even though they are, at root, the same language. (p. 95)

It might be helpful to think of translators and interpreters as cultural brokers who must be highly sensitive to the contexts of intercultural communication.

We often assume that anyone who knows two languages can be a translator or an interpreter. Research has shown, however, that high levels of fluency in two languages do not necessarily make someone a good translator or interpreter. The task obviously requires the knowledge of two languages. But that's not enough. Think about all of the people you know who are native English speakers. What might account for why some of them are better writers than others? Knowing English, for example, is a prerequisite for writing in English, but this knowledge does not necessarily make a person a good writer. Because of the complex relationships between people, particularly in intercultural situations, translation and interpretation involve far more than linguistic equivalence, which traditionally has been the focus.

In his 1993 book *Contemporary Translation Theories*, linguist Edwin Gentzler speculates that the 1990s "might be characterized as experiencing a boom in translation theory" (p. 181). In part, this "boom" was fueled by a recognition that the traditional focus in translation studies is too limiting to explain the wide variety of ways that meanings might be communicated. Gentzler concludes, "With such insight, perhaps we will be less likely to dismiss that which does not fit into or measure up to our standards, and instead open ourselves to alternative ways of perceiving—in other words, to invite real intra- and intercultural communication" (p. 199).

The field of translation studies is rapidly becoming more central to academic inquiry as it moves from the fringes to an area of inquiry with far-reaching consequences for many disciplines. These developments will have a tremendous impact on how academics approach intercultural communication. Perhaps intercultural communication scholars will begin to play a larger role in the developments of translation studies.

LANGUAGE AND IDENTITY

In the previous chapter, we discussed cultural identity and its complexities. One part of our cultural identity is tied to the language(s) that we speak. As U.S. Americans, we are expected to speak English. If we travel to Nebraska, we assume the people there speak English. When we travel around the world, we expect Russians to speak Russian, Koreans to speak Korean, and Indonesians to speak Indonesian. But things get more involved, as we noted in Chapter 4, when we consider why Brazilians speak Portuguese, Congolese speak French, and Australians speak English. The relationship between language and culture becomes more complicated when we look at the complexity of cultural identities at home and abroad.

Language and Cultural Group Identity

When Tom was at the Arizona Book Festival recently, a white man held up a book written in Chinese and asked Tom what it was about. "I don't read Chinese," Tom replied. "Well, you should," he retorted and walked away. Two assumptions seem to be at work here: (1) Anyone who looks Asian must be Chinese, and (2) Asian Americans should be able to speak their ancestral languages. This tension has raised important identity questions for Asian Americans. Writer Henry Moritsugu (1992), who was born and raised in Canada and who later immigrated to the United States, explains,

> There is no way we could teach our children Japanese at home. We speak English. It wasn't a conscious effort that we did this. . . . It was more important to be accepted. . . . I wish I could speak the language better. I love Japanese food. I love going to Japanese restaurants. Sometimes I see Japanese groups enjoying themselves at karaoke bars . . . I feel definitely Western, more so than Asian. . . . But we look Asian, so you have to be aware of who you are. (p. 99)

The ability to speak another language can be important in how people view their group membership.

Many Chicana/os also have to negotiate a relationship to Spanish, whether or not they speak the language. Communication scholar Jacqueline Martinez (2000) explains,

> It has taken a long time for me to come to see and feel my own body as an ethnic body. Absent the capacity to express myself in Spanish, I am left to reach for less tangible traces of an ethnic self that have been buried under layers of assimilation into Anglo culture and practice. . . . Yet still there is a profoundly important way in which, until this body of mine can speak in Spanish, gesture in a "Spanishly" way, and be immersed in Spanish-speaking communities, there will remain ambiguities about its ethnic identification. (p. 44)

Although some people who migrate to the United States retain the languages of their homelands, many other U.S. American families no longer speak the language of their forebears. Historically, bilingualism was openly discouraged in the United States. Writer Gloria Anzaldúa (1987) recalls how she was discouraged from speaking Spanish:

> I remember being caught speaking Spanish at recess—that was good for three licks on the knuckles with a sharp ruler. I remember being sent to the corner of the classroom for "talking back" to the Anglo teacher when all I was trying to do was tell her how to pronounce my name. If you want to be American, speak "American." If you don't like it, go back to Mexico where you belong. (p. 53)

Even today we often hear arguments in favor of making English the official language of the nation. The interconnections between cultural identity and language are indeed strong.

Another intersection between identity and language occurred in 2006, when a controversy arose over the release by some Latino pop stars of a Spanish version anguages develop in relation to their environments. Changes in the global climate are bringing vast changes to the environment of the Arctic regions. Note how the indigenous languages are working to adapt to these changes.

What are the words used by indigenous peoples in the Arctic for "hornet," "robin," "elk," "barn owl" or "salmon?"

If you don't know, you're not alone.

Many indigenous languages have no words for legions of new animals, insects and plants advancing north as global warming thaws the polar ice and lets forests creep over tundra.

"We can't even describe what we're seeing," said Sheila Watt-Cloutier, chair of the Inuit Circumpolar Conference, which says it represents 155,000 people in Canada, Alaska, Greenland and Russia.

In the Inuit language Inuktitut, robins are known just as the "bird with the red breast," she said. Inuit hunters in north Canada recently saw some ducks but have not figured out what species they were, in Inuktitut or any other language.

[. . .]

In Arctic Europe, birch trees are gaining ground and Saami reindeer herders are seeing roe deer or even elk, a forest-dwelling cousin of moose, on former lichen pastures.

"I know about 1,200 words for reindeer—we classify them by age, sex, color, antlers," said Nils Isak Eira, who manages a herd of 2,000 reindeer in north Norway.

"I know just one word for elk—'sarvva'," said 50-year-old Eira. "But the animals are so unusual that many Saami use the Norwegian word 'elg.' When I was a child it was like a mythical creature."

Source: From A. Doyle, "As Ice Melts, Arctic People at Loss for Words." MSNBC, November 24, 2004. Available at http://www.msnbc.msn.com/id/6530026.

of the U.S. national anthem ("Star Spangled Banner"), with somewhat different lyrics ("The time has come to break the chains"), called *Nuestro Himno* (Our Anthem). For the song's producer and singers, it was about trying to help engage immigrants, as a tribute to the United States. For others, the national anthem was a symbol of unity that should be sung only in English. Here we see the importance of contexts. What many people don't know is that the national anthem was translated into Spanish (and many other languages) by the Bureau of Education and has been available in those languages since 1919—with no controversy until the issue becomes related to the current immigration debate (Goldstein, 2006).

What about the challenges facing cultural groups whose languages are nearing extinction? Whereas millions of people speak Chinese, Japanese, and Spanish, some languages are spoken by only a handful of people. One Osage Indian laments,

*Even though I am painfully aware of what needs to be said and how to say it, my
words usually fall upon noncomprehending ears, for only a handful of Osage Indians
can speak or understand our tribal language. And, after each such occasion,
I often silently lament that this may be the last time the Osage language is publicly
spoken and that within a mere 10 years it might not ever be heard again. (quoted
in Pratt & Buchanan, 2000, p. 155)*

Many Native American tribes are currently working to save their tribal languages, but they face enormous challenges. Yet it is their culture and identity
that are at risk.

The languages we speak and the languages others think we should speak can
create barriers in intercultural communication. Why might some U.S. Americans
assume that someone whose ancestors came from China continues to speak
Chinese, while someone whose ancestors came from Germany or Denmark is
assumed to no longer speak German or Dutch? Here, again, we can see how
identity, language, and history create tensions between who we think we are and
who others think we are.

Code Switching

Code switching is a technical term in communication that refers to the phenomenon of changing languages, dialects, or even accents. People code switch
for several reasons: (1) to accommodate the other speakers, (2) to avoid accommodating others, or (3) to express another aspect of their cultural identity.

Linguistics professor Jean-Louis Sauvage (2002) studied the complexity of
code switching in Belgium, which involves not only dialects but languages as
well. He explains the practical side of code switching:

*For example, my house was built by a contractor who sometimes resorted to
Flemish subcontractors. One of these subcontractors was the electrician. I spoke
Dutch to him but had to use French words when I referred to technical notions
that I did not completely understand even in French. This was not a problem for
the electrician, who knew these terms in Dutch as well as in French but would
have been unable to explain them to me in French. (p. 159)*

Given the complex language policies and politics in Belgium, code switching takes on particularly important political meaning. Who code switches and
who does not is a frequent source of contestation.

In her work on code switching, communication scholar Karla Scott (2000)
discusses how the use of different ways of communicating creates different cultural contexts and different relationships between the conversants. Based on a
series of interviews with black women, she notes "the women's shared recognition that in markedly different cultural worlds their language use is connected
to identity" (p. 246). She focuses on the use of the words *girl* and *look* as they
relate to communicative practices in different contexts. She identifies three areas
in which code switching occurs with *girl*: "(1) in discourse about differences
between Black and White women's language use, (2) in discourse about being

code switching A
technical term in communication that refers to the
phenomenon of changing
languages, dialects, or even
accents.

with other Black women, and (3) in uses of '*girl*' as a marker in discourse among participants during the interview" (p. 241). The use of *look* in code switching occurs in three contexts as well: "(1) in discussions and descriptions of talking like a Black woman versus White women's talk, (2) in the women's reports of interactions with Whites, both male and female, and (3) in the women's reports of interactions with Black men" (p. 243). *Girl* creates a sense of solidarity and shared identity among black women, whereas *look* is particularly important in white-dominated contexts because it asserts a different identity. Thus, code switching between these two words reflects different ways of communicating and different identities and relationships among those communicating.

There are similar examples of code switching between English and Spanish, as increasing numbers of U.S. Americans speak both languages—18 million now according to the U.S. census (Silverstein, 2007). Scholar Holly Cashman (2005) investigated how a group of bilingual women code switched during a game of *lotería* (Mexican bingo). She makes the point that code switching does not just demonstrate linguistic competence but, as in Scott's (2000) study, also communicates important information about ethnic identities and social position. Throughout the game, the women's choices to speak Spanish and/or English demonstrated various identifications and social places. When they preferred to speak Spanish, they were identifying inclusively with both English and Spanish speakers. In correcting other's language choices, they were also identifying as not just bilingual, but as arbiters of the spoken language. And in rejecting others' corrections of their language use, they were also asserting certain identifications, as when one woman in refusing another's correction of her Spanish "categorizes herself as 'Chicana,' bringing about a bilingual, oppositional social identity, and rejecting the social structures previously talked into being" (p. 313).

This discussion of code switching and language settings brings up the question of how does a bilingual person decide which language to speak in a setting where there are multiple languages spoken? Is it rude to switch between two languages when some people in the room only understand one language? As our student Liz describes (in the Student Voice box), this is not always an easy question to answer. A helpful theory here is Communication Accommodation Theory (CAT), discussed in Chapter 2. As you might remember, this theory posits that in some situations individuals change their communication patterns to accommodate others—depending on the situation and the attitude of the speaker toward other people. So, for example, if the situation is a neutral one and the speaker feels positively toward others, they will more likely accommodate others. This seems to be the case in Liz's family. Her father instructed her to accommodate everyone in the situation. Liz's experience at a recent party was different. Here, the Serbian speakers did not want to accommodate Liz. At the Salsa party, she tried to accommodate everyone, but it was difficult and her friends did not follow her lead. What is important to remember is that the outcome of accommodation is usually a positive feeling. However, in some situations (like high threat) speakers may not want to accommodate, may even want to accentuate their linguistic differences, or perhaps, as in Liz's Salsa party experience, the effort of accommodating is too challenging.

s it rude to code switch between languages when someone in the room only understands one of the languages?

Growing up in a household that predominately spoke Spanish was challenging when I brought friends over. Not everyone in my family spoke English and not all of my friends spoke Spanish. For as long as I can remember, my father expected me to translate everything that my friends and I said when family members were around us, even if they were not a part of the conversation. My father instilled the importance of respecting people around me by ensuring that everyone was included in the conversation, and to be sensitive to those around me who do not understand the language by giving them a general idea of what was being said.

As I have gotten older, I wonder when is it appropriate to switch languages when someone in the room does not understand the language being spoken. The first time that I really thought about this was when I attended a dinner at a friend's house. All of the people, excluding myself, were from Serbia. When one of the guests realized that I did not speak Serbian, she said, "Oh, so we will have to speak English all night?" My immediate reaction was that I did not think that everyone had to adjust to my needs. After all, this was their time to share food and conversations in their language.

However, I recently went Salsa dancing with a friend who did not speak Spanish. Knowing that most of the people around us were bilingual, I asked people if they could speak in English so that we did not exclude my friend. Most people would start speaking in English, but then break out into conversations in Spanish, which frustrated me. I ended up interpreting conversations for him and felt bad that he was excluded from the conversation. As I apologized to him, my friend said, "Don't feel bad. It is my fault that I do not speak Spanish."

Reflecting on these situations, I wondered when is it appropriate to code switch between languages when someone in the room only understands one of the languages? Why did I not think it was offensive in a situation where I was the one who did not understand and offensive when it was a friend of mine who did not?

—Liz

LANGUAGE POLITICS AND POLICIES

Nations can enact laws recognizing an official language, such as French in France or Irish in Ireland (despite the fact that more Irish speak English than Irish). Some nations have multiple official languages. For instance, Canada has declared English and French to be the official languages. Here in the United States, there is no official national language, although English is the de facto national language. Yet the state of Hawai'i has two official languages, English

FIGURE 6-2 Tensions between English and French speakers—shown by this photo taken near Montreal's Olympic Stadium—have led to the creation of language policies in Quebec. Some U.S. states have attempted to implement language policies as "English-only" laws. Do these language policies reduce or exacerbate intercultural communication problems? Why do some languages face more difficulty in their survival than others? (*Courtesy T. K. Nakayama*)

and Hawaiian. Other U.S. entities have also declared official languages, such as Guam (Chamorro and English), New Mexico (English and Spanish), and Samoa (English and Samoan). Laws or customs that determine which language is spoken where and when are referred to as **language policies.** These policies often emerge from the politics of language use. As mentioned previously, the court of Catherine the Great of Russia used not Russian but French, which was closely tied to the politics of social and economic class. The history of colonialism also influences language policies. Thus, Portuguese is the official national language of Mozambique, and English and French are the official national languages of Cameroon. (See Figure 6-2.)

language policies Laws or customs that determine when and where which language will be spoken.

Language policies are embedded in the politics of class, culture, ethnicity, and economics. They do not develop as a result of any supposed quality of the language itself. There are different motivations behind the establishment of language policies that guide the status of different languages in a place. Sometimes nations decide on a national language as part of a process of driving people to assimilate into the national culture. If the state wishes to promote assimilation, language policies that encourage everyone to speak the official language and conduct business in that language are promoted. One such group, U.S. English, Inc., has been advocating for the establishment of English as the official language of the United States.

Sometimes nations develop language policies as a way of protecting minority languages so these languages do not disappear. Welsh in Wales is one example, but Irish in Ireland and Frisian in Germany and the Netherlands are legally protected languages. Some language policies recognize the language rights of its citizens wherever they are in the nation. One example of this is Canada (English and French). Another is Kenya (Swahili and English). Government services are available in either language throughout the nation.

Other language policies are governed by location. In Belgium, Dutch (Flemish) is the official language in Flanders in the north part of the country. French is the official language in Wallonia in the South, and German is the official language in the Eastern Cantons bordering Germany. Thus, if you are boarding a train to go from Antwerp to Liège, you would need to look for "Luik" in the Antwerp train station. When you returned to the train station in Liège to go back, you would look for the train to "Anvers." The signs would not be posted in both languages, except in the Brussels-Capital region (the only bilingual part of the nation).

In Quebec, Canada, Law 101—passed in the early 1980s—required all Quebec students to attend French-speaking schools (unless their parents went to an English-speaking school in Quebec). So lots of immigrants from all over the world, few of whom spoke French, were required to attend French-speaking schools. Years later, these former students talked about this experience and how this law is changing Quebec. It's creating a more multicultural identity in contrast to previous years when most immigrants would choose English, leaving French to be spoken only by a small, relatively isolated group (Roy, 2007).

Sometimes language policies are developed with language parity, but the implementation is not equal. In Cameroon, for example, English and French are both official languages, although 247 indigenous languages are also spoken. Although Germany was the initial colonizer of Cameroon, Britain and France took over in 1916—with most of the territory going to France—and these "new colonial masters then sought to impose their languages in the newly acquired territory" (Echu, 2003, p. 34). At independence in 1960, French Cameroon established French as its official language and English became the official language in the former British Cameroon areas once they joined together to form Cameroon. Once united in 1961, Cameroon established both languages as official languages. Because French speakers are far more numerous than English speakers, "French has a de facto dominance over English in the areas of administration, education and the media. In fact, it is not an exaggeration to say that French influence as expressed in language, culture and political policy prevails in all domains" (p. 39). So although Cameroon is officially bilingual, French dominates in nearly all domains, because most of the people are French speakers. Thus, "what appears to be a language policy for the country is hardly clearly defined, in spite of the expressed desire to promote English-French bilingualism and protect the indigenous languages" (p. 44). European colonialism has left its mark in this African nation, and the language policy and language realities remain to be worked out.

We can view the development of language policies as reflecting the dialectical tensions between the nation's history and its future, between the various language communities, and between economic and political relations inside and outside the nation. Language policies can help resolve or exacerbate these tensions.

After interviewing many bilinguals, this author provides some general guidelines to help bilinguals know when to code switch.

CONVERSING IS NO SIMPLE MATTER FOR THE BILINGUAL

Cuban-born Maria Carreira, the co-author of two college Spanish textbooks, can glide easily between her native tongue and English. But in her daily life in Southern California, picking which language to speak can be very compli-cado. Such as the time when she was at a taco stand where everyone seemed to be ordering and chatting in Spanish. Carreira started placing her order en espanol, but she quickly switched to English after she got a look at the young employee behind the counter. "He had the bluest eyes," Carreira said. . . . Although the counterman responded in English, it dawned on her that he had been capably handling orders in Spanish. Yet her flub reflects a language-etiquette question confronted daily by the nation's growing ranks of English-Spanish bilinguals: When to use ingles and when to speak Spanish? . . . Still, among the estimated 18 million Americans proficient in both languages, according to the U.S. Census in September, the issue isn't whether to speak English or Spanish, but when. There's the delicate matter of courtesy—and avoiding bruised feelings. Occasionally, Carreira said, "it's a land mine." For example, switching to Spanish might seem rude if it suggests the other speaker is inept in English. Yet among Hispanics proud of their ethnic heritage, completely avoiding Spanish can come across as standoffish. Experts such as Carreira say the language decision among bilinguals is often made in a split second, based on cues such as age, clothing and apparent social status—along with skin, eye and hair color. Names can be giveaways—or traps. When University of California, Los Angeles student Maricruz Cecena introduced herself with a friendly hola to one of her freshman-year dormitory roommates, Laura Sanchez, and then tried to strike up a phone conversation in Spanish, all she got was an earful of English . . . . Sanchez can get by fairly well in Spanish but is much more comfortable in English, which was the primary language in her upper-middle-class Mexican-American home. She said she sometimes is intimidated by friends and acquaintances who speak Spanish better than she does. . . .

LANGUAGE AND GLOBALIZATION

In a world in which people, products, and ideas can move easily around the globe, rapid changes are being made in the languages spoken and learned. Globalization has sparked increased interest in some languages while leaving others to disappear.

The dream of a common international language has long marked Western ways of thinking. Ancient Greeks viewed the world as filled with Greek speakers or those who were *barbaroi* (barbarians). The Romans attempted to establish

As with all etiquette, making the other person comfortable is key.

K. C. McAlpin recalls making small talk recently with a night-crew janitor from Central America who was working at his office. The conversation started in English, but McAlpin, who grew up in Texas and worked in Latin America in the 1970s, decided to help the janitor when "she got hung up on some word." The conversation then resumed in Spanish. . . .

Although Carreira regrets the incident with the blue-eyed counterman, she has a finely honed sense of Spanish-English etiquette that leads her to use Spanish sparingly in public, unless she is approached in Spanish. . . . *Say Carreira needs directions and bumps into somebody who appears Hispanic. She'll ask in English and stick with the language even if the other person speaks with a heavy accent. Switching quickly to Spanish, Carreira reasons, would be "sort of saying, 'Huh, I get it. You can't speak English.' " But by refusing to speak Spanish, "you also risk coming across as aloof or superior, more Americanized, or not one of them," she said. The solution? Carreira will* continue an exchange in English to avoid insult but will toss in a well-pronounced gracias or por favor as "a way of being gracious and showing solidarity."

Among Hispanics, trying a little Spanish sometimes can defuse hostility. . . . *English-speakers struggling to use a few words of Spanish can, in some circumstances, come across very well. . . . But all too often, . . . English-speakers offend with fractured "mock Spanish" that [can be] considered racist—including "no problemo" and "comprendee?" . . .*

Source: From S. Silverstein, "Conversing Is No Simple Matter for the Bilingual, *Los Angeles Times,* November 15, 2007.

Latin and Greek, which led to the subsequent establishment of Latin as the learned language of Europe. Latin was eventually replaced by French, which was spoken, as we have noted, throughout the elite European communities and became the **lingua franca** of Europe. More recently, Esperanto was created as an international language, and although there are Esperanto speakers, it has not attained wide international acceptance. Today, Ancient Greek and Latin, as well as French, still retain some of their elite status, but "English is the de facto language of international communication today" (Tsuda, 1999, p. 153).

lingua franca A commonly shared language that is used as a medium of communication between people of different languages.

Many native English speakers are happy with the contemporary status of the language. They feel much more able to travel around the world, without the burden of having to learn other ways of communicating, given that many people around the world speak English. Having a common language also facilitates intercultural communication, but it can also create animosity among those who must learn the other's language. Dominique Noguez (1998) explains,

In these language affairs, as in many other moral or political affairs— tolerance, for example—is the major criteria for reciprocity. Between comparable

Harumi Befu, emeritus professor at Stanford University, discusses the consequences of English domination for monolingual Americans.

Instead of language enslavement and intellectual imperialism, however, one more often is told of the benefit of learning a second language, such as English. For example, non-native English speakers can relativize their own language and appreciate each language on its own terms. It was Goethe who said that one who does not know a foreign language does not know his/her own language. . . .

Thanks to the global dominance of their country, American intellectuals have acquired the "habitus" (Bourdieu) of superiority, whereby they exercise the license of expressing their thoughts in English wherever they go instead of showing respect to locals through expending efforts to learn their language. This privileged position, however, spells poverty of the mind.

For their minds are imprisoned in a single language; they are unable to liberate their minds through relativizing English. In short, other things being equal, monolingual Americans (not all Americans are monolingual) are the most provincial and least cosmopolitan among those who traffic in the global interlinguistic community—a price they pay for the strength of the country backing them.

Source: From H. Befu, "English Language Intellectual Imperialism and Its Consequences," *Newsletter: Intercultural Communication, 37* (Intercultural Communication Institute, Kanda University of International Studies, Japan), June 2000, p. 1.

languages and equal countries, this must be: I speak and learn your language and you speak and learn mine. Otherwise, it's sadomasochism and company—the sadist being simply the one with the gall to say to another: "I am not speaking your language, therefore speak mine!" This is what Anglo-Saxons have been happily doing since at least 1918. (p. 234)

(En ces affaires de langue, comme en bien d'autres affaires morales ou politiques—la tolérance, par exemple—le critère majeur, c'est la réciprocité. Entre langues comparables et pays égaux, ce devrait être: je parle et enseigne votre langue et vous parlez et enseignez la mienne. Autrement, c'est sadomasochisme et compagnie—le sadique étant tout simplement celui qui l'aplomb de declarer à l'autre: "Je ne parle pas votre langue, parlez donc la mienne!" C'est ce que font, avec assez de bonheur, les Anglo-Saxons depuis au moins 1918.)

Learning a foreign language is never easy, of course, but the dominance of English as the lingua franca raises important issues for intercultural communication.

What is the relationship between our four touchstones and this contemporary linguistic situation? That is, how do culture, communication, power, and context play out in the domination of English? First, the intimate connections between language and culture mean that the diffusion of English is tied to the olonial histories have influenced how people communicate. In Brazil, colonialists developed their own language to communicate across the many indigenous communities they colonized. Although imposed by colonists, today this general language is used to resist domination by Portuguese. How does a language serve political ends? What are the politics of speaking English in the world today?

When the Portuguese arrived in Brazil five centuries ago, they encountered a fundamental problem: the indigenous peoples they conquered spoke more than 700 languages. Rising to the challenge, the Jesuit priests accompanying them concocted a mixture of Indian, Portuguese and African words they called "língua geral," or the "general language," and imposed it on their colonial subjects.

Elsewhere in Brazil, língua geral as a living, spoken tongue died off long ago. But in this remote and neglected corner of the Amazon where Brazil, Colombia and Venezuela meet, the language has not only managed to survive, it has made a remarkable comeback in recent years. [. . .]

Two years ago, in fact, Nheengatú, as the 30,000 or so speakers of língua geral call their language, reached a milestone. By vote of the local council, São Gabriel da Cachoeira became the only municipality in Brazil to recognize a language other than Portuguese as official, conferring that status on língua geral and two local Indian tongues.

As a result, Nheengatú, which is pronounced neen-gah-TOO and means "good talk," is now a language that is permitted to be taught in local schools, spoken in courts and used in government documents. People who can speak língua geral have seen their value on the job market rise and are now being hired as interpreters, teachers and public health aides. [. . .]

"Nheengatú came to us as the language of the conqueror," explained Renato da Silva Matos, a leader of the Federation of Indigenous Organizations of the Rio Negro. "It made the original languages die out" because priests and government officials punished those who spoke any language other than Portuguese or Nheengatú.

But in modern times, the language acquired a very different significance. As the dominion of Portuguese advanced and those who originally imposed the language instead sought its extinction, Nheengatú became "a mechanism of ethnic, cultural and linguistic resistance," said Persida Miki, a professor of education at the Federal University of Amazonas.

Source: From L. Rohter, "Language Born of Colonialism Thrives Again in Amazon," *New York Times*, August 28, 2005, p. A6.

spread of U.S. American culture around the world. Is this a new form of colonialism? If we consider issues of power, what role does the United States play in the domination of English on the world scene? How does this marginalize or disempower those who are not fluent in English in intercultural communication?

WHERE DOES THAT LEAVE FRENCH?

This author argues (regretfully) that out of necessity, the United States needs to stop teaching so much French (and German) in high schools and colleges and concentrate more on other languages.

The United Nations General Assembly has proclaimed 2008 the International Year of Languages. . . . The U.S. needs to establish a longer-range strategic emphasis on the study of cultures, and widespread educational use of languages, to prevent such crises from occurring in the first place. How do we achieve these goals? Should we restore and expand upon the pattern of high school and college language instruction that existed in my youth, when four times as many college students studied "foreign languages"? The present essay lays out a position to which I have gradually and grudgingly been arriving over my nearly 50-year career as a student and teacher of languages and cultures. I was spurred to express this position publicly by recent global and national initiatives in the area of language education but also by an e-mail I received nearly a year ago:

> I teach French, Spanish, and an Intro to World Languages class at a public middle school in a rural community in Virginia. . . . I understand the rise of Spanish in light of the USA's changing demographics, and the wave of Arabic, Chinese, and Japanese with regard to global commerce and homeland security, BUT WHERE DOES THAT LEAVE FRENCH? Do you believe the need for French in the American classroom will continue to decline and become obsolete?

What follows is my latest, fullest response to this question, which I have been pondering ever since. Despite this deep-seated allegiance, I do regretfully conclude that the recent and projected continuing decline of French as one of the most widely studied languages in the U.S. is both inevitable and appropriate. So where does that leave French? . . . The French-speaking world uses not only European French but also the Frenches of the Canadian Québecois and of the numerous former French colonies in Africa and on many islands around the world. Spanish, though instructors also need to recognize Spanish dialect diversity, is probably the only one of the Big Three that will remain in the top 10 in U.S. education by the end of the 21st century. Likely members by then include Arabic, Bengali, Hindi/Urdu, Indonesian, Japanese, Korean, Mandarin, Portuguese, Russian, and Turkish.

Source: From H. S. Straight, 'But Where Does That Leave French?' *Inside Higher Ed. Com.* Retrieved May 9, 2008 from http://www.insidehighered.com/layout/set/print/views/2008/05/05/straight.

What kinds of resentment might be fostered by forcing people to recognize their disempowerment?

In what intercultural contexts is it appropriate to assume that others speak English? For English speakers, this is a particularly unique context. Latvians, for example, cannot attend international meetings and assume that others will speak

Latvian; and Albanians will have difficulty transacting international trade if they assume that others know their language.

This brings up the question of what languages U.S. Americans should be studying in order to communicate better with others in global contexts. For many years, the most studied languages in high schools and colleges in the United States were French, Spanish, and German (see the Point of View box "But Where Does That Leave French?"). However, some suggest that, in order for the United States to remain a key player on the global stage, its citizens should be studying Chinese and Arabic. Experts estimate that by the year 2015 China will have overtaken the United States as the predominant actor in the major power system (Kissane, 2005).

In his study of the developing use of English in Switzerland, Christof Demont-Heinrich (2005) focused on Switzerland in global and local contexts, cultural and national identity issues, power, and communication. The nation recognizes four national languages—French, German, Italian, and Romansh. Three of these are recognized as official languages—German, French, and Italian—which means that all national government materials are available in the three official languages. Some of the power differences among these language communities are reflected in the demographics from the 2000 census in which "63.9% of respondents named German, 19.5% listed French, 6.6% claimed Italian, and 0.5% named Romansch as their first language" (p. 72). In this context, English has become more influential, not only among the banking and financial sectors but increasingly in "consumer and pop culture" (p. 74). Recently, at the initiation of the Zürich canton, a proposal was made to allow English to be the first foreign language taught in school (rather than one of the national languages), and eight other German-speaking cantons quickly aligned themselves with this idea. The Swiss Conference of Cantonal Ministers of Education decided that by 2012 all Swiss students must study two foreign languages, but only one must be a national language. Given the value of English in the global economy and the use of English to communicate with other Swiss, one can see why there would be support for the Zürich position. Given the importance of Swiss national identity and their multilingual identity that is shaped by the languages spoken by other Swiss, one can also see why some French-speaking politicians preferred a policy where one of the other national languages would be the first foreign language. Zürich and other cantons are now proposing a ballot initiative that would "require just one foreign language to be taught, ideally English, at the primary school level" (p. 76), which would leave the other national language to be taught in secondary school. Demont-Heinrich concludes by noting that Romansh is likely headed for linguistic extinction, but what will happen to Switzerland? Can Swiss national identity be maintained with English? And what about the world? "Can such a colossal human social order sustain the diverse forms of human linguistic expression" (p. 81), or must humanity reduce its linguistic expression to a few dominant languages that facilitate economic trade? In the era of globalization, where economic growth is driven by external relations and trade, should we be studying Chinese?

http://anthro.palomar.edu/language/default.htm
This Web resource is an interactive guide to the relationships between language and culture. The site contains standard information on topics like "Language and Thought Processes." However, it also includes audio files that highlight regional differences in pronunciation and dialect.

www.aber.ac.uk/media/Documents/S4B/semiotic.html
This is an excellent resource for students seeking additional information on semiotics. This semiotics guide is complete with charts, easy-to-understand text, and lists of other resources. For those of you looking to write a paper using semiotics, the last chapter listed is a "do-it yourself" guide to semiotics analysis!

www.us-english.org/
www.lsadc.org/
These two Web sites contain very different views on the "English-only" issue in the United States. The group US English is a strong advocate for English-only within the United States. Its Web site contains lots of information about the group's legislative activities and political agenda. The second Web site is the home page of the Linguistic Society of America. This group was not formed to counter English-only policies, but it is a strong advocate of a multilingual society. The group's statement on language rights can be found at www.smo.uhi.ac.uk/saoghal/mion-chanain/LSA_statement.txt.

http://babelfish.altavista.digital.com/translate.dyn
This Web site is an example of one of the ways that technology is changing translation. The "Babel" feature, which can be added to Web content, translates from a great number of languages to a great number of languages. A similar feature is also available in the on-line community of Second Life. What opportunities and challenges does automated translation present for intercultural communication?

- The social science approach focuses on individual aspects of language. The interpretive approach focuses on contextual aspects of language. The critical approach emphasizes the role of power in language use.

- There are different positions on the relationship between language and our perceptions. The nominalist position feels that our perception is not shaped by the language we speak. The relativist position argues that our perception is determined by the language we speak. The qualified relativist position argues that language influences how we perceive.

- Communication styles can be high context or low context, more direct or indirect, or more elaborate or understated.

- Co-cultural groups may use one of three orientations to dealing with dominant groups—assimilation, accommodation, or separation. Within each of these approaches are nonassertive, assertive, and aggressive strategies. Each of these strategies comes with benefits and costs to the co-cultural individual.
- We use language from our social positions, and the power of our language use and labels comes from that social position.
- People can be bilingual or multilingual, and they may engage in code switching or changing languages in different situations, depending on the contexts.
- Translation refers to expressing what was said in another language in a written text. Interpretation is the same process but is oral rather than written.
- Language policies are instituted with different goals. Sometimes language policies are meant to encourage assimilation into a language and national identity. Sometimes language policies are meant to provide protection to minority languages. Sometimes language policies regulate language use in different parts of a nation.
- Globalization has meant that English has become more important worldwide but also has created other intercultural communication conflicts.

DISCUSSION QUESTIONS

1. Why is it important for intercultural communication scholars to study both language and discourse?
2. What is the relationship between our language and the way we perceive reality?
3. What are some cross-cultural variations in language use and communication style?
4. What aspects of context influence the choice of communication style?
5. What does a translator or an interpreter need to know to be effective?
6. Why is it important to know the social positions of individuals and groups involved in intercultural communication?
7. Why do some people say that we should not use labels to refer to people but should treat everybody as individuals? Do you agree?
8. Why do people have such strong reactions to language policies, as in the "English-only" movement?
9. In what ways is the increasing and widespread use of English around the world both a positive and a negative change for U.S. Americans?

Go to the self-quizzes on the Online Learning Center at www.mhhe.com/ martinnakayama5 to further test your knowledge.

ACTIVITIES

1. *Regional Language Variations.* Meet in small groups with other class members and discuss variations in language use in different regions of the United States (accent, vocabulary, and so on). Identify perceptions that are associated with these variations.

2. *"Foreigner" Labels.* Meet in small groups with other class members and generate a list of labels used to refer to people from other countries who come to the United States—for example, "immigrants" and "aliens." For each label, identify a general connotation (positive, negative, mixed). Discuss how connotations of these words may influence our perceptions of people from other countries. Would it make a difference if we referred to them as "guests" or "visitors"?

3. *Values and Language.* Although computer-driven translations have improved dramatically over earlier attempts, translation is still intensely cultural. Communication always involves many layers of meaning, and when you move between languages, there are many more opportunities for misunderstanding. Try to express some important values that you have (e.g., freedom of the press) on this Web site, and see how they are retranslated in five different languages: http://www.tashian.com/multibabel/.

KEY WORDS

bilingual (241)	International Phonetic	multilingual (241)
co-cultural groups (234)	Alphabet (IPA) (220)	nominalist position
code switching (249)	interpretation (243)	(221)
communication	language	qualified relativist
style (228)	acquisition (224)	position (223)
equivalency (243)	language policies (252)	relativist position (222)
high-context	lingua franca (255)	social positions (237)
communication (228)	low-context	source text (243)
honorific (227)	communication (228)	target text (243)
interlanguage (242)	metamessage (228)	translation (243)

The Online Learning Center at www.mhhe.com/martinnakayama5 features flashcards and crossword puzzles based on these terms and concepts.

REFERENCES

Anzaldúa, G. (1987). *Borderlands/la frontera: The new mestiza.* San Francisco: Spinsters/Aunt Lute.

Au, T. K. (1983). Chinese and English counterfactuals: The Sapir-Whorf hypothesis revisited. *Cognition, 15,* 155–187.

Au, T. K. (1984). Counterfactuals: In reply to Alfred Bloom. *Cognition, 17,* 239–302.

Au, T. K. (1985). Language and cognition. In L. L. Lloyd & R. L. Schiefelbusch (Eds.), *Language perspectives II.* Baltimore: University Park Press.

Barthes, R. (1980). *Elements of semiology* (A. Lavers & C. Smith, Trans.). New York: Hill & Wang. (Original work published 1968)

Befu, H. (2000, June). English language intellectual imperialism and its consequences. *Newsletter: Intercultural Communication, 37* (Intercultural Communication Institute, Kanda University of International Studies, Japan), p. 1.

Boxer, D. (2002). Nagging: The familial conflict arena. *Journal of Pragmatics, 34,* 49–61.

Cashman, H. (2005). Identities at play: Language preference and group membership in bilingual talk in interaction *Journal of Pragmatics, 37,* 301–315.

Cruz-Janzen, M. (2002). Lives on the crossfire: The struggle of multiethnic and multiracial Latinos for identity in a dichotomous and racialized world. *Race, Gender & Class, 9*(2), 47–62.

Daniel, J. L., & Smitherman, G. (1990). How I got over: Communication dynamics in the Black community. In D. Carbaugh (Ed.), *Cultural communication and intercultural contact* (pp. 27–40). Hillsdale, NJ: Lawrence Erlbaum.

Dehaene, S., Izard, V., Pica, P., & Spelke, E. (2006). Core knowledge of geometry in an Amazonian indigene group. *Science, 311,* 381–384.

Demont-Heinrich, C. (2005). Language and national identity in the era of globalization: The case of English in Switzerland. *Journal of Communication Inquiry, 29,* 66–84.

Desnoes, E. (1985). The death system. In M. Blonsky (Ed.), *On signs* (pp. 39–42). Baltimore: Johns Hopkins University Press.

Echu, G. (2003). Coping with multilingualism: Trends in the evolution of language policy in Cameroon. *PhiN, 25,* 31–46. Available at http://web.fuberlin .de/phin/phin25/p25t2.htm#ech99b

Gale, T., & Cosgrove, D. (2004). 'We learnt that last week': Reading into the language practices of teachers. *Teachers and Teaching: Theory and Practice, 10*(2), 125–134.

Gentzler, E. (1993). *Contemporary translation theories.* New York: Routledge.

Goldstein, D. (2006, May 6). National anthem in other languages? Heard this before. *Seattle Times.* Retrieved April 28, 2008 from http://seattletimes .nwsource.com/html/nationworld/ 2002975852_anthem06.html.

Grice, H. (1975). Logic and conversation. In P. Cole & J. Morgan (Eds.), *Syntax and semantics: Vol. 3. Speech acts.* New York: Academic Press.

Gudykunst, W. B., & Matsumoto, Y. (1996). Cross-cultural variability of communication in personal relationships. In W. B. Gudykunst, S. Ting-Toomey, & T. Nishida (Eds.), *Communication in personal relationships across cultures* (pp. 19–56). Thousand Oaks, CA: Sage.

Gudykunst, W. B., & Ting-Toomey, S. (2003). *Communicating with strangers: An approach to intercultural communication* (4th ed.). New York: McGraw-Hill.

Hall, E. T. (1976). *Beyond culture.* Garden City, NY: Doubleday.

Hill, P., & Van Zyl, S. (2002). English and multilingualism in the South African engineering workplace, *World Englishes, 21*(1) 23–35.

Hoijer, H. (1994). The Sapir-Whorf hypothesis. In L. Samovar & R. E. Porter (Eds.), *Intercultural communication: A reader* (pp. 194–200). Belmont, CA: Wadsworth.

Jameson, F. (1972). *The prisonhouse of language.* Princeton, NJ: Princeton University Press.

Kaplan, A. (1993). *French lessons: A memoir.* Chicago: University of Chicago Press.

Karlson, D. (2005, December 2). Swastika on sign unnerves residents. *The Cape Codder.* http://www .townonline.com/brewster/localRegional/view .bg?articleid=382002&format=&page=1

Kenneally, C. (2008, April 22). When language can hold the answer. *The New York Times,* p. F1.

Kissane, D. (2005). 2015 and the rise of China: Power cycle analysis and the implications for Australia, *Security Challenges, 1*(1), 105–121.

Kövecses, Z. (2005). *Metaphor in culture: Universality and variation.* Cambridge: Cambridge University Press.

Lakoff, G. (1989). Some empirical results about the nature of concepts. *Mind & Language, 4,* 103–129.

Lakoff, G. (1992). The contemporary theory of metaphor. In Ortony, A. (Ed.), *Metaphor and thought* (2nd ed.) (pp. 202–251). New York: Cambridge University Press.

Li, P., & Gleitman, L. (2002). Turning the tables: Language and spatial reasoning. *Cognition,* 265–294.

Martin, J. N., Krizek, R. L., Nakayama, T. K., & Bradford, L. (1996). Exploring whiteness: A study of self-labels for White Americans. *Communication Quarterly, 44,* 125–144.

Martinez, J. (2000). *Phenomenology of Chicana experience and identity: Communication and transformation in praxis.* Lanham, MD: Rowan & Littlefield.

Marx, E. (1999). *Breaking through culture shock.* London: Nicholas Brealey.

Meléndez, M. (2002, April 7). Police try to connect, reach out in Spanish. *The Arizona Republic,* p. B1.

Mendoza-Denton, N. (1999). Fighting words: Latina girls, gangs and language attitudes. In D. G. Galindo & M. D. Gonzales (Eds.), *Speaking Chicana: Voice, power, and identity* (pp. 39–56). Tucson: University of Arizona Press.

Moritsugu, H. (1992). To be more Japanese. In J. F. J. Lee (Ed.), *Asian Americans* (pp. 99–103). New York: New Press.

Nakayama, T. K. (1997). Les voix de l'autre. *Western Journal of Communication, 61*(2): 235–242.

Noguez, D. (1998). *La colonisation douce: Feu la langue française, carnets, 1968–1998*. Paris: Arléa.

Orbe, M. P. (1998). *Constructing co-cultural theory: An explication of culture, power, and communication.* Thousand Oaks, CA: Sage.

Pinker, S. (2007). *The stuff of thought: Language as a window into human nature.* New York: Viking.

Pratt, S. B., & Buchanan, M. C. (2000). Wa-zha-zhe-i-e: Notions on a dying ancestral language. In A. Gonzàley, M. Houston, & U. Chen (Eds.), *Essays in culture, ethnicity, and communication* (3rd ed., pp. 155–163). Los Angeles: Roxbury.

Pullum, G. K. (1991). *The great Eskimo vocabulary hoax and other irreverent essays on the study of language.* Chicago, IL: University of Chicago Press.

Rhodda, M., & Grove, C. (1987). *Language, cognition, and deafness.* Hillsdale, NJ: Lawrence Erlbaum.

Roy, J-H. (2007, September 15). *Les enfants de la loi 101* (Children of Law 101). *L'actualite, 32*(14), 34–50.

Sapir, E. (Ed.). (1921). *Language: An introduction to the study of speech.* New York: Harcourt, Brace & World.

Saussure, F. de. (1966). *Course in general linguistics* (C. Bally & A. Sechehaye, Eds. W. Baskin, Trans.). New York: McGraw-Hill.

Sauvage, J.-L. (2002). Code-switching: An everyday reality in Belgium. In J. N. Martin, T. K. Nakayama, & L. A. Flores (Eds.), *Readings in intercultural communication: Experiences and contexts* (2nd ed., pp. 156–161). New York: McGraw-Hill.

Scott, K. D. (2000). Crossing cultural borders: "Girl" and "look" as markers of identity in Black women's language use. *Discourse & Society, 11*(2): 237–248.

Silverstein, S. (2007, November 12). Biding their tongues. *Los Angeles Times,* p. A1.

Straight, H. S. (2008, May 5). 'But where does that leave French?' From *Inside Higher Ed. Com.* Retrieved May 9, 2008 from http://www .insidehighered.com/layout/set/print/ views/2008/05/05/straight.

Strobel, W. P. (2001, November 16). Language, cultural void: CIA urgently seeks Afghan, central Asian linguists. *Detroit Free Press.* www.freep.com/ news/nw/terror2001/spies16_20011116.htm

Sue, S. (1992). Growing up in Mississippi. In J. F. J. Lee (Ed.), *Asian Americans* (pp. 3–9). New York: New Press.

Tsuda, Y. (1999). The hegemony of English and strategies for linguistic pluralism: Proposing the ecology of language paradigm. In M. Tehranian (Ed.), *Worlds apart: Human security and global governance* (pp. 153–167). New York: Tauris.

Ueda, K. (1974). Sixteen ways to avoid saying "no" in Japan. In J. C. Condon & M. Saito (Eds.), *Intercultural encounters with Japan* (pp. 185–192). Tokyo: Simul Press.

Vinay, J. P., & Darbelnet, J. (1977). *Stylistique comparée du français et de l'anglais: Méthode de traduction.* Paris: Marcel Didier.

West, F. (1975). *The way of language: An introduction.* New York: Harcourt Brace Jovanovich.

Whorf, B. L. (1956). *Language, thought and reality.* Cambridge, MA: MIT Press.

Yellow Bird, M. (1999). What we want to be called. *American Indian Quarterly, 23*(2), 1–20.

NONVERBAL CODES AND CULTURAL SPACE

CHAPTER OBJECTIVES

After reading this chapter, you should be able to:

1. Understand how verbal and nonverbal communication differ.
2. Discuss the types of messages that are communicated nonverbally.
3. Identify cultural universals in nonverbal communication.
4. Explain the limitations of some cross-cultural research findings.
5. Define and give an example of cross-cultural differences in facial expressions, proxemics, gestures, eye contact, paralanguage, chronemics, and silence.
6. Discuss the relationship between nonverbal communication and power.
7. Define cultural space.
8. Describe how cultural spaces are formed.
9. Explain why it is important to understand cultural spaces in intercultural communication.
10. Understand the differences between the modernist and postmodern views of cultural spaces.

Nonverbal elements of cultural communication are highly dynamic and play an important role in understanding intercultural communication. Consider misunderstandings based on differing expectations for spatial distance. For example, a new co-worker from Mexico who is accustomed to closer spatial distances stands closer to you than you are comfortable with and you back up to become comfortable, what does this action communicate to your co-worker? The consequences for this encounter may be a bit awkward, but in some other instances, understanding nonverbal communication can be a key to survival. A recent news story published by the *Institute for War and Peace Reporting* describes how nonverbal behaviors at military checkpoints in Baghdad play an important role in the safety and security of Iraqi civilians:

> *A Sunni driver coming up to a security post he believes is under Shia control should not only have the right ID to hand over, but should also push in a tape playing Shia religious songs and turn up the volume. He should hang a picture of Imam Ali, the son-in-law of the Prophet Muhammad and the most revered figure in the Shia faith, from the rear-view mirror. He might also slip on the large silver ring worn only by Shias, especially those considered to be descendants of the Prophet, and perhaps carry a "torba," the round piece of clay that Shias often place on their foreheads when they bow down in prayer. These and other handy tips are given on the Iraqi Rabita website, designed to advise Sunnis on how to get through Shia checkpoints. (Checkpoints: Baghdad's Russian Roulette, 2007)*

In another instance, military investigators asked U.S. soldiers if they had shot at women and children in cars at checkpoints, and one soldier answered, "Yes." Asked why, he replied, "They didn't respond to the signs [we gave], the presence of troops or warning shots. Basically, we were at a checkpoint, we had two Arabic signs that said to turn around or be shot. Once [they passed] . . . the first sign, they fired a warning shot. If they passed the second sign, they shot the vehicle. Sometimes it bothers me, "What if they couldn't read the signs?" (Smith & Tyson, 2005).

You may never need to know the right nonverbal behavior to pass through a military checkpoint (see Figure 7-1), but you certainly will find yourself in many intercultural communication situations and cultural spaces. Your own nonverbal communication may create additional problems and, if the behaviors are inappropriate for the particular cultural space, may exacerbate existing tensions. In other cases, your use of nonverbals might reduce tension and confusion.

The first part of this chapter focuses on the importance of understanding nonverbal aspects of intercultural communication. We can examine nonverbal communication in terms of the personal–contextual and the static–dynamic dialectics. Although nonverbal communication can be highly dynamic, personal space, gestures, and facial expressions are fairly static patterns of specific nonverbal communication codes. These patterns are the focus of the second part of this chapter. Finally, we investigate the concept of cultural space and the ways in which cultural identity is shaped and negotiated by the cultural spaces (home, neighborhood, and so on) that people occupy.

There are no guidebooks for reading everyday nonverbal behaviors, and nonverbal communication norms vary from culture to culture; therefore, we

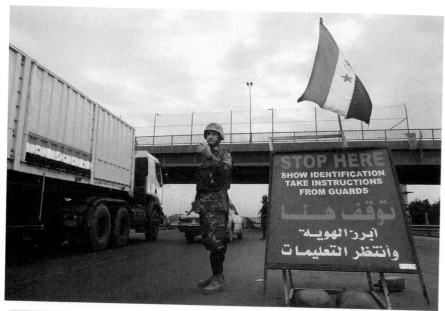

FIGURE 7-1   Nonverbal behaviors at military checkpoints in Iraq play an important role in the safety and security of Iraqi civilians. (© *Wathiq Khuzaie/Getty Images*)

believe it is useless to list nonverbals to memorize. Instead, it will be more beneficial for you to learn the framework of nonverbal communication and cultural spaces so you can tap into the nonverbal systems of whatever cultural groups become relevant to your life. Understanding communication is a matter of understanding how to think dialectically about *systems* of meaning, and not discrete elements. Nonverbal intercultural communication is no exception.

THINKING DIALECTICALLY ABOUT NONVERBAL COMMUNICATION: DEFINING NONVERBAL COMMUNICATION

In this chapter, we discuss two forms of communication beyond speech. The first includes facial expression, personal space, gestures, eye contact, paralanguage, use of time, and conversational silence. (What is not said is often as important as what is spoken.) The second includes the cultural spaces that we occupy and negotiate. **Cultural spaces** are the social and cultural contexts in which our identity forms—where we grow up and where we live (not necessarily the physical homes and neighborhoods, but the cultural meanings created in these places).

In thinking dialectically, we need to consider the relationship between the nonverbal behavior and the cultural spaces in which the behavior occurs, and

cultural space The particular configuration of the communication that constructs meanings of various places.

between the nonverbal behavior and the verbal message. Although there are patterns to nonverbal behaviors, they are not always culturally appropriate in all cultural spaces. Remember, too, that some nonverbal behaviors are cultural, whereas others are idiosyncratic, that is, peculiar to individuals.

Comparing Verbal and Nonverbal Communication

Recognizing Nonverbal Behavior   Both verbal and nonverbal communication are symbolic, communicate meaning, and are patterned—that is, they are governed by contextually determined rules. Societies have different nonverbal languages, just as they have different spoken languages. However, some differences between nonverbal and verbal communication codes have important implications for intercultural interaction.

Let's look at some examples of these differences. The following incident occurred to Judith when she was new to Algeria, where she lived for a while. One day she stood at her balcony and waved to one of the young Algerian teachers, who was walking across the school yard. Several minutes later, the young teacher knocked on the door, looking expectantly at Judith, as if summoned. Because Judith knew that it was uncommon in Algeria for men to visit women they didn't know well, she was confused. Why had he come to her door? Was it because she was foreign? After a few awkward moments, he left. A few weeks later, Judith figured it out. In Algeria (as in many other places), the U.S. "wave" is the nonverbal signal for "come here." The young teacher had assumed that Judith had summoned him to her apartment. As this example illustrates, rules for nonverbal communication vary among cultures and contexts.

Let's consider another example. Two U.S. students attending school in France were hitchhiking to the university in Grenoble for the first day of classes. A French motorist picked them up and immediately started speaking English to them. They wondered how he knew they spoke English. Later, when they took a train to Germany, the conductor walked into their compartment and berated them in English for putting their feet on the opposite seat. Again, they wondered how he had known that they spoke English. As these examples suggest, nonverbal communication entails more than gestures—even our appearance can communicate loudly. The students' appearance alone probably was a sufficient clue to their national identity. One of our students explains,

> *When I studied abroad in Europe, London more specifically, our clothing as a nonverbal expression was a dead giveaway that we were from America. We dressed much more casual, wore more colors, and had words written on our T-shirts and sweatshirts. This alone said enough; we didn't even have to speak to reveal that we were Americans.*

As these examples also show, nonverbal behavior operates at a subconscious level. We rarely think about how we stand, what gestures we use, and so on.

I have a couple of good friends who are deaf, and it is evident that body language, eye contact, and visual communication are far more important in our conversations than between two hearing people. I found that both of my friends, who lived very close to me, would much rather stop by my house than call me on the relay. I can see the cultural implications of space and distance. We keep in touch mostly by using e-mail. It's funny because the e-mails that I get from those guys have more commonly used slang words than most of my hearing friends use. The question is: Do my friends understand the slang, make it a part of their language, and create a sign for it, or do they know the words through somewhat of a verbal exchange with the hearing?
   —Andrea

Occasionally, someone points out such behaviors, which brings them to the conscious level. Consider one more example, from our student Suzanne:

I was in Macedonia and I was traveling in a car, so I immediately put on my seat belt. My host family was very offended by this because buckling my seat belt meant I didn't trust the driver. After that I rode without a seat belt.

When misunderstandings arise, we are more likely to question our verbal communication than our nonverbal communication. We can search for different ways to explain verbally what we mean. We can also look up words in a dictionary or ask someone to explain unfamiliar words. In contrast, it is more difficult to identify nonverbal miscommunications or misperceptions.

Learning Nonverbal Behavior Whereas we learn rules and meanings for language behavior in grammar and language arts lessons, we learn nonverbal meanings and behaviors by more implicit socialization. No one explains, "When you talk with someone you like, lean forward, smile, and touch the person frequently, because that will communicate that you really care about him or her." In many contexts in the United States, such behaviors communicate immediacy and positive meanings (Jones, 2004; Rocca, 2004). But how is it interpreted if someone does not display these behaviors?

Sometimes, though, we learn strategies for nonverbal communication. Have you ever been told to shake hands firmly when you meet someone? You may have learned that a limp handshake indicates a weak person. Likewise, many young women learn to cross their legs at the ankles and to keep their legs together when they sit. These strategies combine socialization and the teaching of nonverbal codes.

Coordinating Nonverbal and Verbal Behaviors Nonverbal behaviors can reinforce, substitute for, or contradict verbal behaviors. For example, when we shake our heads and say "no," we are reinforcing verbal behavior. When we point instead of saying "over there," we are substituting nonverbal behavior for verbal communication. If we tell a friend, "I can't wait to see you," and then don't show up at the friend's house, our nonverbal behavior is contradicting the verbal message. Because nonverbal communication operates at a less conscious level, we tend to think that people have less control over their nonverbal behavior. Therefore, we often think of nonverbal behaviors as conveying the "real" messages.

What Nonverbal Behavior Communicates

relational messages
Messages (verbal and non-verbal) that communicate how we feel about others.

Although language is an effective and efficient means of communicating explicit information or content, every communication also conveys **relational messages**—information on how the talker wants to be understood and viewed by the listener. These messages are communicated not by words, but through nonverbal behavior, including facial expressions, eye gaze, posture, and even our tone of voice (Watzlawick, Beavin, & Jackson, 1967). Nonverbal behavior also communicates **status** and power. For example, a supervisor may be able to touch subordinates, but it is usually unacceptable for subordinates to touch a supervisor. Broad, expansive gestures are associated with high status; conversely, holding the body in a tight, closed position communicates low status.

status The relative position an individual holds in social or organizational settings.

deception The act of making someone believe what is not true.

In addition, nonverbal behavior communicates **deception.** Early researchers believed that some nonverbal behaviors (e.g., avoiding eye contact or touching or rubbing the face) indicated lying. However, as more recent research has shown, deception is communicated by fairly idiosyncratic behaviors and seems to be revealed more by inconsistency in nonverbal communication than by specific nonverbal behaviors (Henningsen, Cruz, & Morr, 2000; Lock, 2004; Vrij, 2004).

Most nonverbal communication about affect, status, and deception happens at an unconscious level. For this reason, it plays an important role in intercultural interactions. Both pervasive and unconscious, it communicates how we feel about each other and about our cultural groups.

expectancy violation theory The view that when someone's nonverbal behavior violates our expectations, these violations will be perceived positively or negatively depending on the specific context and behavior.

A useful theory in understanding nonverbal communication across cultures is **expectancy violation theory.** This theory suggests that we have expectations (mostly subconscious) about how others should behave nonverbally in particular situations. When these expectations are violated (e.g., when someone stands too close to us), we will respond in specific ways. If an act is unexpected and interpreted negatively, for example, when someone stands too close to us at a religious service, we tend to regard the person and the relationship rather negatively. However, if the act is unexpected and interpreted positively (e.g., an attractive person stands close at a party), we will probably regard the relationship rather favorably; in fact, more favorably than if someone stands the exact "expected" distance from us at a religious service or party. Because nonverbal communication occurs at a subconscious level, our negative or positive feelings toward someone may be due to the fact that they violated our expectations—without our realizing it (Burgoon, 1995; Floyd, Ramirez, & Burgoon, 2008).

THE UNIVERSALITY OF NONVERBAL BEHAVIOR

Most traditional research in intercultural communication focuses on identifying cross-cultural differences in nonverbal behavior. How do culture, ethnicity, and gender influence nonverbal communication patterns? How universal is most nonverbal communication? Research traditionally has sought to answer these questions.

As we have observed in previous chapters, it is neither beneficial nor accurate to try to reduce individuals to one element of their identity (gender, ethnicity, nationality, and so on). Attempts to place people in discrete categories tend to reduce their complexities and to lead to major misunderstandings. However, we often classify people according to various categories to help us find universalities. For example, although we may know that not all Germans are alike, we may seek information about Germans in general to help us communicate better with individual Germans. In this section, we explore the extent to which nonverbal communication codes are universally shared. We also look for possible cultural variations in these codes that may serve as tentative guidelines to help us communicate better with others. (See Figure 7-2.)

Recent Research Findings

Research investigating the universality of nonverbal communication has focused on four areas: (1) the relationship of human behavior to that of primates (particularly chimpanzees), (2) nonverbal communication of sensory-deprived children who are blind or deaf, (3) facial expressions, and (4) universal functions of nonverbal social behavior.

Chimpanzees and humans share many nonverbal behaviors. For example, both exhibit the eyebrow flash—a slight raising of the eyebrow that communicates recognition—one of the most primitive and universal animal behaviors. Primates and humans also share some facial expressions, and very recent research reveals another gesture shared by chimps and humans—the upturned palm, meaning "gimme." Chimps have been observed using it in the wild and in captivity, to ask other chimps to share food, for help in a fight, or to request a grooming session (Pollick, Jeneson, & de Waal, 2008). There do seem to be compelling parallels between specific facial expressions and gestures displayed by human and nonhuman primates, universally interpreted to hold similar meanings. However, it still remains true that communication among nonhuman primates, like chimps and monkeys, appears to be less complex than among humans (Preuschoft, 2000; Tierney, 2007)

Recent studies compared the facial expressions of children who were blind with those of sighted children and found many similarities. Even though the children who were blind couldn't see the facial expressions of others to mimic them, they still made the same expressions. This suggests some innate, genetic basis for these behaviors (Galati, Sini, Schmidt, & Tinti, 2003).

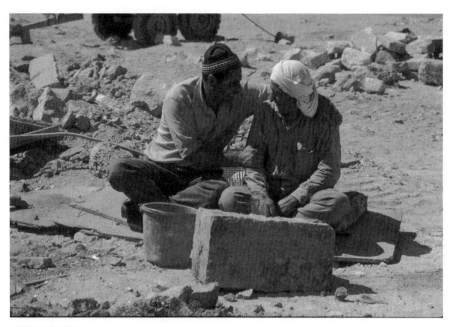

FIGURE 7-2 Nonverbal behavior can vary among cultures, in different settings, and with gender. In this photo, two men are conversing in Israel. Note the nonverbal behavior of these men—their postures, eye contact, physical contact, and facial expressions. These behaviors convey an informal social relationship among friends. How might these same nonverbal behaviors be interpreted in different settings? With strangers? (© Frank Siteman/Stock.Boston)

facial expressions
Facial gestures that convey emotions and attitudes.

Indeed, many cross-cultural studies support the notion of some universality in nonverbal communication, particularly in **facial expressions.** Several facial gestures seem to be universal, including the eyebrow flash just described, the nose wrinkle (indicating slight social distancing), and the "disgust face" (a strong sign of social repulsion). It is also possible that grooming behavior is universal (as it is in animals), although it seems to be somewhat suppressed in Western societies (Schiefenhovel, 1997). Recent findings indicate that at least six basic emotions—including happiness, sadness, disgust, fear, anger, and surprise—are communicated by similar facial expressions in most societies. Expressions for these emotions are recognized by most cultural groups as having the same meaning (Ekman, 2003; Matsumoto, Franklin, Choi, Rogers, & Tatani, 2002).

Recent research on the universality of nonverbal behavior has also focused on how some nonverbal behavior fills universal human social needs for promoting social affiliation or bonding. For example, according to this research, laughter is not just a message about the positive feeling of the sender but an attempt to influence others, to make them feel more positive toward the sender. Similarly, the social purpose of mimicry—when interaction partners adopt similar postures, gestures, and mannerisms—is to create an affective or social bond with others. Researchers point out that people in all cultures use these nonverbal behaviors to influence others, and over time, these behaviors that contributed to positive relationships were favored and eventually became automatic and non-conscious (Montepare, 2003; Patterson, 2003).

Although research may indicate universalities in nonverbal communication, some variations exist. The evoking stimuli (i.e., what causes the nonverbal behavior) may vary from one culture to another. Smiling, for example, is universal, but what prompts a person to smile may be culture-specific. Similarly, there are variations in the rules for nonverbal behavior and the contexts in which nonverbal communication takes place. For example, people kiss in most cultures, but there is variation in who kisses whom and in what contexts. When French friends greet each other, they often kiss on both cheeks but never on the mouth. Friends in the United States usually kiss on greeting only after long absence, with the kiss usually accompanied by a hug. The rules for kissing also vary along gender lines.

Finally, it is important to look for larger cultural patterns in the nonverbal behavior, rather than trying simply to identify all of the cultural differences. Researcher David Matsumoto (1990) suggests that although cultural differences in nonverbal patterns are interesting, noting these differences is not sufficient. Studying and cataloging every variation in every aspect of nonverbal behavior would be an overwhelming task. Instead, he recommends studying nonverbal communication patterns that vary with other cultural patterns, such as values.

For example, Matsumoto links cultural patterns in facial expressions with cultural values of power distance and individualism versus collectivism. Hypothetically, cultural groups that emphasize status differences will tend to express emotions that preserve these status differences. Matsumoto also suggests that within individualistic cultures the degree of difference in emotional display between ingroups and outgroups is greater than the degree of difference between the same groups in collectivistic societies. If these theoretical relationships hold true, we can generalize about the nonverbal behavior of many different cultural groups.

Nonverbal Codes

Facial Expressions As noted earlier, there have been many investigations of the universality of facial expressions. Psychologists Paul Ekman and Wallace Friesen (1987) conducted extensive and systematic research in nonverbal communication. They showed pictures of U.S. Americans' facial expressions reflecting six emotions thought to be universal to people in various cultural groups. They found that people in these various cultures consistently identified the same emotions reflected in the facial expressions in the photographs.

However, Ekman and Friesen's studies have been criticized for a few reasons. First, the studies don't tap into universality; that is, people may be able to recognize and identify the six emotions because of exposure to media. Also, the researchers presented a limited number of responses (multiple-choice answers) when they asked respondents to identify emotions expressed.

Later studies improved on this research. Researchers took many photographs, not always posed, of facial expressions of members from many different cultural groups; then they asked the subjects to identify the emotion conveyed by the facial expression. They showed these photographs to many different individuals in many different countries, including some without exposure to media. Their conclusion supports the notion of universality of facial expressions. Specifically, basic human emotions are expressed in a fairly finite number of facial expressions, and these expressions can be recognized and identified universally (Boucher & Carlson, 1980; Ekman, 2003).

Proxemics   Unlike facial expressions, the norms for personal space seem to vary considerably from culture to culture. As you may recall from Chapter 2, proxemics is the study of how people use various types of space in their everyday lives: fixed feature space, semifixed space, and informal space. Fixed feature space is characterized by set boundaries (divisions within an office building); semifixed feature space is defined by fixed boundaries such as furniture. Informal space, or personal space, is characterized by a personal zone or "bubble" that varies for individuals and circumstances. The use of each of these spatial relationships can facilitate or impede effective communication across cultures; the area that humans control and use most often is their informal space.

O. M. Watson (1970), a proxemics specialist, investigated nonverbal communication between Arab and U.S. students after hearing many complaints from each group about the other. The Arab students viewed the U.S. students as distant and rude; the U.S. students saw the Arab students as pushy, arrogant, and rude. As Watson showed, the two groups were operating with different rules concerning personal space. Watson's research supports Edward Hall's (1966) observations about the cultural variations in how much distance individuals place between themselves and others. Hall distinguished contact cultures from noncontact cultures. He described **contact cultures** as those societies in which people stand closer together while talking, engage in more direct eye contact, use face-to-face body orientations more often while talking, touch more frequently, and speak in louder voices. He suggested that societies in South America and southern Europe are contact cultures, whereas those in northern Europe, the United States, and the Far East are **noncontact cultures**—in which people tend to stand farther apart when conversing, maintain less eye contact, and touch less often. Subsequent research seems to confirm Hall's and Watson's early studies (Andersen, Hecht, Hoobler, & Smallwood, 2002).

Of course, many other factors besides regional culture determine how far we stand from someone. Gender, age, ethnicity, context, and topic all influence the use of personal space. In fact, some studies have shown that regional culture is perhaps the least important factor. For example, in many Arab and Muslim societies, gender may be the overriding factor, because unmarried men and women rarely stand close together, touch each other, or maintain direct eye contact. In contrast, male friends may stand very close together, kiss on the cheek, and even hold hands—reflecting loyalty, great friendship, and, most important, equality in status, with no sexual connotation (Fattah, 2005; Khuri, 2001).

Gestures   Gestures, perhaps even more so than personal space, vary greatly from culture to culture. (See Figure 7-3.) The consequences for this variation

contact cultures
Cultural groups in which people tend to stand close together and touch frequently when they interact—for example, cultural groups in South America, the Middle East, and southern Europe. (See **noncontact cultures.**)

noncontact cultures
Cultural groups in which people tend to maintain more space and touch less often than people do in contact cultures. For instance, Great Britain and Japan tend to have noncontact cultures. (See **contact cultures.**)

POTENTIALLY EMBARRASSING GESTURAL MIXUPS

U.S. Gesture	Other Interpretations
Waving good-bye	Come here (Japan)
Good luck sign	Boyfriend (Japan)
Screw you sign	I don't believe you (Uruguay)
OK sign	Money (Japan) Sex (Mexico) Homosexual (Ethiopia)
Slash across the throat	Lost job (Japan)

Source: From D. Archer, (1997), "Unspoken Diversity: Cultural Differences in Gestures, *Qualitative Sociology, 20:* 81.

can be quite dramatic, as President G. W. Bush discovered when he gave the "hook 'em horns" greeting to the University of Texas Longhorn marching band during his inauguration. The photos of this greeting were met with confusion in Norway, where the gesture is considered a salute to Satan ("Norwegians Confused by Bush 'Horns' Salute," 2005).

Researcher Dane Archer (1997) describes his attempt to catalogue the various gestures around the world on video. He began this video project with several hypotheses: first, that there would be great variation, and this he found to be true. However, more surprising, his assumption regarding the existence of some universal gestures or at least some universal *categories* of gestures (e.g., every culture must have an obscene gesture) was not confirmed.

He gathered his information by visiting English as a Second Language classes and asking international students to demonstrate gestures from their home cultures, resulting in the documentary *A World of Gestures: Culture and Nonverbal Communication.* He drew several conclusions from his study: first, that gestures and their meaning can be very subtle (see the box "Potentially Embarrassing Gestural Mix-ups"). His work "often elicited gasps of surprise, as ESL students from one culture discovered that what at first appeared to be a familiar gesture actually means something radically different in another society" (p. 87). For example, in Germany, and many other European cultures, the gesture for "stupid" is a finger on the forehead, the American gesture for "smart" is nearly identical, but the finger is held an inch to the side, at the temple. Similarly, the American raised thumb gesture of "way to go" is a vulgar gesture, meaning "sit on this" in Sardinia and "screw you" in Iran. And of course, we've already mentioned the difference between the the "hook 'em horns" gesture and the salute to Satan.

Second, Archer emphasizes that gestures are different from many other nonverbal expressions in that they are accessible to conscious awareness—they can be explained, illustrated, and taught to outsiders. Finally, as noted earlier, he had assumed there would be some universal categories—a gesture for "very good,"

FIGURE 7-3   Cultural groups vary in their norms for nonverbal greetings, e.g. a handshake, a bow. (© STOCK4B-RF/Getty Images)

a gesture for "crazy," an obscene gesture. Not so. A number of societies (e.g., the Netherlands, Norway, Switzerland) have no such gesture. In the end, he concludes that through making the video, "We all acquired a deeply enhanced sense of the power, nuances, and unpredictability of cultural differences" (p. 87). And the practical implication of the project was to urge travelers to practice "gestural humility"—assuming that the familiar gestures of our home culture will not mean the same things abroad and also "that we cannot infer or intuit the meaning of any gestures we observe in other cultures" (p. 80).

eye contact A nonverbal code, eye gaze, that communicates meanings about respect and status and often regulates turn-taking during interactions.

Eye Contact   **Eye contact** often is included in proxemics because it regulates interpersonal distance. Direct eye contact shortens the distance between two people, whereas less eye contact increases the distance. Eye contact communicates meanings about respect and status and often regulates turn-taking.

Patterns of eye contact vary from culture to culture. In many societies, avoiding eye contact communicates respect and deference, although this may vary from context to context. For many U.S. Americans, maintaining eye contact communicates that one is paying attention and showing respect.

When they speak with others, most U.S. Americans look away from their listeners most of the time, looking at their listeners perhaps every 10 to 15 seconds. When a speaker is finished taking a turn, he or she looks directly at the listener to signal completion. However, some cultural groups within the United States use even less eye contact while they speak. For example, some Native Americans tend to avert eye gaze during conversation.

ife-or-death decisions sometimes depend on subtle nonverbal signals like tone of voice. According to cross-cultural psychologist Harry Triandis (1994), the first Gulf War could have been avoided if not for a misinterpretation of paralinguistic cues.

In January, 1991, James Baker, then the United States Secretary of State, met with Tariq Aziz, the foreign minister of Iraq. They met in an effort to reach an agreement that would prevent a war. Also present in the room was the half-brother of Saddam Hussein, whose role included frequent calls to Hussein with updates on the talks. Baker stated, in his standard calm manner, that the U.S. would attack if Iraq did not move out of Kuwait. Hussein's half-brother heard these words and reported that "the Americans will not attack. They are weak. They are calm. They are not angry. They are only talking." Six days later Iraq saw Desert Storm and the loss of about 175,000 of their citizens. Triandis argued that Iraqis attend to how something is said more than what is said. He further suggests that if Baker had pounded the table, yelled, and shown outward signs of anger, the outcome may have been entirely different.

Source: H. C. Triandis, *Culture and Social Behavior.* (New York: McGraw-Hill, 1994). Cited in J. J. Blascovich and C. R. Hartel (Eds.), *Human Behavior in Military Contexts.* (National Research Council: The National Academies Press (Committee on opportunities in Research in Behavioral and Social Sciences for the U.S. Military), 2008).

Paralinguistics **Paralinguistics** refers to the study of paralanguage—vocal behaviors that indicate *how* something is said, include speaking rate, volume, pitch, and stress, among others. Saying something very quickly in a loud tone of voice will be interpreted differently from the same words said in a quieter tone of voice at a slower rate, as shown in the Point of View box describing the encounter between U.S. and Iraqi officials prior to the first Gulf War. There are two types of vocal behavior—voice qualities and vocalizations (Alberts, Nakayama, & Martin, 2007).

Voice qualities—or the nontechnical term, tone of voice—means the same thing as vocal qualities. Voice qualities include speed, pitch, rhythm, vocal range, and articulation; these qualities make up the "music" of the human voice. We all know people whose voice qualities are widely recognized. For example, the voice of actor Fran Drescher, who starred in the TV sitcom *The Nanny*, has been frequently remarked upon. Her trademark whiny chuckle and nasal voice allow her to be recognized no matter where she is. Speakers also vary in how they articulate sounds, that is, how distinctly they pronounce individual words and sounds. We tend not to notice these paralinguistic features unless someone articulates very precisely or very imprecisely. Paralinguistics often lead people to negatively evaluate speakers in intercultural communication contexts even when they don't understand the language. For example, Chinese speakers often sound rather musical and nasal to English speakers; English speakers sound rather harsh and guttural to French speakers.

paralinguistics The study of vocal behaviors include voice qualities and vocalization.

voice qualities The "music" of the human voice, including speed, pitch, rhythm, vocal range, and articulation.

vocalizations The sounds we utter that do not have the structure of language.

Vocalizations are the sounds we utter that do not have the structure of language. Tarzan's yell is one famous example. Vocalizations include vocal cues such as laughing, crying, whining, and moaning as well as the intensity or volume of one's speech. They also include sounds that aren't actual words but that serve as fillers, such as "uh-huh," "uh," "ah," and "er." The paralinguistic aspects of speech serve a variety of communicative functions. They reveal mood and emotion; they also allow us to emphasize or stress a word or idea, create a distinctive identity, and (along with gestures) regulate conversation. Paralanguage can be a confusing factor in intercultural communication. For example, Europeans interpret the loudness of Americans as aggressive behavior, while Americans might think the British are secretive because they talk quietly. The amount of silence in conversations and also the speaking rate differ among cultures. For instance, the Finnish and Japanese are comfortable having pauses in their conversations, while most U.S. Americans are seen to talk rapidly and are pretty uncomfortable with silences.

chronemics The concept of time and the rules that govern its use.

monochronic An orientation to time that assumes it is linear and is a commodity that can be lost or gained.

Chronemics   **Chronemics** concerns concepts of time and the rules that govern its use. There are many cultural variations regarding how people understand and use time. Edward Hall (1966) distinguished between monochronic and polychronic time orientation. People who have a **monochronic** concept of time regard it as a commodity: time can be gained, lost, spent, wasted, or saved. In this orientation, time is linear, with one event happening at a time. In general, monochronic cultures value being punctual, completing tasks, and keeping to schedules. Most university staff and faculty in the United States maintain a monochronic orientation to time. Classes, meetings, and office appointments start when scheduled; faculty members see one student at a time, hold one meeting at a time, and keep appointments except in the case of emergency. Family problems are considered poor reasons for not fulfilling academic obligations—for both faculty and students.

polychronic An orientation to time that sees it as circular and more holistic.

In contrast, in a **polychronic** orientation, time is more holistic, and perhaps more circular: Several events can happen at once. Many international business negotiations and technical assistance projects falter and even fail because of differences in time orientation. For example, U.S. businesspeople often complain that meetings in the Middle East do not start "on time," that people socialize during meetings, and that meetings may be canceled because of personal obligations. Tasks often are accomplished *because* of personal relationships, not in spite of them. International students and business personnel observe that U.S. Americans seem too tied to their schedules; they suggest that U.S. Americans do not care enough about relationships and often sacrifice time with friends and family to complete tasks and keep appointments.

Silence   Cultural groups may vary in the degree of emphasis placed on silence, which can be as meaningful as language (Acheson, 2007). One of our students recalls his childhood:

> *I always learned while growing up that silence was the worst punishment ever. For example, if the house chore stated clearly that I needed to take the garbage out,*

Giving gifts seems to be a universal way to please someone, if the gift is appropriate. One colleague of mine, Nishehs, once tried to impress our boss, Joe. Nishehs brought a well-wrapped gift to Joe when they first met with each other in person. Joe was indeed pleased as he received the gift from Nishehs, but his smile faded away quickly right after he opened the gift. Joe questioned Nishehs angrily, "Why is it green?" Shocked and speechless, Nishehs murmured, "What's wrong with a green hat?"

The miscommunication resulted from the cultural differences between them. Nishehs is an Indian, whereas Joe is Chinese. For the Chinese, a green hat means one's wife is having an extramarital affair.
—Chris

and I had not done so, then my mother would not say a word to me. And I would know right away that I had forgotten to do something.

In most U.S. American contexts, silence is not highly valued. Particularly in developing relationships, silence communicates awkwardness and can make people feel uncomfortable. According to scholar William B. Gudykunst's (1985, 2005) uncertainty reduction theory, the main reason for communicating verbally in initial interactions is to reduce uncertainty. In U.S. American contexts, people employ active uncertainty reduction strategies, such as asking questions. However, in many other cultural contexts, people reduce uncertainty using more passive strategies—for example, remaining silent, observing, or perhaps asking a third party about someone's behavior.

In a classic study on the rules for silence among the western Apache in Arizona, researcher Keith Basso (1970) identified five contexts in which silence is appropriate: (1) meeting strangers, (2) courting someone, (3) seeing friends after a long absence, (4) getting cussed out, and (5) being with people who are grieving. Verbal reticence with strangers is directly related to the conviction that the establishment of social relationships is a serious matter that calls for caution, careful judgment, and plenty of time.

Basso hypothesized that the underlying commonality in these social situations is that participants perceive their relationships vis-à-vis one another to be ambiguous and/or unpredictable and that silence is an appropriate response to uncertainty and unpredictability. He also suggested that this same contextual rule may apply to other cultural groups.

Communication scholar Charles Braithwaite (1990) tried to find out if Basso's rule applied to other communities. He compiled ethnographic accounts from 13 speech communities in which silence seems to play a similar role; these groups included Warm Springs (Oregon) Indians, Japanese Hawaiians, and 17th-century Quakers. Braithwaite extended Basso's rule when he determined that in many communities silence is not simply associated with uncertainty. Silence also is associated with social situations in which a known and unequal distribution of power exists among participants.

Recently, scholar Covarrubias (2007) points out that some of the early investigations of silence in American Indian communities did not fully value the communicative importance of silence in these and other cultures. She now encourages communication scholars to rethink the way they view silence, to see it not "as an absence, but, rather, as a fullness of opportunity for being and learning" (p. 270) and perhaps ask what can American Indian perspectives contribute to our knowledge of communication, "particularly to the much underengaged and much needed inquiry into the worlds humans create within silence?" (p. 271)

Recent research has found similar patterns in other cultures. For example, researchers have described the *Asaillinen* (matter-of-fact) verbal style among Finnish people that involves a distrust of talkativeness as "slickness" and a sign of unreliability (Carbaugh & Berry, 2001; Sajavaara & Lehtonen, 1997). Silence, for Finns, reflects thoughtfulness, appropriate consideration, and intelligence, particularly in public discourse or in educational settings like a classroom. In an ethnographic study investigating this communication pattern, Wilkins (2005) reports two excerpts from interviews that illustrate this pattern—one interview with a Finnish student and one with an American student:

Excerpt 1

Finnish Student: I have been to America.

Wilkins: Can you tell me what the experience was like?

Student: The people and the country were very nice.

Wilkins: Did you learn anything?

Student: No.

Wilkins: Why not?

Student: Americans just talk all the time.

Excerpt 2

Wilkins: Do you like Finland?

American Student: Oh yes, I like it a lot.

Wilkins: How about the people?

Student: Sure, Finns are very nice.

Wilkins: How long have you been at the university?

Student: About nine months already.

Wilkins: Oh, have you learned anything?

Student: No, not really.

Wilkins: Why not?

Student: Finns do not say anything in class.

In addition to a positive view of silence, nonverbal facial expressions in the *Asaillinen* style tend to be rather fixed—and expressionless. The American student, of course, did not have the cultural knowledge to understand what can be accomplished by thoughtful activity and silence.

Other scholars have reported similar distrust of talk in Japanese and Chinese cultures influenced by Confucianism and Taoism. Confucius rejected eloquent speaking and instead advocated hesitancy and humble talk in his philosophy of the ideal person (Chang, 1997; Kim, 2001). As one of our Taiwanese students told us, "In America, sometimes students talk about half the class time. Compared to my classes in Taiwan, if a student asked too many questions or expressed his/her opinions that much, we would say that he or she is a show-off."

In a recent review of scholarly research on silence, communication scholar Kris Acheson (2007) acknowledges that silence in the United States has often been associated with negative, unhealthy relationships, or with disempowerment, for example, when women and/or minorities feel their voices are not heard. However, she tells us that increasingly U.S. Americans recognize the positive and sometimes powerful uses of silences in certain contexts. For example, nurses and doctors are encouraged to honor silent patients and learn to employ silence in their ethical care; young people are advised to seek out silence in their lives for the sake of health and sanity, to even noiseproof their homes in an attempt to boost health. In business contexts, sometimes keeping quiet is the best strategy and talking too much can kill a business deal. In education, teachers can create a space for understanding rather than counterarguments by asking for silent reflection after comments or performances. Finally, she admits that in some contexts, like politics and law, silence is still seen as completely negative; for example, pleading the Fifth equates silence with guilt, silence by politicians is often viewed as too much secrecy.

Stereotype, Prejudice, and Discrimination

As noted previously, one of the problems with identifying cultural variations in nonverbal codes is that it is tempting to overgeneralize these variations and stereotype people. For example, psychologist Helmut Morsbach (1988) cautions us about comparing Japanese and Western attitudes toward silence. Based on his research and extensive experience in Japan, he identifies some of the subtleties of cultural patterns of silence. For instance, the television is on continuously in many Japanese homes, and tape-recorded comments about beauty are transmitted at Zen gardens. So, although many scholars suggest that silence might be a cultural ideal, things may be different in practice. In very specific situations (such as in mother–daughter relationships or in the hiding of true feelings), there may be more emphasis on silence in Japan than in comparable U.S. situations. Also, when communicating with strangers, the Japanese view silence as more negative than it is in the United States (Hasegawa & Gudykunst, 1998).

In any case, we would be wise to heed Morsbach's warning about generalizations. Cultural variations are tentative guidelines that we can use in intercultural interaction. They should serve as examples, to help us understand that there is a great deal of variation in nonverbal behavior. Even if we can't anticipate how other people's behavior may differ from our own, we can be flexible when we do encounter differences in how close someone stands or how she or he uses eye contact or conceptualizes time.

SOCIAL VERSUS PSYCHOLOGICAL DEFINITIONS OF RACISM: THE LESSONS OF KATRINA

Of the many sorry things about the contemporary United States that Hurricane Katrina made plain, perhaps none was more depressing than what it showed about the profound divide in how Americans think about race and racism.

This essay suggests that the debate over the racial meaning of Katrina exposes a public disagreement about the meaning of racism itself. The fundamental divide in the debate over racism in the United States today is between those who regard racism as essentially a question of individual psychology *as opposed to those who consider it a* social, structural *phenomenon.*

One of the things that makes discussing racism fundamentally challenging is the tendency . . . to equate racism with racial prejudice. . . . In this definition, racism is not a social condition but rather is something that exists in the minds of "racists."

It is widely and correctly observed that this sort of racial prejudice, or bigotry, has abated greatly in the last half century. Though racial prejudice certainly still exists, many fewer people despise others simply because of their skin color. . . .

The problem with equating racism with prejudice is that such a definition of racism fails to address the fact that racial discrimination takes place not merely through intentional (though perhaps unselfconscious) interactions between individuals, but also as a result of deep social and institutional practices and habits. . . .

The continued exclusion of blacks from certain prestigious, purely social organizations is the archetype for this sort of racism. Consider the stereotype of the all-white country club. The barrier to entry for blacks into these sorts of institutions is rarely an active rule *banning blacks from joining. Rather, what excludes blacks is that the club members know few if any black people as social equals* outside *the club. Now, it would be a mistake to conclude from this lack of black friends that the club members are necessarily prejudiced against black people. Rather, the club is simply an institutional manifestation of a longstanding social network of upper-class whites. For such a social set, it's not that they're against socializing with blacks (though maybe their parents or grandparents were), it's just that* as a matter of fact they don't *socialize with blacks. In the meanwhile, the club facilitates the making of money (within its narrow social circle), the reproduction of the elite (within the same narrow social circle), and thus generally works to assure the social replication of the longstanding racialist pattern,* all without a discriminatory thought ever entering anyone's head.

Moreover, it should be stressed that racism can replicate itself via a mere unwillingness to challenge such racialized institutions and patterns. . . . In the case of Katrina, the result was a huge gap between blacks and whites in their understanding of the meaning of the catastrophe: for blacks, the visible disproportion of blacks among Katrina's victims signified how the government and the American people systematically ignore the plight of their communities; by contrast, the large majority of whites considered race to be more or less irrelevant to the meaning of Katrina.

Here we arrive at the fulcrum of the contemporary political debate about racism. It cannot be repeated often enough that racial exclusion, e.g. racism, today happens not so much through active bigotry as it does through the tacit exclusions created by these sorts of unstated, unconsidered social habits. The fundamental point is one that is deeply uncomfortable for large sectors of this country: if your social network is, for purely historical reasons, defined by color lines that were drawn long ago in a different and undeniably widely bigoted age, then you don't have to be a bigot yourself to be perpetuating the institutional structures of racial exclusion, e.g. racism. *This was exactly Illinois Senator Barack Obama's point when he declared on the Senate floor that the poor response to Katrina was not "evidence of active malice," but merely the result of "a continuation of passive indifference."[1] . . .*

When two thirds of blacks believe that "racism continues to be a problem" in this country, while two thirds of whites believe that it is not, the divide in good measure can be explained by the competing understandings of what constitutes racism. . . . the reason disproportionately many black folks suffered at the hands of Katrina was not because white people (or George Bush) disliked *the black people in New Orleans; it was because they didn't regard blacks and blackness as a meaningful social categories worthy of special attention. It was precisely that history of neglect, that failure to care, that underpinned the racial aspect of the Katrina disaster. . . .*

In sum, Katrina provides an unprecedented opportunity to communicate that "racism" is not just a matter of the psychology of hatred but is instead also a matter of the racial structure of political and economic inclusion and exclusion. Moreover, we should not blinker ourselves: this message is one that is deeply opposed by powerful political forces in the United States today. Those who deny the social nature of racism may not be bigots, but they are undoubtedly abettors of racism in the social sense of the word.

1. "Statement of Senator Barack Obama on Hurricane Katrina Relief Efforts," http://obama.senate.gov/statement/050906-statement_of_senator_barack_obama_ on_hurricane_katrina_relief_efforts/ (September 6, 2005).

Source: From N. Gilman, "What Katrina Teaches About the Meaning of Racism." Social Science Research Council, September 14, 2005. Available from http://understandingkatrina .ssrc.org/Gilman/.

Prejudice is often based on nonverbal aspects of behavior. That is, the negative prejudgment is triggered by physical appearances or behavior. The following report from a Web site that tracks hate crimes underscores the importance of physical appearances in prejudice:

> *On September 26, 2005, in Marysville, California, Daniel J. Farris, 18, was charged with assault with a deadly weapon, causing pain, suffering or injury to an elder or dependent adult and hate crime for allegedly beating an elderly black man while yelling racial slurs. (Accessed at http.//www.splcenter.org/intel/hatewatch/fortherecord.jsp)*

As in many instances of hate crimes, the victim's appearance was more significant than his specific cultural heritage. From these kinds of experiences with prejudice, victims can often spot prejudicial behavior and people with surprising accuracy. In an interesting study, blacks were able to detect prejudiced people (identified previously by objective survey measurement) after only 20 seconds of observation, with much higher accuracy than whites (Richeson & Shelton, 2005). Victims may also then develop imaginary "maps" that tell them where they belong and where they are likely to be rejected. They may even start to avoid places and situations in which they do not feel welcome (Marsiglia & Hecht, 1998). Can you identify places you've been where you or others were not welcome?

Stereotyping or prejudice can lead to overt nonverbal actions to exclude, avoid, or distance and are called **discrimination**. Discrimination may be based on race (racism), gender (sexism), or any of the other identities discussed in Chapter 5. It may range from subtle, nonverbal behavior such as lack of eye contact or exclusion from a conversation, to verbal insults and exclusion from jobs or other economic opportunities, to physical violence and systematic exclusion. To see how exclusion and avoidance can be subtle, consider all the communication choices people can make that affect whether other people feel welcome or valued or like outsiders who don't belong (Johnson, 2001, p. 59):

- Whether we look at people when we talk with them
- Whether we smile at people when they walk into the room or stare as if to say "What are you doing?" or stop the conversation with a hush they have to wade through to be included in the smallest way
- Whether we listen and respond to what people say, or drift away to someone or something else; whether we talk about things they know about, or stick to what's peculiar to the "in-group"
- Whether we acknowledge people's presence, or make them wait as if they weren't there; whether we avoid touching their skin when giving or taking something; how closely we watch them to see what they're up to
- Whether we avoid someone walking down the street, giving them a wide berth when we pass or even cross to the other side
- Whether we share with new colleagues the informal rules that you have to know to succeed, belong, or get along—or turn the conversation to something light and superficial when they're around
- Whether we invite people to our home or out for a drink and talk

discrimination Behaviors resulting from stereotypes or prejudice that cause some people to be denied equal participation or rights based on cultural-group membership, such as race.

Discrimination may be interpersonal, collective, or institutional. In recent years, interpersonal racism has become not only more subtle and indirect but also more persistent. Equally persistent is institutionalized or collective discrimination whereby individuals are systematically denied equal participation in society or equal access to rights in informal and formal ways (Maluso, 1995).

A study by the U.S. Justice Department found that black, Latino/a, and white motorists are equally likely to pulled over by police, but blacks and Latinos are much more likely to be searched, handcuffed, arrested, and subjected to force or the threat of it. Handcuffs were used on a higher percentage of black (6.4%) and Latino/a motorists (5.6%) than white (2%). Also, blacks (2.7%) and Latinos (2.4%) were far more likely than whites (0.8%) to report that police used force or the threat of force (Sniffen, 2005).

Semiotics and Nonverbal Communication

The study of **semiotics,** or semiology, offers a useful approach to examining how different signs communicate meaning. While semiotics is often used for analyzing language/discourse, we find it more useful in analyzing nonverbals and cultural spaces. A particularly useful framework comes from literary critic Roland Barthes (1980). In his system, **semiosis** is the production of meaning and is constructed through the interpretation of **signs**—the combination of signifiers and signified. **Signifiers** are the culturally constructed arbitrary words or symbols we use to refer to something else, the **signified.** For example, the word *man* is a signifier that refers to the signified, an adult male human being.

Obviously, *man* is a general signifier that does not refer to any particular man. The relationship between this signifier and the sign (the meaning) depends on how the signifier is used (for example, as in the sentence, "There is a man sitting in the first chair on the left.") or on our general sense of what *man* means. The difference between the signifier *man* and the sign rests on the difference between the word *man* and the meaning of that word. At its most basic level, *man* means an adult human male, but the semiotic process does not end there. *Man* carries many other layers of meaning. *Man* may or may not refer to any particular adult male, but it provides a concept that you can use to construct particular meanings based on the way the sign *man* functions. What does *man* mean when someone says, "Act like a real man!"

What do you have in mind when you think of the term *man*? How do you know when to use this signifier (and when not to use it) to communicate to others? Think of all of the adult males you know. How do they "fit" under this signifier? In what ways does the signifier reign over their behaviors, both verbal and nonverbal, to communicate particular ideas about them? We are not so much interested in the discrete, individual signifiers, but rather the ways that signifiers are combined and configured. The goal is to establish entire systems of semiosis and the ways that those systems create meaning. Semiotics allows us one way to "crack the codes" of another cultural framework.

The use of these semiotic systems relies on many codes taken from a variety of contexts and places: economic institutions, history, politics, religion, and so

semiotics The analysis of the nature of and relationship between signs.

semiosis The process of producing meaning.

signs In semiotics the meanings that emerge from the combination of the signifiers and signifieds.

signifiers In semiotics, the culturally constructed arbitrary words or symbols that people use to refer to something else.

signified In semiotics, anything that is expressed in arbitrary words or signifiers.

A close friend I used to have in high school was very intelligent. He took honors classes and did great in school. He was Hispanic and dressed more or less like a "cholo," with baggy pants and long shirts. When he went to speak with his counselor upon entering university, the counselor came to the conclusion that my friend was going to take easy classes rather than honors classes. His mother, who had accompanied him to the advising meeting, couldn't believe what the counselor was saying! My friend's appearance obviously caused the counselor to come to a conclusion about who and what type of person my friend was.

—Adriana

on. For example, when Nazi swastikas were spray-painted on Jewish graves in Lyon, France, in 1992, the message they communicated relied on semiotic systems from the past. The history of the Nazi persecution of Jews during World War II is well known: The power behind the signifier, the swastika, comes from that historical knowledge and the codes of antisemitism that it invokes to communicate its message. Relations from the past influence the construction and maintenance of intercultural relations in the present. Semiotics is a useful tool for examining the various ways that meaning is created in advertisements, clothing, tattoos, and other cultural artifacts. Semioticians have been attentive to the context in which the signifiers (words and symbols) are placed to understand which meanings are being communicated. For example, wearing certain kinds of clothes in specific cultural contexts may communicate unwanted messages, as shown in the "Student Voice" box. Or not wearing a particular artifact can also communicate meaning, as illustrated by the controversy over Senator Barack Obama's choosing not to wear a flag lapel pin (see Point of View box "Obama's Lapels"). Color symbolism also varies from culture to culture and context to context. For example, in China, the color red symbolizes good luck and celebration; in India it denotes purity; however, in South Africa, red is the color of mourning. In Egypt, yellow is the color of mourning; and in Japan, yellow symbolizes courage (Kyrnin, 2008). In the U.S., black clothing can hold various meanings depending on the context: In some high schools, black is considered to denote gang membership; an elegant black dress is suitable for a formal dinner event but probably has a different meaning if worn by a bride's mother at her wedding.

Yet cultural contexts are not fixed and rigid. Rather, they are dynamic and fleeting, as Marcel Proust (1981) noted in writing about Paris in *Remembrance of Things Past:*

The reality that I had known no longer existed. It sufficed that Mme Swann did not appear, in the same attire and at the same moment, for the whole avenue to be altered. The places we have known do not belong only to the world of space on which we map them for our own convenience. None of them was ever more than a thin slice, held between the contiguous impressions that composed our life at that time; the memory of a particular image is but regret for a particular moment; and houses, roads, avenues are as fugitive, alas, as the years. (p. 462)

As this excerpt shows, there is no "real" Paris. The city has different meanings at different times for different people, and for different reasons. For example, executives of multinational corporations moving into Paris see the city quite differently from immigrants arriving in Paris for personal reasons. Remember the tremendous unrest in the suburbs of Paris in the fall of 2005? Therefore, to think about cultural contexts as dynamic means that we must often think about how they change and in whose interests they change.

DEFINING CULTURAL SPACE

At the beginning of this book, we provided some background information about where we grew up. Our individual histories are important in understanding our identities. As writer John Preston (1991) explains, "Where we come from is important to who we are" (p. xi). There is nothing in the rolling hills of Delaware and Pennsylvania or the red clay of Georgia that biologically determined who Judith and Tom are. However, our identities are constructed, in part, in relation to the cultural milieu of the Mid-Atlantic region or the South. Each region has its own histories and ways of life that help us understand who we are. Our decision to tell you where we come from was meant to communicate something about who we think we are. So, although we can identify precisely the borders that mark out these spaces and make them real, or material, the spaces also are cultural in the ways that we imagine them to be.

The discourses that construct the meanings of cultural spaces are dynamic and ever changing. For example, the Delaware that Judith left behind and the Georgia that Tom left behind are not characterized by the same discourses that construct those places now. In addition, the relationship between those cultural spaces and our identities is negotiated in complex ways. For example, both of us participated in other, overlapping cultural spaces that influenced how we think about who we are. Thus, just because someone is from, say, Rhode Island or Samoa or India does not mean that his or her identity and communication practices are reducible to the history of those cultural spaces.

What is the communicative (discursive) relationship between cultural spaces and intercultural communication? Recall that we define cultural space as the particular configuration of the communication (discourse) that constructs meanings of various places. This may seem like an unwieldy definition, but it underscores the complexity of cultural spaces. A cultural space is not simply a particular location that has culturally constructed meanings. It can also be a metaphorical place from which we communicate. We can speak from a number of social locations, marked on the "map of society," that give added meaning to our communication. Thus, we may speak as parents, children, colleagues, siblings, customers, Nebraskans, and a myriad of other "places." All of these are cultural spaces.

OBAMA'S LAPELS

In a television interview in Fall 2007, presidential candidate Barack Obama was asked why he wasn't wearing an American flag lapel pin worn by many politicians. Some in the audience felt that wearing a flag pin is a sign of patriotism and shows visible support for the United States in a time of war—a prerequisite for being a viable candidate for the office of the president of the United States.

> *"The truth is that right after 9/11 I had a pin," Mr. Obama replied. "Shortly after 9/11, particularly because as we're talking about the Iraq war, that became a substitute for, I think, true patriotism, which is speaking out on issues that are of importance to our national security." "I decided I won't wear that pin on my chest," he added. "Instead I'm gonna' try to tell the American people what I believe what will make this country great and hopefully that will be a testimony to my patriotism. . . . . My attitude is that I'm less concerned about what you're wearing on your lapel than what's in your heart. And you show your patriotism by how you treat your fellow Americans, especially those who served."*

Source: From J. Zeleny, (2007, October 4). "Obama's Lapels." *New York Times.* Retrieved March 21, 2008 from http://thecaucus.blogs.nytimes.com/2007/10/04/obamas-lapels/.

Cultural Identity and Cultural Space

Home Cultural spaces influence how we think about ourselves and others. One of the earliest cultural spaces we experience is our home. As noted previously, nonverbal communication often involves issues of status. The home is no exception. As English professor Paul Fussell (1983) notes, "Approaching any house, one is bombarded with class signals" (p. 82). Fussell highlights the semiotic system of social class in the American home—from the way the lawn is maintained, to the kind of furniture within the home, to the way the television is situated. These signs of social class are not always so obvious from all class positions, but we often recognize the signs.

Even if our home does not reflect the social class to which we aspire, it may be a place of identification. We often model our own lives on the patterns from our childhood homes. Although this is not always the case, the home can be a place of safety and security. African American writer bell hooks (1990) remembers:

> *When I was a young girl the journey across town to my grandmother's house was one of the most intriguing experiences. . . . I remember this journey not just because of the stories I would hear. It was a movement away from the segregated blackness of our community into a poor white neighborhood [where] we would have to pass that terrifying whiteness—those white faces on porches staring down on us with hate. . . . Oh! that feeling of safety, of arrival, of homecoming when we finally reached the edges of her yard. (p. 41)*

Home, of course, is not the same as the physical location it occupies or the building (the house) at that location. Home is variously defined in terms of specific addresses, cities, states, regions, and even nations. Although we might have historical ties to a particular place, not everyone has the same relationship between those places and their own identities. Indeed, the relationship between place and cultural identity varies. Writer Steven Saylor (1991) explains,

> *Texas is a long way, on the map and otherwise, from San Francisco. "Steven," said my mother once, "you live in another country out there." She was right, and what I feel when I fly from California to Texas must be what an expatriate from any country feels returning to his childhood home. . . . Texas is home, but Texas is also a country whose citizenship I voluntarily renounced. (p. 119)*

The discourses surrounding Texas and giving meaning to Texas no longer "fit" Saylor's sense of who he is or wants to be. We all negotiate various relationships to the cultural meanings attached to the particular places or spaces we inhabit. Consider writer Harlan Greene's (1991) relationship to his hometown in South Carolina:

> *Now that I no longer live there, I often think longingly of my hometown of Charleston. My heart beats faster and color rushes to my cheek whenever I hear someone mentioning her; I lean over and listen, for even hearing the name casts a spell. Mirages rise up, and I am as overcome and drenched in images as a runner just come from running. I see the steeples, the streets, the lush setting. (p. 55)*

Despite his attachment to Charleston, Greene does not believe that Charleston feels the same way toward him. He explains, "But I still think of Charleston; I return to her often and always will. I think of her warmly. I claim her now, even though I know she will never claim me" (p. 67).

The complex relationships we have between various places and our identities resist simplistic reduction. These three writers—hooks, Saylor, and Greene—have negotiated different sentiments toward "home." In doing so, each demonstrates the complex dialectical tensions that exist between identity and location.

Neighborhood   One significant type of cultural space that emerged in U.S. cities in the latter 19th and early 20th centuries was the ethnic or racial neighborhood. (See Figure 7-4.) Historical studies show, however, that the ethnic neighborhoods of the European immigrants were rarely inhabited by only one ethnic group, despite memories to the contrary. According to labor historian D. R. Roediger (2005), even the heart of Little Italy in Chicago was 47% nonItalian, and "No single side of even one square block in the street between 1890 and 1930 was found to be 100 percent Italian. . . . The percentage of Russians, Czechs, Italians and Poles living in segregated neighborhoods ranged from 37 percent to 61 percent" (p. 164). However, this type of real segregation was reserved for the African Americans—where 93 percent of African Americans lived in ghettos. By law and custom, and under different political pressures, some cities developed segregated neighborhoods. Malcolm X (Malcolm X & Haley, 1964), in his

FIGURE 7-4   Many cities abound with multiple cultural spaces. In this photo, several different cultural contexts are adjacent and emphasize the increasing significance of multiculturalism. How would people in this urban place experience cultural spaces differently from people who live in less diverse cultural spaces? How might it influence their intercultural communication patterns? (© Robert Brenner/PhotoEdit, Inc.)

autobiography, tells of the strict laws that governed where his family could live after their house burned down:

> *My father prevailed on some friends to clothe and house us temporarily; then he moved us into another house on the outskirts of East Lansing. In those days Negroes weren't allowed after dark in East Lansing proper. There's where Michigan State University is located; I related all of this to an audience of students when I spoke there in January, 1963. . . . I told them how East Lansing harassed us so much that we had to move again, this time two miles out of town, into the country. (pp. 3–4)*

The legacy of "white-only" areas pervades the history of the United States and the development of its cultural geography. The segregation of African Americans was not accidental. Beginning in 1890 until the late 1960s (the fair-housing legislation), whites in America created thousands of whites-only towns, commonly known as "sundown towns," a reference to the signs often posted at their city limits that warned, as one did in Hawthorne, California, in the 1930s: "Nigger, Don't Let the Sun Set on YOU in Hawthorne." In fact, historian J. Loewen (2005) claims that, during that 70-year period, "probably a majority of all incorporated places [in the United States] kept out African Americans."

Neighborhoods exemplify how power influences intercultural contact. Thus, some cultural groups defined who got to live where and dictated the rules by which other groups lived. These rules were enforced through legal means and by harassment. For bell hooks and Malcolm X, the lines of segregation were clear and unmistakable.

In San Francisco, different racial politics constructed and isolated Chinatown. The boundaries that demarcated the acceptable place for Chinese and Chinese Americans to live were strictly enforced through violence:

> *The sense of being physically sealed within the boundaries of Chinatown was impressed on the few immigrants coming into the settlement by frequent stonings which occurred as they came up Washington or Clay Street from the piers. It was perpetuated by attacks of white toughs in the adjacent North Beach area and downtown around Union Square, who amused themselves by beating Chinese who came into these areas. "In those days, the boundaries were from Kearny to Powell, and from California to Broadway. If you ever passed them and went out there, the white kids would throw stones at you," Wei Bat Liu told us. (Nee & Nee, 1974, p. 60)*

In contrast to Malcolm X's exclusion from East Lansing, the Chinese of San Francisco were forced to live in a marked-off territory. Yet we must be careful not to confuse the experience of Chinese in San Francisco with the experiences of all Chinese in the United States. For example, a different system developed in Savannah, Georgia, around 1900:

> *Robert Chung Chan advised his kinsmen and the other newly arrived Chinese to live apart from each other. He understood the distrust of Chinatowns that Caucasians felt in San Francisco and New York. . . . Robert Chung Chan, probably more than anyone else, prevented a Chinatown from developing in Savannah. (Pruden, 1990, p. 25)*

Nor should we assume that vast migrations of Chinese necessarily led to the development of Chinatowns in other cities around the world. The settlement of Chinese immigrants in the 13th Arrondissement of Paris, for example, reflects a completely different intersection between cultures: "There is no American-style Chinatown [*Il n'y a pas de Chinatown à la américaine*]" in Paris (Costa-Lascoux & Yu-Sion, 1995, p. 197).

Within the context of different power relations and historical forces, settlement patterns of other cultural groups created various ethnic enclaves across the U.S. landscape. For example, many small towns in the Midwest were settled by particular European groups. Thus, in Iowa, Germans settled in Amana, Dutch in Pella, and Czechs and Slovaks in Cedar Rapids. Cities, too, have their neighborhoods, based on settlement patterns. South Philadelphia is largely Italian American, South Boston is largely Irish American, and Overtown in Miami is largely African American. Although it is no longer legal to mandate that people live in particular districts or neighborhoods based on their racial or ethnic backgrounds, the continued existence of such neighborhoods underscores their historical development and ongoing functions. This is especially true in Detroit, Michigan—the most segregated metropolitan region in the country—where the 8-mile road was made famous by the title and the location of the film starring Detroit hip-hop artist Eminem. The eight-mile, eight-lane road separates one city that is 91% white from the other that is overwhelmingly African American

EIGHT MILE ROAD

Sometimes called Detroit's mini Berlin Wall, sometimes called the Wailing Wall, this seemingly innocent looking wall in Joe Louis Park does little to betray its shameful past.

After World War I, some black residents of Detroit moved into a then rural and vacant area near the intersection of Wyoming and Eight Mile. In 1940, a developer sought to build homes for middle income whites in a nearby area. However, the Federal Housing Administration's policies of that era precluded their approving loans in racially mixed areas. To secure FHA approval, this developer put up a wall six feet high, one foot in width and one half mile in length, to clearly demark the white and black areas. His wall led FHA to approve loans for his project.

Built in 1940, this wall presaged the racial divisions that have come to be symbolized by Eight Mile Road. (© *Clayton Sharrard/PhotoEdit, Inc.*)

Source: http://detroityes.com/webisodes/2002/8mile/021106-04-8mile-berlin-wall.htm.

(Chinni, 2002). (See Point of View box.) Economics, family ties, social needs, and education are some factors in the perpetuation of these cultural spaces.

Similar spaces exist in other countries as well. Remember the days of rioting and car burning that took place in the Parisian suburbs in the fall of 2005? Guillaume Parmentier, the head of the French Institute, commented on the relationship between place and human relations: "We are the victims of our architecture," he said, referring to the sterile high-rise ghettos populated by France's Muslim immigrants. They are the French equivalent of ghettos or "*zones de no-droit*" (lawless areas) where police do not go as a matter of policy. Instead, there are checkpoints on the perimeter of these high-rise islands, and those who live there are left to fend for themselves (Hoagland, 2005).

The relationships among identity, power, and cultural space are quite complex. Power relations influence who (or what) gets to claim who (or what), and under what conditions. Some subcultures are accepted and promoted within a particular cultural space, others are tolerated, and still others may be unacceptable. Identifying with various cultural spaces is a negotiated process that is difficult (and sometimes impossible) to predict and control. The key to understanding the relationships among culture, power, people, and cultural spaces is to think dialectically.

Regionalism   Ongoing regional and religious conflict, as well as nationalism and ethnic revival, point to the continuing struggles over who gets to define whom. Such conflicts are not new, though. In fact, some cultural spaces (such as Jerusalem) have been sites of struggle for many centuries.

Although regions are not always clearly marked on maps of the world, many people identify quite strongly with particular regions. **Regionalism** can be expressed in many ways, from symbolic expressions of identification to armed conflict. Within the United States, people may identify themselves or others as southerners, New Englanders, and so on. In Canada, people from Montreal might identify more strongly with the province of Quebec than with their country. Similarly, some Corsicans might feel a need to negotiate their identity with France. Sometimes people fly regional flags, wear particular kinds of clothes, celebrate regional holidays, and participate in other cultural activities to communicate their regional identification. However, regional expressions are not always simply celebratory, as the conflicts in Kosovo, Chechnya, Eritrea, Tibet, and Northern Ireland indicate.

National borders may seem straightforward, but they often conceal conflicting regional identities. To understand how intercultural communication may be affected by national borders, we must consider how history, power, identity, culture, and context come into play. Only by understanding these issues can we approach the complex process of human communication.

regionalism Loyalty to a particular region that holds significant cultural meaning for that person.

Changing Cultural Space

Chapter 8 discusses in greater detail the intercultural experiences of those who traverse cultural spaces and attempt to negotiate change. In this chapter, however, we want to focus on some of the driving needs of those who change cultural spaces.

Travel   We often change cultural spaces when we travel. Traveling is frequently viewed as an unimportant leisure activity, but it is more than that. In terms of his student explains her difficulty in knowing when she is in Japan as she moves through the airport and onto the airplane. How are these cultural spaces different from national borders?

Whenever I am at LAX [Los Angeles International Airport] on the way back to Japan, my sense of space gets really confused. For example, I fly into LAX from Phoenix, and as I line up at the Korean Air check-in counter, I see so many Asian-looking people (mostly Japanese and Koreans). Then, as I proceed, getting past the stores (e.g., duty-free shop) and walk farther to the departure gate, I see a lot less Americans and, eventually and practically, NOBODY but Asian-looking people (except for a very limited number of non-Asian-looking passengers on the same flight). So, when I wait at the gate, hearing Japanese around me, I get confused— "Where am I? Am I still in the U.S.? Or am I already back in Japan?" This confusion gets further heightened when I go aboard and see Japanese food served for meals and watch a Japanese film or TV program on the screen. So, to me, arriving at the Narita International Airport is not the moment of arriving in Japan. It already starts while I am in the U.S. This is just one of the many examples of postmodern cultural spaces that I have experienced in my life.
—Sakura

intercultural communication, traveling changes cultural spaces in ways that often transform the traveler. Changing cultural spaces means changing who you are and how you interact with others. Perhaps the old saying "When in Rome, do as the Romans do" holds true today as we cross cultural spaces more frequently than ever.

On a recent trip to Belgium, Tom flew nonstop on British Airways from Phoenix to London and then on to Brussels. Because the entire flight was conducted in English, Tom did not have a sense of any transition from English to French. Unlike flying the now defunct Sabena (Belgian National Airlines) from the United States to Belgium, flying British Airways provided no cultural transition space between Arizona and Belgium. Thus, when he got off the plane in Brussels, Tom experienced a more abrupt cultural and language transition, from an English environment to a Flemish/French environment.

Do you alter your communication style when you encounter travelers who are not in their traditional cultural space? Do you assume they should interact in the ways prescribed by your cultural space? These are some of the issues that travel raises.

Migration   People also change cultural spaces when they relocate. Moving, of course, involves a different kind of change in cultural spaces than traveling. In traveling, the change is fleeting, temporary, and usually desirable; it is something that travelers seek out. However, people who migrate do not always seek out this change. For example, in recent years, many people have been forced from their strife-torn homelands in Rwanda and in Bosnia and have settled elsewhere. Many immigrants leave their homelands simply so they can survive. But they often find it difficult to adjust to the change, especially if the language and customs of the new cultural space are unfamiliar.

Even within the United States, people may have trouble adapting to new surroundings when they move. Tom remembers that when northerners moved to the South they often were unfamiliar with the custom of banks closing early on Wednesday or with the traditional New Year's Day foods of black-eyed peas and collards. Ridiculing the customs of their new cultural space simply led to further intercultural communication problems.

Postmodern Cultural Spaces

Space has become increasingly important in the negotiation of cultural and social identities, and so to culture more generally. As Leah Vande Berg (1999) explains, scholars in many areas "have noted that identity and knowledge are profoundly spatial (as well as temporal), and that this condition structures meaningful embodiment and experience" (p. 249). **Postmodern cultural spaces** are places that are defined by cultural practices—languages spoken, identities enacted, rituals performed—and they often change as new people move in and out of these spaces. Imagine being in a small restaurant when a large group of people arrives, all of whom are speaking another language. How has this space changed? Whose space is it? As different people move in and out of this space, how does the cultural character change?

In his study of listening among the Blackfeet, Donal Carbaugh (1999) reports that listening is intimately connected to place as a cultural space. It is both a physical location and a cultural phenomenon. Through his cultural informant, Two Bears, Carbaugh notes that

> *in his oral utterance to us about "listening," in this landscape, he is commenting about a non-oral act of listening to this landscape. This nonverbal act is itself a deeply cultural form of action in which the Blackfeet persona and the physical place become intimately linked, in a particularly Blackfeet way. (p. 257)*

But these places are dynamic, and "listening" is not limited to fixed locations: "Some kinds of places are apparently more appropriate for this kind of Blackfeet 'listening' than are others, although—according to Two Bears—'just about anywhere' might do" (p. 257). Physical place, in this sense, can become a cultural space in that it is infused with cultural meanings. Think about how the same physical place might have a different meaning to someone from a different cultural group.

Another set of postmodern spaces that are quite familiar are those of the Internet. There are MOOs (multiobject domains) and MUDs (multiuser domains) and chat rooms where people meet in real time and interact primarily for recreational purposes—assuming their own or another identity (Herring, 2004). There are other Internet spaces like message boards, instant messengers (IMs), and blogs for asynchronous communication (Herring, 2004). People meet in these places for fun, to gain information, or as a place to experience a supportive community (e.g., an online chat room where Japanese elderly meet for

postmodern cultural spaces Places that are defined by cultural practices—languages spoken, identities enacted, rituals performed—and that often change as new people move in and out of these spaces.

support [Kanayama, 2003], or a bulletin board where gay, lesbian, and transgendered people can offer support and exchange useful information). And increasingly, social network sites (SMS) like MySpace and Facebook are places where young people socialize (Boyd, 2007). See Point of View box "Social Network Sites Around the World."

Communication scholars have investigated how these virtual place/spaces affect the communication that occurs there. Teske (2002) explores the implications of this communication that is disembodied—unconnected to time and physical space—and suggests that interacting in these spaces makes us increasingly individualistic and isolated, in spite of communicating through a great medium for *connecting* people. Others suggest that virtual spaces offer a different space for interacting and that cyber relationships are formed, maintained, and dissolved in much the same way (Carter, 2004). We'll explore cyber relationships further in Chapter 10.

The fluid and fleeting nature of cultural space stands in sharp contrast to the 18th- and 19th-century notions of space, which promoted land ownership, surveys, borders, colonies, and territories. No passport is needed to travel in the postmodern cultural space, because there are no border guards. The dynamic nature of postmodern cultural spaces underscores its response to changing cultural needs. The space exists only as long as it is needed in its present form.

Postmodern cultural spaces are both tenuous and dynamic. They are created within existing places, without following any particular guide. There is no marking off of territory, no sense of permanence or official recognition. The postmodern cultural space exists only while it is used.

The ideology of fixed spaces and categories is currently being challenged by postmodernist notions of space and location. Phoenix, for example, which became a city relatively recently, has no Chinatown, or Japantown, or Koreatown, no Irish district, or Polish neighborhood, or Italian area. Instead, people of Polish descent, for example, might live anywhere in the metropolitan area but congregate for special occasions or for specific reasons. On Sundays, the Polish Catholic Mass draws many people from throughout Phoenix. When people want to buy Polish breads and pastries, they can go to the Polish bakery and also speak Polish there. Ethnic identity is only one of several identities that these people negotiate. When they desire recognition and interaction based on their Polish heritage, they can meet that wish. When they seek other forms of identification, they can go to places where they can be Phoenix Suns fans, or community volunteers, and so on. Ethnic identity is neither the sole factor nor necessarily the most important one at all times in their lives.

The markers of ethnic life in Phoenix are the urban sites where people congregate when they desire ethnic cultural contact. At other times, they may frequent different locations in expressing aspects of their identities. In this sense, the postmodern urban space is dynamic and allows people to participate in the communication of identity in new ways (Drzewiecka & Nakayama, 1998).

Cultural spaces can also be metaphorical, with historically defined places serving as sources of contemporary identity negotiation in new spaces. In her

SOCIAL NETWORK SITES AROUND THE WORLD

While MySpace and Facebook are popular in the United States, social network sites (SNS) like Tagworld, Bebo, Piczo, Faceparty, and Mixi took off in places such as the United Kingdom, New Zealand, Australia, and Japan. In China, an instant messaging service called QQ added social network site features, as did the popular Korean community site Cyworld; both are popular across all age groups in China and South Korea.

Participation tends to follow cultural and linguistic lines, although some draw users from different world regions; the two with the most "balanced" user bases worldwide are Tagged and Hi5. Thirty percent of Tagged users are from Asia and the Pacific region, 22% from North America, 14% from Latin America, 23% from Europe, 10% from Africa and the Middle East. Hi5, similarly, has 31% European users, 24% Latin American, 21% Asia-Pacific, 15% North American, and 8% African/Middle Eastern.

MySpace and Facebook both have large percentages of their users in North America (around 65%) with sizeable portions in Europe (15%–25%) and single-digit numbers in all other regions. Bebo, most popular in the U.K., is largely the opposite, with a 62% European base and a 22% North American base. Orkut has about a 50% user base in Latin America, the same in Asia-Pacific, and almost none anywhere else. Friendster, meanwhile, leans the most toward a single geographic market: about 90% users in the Asia-Pacific region.

Sources: From D. Boyd, "Why Youth (heart) Social Network Sites: The Role of Networked Publics in Teenage Social Life." In D. Buckingham (Ed.), *Youth, Identity, and Digital Media* (MacArthur Foundation Series on Digital Learning). (Cambridge, MA: MIT Press, 2007.) And C. McCarthy (2007, July 31), *ComScore's Latest Numbers: Worldwide Social-Networking Growth*. Retrieved March 21, 2008 from http://www.news.com/8301-13577_3-9752857-36.html.

study of academia, Olga Idriss Davis (1999) turns to the historical role of the kitchen in African American women's lives and uses the kitchen legacy as a way to rethink the university. She notes that "the relationship between the kitchen and the Academy [university] informs African American women's experience and historically interconnects their struggles for identity" (p. 370). In this sense, the kitchen is a metaphorical cultural space that is invoked in an entirely new place, the university. Again, this postmodern cultural space is not material but metaphoric, and it allows people to negotiate their identities in new places.

INTERNET RESOURCES

http://nonverbal.ucsc.edu/
This Web site provided by the University of California-Santa Cruz allows students to explore and test their ability to read and interpret nonverbal

communication. The site provides videos that examine nonverbal codes, including personal space and gestures, to better understand cross-cultural communication.

www.cba.uni.edu/buscomm/nonverbal/Culture.htm
This Web site provided by the University of Northern Iowa outlines how nonverbal communication varies across cultures in relation to Hofstede's value dimensions.

http://nonverbal.ucsc.edu/gest.html
This link from a Web site provided by the University of California-Santa Cruz allows students to explore and test their ability to read and interpret nonverbal communication and culture.

http://webdesign.about.com/od/color/a/bl_colorculture.htm
This Web page is dedicated to providing information pertaining to the color symbolism that exists throughout different cultures. Its purpose is to allow Web page designers to understand how their usage of color might be interpreted by different groups and world regions. The page also provides informative links on how gender, age, class, and current trends also play a factor in the meaning of color.

SUMMARY

- Nonverbal communication differs from verbal communication in two ways: It is more unconscious and learned implicitly.
- It can reinforce, substitute for, or contradict verbal communication.
- Nonverbal communication communicates relational meaning, status, and deception.
- Research investigating the universality of nonverbal behaviors includes comparison of primate behavior, behavior of deaf/blind children, cross-cultural studies, and search for universal social needs filled by nonverbal behaviors.
- Nonverbal codes include facial expressions, eye contact, gestures, paralanguage, chronemics, and silence.
- Sometimes cultural differences in nonverbal behaviors can lead to stereotyping of others and overt discrimination.
- Cultural space influences cultural identity and includes homes, neighborhoods, regions, and nations.
- Two ways of changing cultural spaces are travel and migration.
- Postmodern cultural spaces, like cyberspace, are tenuous and dynamic.

1. How does nonverbal communication differ from verbal communication?
2. What are some of the messages that we communicate through our nonverbal behaviors?
3. Which nonverbal behaviors, if any, are universal?
4. How do our cultural spaces affect our identities?
5. What role does power play in determining our cultural spaces?
6. What is the importance of cultural spaces to intercultural communication?
7. How do postmodern cultural spaces differ from modernist notions of cultural space?

 Go to the self-quizzes on the Online Learning Center at www.mhhe.com/ martinnakayama5 to further test your knowledge.

ACTIVITIES

1. *Cultural Spaces.* Think about the different cultural spaces in which you participate (clubs, churches, concerts, and so on). Select one of these spaces and describe when and how you enter and leave it. As a group, discuss the answers to the following questions:

    a. Which cultural spaces do many students share? Which are not shared by many students?

    b. Which cultural spaces, if any, are denied to some people?

    c. What factors determine whether a person has access to a specific cultural space?

2. *Nonverbal Rules.* Choose a cultural space that you are interested in studying. Visit this space on four occasions to observe how people there interact. Focus on one aspect of nonverbal communication (e.g., eye contact or proximity). List some rules that seem to govern this aspect of nonverbal communication. For example, if you are focusing on proximity, you might describe, among other things, how far apart people tend to stand when conversing. Based on your observations, list some prescriptions about proper (expected) nonverbal behavior in this cultural space. Share your conclusions with the class. To what extent do other students share your conclusions? Can we generalize about nonverbal rules in cultural spaces? What factors influence whether an individual follows unspoken rules of behavior?

KEY WORDS

chronemics (278)
contact cultures (274)
cultural space (267)
deception (270)
discrimination (284)
eye contact (276)
expectancy violation
    theory (270)
facial expressions (272)

monochronic (278)
noncontact cultures
    (274)
paralinguistics (277)
polychronic (278)
postmodern cultural
    spaces (295)
regionalism (293)
relational messages (270)

semiosis (285)
semiotics (285)
signified (285)
signifiers (285)
signs (285)
status (270)
vocalizations (278)
voice qualities
    (277)

The Online Learning Center at www.mhhe.com/martinnakayama5 features
flashcards and crossword puzzles based on these terms and concepts.

REFERENCES

Acheson, C. (2007). Silence in dispute. In C. S. Beck (Ed.), *Communication Yearbook 31* (pp. 2–59), New York: Lawrence Erlbaum Associates.

Alberts, J. K., Nakayama, T. K., & Martin, J. N. (2007). *Human communication in society.* Boston: Allyn-Bacon.

Andersen, P. A., Hecht, M. L., Hoobler, G. D., & Smallwood, M. (2002). Nonverbal communication across cultures. In W. B. Gudykunst & B. Mody (Eds.), *Handbook of international and intercultural communication* (2nd ed., pp. 89–106). Thousand Oaks, CA: Sage.

Archer, D. (1997). Unspoken diversity: Cultural differences in gestures. *Qualitative Sociology, 20,* 79–105.

Basso, K. (1970). "To give up on words": Silence in western Apache culture. *Southwestern Journal of Anthropology, 26,* 213–320.

Boucher, J. D., & Carlson, G. E. (1980). Recognition of facial expression in three cultures. *Journal of Cross Cultural Psychology, 11,* 263–280.

Boyd, D. (2007). Why youth (heart) social network sites: The role of networked publics in teenage social life. In D. Buckingham (Ed.), *Youth, identity, and digital media* (MacArthur Foundation Series on Digital Learning). Cambridge, MA: MIT Press.

Braithwaite, C. A. (1990). Communicative silence: A cross-cultural study of Basso's hypothesis. In D. Carbaugh (Ed.), *Cultural communication and intercultural contact* (pp. 321–327). Hillsdale, NJ: Lawrence Erlbaum.

Burgoon, J. K. (1995). Cross-cultural and intercultural applications of expectancy violations theory. In R. L. Wiseman (Ed.), *Intercultural communication theory* (International and Intercultural Communication Annual, Vol. 19, pp. 194–214). Thousand Oaks, CA: Sage.

Carbaugh, D. (1999). "Just listen": "Listening" and landscape among the Blackfeet. *Western Journal of Communication, 63*(3), 250–270.

Carbaugh, D., & Berry, M. (2001). Communicating history, Finnish and American discourses: An ethnographic contribution to intercultural communication inquiry. *Communication Theory, 11,* 352–366.

Carter, D. M. (2004). Living in virtual communities: Making friends online. *Journal of Urban Technology, 11,* 109–136.

Chang, H. (1997). Language and words: Communication in the analects of Confucius. *Journal of Language and Social Psychology, 16,* 107–131.

Checkpoints: Baghdad's Russian Roulette. (2007, September 5). Institute for War and Peace Reporting. Retrieved March 17, 2008 from http://www.iwpr.net/?p=icr&s=f&o=337693&apc_state=henficr337691.

Chinni, D. (2002, November 15). Along Detroit's Eight Mile Road, a stark racial split. *Christian Science Monitor.* Accessed at http://www.csmonitor.com/2002/1115/p01s02-ussc.htm

Costa-Lascoux, J., & Yu-Sion, L. (1995). *Paris-XIIIe, lumières d'Asie.* Paris: Éditions Autrement.

Covarrubias, P. (2007). (Un)Biased in Western theory: Generative silence in American Indian communication. *Communication Monographs, 74*(2), 265–271.

Davis, O. I. (1999). In the kitchen: Transforming the academy through safe spaces of resistance. *Western Journal of Communication, 63*(3), 364–381.

Drzewiecka, J. A., & Nakayama, T. K. (1998). City sites: Postmodern urban space and the communication of identity. *Southern Communication Journal, 64,* 20–31.

Ekman, P. (2003). *Emotions revealed: Recognizing faces and feelings to improve communication and emotional life.* New York: Times Books.

Ekman, P., & Friesen, W. V. (1987). Universals and cultural differences in the judgments of facial expressions of emotion. *Journal of Personality and Social Psychology, 53,* 712–717.

Fattah, H. M. (2005, May 1). Why Arab men hold hands. *New York Times,* Week in Review, 2.

Fletcher, C. (1992). The semiotics of survival: Street cops read the street. *Howard Journal of Communications, 4*(1, 2), 133–142.

Floyd, K., Ramirez, A., & Burgoon, J. K. (2008). Expectancy violations theory. In L. K. Guerrero, J. A. DeVito, & M. L. Hecht (Eds.), *The nonverbal communication reader: Classic and contemporary readings* (3rd ed., pp. 503–510). Prospect Heights, IL: Waveland.

Fussell, P. (1983). *Class.* New York: Ballantine Books.

Galati, D., Sini, B., Schmidt, S., & Tinti, C. (2003). Spontaneous facial expressions in congenitally blind and sighted children aged 8–11. *Journal of Visual Impairment and Blindness, 97,* 418–428.

Greene, H. (1991). Charleston, South Carolina. In J. Preston (Ed.), *Hometowns: Gay men write about where they belong* (pp. 55–67). New York: Dutton.

Gudykunst, W. B. (1985). A model of uncertainty reduction in intergroup encounters. *Journal of Language and Social Psychology, 4,* 79–98.

Gudykunst, W. B. (2005). An anxiety/uncertainty management (AUM) theory of effective communication: Making the mesh of the net finer. In W. B. Gudykunst (Ed.), *Theorizing about intercultural communication* (pp. 281–323). Thousand Oaks, CA: Sage.

Hall, E. T. (1966). *The hidden dimension.* New York: Anchor Books.

Harper, M., & Jones, T. (2005, November 23). Blackface costumes spark Stetson diversity lesson. *Daytona Beach News-Journal* online. Accessed at http://www.news-journalonline.com/NewsJournalOnline/News/Headlines/03NewsHEAD04112305.htm

Hasegawa, T., & Gudykunst, W. B. (1998). Silence in Japan and the United States. *Journal of Cross-Cultural Psychology, 29,* 668–684.

Henningsen, D. D., Cruz, M. G., & Morr, M. C. (2000). Pattern violations and perceptions of deception. *Communication Reports, 13,* 1–9.

Herring, S. C. (2004). Slouching toward the ordinary: Current trends in computer mediated communication. *New Media & Society, 6,* 26–31.

Hoagland, J. (2005, November 9). French lessons. *The Washington Post,* p. A31. Accessed at http://www.washingtonpost.com/wp-dyn/content/article/2005/11/08/AR2005110801257

hooks, b. (1990). *Yearning: Race, gender, and cultural politics.* Boston: South End Press.

Johnson, A. (2001). *Privilege, power and difference.* Boston: McGraw-Hill.

Jones, S. (2004). Putting the person into person-centered and immediate emotional support: Emotional change and perceived helper competence as outcomes of comforting in helping situations. *Communication Research, 31,* 338–360.

Kanayama, T. (2003). Ethnographic research on the experience of Japanese elderly people online. *New Media & Society, 5,* 267–288.

Kim, M.-S. (2001). *Non-Western perspectives on human communication.* Thousand Oaks, CA: Sage.

Khuri, F. I. (2001). *The body in Islamic culture.* London: Saqi Books.

Kyrnin, J. Color symbolism chart by culture. Retrieved March 3, 2008 from http://webdesign.about.com/od/color/a/bl_colorculture.htm

Lock, C. (2004, July 31). Deception detection. *Science News, 166,* 72–73.

Loewen, J. (2005). *Sundown towns: A hidden dimension of American racism.* New York: New Press.

Malcolm X, & Haley, A. (1964). *The autobiography of Malcolm X.* New York: Grove Press.

Maluso, D. (1995). Shaking hands with a clenched fist: Interpersonal racism. In B. Lott & D. Maluso (Eds.), *The social psychology of interpersonal discrimination* (pp. 50–79). New York: Guilford.

Marsiglia, F. F., & Hecht, M. L. (1998). Personal and interpersonal interventions. In M. L. Hecht (Ed.), *Communicating prejudice* (pp. 287–301). Thousand Oaks, CA: Sage.

Matsumoto, D. (1990). Cultural influences on facial expressions of emotion. *Southern Communication Journal, 56,* 128–137.

Matsumoto, D., Franklin, B., Choi, J.-W., Rogers, D., & Tatani, H. (2002). Cultural influences in the expression and perception of emotion. In W. B. Gudykunst & B. Mody (Eds.), *Handbook of international and intercultural communication* (2nd ed., pp. 107–127). Thousand Oaks, CA: Sage.

Montepare, J. M. (2003). Evolution and nonverbal behavior: Adaptive social interaction strategies. *Journal of Nonverbal Behavior, 27,* 141–143.

Morsbach, H. (1988). The importance of silence and stillness in Japanese nonverbal communication: A cross cultural approach. In F. Poyatos (Ed.), *Cross cultural perspectives in nonverbal communication* (pp. 201–215). Lewiston, NY: Hogrefe.

Nee, V. G., & Nee, B. D. B. (1974). *Longtime Californ': A documentary study of an American Chinatown.* Boston: Houghton Mifflin.

Norwegians confused by Bush "homs" salute. (2005, December 1). *USAToday.* Accessed at http://www .usatoday.com/news/washington/ 2005-01-21-bush-norwegians_x.htm? csp=34& POE=click-refer

Patterson, M. L. (2003). Commentary: Evolution and nonverbal behavior: Functions and mediating processes. *Journal of Nonverbal Behavior, 27,* 201–207.

Pollick, A.S., Jeneson, A., & de Waal, F.B.M. (2008) Gestures and multimodal signaling in bonobos. In T. Furuichi & J. Thompson (Eds.), *Bonobos: Behaviour, ecology, and conservation,* New York: Springer.

Preston, J. (1991). Introduction. In J. Preston (Ed.), *Hometowns: Gay men write about where they belong* (pp. xi–xiv). New York: Dutton.

Preuschoft, S. (2000). Primate faces and facial expressions. *Social Research, 67,* 245–271.

Proust, M. (1981). *Swann in love: Remembrance of things past* (C.K.S. Moncrieff & T. Kilmartin, Trans.). New York: Vintage.

Pruden, G. B., Jr. (1990). History of the Chinese in Savannah, Georgia. In J. Goldstein (Ed.), *Georgia's East Asian connection: Into the twenty-first century: Vol. 27. West Georgia College studies in the social sciences* (pp. 17–34). Carrollton: West Georgia College.

Richeson, J., & Shelton, J. N. (2005). Brief report: Thin slices of racial bias. *Journal of Nonverbal Behavior, 29,* 75–86.

Rocca, K. (2004). College student attendance: Impact of instructor immediacy and verbal aggression. *Communication Education, 53,* 185–195.

Roediger, D. R. (2005). *Working toward whiteness: How America's immigrants became white.* New York: Basic Books, 2005.

Sajavaara, K., & Lehtonen, J. (1997). The silent Finn revisited. In A. Jaworski (Ed.), *Silence: Interdisciplinary perspectives* (pp. 263–283). New York: Mouton de Gruyter.

Saylor, S. (1991). Amethyst, Texas. In J. Preston (Ed.), *Hometowns: Gay men write about where they belong* (pp. 119–135). New York: Dutton.

Schiefenhovel, W. (1997). Universals in interpersonal interactions. In U. Segerstråle & P. Molnár (Eds.), *Nonverbal communication: Where nature meets culture* (pp. 61–79). Mahwah, NJ: Lawrence Erlbaum.

Smith, R. J., & Tyson, A. S. (2005, March 7). Shootings by U.S. at Iraq checkpoints questioned page. *Washington Post,* p. A01. Retrieved March 17, 2008 from http://www.washingtonpost.com/ wp-dyn/articles/A12507-2005Mar6.html

Sniffen, M. J. (2005, August 24). Race disparity seen during traffic stops. The Associated Press News Service.

Sudip, M. (2004, January 26). A hairy situation. *Newsweek,* p. 12.

Suomi, S. J. (1988). Nonverbal communication in non-human primates: Implications for the emergence of culture. In U. Segerstråle & P. Molnár (Eds.), *Nonverbal communication: Where nature meets culture* (pp. 131–150). Mahwah, NJ: Lawrence Erlbaum.

Teske, J. A. (2002). Cyberpsychology, human relationships and our virtual interiors. *Zygon, 37,* 677–700.

Tierney, J. (2007, August 28). A world of eloquence in an upturned palm. *The New York Times.* Retrieved March 26, 2008, from http://www.nytimes .com/2007/08/28/science/ 28tier.html?_r=1&oref=slogin.

Vande Berg, L. R. (1999). An introduction to the special issue on "spaces." *Western Journal of Communication, 63* (3), 249.

Vrij, A. (2004). Why professionals fail to catch liars and how they can improve. *Legal and Criminological Psychology, 9,* 159–181.

Watson, O. M. (1970). *Proxemic behavior: A cross cultural study.* The Hague: Mouton.

Watzlawick, P., Beavin, J. H., & Jackson, D. D. (1967). *Pragmatics of human communication.* New York: W. W. Norton.

Wilkins, R. (2005). The optimal form: Inadequacies and excessiveness within the *Asiallinen* [matter of fact] nonverbal style in public and civic settings in Finland. *Journal of Communication, 55,* 383–401.

PART III

Intercultural Communication Applications

UNDERSTANDING INTERCULTURAL TRANSITIONS

CHAPTER OBJECTIVES

After reading this chapter, you should be able to:

1. Describe a dialectical approach to cultural transitions.
2. Identify four types of migrant groups.
3. Define cultural adaptation.
4. Identify three approaches to understanding cultural adaptation.
5. Identify individual characteristics that may influence how people adapt.
6. List outcomes of the adaptation process.
7. Define and describe the occurrence of culture shock.
8. Describe the reentry process and how it differs from adaptation to a host culture.
9. Describe a phenomenological approach to understanding cultural adaptation.
10. Describe how the adaptation process is influenced by contextual elements.
11. Explain how different approaches to adaptation are related to cultural identity.
12. Discuss the effect on the identity of living on the border and making multiple returns.

In Chapter 7, we discussed how we define and move through various cultural spaces. In this chapter, we look more specifically at how we move between cultural contexts. People may travel for work, study, or adventure, or in response to political or other events. Consider the following migration stories:

> *My name is Valdimir. At first when I emigrate[d] to the United States . . . [from Mexico] I had many struggles . . . I did not know anybody here, did not have enough money for rent, a place to live, and pay for food; I did not understand and speak English. . . . After two weeks I got a job and my life changed; I started to earn money and rented a place to live. Then I saw that it is important to learn English, and two months later I started school. (From http://www.otan.us/ webfarm/emailproject/grace.htm)*

> *My name is Tamara. My great-grandparents came from southern Italy to the U.S. in the early 1900s. They came for economic reasons; the village they lived in was very poor and they wanted a better life for their children. They faced lots of discrimination when they first arrived; but my great-grandfather had been trained as a shoemaker, and he set up a shoe repair shop in Greenwich, Connecticut, and eventually they made a good life for themselves.*

> *My name is Dashawn. I studied in Australia for six months. This was the most amazing and surreal experience I have had thus far in my twenty-one years of life. I would have to say that the people of Australia stand out to me the most . . . outrageously friendly. My experience taught me that there is so much more to our world than the U.S. Traveling is the best way to learn about oneself and others.*

Throughout history people have traveled across cultural boundaries for many different reasons. According to experts, there have been three great waves of global migration. The first wave was motivated by a search for resources and military conquest and lasted into the 16th century. The second, illustrated by Tamara's great-grandparents' arrival in the United States, was dominated by the European migration into poorer "empty territories" of the new world and led to the colonization of Africa, Asia, and America; it lasted until the middle of the 20th century. Valdimir's story illustrates the third and most recent wave. This wave—reversing the European colonization from the poorer countries of Asia, Africa, and South America to the richer ones in the postwar period—is more complex and multidimensional (Tehranian, 2004, p. 20).

Experts estimate that 25 people cross national borders every second, one billion journeys per year (Numbers, 2008). They leave their countries for many reasons, including national revolutions and civil wars (Afghanistan Yugoslavia, Rwanda, Sudan). In addition, millions of global nomads are roaming around the world as transnational corporate or government employees, guest workers, refugees, tourists, or study-abroad students, like Dashawn (see Figure 8-1). In 2006, the foreign-born population in the United States reached an all-time high of 37 million (Mather, 2007). And there are internal migrations—where people move from one place to another within national boundaries—often for the same reasons: for better economic opportunities or because of war or famine.

FIGURE 8-1   People have always traveled from their homelands, but with the increasing technological ease of travel, people are moving much more than ever before. Sojourners, business travelers, tourists, immigrants, and refugees have very different reasons for traveling. These people are waiting for international arrivals at the Atlanta airport. How might reasons for traveling shape intercultural experiences? (© Jeff Greenberg/PhotoEdit, Inc.)

Perhaps you can look at your own family and think about your migration history. Perhaps your ancestors came to the United States in the second wave, from western Europe in the 1800s, or perhaps in the third wave, from Europe, Asia, or Latin or South America. Perhaps you've had a global nomad experience of studying abroad or living abroad as an exchange student.

THINKING DIALECTICALLY ABOUT INTERCULTURAL TRANSITIONS

Understanding the process of adaptation in intercultural transitions depends on several dialectical tensions. Unfortunately, there are no easy answers. Think about how the privilege–disadvantage dialectic structures some kinds of intercultural transitions. For example, businesspeople who live abroad while working for transnational corporations often are economically privileged: They receive additional pay, housing relocation money, and so on. They also meet many people through work and can afford to travel in their new host location. In contrast, refugees often lack financial resources in their new host location, which

INTERNATIONAL MIGRATION TODAY

- International migration is the exception, not the rule. Most people do not want to move away from family and friends and most governments try to regulate border crossings.

- International immigration is at an all-time high and likely to increase due to persistent demographic and economic inequalities—191 million migrants in 2005.

- Migration generally flows from developing countries—about equally to other developing countries and more industrialized countries.

- There are increasing numbers of women who migrate; partly due to entry of women into the labor force; also women are preferred by the host countries as house workers, concubines, or prostitutes.

- Migration is increasingly politicized. Migrants can pose sensitive political issues (jobs, language, legality) and lead to the rise of anti-immigrant feelings.

- Migration is increasingly commodified, reminiscent of the colonial period when large numbers of slaves or immigrants were brought by the colonists to provide labor for their plantations. Today, agencies bring women and children from abroad to serve their new masters as servants and concubines; also sweatshops in New York and Los Angeles employ illegal immigrants with few human rights.

Source: Adapted from M. Tehranian, "Cultural Security and Global Governance: International Migration and Negotiations of Identity." In J. Friedman and S. Randeria (Eds.), *Worlds on the Move: Globalization, Migration and Cultural Security* (pp. 3–22). (New York: I. B. Tauris, 2004) and P. Martin and G. Zürcher (2008) "Managing Migration: The Global Challenge," *Population Bulletin, 63*(1): 1–18.

may have been chosen out of sheer necessity. They may have few opportunities to meet other people, travel in their new homeland, or purchase basic necessities. In this way, they may not view their new environment in the same way as a more privileged migrant. These dialectical differences shape the intercultural migrant's identity and the changes that this identity undergoes.

We might also invoke the personal–contextual dialectic. Often, in adapting to new cultural contexts, people may find themselves challenged to be culturally competent by behaving in ways that may be contradictory to their personal identities. For example, a Muslim woman may feel that she can't wear her chador in certain U.S. contexts and thus can't express her religious identity. The dialectic calls for a balance between the individual and contextual demands.

What can we learn about cultural transitions from these particular intercultural experiences? Why are some transitions easy for some people and more difficult for others? Why do some people choose to adapt and others resist

"LESS THAN GENEROUS"

This author describes the humanitarian crisis in Iraq and decries the lack of assistance from other countries:

> *In the recent years about 4 million Iraqis have been displaced, 50% still inside the country. The office of the UN high Commission for Refugees says that 80,000–100,000 are deemed to be extremely vulnerable, and in pressing need of resettlement outside the region. Some are at risk because they, or members of their families, worked for the American-led administration of Iraq, or for Western humanitarian agencies. Others belong to ethnic or religious minorities: these include Christians and Palestinians who are seen by some Iraqis as collaborators with the old regime. . . .But few have found new homes. . . . Only 2,600 Iraqis were resettled in America last year and that was a jump from previous years. . . .Some states have recently shown sign of responding to moral pressure. Britain and Denmark have offered more places for people who helped their military missions in Iraq; Poland will do likewise. But since the 2004 UN resolution which transferred power to Iraq's elected rulers, the whole world has in theory been committed to helping that country; more kindness from a few more countries wouldn't go amiss.*

Source: "Less than Generous." (2008, February 23). *The Economist, 386*(8568): 78–79.

adaptation? What can we learn about culture and communication from these experiences?

We begin this chapter by discussing four groups of travelers (migrants), and using a dialectical approach, we describe five ways in which migrants and hosts can relate. Then we turn our attention to the individual experience of dealing with cultural adaptation and describe three social science models of adaptation: the AUM model, the transition model, and the integrated theory of communication and cultural adaptation model. Interpretive approaches follow, which focus more on in-depth analysis and description of cultural adaptation, including culture shock and the reentry shock process. Finally, employing a critical lens, we describe the contextual elements (social institutions and political, historical, and economic structures) that influence cultural adaptation.

TYPES OF MIGRANT GROUPS

A dialectical perspective requires that we examine intercultural transitions on both a personal and a contextual level (Berry, 1992). On the personal level, we can look at individual experiences of adapting to new cultural contexts. But we also can examine the larger social, historical, economic, and political contexts in which these personal transitions occur. To understand cultural transitions,

TABLE 8-1 FOUR TYPES OF MIGRANT GROUPS		
Motivation for Migration	**Short-Term Duration**	**Long-Term Duration**
Voluntary	Sojourners	Immigrant
Involuntary (Forced)	Short-term refugee	Long-term refugee

we must simultaneously consider both the individual migrant groups and the contexts in which they travel.

Migration may be long term or short term and voluntary or involuntary. A **migrant** is an individual who leaves the primary cultural contexts in which he or she was raised and moves to a new cultural context for an extended period. For instance, exchange-students' sojourns are relatively short term and voluntary, and these transitions occur within a structured sociopolitical context. In contrast, the experience of being forced to relocate because of an unstable sociopolitical context would make the sojourn a long-term one. Cultural transitions may vary in length and in degree of voluntariness. We can identify four types of migrant groups based on these criteria. (See Table 8-1.)

Voluntary Migrants

There are two groups of voluntary travelers: sojourners and immigrants. **Sojourners** are those travelers who move into new cultural contexts for a limited time and a specific purpose. They are often people who have freedom and the means to travel. This includes international students who go abroad to study and technical assistance workers, corporate personnel, and missionaries who go abroad to work for a specific period. Some domestic sojourners move from one region to another within their own country for a limited time to attend school or work (e.g., Native Americans who leave their reservations).

Another type of voluntary traveler is the **immigrant,** first discussed in Chapter 1. Families who voluntarily leave one country to settle in another exemplify this type of migrant. Although many U.S. Americans believe that most immigrants come to the United States in search of freedom, the truth is that the primary reason people come to the United States is to join other family members; two other primary reasons are for employment and to escape from war, famine, or poverty. There is often a fluid and interdependent relationship between the countries that send and those that receive immigrants. Countries like the United States welcome working immigrants, even issuing special visas and developing programs (such as the *bracero* program of the 1940s between the United States and Mexico) during times of economic prosperity. Currently, only five major countries officially welcome international migrants as permanent residents: the United States, Canada, Australia, Israel, and New Zealand. Altogether, these countries accept 1.2 million immigrants a year, a small percentage of the estimated annual global immigration—and these countries can quickly restrict immigration during economic downturns (Martin & Zürcher, 2008). However, most migrants who move to another country are not accepted

migrant An individual who leaves the primary cultural context in which he or she was raised and moves to a new cultural context for an extended time. (See also **immigrant** and **sojourners**.)

sojourners People who move into new cultural contexts for a limited period of time and for a specific purpose, such as for study or business.

immigrants People who come to a new country, region, or environment to settle more or less permanently.

as official immigrants. And because of shifts in economic and political policy, family members of migrants may be trapped in the home country, unable to join the rest of the family in the new home country.

There are two kinds of migrant labor: cheap manual labor and highly skilled intellectual labor. Newly industrializing countries need trained labor for routine and repetitive tasks, and also newly rich countries and individuals are in need of domestic services. As shown in the "Point of View" box, increasing numbers of immigrant workers are women. Because they are often more reliable than men, they are increasingly doing manual work and employed as domestics. Ehrenreich and Hochschild (2003) label this recent pattern of female migration a "worldwide gender revolution" in their book *Global Woman*. They describe how millions of women from poor countries in the south (Philippines, Sri Lanka, and India) migrate to do the "women's work" of the north (North America, Europe, and the Middle East)—work that middle- and upper-class women are no longer able or willing to do. For example, Mexican and Latin American women are the domestics for U.S. women; Asian migrant women work in British homes; North African women work in French homes; Turkish women in German homes; Filipinas work in Spain, Italy, and Greece; and Filipino, Indian, and Sri Lankan women travel to Saudi Arabia to work. Ehrenreich and Hochschild raise many issues concerning this migration, one of which is who is taking care of the nanny's children. Most of these women leave their own children to care for the children of their employer.

More and more people are moving temporarily. Overseas study options are increasing, and today some 40% of Australia's skilled migrants are drawn from the overseas student cohort, with similar trends in Canada, the United States, and Europe. A core principle of the 27 countries who belong to the European Union (EU) is "freedom of movement," meaning that an EU national may travel to another EU member state and live, study, or work on an equal basis with native-born residents. For example, a French worker who applies for a job at Volkswagen in Germany must be treated just like a German applicant and can complain if a private employer discriminates in favor of local workers (Martin & Zürcher, 2008).

Involuntary Migrants

As shown in Table 8-1, two types of migrants move involuntarily: **long-term refugees** and **short-term refugees.** According to the United Nations High Commissioner for Refugees, there were 9.9 million refugees in 2006, the highest in four years. Most refugees are from developing countries and flee to other nearby developing countries. For example, in 2006, the highest numbers of refugees came from Afghanistan and Iraq and the countries who hosted the largest numbers of refugees were their neighboring countries, Pakistan and Iran. In Africa, conflict between the Muslim north and the Christian south of Sudan moved refugees to Chad, Kenya, and other neighboring countries. Similarly, in Somalia and the Democratic Republic of Congo, internal conflicts have sent refugees fleeing over the last decade.

At the start of 2006, there were an estimated 23.7 million "internally displaced people" (IDP) worldwide—people who migrate involuntarily within their

long-term refugees
People who are forced to relocate permanently because of war, famine, and oppression.

short-term refugees
People who are forced for a short time to move from their region or country.

FIGURE 8-2   Voluntary international migration can be very challenging and is usually a carefully considered individual or family decision. (© *Reuters/Corbis*)

own country, usually because of civil war or famine—many from Africa (Sudan, Somalia, and Liberia), the former Soviet Union (Azerbaijan, Russia, Georgia), the former Yugoslavia (Serbia and Montenegro), and Iraq and Afghanistan (*UNHCR Statistical Yearbook 2006*).

Most refugees, whether they have migrated domestically or internationally, want to return home as soon as possible, and an unprecedented number have done just that in the last four years—an estimated 6 million. In 2004, almost a million Afghanis and 200,000 Iraqis returned to their homes (*UNHCR Statistical Yearbook, 2006*).

One of our students, Naida, describes how her family fled Bosnia to become refugees and then immigrants in the United States:

During the year 1992, civil war erupted in my home country, Bosnia. Overnight my life shifted from a peaceful existence to fear, persecution, and anxiety. My family and I were forcefully taken to a concentration camp, where we witnessed the blind rage of mankind expressed through physical and mental abuses, humiliation, destruction, rapes, and killings. Six months later, we were among the 5,000 people released. We returned home to fight for simple survival. At the age of 16, I found myself spending my days planning ways for my family to escape. My family and I were again forced from our home and experienced three years of uncertainty, fear

OH, YOU MEAN THOSE IMMIGRANTS

I am married to an immigrant who also happens to have the same last name as one of the most despised men in modern history (Milosevic, the "Butcher of the Balkans"; the name Milosevic in Serbia was as common as Smith here).

Several times since 9/11, I have been present when someone starts a harangue about the "problem with immigrants." Once I was in the Southwest, and someone said, "They aren't like us, and they take our jobs." I pointed out that Mexicans had been in the Southwest for hundreds of years before Anglos, if that was the "they" this person was talking about, and the jobs they "took" were often jobs no one else would do. Plus, "I'm married to an immigrant."

"Oh, well, I didn't mean immigrants like him," she said.

"Why? Because he's European?"

A great deal of stammering ensued.

Another time someone said we "really need to be wary of immigrants. They come from different cultures, and they don't understand our culture." Again I said, "My husband is an immigrant."

"Oh, I didn't mean him."

"Why? Because he's white?"

"Well, he's . . . Actually, I didn't know he was an immigrant."

I always end these conversations with "All of us are immigrants on this continent or descendants, with the possible exception of Native Americans."

That particular argument never wins me any points. We are here now, people say; so they need to adapt to our ways. Whoever "they" are.

Source: From http://www.sentimentalrefugee.com/thoseimmigrants.html.

and anger. The life we knew and had taken for granted was abruptly changed by others' political agendas. Having our basic human rights violated was the experience that literally changed my life.

Her family was eventually rescued by the International Red Cross in 1995 and transported to Phoenix, Arizona.

There are also cases of domestic refugees who are forced, for short or indefinite periods, to move within a country. Examples include the Japanese Americans sent to internment camps during World War II; the Cherokees forcibly removed in 1838 from their own nation, New Echota, to Oklahoma (the devastating Trail of Tears); and the Mormons, who fled the East and eventually settled in Utah and elsewhere in the West. Populations also relocate temporarily because of natural disasters, such as hurricanes or floods. This mass migration of refugees presents complex issues for intercultural communication, pointing to the importance of the relationship between the migrants and their host cultures.

MIGRANT-HOST RELATIONSHIPS

The relationships between immigrants and their hosts are very complex, and understanding these relationships requires a dialectical approach. International migration is usually a carefully considered individual or family decision (see Figure 8-2). The major reasons to migrate can involve economic and/or noneconomic reasons and complex push-pull (dialectical) factors. An economic migrant may be encouraged to move by a host employer recruiter—pulling him or her to migrate, or a push factor might be lack of jobs in the home country. Migrants crossing borders for noneconomic reasons may be moving to escape persecution—a push factor. One of the most important noneconomic motivations for crossing national borders is family unification—a pull factor for family migration (Martin & Zürcher, 2008). Once in the host country, the migrant may face a range of reactions from people there. For example, in Arizona and many other states, business interests depend on cheap labor provided by Mexican immigrants; the general economy also depends on dollars spent by immigrants. At the same time, citizens may fear the consequences of rising illegal immigration and the pressure on the medical, social, and educational systems. The immigrants may be simultaneously accepted and rejected, privileged and disadvantaged, and relationships may be both static and dynamic. These relationships have implications for intercultural communication.

Migrant-host relationships exist in multiple tensions: The migrants want to cherish and retain their own culture as well as value their host culture. The host culture also may be motivated to accept or reject the new migrants. Social psychologist John Berry (1992) developed a framework that considers the relationship of migrants and hosts and their attitude toward each other's cultures, resulting in four types of relationships (see Table 8-2). When migrants value the host culture more than their own, they assimilate. When migrants value their heritage culture more than the host, they separate. When migrants value both the host and their heritage culture, they integrate, and when migrants value neither their host nor their heritage culture, they are marginalized. Of course, we must also consider the reception of the host culture toward the migrants. Scholars point out that many migrant experiences do not fit neatly into one of these four types—migrants may shift from one to the other depending on the context—resulting in a fifth mode, cultural hybridity (Rosenau, 2004). Let's examine each of these relationships more closely.

Assimilation

assimilation A type of cultural adaptation in which an individual gives up his or her own cultural heritage and adopts the mainstream cultural identity. (See **cultural adaptation.**)

In an **assimilation** mode, the individual does not want to maintain an isolated cultural identity but wants to maintain relationships with other groups in the new culture. The migrant is more or less welcomed by the new cultural hosts. When this course is freely chosen by everyone, it creates the archetypal "melting pot." The central focus in assimilation is not on retaining one's cultural heritage. Many immigrant groups, particularly those from Europe, follow this mode of adapting in North America. For them, assimilating may not require adjusting

TABLE 8-2 MIGRANT–HOST RELATIONSHIPS

	Migrants Value Host/Majority Culture		Migrants Devalue Host/Majority Culture
Migrants devalue own/ minority culture	Assimilation		Marginalization
		Hybridity	
Migrants value own/ minority culture	Integration		Separation

to new customs. The same religions dominate, eating practices (the use of forks, knives, and spoons) are the same, and many other cultural practices (clearly originated in Europe) are already familiar. However, when the dominant group forces assimilation, especially on immigrants whose customs are different from those of the host society, it creates a "pressure cooker." This mode of relating often entails giving up or losing many aspects of the original culture, including language. One of our students, Rick, describes the process:

> *I am Mexican American and I grew up in a household where we took part in cultural events, but we never discussed why we did them. I am always asked if I know how to speak Spanish. I guess people ascribe this to my appearance. My parents speak Spanish fluently, as well as English, but they never taught my siblings or myself because they did not want us to have any problems when we entered school, as they did.*

Some people question why immigrants need to give up so much to assimilate. As one of our students said, "Why must we lose our history to fit into the American way of life? I suppose that, because race is such a sensitive issue in our country, by not discussing culture and race we feel it makes the issue less volatile." A recent study of African Americans and Hispanic Americans showed the effects of society's pressure on groups to assimilate. According to the study, the more experiences people had with ethnic or racial discrimination (on the job, in public settings, in housing, and in dealings with police), the less importance they assigned to maintaining their own cultural heritage. This suggests that heavy doses of discrimination can discourage retention of immigrants' original cultural practices (Ruggiero, Taylor, & Lambert, 1996).

Separation

There are two forms of **separation.** The first is when migrants choose to retain their original culture and avoid interaction with other groups. This is the mode followed by groups like the Amish, who came to the United States from Europe in the 18th century. They maintain their own way of life and identity and avoid prolonged contact with other groups. Many strict religious groups actively resist the influence of the dominant society. The Amish, for example, do not

separation A type of cultural adaptation in which an individual retains his or her original culture while interacting minimally with other groups. Separation may be initiated and enforced by the dominant society, in which case it becomes segregation.

participate in U.S. popular culture; they don't have televisions or radios, go to movies, or read mainstream newspapers or books. An important point here is that these groups choose separation, and the dominant society respects their choice.

However, if such separation is initiated and enforced by the dominant society, the condition constitutes a second type of separation, **segregation** (see Figure 8-3). Many cities and states in the United States historically had quite restrictive codes that dictated where members of various racial and ethnic groups could and could not live. For example, Oregon passed legislation in 1849 excluding blacks from the state; it was not repealed until 1926 (Henderson, 1999, p. 74). You may recall the excerpt in Chapter 7 from Malcolm X's autobiography in which he notes that his family could not live in East Lansing, Michigan, because it was for whites only. An example of de facto segregation is the practice of redlining, in which banks refuse loans to members of particular ethnic groups. This practice perpetuates ethnic segregation.

Many migrants from Latin America and the Caribbean experience prejudice and discrimination as they strive to make it in the United States. For example, a recent longitudinal study shows that many of today's Latino immigrants, in comparison to previous generations, are struggling more educationally and economically and tend to live in more segregated neighborhoods. The authors blame the loss of middle-class manufacturing jobs, prejudice fueled by the immigration debate, and a decline in public education (Telles & Ortiz, 2008).

Some people, realizing they have been excluded from the immigrant advancement version of the melting pot by legal or informal discriminatory practices, in turn promote a separate mode of relating to the host culture. They may demand group rights and recognition but not assimilation.

segregation The policy or practice of compelling groups to live apart from each other.

Integration

Integration occurs when migrants have an interest both in maintaining their original culture and language and in having daily interactions with other groups. This differs from assimilation in that it involves a greater interest in maintaining one's own cultural identity. Immigrants can resist assimilation in many ways— for example, by insisting on speaking their own language in their home. One immigrant from Ghana, Meri, describes her home:

integration A type of cultural adaptation in which individuals maintain both their original culture and their daily interactions with other groups. (See also **cultural adaptation.**)

> *"English was spoken only in the presence of people who could not communicate in any of our languages (Ga or Twi). It wasn't as if my parents forbade me to speak English, but if I addressed either of them in English, the response I got was always in Ga. . . . My mother still insists upon conversing with me in Ga. When it appeared as though I was losing fluency, she became adamant and uncompromising about this; in her mind, to forget one's mother tongue was to place the final sever in the umbilical cord. I do believe that she was right, but over the years I have praised and cursed her for this." (quoted in O'Hearn, 1998, p. 102)*

FIGURE 8-3 This photo depicts the practice of segregation. At the Greene County fair in Greensboro, Georgia, white students were admitted free one day and black students the next day. (*Library of Congress*)

Meri also describes how her family participated in other aspects of American life, such as enjoying American music: "We listened to reggae, calypso, high life, jazz and sometimes R&B. We listened to country music—Kenny Rogers and Willie Nelson" (p. 103).

Other immigrants, like Asian Indians in the United States, maintain a strong sense of their ethnic identity by celebrating Indian holidays like Navarātrī, the Hindu festival that celebrates cosmic good over evil. Communication scholar Radha Hegde (2000) describes how these kinds of celebrations

provide a connection and sense of affirmation to immigrants, playing an important part in the process of redefining selfhood and establishing a sense of community in the new environment. . . . To immigrants like myself, these are opportunities to enjoy being Indian and to savor the colors, clothes, tastes, and sounds of a home left behind. (p. 129)

Migrant communities can actively resist assimilation in many ways. They may refuse to consume popular culture products (TV, radio, movies) or the fashions of the host society, often for many generations. In any case, integration depends on the openness and willingness of those in the dominant society to accept and accommodate somewhat the cultures of others. For example, an interesting debate is occurring in the multicultural city of Liverpool, England. There are currently 122 ethnic support groups, from the Afro-Caribbean lunch club to a forum for Chinese diabetics, and local state-funded "faith schools" can select students according to their religious background. However, when the town was considering "women only" nights at the local swimming pools (in deference to the religious traditions of local Muslims), city officials published guidelines to restrict using public money on projects that "might unnecessarily keep people apart." The challenge for host and immigrant groups is to find the balance of "integration," somewhere between segregation and assimilation ("The search for social glue," 2008).

Marginalization

marginalization A type of cultural adaptation in which an individual expresses little interest in maintaining cultural ties with either the dominant culture or the migrant culture. (See **cultural adaptation**.)

Marginalization occurs when individuals or groups express little interest in maintaining cultural ties with either the dominant culture or the migrant culture. This situation of being out of touch with both cultures may be the result of actions by the dominant society—for example, when the U.S. government forced Native Americans to live apart from other members of their nations. However, the term *marginalization* has come to describe, more generally, individuals who live on the margin of a culture, not able to participate fully in its political and social life as a result of cultural differences. For example, women from overseas who marry U.S. military men may find themselves living in relatively isolated parts of the country upon their husbands' return to the States. These women, sometimes called "war brides," become marginalized by the dominant society. They cannot find a local community of people with whom to share their native culture and language, nor can they participate in U.S. culture as a result of linguistic, cultural, and sometimes prejudicial barriers. These women may also be rejected by their husbands' families, leading to further marginalization.

Cultural Hybridity

Migrants and their family often combine these four different modes of relating to the host society—at times assimilating, other times integrating, and still other times separating, or marginalizing, forming a cultural hybridity relationship with the host culture. They may desire economic assimilation (via employment), linguistic integration (bilingualism), and social separation (marrying someone from the same group and socializing only with members of their own group), producing not the "melting pot" society where everyone was supposed to try to become the same, but rather a "salad" society, where each group retains a distinctive flavor but blends together to make up one great society.

Many people in today's world who consider themselves the product of many cultures, not easily fitting into any of the categories, are also cultural hybrids. Consider the case of Virginia:

> *I was born in Argentina, my entire family is Argentinean, and culturally I have been raised Argentinean. Yet at age four I moved out of Argentina and only returned on vacations. I grew up in Panama until I was thirteen and then moved to California. So where does that leave me? I speak perfect English and Spanish. Physically, I can pass as Californian, Panamanian, or Argentinean. I know many people who are in my same situation. In a sense, we identify with each other. We have created our own territory, imagined, but a territory nonetheless.*

In some families, individual members choose different paths of relating to the larger culture. This can cause tensions when children want to assimilate and parents prefer a more integrative mode.

One of the more difficult aspects of adaptation involves religion. How do immigrants pass on their religious beliefs to their children in a host country with very different religious traditions? Or should they? Aporva Dave, an honors student at Brown University, was curious about this question and conducted (along with another student) a study as an honors thesis. He interviewed members of South Asian Indian families that, like his own, had immigrated to the United States. He was curious about how strictly the parents followed the Hindu religion, how strongly they wanted their children to practice Hinduism in the future, and how the children felt about following the religious practices of their parents. In general, as expected, the children had a tendency to move away from the traditional practices of Hinduism, placing more emphasis on Hindu values than on Hindu practices (e.g., prayer). Although many of the parents themselves prayed daily, most were more concerned that their children adopt the morals and values of Hinduism. The parents seemed to understand that assimilation requires a move away from strict Hindu practices. Most viewed Hinduism as a progressing, "living" religion that would change but not be lost. And many spoke of Hinduism as becoming more attractive as a religion of the future generation.

However, the study also revealed that children raised in the same house could have very different attitudes toward adaptation and religion. For example, two sisters who participated in the study were raised with "moderately" religious parents who worship weekly, read religious articles, and spend much time thinking about God. One sister followed the traditions of the parents: She prays every day, spends time reading religious scriptures, and is committed to marrying a Hindi. The other sister does not practice Hinduism and places emphasis on love in making a marriage decision. These kinds of differences can sometimes make communication difficult during the adaptation process.

As individuals encounter new cultural contexts, they have to adapt to some extent. This adaptation process occurs in context, varies with each individual, and is circumscribed by relations of dominance and power in so-called host cultures. Let's look more closely at this process.

TABLE 8-3	CONTRIBUTIONS OF THREE APPROACHES TO CULTURAL ADAPTATION	
Social Science	**Interpretive**	**Critical**
Role of individual migrant characteristics and background; theories of culture shock and reentry shock; outcomes of adaptations	In-depth analysis of adaptation experience	Importance of history, politics, and societal structures in migrant adaptation and identity

CULTURAL ADAPTATION

cultural adaptation A process by which individuals learn the rules and customs of new cultural contexts.

Cultural adaptation is the long-term process of adjusting to and finally feeling comfortable in a new environment (Y. Y. Kim, 2001, 2005). How one adapts depends to some extent on the host environment—whether it is welcoming or hostile. There are three communication approaches to studying cultural adaptation, and they vary in the degree to which they emphasize individual or contextual/environmental influences in the adaptation process. A dialectical perspective incorporates both the individual and the contextual. As shown in Table 8-3, the social science approach emphasizes the role of personal characteristics of the migrant; the interpretive focuses on the experience of the migrant in the adaptation context; the critical explores the role of larger contexts that influence cultural adaptation: social institutions and history, politics, and economic structures.

Social Science Approach

The social science approach focuses on the individual in the adaptation process, individual characteristics and background of the migrant, and the individual outcomes of adaptation. It includes three models: the anxiety and uncertainty management (AUM) model, the transition model, and the integrative model.

Individual Influences on Adaptation   Many individual characteristics—including age, gender, preparation level, and expectations—can influence how well migrants adapt (Ward, 1996). But there is contradictory evidence concerning the effects of age and adaptation. On the one hand, younger people may have an easier time adapting because they are less fixed in their ideas, beliefs, and identities. Because they adapt more completely, though, they may have more trouble when they return home. On the other hand, older people may have more trouble adapting because they are less flexible. However, for that very reason, they may not change as much and so have less trouble when they move back home (Kim, 2001).

Level of preparation for the experience may influence how migrants adapt, and this may be related to expectations. Many U.S. sojourners experience more culture shock in England than in other European countries because they expect arco's parents sent him to the United States in 1993 because they thought it would be easier to combine sports and academic studies in a U.S. high school than a German high school. Marco's career goal is to become a professional tennis player. He describes his initial culture shock and his ultimate adaptation to life here.

The first semester at an American high school, I experienced culture shock, even though I had visited the States several times before with my parents. . . . Even though I studied English since the fifth grade in Germany and understood most of what people said, it was hard to get used to the American slang. I was really close to going back home to Germany, because I was frustrated and had to get used to the new living conditions. . . .

Sometimes it confuses me, and I don't know in which of these two worlds I belong, because I wonder where in 10 years I am going to be living and working. First, I was intimidated by the unfamiliarity of the school, but I recovered from culture shock soon, because I adapted to the new cultural situation and living arrangements with my new family and the language. I have lived here in the United States for about a fourth of my life, and sometimes I feel like I am American even though I am still a German citizen. At the same time, my friends in Germany refer to me as the "American," but here I am perceived as being German. Living here in the U.S. has taught me a great deal about being German—maybe more than I could have found out living in Germany, because here I see everything through different eyes. . . .

I still consider myself German . . . but if people ask me where I am from I sometimes answer that I am from California, and they would never find out that I was not. I don't even consider the fears I once had about coming to the U.S. and experiencing another culture anymore, because over the years it has become such a ritual to me that it is no longer a big issue. It feels like I am able to switch back and forth between two different cultures without having anxiety.

—Marco

little difference between life there and life here in the United States (Weissman & Furnham, 1987). In contrast, sojourners traveling to cultures that are very different expect to experience culture shock. The research seems to show that overly positive and overly negative expectations lead to more difficulty in adaptation; apparently, positive but realistic or slightly negative expectations prior to the sojourn are best (Martin, Bradford, & Rohrlich, 1995).

Anxiety and Uncertainty Management Model Communication theorist William Gudykunst (1995, 1998, 2005) stresses that the primary characteristic of relationships in intercultural adaptation is ambiguity. The goal of effective intercultural communication can be reached by reducing anxiety and seeking information, a

uncertainty reduction
The process of lessening
uncertainty in adapting to
a new culture by seeking
information.

predictive uncertainty
A sense of uncertainty that
stems from the inability to
predict what someone will
say or do.

explanatory
uncertainty   In the
process of cultural adap-
tation, uncertainty that
stems from the inability
to explain why people
behave as they do. (See
cultural adaptation.)

process known as **uncertainty reduction.** There are several kinds of uncertainty. **Predictive uncertainty** is the inability to predict what someone will say or do. We all know how important it is to be relatively sure how people will respond to us. **Explanatory uncertainty** is the inability to explain why people behave as they do. In any interaction, it is important not only to predict how someone will behave but also to explain why the person behaves in a particular way. How do we do this? Usually, we have prior knowledge about someone, or we gather more information about the person. One of our students, Linda, describes her interactions with a Swedish exchange student:

> I remember feeling very uncomfortable and unsure about how to communicate with her. . . . I can remember asking simple questions about her hobbies, her family, and why she wanted to be a foreign exchange student. Basically, I was seeking to reduce my own uncertainty so that I could better predict her behavior. . . . The experience was a very positive one.

Migrants also may need to reduce the anxiety that is present in intercultural contexts. Some level of anxiety is optimal during an interaction. Too little anxiety may convey that we don't care about the person, and too much causes us to focus only on the anxiety and not on the interaction. One student recalls her anxiety about communicating during a visit to Italy: "Once I decided to let go of my anxiety and uncertainty, I was much better at assessing behavior and attitudes [of Italians] and thereby increasing my understanding of aspects of the Italian culture."

This model assumes that to communicate effectively we will gather information to help us reduce uncertainty and anxiety. How do we do this? The theory is complicated; however, some general suggestions for increasing effectiveness are useful. The theory predicts that the most effective communicators (those who are best able to manage anxiety and predict and explain others' behaviors) (1) have a solid self-concept and self-esteem, (2) have flexible attitudes (a tolerance for ambiguity, empathy) and behaviors, and (3) are complex and flexible in their categorization of others (e.g., able to identify similarities and differences and avoid stereotypes). The situation in which communication occurs is important in this model. The most conducive environments are informal, with support from and equal representation of different groups. Finally, this model requires that people be open to new information and recognize alternative ways to interpret information.

Of course, these principles may operate differently according to the cultural context; the theory predicts cultural variability. For example, people with more individualistic orientations may stress independence in self-concepts and communities; self-esteem may become more important in interactions. Individualists also may seek similarities more in categorizing. (See also Witte, 1993.)

The Transition Model   Culture shock and adaptation have been viewed as a normal part of human experience, as a subcategory of transition shock. Janet Bennett (1998), a communication scholar, suggests that culture shock and adaptation are just like any other "adult transition." Adult transitions include going n this essay, Grant Pearse, a New Zealander of mixed ethnicity, writes about his experience as a student in the United States. Note his description of conflicting feelings: simultaneously missing his home, enjoying his life in his host country, and feeling uncomfortable with the emphasis on individuality.

AN INDIVIDUAL, BUT NOT TOTALLY

Whatever the reason people come to the United States, whether it is for escape from economic, political or social unrest, or for adventure or just to experience another country, we're all faced with one thing and that is that our home culture is different from the one we experience here. . . .

I think of when my mother died in New Zealand and I went back. While standing in line at the supermarket, my mother's best friend came up to me and we embraced for about 10 minutes, just standing there in line at the supermarket, hugging and weeping. Then this friend invited me to her home for a special New Zealand meal, so that I wouldn't forget that this was my home.

In the Maori traditions, the body lies in the house, just as my mother did, with a Tongan tapa cloth draped over our sturdy coffee table, and the casket on top. Then people come and visit, bring food and gifts of money. I miss the singing, the vehemence, the subtle harmonies so unrehearsed and yet so moving as to bring change into a soul. I miss the participation at the grave site, each of the family shoveling the earth onto the coffin in the final gesture of love.

Yet I love my new home here in the United States with its beauty and excitement, but am torn by its adoration of individuality and lack of community. I believe that I am an individual but not totally, as I can never separate myself from my relationship to a family, a community, the earth and God. What I do enhances these groups, and what I fail to do, fails these groups. I can't give up the Polynesian attitude that if everyone else can't rise with me, it is not worth rising at all.

Source: From C. C. Ottesen, *L.A. Stories: The Voices of Cultural Diversity* (Yarmoutri, ME: Intercultural Press, 1993), p. 39.

away to college for the first time, getting married, and moving from one part of the country to another. These experiences share common characteristics and provoke the same kinds of responses.

All transition experiences involve change, including some loss and some gain, for individuals. For example, when people marry, they may lose some independence, but they gain companionship and intimacy. When international students come to the United States to study, they leave their friends and customs behind but find new friends and new ways of doing things.

Cultural adaptation depends in part on the individual. Each person has a preferred way of dealing with new situations. Psychologists have found that

flight approach A strategy to cope with a new situation, being hesitant or withdrawn from the new environment. (Compare with **fight approach.**)

fight approach A trial-and-error approach to coping with a new situation. (Compare with **flight approach.**)

most individuals prefer either a "flight" or a "fight" approach to unfamiliar situations. Each of these approaches may be more or less productive depending on the context. Migrants who prefer a **flight approach** when faced with new situations tend to hang back, get the lay of the land, and see how things work before taking the plunge and joining in. Migrants who take this approach may hesitate to speak a language until they feel they can get it right, which is not necessarily a bad thing. Taking time out from the stresses of intercultural interaction (by speaking and reading in one's native language, socializing with friends of similar background, and so on) may be appropriate. Small periods of "flight" allow migrants some needed rest from the challenges of cultural adaptation. However, getting stuck in the "flight" mode can be unproductive. For example, some U.S. students abroad spend all of their time with other American students and have little opportunity for intercultural learning.

A second method, the **fight approach,** involves jumping in and participating. Migrants who take this approach use the trial-and-error method. They try to speak the new language, don't mind if they make mistakes, jump on a bus even when they aren't sure it's the right one, and often make cultural gaffes. For example, Bill, a U.S. exchange teacher in France, took this approach. His French was terrible, but he would speak with anyone who would talk to him. When he and his wife first arrived in their town late at night, he went to the Hôtel de Ville (City Hall) and asked for a room! His wife, Jan, was more hesitant. She would speak French only when she knew she could get the grammar right, and she would study bus schedules for hours rather than risk getting on the wrong bus or asking a stranger. Getting stuck in the "fight" mode can also be unproductive. Migrants who take this approach to the extreme tend to act on their surroundings with little flexibility and are likely to criticize the way things are done in the new culture.

Neither of these preferences for dealing with new situations is inherently right or wrong. Individual preference is a result of family, social, and cultural influences. For example, some parents encourage their children to be assertive, and others encourage their children to wait and watch in new situations. Society may encourage individuals toward one preference or the other. A third alternative is the "flex" approach, in which migrants use a combination of productive "fight" or "flight" behaviors. The idea is to "go with the flow" while keeping in mind the contextual elements. Hostile contexts (such as racism or prejudice) may encourage extreme responses, but a supportive environment (tolerance) may encourage more productive responses.

The Integrative Model   The three approaches discussed so far concentrate on the psychological feelings of migrants, on how comfortable they feel. What role does communication play in the adaptation process? For an answer, we turn to a model of adaptation developed by communication scholar Young Yun Kim (2001, 2005). Kim suggests that adaptation is a process of stress, adjustment, and growth. As individuals experience the stress of not fitting in with the environment, the natural response is to seek to adjust. This process of adjustment represents a psychic breakdown of previously held attitudes and behaviors—ones that worked in original cultural contexts. This model fits very well with our dialectical approach in its emphasis on the interconnectedness of individual and context in the adaptation process.

Adaptation occurs through communication. That is, the migrant communicates with individuals in the new environment and gradually develops new ways of thinking and behaving. In the process, the migrant achieves a new level of functioning and acquires an intercultural identity. Of course, not everyone grows in the migrant experience. Some individuals have difficulty adapting to new ways. According to the cognitive dissonance theorists of the 1950s, individuals typically have three options when confronting ideas or behaviors that do not fit with previously held attitudes: They can (1) reject the new ideas, (2) try to fit them into their existing frameworks, or (3) change their frameworks (Festinger, 1957).

Communication may have a double edge in adaptation: Migrants who communicate frequently in their new culture adapt better but also experience more culture shock. Beulah Rohrlich and Judith Martin (1991) conducted a series of studies of U.S. American students living abroad in various places in Europe. They discovered that those students who communicated the most with host culture members experienced the most culture shock. These were students who spent lots of time with their host families and friends in many different communication situations (having meals together, working on projects together, socializing, and so on). However, these same students also adapted better and felt more satisfied with their overseas experience than the students who communicated less. Along the same lines, communication scholar Stephanie Zimmerman (1995) found that international students who interacted most often with U.S. American students were better adapted than those who interacted less.

Another dimension of communication is the important role of social support. When migrants leave their home countries they are deprived of important others who endorse their sense of self. When feelings of helplessness and inadequacy arise during the cultural adaptation, **social support** from friends can play an important role in helping the newcomer reduce stress, clarify uncertainty, and increase a sense of identity and self-esteem (Adelman, 1988). However, the social support system needs to include individuals both from the home culture and from the host culture. For example, studies show that international students' relationships with host culture members and also with other international students lead to better adjustment in general (Kashima & Loh, 2006).

Dan Kealey (1996), who worked for many years with the Canadian International Development Agency, conducted studies of overseas technical assistance workers in many different countries. Kealey and his colleagues tried to understand what characterized effective workers and less effective workers. They interviewed the Canadian workers, their spouses, and their host country co-workers. They discovered that the most important characteristics in adaptation were the interpersonal communication competencies of the workers.

In one study, Kealey (1989) found that those who communicated more in the host country experienced a greater degree of culture shock and had more initial difficulty in adapting to the new country. These people also were rated by

social support Ties with other people that play a significant part in mediating psychological health over time.

their host country co-workers as more successful. As with the student sojourners, for these workers, communication and adaptation seem to be a case of "no pain, no gain." Intercultural interaction may be difficult and stressful but ultimately can be highly rewarding.

Outcomes of Adaptation Much of the early research on cultural adaptation concentrated on a single dimension. More recent research emphasizes a multidimensional view of adaptation and applies best to voluntary transitions. There are at least three aspects, or dimensions, of adaptation: (1) psychological health, (2) functional fitness, and (3) intercultural identity (Kim, 2001). Again, we must note that these specific aspects are dialectically related to the contexts to which individuals adapt.

Part of adapting involves feeling comfortable in new cultural contexts. **Psychological health** is the most common definition of adaptation, one that concentrates on the emotional state of the individual migrant (Berry, Kim, Minde, & Mok, 1987). Obviously, the newcomer's psychological well-being will depend somewhat on members of the host society. As mentioned previously, if migrants are made to feel welcome, they will feel more comfortable faster. But if the host society sends messages that migrants don't really belong, psychological adjustment becomes much more difficult.

Achieving psychological health generally occurs more quickly than the second outcome, **functional fitness,** which involves being able to function in daily life in many different contexts (Ward, 1996). Some psychologists see adaptation mainly as the process of learning new ways of living and behaving (Ward, Bochner, & Furnham, 2001). That is, they view the acquisition of skills as more important than psychological well-being. They have tried to identify areas of skills that are most important for newly arrived members of a society to acquire. Specifically, newcomers to a society should learn the local rules for politeness (e.g., honesty), the rules of verbal communication style (e.g., direct, elaborate), and typical use of nonverbal communication (e.g., proxemic behavior, gestures, eye gaze, facial expressions).

Obviously, this outcome of becoming functionally fit takes much longer and also depends on the cooperation of the host society. Newcomers will become functionally fit more quickly if host members are willing to communicate and interact with them. Even so, it takes most migrants a long time to function at an optimal level in the new society.

Another potential outcome of adaptation is the development of an **intercultural identity,** a complex concept. Social psychologist Peter Adler (1975) writes that the multicultural individual is significantly different from the person who is more culturally restricted. One student describes her change in identity after living abroad for a year:

> *The year I studied abroad in France was crucial to developing my identity. Not only was I interacting among French people, but I also dealt with intercultural relations among other international students and American exchange students. I developed a new identity of myself and braved a complete transformation of self.*

psychological health The state of being emotionally comfortable in a cultural context.

functional fitness The ability to function in daily life in many different contexts.

intercultural identity Identity based on two or more cultural frames of reference.

All my intercultural experiences have helped me to become a more competent and understanding person.

The multicultural person is neither a part of nor apart from the host culture; rather, this person acts situationally. But the multicultural life is fraught with pitfalls and difficulty. Multicultural people run the risk of not knowing what to believe or how to develop ethics or values. They face life with little grounding and lack the basic personal, social, and cultural guidelines that cultural identities provide.

Interpretive Approach

The interpretive approach focuses on in-depth descriptions of the adaptation process, often employing a phenomenological approach (see Table 8-3). Scholars using this approach explore the essential structures of lived experience through careful and systematic analysis of interview data and participant observation. Whereas the social science approach tends to see the adaptation experience in terms of stable categories like phases and variables like age, gender, and so on, that affect adaptation, an interpretive approach emphasizes the complex and continuous nature of cultural adaptation. To understand this process, researchers generally employ qualitative research methods—like interviewing and focus groups. There are three such interpretive models: the U-curve model, W-curve model, and phenomenological model.

U-Curve Model Many theories describe how people adapt to new cultural environments. The pattern of adaptation varies depending on the circumstances and the migrant, but some commonalities exist. The most common theory is the **U-curve theory** of adaptation. This theory is based on research conducted by a Norwegian sociologist, Sverre Lysgaard (1955), who interviewed Norwegian students studying in the United States. He was interested in understanding the experience of cultural adaptation. His results have been confirmed by many other subsequent studies and have been applied to many different migrant groups.

> **U-curve theory** A theory of cultural adaptation positing that migrants go through fairly predictable phases—excitement/anticipation, shock/disorientation, adjustment—in adapting to a new cultural situation.

The main idea is that migrants go through fairly predictable phases in adapting to a new cultural situation. They first experience excitement and anticipation, followed by a period of shock and disorientation (the bottom of the U curve); then they gradually adapt to the new cultural context. Although this framework is simplistic and does not represent every migrant's experience, most migrants experience these general phases at one time or another.

Anticipation: The first phase is the anticipation or excitement phase. When a migrant first enters a new cultural context, he or she may be excited to be in the new situation and only a little apprehensive. This was the case for Helga María, who moved from Iceland to the United States so that her mother could attend graduate school in Florida. She describes the excitement of moving to the States:

> *The travel date finally arrived. My grandma cried as we walked toward our gate at the airport, but I still felt as if we were just going on a long, fun vacation. . . .*

I remember how huge the supermarket was, the first time we went buying groceries. Every aisle had more and more food and I wanted to taste all the different types of candy and cakes. Even the bread was different, so soft and it felt like a pillow.

Although moving was mostly fun for Helga María, someone adapting to a new job in a new region of the country may experience more apprehension than excitement during the first part of the transition. The same would be true for, say, an international student from East Africa who experiences prejudice in the first months at a U.S. college, or for refugees who are forced to migrate into new cultural contexts.

Culture Shock: The second phase, culture shock, happens to almost everyone in intercultural transitions. Individuals face many challenges of transition in new cultural contexts. **Culture shock** is a relatively short-term feeling of disorientation, of discomfort due to the unfamiliarity of surroundings and the lack of familiar cues in the environment. Kalvero Oberg, the anthropologist who coined the term *culture shock*, suggests it is like a disease, complete with symptoms (excessive hand washing, irritability, and so on). If it is treated properly (that is, if the migrant learns the language, makes friends, and so on), the migrant can "recover," or adapt to the new cultural situation and feel at home (Oberg, 1960).

Although most individuals experience culture shock during the period of transition to a new culture, they are less likely to experience it if they maintain separateness because culture shock presumes cultural contact. For instance, military personnel who live abroad on U.S. bases and have very little contact with members of the host society often experience little culture shock. However, in more recent military operations (e.g., Iraq and Afghanistan), soldiers are having much more contact with civilians, experiencing strong culture shock and some negative outcomes—searching homes without the presence of a male head of household and males conducting body searches of females—very inappropriate behavior in these Muslim contexts. Almost all migrants who cross cultural boundaries, whether voluntarily or not, experience culture shock. And training before encountering a new culture, can help with a smoother transition. For example, incidents of disrespect by American soldiers suggest a need for cultural training and better cultural understanding, since "issues of ethnocentrism and analytical bias can affect tactical, operations, and strategic success" (Chandler 2005, p. 21). High-ranking military personnel very recently emphasized that U.S. advisors need to understand the Iraqi perspective by being trained in "general knowledge of the history of the Middle East with a specific focus on the development of Islam and Arab history—which are not the same thing . . .they need to understand the overlapping and competing spheres of influence at play in this complex culture . . . to see the informal networks behind the formal bureaucracy . . . to more effectively comprehend and influence the behavior of the Iraqi counterparts . . . ." (Allardice & Head, 2008).

For many individuals, long-term adaptation is not easy. Some people actively resist assimilation in the short term. For example, many students from Muslim

culture shock A relatively short-term feeling of disorientation and discomfort due to the lack of familiar cues in the environment.

countries, especially females, often continue to wear traditional clothing while living in the United States, thus actively resisting participating in U.S. popular culture. Others resist assimilation in the long term, as is the case with some religious groups, like the Amish and the Hutterites. Some would like to assimilate but are not welcome in the new culture, as is the case with many immigrants to the United States from Latin America. And some people adapt to some aspects of the new culture but not to others.

For Helga María, culture shock happened pretty quickly:

After a few weeks, when my school started, the heat became rather
tiring. I could hardly be outside for more than five minutes without looking like
I just came out of the shower. . . . I walked around from class to class feeling almost
invisible. Thankfully, I could understand some of what people were saying, but not
communicate back to them.

For Helga María's mother, Erla, it was even harder:

The first semester in Pensacola was one of the hardest in our lives. . . . I missed
my colleagues, my work, and my family at home. I felt so ignorant, unintelligent,
and old when I first started. I walked from one building to another, between
classes. I kept my mouth shut, and when I tried to speak, the southern instructors
often didn't understand what I was trying to say. This was awful. . . . Maybe my
friends were right after all; I was being crazy and selfish. But here we were, and
not about to give up.

Not everyone experiences culture shock when they move to a new place. For example, migrants who remain isolated from the new cultural context may experience minimal culture shock. As noted previously, U.S. military personnel, as well as diplomatic personnel, often live in compounds overseas where they associate mainly with other U.S. Americans and have little contact with the indigenous cultures. Similarly, spouses of international students in the United States sometimes have little contact with U.S. Americans. In contrast, corporate spouses may experience more culture shock because they often have more contact with the host culture: placing children in schools, setting up a household, shopping, and so on.

During the culture shock phase, migrants like Helga María and her family may experience disorientation and a crisis of identity. Because identities are shaped and maintained by cultural contexts, experiences in new cultural contexts often raise questions about identities. For example, Judy, an exchange teacher in Morocco, thought of herself as a nice person. Being nice was part of her identity. But when she experienced a lot of discipline problems with her students, she began to question the authenticity of her identity. When change occurs to the cultural context of an identity, the conditions of that identity also change.

Adjustment: The third phase in Lysgaard's model is adjustment, in which migrants learn the rules and customs of the new cultural context. As Erla says, "After the first semester, we started adapting pretty well. My daughters made new

STRATEGIES FOR FACILITATING GROWTH

Communication scholar Shelly Smith provides the following strategies to help sojourners gain maximum benefits from long-term living, working, or studying abroad:

1. *When your cultural assumptions are challenged, try to suspend judgment until you understand the reasons for your reaction. Reactions can be emotional and intense. When it is hardest to be rational, it is important to stop, take a deep breath and figure out why you feel as you do.*

2. *Try to remember that not all values are created equal. Many differences can be accepted, embraced and enjoyed over time but others remain inviolable. . . . Being able to engage in mindfulness allows you to understand it's a personal choice . . . and OK that others embrace behaviors you cannot.*

3. *Be willing to engage the culture. Genuine interest, curiosity, and a willingness to take risks involves the possibility of making mistakes and looking foolish . . . but it's inevitable and OK.*

4. *Keep a sense of humor. The mistakes one makes will make the best stories later and if you can laugh at yourself, adjustment becomes much easier.*

5. *Be patient. Adjusting to a new culture takes time and happens in increments.*

6. *It's OK to temporarily retreat and embrace your emotions. All sojourners experience moments of anger, frustration, confusion and occasionally even contempt. It's better to take a break than explode needlessly in front of your hosts.*

7. *Remember that successful adaptation involves identity change that will affect your reentry. Take account of how you changed and what you've learned and this will help you explain your experiences to others back home, making reentry a little easier.*

Source: Adapted from S. Smith, "The Cycle of Cross-Cultural Adaptation and Reentry." In J. Martin, T. K. Nakayama, and L. A. Flores (Eds.), *Readings in Intercultural Communication* (Boston: McGraw-Hill, 2002), pp. 253–255.

friends and so did my husband and I. I got used to studying, and started looking at it as any other job. My daughters learned how to speak English very well." Like Helga María, Erla, and the rest of their family, many migrants learn a new language, and they figure out how much of themselves to change in response to the new context. Remember Naida, the immigrant from Bosnia? After several years here in the States, she, too, has adapted. But she also acknowledges that life here still has its challenges:

> *I need to be thankful that I have a stable and peaceful life, a roof over my head, and food to eat. Unlike in some other parts of the world, here I have the opportunity to educate myself, and to make things better, and I must take advantage of it and appreciate it. I should know. I also know that I am going to experience many*

setbacks, disappointments, and emotional crises in my life, but I want to look forward, beyond that and learn.

However, this phase may be experienced very differently if the sociopolitical context is not conducive to individual adaptation. This was the experience of Maria and her sister, who migrated from Greece to Germany:

Unfortunately, I am also the victim of discrimination at the moment. I am applying for a job here in Germany, and although I have finished the German university with an excellent grade and I have the permission to work here, I always get rejected because of my nationality! All the other students from my university have already found a job, only because they are German!! The same experience I had in the UK. And I was only looking for a temporary job!! . . . I think that a cultural adaptation will only take place if we all first learn to respect one another!!

Although the U curve seems to represent the experiences of many short-term sojourners, it may be too simplistic for other types of migrants (Berry, 1992). A more accurate model represents long-term adaptation as a series of U curves. Migrants alternate between feeling relatively adjusted and experiencing culture shock; over the long term, the sense of culture shock diminishes.

W-Curve Model   When migrants return home to their original cultural contexts, the same process of adaptation occurs and may again involve culture, or reentry, shock depicted by the W-curve model (Gullahorn & Gullahorn, 1963). Sometimes this adaptation is even more difficult because it is so unexpected. Coming home, we might think, should be easy. However, students who return home from college, businesspeople who return to corporate headquarters after working abroad, and Native Americans who return to their nations all notice the difficulty of readjusting (Martin & Harrell, 2004).

Scholars refer to this process as the **W-curve theory** of adaptation because sojourners seem to experience another U curve: the anticipation of returning home, culture shock in finding that it's not exactly as expected, and then gradual adaptation (Storti, 2001). Other terms for the process of readapting to one's home culture include: *reverse culture shock*, *reentry shock*, and *repatriation*. Recall Helga María, who migrated from Iceland to Florida with her family. She returned home to Iceland for a short visit and found it was not what she expected:

W-curve theory A theory of cultural adaptation that suggests that soujourners experience another U curve upon returning home. (See **U-curve theory** and **sojourners**.)

We were all pretty excited about going back and seeing our friends and family again. We kind of expected everything to be the same, but it wasn't. My sister and I still talked English to each other. Even when I talked my own language, people said I had an American accent. I never thought that could happen. Being there, I felt more like a visitor, instead of it being my home country.

There are two fundamental differences between the first and second U curves, related to issues of personal change and expectations (Martin, 1984). In the initial curve or phase, the sojourner is fundamentally unchanged and is experiencing new cultural contexts. In the reentry phase, the sojourner has changed orporate management often neglects to take advantage of the skills that many returning workers have acquired in overseas assignments. Cross-cultural specialist Craig Storti identifies specific skills that these returnees can offer the home organization.

WHAT RETURNEES OFFER THEIR ORGANIZATION

Anyone who has been posted abroad comes home with some old skills greatly enhanced and some skills that are new to the organization. Management should highlight these skills and take advantage of them.

1. The returnee may have invaluable knowledge of certain regions, countries, or markets with which the company or organization does business or competes.

2. The returnee brings a different, perhaps unique perspective to issues, discussions, and problem solving.

3. The returnee is likely to be more flexible in dealing with others and more open to new ideas, more likely to try something that hasn't been tried before.

4. The returnee has increased tolerance for different ideas, behaviors, and opinions and, hence, an increased ability to work with or manage a culturally or ethnically diverse workforce.

5. The returnee is more able to compromise, to be more humble and less rigid.

6. The returnee understands the home culture better, can step outside it and observe objectively how it influences decisions and other organizational behavior.

7. The returnee has more self-confidence, having survived and prospered in a challenging environment.

Source: From Craig Storti, *The Art of Coming Home* (2nd ed.) (Yarmoutri, ME: Nicolas Brealey/Intercultural Press, 2001), p. 92.

through the adaptation process and has become a different individual. The person who returns home is not the same person who left home. Helga María's mother, Erla, describes how much she had changed as a result of her sojourn in the United States and how these changes affected her reentry to Iceland:

Surprisingly, I felt like a stranger in my own country; everything seemed so small, the streets, houses, road signs, and I saw my home city in a completely new light. And when I tried to describe all these wonderful, dreadful, amazing, beautiful, and funny things that I had experienced, it seemed like my family and friends weren't interested. Whatever bliss I might have had was quickly blown away, and

I felt that I didn't fit into my own culture. I realized that I had changed and so had my previous friends. . . . This was quite a shock for me.

International students who return home also talk about how their friends and families expect them to be a little different (more educated) but basically the same as before they went off to school (Martin, 1986). This lack of interest on the part of friends and family can be especially detrimental for corporations that send employees overseas. The home corporation often does not take advantage of the knowledge and skills that returnees have acquired during their overseas assignments. Rather, employees in the home office often expect the returnees to fit back in, as if the overseas assignment had never happened (Black & Gregersen, 1999).

Like other sojourners and migrants, the reentry for military personnel can be very stressful, even more stressful than deployment. For example, the Web site for reservists and their families has extensive information to facilitate the homecoming, including the importance of communication, transitional health care benefits, reemployment rights, as well as emotional issues associated with a reunion. It also acknowledges the importance of recognizing changes undergone by soldiers and their families and the need to have realistic expectations (Army reserve family programs, 2008).

Returnees also need to recognize that the cultural context of reentry is different from being overseas. Depending on how long the person was away, political figures, popular culture, family, technology, and even language may have changed. For instance, when Tom's father went to Japan for the first time, a Japanese taxi driver said to him, "I don't know where you are from, but you have been away for a long, long time." Tom's father had never been to Japan before, so the taxi driver was responding to his use of Japanese. Many words in the Japanese language have changed from the 19th century when Tom's family immigrated to the United States, but many now archaic words and structures remain in use by Japanese speakers in the United States.

Sojourners who leave their countries during times of political upheaval and return when peace is reestablished may have to contend with the ambivalence many of those who stayed have toward those who left. In this excerpt, a Lebanese woman describes her feelings toward a friend who had left during the civil war but who has now returned:

> *When you tried to be one of us again, the dominant expression on your face was pity, for everyone who'd stayed here. As you moved you clasped people to you, then touched their faces, then held them again, as if you were saying, "I know what you're suffering." Why were you so sure that those who stayed were the only ones suffering? (Al-Shaykh, 1995, p. 8)*

Phenomenological Model Using a **phenomenological approach**, Chen (2000) interviewed Chinese international students and described in depth how they *experienced and made sense* of the adaptation process. She describes three phases: taking things for granted, making sense of new patterns, and coming to understand new information.

phenomenological approach A research approach that seeks in-depth explanations of human experiences.

In the first phase, migrants realize that their assumptions are wrong and need to be altered. Chen describes the experiences of one of the students she interviewed, Mr. An. He was arriving in the middle of the night at his new U.S. university, but he wasn't worried. In China, student housing is always arranged for by university officials. However, in conversations on the plane with a friendly seatmate named Alice, he began to realize that his expectations of having a place to stay were probably a mistake. He was grateful when Alice offered her home. Mr. An explained, "Alice said she could put me up for the night, that I could live in her house until I found a place. . . . I was surprised but also very grateful" (Chen, 2000, p. 221).

In the second stage, migrants slowly begin to make sense of new patterns, through communication experiences. The first step in making sense for Mr. An took place the next day when he went to the International Students Office. A clerk handed him a map and told him to find his own housing. Although he had heard that people in the United States were individualistic and independent, this cultural pattern was now a living experience for him. The dorms were full, but Mr. An learned how to seek alternatives. He explained how he began to make sense of the experience: "I started to better understand the meaning of independence. I felt I really understood America and was overjoyed [to find] there was a Chinese Student Association on campus. This meant that maybe I could get help from them" (p. 224).

As migrants begin to make sense of their experiences and interactions in new cultural contexts, they come to understand them in a more holistic way. This enables them to fit the new information into a pattern of cultural understanding. Again, this happens through communication with members of the host country and others who implicitly or explicitly explain the new cultural patterns. Mr. An stayed in touch with Alice for a while, but this changed over time. He explained,

> *One day I realized I had not called Alice in a long time, then it occurred to me that she rarely called me; I was the one who usually made the calls. . . . I just didn't get around to calling her again, but now I don't feel guilty about it. She didn't seem to mind one way or the other. I've learned that many Americans are ready to help others, but never see them again afterwards. (p. 226)*

At that point, Mr. An understood the U.S. cultural emphasis on helpful intervention, and he was able to make sense of his friendship with Alice—as a momentary helping relationship. As Chen notes, "Coming to a tentative understanding is the last stage in a cycle of sense-making. . . . In the long run, however, this new perspective will never be completely fulfilled by one's accumulation of knowledge" (p. 227). As Chen points out, there are always more sense-making cycles.

In a more recent study, Kristjánsdóttir (2009) explored the adaptation experience of a group of undergraduate chemistry majors who worked in French chemistry labs during their summer break. Using a phenomenological approach, she interviewed the students several times before they left, during their sojourn in France, and after they returned to the States. Her findings reflect the embodied, visceral experience of their cultural adaptation—specifically in struggles

When I first arrived in Belgium, I watched a lot of TV. I always liked to watch TV before I left the United States, so it was a good way for me to learn French. And it was certainly a lot easier and less painful than trying to talk with Belgians. I always hated that pained look they got on their faces when I would screw up the language in my halting speech.
—Jesse

with the language, their experience of their national and ethnic identity, and their acquired knowledge.

The students described vividly their struggles with the language, how the inability to speak French made their stay in France difficult and how their inability to "read" the social context added to the stress of being misunderstood. One student said, "I feel kind of stupid." Others talked about feeling alone and isolated because no one seemed to want to interact with them. As Kristjánsdóttir describes it, "Due to the language barrier, their embodied relation to the world became problematic. Their self-esteem dropped and they became very self-conscious about themselves. Their whole bodies were entrenched in this effort of trying [to communicate] in French. For the students, it was a laborious and involved process that was connected to all aspects of themselves, being, human sensibilities, and human existence."

The students' experience of their national and ethnic identity was also important in their adaptation process and is described as an experience of feeling invisibility and visibility. Specifically, the white students found that they were often disliked just because they were from the United States—adding stress in the adaptation process. They sometimes feared to talk, knowing their accent would reveal their nationality, and so they would often choose to remain "invisible." They described the experience as a "feeling of being suffocated" because of their Americanness and then a feeling of being extremely visible and standing out when they spoke. Because of their whiteness, they experienced both invisibility and visibility.

In contrast, the students of color did not have the option of experiencing invisibility, and they described their feeling of "standing out" and being extremely visible all the time. They felt their race/ethnicity was adding another layer of stress, of not fitting in the French cultural space. Their "differentness" was apparent even before they opened their mouths to speak, although their nationality might not be entirely obvious. One African American student said, "People are going to look at you . . . they might stare, if they see me looking, and all of a sudden they stare at you all the time." This caused him to feel very uneasy, especially when he was sharing a table with someone at a restaurant or at the university cafeteria. The other students of color described similar experiences.

Having lived through the experience of being rejected enabled the white students to understand a little how it feels to belong to a minority group in the

United States. The students' bodily experience of not having a voice in society and the feeling of being invisible created a new embodied relation to their Americanness. Learning about the French value system aided them in erasing stereotypes they used to have about the French people being lazy. The students' intercultural experience of living in France was eye opening; they not only learned about a new culture but, more importantly, learned about themselves as persons and their home culture of the United States.

These interpretive phenomenological studies help flesh out the social science studies—helping us understand the visceral, embodied experience of cultural adaptation, as shown in Table 8-3.

Mass media also play a role in helping sojourners and immigrants adapt. Radio, television, movies, and so on, are powerful transmitters of cultural values and readily accessible as sources of socialization for newcomers. The mass media may play an especially important role in the beginning stages of adaptation. When sojourners or immigrants first arrive, they may have limited language ability and limited social networks. Listening to the radio or watching TV may be the primary source of contact at this stage, one that avoids negative consequences of not knowing the language (Nwanko & Onwumechili, 1991).

Critical Approach: Contextual Influences

The critical approach reminds us that cultural adaptation depends on the context. Some contexts are easier to adapt to than others, and some environments are more accepting. Young Yun Kim (2001) writes about the receptivity of the host environment and the degree to which the environment welcomes newcomers. She maintains that in a country like Japan, which emphasizes homogeneity, people may be less welcoming toward outsiders than in less homogeneous settings, as in many contexts in the United States. Communication scholar Satoshi Ishii (2001) explains the ambivalent feelings of contemporary Japanese toward foreigners and traces their historical roots: "Since ancient times the Japanese have consistently held not positive–negative dichotomous feelings but the conventional welcome–nonwelcome and inclusion–exclusion ambivalence in encountering and treating . . . strangers" (p. 152). Similarly, many Muslim societies tend to be fairly closed to outsiders. In these societies, the distinction between ingroup (family and close friends) and outgroup (everyone else) is very strong.

Institutional, Political, and Class Influences   Local institutions, like schools, religious institutions, and social service agencies, can facilitate or hinder immigrants' adaptation. For example, schools can help immigrant children to adapt by offering language classes to bring them up to speed. In the United States today, there are approximately 3.5 million schoolchildren with limited English ability, and most are concentrated in a small number of schools. Some regions offer language programs; however, many are cutting their bilingual programs as part of the English-only movement. In Arizona, for example, Proposition 203 banned bilingual education and required schools to use mostly English immersion to teach children with limited English proficiency (Gonzalez, 2005). Some schools *met Ayla Yildirim on February 28, 2003. If I had to say what immediately caught my attention, I would have to smile and say it was it was her accent. The night we met at The Egyptian Club in Portland, Oregon, was the beginning of something new for both of us. We talked and danced and got to know each other. As we started dating, I realized that this was the woman that I had finally been searching for. Her love and kindness filled a void in my heart that had been broken. Soon we began talking and making plans for a commitment ceremony and chose June 14, 2003, as our special day.*

Ayla had come to the United States in 1989 from Turkey. In 2002 she filed for political asylum to remain in the United States. She told me that it would not be fair for me not to know her situation and was unsure if she would be able to remain here. She said I could just walk away and she would understand. I did not know much about immigration laws but knew that I loved her and did not want to end the relationship that we had started. I told her that we would fight this thing together and if ultimately she could not remain here that I would go with her. It is now 2004 and we again made that commitment on March 12, 2004, when marriage licenses were being issued in Portland, Oregon. The one-year deadline to file asylum passed by Congress will make it very difficult to win asylum in her case. Turkey is a country very hostile towards gays and lesbians, but the information regarding persecution of lesbians in Turkey is practically nonexistent, making future persecution difficult to prove as well.

The psychological and financial burden this has placed in our lives has been overwhelming. We dare not make any plans for the long-term future because we don't even know where our future will be. . . . The tremendous injustice of our laws has made me very angry. I feel helpless and like a second-class citizen.

While heterosexual US citizens can get married on a whim and even file a fiancee application for their foreign-born partner, binational same-sex couples are not afforded this same relief. Ultimately binational couples are made to choose their own country, the country of their partner, or a safe third country that will allow both partners to emigrate. . . . Time is a binational couples' best friend and now is the time for change. My heart goes out to all of the couples out there who are suffering the same cruel injustice and sense of impermanence.

Source: From http://www.immigrationequality.net/haxall/stories.html?&mimid=NVNOX8
7RRE598PP346X3JWJ298FQ6ED8&cid=986.

are working hard to mainstream these students, reaching out to parents and community leaders to ease the students' linguistic and social adaptation (Reid, 2005). Others are leading the fight to cut such programs. In Australia, children of undocumented parents have been removed from school and placed in detention (Sedgman, 2005). Similar situations occur in the United States (Garcia, 2005).

When I moved to Arizona from San Francisco to go to school, it was a big shock. I was used to seeing many different kinds of people—Asian Americans, African Americans. At my new university in Phoenix, almost everyone is white. And I was treated differently in Phoenix than I was at home. I often got passed by at the supermarket while the clerk waited on someone who was white. Some of the children who lived in my apartment complex followed me one day, yelling, "Chink, Chink, Chinaman."
    —Lois

Religious institutions can also play an important role in assisting immigrants. Many churches, synagogues, and mosques delivered aid to the victims of Hurricane Katrina. Muslims in the United States have a long tradition of assisting new immigrants financially and socially, through local mosques and civic organizations (Bahadur, 2005). Religious institutions, in turn, can be revitalized by immigrants. For example, a Baptist church in St. Paul, Minnesota, reached out to immigrants from Myanmar, providing them accommodations and airport pickups. People in the church bring donations of food and clothes. The downtown church, with dwindling membership, has been revitalized with the new immigrants (Pratik, 2005). Synagogues in South Florida have been revitalized by Russian immigrants who fled Russia and the religious oppression there (Collie, 2005).

But religious institutions do not always play facilitative roles in migrant transitions. Many Christian organizations in the United States, Canada, and Australia victimized indigenous children by requiring them to attend church schools far away from their homes in an attempt to "drum their native culture from their psyches," where they were often abused and maltreated. Fortunately, some churches are now seeking to redress these abuses (Duff-Brown, 2005).

The relative status and power of sojourners and host groups also influence adaptation. Several recent studies have found that Asian, African, and Latino students in the United States report experiences of discrimination and hostility based on their race/ethnicity while white international students report very few such experiences. These difficulties make it very difficult to adapt to a new country and range from being ignored to verbal insults, confrontation, and even physical assaults—in a variety of contexts, both in and outside the classroom, by peers, faculty, and members of the local community (Lee & Rice, 2007; Poyrazli & Lopez, 2007).

The authors of the studies point to the institutional accountability for international student satisfaction and, ultimately, for positive relations with potential future students in the internationals' home countries:

We recommend that members of the educational community be made aware of this issue and their responsibility in creating intellectual environments that foster cross-national acceptance and learning . . . [and] that guidelines concerning teaching and working with international students be articulated so that administrators and

> *faculty are aware of their responsibility in providing a safe and welcoming*
> *environment for international students (Lee & Rice, p. 405).*

Similarly, it can be difficult for women to adapt in many contexts because of their relatively lower status.

Class issues often enter into the picture. Sometimes immigrant workers are seen as necessary but are not really welcomed into the larger society because of their class (which is often fused with racial differences). And sometimes the discrimination and class issues result in conflict between recent migrants and emigrants from the same country who have been in the host country for a long time. For example, Mexicans have come in increasing numbers to work in the carpet plants in the Southeast and in the meatpacking plants in the Midwest. This has led to tension between those Latinos/as, who have worked hard to achieve harmony with whites and to attain middle-class status, and the newcomers, who are usually poor and have lower English proficiency. The older Latinos/as feel caught between the two—ridiculed by whites for not speaking English correctly and now by recently arrived Mexicans for mangling Spanish. This resentment between old and new immigrants has always been present in America—from the arrival of the first Europeans.

However, there is an upside to the arrival of these new immigrants. Journalist Arian Campo-Flores (2001), writing about the relationships between these two groups in one Midwest town, observes,

> *Cultural collisions can be as enriching as they are threatening. . . . Older Chicanos*
> *have learned to adjust, too. In fact many say that the fresh infusion of Hispanic*
> *culture brought by immigrants has revitalized their identity as Latinos. Their*
> *girls are celebrating* quinceaneras, *the equivalent of "sweet 16" parties. They're*
> *singing to their departed relatives at the cemetery. They've resuscitated their*
> *language . . . both communities have recognized that their complexions will*
> *become only more richly hued. And Chicanos, who in a way are the arbiters*
> *between what the towns used to be and what they've become, are uniquely*
> *qualified to lead. (p. 51)*

The United States is not the only country grappling with an influx of new workers. When Germany needed low-cost laborers, the country brought in many Turkish guest workers, but these immigrants were not necessarily welcomed into German society. Citizenship and other signs of entry into German society were not easily obtainable, and many immigrants (or those perceived to be immigrants) were victims of violent attacks. In fact, all over Europe, people of color seem to be facing increasing trends in racism that make life more difficult than it is for the average citizen in any of these countries (Akwani, 2006). Economic changes that resulted from the reuniting of East and West Germany have reduced the need for guest workers.

Which groups of migrants do you think have a positive image in the United States? Which groups do you think have a negative image? Which groups of international students do you think U.S. students would want to meet and socialize with? Which groups would students not want to meet? The stereotypes of various cultural groups should make it easy for you to sense which groups would face resistance from U.S. Americans in trying to adapt to U.S. culture.

Identity and Adaptation   How individual migrants develop multicultural identities depends on three issues. One is the extent to which migrants want to maintain their own identity, language, and way of life compared to how much they want to become part of the larger new society. Recall that the immigrant–host culture relationship can be played out in several ways. Immigrants to the United States often are encouraged to "become American," which may entail relinquishing their former cultural identity. For example, Mario and his family emigrated from Mexico to Germany when Mario's father took a new job. Mario and his siblings have taken different paths with respect to their relationship to Mexican culture. Mario, the oldest child, has tried to keep some Mexican traditions. His brother, who was very young when the family migrated to Germany, did not learn to speak Spanish at home but is now trying to learn it in college.

The second issue that affects how migrants develop multicultural identities is the extent to which they have day-to-day interactions with others in the new society. Some migrants find it painful to deal with the everyday prejudices that they experience and so retreat to their own cultural groups.

The third issue that affects how migrants relate to their new society involves the ownership of political power. In some societies, the dominant group virtually dictates how nondominant groups may act; in other societies, nondominant groups are largely free to select their own course. For instance, Tom learned that when his mother first went to grammar school she had to pick an "American name" because her own name "was too hard to pronounce." As a first grader, she chose the name "Kathy" because she thought it sounded pretty. This kind of forced assimilation reflects the power of dominant groups over nondominant groups. In this case, *American* means "English" or "British," even though we are a nation of emigrants from all parts of the world. Looking at how migrants deal with these identity issues in host culture contexts can help us understand different patterns of contact (Berry, 1992).

Living on the Border   As international migration increases and more and more people travel back and forth among different cultures, the lines between adaptation and reentry become less clear (Onwumechilia, Nwosu, Jackson, & James-Huges, 2003). More and more people are living on the border physically, making frequent trips between countries, or living on the border psychologically between bicultural identities.

The experience of living on the border was described by Anthropologist Victor Turner (1969) as the experience of **liminality.** According to Turner, liminal people are "threshold people"; they are neither "here nor there," they are "betwixt and between various cultural positions . . . frequently likened to death, to being in the womb, to invisibility, to bisexuality" (p. 95). The trend calls for a new view of cultural boundaries and adaptation.

liminality The experience of being between two or more cultural positions.

> *The emerging "interethnic identity" is a special kind of mindset that promises greater fitness in our increasingly interfaced world. It represents a continuous struggle of searching for the authenticity in self and others within and across*

ethnic groups. . . . A particular emphasis has been placed on the possibility of identity development from a monoethnic identity to a more interethnic identity, from a categorical identity to a more flexible and inclusive identity of individuated and universalized self-other orientation. (Kim, 2006, pp. 292, 295)

This **transnationalism** calls into question comforting notions like nation-states, national languages, and coherent cultural communities. People who move back and forth between cultural worlds often develop a **multicultural identity**, as discussed in Chapter 5. Denis, an international student from France, describes this transnational experience:

> *I have been living outside my home country for several years now, and it seems that the returns home are not as hard as they were in the past. . . . I have learned to just take things as they come and become nonjudgmental regarding people's actions and behaviors. . . . to be able to step back and also realize that in most interactions problems are rarely with the people who live in a country, but rather they are within your own framework of beliefs and behaviors that you have to mentally put aside in order to see the other culture or your own.*

Communication scholar Radha Hegde (1998) uses the metaphor of swinging on a trapeze to describe the immigrant's experience of vacillating between the cultural patterns of the homeland and the new country. Writer Gloria Anzaldúa (1999) also stresses the fluidity and the active roles that individuals must take when living on the borders. She thinks that we need to resist being placed in set categories—like "Chicano/a" or "black" or "Asian American." She also insists that all our identities are in flux and interact with each other. Anzaldúa herself is Chicana, gay, and female. She describes how she has struggled to reconcile the indigenous with the Spanish, the male with the female, and her rather patriarchal Catholic upbringing with her spiritual and sexual identity. The result is the "mestiza"—a person who has actively confronted the negative aspects of identity, such as being silenced as a woman in a patriarchal Mexican-Catholic context, and then constructed a provisional identity:

> *The new mestiza copes by developing a tolerance for contradictions, a tolerance for ambiguity. She learns to be an Indian in Mexican culture, to be Mexican from an Anglo point of view. She learns to juggle cultures. She has a plural personality, she operates in a pluralist mode—nothing is thrust out, the good the bad and the ugly, nothing rejected, nothing abandoned. Not only does she sustain contradictions, she turns the ambivalence into something else. (p. 101)*

This "something else" is the construction of her own historical legacy, a transformation that involves facing her fear of change. Once she accomplishes her personal inner journey, she comes to recognize her multiple identities. In her writing, she demonstrates the many facets of her many identities—writing in several languages (Spanish, English, and Nuhuatl), and in prose (the academic) and poetry (the artistic and spiritual):

> *I will no longer be made to feel ashamed of existing. I will have my voice: Indian, Spanish, white. I will have my serpent's tongue—my woman's voice, my sexual voice, my poet's voice. I will overcome the tradition of silence. (p. 81)*

transnationalism The activity of migrating across the borders of one or more nation-states.

multicultural identity A sense of in-betweenness that develops as a result of frequent or multiple cultural border crossings.

Technological developments have made global travel much easier, and we can change cultural contexts as never before. Yet the movement between cultures is never as simple as getting on a plane (Clifford, 1992). David Mura (1991), a Japanese American from the Midwest, went to live in Japan and wrote about his experiences there:

> *Japan helped me balance a conversation which had been taking place before I was born, a conversation in my grandparents' heads, in my parents' heads, which, by my generation, had become very one-sided, so that the Japanese side was virtually silenced. My stay helped me realize that a balance, which probably never existed in the first place, could no longer be maintained. In the end, I did not speak the language well enough; I did not have enough attraction to the culture. In the end, the society felt to my American psyche too cramped, too well defined, too rule-oriented, too polite, too circumscribed. I could have lived there a few more years if I had had the money and the time, but eventually I would have left.*

The entanglements of history, identity, language, nonverbal communication, and cultural spaces are all salient concerns for understanding these global movements.

INTERNET RESOURCES

www.state.gov/m/dghr/flo/c21995.htm
This Web page provided by the U.S. Department of State provides information on third-culture kids. It provides resources, publications, and Web links on the topic, including one for transition workshops designed for third-culture kids—children whose parents live/work internationally.

www.migrationinformation.org/index.cfm
This Web page provided by Migration Information Source gives "Fresh thought, Authoritative Data, Global Reach" and provides information regarding immigration flows, what to expect when immigrating to certain countries, U.S. perspective, etc.

www.interchangeinstitute.org/html/about.htm
This Web site offers advice, information, and support for transitioning to the United States. It provides insights on the migration experience and also describes the types of support systems that are available for migrants and travelers.

www.arfp.org/skins/ARFP/home.aspx?AllowSSL=true
This Army Reserve Family Programs Online page provides various links that offer services for army personnel and their families. Among these links you will find the "Army Family Action Plan" and "Child and Youth Services." It provides extensive information and guidelines for both returning soldiers and their families to facilitate the often stressful time of homecoming and reunion.

SUMMARY

- A dialectical perspective on transitions reveals the tension between the individual and societal level of cultural adaptation.
- The four types of migrants are sojourners, immigrants, short-term refugees, and long-term refugees.
- There are five modes of host–migrant relationships: assimilation, separation, integration, marginalization, and hybridity.
- A social science approach to adaptation emphasizes individual influences and outcomes and includes the AUM model, the transition model, and the integrative model.
- An interpretive approach emphasizes the lived experience and includes the U-curve theory, the W-curve theory, and phenomenological studies.
- A critical approach emphasizes the contextual influences on adaptation: social institutions, and political, historical, and economic structures.
- Cultural identity and adaptation are related in many ways.
- Those who live "on the borders" often develop multicultural identities.

DISCUSSION QUESTIONS

1. Why does culture shock occur to people who make cultural transitions?
2. Why are adaptations to cultures difficult for some people and easier for others?
3. What is the role of communication in the cultural adaptation process?
4. How do relations of power and dominance affect adaptation?
5. What factors affect migration patterns?
6. What dialectical tensions can you identify in the process of adapting to intercultural transitions?

Go to the self-quizzes on the Online Learning Center at www.mhhe.com/ martinnakayama5 to further test your knowledge.

ACTIVITIES

Culture Shock. Meet with other students in your class in small groups and explore your own experiences of cultural adaptation. Find out how many students experienced culture shock during the first year of college. What did it feel like? How many experienced culture shock when traveling abroad? How about reentry shock? If there are differences in students' experience, explore why these differences exist. Are they related to differences in individual experience? In contexts?

assimilation (314)
cultural adaptation (320)
culture shock (328)
explanatory
    uncertainty (322)
fight approach (324)
flight approach (324)
functional fitness (326)
immigrants (310)
integration (316)
intercultural
    identity (326)

liminality (340)
long-term refugees (311)
marginalization (318)
migrant (310)
multicultural identity
    (341)
phenomenological
    approach (333)
predictive uncertainty
    (322)
psychological health
    (326)

segregation (316)
separation (315)
short-term
    refugees (311)
social support (325)
sojourners (310)
transnationalism
    (341)
U-curve theory (327)
uncertainty
    reduction (322)
W-curve theory (331)

 The Online Learning Center at www.mhhe.com/martinnakayama5 features flashcards and crossword puzzles based on these terms and concepts.

REFERENCES

Adelman, M. B. (1988). Cross-cultural adjustment: A theoretical perspective on social support. *International Journal of Intercultural Relations, 12,* 183–204.

Adler, P. (1975). The transition experience: An alternative view of culture shock. *Journal of Humanistic Psychology, 15,* 13–23.

Allardice, R. R., & Head, K. (2007, Winter). The coalition Air Force Transition Team. *Air & Space Power Journal.* Retrieved April 2, 2008, from http://www.airpower.maxwell.af.mil/airchronicles/apj/apj07/win07/allardice.html

Akwani, O. (2006, June 10). Racism against blacks is a growing trend in Europe. Global News Digest. Retrieved March 28, 2008 from http://imdcontentnew.searchease.com/villages/global/civil_human_equal_rights/RacismagainstBlacksinEurope.asp

Al-Shaykh, H. (1995). *Beirut blues.* New York: Anchor Books.

Anzaldúa, G. (1999). *Borderlands/La frontera: The new mestiza* (2nd ed.). San Francisco: Aunt Lute Press.

Army reserve family programs (Web site). Retrieved April 2, 2008 from http://www.arfp.org/skins/ARFP/home.aspx?AllowSSL=true

Bahadur, G. (2005, August 7). Muslims here balance between two cultures. *Philadelphia Inquirer,* p. B01.

Bennett, J. M. (1998). Transition shock: Putting culture shock in perspective. In M. J. Bennett (Ed.), *Basic concepts in intercultural communication: Selected readings* (pp. 215–224). First published in 1977, in N. C. Jain (Ed.), *International and Intercultural Communication Annual, 4,* 45–52.

Berry, J. W. (1992). Psychology of acculturation: Understanding individuals moving between two cultures. In R. W. Brislin (Ed.), *Applied cross cultural psychology* (pp. 232–253). Newbury Park, CA: Sage.

Berry, J. W., Kim, U., Minde, T., & Mok, D. (1987). Comparative studies of acculturative stress. *International Migration Review, 21,* 491–511.

Black, J. S., & Gregersen, H. B. (1999). *So you're coming home.* San Diego: Global Business.

Campo-Flores, A. (2001, September 18). Brown against brown. *Newsweek,* pp. 49–51.

Chandler, J. V. (2005). *Why culture matters: An empirically-based pre-deployment training program.* Masters Thesis, Naval Postgraduate School.

Chen, L. (2000). How we know what we know about Americans: How Chinese sojourners account for their experiences. In A. González, M. Houston, & V. Chen (Eds.), *Our voices: Essays in culture, ethnicity and communication* (3rd ed., pp. 220–227). Los Angeles: Roxbury.

Clifford, J. (1992). Traveling cultures. In L. Grossberg, C. Nelson, & P. Treichler (Eds.), *Cultural studies* (pp. 96–116). New York: Routledge.

Collie, T. (2005, October 30). Rediscovering Judaism: Synagogues, religious schools are booming as Russian Jews reclaim their culture. *South Florida Sun-Sentinel,* p. 3J.

Danquah, M. N.-A. (1998). Life as an alien. In C. C. O'Hearn (Ed.), *Half + half.* New York: Pantheon Books.

Doyle , M. W. (2004). The challenge of worldwide migration. *Journal of International Affairs, 57*(2), 1–5.

Duff-Brown, B. (2005, November 24). Canada, Aboriginals discuss redress plan. Associated Press News Service.

Ehrenreich, B., & Hochschild, A. R. (2003). Introduction. In B. Ehrenreich & A. R. Hochschild (Eds.), *Global woman: Nannies, maids, and sex workers* (pp. 1–14). New York: Metropolitan Books.

Festinger, L. (1957). *A theory of cognitive dissonance.* Stanford, CA: Stanford University Press.

Gonzalez, D. (2005, October 12). Language gap grows. Studies: Schools face increased challenges. *Arizona Republic*, p. B1.

Gudykunst, W. B. (1995). Anxiety uncertainty management (AUM) theory: Current status. In R. L. Wiseman (Ed.), *Intercultural communication theory* (pp. 8–58). Newbury Park, CA: Sage.

Gudykunst, W. B. (1998). Applying anxiety/uncertainty management (AUM) theory to intercultural adjustment training. *International Journal of Intercultural Relations, 22*, 187–227.

Gudykunst, W. B. (2005). An anxiety/uncertainty management (AUM) theory of effective communication: Making the mesh of the net finer. In W. B. Gudykunst (Ed.), *Theorizing about intercultural communication* (pp. 281–323). Thousand Oaks, CA: Sage.

Gullahorn, J. T., & Gullahorn, J. E. (1963). An extension of the U-curve hypothesis. *Journal of Social Issues, 19*, 33–47.

Hegde, R. S. (1998). Swinging the trapeze: The negotiation of identity among Asian Indian immigrant women in the United States. In D. V. Tanno & A. González (Eds.), *Communication of identity across cultures* (pp. 34–55). Thousand Oaks, CA: Sage.

Hegde, R. S. (2000). Hybrid revivals: Defining Asian Indian ethnicity through celebration. In A. González, M. Houston, & V. Chen (Eds.), *Our voices: Essays in culture, ethnicity and communication* (3rd. ed., pp. 133–138). Los Angeles: Roxbury.

Henderson, M. (1999). *Forgiveness: Breaking the chain of hate.* Wilsonville, OR: Book-Partners.

Ishii, S. (2001). The Japanese welcome-nonwelcome ambivalence syndrome toward Marebito (Ijin) Gaijin strangers: Its implications for intercultural communication research. *Japan Review, 13*, 145–170.

Kashima, E. S., & Loh, E. (2006). International students' acculturation: Effects of international, conational, and local ties and need for closure. *International Journal of Intercultural Relations, 30*, 471–486.

Kealey, D. J. (1989). A study of cross-cultural effectiveness: Theoretical issues, practical applications. *International Journal of Intercultural Relations, 13*, 387–427.

Kealey, D. J. (1996). The challenge of international personnel selection. In D. Landis & R. S. Bhagat (Eds.), *Handbook of intercultural training* (2nd ed., pp. 81–105). Thousand Oaks, CA: Sage.

Kim, M.-S. (2002). Models of acculturative communication competence: Who bears the burden of adaptation? In *Non-western perspectives on human communication* (pp. 141–154). Thousand Oaks, CA: Sage.

Kim, Y. Y. (2001). *Becoming intercultural: An integrative theory of communication and cross-cultural adaptation.* Thousand Oaks, CA: Sage.

Kim, Y. Y. (2005). Adapting to a new culture: An integrative communication theory. In W. B. Gudykunst (Ed.), *Theorizing about intercultural communication* (pp. 375–400). Thousand Oaks, CA: Sage.

Kim, Y. Y. (2006). From ethnic to interethnic: The case for identity adaptation and transformation. *Journal of Language and Social Psychology, 25*(3), 283–300.

Kim, Y. Y., & Gudykunst, W. B. (Eds.). (1988). *Cross cultural adaptation: Current approaches.* International and Intercultural Communication Annual 11. Newbury Park, CA: Sage.

Kristjánsdóttir, E. S. (2009). Invisibility dreaded and desired: Phenomenological inquiry of sojourners' cross-cultural adaptation. *Howard Journal of Communications, 20*(22).

Lee, J. J., & Rice, C. (2007). Welcome to America? International student perceptions of discrimination, *Higher Education, 53*, 381–409.

Lysgaard, S. (1955). Adjustment in a foreign society: Norwegian Fulbright grantees visiting the United States. *International Social Science Bulletin, 7*, 45–51.

Martin, J. N. (1984). The intercultural reentry: Conceptualizations and suggestions for future research. *International Journal of Intercultural Relations, 8*, 115–134.

Martin, J. N. (1986). Communication in the intercultural reentry: Student sojourners' perceptions of change in reentry relationships. *International Journal of Intercultural Relations, 10*, 1–22.

Martin, J. N., Bradford, L., & Rohrlich, B. (1995). Comparing predeparture expectations and post-sojourn reports: A longitudinal study of U.S. students abroad. *International Journal of Intercultural Relations, 19*, 87–110.

Martin, J. N., & Harrell, T. (2004). Intercultural reentry of students and professionals: Theory and practice. In D. Landis, J. M. Bennett, & M. J. Bennett (Eds.), *Handbook of intercultural training* (3rd ed., pp. 309–336). Thousand Oaks, CA: Sage.

Martin, P., & Zürcher, G. (2008) Managing migration: The global challenge. *Population Bulletin, 63*(1), 1–18.

Mather, M. (2007). Education and occupation separates two kinds of immigrants in the United States. Population Reference Bureau. Retrieved March 28, 2008 from http://www.prb.org/Articles/2007/EducationAndOccupationSeparatesUSImmigrants.aspx

Mead, J. C. (2003, September 28). In Island's wealthiest area, backlash against the poorest, *The New York Times*, Section 14LI, p. 1.

Mura, D. (1991). *Turning Japanese: Memoirs of a sansei*. New York: Anchor Books.

Numbers. (2008, February 4). *Time*, p. 18.

Nwanko, R. N., & Onwumechili, C. (1991). Communication and social values in cross-cultural adjustment. *Howard Journal of Communications, 3*, 99–111.

Oberg, K. (1960). Cultural shock: Adjustment to new cultural environments. *Practical Anthropology, 7*, 177–182.

O'Hearn, C. C. (ed). (1998). *Half and Half: Writers on growing up biracial and bicultural*. New York: Pantheon Books.

Omelaniuk, I., & Weiss. T. L. (2005). Introduction. In I. Omelaniuk (Ed.), *World migration 2005: Costs and benefits of international migration (pp. 13–22)*. Geneva, Switzerland: International Organization for Migration.

Onwumechilia, C., Nwosu, P. O., Jackson, R. L., & James-Huges, J. (2003). In the deep valley with mountains to climb: Exploring identity and multiple reacculturation. *International Journal of Intercultural Relations, 27*, 41–62.

Poyrazli, S., & Lopez, M. D. (2007). An exploratory study of perceived discrimination and homesickness: A comparison of international students and American students. *The Journal of Psychology, 141*(3), 263–280.

Pratik, J. (2005, May 15). Refugees renew church. *St. Paul Pioneer Press*, p. C1.

Reid, B. (2005, November 10). Options are available for students, parents: Finding the right fit for English learners. *Arizona Republic*, p. B3.

Rohrlich, B., & Martin, J. N. (1991). Host country and reentry adjustment of student sojourners. *International Journal of Intercultural Relations, 15*, 163–182.

Rosenau, J. N. (2004). Emergent spaces, new places, and old faces: Proliferating identities in a globalizing world. In J. Friedman & S. Randeria (Eds.), *Worlds on the move: Globalization, migration and cultural security* (pp. 23–62). New York: I. B. Tauris.

Ruggiero, K. M., Taylor, D. M., & Lambert, W. E. (1996). A model of heritage culture maintenance. *International Journal of Intercultural Relations, 20*, 47–67.

Santos, B. (2004). Transnational third world. In J. Friedman & S. Randeria (Eds.), *Worlds on the move: Globalization, migration and cultural security* (pp. 293–318). New York: I. B. Tauris.

Search for social glue. (2008, February 23). *The Economist, 386*(8568), 74.

Sedgman, J. M. (2005, March 16). Children removed from schools by immigration officials. *The World Today, ABC Online*. Accessed at http://www.abc.net.au/cgi-bin/common/printfriendly.pl?http://www.abc.net.au/worldtoday/content/2005/s1324795.htm

Storti, C. (2001). *The art of coming home* (2nd ed.). Yarmouth, ME: Nicholas Brealey/Intercultural Press.

Sullivan, K. (1997, December 6). "White" Australia in identity crisis: Many fear Asian immigrants are taking away jobs, culture. *Washington Post*, p. A1.

Tehranian, M. (2004). Cultural security and global governance: International migration and negotiations of identity. In J. Friedman & S. Randeria (Eds.), *Worlds on the move: Globalization, migration and cultural security* (pp. 3–22). New York: I. B. Tauris.

Telles, E. E., & Ortiz, V. (2008). *Generations of exclusion: Mexican Americans, assimilation, and race*. New York: Russell Sage Foundation.

Turner, V. W. (1969). *The ritual process*. Chicago: Aldine Publishing Company.

UNHCR Statistical Yearbook 2006, United Nations High Commissioner for Refugees. Retrieved March 27, 2008 from http://www.unhcr.org/statistics/STATISTICS/478cda572.html

Vanderpool, T. (2002, April 2). Lesson no. 1: Shed your Indian identity. *Christian Science Monitor*, p. 14.

Ward, C. (1996). Acculturation. In D. Landis & R. S. Bhagat (Eds.), *Handbook of intercultural training* (2nd ed., pp. 125–147). Thousand Oaks, CA: Sage.

Ward, C., Bochner, S., & Furnham, A. (2001). *The psychology of culture shock* (2nd ed.). East Sussex: Routledge. (Simultaneously published in the United States by Taylor & Francis, Philadelphia, PA.)

Weissman, D., & Furnham, A. (1987). The expectations and experiences of a sojourning temporary resident abroad: A preliminary study. *Human Relations, 40*, 313–326.

Witte, K. (1993). A theory of cognitive and negative affect: Extending Gudykunst and Hammer's theory of uncertainty and anxiety reduction. *International Journal of Intercultural Relations, 17*, 197–216.

Zimmerman, S. (1995). Perceptions of intercultural communication competence and international student adaptation to an American campus. *Communication Education, 44*, 321–335.

POPULAR CULTURE AND INTERCULTURAL COMMUNICATION

CHAPTER OBJECTIVES

After reading this chapter, you should be able to:

1. Differentiate between high and low culture.
2. Discuss the importance of popular culture as a public forum.
3. Identify the four characteristics of popular culture.
4. Identify some patterns of how people consume popular culture.
5. Identify some ways that people resist popular culture.
6. Describe some of the ways that popular culture influences how people understand another culture.
7. Explain the role of popular culture in stereotyping.
8. Explain how the global movement of popular culture influences people around the world.
9. Discuss the concerns of some governments about the influence of foreign media in their countries.

Originally broadcast in the Netherlands, *Big Brother* has expanded around the world from the U.S. and U.K. to Australia and Nigeria.. The 2007 season of *Big Brother* Australia features a diverse cast of participants, all of whom are Australian. Yet, because not all of them are white, one of the contestants wanted them evicted:

> *"Aussies, I don't think there are enough Aussies in the house," big brother contestant, Andrew said. The "Big Brother" contestant appeared to have analyzed the appearance of housemates in the house before declaring that maybe "Big Brother" should have a special eviction to non-appearing Australians in the house because according to him the "Aussies" seemed to be numbered by darker looking housemates. (Harris, 2007).*

Charges of racism and racist remarks in the Australian version have followed similar charges in the U.K. version. In discussing the racist comments made on the U.K. version of *Big Brother*, sociologist Steve Spencer observes: "Yes this is racism—the sort of everyday racism which is normally invisible—not overt, but in the private domain of the general population. Racist and xenophobic reactions like these 'private' conversations which are broadcast to a mass audience are a bizarre inversion of the everyday racism—the sneering comments, the cultural ignorance and intolerance which is commonplace in our society" (quoted in "Big Brother," 2007).

The popularity of *Big Brother* and reality television more generally opens up the private space of the home and interpersonal relationships to the public arena. The kinds of intercultural interaction and intercultural conflicts that take place in reality television are broadcast widely to a very large audience. These shows bring some of these cultural tensions into public discussion on various discussion boards, Web pages, newspapers, and other outlets.

This chapter explores one type of culture that is often overlooked by intercultural communication scholars but that plays an important role in the construction, maintenance, and experience of culture, particularly in intercultural interactions. This type of culture is popular culture.

LEARNING ABOUT CULTURES WITHOUT PERSONAL EXPERIENCE

As discussed in Chapter 8, people can experience and learn about other cultures by traveling to and relocating and living in other regions. But there will always be many places around the world that we have not visited and where we have not lived. How do we know about places we have never been? Much of what we know probably comes from popular culture—the media experience of films, television, music, videos, books, and magazines that most of us know and share. How does this experience affect intercultural communication?

The Power of Popular Culture

Neither Tom nor Judith has ever been to Brazil, Nigeria, India, Russia, or China. Yet both of us hold tremendous amounts of information about these places from the news, movies, TV shows, advertisements, and more. The kind and quality of information we all have about other places are influenced by popular culture. But the views that the media portray supplement the information we get from other sources. For example, audiences that see the movie *Jarhead* are likely to be familiar with the military mission in Iraq, even if they have not been in military service there. In this sense, popular culture is pervasive.

The complexity of popular culture is often overlooked. People express concern about the social effects of popular culture—for example, the influence of television violence on children, the role of certain kinds of music in causing violent behavior by some youths, and the relationship between heterosexual pornography and violence against women. Yet most people look down on the study of popular culture, as if this form of culture conveys nothing of lasting significance. So, on the one hand, we are concerned about the power of popular culture; on the other, we don't look on popular culture as a serious area of academic research. This inherent contradiction can make it difficult to investigate and discuss popular culture.

As U.S. Americans, we are in a unique position in relationship to popular culture. Products of U.S. popular culture are well known and circulate widely on the international market. The popularity of U.S. movies such as *Transformers* and *Spider Man 3*, of U.S. music stars such as Shakira and Carrie Underwood, and of U.S. television shows from *Grey's Anatomy* to *CSI* and *Desperate Housewives* creates an uneven flow of texts between the United States and other nations. Scholars Elihu Katz and Tamar Liebes (1987) have noted the "apparent ease with which American television programs cross cultural and linguistic frontiers. Indeed, the phenomenon is so taken for granted that hardly any systematic research has been done to explain the reasons why these programs are so successful" (p. 419).

In contrast, U.S. Americans are rarely exposed to popular culture from outside the United States. Exceptions to this largely one-way movement of popular culture include pop music stars who sing in English, such as Wyclef Jean (Haitian), Shakira (Colombian), and Céline Dion (French Canadian). Consider how difficult it is to find foreign films or television programs throughout most of the United States. Even when foreign corporations market their products in the United States, they almost always use U.S. advertising agencies—collectively known as "Madison Avenue." The apparent imbalance of cultural texts globally not only renders U.S. Americans more dependent on U.S.-produced popular culture but also can lead to cultural imperialism, a topic we discuss later in this chapter.

The study of popular culture has become increasingly important in the communication field. Although intercultural communication scholars traditionally have overlooked popular culture, we believe that it is a significant influence in intercultural interaction.

I was on my way to Rome from Newark last summer. Since I took the Polish Airlines, I had to make a stopover there in Warsaw. During my first morning in Warsaw, I got up, took a shower, and turned on the TV, just out of curiosity to see what was showing. I guess I expected to hear Polish, some local news and dramas, etc.

The first thing that jumped at me from the TV screen was Ricky Martin! Then followed Destiny's Child! I was shocked! U.S. popular culture really is everywhere! And I thought I already knew that! But I didn't expect it, all the way in Poland.

— Mina

What Is Popular Culture?

The 19th-century essayist and poet Matthew Arnold, who expressed concern about protecting civilization, defined *culture* as "the best that has been thought and said in the world"—a definition that emphasizes quality. In this context, many Western societies distinguish "high culture" from "low culture."

High culture refers to those cultural activities that are often the domain of the elite or the well-to-do: ballet, symphony, opera, great literature, and fine art. These activities sometimes are framed as *international* because supposedly they can be appreciated by audiences in other places, from other cultures, in different time periods. Their cultural value is seen as transcendent and timeless. To protect these cultural treasures, social groups build museums, symphony halls, and theaters. In fact, universities devote courses, programs, and even entire departments to the study of aspects of high culture.

In opposition to high culture is low culture, which refers to the activities of the nonelite: music videos, game shows, professional wrestling, stock car racing, graffiti art, TV talk shows, and so on. Traditionally, low-culture activities have been seen as unworthy of serious study—and so of little interest to museums or universities. The cultural values embedded in these activities were considered neither transcendent nor timeless.

The elitism reflected in the distinction between high and low culture points to the tensions in Western social systems. In recent decades, however, this distinction has begun to break down. Rapid social changes propelled universities to alter their policies and also have affected how we study intercultural communication. For example, the turbulent 1960s brought to the university a powerful new interest in ethnic studies, including African American studies and women's and gay and lesbian issues. These areas of study did not rely on the earlier distinctions between high and low culture. Rather, they contributed to a new conceptual framework by arguing for the legitimacy of other cultural forms that traditionally would have been categorized as low culture but were now framed as **popular culture.** Because of this elitist view of culture, the distinction between "high culture" and "low culture" has led to low culture being reconceptualized

popular culture A new name for *low culture*, referring to those cultural products that most people share and know about, including television, music, videos, and popular magazines.

350

as popular culture. Barry Brummett (1994), a contemporary rhetorician, offers the following definition: "Popular culture refers to those systems or artifacts that most people share and that most people know about" (p. 21). According to this definition, television, music videos, YouTube, Disney, advertising, soap operas, and popular magazines are systems of popular culture. In contrast, the symphony and the ballet do not qualify as popular culture because most people cannot identify much about them unless they have studied them.

So, popular culture often is seen as populist—including forms of contemporary culture that are made popular by and for the people. John Fiske (1989), professor of communication arts, explains,

> *To be made into popular culture, a commodity must also bear the interests of the people. Popular culture is not consumption, it is culture—the active process of generating and circulating meanings and pleasures within a social system: culture, however industrialized, can never be adequately described in terms of the buying and selling of commodities. (p. 23)*

In his study of popular Mexican American music in Los Angeles, ethnic studies professor George Lipsitz (1990) highlights the innovative, alternative ways that marginalized social groups are able to express themselves. In this study, he demonstrates how popular culture can arise by mixing and borrowing from other cultures: "The ability of musicians to learn from other cultures played a key role in their success as rock-and-roll artists" (p. 140). The popular speaks to—and resonates from—the people, but it does so through multiple cultural voices. Lipsitz continues,

> *The marginality of Chicano rock-and-roll musicians has provided them with a constant source of inspiration and a constant spur toward innovation that gained them the attention of mainstream audiences. But this marginal sensibility amounts to more than novelty or personal eccentricity; it holds legitimacy and power as the product of a real historical community's struggle with oppression. . . . As Chicano musicians demonstrate in their comments about their work, their music reflects a quite conscious cultural politic that seeks inclusion in the American mainstream by transforming it. (p. 159)*

Intercultural contact and intercultural communication play a central role in the creation and maintenance of popular culture. Yet, as Lipsitz points out, the popular is political and pleasurable, which further complicates how we think about popular culture.

There are four significant characteristics of popular culture: (1) It is produced by culture industries, (2) it differs from **folk culture,** (3) it is everywhere, and (4) it fills a social function. As Fiske (1989) points out, popular culture is nearly always produced within a capitalist system that sees the products of popular culture as commodities that can be economically profitable. They are produced by what are called **culture industries.** The Disney Corporation is a noteworthy example of a culture industry because it produces amusement parks, movies, cartoons, and a plethora of associated merchandise.

folk culture Traditional and nonmainstream cultural activities that are not financially driven.

culture industries Industries that produce and sell popular culture as commodities.

TABLE 9-1 THIS CHART HIGHLIGHTS SOME OF THE DISTINCTIONS BETWEEN HIGH CULTURE, FOLK CULTURE, AND POPULAR CULTURE

Type	Definition	Who Knows It?	What Does It Look Like?
High culture	Elite aristocratic expressions of culture	Rich members of the political establishment	Opera, classic sculpture, symphony performances
Folk culture	Traditional and nonmainstream cultural activities that are not financially driven	Most cultural groups, but especially middle-class groups	Folk music
Popular culture	Ever-present cultural products designed for profitable consumption	Almost everyone in a social group	Mainstream music, movies, television, romance novels

More recently, communication scholars Joshua Gunn and Barry Brummett (2004) have challenged the second point that there is an important difference between folk culture and popular culture. They suggest, "We write as if there is a fundamental difference between a mass-produced and mass-marketed culture and a more authentic 'folk' culture or subculture. Such a binary is dissolving into a globally marketed culture. A few remaining pockets of folk culture remain here and there: on the Sea Islands, in Amish country, in departments of English. The rest of folk culture is now 50% off at Wal-Mart" (p. 707). In the new context of globalization, whatever happened to folk traditions and artifacts? Have they been unable to escape being mass-produced and marketed around the globe? Where would you look for folk culture today? Whatever happened to traditional folk dancing, quilting bees, and other forms of folk culture?

Popular culture is ubiquitous. We are bombarded with it, every day and everywhere. On average, U.S. Americans watch more than 40 hours of television per week. Movie theaters beckon us with the latest multimillion-dollar extravaganzas, nearly all U.S. made. Radio stations and music TV programs blast us with the hottest music groups performing their latest hits. (See Figure 9-1.) And we are inundated with a staggering number of advertisements and commercials daily.

It is difficult to avoid popular culture. Not only is it ubiquitous but it also serves an important social function. How many times have you been asked by friends and family for your reaction to a recent movie or TV program? Academicians Horace Newcomb and Paul Hirsch (1987) suggest that television serves as a cultural forum for discussing and working out our ideas on a variety of topics, including those that emerge from the programs themselves. Television, then, has a powerful social function—to serve as a forum for dealing with social issues.

FIGURE 9-1 Shakira is a multilingual Colombian singer whose songs have hit the charts in many countries, including Turkey and the United States. She exemplifies non-U.S. popular culture making an impact internationally. (© *Chris Polk/FilmMagic/Getty Images*)

In his study of the role of the local newspaper, *The Newsboy*, in restoring the image of Jasper, Texas, after the dragging murder of James Byrd, Jr., Jack Glascock (2004) found that the newspaper's editorials played an important role in guiding the community response to the hate crime. He notes that the "paper's involvement in community affairs at the outset allowed it to convey the agreed-upon objectives of the crisis discourse to the rest of the community. As the crisis played out the paper extended its leadership role by continuing, dropping or modifying its strategies. The paper's opinion pages also provided a forum for the community to participate, primarily by bolstering the town's image, both within the community [and] to outsiders" (p. 45). In this case, the paper is both a forum for public discussion and a leader in community restoration.

In a similar study, communication scholars Dreama Moon and Tom Nakayama (2005) analyzed newspaper accounts of the murder of Arthur "J. R." Warren in West Virginia. Although the small town where he was murdered did not have a local paper, they found that the media coverage did highlight significant differences in how African Americans, gays and lesbians, and white heterosexual residents experienced and perceived life there. Through the media, African Americans and gays and lesbians were able to offer an alternative view that differed from the dominant view of idealized small-town life. Again, newspapers served as a forum for discussion of this tragic event and related aspects of everyday life and community in this small West Virginia town.

In contrast, not all popular culture may serve as a forum for public deliberation. In his study of baseball tributes in ballparks after the attacks of September 11, 2001, Michael Butterworth (2005) found that these rituals tended to discourage expression of opinions that differed from a nationalistic patriotism at the expense of democratic deliberation. Butterworth describes these baseball tributes and notes, "If baseball can be understood as a representative institution of American democratic culture, then the ways in which it performs (or fails to perform) democratically merit scrutiny and criticism. In the aftermath of unprecedented tragedy (for Americans), baseball could have been a site not only for communal healing but also for productively engaging the pluralism that the game does or should represent" (p. 122). Baseball tributes, then, are a form of popular culture that does not serve a cultural forum for the democratic exchange of ideas.

The ways that people negotiate their relationships to popular culture are complex, and it is this complexity that makes understanding the role of popular culture in intercultural communication so difficult. Clearly, we are not passive recipients of this deluge of popular culture. We are, in fact, quite active in our consumption of or resistance to popular culture, a notion that we turn to next.

CONSUMING AND RESISTING POPULAR CULTURE

Consuming Popular Culture

cultural texts Popular culture messages whether television shows, movies, advertisements, or other widely disseminated messages.

Faced with this onslaught of **cultural texts,** people negotiate their ways through popular culture in quite different ways. Popular culture texts do not have to win over the majority of people to be "popular." People often seek out or avoid specific forms of popular culture. For example, romance novels are the best-selling form of literature, but many readers have no interest in such books. Likewise, whereas many people enjoy watching soap operas or professional wrestling, many others find no pleasure in those forms of popular culture.

Stuart Hall's (1980) encoding/decoding model might be helpful here. Hall is careful to place "meaning" at several stages in the communication process, so that it is never fixed but is always being constructed within various contexts. Thus, in his model, he places **encoding**—or the construction of textual meaning by popular culture institutions—within specific social contexts. **Decoding**—the interpretation of the text's meaning by receivers—is performed by various audiences in different social contexts, whose members have different interests at stake. In this way, the meaning(s) of various popular culture texts can be seen as negotiated throughout the communication process. The "real meaning" of any popular culture text cannot simply be located in either the senders or the receivers. Although this model may seem to suggest tremendous unpredictability in popular culture, people do not create just any meaning out of these texts. We are always enmeshed in our social identities, which help guide our interpretations as decoders. Encoders, in turn, rely on these larger identity formations to help them fashion their texts to sell to particular markets. (See Figure 9-2.)

encoding The process of creating a message for others to understand.

decoding The process of interpreting a message.

For example, communication researcher Antonio La Pastina (2004) did an interpretive study of how people in a rural Brazilian community, Macambira in northeastern Brazil, decoded the meanings of the telenovela *The Cattle King.*

Meaningful discourse

Encoding

Decoding

Production of meaning I

Production of meaning II

Social context

Social context

FIGURE 9-2   Stuart Hall's encoding/decoding model. Try to use this model to discuss how different people might arrive at different interpretations of your favorite TV show.

This telenovela is set in urban Brazil and features many melodramatic stories about socioeconomic class, romance, and sexuality. In interviewing the people of this very rural and isolated community, he found that these viewers tended to interpret the telenovelas based on their own cultural values about gender, relationships, and sexuality. He also found that these telenovelas tended to shape how the viewers saw urban life in Brazil. Although the producers of this tele-novela may not have encoded the shows with this audience in mind when they wrote and produced these narratives, the viewers in this community used their own cultural values to decode their own meanings of the shows.

There is some unpredictability in how people navigate popular culture. After all, not all men enjoy watching football, and not all women like to read romance novels. However, some profiles emerge. Advertising offices of popular magazines even make their **reader profiles** available to potential advertisers. These reader profiles portray what the magazine believes its readership "looks" like. Although reader profiles do not follow a set format, they generally detail the average age, gender, individual and household incomes, and so on, of their readership. The reader profile for *Vogue*, for example, will not look like the reader profile for *Esquire*.

reader profiles Por-trayals of readership demographics prepared by magazines.

Each magazine targets a particular readership and then sells this readership to advertisers. The diversity of the U.S. American population generates very different readerships among a range of magazines, in several ways. Let's explore some of the ways this diversity is played out in the magazine market.

How Magazines Respond to the Needs of Cultural Identities   A wide range of magazines respond to the different social and political needs of groups with different cultural identities. You may already be familiar with magazines geared toward a male or a female readership. But many other kinds of magazines serve important functions for other cultural groups. For example, *Ebony* is one of many magazines that cultivate an African American readership. Similar magazines exist for other cultural identities. *Hispanic Magazine*, published in Florida, targets a Latino/a audience; *The Advocate* claims to be the national newsmagazine for gays and lesbians. These magazines offer information and viewpoints that are generally unavailable in other magazines. They function as a discussion forum for concerns that mainstream magazines often overlook. They also tend to affirm, by their very existence, these other cultural identities, which sometimes are invisible or are silenced in the mainstream culture.

In addition, many non-English-language newspapers circulate among readers of specific ethnic groups, serving the same functions as the magazines just mentioned. However, because their production costs are low, they are better able to survive and reach their limited readerships. For instance, newspapers printed in Cantonese, Spanish, Vietnamese, Japanese, French, Korean, Arabic, Polish, Russian, and other languages reach non-English-speaking readers in the United States.

How Readers Negotiate Consumption   Readers actively negotiate their way through cultural texts such as magazines—consuming those that fulfill important cultural needs and resisting those that do not. Hence, it is possible to be a reader of magazines that reflect various cultural configurations; that is, someone might read several women's magazines and Spanish-language newspapers and magazines, as well as *Newsweek* and *Southern Living*.

Cultural Texts Versus Cultural Identities   We must be careful not to conflate the magazines with the cultural identities they are targeting. After all, many publications offer different points of view on any given topic. Thus, there is no single, unified "Asian American position" on immigration reform or any "Latino position" on affirmative action. Rather, there can be a preponderance of opinions on some issues. These often are played out through popular culture forums.

People come together through cultural magazines and newspapers to affirm and negotiate their relationships with their cultural identities. In this way, the texts resemble cultural spaces, which we discussed in Chapter 7. However, magazines are but one example of how popular culture can function. Not all popular culture texts are easily correlated to particular cultural groups. Think about the various TV programs, movies, mass-market paperbacks, and tabloids that flood our everyday lives. The reasons that people enjoy some over others cannot easily be determined. People negotiate their relationships to popular culture in complex ways.

Resisting Popular Culture

Sometimes people actively seek out particular popular culture texts to consume; other times they resist cultural texts. But resistance to popular culture is a complex process. Avoiding certain forms of popular culture is one kind of resistance, but resistance can occur in a variety of ways.

Let's look at the ongoing controversy over the use of the logo of the University of North Dakota's Fighting Sioux. In August 2005, the National Collegiate Athletic Association (NCAA) placed "a ban on Indian imagery that it considers 'hostile or abusive'" (Borzi, 2005, p. B15) in postseason play. In appealing the NCAA division, the University of North Dakota and the NCAA have settled this dispute. This settlement means that "the university will have three years to obtain approval of the mascot from the two Sioux tribes with a significant presence in the state" (U. of North Dakota, 2007). If they do receive tribal support, the university can keep the mascot. If not, then they must change the mascot.

Let's look at how this logo creates strong feelings on both sides and how people are responding to the NCAA decision. There is mixed reaction to the meaning of the way the logo is used. Among American Indians as well there is disagreement about the use of the logo. It is important to recognize that all members of any cultural group have diverse reactions to popular images. For example, not all women are offended by the Hooters restaurant/bar chain that features scantily clad waitresses. Some women, however, do not like the way that women are represented at Hooters.

If we return to our touchstones to examine this controversy, we can see how communication, culture, power, and context play out in this example. American Indians are a relatively small segment of the population. At the University of North Dakota, there were 378 American Indian students out of 12,954 students in the 2005–2006 academic year (http://www.und.edu/profile/). They are the largest minority group at UND, but only about 3% of the student population. The U.S. census taken in 2000 shows that 642,200 people live in the state of North Dakota, and 31,329 are American Indian, or about 4.9% of the population (http://www.census.gov/prod/2002pubs/c2kbr01-15.pdf). To whom, then, is this logo communicating? Which groups have a dominant voice in how the logo is interpreted? Think about who is communicating with whom. What kind of power differential is at work here when primarily non–American Indians choose and circulate these images to mostly non–American Indians?

The University of North Dakota's Web page describes the image in this way: "Since the early 1930s, the University of North Dakota athletic teams have been known as the Fighting Sioux and have used an American Indian head representation as their symbol. UND officially adopted the name 'Fighting Sioux' in honor of the first inhabitants of the region and some of the American Indian tribes of the state" (http://www.universityrelations.und.edu/logoappeal/history .html). The president of the university, Charles Kupchella, says, "I don't have a clue why anyone would take offense to something done respectfully and clearly meant as an honor" (quoted in Borzi, p. B16).

The context is important as well. As we noted earlier in this book, we need to consider the historical context as one important frame that helps us understand how meaning is created in intercultural contexts. The history of American Indian imagery is reflected in a distorted media image: "The Hollywood Indian is a mythological being who exists nowhere but within the fertile imaginations of its movie actors, producers, and directors" (Jojola, 1998, p. 12). How might these other distorting images influence the reading of this logo?

Because some of these stereotypes are negative, they have negative consequences for members of that social group. In his study of the controversy at the University of North Dakota over their mascot, the Fighting Sioux, communication scholar Raúl Tovares (2002) points to the climate at sporting events, which highlights the ways in which stereotypes, cultural values, and popular culture images can come together. (See Figure 9-3.) He explains,

> *Hockey and football games have become sites where offensive images of Native Americans are common. Students from NDSU [North Dakota State University] show up at athletic events with cartoonish images of bison forcing themselves sexually on Native Americans. At "sporting" events, it is not uncommon to hear phrases such as "kill the Sioux," "Sioux suck," "f———k the Sioux," and "rape Sioux women." Such phrases, many Native American students claim, are a direct result of the Fighting Sioux logo. (p. 91)*

Now a Division I school, NDSU (North Dakota State University) is not scheduled to play the University of North Dakota in football. North Dakota State does not currently host a men's hockey team. Think about the ways that this mascot might circulate on jackets, T-shirts, cartoons, and other popular culture forms. How does popular culture represent an important site for negotiating this cultural identity? Why do non–Native Americans have a dominant voice and more power in these representations?

Finally, an interpretivist who is studying the logo controversy might go to the University of North Dakota and speak to the people there. One professor highlights this aspect of the controversy: "'Unless you're here, you don't know what it's like and how nasty it can get,' said a psychology professor, Doug McDonald, who is Sioux. 'I've had students in my office in tears because of the harassment we get'" (quoted in Borzi, 2005, pp. B15–B16). The logo and associated meaning (e.g., the sale of "Sioux-per dogs") create an environment in which some students clearly see negative meanings.

Here we saw a clear example of a group's resistance to popular culture and popular images because they construct American Indian identity in undesirable ways. Indeed, people often resist particular forms of popular culture by refusing to engage in them. For example, some people feel the need to avoid television and even decide not to own televisions. Some people refuse to go to movies that contain violence or sexuality because they do not find pleasure in such films. In this case, these kinds of conscious decisions are often based on concerns about the ways that cultural products should be understood as political.

Resistance to popular culture can also be related to social roles. Likewise, some people have expressed concern about the supposedly homophobic or racist ideologies embedded in Disney films such as *Aladdin* (Boone, 1995). *Aladdin* plays into Western fears of homosexuality and the tradition of projecting those concerns on Arab culture. Resistance stems mainly from concerns about the representation of various social groups. Popular culture plays a powerful role in how we think about and understand other groups. The Disney film *Pocahontas* was criticized for its rewriting of the European encounters with Native Americans. According to communication scholars Derek Buescher and Kent Ono (1996),

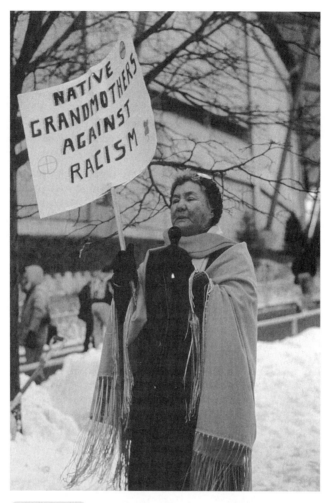

FIGURE 9-3   Concern about sports mascots centers on issues of how they are interpreted and how they create barriers to intercultural communication. This woman's concern that Indian mascots reflect racism is not always understood by sports fans. Although many people know that these mascots are offensive to some, what might drive people to resist changing sports mascots? How does this conflict demonstrate the diversity that resides within U.S. culture? (© *Steve Skjold/ PhotoEdit, Inc.*)

this film "helps audiences unlearn the infamous history of mass slaughter by replacing it with a cute, cuddly one" (p. 128).

Sometimes resistance is targeted at the profits of popular culture corporations. For example, in Iraq, many Iraqis buy pirated DVDs of U.S. films. These pirated DVDs are sold on the black market and the U.S. film corporations do not

NIKE IN CHINA

Consider again the Nike ad covered in Chapter 1. To understand why the Chinese government and many Chinese people were upset by this advertisement, think about the history of European imperialism in China as one frame for understanding this controversy. If people are upset about an advertisement in the United States, how might they appeal to get an advertisement pulled?

China has banned a Nike television commercial showing U.S. basketball star LeBron James in a battle with an animated cartoon kung fu master, saying the ad insults Chinese national dignity.

The commercial, titled Chamber of Fear, was broadcast on local Chinese stations and on state television's national sports channel before being pulled last month. It shows James, the Cleveland Cavaliers' reigning NBA rookie of the year, in a video game-style setting defeating the kung fu master, two women in traditional Chinese attire and a pair of dragons, considered a sacred symbol in traditional Chinese culture.

The advertisement "violates regulations that mandate that all advertisements in China should uphold national dignity and interest and respect the motherland's culture," the State Administration for Radio, Film and Television said on a statement posted Monday on its Web site.

"It also goes against the rules that require ads not to contain content that blasphemes national practices and cultures."

The statement added: "The ad has received an indignant response from Chinese viewers."

Source: From Audra Ang, "China Bans Nike Commercial," *Miami Herald*, December 7, 2004, p. 5C.

earn profits from these sales. One storeowner explains that: "The best-pirated movies come from Malaysia, says Milad Tareq, 21, who runs the Option CDs shop. Among the more popular movies in the Iraqi capital are those starring Robert DeNiro, Tom Hanks or Julia Roberts, he says" (Sabah, 2006). While this kind of resistance may be oriented toward the storeowner making a profit than undercutting the U.S. film corporations, these sales both spread U.S. popular culture, as well as hurt the potential profits of the filmmakers.

REPRESENTING CULTURAL GROUPS

As noted at the beginning of this chapter, people often are introduced to other cultures through the lens of popular culture. These introductions can be quite intimate, in ways that tourists may not experience. For example, movies may portray romance, familial conflict, or a death in the family; the audience experiences

Belgian student describes his first impressions on arriving in the United States.

When I first landed at JFK Airport, I felt like I was going crazy. When I was younger, I only knew about America through television, radio, books, and movies. Even if people don't like America, it is still like a dream-land because it is a place where everything is big, where movies are made, especially police movies. American movies are very well made, with special effects, and so the first time I saw the real America, it was like in the movies. The police in the airport were like cowboys, wearing sunglasses, big mustaches, with badges everywhere and they were big and unafraid, like cowboys. You must respect the customs lines, and all the rules are very strict.

When we left the airport to go to Manhattan, we saw really poor neighborhoods near the airport. I wondered, is America really so poor with small houses? The houses look like they are made of wood and flimsy, unlike the brick ones in Belgium. Once you cross into Manhattan, however, you understand that in America you either have money or you don't. There are majestic cities and poverty; you can get lots of money or nothing. It is another way of living. In Belgium, you do not have to struggle so much for money. Once you have a job in Belgium, there are lots of job protections. In Belgium, if you want to live, you don't have to work.

— Christophe

the private lives of people they do not know, in ways that they never could simply as tourists.

Yet we must also think about how these cultural groups are portrayed through that lens of popular culture. Not everyone sees the portrayal in the same way. For example, you may not think that the TV shows *Desperate Housewives* and *Two and a Half Men* represent quintessential U.S. American values and lifestyles. But some viewers may see it as their entree into how U.S. Americans (or perhaps European Americans) live.

In a social science study on television coverage of affirmative action and African Americans, communication researchers Alexis Tan, Yuki Fujioka, and Gerdean Tan (2000) found that more negative coverage increased negative stereotypes about African Americans. However, they also found that "positive TV portrayals did not lead to positive stereotypes, nor did they influence opinions" (p. 370). They conclude that "negative portrayals are remembered more than positive portrayals, are more arousing and therefore are more influential in the development of stereotypes" (p. 370). Given this dynamic, it is clear how TV news coverage can continue to marginalize and reinforce negative stereotypes, even if the reports also present positive information about minority groups.

In a more recent social science study, Mary Beth Oliver and her colleagues (2004) examined news readers' memories of racial facial features of people in the news. They presented one of four different kinds of news stories—nonstereotyped, stereotyped/noncrime, nonviolent crime, and violent crime—with the same photograph of the individual in the story. Participants were asked to recall this individual's facial features on a computer screen. They conclude, in part, that "[w]hen the stories pertained to crime, Afrocentric features were significantly more pronounced than the actual photograph depicted, whereas when the stories were unrelated to crime, the selected features did not differ significantly from the photograph actually seen" (p. 99). They suggest that certain topics might activate stereotypes and thus influence how these news stories are interpreted.

Migrants' Perceptions of Mainstream Culture

Ethnographers and other interpretive scholars have crossed international and cultural boundaries to examine the influence of popular culture. In an early study, Elihu Katz and Tamar Liebes (1987) set up focus groups to see how different cultural groups perceived the popular 1980s TV drama *Dallas*:

> There were ten groups each of Israeli Arabs, new immigrants to Israel from Russia, first and second generation immigrants from Morocco, and kibbutz members. Taking these groups as a microcosm of the worldwide audience of Dallas, *we are comparing their readings of the program with ten groups of matched Americans in Los Angeles. (p. 421)*

Katz and Liebes found that the U.S. Americans in Los Angeles were much less likely to perceive *Dallas* as portraying life in the United States. In contrast, the Israelis, Arabs, and immigrants were much more inclined to believe that this television show was indeed all about life in the United States. Katz and Liebes note, "What seems clear from the analysis, even at this stage, is that the non-Americans consider the story more real than the Americans. The non-Americans have little doubt that the story is about 'America'; the Americans are less sure" (p. 421). The results of this study are not surprising, but we should not overlook what they tell us about the intercultural communication process. We can see that these popular culture images are often more influential in constructing particular ways of understanding other cultural groups than our own.

Another study (Lee & Cho, 1990) that focused on immigrants to the United States yielded similar results. The researchers asked female Korean immigrants why they preferred watching Korean TV shows (which they had to rent at the video store) instead of U.S. programs. The respondents stated that, because of the cultural differences, the Korean shows were more appealing. Yet, as one respondent noted,

> *I like to watch American programs. Actors and actresses are glamorous and the pictures are sleek. But the ideas are still American. How many Korean women are that independent? And how many men commit incest? I think American*

programs are about American people. They are not the same as watching the Korean programs. But I watch them for fun. And I learn the American way of living by watching them. (p. 43)

Here, both consumption of and resistance to U.S. television are evident. This woman uses U.S. television to learn about the U.S. American "way of living," but she prefers to watch Korean shows because they relate to her cultural identity. As she says, "I like the Korean programs because I get the sense of what's going on in my country" (p. 43).

The use of popular culture to learn about other cultures should not be surprising. After all, many teachers encourage their students to use popular culture in this manner, not only to improve their language skills but also to learn many of the nuances of another culture. When Tom was first studying French, his French professor told the students that *Le dernier métro* (*The Last Metro*), a film by director François Truffaut, was playing downtown. The point, of course, was to hear French spoken by natives. But Tom remembers being amazed at the subtle references to anti-Semitism, the treatment of lesbianism, and the film's style, which contrasted sharply with that of Hollywood films.

Popular Culture and Stereotyping

In what ways does reliance on popular culture create and reinforce stereotypes of different cultures? As we noted at the outset of this chapter, neither author has had the opportunity to travel all over the world. Our knowledge about other places, even places we have been, is largely influenced by popular culture. For people who do not travel and who interact in relatively homogeneous social circles, the impact of popular culture may be even greater.

Film studies scholar Richard Dyer (1993) tells us that

the effectiveness of stereotypes resides in the way they invoke a consensus. . . . The stereotype is taken to express a general agreement about a social group, as if that agreement arose before, and independently of, the stereotype. Yet for the most part it is from stereotypes that we get our ideas about social groups. (p. 14)

Dyer makes an important observation that stereotypes are connected to social values and social judgments about other groups of people. These stereotypes are powerful because they function to tell us how "we" value and judge these other groups.

Many familiar stereotypes of ethnic groups are represented in the media. Scholar Lisa Flores (2000) describes the portrayal of a diverse group of high school students in the television show *Matt Waters.* Flores focuses her analysis on Angela, a Puerto Rican student. According to Flores, there is a strong theme of assimilation at work in this show. She notes,

to follow the seeming logic of this assimilationist politics requires an initial belief in the goal of a single, unified American culture expressed in a harmonious community such as that found within the Matt Waters *community. The assimilationist*

I see plenty of ethnic groups on the television. Asians are portrayed as highly paid, intelligent, yet quiet individuals. Whites are portrayed mostly as middle to upper class individuals, also well paid. Most blacks and Hispanics are seen as criminal and poor, mostly on welfare. Arabs and other Middle Eastern peoples are seen as terrorists or in subservient roles, but almost always seen as outsiders. I think that urban Blacks as well as Asians are portrayed in the most fair light. While their portrayal might still be stereotypical, I think that it sums up what I see on a daily basis pretty accurately.

The portrayals of race and socioeconomic status on television seriously affects intercultural communication between members of other groups in a negative way. People internalize the stereotypical portrayals of these groups and communicate based on them, in ways that affect the feelings of other groups.

— Michael

perspective also mandates an assumption that ethnic minorities cannot maintain cultural difference except in rejection of all of dominant or mainstream society. (pp. 37–38)

She turns to Chicana feminism to show how we can resist these popular culture representations.

African American women also traditionally have been portrayed stereotypically on TV, especially in the 1950s and 1960s, when the roles they held were secondary (e.g., as domestics). Scholar Bishetta Merritt (2000) also reminds us of the African American female characters who often appear as background scenery: the person buying drugs, the homeless person on the sidewalk, the hotel lobby prostitute. Merritt points out that these women still project images, even if they aren't the focus:

If the majority of black women the television audience is exposed to are homeless, drug-addicted, or maids, and if viewers have no contact with African American women other than through television, what choice do they have but to believe that all women of this ethnic background reflect this television image? . . . It is, therefore, important, as the twenty-first century approaches and the population of this country includes more and more people of color, that the television industry broaden the images of African American women to include their nuances and diversity. (p. 53)

In her more recent study of local news coverage of Freaknik, an annual African American spring break event in Atlanta that ended in 2000, communication scholar Marian Meyers (2004) studied the ways that the violence perpetrated by African American men on African American women was represented. She found that the media coverage brought together issues of race, class, and gender and therefore tended to identify the perpetrators as nonstudent local troublemakers rather than as students. The news coverage also "minimizes the seriousness of the violence and his essay points out the problem of stereotypes perpetuated by the media.

WHAT'S AMERICAN?

Say the words "quintessentially American kid" to most anyone, and the image that comes to mind is one of a white American—blond-haired, blue-eyed, etc.

Why is it that an African-American kid is never referred to as a quint-essentially American kid? Why not a Hispanic child, an Asian child or an Indian child? Are they not just as American? Part of the reason for the slight is that stereotyping is ages old, as compelling as it is devastating.

In the wake of the recent school shootings that have rocked America, the hypocrisy of stereotyping people reached another insulting crescendo. . . .

Kip Kinkel, the 15-year-old boy who allegedly killed his parents and two classmates in Oregon last month, was described in Newsweek *magazine as having "an innocent look that is part Huck Finn and part Alfred E. Newman—boyish and quintessentially American."*

You knew he was white. . . .

The New York Times *and* Newsweek *also described Kinkel with words such as "skinny," "slight," "diminutive," "freckle-faced," with an "innocent look." Luke Woodham, convicted recently in Mississippi of killing two students, was the "chubby, poor kid at Pearl High School who always seemed to get picked on." Mitchel Johnson and Andrew Golden, who allegedly killed four girls and a teacher in Jonesboro, Arkansas, were "little boys." Andrew Wurst, who allegedly killed a teacher in Edinboro, Pennsylvania, was a "shy and quirky eighth grader with an offbeat sense of humor." . . .*

When's the last time a black child who allegedly committed a comparable crime was described in such wholesome detail, instead of as cold or adultlike?

The danger in such description is that black children are demonized in people's minds, making it easier to dismiss their humanity and easier to mete out more harsh and unfair judgments and punishment than whites receive.

Source: From "What's American? When Is the Last Time You Heard a Young Black Suspect Described as 'Innocent-Looking' or 'Shy'?" *The Post Standard,* July 3, 1998, p. A6.

portrays its victims primarily as stereotypic Jezebels who provoke male violence through their own behavior" (p. 96). The continued use of this sexualized stereotype for African American women displaces responsibility for what happened from the male perpetrators to the women who were attacked.

What about those ethnic groups that simply don't appear except as infrequent stereotypes—for example, Native Americans and Asian Americans? How do these stereotypes influence intercultural interaction? Do people behave any differently if they don't hold stereotypes about people with whom they are interacting? Two communication researchers, Valerie Manusov and Radha Hegde n celebration of Black History Month *Time* magazine chronicled the most important movies that dealt with race. This excerpt is important, but how would a similar piece on Asian or Latin cinema read?

Look around, and you'll see how African Americans have emerged as the big screen's most reliable stars. Will Smith is the one demonstrable megastar. Morgan Freeman's quiet dignity gets him designated as the face of God and the soul of humanity. And the achievements of blacks are regularly honored by Hollywood. In the past seven years, blacks have won Academy Awards in every acting category. Halle Berry took Best Actress for Monster's Ball, *Freeman Best Supporting Actor for* Million Dollar Baby, *Jennifer Hudson Best Supporting Actress for* Dreamgirls. *In Best Actor, three of the last six Oscars have gone to African Americans: Denzel Washington for* Training Day, *Jamie Foxx for* Ray *and Forest Whitaker for* The Last King of Scotland. *In these glamorous categories, blacks have achieved a kind of parity. Hmmm, that didn't take long — only* 100 *years.*

To celebrate Black History Month, we've chosen 25 movies to honor the artistry, appeal and determination of African Americans on and behind the screen. The films span nine decades, and reveal a legacy that was tragic before it was triumphant. At first, blacks were invisible; when they were allowed to be seen, it was mostly as derisive comic relief. The 1950s ushered in the age of the noble Negro, in the imposing person of Sidney Poitier — the Jackie Robinson of movies. Only when Hollywood realized that a sizable black audience would pay to see films more reflective of their lives, whether funny, poignant or violent, were they given control of the means of production.

Source: From "Hollywood on Race" (2008), *Time.* Retrieved on May 15, 2008 from http://www.time.com/time/specials/2007/article/0,28804,1709148_1709143,00.html

(1993), investigated these questions in a study in which they identified two groups of college students: those who had some preconceived ideas about India (which were fairly positive) and those who didn't. Manusov and Hegde asked all of the students to interact, one at a time, with an international student from India who was part of the study.

When the students with preconceptions talked with the Indian student, they interacted differently from those who had no expectations. Specifically, students from the former group relied less on small talk, covered more topics, and asked fewer questions within each topic. Overall, their conversations were more like those between people who know each other. The students with the preconceptions also were more positive about the conversation.

What can we learn from this study? Having some information and positive expectations may lead to more in-depth conversations and positive outcomes than having no information. But what happens when negative stereotypes are present? It is possible that expectations are fulfilled in this case too.

For example, in several studies at Princeton University, whites interviewed both white and black "job applicants" who were actually part of the study and were trained to behave consistently, no matter how interviewers acted toward them. The interviews were videotaped. The interviewers clearly behaved differently toward blacks: Their speech deteriorated, they made more grammatical errors, they spent less time, and they showed fewer "immediacy" behaviors—that is, they were less friendly and less outgoing. In a second study, interviewers were trained to be either "immediate" or "nonimmediate" as they interviewed white job applicants. A panel of judges watched the videotapes and agreed that those applicants interviewed by the "nonimmediate" interviewer performed less well and were more nervous. This suggests that the African American applicants in the first study never had a chance: They were only reacting to the nonimmediate behavior of the interviewers. Mark Snyder (1998) summarizes: "Considered together, the two investigations suggest that in interracial encounters, racial stereotypes may constrain behavior in ways to cause both blacks and whites to behave in accordance with those stereotypes" (p. 455).

U.S. POPULAR CULTURE AND POWER

One of the dynamics of intercultural communication that we have highlighted throughout this text is power. In considering popular culture, we need to think about not only how people interpret and consume popular culture but also how these popular culture texts represent particular groups in specific ways. If people largely view other cultural groups through the lens of popular culture, then we need to think about the power relations that are embedded in these popular culture dynamics.

Global Circulation of Images and Commodities

As noted previously, much of the internationally circulated popular culture is U.S. popular culture. U.S.-made films, for example, are widely distributed by an industry that is backed by considerable financial resources. Some media scholars have noted that the U.S. film industry earns far more money outside the United States than from domestic box office receipts (Guback, 1969; Guback & Varis, 1982). This situation ensures that Hollywood will continue to seek overseas markets and that it will have the financial resources to do so. The film *Spider-Man* exemplifies this economic position of Hollywood. Although the producers and distributors certainly made a considerable amount of money from the domestic screenings, they earned significant amounts of money from non-U.S. showings as well. (See Figure 9-4.)

Many other U.S. media are widely available outside the United States, including television and newspapers. For example, MTV and CNN are broadcast internationally. And the *International Herald Tribune*, published jointly by the *New York Times* and the *Washington Post*, is widely available in some parts of

FIGURE 9-4   James Dean remains a popular cultural icon in the United States and abroad. This 1996 photo shows that one of his films, *East of Eden,* continues to play in Tokyo. How does Dean's popularity in Japan contrast with the absence of a similarly popular Japanese male star in the United States? What might explain this disparity? Think about the issues of cultural imperialism raised in this chapter. (*Courtesy T. K. Nakayama*)

the world. The implications of the dominance by U.S. media and popular culture have yet to be determined, although you might imagine the consequences. India produces more films than the United States but makes less money in box office receipts. (See "Point of View" box on page 372.)

Not all popular culture comes from the United States. For example, James Bond is a British phenomenon, but the famous character has been exported to the United States. In their study of the popularity of the Bond series, scholars Tony Bennett and Janet Woollacott (1987) note that in the Bond film *A License to Kill* "the threat to the dominance of white American male culture is removed not by a representative of that culture, and certainly not by a somewhat foppish English spy, but by the self-destruction of the forces ranged against it" (pp. 293–294). Here, a British character becomes a hero for U.S. and international audiences through the U.S. film industry. It is not always easy to know what is and what is not U.S. popular culture.

Recently, the *Korean Wave* (*Hallyu*) has demonstrated the profitability of South Korean popular culture. This popular culture phenomenon has "become a rallying cry within Korea for the perceived success of its cultural industries in Asia" (J. Kim, 2007, p. 48). *The Korea Times* reports that "according to the Ministry of Culture, Sports and Tourism, the nation exported about $1.4 billion

Ethnic groups are starting to be portrayed a lot in television shows. I think that is due to the diversity of different cultures in different societies. However, the ethnic groups are not shown in any major roles. Most of the roles that they tend to occupy are ones of lower class or the poor. It is very rare to see a person of a different race in a very high position in television shows. However, that is starting to become common now as compared to before. To me, I think that people of Asian descent are shown as having a lot of different roles on TV. I personally do not think that the way media or television portrays different ethnic groups has any sort of effect on the way they are treated.
    — Sadaf

I think for the most part, the lower class isn't even represented on TV. Yet when they are, its usually in a negative light. They are criminals or drug addicts on Law and Order. *My favorite show,* Sex and the City, *never even shows a person who doesn't wear designer clothes or is a politician. I think it's sad and is a misrepresentation of the real world. I guess that's why we like to watch it!*
    — Alexia

worth of entertainment products last year" (Kim, 2008). While primarily popular in Asia, *Hallyu* has even made the city of Chuncheon a popular tourist destination, as the local drama "Winter Sonata" (2002) gained popularity abroad (S.-Y. Kim, 2008).

Key to this South Korean phenomenon, however, is the global circulation of popular culture. Thus, "Hallyu is a term that can *only* be applied to a cultural product once it has been exposed to foreign audiences. In other words, not every Korean drama, film or pop song, no matter how popular in Korea, will be labeled Hallyu—only those that have been exported and done so successfully" (J. Kim, 2007, pp. 49–50). The focus of *Hallyu*, however, is on "Asian rather than global domination" (p. 55). In any case, the international circulation of Korean popular culture has important implications for the production of Asian standards of beauty and relationships, as well as international trade.

Much popular culture that is expressed in non-English languages has a difficult time on the global scene. Although Céline Dion, who sings in English, has been able to reach a worldwide audience, a fellow French Canadian, Garou, who sings in French, has not reached the same level of notoriety. Still, Garou (Pierre Garand) is extremely popular in the francophone world. Have you ever heard of Garou? To reach a worldwide audience, must he sing in English? Garou released his next CD, *Reviens*, in 2003 and decided that because of "the generosity of his French-speaking public . . . [the album] would be written and sung in French" (www.garouland.com/Reviens/english/bio_08.html). What does this tell us about popular culture? What does it tell us about the unequal power relations that are evident in popular culture? How does it influence how we think about the world?

TABLE 9-2	U.S. POPULAR CULTURE IS PROFITABLE INTERNATIONALLY. SOME PLACES ENJOY CONSUMING U.S. PRODUCTS WHILE OTHERS RESIST THESE PRODUCTS.

United States International Pop Culture Influence

Product	Destination	Impact
Titanic (film)	Worldwide	*Titanic* was a huge success in the United States, but over 2/3 of its eventual 1.8 billion dollar gross was acquired overseas (boxofficemojo).
A.L.F. (television show)	Russia	*A.L.F.* was a mildly popular situation comedy featuring an alien (hand-puppet) who lived with a suburban family. The show is hugely popular in Russia (Havens, 2002).
The film industry	Iran	Iran's fledgling film industry has been sheltered by a protective government unwilling to air many American films. There is broad concern that American films will "overwhelm" Iranian industry and "debase" the moral foundations of the nation. As a result, many popular international films are simply unavailable in Iran (Crothers, 2007).

Sources: All time international box office. Retrieved on May 15, 2008 from http://www.boxofficemojo.com/alltime/world/; Timothy Havens, (2002). "It's Still a White World Out There": The Interplay of Culture and Economics in International Television Trade, *Critical Studies in Media Communication,* 19: 377–397; Lane Crothers, *Globalization and American Popular Culture.* Plymouth U.K.: Rowman & Littlefield Publishers, 2007.

Cultural Imperialism

It is difficult to measure the impact of the U.S. and Western media and popular culture on the rest of the world, but we do know that we cannot ignore this dynamic. The U.S. government in the 1920s believed that having U.S. movies on foreign screens would boost the sales of U.S. products because the productions would be furnished with U.S. goods. The government thus worked closely with the Hays Office (officially, the Motion Picture Producers and Distributors of America) to break into foreign markets, most notably in the United Kingdom (Nakayama & Vachon, 1991).

media imperialism
Domination or control through media.

electronic colonialism
Domination or exploitation utilizing technological forms.

cultural imperialism
Domination through the spread of cultural products.

Discussions about **media imperialism, electronic colonialism,** and **cultural imperialism,** which began in the 1920s, continue today. The interrelationships among economics, nationalism, and culture make it difficult to determine with much certainty how significant cultural imperialism might be. The issue of cultural imperialism is complex because the definition is complex. In his survey of the cultural imperialism debates, scholar John Tomlinson (1991) identifies

FIGURE 9-5   South Korean actor Bae Yong Joon is shown arriving at the Tokyo airport with thousands of fans awaiting his arrival. He is a very popular television drama star who is part of the Korean Wave. The Korean Wave highlights how non-U.S. popular culture can circulate and become very marketable in other parts of the world. (© *Katsumi Kasahara/AP Images*)

five ways of thinking about cultural imperialism: (1) as cultural domination, (2) as media imperialism, (3) as nationalist discourse, (4) as a critique of global capitalism, and (5) as a critique of modernity (pp. 19–23). Tomlinson's analysis underscores the interrelatedness of issues of ethnicity, culture, and nationalism in the context of economics, technology, and capitalism—resources that are distributed unevenly throughout the world. To understand the concerns about cultural imperialism, therefore, it is necessary to consider the complexity of the impact of U.S. popular culture. (See Table 9-2.) There is no easy way to measure the impact of popular culture, but we should be sensitive to its influences on intercultural communication. Let's look at some examples.

Some governments have become concerned about the amount of popular culture coming into their countries. The French government, for example, has expressed dismay about the domination of the English-language broadcasting of CNN because it feels it projects a view of the world it does not share. In order to challenge this view, the French are launching their own international broadcasting network to present their views on the world. Although informally referred to as "CNN à la française," this new "channel would promote a vision of a 'multipolar' world that is not dominated by one superpower, such as the United States" (Louet, 2005). This new channel will not initially be available in the United States, but it hopes to expand from Europe, Africa, and the Middle

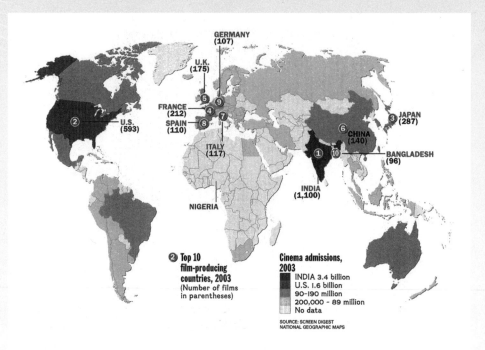

GERMANY
(107)

U.K.
(175)

FRANCE
(212)
SPAIN
(110)

U.S.
(593)

ITALY
(117)

NIGERIA

JAPAN
(287)

CHINA
(140)

BANGLADESH
(96)

INDIA
(1,100)

Top 10
film-producing
countries, 2003
(Number of films
in parentheses)

Cinema admissions,
2003
INDIA 3.4 billion
U.S. 1.6 billion
90-190 million
200,000 - 89 million
No data

SOURCE: SCREEN DIGEST
NATIONAL GEOGRAPHIC MAPS

THE REEL WORLD

Nigerians don't go to the movies; the movies come to them. With few operating cinemas in Nigeria's largest city of Lagos, screenings often occur in local restaurants and private homes; videos are sold at market stands and sometimes hawked to motorists caught in traffic. This distribution of films from "Nollywood," as the country's ultralow-budget industry is known, may seem unusual, but it still satisfies the demand for movies—an obsession shared by people around the world.

In 2003, according to film industry source *Screen Digest*, some seven billion movie tickets were sold worldwide, earning an estimated 22 billion dollars. The greatest share of these global box-office receipts—more than 43 percent—came from U.S. theaters. Japanese theaters charged the most for tickets: Reserved seats can cost up to $25. Though India made more films than Hollywood, it

East to Asia, South America, and the United States later. This will allow the French to compete with CNN, the BBC, and A1 Jazeera as international broadcasting networks.

In a study on this tension between global networks and local networks, Jonathan Cohen (2005) examined the situation in Israel. He looked at Israel's 99 channels and identified six different ways that these channels function in the global and local environment. He then noted, "Foreign television is often thought to be harmful because it separates people from their national communities"

(© William Albert Allard/National Geographic Image Collection)

made less money from them; the price of admission to an Indian theater averaged just 20 cents.

Many American blockbusters rake in more money internationally than at home. *Titanic*, the highest grossing film of all time, made two-thirds of its 1.8-billion-dollar take overseas. American movies have long been retooled for foreign sale. In the 1930s stars such as the comedy team Laurel and Hardy reshot their films in German and other languages—coached with phonetically spelled cue cards. Now native speakers are recorded over original actors' voices with varying success. In the French version of *Star Wars*, the villain's voice is considerably less menacing, and his name's been changed to Dark Vador.

American movies may be popular abroad, but foreign concession stands still cater to local tastes. Some European audiences wash their popcorn down with beer. In China the popcorn's sweetened. Other film snack favorites there—spicy cabbage, salted plums, dried squid shreds—have a flavor all their own.

Source: From Scott Elder, "The Reel World," Geographica, *National Geographic*, March 2005.

(p. 451), but he warned that we should not so easily view foreign television in this way. He doesn't think it is yet clear that watching U.S. television shows "like *Sex and the City* or *The Apprentice* weakens viewers' connections to Israeli culture or strengthens them by providing a stark contrast to viewers' lives" (p. 451). Think back to Stuart Hall's encoding and decoding model. Cohen is emphasizing that we cannot assume people who watch certain shows will decode them in any particular way. The influence of media is more complex than a simple imposition of meaning from abroad.

Sometimes the Western images are imported and welcomed by the ruling interests in other countries. For example, the government of the Ivory Coast in West Africa has used foreign (mostly French) media to promote its image of a ome people seek out foreign films; others avoid them. In choosing either response to foreign films, are you choosing films based on the narrative or the subtitles?

I do not like foreign films because I have a hard time understanding what is going on even with the subtitles. I can't understand a lot of the humor in foreign movies. I also don't think that all languages translate to English exactly, and it makes it hard to understand these movies.
—Elizabeth

Foreign films seem to paint a picture that rings more true to me than Hollywood films. In Hollywood films, there seems to be recurring themes: the strong man, the materialistic woman, heterosexuality, white stars with a token minority. They seldom get a role free of the most ridiculous stereotypes. The foreign independent films seem to have more diversity, more balance, a better depiction of the world.
— Sam

"new" Ivoirien cultural identity. The government purchased a satellite dish that permits 1,400 hours of French programming annually, which represents 77% of all programming. But it has been criticized by many for borrowing heavily from the Western media—for inviting cultural imperialism:

> While television, as mirror, sometimes reflects multiple Ivoirien cultures, the latter are expected to acquiesce to a singular national culture in the image of the Party, which is also synonymous with a Western cultural image. . . . The cultural priority is openness for the sake of modernization in the quest of the Ivoirien national identity. (Land, 1992, p. 25)

In another take on globalization, communication scholar Radhika Parameswaran (2004) undertook a textual analysis of Indian newspaper and magazine coverage of India's six Miss Universe and Miss World titleholders. In the context of a global economy, these women are upheld as role models who are ordinary women who worked hard to become a beauty queen while maintaining their national identities. Noting that "the therapeutic vocabulary of the beauty queen as role model, a recent construct of liberal individualism in South Asia, induces amnesia and insulates middle class citizens from the contradictions that such individualized discourses of empowerment can conceal. . . . [G]lobalization's ideologies of prosperity in India offer no recourse for the vast majority of poor citizens to attain even the humble ordinariness of the middle class consumer who desires the status of the global beauty queen" (p. 367). By asking what social functions these narratives serve, this critical study argues that they serve the more elite segments of society in India.

In all of these examples, popular culture plays an enormous role in explaining relations around the globe. It is through popular culture that we try to understand the dynamics of other cultures and nations. Although these representations are problematic, we also rely on popular culture to understand many kinds of issues: the conflict in Kashmir between India and Pakistan, the sex abuse scandals in the Catholic Church, the conflict in the West Bank between Israelis and Palestinians, and global warming. For many of us, the world exists through popular culture.

INTERNET RESOURCES

www.racialicious.com/
This Web site is a privately run blog pertaining to the intersections of race and popular culture. The blog contributors compile a diverse array of information about music, television, film, print media, and other pop culture outlets. Most blog entries engage in some sort of analysis of the merits of or story surrounding a particular cultural artifact. Along with written resources, this blog contains www.Youtube.com entries as well.

www.npr.org/templates/topics/topic.php?topicId=1048
National Public Radio hosts a Web page devoted to identifying and commenting on popular culture trends. This resource is not specifically about intercultural issues, but these issues are covered. The Web site is a good mix of information and political commentary for students doing research on emerging popular culture issues.

www.uiowa.edu/~commstud/resources/POP-Culture.html
The well-respected communication department at the University of Iowa has compiled a wonderful resource for students doing popular culture research. This Web site lists and direct links to hundreds of communication-oriented articles on pop culture subjects ranging from Bazooka Joe to Madonna. The articles are categorized and easily accessible.

www.wsu.edu/~amerstu/pop/race.html#articles
Washington State University hosts this Web resource. This Web site is a compilation of academic and popular press articles related to the intersection of popular culture and race. It contains direct links to articles, a directory of other Web sites, and a useful bibliography.

www.mediaed.org/videos/MediaRaceAndRepresentation/
CulturalCriticismandTransformation/#
This is the Web resource for the bell hooks video on *Cultural Criticism and Transformation*, a 1997 edited interview with cultural critic bell hooks. The video is not available in its full form online (though sections are available on www.Youtube.com/), but this site does contain related articles and a section for comments.

SUMMARY

- We learn about other cultures through popular culture.
- Popular culture is popular because of its wide dissemination and easy access to many people.
- Popular culture is produced by culture industries, is not folk culture, is ubiquitous, and serves social functions.
- Popular culture can serve as a public forum.
- Cultural texts are not the same as cultural identities.
- People can seek out or resist popular culture.
- Cultural groups are often represented in ways that can play into stereotypes.
- Migrants can learn about other cultures through popular culture.
- The United States still dominates global production of popular culture, but other nations produce significant amounts that are important locally.
- Concerns about cultural imperialism need to be considered.

DISCUSSION QUESTIONS

1. Why do people select some popular culture forms over others?
2. How do the choices you make about what forms of popular culture to consume influence the formation of your cultural identity?
3. What factors influence culture industries to portray cultural groups as they do?
4. How does the portrayal of different cultural groups by the media influence intercultural interactions with those groups?
5. What stereotypes are perpetuated by U.S. popular culture and exported to other countries?
6. How do our social roles affect our consumption of popular culture?
7. What strategies can people apply to resist popular culture?

 Go to the self-quizzes on the Online Learning Center at www.mhhe.com/martinnakayama5 to further test your knowledge.

ACTIVITIES

1. *Popular Culture.* Meet with other students in small groups and answer the following questions:
   a. Which popular culture texts (magazines, TV shows, and so on) do you watch or buy? Why?

b. Which popular culture texts do you choose *not* to buy or watch? Which do you *not* like? Why?

c. Think about and discuss why people like some products compared to others. (For example, do they support our worldview and assumptions?)

2. *Ethnic Representation in Popular Culture.* For a week, keep a log of the TV shows you watch. Record the following information for each show and discuss in small groups:

a. How many different ethnic groups were portrayed in this show?

b. What roles did these ethnic groups have in the show?

c. What ethnic groups were represented in the major roles?

d. What ethnic groups were represented in the minor roles?

e. What ethnic groups were represented in the good-guy roles?

f. What ethnic groups were represented in the bad-guy roles?

g. What types of roles did women have in the show?

h. What intercultural interaction occurred in the show?

i. What was the outcome of the interaction?

j. How do the roles and interactions support or refute common stereotypes of the ethnic groups involved?

KEY WORDS

cultural imperialism (370)
cultural texts (354)
culture industries (351)
decoding (354)

electronic colonialism (370)
encoding (354)
folk culture (351)

media imperialism (370)
popular culture (350)
reader profiles (355)

 The Online Learning Center at www.mhhe.com/martinnakayama5 features flashcards and crossword puzzles based on these terms and concepts.

REFERENCES

Arseneault, M. (2001, December 15). Il chante avec les loups. *L'actualité*, pp. 76–82.

Bennett, T., & Woollacott, J. (1987). *Bond and beyond: The political career of a popular culture hero.* New York: Methuen.

Big Brother has exposed 'everyday racism.' (2007, January 19). *Social Science News.* Sheffield Hallam University. (Retrieved May 15, 2008) from http://www.shu.ac.uk/social/news2.html

Boone, J. A. (1995). Rubbing Aladdin's lamp. In M. Dorenkamp & R. Henke (Eds.), *Negotiating lesbian and gay subjects* (pp. 149–177). New York: Routledge.

Borzi, P. (2005, November 26). A dispute of great spirit rages on: North Dakota fights to keep a logo, Indians consider its use profane. *New York Times*, pp. B15–B16.

Brummett, B. (1994). *Rhetoric in popular culture.* New York: St. Martin's Press.

Buescher, D. T., & Ono, K. A. (1996). Civilized colonialism: *Pocahontas* as neocolonial rhetoric. *Women's Studies in Communication, 19,* 127–153.

Butterworth, M. (2005). Ritual in the 'church of baseball': Suppressing the discourse of democracy after 9/11. *Communication & Critical/Cultural Studies, 2,* 107–129.

Cohen, J. (2005). Global and local viewing experiences in the age of multichannel television: The Israeli experience. *Communication Theory, 15,* 437–455.

Dyer, R. (1993). *The matter of images: Essays on representations.* New York: Routledge.

Fiske, J. (1989). *Understanding popular culture.* New York: Routledge.

Flores, L. (2000). Challenging the myth of assimilation: A Chicana feminist perspective. In Mary Jane Collier (Ed.), *Constituting cultural difference through discourse* (pp. 26–46). International and Intercultural Communication Annual 12. Thousand Oaks, CA: Sage.

Glascock, J. (2004). The Jasper dragging death: Crisis communication and the community newspaper. *Communication Studies, 55,* 29–47.

Guback, T. (1969). *The international film industry: Western Europe and America since 1945.* Bloomington: Indiana University Press.

Guback, T., & Varis, T. (1982). *Transnational communication and cultural industries.* Paris: Unesco.

Gunn, J., & Brummett, B. (2004). Popular culture after globalization. *Journal of Communication, 54,* 705–721.

Hall, S. (1980). Encoding/decoding. In S. Hall, D. Hobson, A. Lowe, & P. Willis (Eds.), *Culture, media, language.* London: Hutchinson.

Harris, A. (2007, June 19). Racism hits "Big Brother" Australia. *NewsBlaze.* Retrieved May 15, 2008 from http://newsblaze.com/story/20070619155951alih .nb/topstory.html

Jojola, T. (1998). Absurd reality II: Hollywood goes to the Indians. In P. C. Rollins & J. E. O'Connor (Eds.), *Hollywood's Indian: The portrayal of the Native American in film* (pp. 12–26). Lexington: University Press of Kentucky.

Katz, E., & Liebes, T. (1987). Decoding *Dallas:* Notes from a cross-cultural study. In H. Newcomb (Ed.), *Television: The critical view* (4th ed., pp. 419–432). New York: Oxford University Press.

Kim, J. (2007). Why does Hallyu matter? The significance of the Korean Wave in South Korea. *Critical Studies in Television, 2,* 47–59.

Kim, S.-Y. (2008, May 5). Korean wave 'Hallyu' abroad waning. *The Korea Times.* Retrieved May 15, 2008 from http://www.koreatimes.co.kr/www/ news/special/2008/05/180_23641.html

La Pastina, A. C. (2004). Telenovela reception in rural Brazil: Gendered readings and sexual mores. *Critical Studies in Media Communication, 21,* 162–181.

Land, M. (1992). Ivoirien television, willing vector of cultural imperialism. *The Howard Journal of Communications, 4,* 10–27.

Lee, M., & Cho, C. H. (1990, January). Women watching together: An ethnographic study of Korean soap opera fans in the U.S. *Cultural Studies, 4*(1), 30–44.

Lipsitz, G. (1990). *Time passages: Collective memory and American popular culture.* Minneapolis: University of Minnesota Press.

Louet, S. (2005, November 30). "French CNN" seen operational by end of 2006. Reuters Business Channel. Retrieved from December 3, 2005. http://today.reuters.com/business/newsArticle. aspx?type=media&storyID=nL30762703

Manusov, V., & Hegde, R. (1993). Communicative outcomes of stereotype-based expectancies: An observational study of cross-cultural dyads. *Communication Quarterly, 41,* 338–354.

Merritt, B. D. (2000). Illusive reflections: African American women on primetime television. In A. González, M. Houston, & V. Chen (Eds.), *Our voices* (3rd ed., pp. 47–53). Los Angeles: Roxbury.

Meyers, M. (2004). African American women and violence: Gender, race, and class in the news. *Critical Studies in Media Communication, 21,* 95–118.

Moon, D. G., & Nakayama, T. K. (2005). Strategic social identities and judgments: A murder in Appalachia. *Howard Journal of Communications, 16,* 1–22.

Nakayama, T. K., & Vachon, L. A. (1991). Imperialist victory in peacetime: State functions and the British cinema industry. *Current Research in Film, 5,* 161–174.

Newcomb, H., & Hirsch, P. M. (1987). Television as a cultural forum. In H. Newcomb (Ed.), *Television: The critical view* (4th ed., pp. 455–470). New York: Oxford University Press.

Oliver, M. B., Jackson, R. L., Moses, N. N., & Dangerfield, C. L. (2004). The face of crime: Viewers' memory of race-related facial features of individuals pictured in the news. *Journal of Communications, 54,* 88–104.

Parameswaran, R. (2004). Global queens, national celebrities: Tales of feminine triumph in post-liberalization India. *Critical Studies in Media Communication, 21,* 346–370.

Sabah, Z. (2006, January 19). Pirated DVDs among hottest items on Iraqi shelves. *USA Today.* Retrieved May 15, 2008 from http://www.usatoday.com/news/ world/iraq/2006-01-19-iraq-dvds_x.htm#

Snyder, M. (1998). Self-fulfilling stereotypes. In P. Rothenburg (Ed.), *Race, class and gender in the United States* (4th ed., pp. 452–457). New York: St. Martin's Press.

Tan, A., Fujioka, F., & Tan, G. (2000). Television use, stereotypes of African Americans and opinions on affirmative action: An affective model of policy reasoning. *Communication Monographs, 67* (4), 362–371.

Tomlinson, J. (1991). *Cultural imperialism.* Baltimore: Johns Hopkins University Press.

Tovares, R. (2002). Mascot matters: Race, history, and the University of North Dakota's "Fighting Sioux" logo. *Journal of Communication Inquiry, 26* (1), 76–94.

U. of North Dakota and NCAA settle lawsuit over 'Fighting Sioux' mascot. (2007, October 26). *The Chronicle of Higher Education.* Retrieved May 15, 2008 from http://chronicle.com/news/article/3317/ u-of-north-dakota-and-ncaa-settle-lawsuit-over-fighting-sioux-mascot

CHAPTER 10

CULTURE, COMMUNICATION, AND INTERCULTURAL RELATIONSHIPS

CHAPTER OBJECTIVES

After reading this chapter, you should be able to:

1. Identify three benefits and three challenges to intercultural relationships.
2. Describe six dialectics of intercultural relationships.
3. Identify three approaches to understanding intercultural relationships.
4. Describe some cultural differences in the notion of friendship.
5. Describe cultural differences in relational development.
6. Describe "turning points" in intercultural friendships.
7. Explain the frequency of intercultural dating today.
8. Identify challenges of intercultural marriages.
9. Identify four interaction styles in intercultural marriages.
10. Identify and describe characteristics of gay and lesbian friendships.
11. Describe how institutional, historical, or political contexts can facilitate or hinder intercultural relationships.

When Frédéric Minvielle got married in 2003, he did not foresee that his international and intercultural marriage would cause him to lose his citizenship. The French newspaper *Libération* observed that "He is no longer French. Born in Lorient 37 years ago, Frédéric Minvielle just lost his citizenship after his marriage"[1] (Rotman). After moving to the Netherlands, he learned the Dutch language and later obtained Dutch citizenship, as he wanted to have dual nationality with France. Had he married a woman, he would have been able to keep his French citizenship; however, Frédéric married a Dutch man. While the Netherlands recognizes same-sex marriages, France does not. Therefore, under French law, Frédéric is not considered married and France abruptly terminated his French citizenship. *Le Journal du dimanche au quotidien* reported: "on December 7, 2007, Frédéric Minvielle received a letter from the French consulate in Amsterdam which announced the decision of the Ministry of Justice to revoke his French citizenship. The new Dutch citizen must return his [French] identity card and his passport—which he refused to do since it expires at the end of 2012—and he was asked to sign a document that he '*would not ask for French citizenship again.*' "[2] In light of this decision, Minvielle said, "I want to keep my citizenship, it's a question of principle. I was born French, in Lorient, all of my family is in France. I feel rejected by my country, but I hope that my case will cause the legal system to change the law"[3] (quoted in "Un Français déchu"). Because of the attention drawn to his case, the French government is changing the Franco-Dutch agreement and Frédéric Minvielle will be eligible to ask for French citizenship after March 2009 (*Têtu*).

We do not often think that our personal relationships might cause us to lose our nationality or other group memberships, but not all cultures recognize or value all relationships. In the case of Frédéric Minvielle, the differences between the Netherlands and France highlight some of the challenges to intercultural relationships, but there are also benefits to developing intercultural relationships, as he learned the Dutch language and now lives in the Netherlands.

How do we develop relationships with people who differ from us in terms of age, ethnicity, religion, class, or sexual orientation? Think about friends who differ from you in any of these ways. How did you get to know them? Are these relationships any different from those that are characterized by similarity? Why do we develop relationships with some people and not with others? There seems to be some truth to *both* adages "Birds of a feather flock together" and "Opposites attract."

---

[1]"Il n'est plus français. Né à Lorient il y a trente-sept ans, Frédéric Minvielle vient d'être déchu de la nationalité française après son marriage."

[2]"le 7 décembre 2007, Frédéric Minvielle reçoit une lettre du consulat français à Amsterdam, qui lui signifie la décision du ministère de la Justice de lui retirer sa nationalité française. Le nouveau Néerlandais doit rendre sa carte d'identité et son passeport—ce qu'il a refusé de faire car ce dernier expirait fin 2012—et est appelé à signer un document dans lequel il s'engagerait "*à ne pas redemander la nationalité française.*"

[3]"Je veux garder ma nationalité, c'est une question de principe. Je suis né Français, à Lorient, toute ma famille est en France. Je me sens rejeté par mon pays mais j'espère que mon cas fera jurisprudence pour changer la loi."

What is the role of communication in intercultural relationships? And how do contexts (social, historical, political) influence our relationships? In this chapter, we explore the benefits and challenges of intercultural relationships, examine how relationships develop over time, and identify some cultural differences in relational development and maintenance. Throughout the chapter, we emphasize a dialectical perspective on intercultural relationships—both friendship and romantic. Contextual issues exist along with individual relational issues, so for each of these topics we'll examine contextual issues.

There are increasing opportunities to meet people from other cultures through the Internet and increasing cultural diversity in many schools and workplaces, yet a recent survey shows that today's first-year college students have less interest in meeting people who are different from them (Farrell, 2005). In surveys, young people repeatedly say they are open to intercultural romantic relationships, yet for some groups, the rate of intercultural dating is exactly the same as it was 20 years ago (Clark-Ibanez & Felmlee, 2004).

Why do some people get involved in intercultural relationships and others not? Why do some intercultural relationships seem to flourish and others not? We think the answer lies in a dialectic: Although individual style and preference may play a large role, the contexts in which people meet and interact have much to contribute to the viability of intercultural friendships and romantic relationships. That is, social, religious, and educational contexts may promote *or* discourage intercultural relationships. Historical and political contexts also play a big role. For example, it was only 50 years ago that it was illegal for whites and African Americans to marry (Root, 2001). This, no doubt, is part of the reason that rates of interracial dating and marriage are the lowest among these two groups when compared to rates for other ethnic and racial groups (Martin, Bradford, Drzewiecka, & Chitgopekar, 2003). Who we choose to befriend is determined both by our individual preferences *and* by social, religious, and political contexts.

In this chapter, we first examine the benefits and challenges of intercultural relationships. Then we describe six dialectics as a way of thinking about intercultural friendships and intercultural romantic relationships. Then we present the contributions of three communication perspectives on intercultural relationships—starting with the social science approach that emphasizes cross-cultural comparisons of relational notions. We then move to the interpretive perspective that has contributed in-depth information about various types of intercultural relationships, and finally we discuss the critical approach that emphasizes the role of context in determining who we form relationships with and how these relationships develop.

BENEFITS AND CHALLENGES OF INTERCULTURAL RELATIONSHIPS

Benefits

intercultural relationships Relationships that are formed between individuals from different cultures.

Most people have a variety of **intercultural relationships** that may feature differences in age, physical ability, gender, ethnicity, class, religion, race, or nationality. The potential rewards and opportunities in these relationships are tremendous. The key to these relationships often involves maintaining a balance between differences and similarities. One example is the relationship between Judith and a Chicana colleague. When they first met, they thought they had little in common, coming as they did from very different ethnic and cultural backgrounds. But once they found commonality in their academic work, they discovered that they actually had a great deal in common. For instance, both come from large religious families, both have parents who contributed a great deal to their communities, and both are close to their older sisters and their nieces. Through the relationship, they also have learned a lot about each other's different worlds.

The benefits of such relationships include (1) acquiring knowledge about the world, (2) breaking stereotypes, and (3) acquiring new skills. You can probably think of a lot more. In intercultural relationships, we often learn specific information about unfamiliar cultural patterns and languages. Nancy, an undergraduate student, describes how she learned about culture and religion through her relationship with her boyfriend:

> *My family and I are Buddhists; however, we are not very religious. We still celebrate the holidays and traditions, but we do not attend the temple often. Anyway, my boyfriend, being Catholic, asked me to go to his church for an Easter celebration one year. I decided to go because I am an open person and not restricted to believing in just one religion. Anyhow, I went to his church, and I must say it was a good learning experience and a fun one, too. I was glad that I went to see what "Catholics" do to celebrate Easter.*

A romance or a close intercultural friendship may be the vehicle through which we learn something about history. Jennifer, a student in one of our classes, told us how she learned more about the Holocaust from her Jewish friends and about the Middle Passage from her African American friends. These are examples of **relational learning**—learning that comes from a particular relationship but generalizes to other contexts. Relational learning is often much more compelling than knowledge gained from books, classes, and so on. And once we develop one close intercultural relationship, it becomes much easier to form others. (See Figure 10-1.)

relational learning
Learning that comes from a particular relationship but generalizes to other contexts.

Intercultural relationships also can help break stereotypes. Andy, a student at Arizona State University, told us about how he used to view Mexicans as lazy. This opinion was formed from media images, discussions with friends, and political speeches about immigration in the Southwest. However, when he met and made friends with emigrants from rural Mexico, his opinion changed. He saw that in everyday life his friends were anything but indolent. They had family responsibilities and sometimes worked two jobs to make ends meet. Later, we'll discuss how breaking stereotypes actually works in relationships.

We often learn how to do new things in intercultural relationships. Through her friendships with students in the United States and abroad, Judith has learned to make paella (a Spanish dish) and *nopalitos con puerca* (a cactus-and-pork stew), to play bridge in French, and to downhill ski. Through intercultural relationships, newcomers to a society can acquire important skills. Andy's immigrant friends often ask him for help with new tasks and activities, such as buying car

FIGURE 10-1   College students often benefit from the experience of forming intercultural relationships. Through these relationships, we can learn about other cultural groups, as well as gain additional insight into our own cultural backgrounds. How often do you come into contact with people who are different from you? How often do you seek out intercultural friendships? (© *Chuck Savage/Corbis*)

insurance or shopping for food. When Tom first moved to France, his new French friends helped him navigate the university cafeteria. All of these potential benefits can lead to a sense of interconnectedness with others and can establish a lifelong pattern of communication across differences. We also hope that it helps us become better intercultural communicators.

Challenges

Intercultural relationships are unique in several ways, and as such present particular challenges. By definition, they are characterized by cultural differences in communication style, values, and perceptions. The dissimilarities probably are most prominent in the early stages of relational development when people tend to exchange less personal information. However, if some commonality is established and the relationship develops beyond the initial stages, these cultural differences may have less of an impact because all relationships become more idiosyncratic as they move to more intimate stages. There seems to be an interplay of both differences and similarities in intercultural relationships. The differences are a given, and the challenge can be to discover and build on the similarities—common interests, activities, beliefs, or goals.

oung people often encounter disapproval for interethnic relationships, sometimes from both sides. Thomas Matthew Pilgrim and Robert Brown, from Athens, Georgia, are good friends. They describe how they got together and how they each get some static from their respective friends and family.

Matthew: *Ask anybody in Athens about me and Robert, they'll say that we are always together. I'm 15. He's 17. We think just alike, act just alike and dress just alike. If he wasn't black and if I wasn't white, people could think that we were brothers. A brother in every sense of the word.*

I'm part Mexican. I'm probably the only white person in Athens with their hair braided. I just did it because it's long; it's hard to keep up with. Most of the people I know are black or Mexican. As far as I know they don't have a problem with me. But there's always got to be an odd person that has to say something. One woman said, "Look, white boy, why you got your hair braided?" I just stopped caring what people think about me. [My] family are just really big———. All they like are people with the same skin as them. But race doesn't matter to me and my sister. And Robert and the other people I hang with don't care that I'm white. They were who I stuck with when I first moved here two and a half years ago. They took to me and really helped me. He's my best friend.

Robert: *I was going to fight him at first. I'm not going to lie. The homeboys I used to hang around with were like, "Hey man, look at that white boy." But my friend Jason knew Matt, so it was cool. I asked him his name. I told him mine. We started chilling from there. All my friends are black except for Matthew. It'd be about 30 of us and Matt. . . . He fits right in with me. He acts like everybody else that I hang around with. I don't care that he's white. If you want to find me, you look for Matt. Every day, all day, we hang out. We play basketball, beat each other up, listen to rap. We have fun. . . .*

Source: From "'Hometown Homeboys,' What They Were Thinking About Race," *New York Times Magazine*, special issue (How Race Is Lived in America), July 16, 2000, p. 26.

Negative stereotyping often comes into play in intercultural relationships. As we discussed in Chapter 5, stereotypes are a way of categorizing and processing information but are detrimental when they are negative and are held rigidly. Sometimes people must work to get information that can counteract the stereotype. Navita Cummings James (2000), a communication scholar, describes the beliefs and stereotypes about white people passed along to her from her family:

- Whites can be violent and treacherous.
- Whites have an inferiority complex that compels them to "put down" blacks and other minorities.

My growing up and my being raised . . . there was all kind of problems out there in the open for black people. And it would be very easy to hate a white person. And at home I didn't sense that hate. I sensed an understanding of what was going on, a dislike for what was going on, but not hate for the individual. And I think I've always had an open mind. My dad had several white friends that would come by and sit around and eat and laugh and talk.

Source: Wilson, in P. C. Rosenblatt et al., *Multiracial Couples: Black and White Voices* (Thousand Oaks, CA: Sage, 1995), p. 44.

- White men are arrogant, and white women are lazy.
- "Good" whites are the exception.

More importantly, James goes on to describe how she did not let these stereotypes become "an intellectual prison of my self identity or beliefs about Whites" (p. 45). Through intercultural relationships and effort, her beliefs evolved and the stereotypes diminished. She learned that race is not a predictor of intelligence but that income and opportunities are. She learned that all people, regardless of color, deserve to be treated with dignity and respect. And she made definite choices about how to relate to others and to cultivate a variety of friends, and not merely African Americans.

Another challenge in intercultural relationships involves the anxiety that people often experience initially. Some anxiety is present in the early stages of any relationship, but the anxiety is greater in intercultural relationships. Anxiety arises from concern about possible negative consequences. We may be afraid that we'll look stupid or that we'll offend someone because we're unfamiliar with that person's language or culture. Differences in age do not usually evoke such anxiety, but differences in physical ability, class, or race are likely to—at least initially. For example, a student describes his experience of being on a soccer team with players from Kenya, Jamaica, Egypt, and Mexico:

In our first meeting, we were to get acquainted with everyone and introduce ourselves. At the end of the meeting, we all stood around talking—reducing anxiety. Eventually, our conversations were directed toward self-disclosure and relating our experiences. I believe this helped me prepare for more experiences along this line.

The level of anxiety may be higher if one or both parties have negative expectations based on a previous interaction or on stereotypes (Stephan & Stephan, 1992). In contrast, intercultural interactions in which one or both parties have few negative expectations and no negative prior contact probably have less anxiety. For example, one student tells of traveling to New Zealand as an 18-year-old on a sports team:

I remember quite vividly experiencing uncertainty and anxiety and being forced to deal with it. Eighteen years old in a foreign land, and forced to deal with factors ommunication plays a key role in intercultural relationships. These intercultural relationships can change who you are and how you see the world. Our student Jessica went to New Zealand:

What an amazing experience. Not only did I get to stay with a family that had three girls, one my age, but I also learned about the Maoris, the first people to inhabit New Zealand. I developed a lifelong relationship with my host family and relished learning the difference and similarities between our cultures. I have fond memories of sitting up late at night drinking tea, not coffee, with my New Zealand mother. We would talk for hours. This was a powerful learning experience.

Although my experiences have for the most part been overseas, I feel they have opened a window for me. My worldview has gone from just me to phenomenally huge. I see things from other people's point of view; I actually try to see things in a different light. I have my experiences with people from other cultures to thank.

—Jessica

I did not know existed. . . . As I look back, I see that I was merely experiencing what I would later come to know as uncertainty and anxiety management.

The student goes on to describe how, with few negative preconceptions and no real language barrier, he quickly found similarity with people he met and had "truly an unforgettable experience."

Writer Letty Cottin Pogrebin (1987) emphasizes that intercultural relationships take more "care and feeding" than do those relationships between people who are very similar. Intercultural relationships are often more work than ingroup relationships. A lot of the work has to do with explaining—explaining to themselves, to each other, and to their respective communities.

First, in some way, conscious or unconscious, we ask ourselves, What is the meaning of being friends with someone who is not like me? Am I making this friend out of necessity, for my job, or because everyone I'm around is different from me in some way? Am I making this friend because I want to gain entry into this group for personal benefit? Because I feel guilty?

Second, we explain to each other. This is the process of ongoing mutual clarification, one of the healthiest characteristics of intercultural relationships. It is the process of learning to see from the other's perspective. For example, Judith discovered that, even when she thought she was being very indirect with her Japanese students, they still thought she was being rather direct. In this way, Judith came to understand that others can interpret events and conversation in very different ways.

Third, people who cross boundaries often have to explain this to their respective communities. Thus, your friends may question your close relationship with someone who is much older or is of a different ethnicity. This may be especially true for those who date someone from a different culture. For example, one of our students recounted how his friend terminated an intercultural relationship because of his parents' attitudes:

My Jewish friend was dating a Christian girl he met during his freshman year in college. He proposed marriage when they both graduated last year. But throughout their relationship, the parents of my friend let it be known that they were not happy with the fact that they were dating. My friend and his girlfriend are no longer seeing one another. My friend has told me he believes the parents' disapproval of the relationship was one of the reasons for their eventual split.

Historically, the biggest obstacles to boundary-crossing friendships have come not from minority communities, but from majority communities (McCullough, 1998). Those in the majority (e.g., whites) have the most to gain by maintaining social inequality and are less likely to initiate boundary-crossing friendships. In contrast, minority groups have more to gain. Developing intercultural relationships can help them survive—economically, professionally, and personally.

Finally, in intercultural relationships, individuals recognize and respect the differences. In these relationships, we often have to remind ourselves that we can never know exactly what it's like to walk in another person's shoes. Furthermore, those in the majority group tend to know less about those in minority groups than vice-versa. As Pogrebin (1992) stated, "Mutual respect, acceptance, tolerance for the faux pas and the occasional closed door, open discussion and patient mutual education, all this gives crossing friendships—when they work at all—a special kind of depth" (p. 318). Perhaps this is especially true of interracial relationships in the United States. Pat, an African American woman, describes the importance of honesty and openness in her relationship with her friend Rose, who is white:

"Rose is one of the few White women that I have an honest, direct relationship with. . . . She is very aware that I am a Black woman and she is a White woman. . . . I care about her very deeply. . . . And I am committed to our friendship and I respect her a whole lot. . . . I like her values. I like how she thinks about people, about nature, her integrity and her principles. . . . It is her willingness to make race her issue." (quoted in McCullough, 1998, p. 193)

THINKING DIALECTICALLY ABOUT INTERCULTURAL RELATIONSHIPS

Researcher Leslie A. Baxter (1993) suggests that a dialectical model explains the dynamics of relationships. She and her colleagues have identified several basic dialectical tensions in relationships: novelty–predictability, autonomy–connection, and openness–closedness (Baxter & Montgomery, 1996). That is, we can simultaneously feel the need to be both connected and autonomous in relationships with our parents, friends, and romantic partners. We may also feel the need simultaneously for novelty and predictability and the need to be open and yet private in our relationships. According to one study, Taiwanese students in close relationships experience these same dialectical tensions (Chen, Drzewiecka, & Sias, 2001). We can extend the notion of dialectical tensions to encompass the entire relational sphere (Chen, 2002; Martin, Nakayama, & Flores, 2002). Let's see how each of these dialectics work.

Personal-Contextual Dialectic

Intercultural relationships are both personal and contextual. There are aspects of the relationship that are personal—consistent from situation to situation—but context also plays a huge role in how intercultural relationships are developed and maintained. For example, are there contexts where you would be more or less comfortable in an intercultural relationship? How do your family, your church, your religious friends react to intercultural relationships? Studies have shown that the number-one predictor of whether individuals engage in intercultural dating is the diversity of their social networks—that is, if you are in contexts where there is diversity, it is more likely you will meet and go out with people from other ethnic/racial backgrounds (Clark-Ibanez & Felmlee, 2004).

Even who we are attracted to is largely determined by cultural contexts. Notions of attractiveness are defined for us and reinforced by what we see on TV and film and in other media. The standard of beauty for American women seems to be white and blond, and at least one study states that 90% of models in U.S. women's magazines are white (Frith, Shaw, & Cheng, 2005). This trend was noticed by one of our students:

I stopped by an airport newsstand and was struck by the similarity of the covers on the popular magazines displayed there (e.g., Vanity Fair, Cosmopolitan, Self). *Out of the 24 magazines, 19 had a white model with long blond hair on their covers! Two magazines had Caucasian brunettes, and two covers featured nonwhite women (one was Jennifer Lopez, the other Oprah Winfrey—on the cover of her* O *magazine).*

At the same time, Asian and Asian American women are often portrayed in popular culture texts and discourses as erotic, exotic, and submissive and thus highly attractive to white men (Root, 2001). One young man, Shane, described his attraction to Asian women:

I think they're so exotic. Really, what concerns me about the girl is the eyes, and Asian women have beautiful eyes, the form and the shape of them. It's a plus for me. I had another Asian girlfriend before. And I like their skin color, tannish, not just white, white, white. A girl with color. It's just different; it's more sexual, it's not just like plain Jane. ("Talking About Race," 2000, p. 59)

This kind of attraction has spawned an entire business of mail-order Asian brides. Communication scholar Rona Halualani (1995) analyzed how these businesses perpetuate and market stereotypes of Asian women as idealized wives—submissive, sexual, and eager to please men. In contrast, Asian men are often stereotyped in ways that downplay their masculinity (Eng, 2001).

Of course, we all want to believe we choose our relational partners outside of the influences of these social discourses. We all want to believe we fell in love with this man or this woman because he or she is "special." Yet if we want to understand the problems and dynamics of intercultural communication, we must be attentive to these large contextual discourses about racial and sexual identities and realize there is the tension of both personal and contextual forces in any intercultural relationship.

Differences-Similarities Dialectic

similarity principle A principle of relational attraction suggesting that individuals tend to be attracted to people they perceive to be similar to themselves.

According to the **similarity principle,** we tend to be attracted to people who we perceive to be similar to ourselves, and evidence indicates that this principle works for many cultural groups (Osbeck & Moghaddam, 1997; Tan & Singh, 1995). Finding people who agree with our beliefs confirms our own beliefs and provides us with **cognitive consistency** (if we like ourselves, we'll probably like others who share our views). In fact, we may explicitly seek partners who hold the same beliefs and values because of deep spiritual, moral, or religious conviction. In intercultural relationships, in contrast, we may be attracted to persons who are somewhat different from ourselves. The differences that form the basis of attraction may involve personality traits and may contribute to complementarity or balance in the relationship. An introverted individual may seek a more outgoing partner, or a spendthrift may be attracted to an individual who is more careful with money. Some individuals are attracted to people simply because they have a different cultural background. Intercultural relationships present intriguing opportunities to experience new ways of living in and looking at the world.

cognitive consistency Having a logical connection between existing knowledge and a new stimulus.

Most of us seek a balance between novelty and predictability in our relationships. Research shows that the most successful relationships have a balance of differences and similarities (Luo & Klohnen, 2005). In intercultural relationships especially, it is important to consider differences and similarities at the same time. Tamie, a student from Japan, explains how this dialectic works in her relationship with her roommate/friend Hong-Ju, a Korean graduate student:

We are both women and about the same age—30. Both of us are pursuing a Ph.D. degree and aspire to become successful professional scholars and educators. When we cook in our apartment, there are several common foods (e.g., rice, dried seaweed) while our eating styles may be different (e.g., Hong-Ju's cooking tends to include more spicy food than mine). We also share some common cultural values (e.g., importance of respect for elders). Yet Hong-Ju is married (a long-distance marriage), and I am single. Finally, we both consider ourselves as "not so typical" Korean or Japanese women. Hong-Ju's long-distance marriage and my staying single even in my 30s are usually considered as nontraditional in our respective countries. Eventually, this "nontraditionalness" creates in both of us a shared and proud sense of identity and bond.

Cultural-Individual Dialectic

Communication in intercultural relationships is both cultural and individual, that is, idiosyncratic. We have described various cultural differences that exist in value orientations, in both nonverbal and verbal communication. Although we have provided some generalizations about how various cultural groups differ, it is important to remember that communication is both cultural and individual. Tamie describes how she deals with this cultural-individual dialectic in her classroom teaching:

> *I have become very aware of cultural differences between U.S. classrooms and Japanese classrooms. In terms of my teaching style, I have noticed myself delivering the course content in a more linear, straightforward, fast-paced manner than I would in Japan. Therefore, there is definitely a certain cultural expectation that I am aware of as I teach in the U.S. However, I am also aware that there are unique individual styles and preferences among U.S. students—some students are outspoken and comfortable in speaking up; others take more time before speaking up, as they reflect and think more holistically. So this cultural–individual dialectic is always at work in my intercultural teaching experience here in the U.S.*

Privilege-Disadvantage Dialectic

We have stressed the importance of (and the difficulty of understanding) power and power differentials in intercultural relationships. People may be simultaneously privileged and disadvantaged, or privileged in some contexts and disadvantaged in others. For example, Laura, a bilingual university student, feels at a greater advantage in settings in which conversations take place in Spanish and English than she does in all-English settings. Her friends who speak only English probably feel the opposite. People in more powerful positions in particular need to be sensitive to power differentials, which may be less obvious to them.

Static-Dynamic Dialectic

This dialectic suggests that people and relationships are constantly in flux, responding to various personal and contextual dynamics. Intercultural relationships are no different in this regard. When Judith first met her friend Patricia (a third-generation, Mexican American, older student), Patricia was single and had just transferred to Arizona State University from a community college. At that time, both were living alone (Judith was in a commuter marriage), but both were close to their families. Patricia is now married, has a daughter, and has almost completed her graduate education. In this context, Judith and Patricia cannot respond to each other as the people they were five years ago but must respond to each other as they are now. Changes occur very slowly sometimes, but we need to remind ourselves that relationships are both static and dynamic.

History/Past–Present/Future Dialectic

Rather than trying to understand relationships by examining the relational partners alone, it is helpful to consider the contexts in which relationships occur. Often, this means the historical context. As noted in Chapter 4, cultural groups have different relationships with each other; some of these relationships are more positive and others more negative. For example, the historical and continuing hostility between the United States and Cuba means that each cultural group has fewer opportunities to meet people from the other nation and thus fewer opportunities to develop relationships. One student, John, gives his views on the past–present dialectic:

> I don't feel as if people should feel guilty about what their family, ethnic group, or country did in the past, but they should definitely empathize with those their ancestors have hurt, understand what they did, understand the implications of what they did, and understand how the past (whether we have ties to it or not) greatly affects the present.

INTERCULTURAL RELATIONSHIPS

As with other topics, there are three communication approaches to studying intercultural relationships, and each makes a unique contribution to our understanding of how we develop and maintain relationships across differences. The social science approach identifies cross-cultural differences in how relationships are defined, initiated, and developed. The interpretive approach explores in depth the nature of these relationships and the role communication plays. The critical approach emphasizes the influence of various contexts—institutional, political, and historical—in facilitating and/or discouraging the development and maintenance of intercultural relationships.

Social Science Approach: Cross-Cultural Differences

The social science approach identifies various cross-cultural differences in relationships—including notions of friendships and the initiation and development of relationships.

Differences in Notions of Friendship What are the characteristics of a friend? How do notions of friendship vary across cultures? To some people, a friend is someone to see or talk with occasionally, someone to do things with—go to a movie, discuss interests, maybe share some problems. This person might be one of many friends. If the friend moves away, the two people might eventually lose contact, and both might make new friends. Other people, however, view friendship much more seriously. For them, a friendship takes a long time to develop, includes many obligations (perhaps lending money or doing favors), and is a lifelong proposition.

Friendships are seen in very different ways around the world. For example, in most Western cultures, these relationships are seen as mostly voluntary and spontaneous, in contrast to family or work relationships. Although our friendships may be more constrained than we think (we do form relationships with people who are often very similar to ourselves), nonetheless, we enter into them voluntarily (Bell & Coleman, 1999).

Cultural differences in notions about friendships are related to ideas discussed earlier—ideas about identity and values. In societies that stress values like individualism and independence, as is the case in most Western cultures, it makes sense to view friendship and romance as voluntary relationships. However, people who view the self always in relation to others—that is, collectivists—hold a notion of friendship that is also less individual oriented and less spontaneous (Carrier, 1999). For example, in China, where the value of collectivism is very strong, friendships are long term and involve obligations:

> The meaning of friendship itself differs from the American version. Chinese make few casual, short-term acquaintanceships as Americans learn to do so readily in school, at work, or while out amusing themselves. Once made, however, Chinese friendships are expected to last and to give each party very strong claims on the other's resources, time and loyalty. (Gates, 1987, p. 6)

Friendship in China cannot be understood without attention to an important related concept, **guanxi**—"relationships of social connection built on shared identities such as native place, kinship or attending the same school" (Smart, 1999, p. 120). It is through *guanxi* that things get done (e.g., jobs acquired or bureaucratic snafus resolved), often "through the back door." Although "connections" are important in the United States, they are not viewed in so positive a light. Here, one should not have to resort to connections to get something done. In China, in contrast, being able to get something done through connections, or *guanxi*, is seen as very positive, and so these relationships are purposefully cultivated. *Guanxi* is not the same thing as friendship, but friendship provides an acceptable base on which *guanxi* can be built (Smart, 1999).

guanxi A Chinese term for relational network

This emphasis in China on cultivating close relationships, filled with obligations (and always open to *guanxi*), can be a bit overwhelming to people from Western cultures, but it can also be rewarding. A prominent journalist, Fox Butterfield (1982), who spent many years in China, describes these rewards:

> Friendship in China offered assurances and an intimacy that we have abandoned in America; it gave the Chinese psychic as well as material rewards that we have lost. We ourselves did feel close to the Wangs [their Chinese friends], but as Westerners, the constant gift giving and obligations left us uneasy. (p. 47)

Differences in Relational Development   Cultural differences often come into play in the very beginning stages of relational development, in initial interactions.

SOME INTERESTING CULTURAL VARIABLES IN RELATIONSHIPS

Brazil: To be invited to a Brazilian's home is an honor. Guests are expected to stay for many hours rather than stop for a brief visit.

China: Face-saving is extremely important in China. Chinese always avoid embarrassing situations and help one another save face and retain self-respect.

France: When French greet people, they tend to be formal. Titles such as Monsieur, Madame, and Mademoiselle are often used. If they know the person, they may give the traditional kiss by the cheek/air.

Spain: The Spanish often invite guests to their home out of courtesy. One should wait until the host insists to accept the invitation.

Germany: Germans tend to be formal. They do not use first names unless they know the person very well.

Egypt: Always use titles such as Doctor or Professor to address people.

Kenya: The Kenyan socialize at the end of the meal, not before the meal.

Greece: Avoid overpraising any item in a Greek home because the host may feel obligated to present it as a gift later.

Source: From M. Mancini, *Selling Destinations: Geography for the Travel Professional*, 4th ed. (Clifton Park, NY: Thomson/Delmar Learning, 2003).

Different cultural rules govern how to regard strangers. In some cultural communities, all strangers are viewed as sources of potential relationships; in others, relationships can develop only after long and careful scrutiny. For example, in traditional German Mennonite society, strangers, especially those outside the religious group, are regarded with suspicion and not as potential friends. In contrast, many U.S. Americans are known to disclose personal information in very public contexts. One international student observes,

> One thing that was very different from what I was used to in Iceland was that people, even people that I didn't know at all, were telling me their whole life stories, or so it felt like. Even some women at the checkout line at the supermarket were talking about how many times they had been married or divorced or about the money they had, which, in my culture, we are not used to just telling anyone about.

The renowned communication scholar Dean Barnlund (1989), along with his colleagues, found many differences in relational development in their students in Japanese and U.S. colleges. Students in both countries were asked about their interactions with strangers and friends and about their views on friendship and more intimate relationships. The U.S. American students were more open and receptive to strangers; they talked to strangers in many different contexts—perhaps at a bus stop, in line at the grocery store, or in classes. In n some societies, the development of relationships is intricately related to issues of status and formality. Communication scholar Wintilo Garcia explains how these issues are expressed in Mexican Spanish.

The Mexican use of the Spanish words tu *and* usted *signals the immediacy and status of the relational partners.* Tu *is the informal application of the pronoun* you. *It is common that individuals refer to their friends, family members, or children by this form of the word. The word* usted *is the formal form of the pronoun* you. *Cultural norms and rules require individuals to use this form when addressing new acquaintances, older people, professional (white-collar) people, and people who possess some sort of power. . . . In Mexico, as relationships become more intimate, the form of address changes. This often occurs over time where people who were once referred to by* usted *will later be referred to by* tu. *. . . Usually this transformation is initiated by the person who holds a perceived higher class. This is reasonable because high class individuals are perceived to possess more power in the relationship. In Mexico, the usual request phrase from the high class player is* tuteame *(interpreted as you "tu" me), which implies a desire for relational equality. In order for this request to be fulfilled, relational players must negotiate the pattern of communication. . . . For example, if a student normally addresses professors by the title* Doctor G *and* Doctor T, *it implies a status and class difference. In general, to change this form of address, the professor must initiate the request.*

Source: From Wintilo Garcia, "Respeto: A Mexican Base for Interpersonal Relationships," in *Communication in Personal Relationships Across Cultures*, edited by W. B. Gudykunst, S. Ting-Toomey, and T. Nishida, (Thousand Oaks, CA: Sage, 1996), pp. 137–155.

contrast, the Japanese students talked to significantly fewer strangers than did U.S. Americans over the same period.

More recently, communication scholar Pei-Wen Lee studied intercultural friendships that arise in a third culture, a culture that is not home to either of the friends. She notes that "the third cultural context serves as a significant backdrop with rules, norms, and events to which the intercultural dyad can relate and refer during their interactions" (2008, p. 66). The influence of a third culture complicates the stage model for intercultural friendships but can serve as a useful background for building these friendships.

Friendships   As relationships develop in **intimacy,** friends share more personal and private information.

intimacy The extent of emotional closeness.

Over a half century ago, Kurt Lewin (1948), a renowned psychologist, conducted a classic cross-cultural study in self-disclosure whose findings still hold true today. Lewin proposed that the personal/private self can be modeled as three concentric circles representing three areas of information we share with others. The first circle is an outer boundary that includes superficial information about ourselves and our lives—our general interests, our daily life, and so on. The raditionally, when studying other cultures, people focus on the differences, appreciating and respecting them. However, the dialectic that includes differences and similarities takes this process one step further. It not only expresses the importance of respecting differences but also points up the basic human needs and wants we all possess. In our multicultural society, it is important to recognize the similarities among ourselves.

It is apparent that most cultures share some common bonds. Human emotions are the same throughout the world. Knowing that someone laughs, cries, and is scared the same as you creates an empathy that is important to understanding other cultures. This point of view allows us to form bonds and brings us closer to the people of the other culture.

Emotions are universal, and being able to see someone as you see yourself can lead to a deep respect and appreciation for the other person. Using this dialectic myself, I have already begun to blur the lines that divide me from people of other cultures. Where I once might have been scared or nervous to approach someone different, I am now curious to see how the person is the same. It is a very rewarding feeling to break down these barriers and become enlightened by someone of a different culture. I've learned that the physical differences that at first seem so apparent begin to fade away as people of different cultures communicate with one another. No matter where we come from, what our language or skin color, we all bleed red, and that makes us the same.

—Danielle

middle circle includes more personal information—perhaps our life history, our family background, and so on. Then there is the inner core, which includes very personal and private information, some of which we share with no one. These spheres of information may correspond with the phases in relational development. Thus, in the exploratory stage, people exchange some personal information, and in the stability phase, they may disclose more intimate information.

According to Lewin, there is the most variation in the extent to which the outer area is more or less permeable. For example, for many European Americans, the outer boundary is highly permeable; they may disclose a wide range of relatively superficial information with many people, even those they don't know well, in many contexts. The middle, or second, area is less permeable; this information is shared with fewer people and in fewer contexts. And information in the inner area is shared with very few. In contrast, for many other cultural and ethnic groups, the outer boundary is much more closed. International students in the United States often remark that U.S. students seem superficial. That is, U.S. students welcome interaction with strangers and share information of a superficial nature—for example, before class or at a party. When some international students experience this, they assume they are moving into the exploratory "friend" phase (the middle circle), only to discover that the U.S. student considers the international student to be merely an acquaintance. A student from Singapore explains,

> *I learned in the first couple months that people are warm yet cold. For example, I would find people saying "Hi" to me when I'm walking on campus or asking me how I am doing. It used to make me feel slighted that even as I made my greeting back to them, they were already a mile away. Then when real interaction occurs— for example, in class—somehow I sense that people tend to be very superficial and false. Yet they disclose a lot of information—for example, talking about personal relationships, which I wasn't comfortable with. I used to think that because of such self-disclosure you would share a special relationship with the other person, but it's not so because the same person who was telling you about her personal relationship yesterday has no idea who you are today. Now I have learned to not be offended or feel slighted by such incidences.*

It's probably more accurate to say that what most people in the world consider simply a "friend" is what a U.S. American would consider a "close friend." A German student explains that in Germany people are hardly able to call somebody a friend, even if they have known that person for more than a year. Only if they have a "special emotional relationship" can they call the person a friend (Gareis, 1995, p. 128). For most U.S. Americans, the "special emotional relationship" is reserved for a so-called good or close friend.

Mary Jane Collier conducted a study with these three groups and Asian Americans in which she investigated conversational rules in close friendships (Collier, 1996). Again, she found many similarities in how these groups thought about close friendship. However, she also found some differences. For instance, Latino/a, Asian American, and African American students said that it took, on average, about a year to develop a close friendship; European Americans felt that it took only a few months. She also found differences in what each group thought was important in close friendships: "Latinos emphasized relational support, Asian Americans emphasized a caring, positive exchange of ideas, African Americans emphasized respect and acceptance and Anglo [European] Americans emphasized recognizing the needs of individuals" (p. 315). Clearly, such distinctions affect how people of different cultural groups develop friendships.

There also are cultural differences in how much nonverbal expression is encouraged. Again, according to Barnlund's and other studies, U.S. Americans expressed much more intimacy nonverbally than did the Japanese respondents (Nishida, 1996).

Romantic Relationships Some intimate relationships develop into **romantic relationships.** Several studies have compared the development of these types of intimate relationships across cultures. For example, communication researcher Gao Ge (1991) compared romantic heterosexual relationships among Chinese and U.S. American young people. Based on interviews with students about their romantic relationships, she identified common themes of openness, involvement, shared nonverbal meanings, and relationship assessment. However, there were some variations between the two groups. The U.S. American students

romantic relationships
Intimate relationships that comprise love, involvement, sharing, openness, connectedness, and so on.

emphasized the importance of physical attraction, passion, and love, which Gao interprets as a reflection of a more individualistic orientation. In contrast, the Chinese students stressed the importance of their partners' connectedness to their families and other relational connections, reflecting a more collectivistic orientation.

In another study, Gao (2001) compared intimacy, passion, and commitment in Chinese and U.S. American heterosexual romantic relationships. Based on her previous research and on cultural values, she predicted that intimacy and passion would be higher for U.S. couples, given that passion and intimacy are more individually centered relationship goals. She also predicted that commitment—a more collectivistic relational value—would be higher for Chinese couples. She found that passion *was* significantly higher in U.S. American couples than in Chinese couples but that the amount of intimacy and commitment did not vary cross-culturally. This may mean that intimacy is a universal dimension of romantic relationships, but the finding about commitment is more puzzling. Gao speculates that this finding may be related to the fact that all the couples in her study were in advanced stages of serious relationship, at which time commitment is more universally expected. Her hypothesis about commitment may have applied to couples in earlier stages in their relationships.

This was confirmed in a similar study comparing North American, Japanese, and Russian beliefs about romantic love. In this study, North Americans emphasized romantic love, passionate love, and love based on friendship more than did the Japanese or Russians. Other, more collectivistic cultural groups emphasized the acceptance of the potential mate by family members and commitment over romantic or passionate love (Sprecher et al., 1994).

Research on the development of romantic relationships in the United States has focused on the importance of the individual's autonomy. Togetherness is important as long as it doesn't interfere too much with a person's freedom. Being open, talking things out, and retaining a strong sense of self are seen as specific strategies for maintaining a healthy intimate relationship. This emphasis on autonomy—trying to balance the needs of two "separate" individuals—in relationships can be difficult. Also, extreme individualism makes it challenging for either partner to justify sacrificing or giving more than she or he is receiving. All of this leads to fundamental conflicts in trying to reconcile personal freedom with relational obligations (Dion & Dion, 1988). In fact, one study found that people who held extremely individualistic orientations experienced less sense of love, care, trust, and physical attraction toward their partners in romantic relationships (Dion & Dion, 1991). These problems are less common in collectivistic societies.

Interpretive Approach: Communicating in Intercultural Relationships

Now that we have considered the contributions of the social science research, let's turn our attention to more in-depth examination of how we communicate across cultural differences. As we've noted, intercultural relationships may be very similar to intracultural relationships. However, there may be some unique characteristics that can guide our thinking about communicating in these relationships.

Based on interviews with U.S. and Japanese students who were friends, researcher Sandra Sudweeks and colleagues (1990) identified competence, similarity, involvement, and turning points as characterizing important aspects of intercultural relationships. For example, the students talked about the importance of linguistic and cultural competence. At first, language was a common issue. Even when people speak the same language, they sometimes have language difficulties that can prevent relationships from flourishing. The same holds true for cultural information. Dissimilarity may account for the initial attraction, but these students mentioned the importance of finding some *similarity* in their relationships that transcended the cultural differences. For example, they looked for a shared interest in sports or other activities. Or they were attracted by similar physical appearance, lifestyle, or attitude. Sometimes shared religious beliefs can help establish common bonds (Graham, Moeai, & Shizuru, 1985).

Relationships take time to develop; students interviewed by Sudweeks and colleagues mentioned how important it was that the other person make time for the relationship. This is one aspect of involvement. Intimacy of interaction is another element, as are shared friendship networks. According to the study, sharing the same friends is more important for Japanese students than for U.S. American students because the Japanese students had left their friendships behind.

Finally, the students mentioned significant occurrences that were related to perceived changes in the relationship—turning points that moved the relationship forward or backward. For example, asking a friend to do a favor or to share an activity might be a turning point. The students remarked that if the other person refused, the relationship often didn't develop beyond that point. However, a turning point of understanding—**self-disclosure**—may move the relationship to a new level.

self-disclosure Revealing information about oneself.

Another communication scholar, Brenda J. Allen (2000), gives us an example of a turning point. She describes her relationship across sexual orientation lines with a colleague in her department:

> *We found that we had similar ideas about issues, activities and improvement on our own critical thinking skills in the classroom. . . . [We] were both baby boomers from the Midwest, only months apart in age. We also came from lower-class families, and religion played a strong role in our childhood. (p. 179)*

Allen describes the turning point in their relationship when her friend revealed that she was gay: "As a heterosexual I had never before given much thought to sexual orientation or gays 'coming out of the closet.' Thanks to Anna, I have become far more sensitive and enlightened" (p. 180).

The process of dealing with differences, finding similarities, and moving beyond stereotypes and prejudice is summed up by a U.S. American student talking about her relationship with a Singaporean friend:

> *"We just had different expectations, different attitudes in the beginning, but at the end we were so close that we didn't have to talk about it. . . . After we erased*

> *all prejudices, that we thought the other person has to be different, after we erased that by talking, we just understood each other." (quoted in Gareis, 1995, p. 136)*

Intercultural Work Relationships   For many people, work is the place where they encounter the most diversity—working with people from different religions, generations, language backgrounds, ethnicity, races, and nationality. These encounters may be face-to-face or mediated—through telephone or computer. Understanding this diversity is especially important as organizations move from an assimilationist perspective ("Hire the quota and let them assimilate to us") to a more integrative perspective. One leading diversity expert refers to the latter as "foxhole diversity," the view that if the enemy is all around, you need people in the foxhole with you to support you; you need to cut through the superfluous and think about what skills and expertise your foxhole colleagues really need to possess as job requirements, not just what you'd prefer. We may prefer that our co-workers look like us and have the same language and religious background, but these preferences are not the same as the requirements for the job (Chozick, 2005). And more and more organizations are seeing the bottom-line payoff for a truly diverse workforce in a global economy—moving beyond concerns of women and minorities to concerns of generational differences, the pressures on gays and lesbians who have to hide part of their lives, and challenges in incorporating disabled workers (Hymowitz, 2005).

So the challenge in the workplace is to get along with people who may be very different, and some of the work relationships may turn into friendships, as one of our students reported:

> *At my job in the Memorial Union, I work with students of all ethnicities, races, and nationalities. At first I was kind of intimidated, but I've found that I've got to know some of them, since work issues always provide an easy topic to discuss and some of the discussions have led to more socializing. While I can't say these are among my closest friends, I probably wouldn't have had the chance to meet so many different people if I weren't working at this job.*

Power, of course, often comes into play because most work relationships are within a hierarchy. There are subordinate–superior relationships and peer relationships, and the nature of the relationship constrains the interaction. If your boss tells you your hairstyle violates company policy, that's one thing. If your office mate, your company peer, tells you the photos on your desk offend her, that's something else. There is more room for negotiation and discussion.

It is difficult when race, ethnicity, and class are all part of the hierarchy—as is common in the tourist and restaurant business. The experience of one of our students is quite common:

> *In the restaurant where I work, all the servers (like me) are female and white, and all the busboys and kitchen help are Latino, who mostly speak Spanish, and the two bosses are white males—who make everyone speak English when they're around. I kind of like to practice my Spanish a little in talking with the Latino workers, and I have a pretty good relationship with them. Some of the other servers really refuse to speak Spanish.*

Because there is a hierarchy, the busboys and kitchen help must speak English—even if the server can speak Spanish whenever she feels like practicing her Spanish.

Intercultural Relationships Online   As we noted in Chapter 1, more and more people are using the Internet to communicate—for fun and for work, so much so that computer-mediated communication (CMC) has become an ordinary part of our daily life (Herring, 2004). The Internet presents us with enormous opportunities to form relationships across cultures and leads us to speculate how online relationships differ from RL (real-life) relationships and whether it is easier or more difficult to communicate across cultures online. The answers to these questions seem to be dialectical. Online communication is both similar to *and* different from RL relationships, and it both facilitates and inhibits the development of intercultural relationships.

Some scholars suggest that online communication can facilitate the development of intercultural relationships because of the filtering of nonverbal cues and the lack of so-called gating. That is, there is no **line of sight** data (information about gender, age, race, or nationality) in online communication. So online relationships are less likely to be "anchored" in these social/cultural conventions, prejudices, or stereotypes (Postmes, Spears, & Lea, 1998). And the reasoning goes, if one can develop a solid online relationship, not based on physical attributes or attractiveness, by the time online friends meet in person, these line of sight data don't matter so much (McKenna, Green, & Gleason, 2002). Of course this doesn't really address the problem of prejudices based on physical appearance. As scholar Radhika Gajjala points out,

line of sight information about other people's identity based upon visible physical characteristics.

> *Why should it be wonderful for women and colored people to be able to hide who they are and to be able to disguise their gender, race, and culture in favor of passing as Caucasian? Why must we be ashamed of being women or colored or both? What's wrong with being colored? What's wrong with being a woman? (p. 84)*

A number of studies show that online relationships are very similar to RL relationships. For example, Denise Carter (2004) studied CMC in "Cybertown"—a virtual "city" where people from all over the world "live" in virtual houses, spend city "cash," visit and socialize in various places around town—the plaza, beach, and café. She visited Cybertown several times a day for several years—and interviewed many of the hundreds of residents. She found that about half the residents transferred their relationship offline. She concludes that these friendships are very much like RL friendships, characterized by freedom, commitment, intimacy, and trust, and very much a part of everyday life. She found that because there was no gating based on line of sight data, cultural differences played a very small role in Cybertown relationships. People from all over the globe interacted; formed friendships based on similar interests, values, and beliefs; and by the time many transferred their relationships offline, there was a solid basis of trust. Other scholars support Carter's conclusions—that the lack of physical cues in CMC helps facilitate cohesion dynamics in international settings, which might not occur in video or face-to-face (FTF) encounters (Gasner, 1999; Henderson & Gilding, 2004; Walther, 1996; Walther & Parks, 2002).

It needs to be pointed out that Cybertown residents, although from different countries, all spoke English, so misunderstandings related to language differences were minimized. Also, many experts point out that language and other cultural differences hold significant challenges for online relationships, particularly in initial stages of relational development. However, very few studies document particular difficulties. You might speculate on some communication challenges in online relationships: language challenges and communication-style challenges.

Language differences can make online communication and relationship development difficult, although the asynchronicity of CMC does allow nonnative speakers more time to compose a message and to decode and respond than is true in FTF interaction. In addition to possible misunderstandings of specific words and phrases, language conventions such as humor can often be misunderstood. Understanding humor in a language often requires a sophisticated understanding of subtle nuances; irony, sarcasm, and cynicism in online communication across cultures should be approached with great caution (St. Amant, 2002). And when humor is misunderstood, it often takes complicated explanations to clarify, as one communication professor discovered:

> One of the classmates in my online course made a remark, meant to be slightly sarcastic and humorous, about one of the group projects he was involved in for our course. However, the remark was perceived by some of the international members of his group to be in poor taste. Some thought it very rude and insulting. Others just found it childish. It took almost half the semester to figure out what had gone wrong, why the remark was misunderstood and to get things back on a good footing. I can't imagine it would have taken even half that long if the interaction had been face-to-face instead of on the Internet.

Sometimes problems caused by language differences are exacerbated because one or both interactants may not be aware of the problem, because confusion or misunderstanding is generally shown nonverbally—by a quizzical look or a raised eyebrow. Online communicators may have to work a little harder to make sure they understand each other and to give the other some leeway in expressing different cultural values and communication styles.

What happens when low-context and high-context communicators interact online? Because the Internet filters out almost all contextual cues (tone of voice, eye gaze, facial expression, etc.), scholars speculate that conversations between low- and high-context communicators might be difficult online (Olaniran, 2001). The low-context communicator might be very comfortable being direct about feelings and opinions, whereas the high-context communicator might feel rather constrained by CMC. When misunderstandings occur, it might be especially difficult to identify the source of misunderstanding and resolve it (Snyder, 2003).

For example, a Korean colleague who teaches at an American university reported that she often feels constrained in e-mail conversations with her U.S. colleagues. Having a preference for high-context communication, she finds the direct, low-context style of her colleagues a bit off-putting. This is especially true when they discuss sensitive issues through e-mail, and her colleagues ask her to give an explicit opinion that might conflict with others' opinions. She reports that she sometimes doesn't respond to these e-mail messages or tries to carry on the discussion with them face-to-face where contextual, nonverbal cues are available to her.

Another possible issue for high- and low-context communication differences concerns identity information. For many high-context cultures, background information of the speaker is part of the contextual information needed to understand and respond to a message, and as St. Amant (2002) explains,

> *However, in CMC, cues essential for determining identity are absent; therefore, it lacks context information that people from certain cultures need to determine how to interact in a given communication situation. As a result, participants from such cultures may feel uncomfortable, frustrated or reserved, because without these identity-based context cues, they cannot determine what is acceptable and what is unacceptable behavior in a given discourse situation. (p. 201)*

Of course, being reserved or quiet in a CMC environment can have implications for how one is perceived—particularly by those with context communication preferences.

Similarly, what are the challenges when someone from a high-power distance culture communicates from a low-power distance culture? The high-power person might be uncomfortable with the informality and relative disregard for hierarchy expressed by the low-power distance person. And depending on preference for face-saving strategies, it might be difficult to discuss communication differences, with interactants choosing different ways to protect or save theirs or the other person's face. For example, one study found that in Japan and Korea using a fax machine was much more popular in corporate communications than e-mail (Lee, 2002). This may be because people from East Asian countries such as Japan, Korea, and China, unlike people in Western countries, share the tradition of Confucianism, which emphasizes the social order in everyday living and showing respect for elders or seniors in the workplace and other contexts. These beliefs influence their use of communication technologies, as illustrated in this report from a Korean marketing specialist, who is a virtual team member:

> *Whenever I want to report something and try to send the document via email, upon turning on a computer email facility, I hesitate and somehow give up and decide to go to see him [boss] in person or make a telephone call or send him a fax or an express surface mail. . . . The thing is that I have this feeling of being rude to him if I send the document via email. . . . In our Confucius culture, one has to show respect to seniors. . . . I think that email cannot convey signs of respect in an effective manner. . . . [S]ending via fax or surface mail at least shows some pains taken in order to give respect to the boss, and that matters. I feel that email might look too easy and casual to the degree that I might look like I don't show enough respect for my boss. (Lee, 2002, pp. 230–231)*

Intercultural Dating   Why do people date others from different cultural backgrounds? Probably for the same reasons we form any intercultural relationship. We are attracted to them, and the relationship offers benefits—increased knowledge about the world and the breaking of stereotypes. This has been the experience of Peiting, a Tawainese American dating Paul, a Danish exchange student: "Dating Paul offers me this whole new perspective of life as a Caucasian and a Dane." Also, she encounters ideas that differ from those of most of her U.S. American friends: "We'll talk for hours about American films, about Danish government, even about variations in our countries attitudes toward drinking" (quoted in Russo, 2001).

Several decades ago, researcher Phillip E. Lampe (1982) investigated inter-ethnic dating among students attending a college in Texas. He discovered that the reasons students gave for dating within and outside their own ethnic group were very similar: They were attracted to the other person, physically and/or sexually. In contrast, the reasons students gave for not dating someone within or outside their own ethnic group were very different. The main reason for not dating *within* the ethnic group was lack of attraction. However, the reasons for not dating *outside* the ethnic group were not having an opportunity to do so and not having thought about it. Lampe interpreted this distinction in responses as reflecting the social and political structure of U.S. American society. That is, most individuals, by the time they reach adolescence, have been taught that it is better to date within one's ethnic and racial group and probably have had very little opportunity to date interethnically.

Have things changed since Lampe's study? It does seem that they have, that U.S. Americans today are much more open to intercultural relationships. For example, in one survey, 77% of those surveyed said it's all right for blacks and whites to date each other—up from 48% who felt this way in 1987. The young are the most accepting; 91% of people questioned who were born after 1976 said that interracial dating is acceptable—compared to 50% of the oldest generation (Taylor, Funk, & Craighill, 2006). This survey showed that attitudes are more tolerant, but do people's behaviors match their attitudes? The results of our own study show that, in some instances, patterns of intercultural dating have not changed a great deal and confirm that individual dating experiences and societal contexts are still closely related (Martin, Bradford, Chitgopekar, & Drzewiecka, 2003). Like Lampe's respondents, about 60% of our respondents said they had dated interculturally, with Mexican Americans doing so more frequently than African Americans or whites. Many of the remaining 40% gave the same reasons as respondents in Lampe's study for not dating interculturally: They had no desire or no opportunity. So, even though Lampe's study was conducted in the early 1980s, the same conditions seem to hold, at least in some parts of the United States, particularly for African Americans and whites. The reality remains that most Americans live, go to school, and worship in segregated groups (Logan, Stults, & Farley, 2004). And this was certainly true in our study, as 80% of the white students said they grew up in all-white neighborhoods.

We also found that the social context and past experiences were a strong influence on whether young people dated interculturally. Not surprisingly, those who did date interculturally were more likely to have grown up in ethnically diverse neighborhoods and to have more ethnically diverse acquaintances and friends. In addition, they came from families in which other family members had

My girlfriend and I are in what fits into the category of intercultural relationships. While we are both Mexican, she is religious (and her family), while I am not at all, nor is my family. At times the religion difference has been a cause for some complications. For instance, she did not want to let her family know that I am Atheist when we began dating because she thought they would dislike me without getting to know me. Not ever having given much thought to religion I thought it would not matter. But to my surprise one of the first times I met her grandmother I was asked about my religion and which church I attended, and when I was baptized. I could see the look on my girlfriend's face as I calmly answered that I was not religious, and almost instantly I could see the looks of her family change and I quickly understood why she was so worried. While I do not believe her family hates me, I know that they remember that conversation.

　—Timothy

dated interculturally. This suggests that family attitudes play a big role. Indeed, other studies confirm that families often instill negative attitudes regarding interracial friendships or romantic relationships (Moore, 2000). And these attitudes are learned at a very young age. As Derryck, a young black child said, when asked about his relationship with his white friend, "Black and white kids can be friends with each other, if you're in the same class. But they can't get married, because they don't match. They can't have a kid together" ("Talking About Race," 2000, p. 47). Interracial friendships may be more accepted in elementary school, but they are less accepted in teenage years (Graham & Cohen, 1997).

Finally, whether individuals date interculturally may also depend on the region of the country in which they grow up. A study conducted in California, for example, showed a slightly higher incidence of intercultural dating there than we found in our study (Tucker & Mitchell-Kernan, 1995). As the 2000 census shows, there is more diversity in the West and Southwest. Given what we know about the influence of context on interpersonal relationships, we would expect more diverse schools and neighborhoods, and thus more opportunity for intercultural contact in these areas.

There are other factors that do not clearly explain intercultural dating patterns. In a recent study of Internet personal ads, Shauna Wilson and her colleagues (2007) found that blacks who knew they did or did not want children were more willing to date other blacks than blacks who were unsure if they wanted children. Also, blacks in the West were less willing to date other blacks than those living in other parts of the country. Also, black smokers were less willing to date other blacks. It isn't clear how these variables are related to intercultural dating. They call for more research to better understand these patterns.

Permanent Relationships　In spite of substantial resistance to intercultural (especially interracial) romantic relationships, increasing numbers of people are marrying across racial and ethnic lines, so much so that scholar Maria P. P. Root ame-sex couples can get married in some places around the world, but these marriages are not recognized by U.S. immigration law. Some nations do recognize same-sex relationships for immigration purposes.

Binational couples refers to couples in which the partners come from different countries. Although 16 nations around the world allow their citizens to sponsor their same sex partners for immigration benefits, unfortunately, the United States does not recognize our relationships for immigration purposes. Because of the Defense of Marriage Act, which defines marriage as between a man and a woman, even same sex couples which have been legally married in Massachusetts, Canada, the Netherlands, or Belgium will not be able to immigrate based on their marriage. Every day we hear from desperate couples, forced to choose between the partner they love and the country they love, which is why we are fighting to change the immigration law and end this discrimination.

Source: From "Immigration Equality." Retrieved on May 13, 2008 from http://www.immigrationequality.org/template.php?pageid=2

(2001) says we are in the midst of a "quiet revolution." Who is most likely to intermarry in the United States? According to Root, women (except for black women) intermarry more than men. Also, older rather than younger people tend to intermarry, except where similar-size groups live in proximity to one another. For example, in Hawaii, California, and Arizona, younger persons are more likely to intermarry. In addition, later generations of immigrants have higher rates of intermarriage than earlier ones. (See Figure 10-2.)

Why are the rates of intermarriage so low for certain groups? The answer has to do with various contextual issues related to gender and social status. For example, there are fewer objections to Asian American–white than to black–white marriages. Gender stereotypes come into play in that Asian women are, even now, viewed as traditionally feminine, subservient, and obedient, as well as petite—making them attractive as partners for white men. This has led to increasing numbers of Asian American women intermarrying. The same is true for Latinas and Native American women, but not black women. As Root observes, blackness for them still has caste connotations, which means they are partnered in intermarriages less than any other group. White women, in contrast, intermarry more frequently.

The larger social discourses on interracial relationships should not be ignored. Columnist Hoyt Sze (1992) notes,

Naturally, people outmarry [marry outside their racial group] for love. But we must ask ourselves how much of this love is racist, unequal love. Unfortunately, interracial love is still inextricably linked to colonialism. How else does one explain the disproportional rates at which Asian American women and African American men marry out? Is it just a coincidence that the mainstream media objectify the

FIGURE 10-2   Weddings are one way that people mark their cultural and relational identities. This is a photo of an Indian wedding in South Africa. Many Indians migrated to South Africa in the 19th century, and today there are more than a million Indian South Africans. How might this relationship face different issues than relationships among majority group members? (© *David Turnley/Corbis*)

same groups as "exotic-erotic" playthings? I know that Asian American men and African American women aren't fundamentally lacking in attractiveness or desirability. (p. 10)

If we try to understand romantic love only on the interpersonal level, how might we explain the high rates of outmarriage by some groups and not others?

In any case, the current trend to intermarry may change things. As the rates of intermarriage continue to increase, these families will produce more children who challenge the current race and gender stereotypes, and the structural barriers to intermarriage will be eroded (Lee & Edmonston, 2005). As Root (2001) observes, "Intermarriage has ripple effects that touch many people's lives. It is a symbolic vehicle through which we can talk about race and gender and reexamine our ideas about race" (p. 12). And the fact is that younger people do have more tolerant attitudes about intermarriage. Although intermarriage will not solve all intercultural problems, the increasing numbers of multicultural people will have a positive impact.

What are the major concerns of couples who marry interculturally? One study compared experiences of inter- and intracultural couples. Their concerns, like those of dating couples, often involved dealing with pressures from their families and from society in general. An additional issue involved raising

Most people describe their reasons for intermarriage in terms of romantic love. Mariel, a 24-year-old Chicana raised in a suburb of Los Angeles, reflected on what influenced her decision to marry her black husband and how fortunate she was that her family approved.

I was really active in La Raza *and feel committed to my people, so I always thought I would marry a Chicano guy. I love my older brothers and even thought I might marry one of their friends. When I went away to college. . . . I was just exposed to so many people. My political ideals didn't change. But I met my husband in my second year. He was very supportive of my commitments. We just started doing things together, studying, talking, going to parties. He fit in well with my friends and I liked his friends. It was like we would go to parties and there were all sorts of people there and I'd find I always had more in common with him than just about anyone in a room. We had really good talks. And music. We both loved music and movies. So one thing led to another. I tried to talk myself out of my feelings for him, thinking I should just keep it as good friends, but then I thought, "Shouldn't the man I marry be my best friend?" My family liked him. I mean, like, if my brothers didn't like him, this would have been real hard. They have a lot of influence on me even though I make up my own mind. We talked a lot about what it meant to marry someone different than your own cultural background. But I realized I didn't have to give up my commitment to my people. We believed in the same issues. Now it might have been different if he was white. I'm not sure how that would have gone over.*

Source: From M. P. P. Root, *Love's Revolution: Interracial Marriage*, (Philadelphia: Temple University Press, 2001), pp. 7–8.

children. Sometimes these concerns are intertwined. Although many couples are concerned with raising children and dealing with family pressures, those in intercultural marriages deal with these issues to a greater extent. They are more likely to disagree about how to raise the children and are more likely to encounter opposition and resistance from their families about the marriage (Graham, Moeai, & Shizuru, 1985).

Writer Dugan Romano (1997) interviewed couples in which one spouse came from another country to identify challenges of these international marriages. Some are common problems faced by most couples, including friends, politics, finances, sex, in-laws, illness and suffering, and children. But some issues are exacerbated in these intercultural marriages; these involve values, eating and drinking habits, gender roles, attitudes regarding time, religion, place of residence, stress, and ethnocentrism.

Of course, every husband and wife develop their own idiosyncratic way of relating to each other, but intercultural marriage poses consistent challenges. Romano also points out that most couples have their own systems for working out the power balance in their relationships, for deciding who gives and who takes. She identifies four styles of interaction: submission, compromise, obliteration, and consensus. Couples may adopt different styles depending on the context.

The **submission style** is the most common. In this style, one partner submits to the culture of the other partner, abandoning or denying his or her own. The submission may occur in public, whereas in private life the relationship may be more balanced. Romano points out that this model rarely works in the long run. People cannot erase their core cultural background, no matter how hard they try.

In the **compromise style,** each partner gives up some of his or her culturally bound habits and beliefs to accommodate the other person. Although this may seem fair, it really means that both people sacrifice things that are important to them. For example, the Christian who gives up having a Christmas tree and celebrating Christmas for the sake of a Jewish spouse may eventually come to resent the sacrifice.

In the **obliteration style,** both partners deal with differences by attempting to erase their individual cultures. They may form a new culture, with new beliefs and habits, especially if they live in a country that is home to neither of them. This may seem to be the only way for people whose backgrounds are completely irreconcilable to survive. However, because it's difficult for people to completely cut themselves off from their own cultural backgrounds, obliteration is not a viable long-term solution.

The style that is the most desirable, not surprisingly, is the **consensus style,** which is based on agreement and negotiation. It is related to compromise in that both partners give and take, but it is not a trade-off; rather, it is a win-win proposition. Consensus may incorporate elements of the other models. On occasion, one spouse might temporarily "submit" to the other's culture or temporarily give up something to accommodate the other. For example, while visiting her husband's Muslim family, a Swiss wife might substantially change her demeanor, dressing more modestly and acting less assertive. Consensus requires flexibility and negotiation. Romano stresses that couples who are considering permanent international relationships should prepare for the commitment by living together, spending extended time with the other's family, learning the partner's language, studying the religion, and learning the cuisine. The couple should also consider legal issues like their own and their children's citizenship, finances and taxation, ownership of property, women's rights, and divorce.

Gay and Lesbian Relationships   Most of the discussion so far was derived from research on heterosexual friendships and romantic relationships. Much less information is available about gay and lesbian relationships. What we do know is that these relationships are a fact of society: homosexuality has existed in every society and in every era (Chesebro, 1981, 1997).

What we know about gay and lesbian relationships is often in contrast to the "model" of heterosexual relationships. Gay and lesbian relationships may be intracultural or intercultural. Although there are many similarities between gay/lesbian and straight relationships, they may differ in several areas, including the

submission style A style of interaction for an intercultural couple in which one partner yields to the other partner's cultural patterns, abandoning or denying his or her own culture. (Compare with **compromise style, consensus style,** and **obliteration style.**)

compromise style A style of interaction for an intercultural couple in which both partners give up some part of their own cultural habits and beliefs to minimize cross-cultural differences. (Compare with **consensus style, obliteration style,** and **submission style.**)

obliteration style A style of interaction for an intercultural couple in which both partners attempt to erase their individual cultures in dealing with cultural differences. (Compare with **compromise style, consensus style,** and **submission style.**)

consensus style A style of interaction for an intercultural couple in which partners deal with cross-cultural differences by negotiating their relationship. (Compare with **compromise style, obliteration style,** and **submission style.**)

roles of same-sex friendships and cross-sex friendships and the relative importance of friendships.

Same-sex friendship relationships may have different roles for gay and straight males in the United States. Typically, U.S. males are socialized toward less self-expression and emotional intimacy. Most heterosexual men turn to women for emotional support; often, a wife or female romantic partner, rather than a same-sex friend, is the major source of emotional support.

This was not always the case in the United States, and it is not the case today in many countries, where male friendship often closely parallels romantic love. In India, for example, "men are as free as women to form intimate friendships with revelations of deep feelings, failures, and worries and to show their affection physically by holding hands" (Gareis, 1995, p. 36). Same-sex friendships and romantic relationships both may involve expectations of undying loyalty, deep devotion, and intense emotional gratification (Hammond & Jablow, 1987). This seems to be true as well for gay men, who tend to seek emotional support from same-sex friendships (Sherrod & Nardi, 1988). However this differentiation doesn't seem to hold for straight women and lesbians, who more often seek intimacy through same-sex friendships. That is, they seek intimate friendships with women more than with men.

The role of sexuality also may be different in heterosexual relationships than in gay and lesbian relationships. In heterosexual relationships, friendship and sexual involvement sometimes seem mutually exclusive. As the character Harry said to Sally in the film *When Harry Met Sally*, "Men can never be friends with women. The sex thing always gets in the way." Cross-sex friendships always seem ambiguous because of the "sex thing."

This ambiguity does not seem to hold in gay and lesbian relationships. Friendships can start with sexual attraction and involvement but endure after sexual involvement is terminated. There is frequently a clear distinction between "lover" and "friend" for both gays and lesbians similar to the "incest taboo" among a family of friends (Nardi, 1992, p. 114). Close friendships may play a more important role for gays than for straights. Gays and lesbians often suffer discrimination and hostility from the straight world (Nakayama, 1998), and they often have strained relationships with their families. For these reasons, the social support from friends in the gay community can play a crucial role. Sometimes friends act as family, as one young man explains,

> *"Friends become part of my extended family. A lot of us are estranged from our families because we're gay and our parents don't understand or don't want to understand. That's a separation there. I can't talk to them about my relationships. I don't go to them; I've finally learned my lesson: family is out. Now I've got a close circle of good friends that I can sit and talk to about anything. I learned to do without the family." (quoted in Nardi, 1992, p. 110)*

Many of the issues in heterosexual romantic relationships apply to gay/lesbian couples as well. However, some relational issues, especially those pertaining to permanence and relational dissolution, are unique to gay partners.

I had a friend who was lesbian and with whom I used to work at a car dealership. In class, we talked about the theory that we are attracted by dissimilarities, but only after we interact with the dissimilar person. I can relate to this theory. When I first met Yvette, I was nervous and wasn't sure whether I wanted to become friends with her. Before I even met her, I made fun of her behind her back, along with my other co-workers. It was only after I got to know her that I realized a person's sexuality is insignificant in developing a relationship. I was threatened by what I didn't understand or know.

After I got to know Yvette, I came to appreciate our differences. She has become a real friend and confidante. I found her sexuality to be not only interesting but refreshingly different. I met her girlfriend and went out to dinner with them. Because I have allowed myself to let down my barriers with her, it has become easier to let down my barriers with other people whose culture is different from mine. However, sometimes I still make the mistake of patronizing on the basis of dissimilarities without fully getting to know the person. This is something I have a feeling we all need to work on!
—Shannon

In the United States, there is little legal recognition of permanent gay and lesbian relationships. At the time of this writing, only six states offer spousal rights to same-sex couples—Vermont, Connecticut, California, New Hampshire, New Jersey, and Oregon. Only Massachusetts issues marriage licenses to same-sex couples. Hawai'i, Maine, Washington, and the District of Columbia offer some spousal rights to same-sex couples. Most U.S. states prohibit same-sex marriage (see page 412). In fact, many states have passed laws stating that only marriages between a man and a woman will be recognized (Neil, 2005). The federal government also has passed the Defense of Marriage Act, which allows states to not recognize same-sex marriages registered in other states. These political and legal actions have implications for the development and maintenance, as well as the termination, of gay and lesbian relationships in the United States.

Some countries, however, formally recognize same-sex relationships and thereby create different social conditions for gay and lesbian relationships (Fish, 2005). Same-sex relationships, like heterosexual relationships, are profoundly influenced by the cultural contexts in which they occur. For example, Vietnam does not stipulate that marriage must be between members of the opposite sex ("Mariage Vietnamien Lesbien," 1998), and King Sihanouk has supported gay marriages in Thailand ("Cambodian King Backs Gay Marriage," 2004). In the Netherlands, Belgium, Spain, South Africa, Canada, and Norway, gay and lesbian couples are allowed to marry with all the same legal rights and responsibilities as heterosexual spouses (Knox, 2005). In many European countries (and also Australia and New Zealand), gay relationships are recognized as legal "partnerships"; in some of these countries (e.g., Denmark, Finland, Iceland, Norway, and Sweden), same-sex couples are provided rights similar to

STATEWIDE MARRIAGE PROHIBITIONS

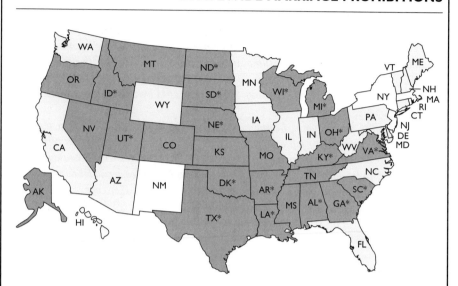

Statewide prohibitions against marriage for same-sex couples are in place in most states—either in the form of statutory law or amendment to the state's constitution. States that explicitly bar same-sex couples from marriage are as follows.

 States with constitutional amendments restricting marriage to one man and one woman. (26 states)

Alabama (2006), Alaska (1998), Arkansas (2004), Colorado, Georgia (2004), Kansas (2005), Idaho (2006), Kentucky (2004), Louisiana (2004), Michigan (2004), Mississippi(2004), Missouri (2004), Montana (2004), Nebraska (2000), Nevada (2002), North Dakota (2004), Ohio (2004), Oklahoma (2004), Oregon (2004), South Carolina (2006), South Dakota (2006), Tennessee (2006), Texas (2005), Utah (2004), Virginia (2006) and Wisconsin (2006).

 States with law restricting marriage to one man and one woman. (19 states)
In addition to those listed above, Arizona, California, Connecticut, Delaware, Florida, Hawaii, Illinois, Indiana, Iowa, Maine, Maryland, Minnesota, New Hampshire, North Carolina, Pennsylvania, Vermont, Washington, West Virginia and Wyoming.

Broader Consequences: *States where the law or amendment has language that does, or may, affect other legal relationships, such as civil unions or domestic partnerships. (17 states): *Alabama, Arkansas, Georgia, Kentucky, Idaho, Louisiana, Michigan, Nebraska, North Dakota, Ohio, Oklahoma, South Carolina, South Dakota, Texas, Utah, Virginia and Wisconsin.*

Pending Legislation: As of this writing, hostile amendments are being considered by legislators in 9 states: Alaska, Delaware, Illinois, Minnesota, New Jersey, North Carolina, Oklahoma, Washington and West Virginia. Keep track of all state legislative action on the HRC website.

those enjoyed by married couples. In other countries (Czech Republic, France, Germany, Luxembourg, Norway, Sweden, and Switzerland) the rights of these partnerships pertaining to health and medical benefits and financial rights (such as tax status and inheritance) are more restricted (ABC Newsonline, 1999; Cole, 2001; Fish, 2005; see also http://www.ilga-europe.org/europe/issues/marriage_and_partnership). However, in many places in the world, the social contexts are much more problematic for gay partners in permanent relationships.

Regardless of one's position on the desirability of gay and lesbian marriage, it is important to understand the implications for same-sex relationships, which include issues of dissolution. The dissolution of heterosexual relationships often is delayed because of family and societal pressures, religious beliefs, child custody battles, and so on. However, some gay relationships probably terminate much earlier because they are not subject to these pressures. This also may mean that even though they are shorter lived, gay and lesbian relationships are happier and more mutually productive (Bell & Weinberg, 1978).

Critical Approach: Contextual Influences

It is important to consider intercultural relationships in the contexts in which they emerge—whether the contexts are supportive or whether they discourage intercultural relationships. Let's examine several of these contextual influences: family and neighborhood, educational and religious institutions, and historical and political contexts.

Family and Neighborhood Contexts   According to Dodd and Baldwin (2002), the first place we learn about communication adaptability and receptivity—how to respond to those who are different and how to respond to new situations—is in the family. Did your family encourage you to seek out intercultural relationships? Did your parents have a culturally diverse set of friends? And some types of relationships are more accepted that others. For example, parents may encourage children to develop friendships across religious, racial, and class lines but discourage romantic relationships with members of these same groups. Parents often play an important role in who their children date—particularly for daughters. In a recent study, it was found that women were much more likely than men to mention pressure from family members as a reason that interethnic dating would be difficult. As one Latina said,

> It would be hard . . . because my parents wouldn't agree with it and neither would my Hispanic friends. They've all told me not to mix blood. Stay with your own. (Clark-Ibanez & Felmlee, 2004, p. 300)

Even more important than what parents say is what they do. In this same study, it was the diversity of parents' friendship network, not the parents' attitudes, that determined the likelihood of the child's dating interethnically. Those whose parents had diverse friends were more likely to date interethnically than those whose parents had less diverse friends.

There are many Internet resources for those seeking international marriages. Think about the power relationships created in these marriages. Is this how you would want to meet your husband or wife? How would this work differently for same-sex relationships?

Mail-Order Relationships

Type	Nationality Specified	Web Site	Gender	Race	Power
International Female	Filipino	http://www.theatavist.com/	This site focuses on relationship building between Western men and Filipina women. There are discussion forums and links to international dating services.	From the site: "I have met so many men with an obsession for Filipina women that I have wondered exactly what it is men seem to find so alluring. Is there some single definitive quality that we can reach consensus on?"	Privileges white Western men who get to choose from a large number of Filipina women.
International Female	Russian and Ukrainian	http://www.anastasia-international.com/newest.html	The sexuality of the women is a primary focus of the photos.	The race of the women is not "featured." In fact, most of the women appear to accentuate their American characteristics.	"Romance tours" are a feature of this site. In these tours, men travel to the Ukraine where women compete for their affection.
International Male	Diverse with an emphasis on the Ukraine	http://www.alovinghusband.com/index.php?page=index	The occupations of the men are featured along with their interests.	Not a focus of the site. However, the language issue seems to be a major one as translation is always available for site users.	There is a lack of information on the potential dynamics of the relationships.

The diversity of one's neighborhood also has a great influence on whether one forms intercultural friendships. Here, the proximity principle comes into play. That is, we are more likely to be attracted to and form relationships with those we see often. How diverse was your childhood neighborhood?

Religious and Educational Contexts   Institutions like schools and churches/synagogues can play a huge part in promoting or discouraging intercultural friendships. It was not that long ago that some colleges banned interracial dating, and an often quoted statistic is that the most segregated hour of the week is Sunday morning—when Christians are in church. At the same time, religious institutions can provide much-needed support. One interracial couple found support by participating in a series of workshops for interracial families sponsored by their church:

> *I think that being in this community helps us a lot . . . being in interracial family*
> *workshops, those kind of things; . . . it's an injection for us and that we value. And*
> *being able to expose ourselves to different types of interracial families. . . .*
> *I feel very interested and involved and somewhat knowledgeable and interested*
> *in the various adoption controversies that are going on and noticing again in this*
> *community the various levels of interracial activity. (Rosenblatt, Karis, & Powell,*
> *1995, p. 271)*

From very recent research, it appears that *integrated* religious institutions and educational institutions provide the best opportunities for intercultural friendships and the best environment to improve attitudes about interracial marriage (Johnson & Jacobson, 2005). For example, a study of six California State University campuses found that the students on these campuses interacted equally, in interracial and intraracial encounters (Cowan, 2005). These campuses are very diverse; no one ethnic or racial group is a majority. On the other hand, neighborhoods and work contexts do not seem to provide opportunities for the *type* of contact (intimate, friendly, equal status interaction) that clearly facilitates intercultural friendships (Johnson & Jacobson, 2005). Having ethnically varied friends has more of an influence on the propensity to engage in an interethnic romance than does being in a diverse social environment in general. "The role of friends is particularly important, perhaps because an individual is most likely to be introduced to a partner by a common friend, and because social approval from one's friends is a potent predictor of relationship stability" (Clark-Ibanez & Felmlee, 2004, p. 301).

Historical and Political Contexts   As noted in Chapter 4, history is an important context for understanding intercultural interactions and relationships. Many U.S. men in military service during various wars have returned to the United States with wives whom they met and married while stationed abroad. And many of the servicemen who experienced such intercultural relationships argued successfully against miscegenation laws, or laws that prohibited interracial marriages.

My aunt is full-blooded Mexican and her husband is full-blooded middle-Eastern. They have been married for about twelve years, and have three beautiful children. Despite many cultural differences, their relationship keeps going strong.

One such difference is the language barrier. She only spoke Spanish, while he spoke Arabic and English. At the beginning of their relationship a friend translated for them in order to understand each other. A year later they got married and my aunt had to learn English to communicate with him and his family, while also trying to learn Arabic. Another difference was their religion. She is Catholic and he is Christian. Together, they have to cope with each other and educate their children. They have learned from each others' culture and are trying to take a little bit of both and combine it for their kids.

—Amilia

An example of the role that history and politics can play in intercultural communication can be seen in the experiences of William Kelly (2006), a communication scholar who lived in Japan for many years. He recounts his experiences when he first went to Japan to teach English 25 years ago. There were few U.S. Americans in Japan, and they were treated with great deference. In retrospect, he realizes that he was quite arrogant in his view of the Japanese:

> *I expected Japanese to assimilate to my culture. I also felt superior to them. Due to their culture, I believed that Japanese would never reach the goals of individual freedom, rational thought in daily life and speaking English like a U.S. American. Therefore they would always remain aspiring U.S. Americans, not capable of achieving equality. (p. 15)*

His relationship with the Japanese can best be understood in the context of the history of U.S.-Japanese relations. As we learned in Chapter 1, Asians in the United States were treated very badly in the late 18th and early 19th centuries. (Remember the Oriental Exclusion Act of 1882 as well as the Johnson-Read Act of 1924, which severely restricted Japanese immigration to the United States.) Then came World War II and the internment of Japanese Americans, followed by the U.S. occupation of Japan. As a result, in the 1960s, 1970s, and 1980s, although the Japanese deferred to U.S. economic and political superiority, there was restrained resentment, and sometimes outright racism, toward U.S. Americans living in Japan. For example, in the 1980s, U.S. Americans in Japan could not enter certain establishments, obtain loans, or have the same jobs as Japanese. This example reveals the importance of the material and the symbolic realm in understanding culture. Kelly explains,

> *It was the material conditions of white U.S. power and privilege that led me to assume a stance of superiority in relation to the Japanese people I encountered. The communication grooves that I unthinkingly entered when I began living in Japan were the outcome of a colonial relationship between the United States and Japan.*

(p. 15) Japanese racial discrimination against whites has often been a defensive measure to keep members of a powerful nation within well-defined spheres. The goal has been to maintain a private area of Japanese people where the overbearing Western presence was absent and where Japanese could be "themselves."
(pp. 16–17)

Over the years, Kelly developed a different way of relating to Japanese. This came about primarily as a result of his encounters with U.S. Americans in Japan who were truly respectful of the Japanese. They learned Japanese, had many Japanese friends, and tried to adapt to the Japanese way of life—thereby achieving a more equal power balance. Eventually, he says, he was able to reach a level of understanding that accepted both similarities and differences between Japan and the United States. Kelly points out that his efforts to communicate with Japanese people in a truly respectful manner were assisted by the diminishing of the unequal power relations between the United States and Japan:

By the 1990s, there were many Japanese who had experienced the West that were no longer so positive about Westerners, and especially Americans. They expected white people to learn the Japanese language and communicate in a more Japanese way. . . . Many Japanese had gone overseas to work or study and there was less of an inferiority complex among Japanese towards white Americans. European Americans had been very gradually losing their place of privilege. (p. 18)

All this points to the effect of power on hierarchical relations of communication. Although power does not determine communication patterns in any simple causal sense, it does have an impact on the direction communication takes within intercultural relations. Although U.S.-Japanese communication is still affected in numerous ways by the legacy of the U.S. occupation of Japan, increased economic power has given the Japanese people a new sense of pride.

There are other examples of how colonial histories framed relationships. The British, for example, constructed myriad intercultural relationships, recognized or not, within the lands they colonized. Writer Anton Gill (1995), in his book *Ruling Passions*, discusses various ways in which the colonialists tried to engage in or to avoid intercultural relations, as well as the legacy of interracial children left in their wake. He was concerned with British social policies in the colonies, particularly as they related to offspring, who were often unwanted and abandoned.

The dialectical tension rests, on the one hand, in the social, political, and economic contexts that make some kinds of intercultural relationships possible and, on the other hand, in the desires and motives of the partners involved. There are no easy explanations for whom we meet, when we meet them, and under what conditions we might have a relationship. Different cultural groups have different demographics, histories, and social concerns. Scholar Harry Kitano and his colleagues (1984) discuss some of these issues for Asian Americans. Scholars Robert Anderson and Rogelis Saenz (1994) apply the demographics of Mexican American communities to argue for the importance of larger structural factors—such as proximity—in understanding interracial marriage.

INTERNET RESOURCES

www.lovingday.org/
This Web site is dedicated to the legal histories of interracial relationships. There is an interactive map of the United States that gives a visual feel for interracial legislation. The site contains stories of interracial couples and their trials and triumphs. Most importantly, the site works to promote June 12 as "Loving Day" in commemoration of the 1967 decision in *Loving* v. *Virginia* that formally legalized interracial marriage.

www.npr.org/templates/story/story.php?storyId=10184979
This is an NPR podcast about negotiating intercultural relationships. The experts provide practical advice with an academic foundation for couples dealing with the tribulations of intercultural issues. The podcast is part of a series of NPR productions revolving around culture.

www.theatavist.com/
This is not a "resource" in the traditional sense. This Web site is designed for Western men who want to be in relationships and/or marry women from the Philippines. Services like this are not uncommon. This Web site is included not as a resource for a paper, but as a typical example of some of the ways intercultural relationships are approached in the West.

www.interfaithfamily.com/ix.php?tid=IF.RL.IR
This is a Web resource designed for Jewish families seeking help negotiating intercultural and interfaith relationships. The inclusion of faith makes this an intercultural topic with added complications. Please note that the articles are written with the idea that the readers are Jewish.

www.youtube.com/watch?v=6Z87iSjZeJ8
This is the first of a series of videos on YouTube where African American women comment on interracial friendships/relationships. The panel format in this series produces interesting results. In addition, the commentary from other YouTube users is always a source of interest and/or frustration.

SUMMARY

- Through relationships, we acquire specific and general knowledge, break stereotypes, and acquire new skills.
- Special challenges of intercultural relationships include coping with differences, tending to stereotype, dealing with anxiety, and having to explain ourselves to others.
- There are six dialectics of intercultural relationships: personal-contextual, differences-similarities, cultural-individual, privilege-disadvantage, static-dynamic, and history/past–present/future.

- There are three communication approaches to understanding intercultural relationships: social science, interpretive, and critical.
- The social science approach emphasizes the individual role in relationships and identifies various cross-cultural differences in notions of friendship and how relationships are developed and maintained.
- The interpretive perspective provides in-depth descriptions of various types of intercultural relationships.
- Intercultural relationships often include competence, similarity, involvement, and turning points.
- Online relationships are both similar to and different from RL (real-life) relationships. Language and communication-style differences can be exacerbated in online communication.
- Relationships at work are characterized by hierarchy and sometimes varying attitudes toward power.
- In gay and lesbian relationships, friendship and sexual involvement are not mutually exclusive.
- Intercultural dating and marriage are increasingly common; however, interracial relationships are still often disapproved of by families and by society.
- Intercultural marriages face challenges of family and societal disapproval and issues of child rearing.
- The critical perspective emphasizes the role of institutions, politics, and history in intercultural relationships.
- Family, schools, and religious institutions can either hinder or discourage intercultural relationships.

DISCUSSION QUESTIONS

1. What are some of the benefits of intercultural relationships?
2. What factors contribute to our forming relationships with some people and not with others?
3. How is the development of intercultural relationships different from that of intracultural relationships?
4. What challenges do intercultural couples face when they decide to make their relationships permanent?
5. What are the advantages of taking a dialectical perspective on intercultural relationships?

Go to the self-quizzes on the Online Learning Center at www.mhhe.com/
martinnakayama5 to further test your knowledge.

1. *Intercultural Relationships.* List all of your friends to whom you feel close. Identify any friends on the list who are from other cultures. Answer the following questions, and discuss your answers with other class members.

   a. Do people generally have more friends from their own culture or from other cultures? Why?

   b. In what ways are intercultural friendships different from or similar to friendships with people from the same culture?

   c. What are some reasons people might have for not forming intercultural friendships?

2. *Friendship Dialectics.* Choose one friend who is different from you. Describe a situation or situations in which you experienced the dialectics discussed in this chapter. (*Hint:* Think of the ways in which the two of you are both similar and different—age, gender, background, interests, personality, and so on. Think of the ways your relationship has both changed and stayed the same—attitudes, experiences, interests, and so on.)

cognitive consistency (390)	intercultural relationships (382)	romantic relationships (397)
compromise style (409)	intimacy (395)	self-disclosure (399)
consensus style (409)	line of sight (401)	similarity principle (390)
guanxi (393)	obliteration style (409)	submission style (409)
	relational learning (383)	

 The Online Learning Center at www.mhhe.com/martinnakayama5 features flashcards and crossword puzzles based on these terms and concepts.

REFERENCES

ABC News Online. (1999, October 14). France grants equal legal rights to gay couples. Australian Broadcasting Corporation.

Allen, B. J. (2000). Sapphire and Sappho: Allies in authenticity. In A. Gonzalez, M. Houston, & V. Chen (Eds.), *Our voices: Essays in culture, ethnicity and communication* (3rd ed., pp. 179–183). Los Angeles: Roxbury.

Anderson, R. N., & Saenz, R. (1994). Structural determinants of Mexican American intermarriage, 1975–1980. *Social Science Quarterly, 75*(2), 414–430.

Barnlund, D. S. (1989). *Communication styles of Japanese and Americans: Images and reality.* Belmont, CA: Wadsworth.

Baxter, L. A. (1993). The social side of personal relationships: A dialectical perspective. In S. Duck (Ed.), *Social context and relationships* (pp. 139–165). Newbury Park, CA: Sage.

Baxter, L. A., & Montgomery, B. (1996). *Relating: Dialogues and dialectics.* New York: Guilford Press.

Bell, A. P., & Weinberg, M. S. (1978). *Homosexualities: A study of diversity between men and women.* New York: Simon & Schuster.

Bell, S., & Coleman, S. (1999). The anthropology of

friendship: Enduring themes and future possibilities. In S. Bell & S. Coleman (Eds.), *The anthropology of friendship* (pp. 1–20). New York: Berg.

Butterfield, F. (1982). *Alive in the bitter sea.* Toronto: Bantam Books.

Cambodian king backs gay marriage. (2004, February 20). BBC News. Accessed at http://news.bbc.co.uk/2/hi/asia-pacific/3505915.stm

Carrier, J. G. (1999). People who can be friends: Selves and social relationships. In S. Bell & S. Coleman (Eds.), *The anthropology of friendship* (pp. 21–28). New York: Berg.

Carter, D. M. (2004). Living in virtual communities: Making friends online. *Journal of Urban Technology, 11,* 109–136.

Chen, L. (2002). Communication in intercultural relationships. In W. B. Gudykunst & B. Mody (Eds.), *Handbook of international and intercultural communication* (pp. 241–258). Thousand Oaks, CA: Sage.

Chen, T. C.-C., Drzewiecka, J. A., & Sias, P. M. (2001). Dialectical tensions in Taiwanese international student friendships. *Communication Quarterly, 49,* 57–66.

Chesebro, J. W. (Ed.). (1981). *Gayspeak: Gay male and lesbian communication.* New York: Pilgrim Press.

Chesebro, J. W. (1997). Ethical communication and sexual orientation. In J. M. Makau & R. C. Arnett (Eds.), *Communication ethics in an age of diversity* (pp. 126–154). Bloomington: University of Illinois Press.

Chozick, A. (2005, November 14). Beyond the numbers. *Wall Street Journal,* p. R4.

Clark-Ibanez, M. K., & Felmlee, D. (2004). Interethnic relationships: The role of social network diversity. *Journal of Marriage and Family, 66,* 229–245.

Cole, D. (2001, July 31). Germany opens door to gay marriage. *Agence Presse.* www.gfn.com/archives/story.phtml?sid=9975

Collier M. J. (1996). Communication competence problematics in ethnic friendships. *Communication Monographs, 63,* 314–346.

Cowan, G. (2005). Interracial interactions of racially diverse university campuses. The *Journal of Social Psychology, 14,* 49–63.

Desnos, M. (2008, May 2). La France rejette un marié gay. *Le Journal du dimanche au quotidien.* Retrieved May 2, 2008 from http://www.lejdd.fr/cmc/societe/200818/la-france-rejette-un-marie-gay_114517.html.

Dion, K. K., & Dion, K. L. (1991). Psychological individualism and romantic love. *Journal of Social Behavior and Personality, 6,* 17–33.

Dion, K. L., & Dion, K. K. (1988). Romantic love: Individual and cultural perspectives. In R. Sternberg & M. Barnes (Eds.), *The psychology of love* (pp. 264–289). New Haven, CT: Yale University Press.

Dodd, C. H., & Baldwin, J. R. (2002). The role of family and macrocultures in intercultural relationships. In J. N. Martin, T. K. Nakayama, & L. A. Flores (Eds.), *Readings in intercultural communication* (2nd ed., pp. 279–289). Boston: McGraw-Hill.

Eng, D. L. (2001). *Racial castration: Managing masculinity in Asian America.* Durham, NC: Duke University Press.

Fahrenthold, D. A. (2005, October 2). Connecticut's first same-sex unions proceed civilly. *The Washington Post,* A3.

Farrell, E. (2005, February 4). More students plan to work to help pay for college. *Chronicle of Higher Education,* pp. A1, A34.

Fiebert, M. S., Nugent, D., Hershberger, S. L., & Kasdan, M. (2004). Dating and commitment choices as a function of ethnicity among American college students in California. *Psychological Reports, 94,* 1293–1300.

Fish, E. (2005). The road to recognition: A global perspective on gay marriage. *Harvard International Review, 27,* 32–35.

«Frédéric Minvielle pourra redevenir Français en 2009», dit le Quai d'Orsay. (2008, May 2). *Têtu.* Retrieved, May 2, 2008 from http://www.tetu.com/rubrique/infos/infos_detail.php?id_news=12881

Frith, K., Shaw, P., & Cheng, H. (2005). The construction of beauty: A cross-cultural analysis of women's magazine advertising. *Journal of Communication, 55,* 56–70.

Gajjala, R. (2004). Negotiating cyberspace/negotiating RL. In A. Gonzalez, M. Houston, & V. Chen (Eds.), *Our voices: Essays in culture, ethnicity and communication* (4th ed., pp. 63–71). Los Angeles: Roxbury.

Gao, G. (1991). Stability of romantic relationships in China and the United States. In S. Ting-Toomey & F. Korzenny (Eds.), *Cross-cultural interpersonal communication* (pp. 99–115). Newbury Park, CA: Sage.

Gao, G. (2001). Intimacy, passion, and commitment in Chinese and U.S. American romantic relationships. *International Journal of Intercultural Relations, 25,* 329–342.

Gareis, E. (1995). *Intercultural friendship: A qualitative study.* Lanham, MD: University Press of America.

Gasner, A. (1999). Globalization: The changing face of the workforce. *Business Today, 36,* 43–44.

Gates, H. (1987). *Chinese working-class lives.* Ithaca, NY: Cornell University Press.

Gill, A. (1995). *Ruling passions: Sex, race and empire*. London: BBC Books.

Graham, J. A., & Cohen, R. (1997). Race and sex factors in children's sociometric ratings and friendship choices. *Social Development, 6*, 355–372.

Graham, M. A., Moeai, J., & Shizuru, L. S. (1985). Intercultural marriages: An intrareligious perspective. *International Journal of Intercultural Relations, 9*, 427–434.

Gudykunst, W. B., & Matsumoto, Y. (1996). Cross-cultural variability of communication in personal relationships. In W. B. Gudykunst, S. Ting-Toomey, & T. Nishida (Eds.), *Communication in personal relationships across cultures* (pp. 19–56). Thousand Oaks, CA: Sage.

Halualani, R. T. (1995). The intersecting hegemonic discourses of an Asian mail-order bride catalog: Pilipina "oriental butterfly" dolls for sale. *Women's Studies in Communication, 18*(1), 45–64.

Hammond, D., & Jablow, A. (1987). Gilgamesh and the Sundance Kid: The myth of male friendship. In H. Brod (Ed.), *The making of masculinities: The new men's studies* (pp. 241–258). Boston: Allen & Unwin.

Harris, T. M., & Kalbfleisch, P. J. (2000). Interracial dating: The implications of race for initiating a romantic relationship. *The Howard Journal of Communications, 11*, 49–64.

Henderson, S., & Gilding, M. (2004). I've never clicked this much with anyone in my life: Trust and hyperpersonal communication in online friendships. *New Media & Society, 6*, 487–506.

Herring, S. C. (2004). Slouching toward the ordinary: Current trends in computer mediated communication. *New Media & Society, 6*, 26–31.

Hymowitz, C. (2005, November 14). The new diversity. *Wall Street Journal*, pp. R1, R3.

Jacobson, C. K., & Johnson, B. R. (2006). Interracial friendship and African Americans' attitudes toward interracial marriage. *Journal of Black Studies, 36*, 570–584.

James, N. C. (2000). When Miss America was always white. In A. González, M. Houston, & V. Chen (Eds.), *Our voices: Essays in culture, ethnicity and communication* (3rd ed., pp. 42–46). Los Angeles: Roxbury.

Johnson, B. R., & Jacobson, C. K. (2005). Context in contact: An examination of social settings on Whites' attitudes toward interracial marriage, *Journal of Social Psychology, 68*, 387–399.

Kelly, W. E. (2006). Applying a critical metatheoretical approach to intercultural relations: The case of U.S.-Japanese communication. *China Media Research, 2*(4), 9–21.

Kitano, H. H. L., Yeung, W.-T., Chai, L., & Hatanaka, H. (1984). Asian-American interracial marriage. *Journal of Marriage and the Family, 56*, 179–190.

Knox, N. (2005, August 11). Religion takes a back seat in Western Europe, *USA Today*, p. 01A.

Lampe, P. (1982). Interethnic dating: Reasons for and against. *International Journal of Intercultural Relations, 6*, 115–126.

Lee, O. (2002). Cultural differences in E-mail use of virtual teams: A critical social theory perspective. *CyberPsychology & Behavior, 5*, 227–232.

Lee, P.-W. (2008). Stages and transitions of relational identity formation in intercultural friendship: Implications for Identity Management Theory. *Journal of International and Intercultural Communication, 1*, 51–69.

Lee, S. M., & Edmonston, B. (2005). New marriages, new families: U.S. racial and Hispanic intermarriage. *Population Bulletin, 60*(2), 3–36.

Lewin, K. (1948). Some social psychological differences between the United States and Germany. In G. Lewin (Ed.), *Resolving social conflicts*. New York: Harper.

Logan, J. R., Stults, B. J., & Farley, R. (2004). Segregation of minorities in the Metropolis. *Demography, 41* 1–22.

Luo, S., & Klohnen, E. C. (2005). Assortative mating and marital quality in newlyweds: A couple-centered approach. *Journal of Personality and Social Psychology, 88*, 301–326.

Mariage vietnamien lesbien. (1998, May). *Illico*, 32–33.

Martin, J. N., Bradford, L. J., Drzewiecka, J. A., & Chitgopekar, A. S. (2003). Intercultural dating patterns among young white U.S. Americans: Have they changed in the past 20 years? *Howard Journal of Communications, 14*, 53–73.

Martin, J. N., Nakayama, T. K., & Flores, L. A. (2002). A dialectical approach to intercultural communication. In J. N. Martin, T. K. Nakayama, & L. A. Flores (Eds.), *Readings in intercultural communication* (2nd ed., pp. 3–13). Boston: McGraw-Hill.

McCullough, M. W. (1998). *Black and White women as friends: Building cross-race friendships*. Cresskill, NJ: Hampton Press.

McKenna, K. Y. A., Green, A. S., & Gleason, M. E. J. (2002). Relationship formation on the Internet: What's the big attraction? *Journal of Social Issues, 58*, 9–31.

Mercer, K. (1994). *Welcome to the jungle*. New York: Routledge.

Moore, R. M. (2000). An exploratory study of interracial dating on a small college campus. *Sociological Viewpoints, 16*, 46–64.

Nakayama, T. K. (1998). Communication of hetero-sexism. In M. L. Hecht (Ed.), *Communication of prejudice* (pp. 112–121). Thousand Oaks, CA: Sage.

Nardi, P. M. (1992). That's what friends are for: Friends as family in the gay and lesbian community. In K. Plummer (Ed.), *Modern homosexualities: Fragments of lesbian and gay experience* (pp. 108–120). New York: Routledge.

Neil, M. (2005). Same-sex benefits bind. *ABA Journal, 91,* 22–24.

Nishida, T. (1996). Communication in personal relationships in Japan. In W. B. Gudykunst, S. Ting-Toomey, & T. Nishida (Eds.), *Communication in personal relationships across cultures* (pp. 102–121). Thousand Oaks, CA: Sage.

Olaniran, B. A. (2001). The effects of computer-mediated communication on transculturalism. In V. H. Milhouse, M. K. Asante, & P. O. Nwosu (Eds.), *Transcultural realities: Interdisciplinary perspectives on cross-cultural relations* (pp. 83–105). Thousand Oaks, CA: Sage.

Osbeck, L. M., & Moghaddam, F. M. (1997). Similarity and attraction among majority and minority groups in a multicultural context. *International Journal of Intercultural Relations, 21,* 113–123.

Pogrebin, L. C. (1987). *Among friends.* New York: McGraw-Hill.

Pogrebin, L. C. (1992). The same and different: Crossing boundaries of color, culture, sexual preference, disability, and age. In W. B. Gudykunst & Y. Y. Kim (Eds.), *Readings on communicating with strangers* (pp. 318–336). New York: McGraw-Hill.

Postmes, T., Spears, R., & Lea, M. (1998). Breaching or building the social boundaries? SIDE-effects of computer-mediated communication. *Communication Research, 25,* 689–715.

Romano, D. (1997). *Intercultural marriage: Promises and pitfalls* (2nd ed.). Yarmouth, ME: Intercultural Press.

Root, M. P. P. (2001). *Love's revolution: Interracial marriage.* Philadelphia: Temple University Press.

Rosenblatt, P. C., Karis, T. A., & Powell, R. D. (1995). *Multiracial couples: Black and white voices.* Thousand Oaks, CA: Sage.

Rotman, C. (2008, May 2). Privé de sa nationalité après un mariage gay. *Libération.* Retrieved May 2, 2008 from http://www.liberation.fr/actualite/societe/324214.FR.php

Russo, R. (2001, February 9). Intercultural relationships flourish despite differences. *The (Georgetown) Hoya.*

Sherrod, D., & Nardi, P. M. (1988). *The nature and function of friendship in the lives of gay men and lesbians.* Paper presented at the annual meeting of the American Sociological Association, Atlanta.

Shibazaki, K., & Brennan, K. (1998). When birds of a different feathers flock together: A preliminary comparison of intra-ethnic and inter-ethnic dating relationships. *Journal of Social & Personal Relationships, 15,* 248–256.

Smart, A. (1999). Expression of interest: Friendship and *quanxi* in Chinese societies. In S. Bell & S. Coleman (Eds.), *The anthropology of friendship* (pp. 119–136). New York: Berg.

Snyder, G. (2003, May). Teams that span time zones face new work rules. Stanford Business. Web site of Stanford Graduate School of Business. Accessed at http://www.gsb.stanford.edu/news/bmag/sbsm0305/feature_virtual_teams.shtml

Sprecher, S., Aron, A., Hatfield, E., Cortese, A., Potapova, E., & Levitskaya, A. (1994). Love: American style, Russian style, and Japanese style. *Personal Relationships, 1,* 349–369.

St. Amant, K. (2002). When cultures and computers collide: Rethinking computer-mediated communication according to international and intercultural communication expectations. *Journal of Business and Technical Communication, 16,* 196–214.

Stephan, W., & Stephan, C. (1992). Reducing intercultural anxiety through intercultural contact. *International Journal of Intercultural Relations, 16,* 89–106.

Sudweeks, S., Gudykunst, W. B., Ting-Toomey, S., & Nishida, T. (1990). Developmental themes in Japanese–North American relationships. *International Journal of Intercultural Relations, 14,* 207–233.

Sze, H. (1992, July 24). Racist love. *Asian Week,* pp. 10, 24.

Talking about race. (2000, July 16). *New York Times Magazine,* special issue (How Race Is Lived in America).

Tan, D., & Singh, R. (1995). Attitudes and attraction. *Personality and Social Psychology Bulletin, 21,* 975–986.

Taylor, P., Funk, C., & Craighill, P. (2006). Guess who's coming to dinner?: 22% of Americans have a relative in a mixed-race marriage. Pew research report. Retrieved December 12, 2008 from http://pewsocialtrends.org/assets/pdf/interracial.pdf

Tucker, M. B., & Mitchell-Kernan, C. (1995). Social structure and psychological correlates of interethnic dating. *Journal of Social and Personal Relationships, 12,* 341–361.

Un Français déchu de sa nationalité française après son mariage avec un Néerlandais. (2008, May 2). *Le Monde.* Retrieved May 2, 2008 from http://www.lemonde.fr/archives/article/2008/05/02/

un-francais-dechu-de-sa-nationalite-francaise-apres-son-mariage-avec-un-neerlandais_1040427_0.html

Walther, J. B. (1996). Computer-mediated communication: Impersonal, interpersonal, and hyperpersonal interaction. *Communication Research, 23*, 3–43.

Walther, J. B., & Parks, M. R. (2002). Cues filtered out, cues filtered in: Computer-mediated communication and relationships. In M. L. Knapp & J. A. Daly (Eds.), *Handbook of interpersonal communication* (pp. 529–563). Thousand Oaks, CA: Sage.

Wilson, S. B., McIntosh, W. D., & Insana, S. P., II. (2007). Dating across race: An examination of African American internet personal advertisements. *Journal of Black Studies, 37*, 964-982.

Yancy, G. (2002). Who interracially dates: An examination of the characteristics of those who have interracially dated. *Journal of Comparative Family Studies, 33*, 177–190.

CULTURE, COMMUNICATION, AND CONFLICT

CHAPTER OBJECTIVES

After reading this chapter, you should be able to:

1. Identify two orientations to conflict.

2. Understand a dialectical approach to these orientations.

3. Be able to discuss three approaches—social science, interpretive, and critical—to studying conflict.

4. Be able to identify five types of interpersonal conflict.

5. Explain the role of gender, ethnicity, values, and conflict styles in interpersonal conflict.

6. Be able to discuss some of the contexts that contribute to social conflict.

7. Explain some strategies for dealing with conflict.

8. Be able to distinguish productive from destructive conflict.

The need to understand intercultural conflict seems more important now than ever. One thing we can be sure of is that conflict is inevitable. Conflicts are happening all around the world, as they always have, and at many different levels: interpersonal, social, national, and international. For example, at the interpersonal level, friends or romantic partners may disagree about their relationship between themselves or with friends and family. At the social level, cultural differences of opinion regarding the importance of preserving the environment compared with the importance of developing industry may fuel conflict between environmentalists and business interests.

Intercultural conflict can also be generational. Recently, attempts to stop young people from loitering in public areas has generated some interesting strategies. In Britain, "they are using a device known as the 'Mosquito,' which emits an irritating, high-pitched sound that can only be picked up by children and people in their early 20s. Young people have complained that it hurts their ears" ("High-pitched sound used to deter teenagers," 2008). In contrast, a section of Sydney, Australia, has turned to playing Barry Manilow's early songs. A councilor noted: "His early songs, that certainly worked. Instead of getting 200 cars in a car park, we probably get about 100 now" (quoted in "High-pitched sound").

An extreme example of conflict on the international level can be seen in an ongoing struggle between Muslims and Christians in Nigeria. In February 2004, early in the morning, about 70 people were praying at the Church of Christ in the small town of Yelwa when they heard gunshots and a call from the loudspeakers of the mosque next door: "Allahu Akhbar, let us go for jihad." The worshippers went outside and saw men dressed in military fatigues who told them they were safe and then herded them back into the church. Then the men (who were not from the government) set the church on fire and killed everyone trying to escape. Two months later, Christian men and boys surrounded and attacked the town of Yelwa. According to Human Rights Watch, 660 Muslims were massacred over the course of the next two days, including the patients in a health clinic. Twelve mosques and 300 houses went up in flames. Young girls were marched to a nearby Christian town and forced to eat pork and drink alcohol. Many were raped, and 50 were killed (Griswold, 2008).

As you can see from this example, conflict is not simply a matter of disagreement. Conflict among cultural groups can escalate into enormous tragedies that reverberate across generations. What is the history of this conflict involving these religions? What role did other nations have in this conflict? What solutions are there to the tragedies that result from conflicts such as these? How do these people overcome conflict and put it behind them? There are no easy answers to these questions, but we must consider these questions, as a part of our understanding of intercultural conflict.

There are three significant approaches to understanding conflict. One is the social science approach, which focuses on how cultural differences cause conflict and influence the management of the conflict on the interpersonal level. The other two approaches—the interpretive and the critical—focus more on intergroup relationships and on cultural, historical, and structural elements as the primary sources of conflict. These three approaches emphasize different aspects of the individual-contextual dialectic.

Understanding intercultural conflict is especially important because of the relationship between culture and conflict. That is, cultural differences can cause conflict, and once conflict occurs, cultural backgrounds and experiences influence how individuals deal with it. Culture shapes what people consider valuable and worth fighting over; it influences official positions taken and interpretations of others' actions (Ross, 1993a). We should say up front that little is known about how to deal effectively with intercultural conflict. Most research to date in the United States applies almost exclusively to majority culture members. Our challenge is to review this body of research, take what can be applied in intercultural contexts, and perhaps suggest some new ways to think about conflict.

In this chapter, then, we identify characteristics of intercultural conflict, extending our dialectical perspective, and outline two broad orientations to conflict. We examine intercultural conflict in interpersonal contexts, incorporating more interpretive and critical theories into our understanding of conflict. We also examine how cultural background can influence conflict management. Finally, we discuss guidelines for viewing and engaging in conflict across cultural borders.

CHARACTERISTICS OF INTERCULTURAL CONFLICT

One way to think about **intercultural conflict** is from a dialectical perspective, applying many of the same dialectics discussed in Chapter 10. Let's see how this works in an actual dispute that arose in France. In late October and into November 2005, riots that began in a suburb of Paris—Clichy-sous-Bois—began to spread throughout the nation to over 300 cities, and, as seen around the world: "A blaze without precedent which stupefies the world, ruins the image of France abroad and becomes more and more dangerous for its inhabitants" (Mandonnet, Pelletier, Pontaut, & Rosso, 2005, p. 22 [*Un embrasement sans précédent, qui stupéfie le monde, ruine l'image de la France à l'étranger et devient de plus en plus dangereux pour ses habitants.*]). As images of cars burning were broadcast, commentators rushed to offer reasons for this social upheaval and social conflict. Many offered comparisons to their own societies. Yet the rioting in France by those marginalized in French society—primarily the children and grandchildren of North African immigrants—underscores the point that disputes are often more complicated than they first appear. We can invoke the various dialectics to illuminate the complexity of this conflict. For example, the dispute has been described as rooted in Islamic discontent with the West. The cover of *U.S. News and World Report's* November 21, 2005, issue asked, "Is it religion or culture?" *The Economist* also noted that "[m]uch of the world's attention over these two weeks has been the role played by Islam" ("France's Failure," p. 11). Yet *The Economist* goes on to suggest that "[a] much greater contributor than Islam to the malaise in the suburbs is the lack of jobs" (p. 11).

intercultural conflict
Conflict between two or more cultural groups.

Other commentators attempted to explain this upheaval in terms of their own national experiences. A writer for the *Washington Post* noted, "The deeper difference is that however ignored or mistreated America's black underclass may be, most Americans do think of its members as Americans. By contrast, I doubt whether most Frenchmen even contemplate the possibility that the African and Arab immigrants and their offspring who make up their underclass, and who are both perpetrators and victims of these riots, could ever be truly French, even if they hold French passports (and millions do)" (Applebaum, 2005, p. A31). The focus on identity and belonging is repeated in a Canadian writer's view of the French riots. In a Toronto newspaper, *The Globe and Mail,* Timothy B. Smith (2005) suggests that

> [t]he French believe that multiculturalism would only privilege individuals by association with their ethnic, religious or racial roots. There is no such concept as Algerian French. By contrast, one can be Chinese Canadian and still be considered a full citizen. Before immigrants to Canada become equal in the economic sense, their culture is already considered equal in the theoretical sense. The one helps lead to the other. Canada is no bed of roses for thousands of recent immigrants toiling at minimum-wage jobs, but history suggests that, in the long run, many of them will enter the lower middle class. And, as the French riots suggest, no jobs are worse than bad jobs. Multiculturalism embodies a message of hope and puts a high ideal in our sights. France tells newcomers that their past belongs in another country. Most Canadians see immigrants in a positive light—they add diversity to the cultural scene, they spice up our cuisine, they make important economic contributions, they will help pay for the boomers' pensions. In the context of chronic high unemployment, a large chunk of the French-born majority sees immigrants as threats to its share of a limited system of spoils.

In a sense, then, the economic contexts, the cultural identities and belongingness, and the political and religious contexts all work together to shape this conflict. Some people do not believe that riots and violence are an appropriate way to change the social problems in French society or any society. Others believe this kind of violence is one of the few ways that society can be provoked into interrogating social inequities and begin the long process of changing any society. As one writer noted, connecting the United States to France, "America's lesson for the French is that they have a long, hard road ahead" (Ignatius, 2005, p. A31).

This "long road" was revealed again when riots broke out once more in the northern Paris suburb of Villiers-le-Bel in November 2007. These riots spread to Toulouse in the south of France. In this round of riots, Reuters reported that "a library, several public buildings and dozens of cars were burned" (Balmforth, 2008). *The Economist* reported that "over two nights of violence, they torched scores of cars and rubbish bins, a police station, a nursery school, a library, shops, a car dealer and a McDonald's. Other *banlieues* [suburbs] north of Paris and in Toulouse saw car-burnings. Some 130 policemen were wounded, several seriously" ("Le Paris flambé," 2007).

The resurgence of rioting points to deep social and cultural conflict. "Local (mainly Socialist) mayors had been warning for a while that tension remained high in the country's banlieues, two years on" ("On the streets, again," 2007). There are no easy solutions to these conflicts, but France has been working hard to change the economic and cultural conditions that led to them. "There has been a heavy injection of public cash, primarily into the renovation of the housing estates that ring the big cities" and through French President Nicolas Sarkozy's inclusion of "other members of ethnic minorities, in his government, he also sent a message of inclusion to the heavily Muslim and ethnic population in the *banlieues*" ("On the streets, again," 2007). As long as these cultural groups remain marginalized, alienated, and largely unemployed in French society, these cultural conflicts are likely to continue.

The point here is that there is no reason to seek a single source for conflict. The riots in France, for example, probably have multiple causes, and, by taking a dialectical approach to thinking about these riots, you can see how these various forces—economic, social, political, religious—may all play different roles at different times. Yet when confronted with such conflicts, how should society respond? How should you respond?

Intercultural conflict may be characterized by ambiguity, which causes us to resort quickly to our default style—the style that we learned growing up—in handling it. If your preferred way of handling conflict is to deal with it immediately, and you are in a conflict situation with someone who prefers to avoid it, the conflict may become exacerbated as you both retreat to your preferred style. As the confronting person becomes increasingly confrontational, the avoider simply retreats further.

Issues surrounding language may be important to intercultural conflict. One student, Stephanie, described a situation that occurred when she was studying in Spain. She went to an indoor swimming pool with her host family sisters. Being from Arizona, she was unaccustomed to swimming in such cold water, so she went outside to sunbathe. Her "sisters" asked her why she didn't swim with them. Stephanie explains,

> *At that point I realized they thought I should really be with them. . . . I didn't know how to express myself well enough to explain to them. . . . I tried, but I don't think it worked very well. So I just apologized. . . . I did basically ignore the conflict. I would have dealt with it, but I felt I did not have the language skills to explain myself effectively, so I did not even try. . . . That is why I had such a problem, because I could not even express what I would have liked to.*

When individuals don't know the language well, it is very difficult to handle conflict effectively. At the same time, silence is not always a bad thing. Sometimes it provides a "cooling off" period, allowing things to settle down. Depending on the cultural context, silence can be very appropriate.

Intercultural conflict also may be characterized by a combination of orientations to conflict and conflict management styles. Communication scholar Sheryl Lindsley (1999) interviewed managers in *maquiladoras*—sorting or lthough forgiveness is often a key element in conflict resolution, it is not always easy to forgive. Sometimes those who are hurt in conflict still live with everyday pain from the conflict, and they do not always find it easy to forgive. In Northern Ireland, the British government is asking many people to forgive the IRA to help build peace there.

Thirty-three years after Sam Malcolmson was shot by an Irish Republican Army gunman, the wound in his side is still open and leaking fluid. He has to change the dressing constantly. He takes morphine four times a day for blinding pain caused by bullet shards lodged in his spine. . . .

"People tell me I should forgive and forget so we can all move on," said Malcolmson, who was a 22-year-old police recruit when the IRA ambushed him in 1972. "They are asking an awful lot."

The British government is asking for such forgiveness on the grounds that it will help seal the peace in Northern Ireland after more than three decades of sectarian violence. . . .

Prime Minister Tony Blair told Parliament that the bill was "a very difficult" but essential part of peacemaking. The measure would follow the IRA's announcement in July that it had laid down its weapons for good.

"I don't minimize the anger there will be in some quarters, or the anguish if you are the relative of a policeman in Northern Ireland who was killed," Blair told legislators. "But I also genuinely believe we need to get this out of the way and dealt with so we can get on with the really tough" task of rebuilding the province's government and institutions.

Northern Ireland Secretary Peter Hain, Blair's top official for the province, said in an interview that the fugitives bill was "painful but necessary to bring closure on the past."

"The history of conflict resolution and this world is that sometimes you have to do things you ideally wouldn't want to, to bring closure," Hain said. Asked what he would tell victims' families, he said he would say that he understands the "appalling horror" of their experience but that "at least you can have the comfort of knowing that there won't be more victims like you in the future."

The measure has met ferocious opposition from people who say Blair is asking too much in the name of peace.

Source: From K. Sullivan, "In Northern Ireland, Forgiveness Is a Bitter Pill," *Washington Post,* December 7, 2005, p. A19.

assembly plants along the Mexican-U.S. border—and found many examples of conflict. For example, Mexican managers thought that U.S. managers were often rude and impolite in their dealings with each other and the workers. The biggest difference between U.S. Americans and Mexicans was in the way that U.S. Americans expressed disagreement at management meetings. One Mexican manager explained,

> *When we are in a meeting together, the U.S. American will tell another manager, "I don't like what you did." . . . Mexicans interpret this as a personal insult. They have a difficult time understanding that U.S. Americans can insult each other in this way and then go off and play golf together. . . . Mexicans would be polite, perhaps tell the person in private, or make a suggestion, rather than confronting. (quoted in Lindsley, 1999, p. 158)*

As Lindsley points out, the conflict between the Mexican and U.S. American managers in their business meetings needs to be understood as a dialectical and "layered" process in which individual, dyadic, societal, and historical forces are recognized.

TWO ORIENTATIONS TO CONFLICT

Is conflict good or bad? Should conflict be welcomed because it provides opportunities to strengthen relationships? Or should it be avoided because it can only lead to problems for individuals and groups? What is the best way to handle conflict when it arises? Should people talk about it directly, deal with it indirectly, or avoid it?

It's not always easy to figure out the best way to deal with conflict. And what does culture have to do with it? To answer some of these questions, we first describe two very different ways of thinking about conflict. Then we outline some of the ways in which culture and conflict are related. (See Figure 11-1.) As you read about these two orientations, try to keep in mind the importance of thinking dialectically. Neither orientation is always the best approach, nor does any culture only utilize one approach to conflict.

Conflict as Opportunity

The "opportunity" orientation to conflict is the one most commonly represented in U.S. interpersonal communication texts. **Conflict** is usually defined as involving a perceived or real *incompatibility* of goals, values, expectations, processes, or outcomes between two or more *interdependent* individuals or groups (Cupach & Canary, 1997; Wilmot & Hocker, 2001). According to theologian and mediator David Augsburger (1992), this approach to conflict is based on four assumptions:

1. Conflict is a normal, useful process.
2. All issues are subject to change through negotiation.
3. Direct **confrontation** and conciliation are valued.

conflict The interference between two or more interdependent individuals or groups of people who perceive incompatible goals, values, or expectations in attaining those ends.

confrontation Direct resistance, often to the dominant forces.

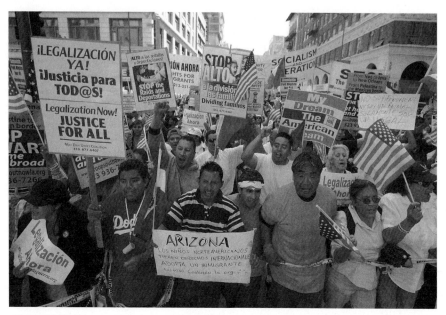

FIGURE 11-1   In Arizona and other border states tensions over immigration often spill into the streets. In this photo, pro-immigration marchers celebrate May Day 2007 with signs highlighting important immigrant contributions to America. These protesters were met by members of anti-illegal immigration groups like the Minutemen. How is conflict over illegal immigration different from other types of cultural conflicts? What groups do you believe are the most invested in immigration issues? (© *David McNew/Getty Images*)

4. Conflict is a necessary renegotiation of an implied contract—a redistribution of opportunity, release of tensions, and renewal of relationships.

Let's examine these assumptions more fully.

Conflict may be a difficult process, but it ultimately offers an opportunity for strengthening relationships. Although this orientation to conflict recognizes that many people don't enjoy conflict, it emphasizes the potentially positive aspects. The main idea is that working through conflict constructively results in stronger, healthier, and more satisfying relationships (Canary, Cupach, & Messman, 1995). From this perspective, there are additional benefits for groups working through conflict: They can gain new information about other people or groups, diffuse more serious conflict, and increase cohesiveness (Filley, 1975).

Consider the second and third assumptions. Individuals should be encouraged to think of creative, and even far-reaching, solutions to conflict. Furthermore, the most desirable response to conflict is to recognize it and work through it in an open, productive way. In fact, many people consider conflict-free relationships to be unhealthy. In relationships without conflict, they suggest, partners are ignoring issues that need to be dealt with (Canary, Cupach, & Messman,

1995). Finally, because conflict represents a renegotiation of a contract, it is worthy of celebration.

This Western-based approach to conflict suggests a neutral-to-positive orientation, but it is not shared by all cultural groups. Let's look at another orientation.

Conflict as Destructive

Many cultural groups view conflict as ultimately unproductive for relationships, a perspective that may be rooted in spiritual or cultural values. Although we must be cautious about generalizing, this viewpoint is generally shared by many Asian cultures (reflecting the influence of Confucianism and Taoism) and in the United States by some religious groups, such as Quakers and the Amish. According to Augsburger (1992), four assumptions underly this perspective:

1. Conflict is a destructive disturbance of the peace.
2. The social system should not be adjusted to meet the needs of members; rather, members should adapt to established values.
3. Confrontations are destructive and ineffective.
4. Disputants should be disciplined.

Again, let's examine these assumptions. Consider the first one: Most Amish, for example, think of conflict not as an opportunity to promote personal growth, but as almost certain to destroy the fabric of interpersonal and community harmony. When conflict does arise, the strong spiritual value of **pacifism** dictates a nonresistant response, such as avoidance or silence. Consider the second assumption, that members of society should adapt to existing values. Among the Amish, the nonresistant stance of *Gelassenheit*, or "yieldedness," forbids the use of force in human relations. Thus, the Amish avoid legal and personal confrontation whenever possible (Kraybill, 1989). This avoidance of conflict extends to a refusal to participate in military activities. For instance, during World War II, the federal government granted alternatives to military service for young Amish men. As a result, most Amish conscientious objectors received agricultural deferments, allowing them to work on their farms or on other agricultural projects. Amish children are instructed to turn the other cheek in any conflict situation, even if it means getting beaten up by the neighborhood bully. This emphasis extends to personal and business relationships; that is, the Amish would prefer to lose face or money than to escalate conflict. Similarly, cultural groups influenced by Buddhist, Taoist, Confucian, and Shinto traditions share a common tendency toward avoidance of confrontation and verbal aggression and absence of direct expression of feelings (Toupin, 1980).

Cultural groups that see conflict as destructive often avoid low-level conflict. However, another appropriate response is to seek intervention from a third party, or **intermediary.** On an informal level, a friend or colleague may be asked to intervene. For example, a Taiwanese student at a U.S. university was offended by the People's Republic of China flag that her U.S. American

pacifism Opposition to the use of force under any circumstances.

intermediary In a formal setting, a professional third party, such as a lawyer, real estate agent, or counselor, who intervenes when two parties are in conflict. Informal intermediaries may be friends or colleagues who intervene.

roommate unwittingly displayed in their dorm room. The Taiwanese student went to the international student adviser and asked him to talk to her roommate about the flag. Intermediaries are also used by those who think that interpersonal conflict provides opportunities, mainly in formal settings. For example, people hire lawyers to mediate disputes or negotiate commercial transactions, or they engage counselors or therapists to resolve or manage relational conflicts. Whereas confronting conflict is ultimately desirable, intervention is a less desirable option.

Finally, consider the fourth assumption, that disputants should be disciplined. Discipline is a means of censuring conflict. After all, communities celebrate their success in regaining harmony; they do not celebrate members' contribution to community change and growth through conflict. An example of how a community censures rather than facilitates conflict involves a Maori who was addressing other Maori from New Zealand. His speech turned nasty; he was using swear words and making scathing comments:

> *A woman went up to him, laying her hand on his arm and speaking softly. He shook her off and continued. The crowd now moved back from him as far as possible, and as if by general agreement, the listeners dropped their gaze to their toes until all he could see was the tops of their heads. The speaker slowed, faltered, was reduced to silence, and then sat down. (Augsburger, 1992, p. 80)*

This emphasis on nonviolence and pacifism may contrast with mainstream U.S. values, but as noted previously, many cultural groups practice a nonviolent approach to human and group relations. What are the basic principles of nonviolence applied to interpersonal relations? As Hocker and Wilmot (1991) point out, our language makes it difficult even to talk about this approach. Words and phrases like *passive resistance* and *pacifism* sound lofty and self-righteous. Actually, nonviolence is not the absence of conflict, and it is not a simple refusal to fight. Rather, it is a difficult (and sometimes risky) orientation to interpersonal relationships. The "peacemaking" approach (1) strongly values other people and encourages their growth, (2) attempts to deescalate conflicts or keep them from escalating once they start, and (3) favors creative negotiations to resolve conflicts when they arise. We'll discuss this approach in detail later.

Researcher Stella Ting-Toomey (1997) describes how these two orientations—conflict as opportunity and conflict as destructive—are based on different underlying cultural values involving identity and face-saving. In the more individualistic approach, espoused by most interpersonal communication textbooks, the concern is how individuals can save their own dignity. The more communal approach espoused by both Amish and Japanese cultures and by other collectivistic groups is more concerned with maintaining interpersonal harmony and saving the dignity of others. For example, in classic Chinese thought, social harmony is the goal of human society—in personal virtue, marriage, family, village, and nation. Writer John C. Wu (1967) explains,

> *If one is entangled in conflict, the only salvation lies in being so clear-headed and inwardly strong that he is always ready to come to terms by meeting the opponent*

halfway. To carry the conflict to the bitter end has evil effects even when one is in the right, because the enmity is then perpetuated. (p. 227)

Cultural Differences in Conflict Views: A Dialectical Perspective

Anthropologists have long been interested in how various cultures differ in the amount of conflict tolerated and the strategies for dealing with conflict. By taking a dialectical perspective, we can see no one approach to conflict is appropriate in all situations. It is important to recognize that these approaches are in dialectical tension with each other, and the best solution is not always one or the other but may lie somewhere in between. So although cultures may be predisposed to one orientation or another to conflict, this does not mean any culture only uses one approach.

Why are some cultures more prone to conflicts, whereas others have a low incidence of conflict? Anthropologist Marc Howard Ross (1993a, 1993b) spent many years investigating this question, studying views and norms regarding conflicts in small preindustrial cultures and in modern industrialized nations. According to Ross, in some cultures, conflict tends to be minimized and dealt with constructively; in other cultures, conflicts abound.

The reasons for this variation seem to lie in both structural and individual and interpersonal characteristics. Take two examples, Northern Ireland and Norway. Northern Ireland has been the scene of conflict for many years between two divided religious groups, Catholic and Protestant, with incompatible interests. These groups live in segregated communities, and members hold powerful stereotypes. In addition to a powerful class and socioeconomic hierarchy, there is a history of discrimination against Catholics in housing and jobs. Reasons for this conflict may also originate from a more personal level, such as male gender identity conflict, the absence of affection and warmth, a lack of social trust, and emotional distance between fathers and children—none of the predispositions useful in dealing with political differences in a democratic society.

In contrast, Norway traditionally has a low incidence of internal conflict, although Norwegians have fought with outsiders in the past. Certainly, social homogeneity is a structural plus (although there are some strong regional differences). There are also extensive "moralnets"—people who provide support to individuals in times of need, such as extended family, friends, and neighbors. Involvement in voluntary associations (characterized by attachments that are more instrumental than emotional) and overlapping social networks make it difficult for communities to divide into permanent factions. A strong collective sense of responsibility is expressed in a variety of ways, including an emphasis on equality and status leveling, attentiveness to community norms, and conformity and participation, with or without personal commitment.

On a more personal level, Norwegians are socialized to avoid conflict. There are high levels of maternal nurturance and supervision, as well as high levels of paternal involvement, and little is demanded of young children. Norwegians learn early in life that overt aggression or even indirect confrontation of others is unacceptable. Emotional self-control over negative feelings is important. And there are few aggressive models in the popular culture—newspapers do not sensationalize crime, television features little violence and no boxing, and films are controlled. For example, *E.T.* was considered too violent for children under age 12 (Ross, 1993b).

Low-conflict societies share several characteristics (Ross, 1993b). These include interpersonal practices that build security and trust; a strong linkage between individual and community interests, and high identification with the community so that individuals and groups in conflict trust that its interests are their own; a preference for joint problem solving, which leaves ultimate control over decisions in the hands of the disputants; available third parties, sometimes in the form of the entire community, to facilitate conflict management; an emphasis on the restoration of social harmony that is often at least as strong as the concern with the substantive issues in a dispute; the possibility of exit as a viable option; and strategies of conflict avoidance.

THE SOCIAL SCIENCE APPROACH TO CONFLICT

Perhaps if everyone agreed on the best way to view conflict, there would be less of it. But the reality is that different orientations to conflict may result in more conflict. In this section, which takes a social science approach, we identify five different types of conflict (see box) and some strategies for responding to conflict.

Strategies and Tactics for Dealing with Conflict

One theory, face negotiation, links cultural values to facework and conflict styles (Ting-Toomey, 2005). **Facework** refers to specific communication strategies we use to "save" our own or another person's face and is a universal concept; how we "do" facework varies from culture to culture and influences conflict styles.

facework Communication strategies used to "save" our own or someone else's "face," or public image.

The ways in which people respond to conflict may be influenced by their cultural backgrounds. Most people deal with conflict the way they learned to while growing up and watching those around them deal with contentious situations. Conflict strategies usually reflect how people manage themselves in relational settings. For example, they may prefer to deal with conflicts directly.

Although individuals have a general predisposition to deal with conflict in particular ways, they may choose different tactics in different situations. People are not necessarily locked into a particular strategy. There are at least five specific styles of managing conflicts (Rahim, 1986; Rahim & Magner, 1995; Thomas & Kilmann, 1974):

- Dominating
- Integrating

Types of Conflict

There are many different types of conflict, and we may manage these types in different ways. Communication scholar Mark Cole (1996) conducted interviews with Japanese students about their views on conflict and found most of the same general categories as those identified in the United States. These categories include the following:

- *Affective conflict* occurs when individuals become aware that their feelings and emotions are incompatible. For example, suppose someone finds that his or her romantic love for a close friend is not reciprocated. The disagreement over their different levels of affection causes conflict.

- *A conflict of interest* describes a situation in which people have incompatible preferences for a course of action or plan to pursue. For example, one student described an ongoing conflict with an ex-girlfriend: "The conflicts always seem to be a jealousy issue or a controlling issue, where even though we are not going out anymore, both of us still try to control the other's life to some degree. You could probably see that this is a conflict of interest." Another example of a conflict of interest is when parents disagree on the appropriate curfew time for their children.

- *Value conflict*, a more serious type, occurs when people differ in ideologies on specific issues. For example, suppose Mario and Melinda have been dating for several months and are starting to argue frequently about their religious views, particularly as related to abortion. Melinda is pro-choice and has volunteered to do counseling in an abortion clinic. Mario, a devout Catholic, is opposed to abortion under any circumstances and is very unhappy about Melinda's volunteer work. This situation illustrates value conflict.

- *Cognitive conflict* describes a situation in which two or more people become aware that their thought processes or perceptions are incongruent. For example, suppose Marissa and Derek argue frequently about whether Marissa's friend Jamal is paying too much attention to her; Derek suspects that Jamal wants to have a sexual encounter with Marissa. Their different perceptions of the situation constitute cognitive conflict.

- *Goal conflict* occurs when people disagree about a preferred outcome or end state. For example, suppose Bob and Ray, who have been in a relationship for 10 years, have just bought a house. Bob wants to furnish the house slowly, making sure that money goes into the savings account for retirement, whereas Ray wants to furnish the house immediately, using money from their savings. Bob's and Ray's individual goals are in conflict with each other.

Conflicts arise for many reasons. Religion is a common cause of conflict in intercultural relationships. Note how this student dealt with religious differences in her marriage.

I just recently got married. I am Caucasian, and my husband is Hispanic. He comes from a large, traditional family. My family background does not include many specific traditions. His family is very religious, and I grew up virtually without religion. When I became pregnant, his family told me that the baby would be baptized Catholic and raised Catholic. They also told me that they did not view our marriage as being legitimate (because we were not "married in God's eyes," that is, the Catholic Church). This was hard for me to deal with at first. I felt that I was being pressured to become someone I wasn't. But I agreed to go to church and learn Catholicism.
—Stacy

- Compromising
- Obliging
- Avoiding

dominating style A conflict management strategy whereby an individual achieves his or her goal at the expense of others' needs.

The **dominating style** reflects high concern for the self and low concern for the other person. It has been identified with having a win-lose orientation and with forcing behavior to win one's position. The behaviors associated with this style include loud and forceful verbalization, which may be counterproductive to conflict resolution. However, this view may indicate a Eurocentric bias because members of some cultural groups (including African Americans) see these behaviors as appropriate in many contexts (Speicher, 1994).

integrating style A conflict management strategy characterized by the open and direct exchange of information in an attempt to reach a solution acceptable to both parties.

The **integrating style** reflects high concern for both the self and the other person and involves an open and direct exchange of information in an attempt to reach a solution acceptable to both parties. This style is seen as effective in most conflicts because it attempts to be fair and equitable. It assumes collaboration, empathy, objectivity, creativity, and recognition of feelings. However, it requires a lot of time and energy (Folger, Poole, & Stutman, 1993).

compromising style A conflict management strategy that involves sharing and exchanging information to the extent that both individuals give up something to find a mutually acceptable decision.

The **compromising style** reflects a moderate degree of concern for both the self and the other person. This style involves sharing and exchanging information in such a way that both individuals give up something to find a mutually acceptable solution. Sometimes this style is less effective than the integrating approach because people feel forced to give up something they value and so have less commitment to the solution.

obliging style A conflict management strategy characterized by playing down differences and incompatibilities while emphasizing commonalities.

The **obliging style** describes a situation in which one person in the conflict plays down the differences and incompatibilities and emphasizes commonalities that satisfy the concerns of the other person. Obliging may be most appropriate when one individual is more concerned with the relationship itself than with specific issues. This is often true of hierarchical relationships in which one person

When I was back home in Singapore, my parents never really taught me about how to deal with conflict. I was never encouraged to voice my opinions, and, I guess because I'm a girl, sometimes my opinions are not highly valued. I think society also taught me to maintain harmony and peace, and that meant avoiding conflict. I practiced silence and had to learn quietly to accept the way things are at school and especially at work.

When I first came to the United States, I tried to be more vocal and to say what was on my mind. But even then I would restrain myself to a point where I couldn't help it any longer, and then I would try to come across as tactfully as possible. I used to think about when I was back in Singapore, when I dealt with conflict in such a way: If I could not remove the situation, then I would remove myself from the situation. But now, after learning to be more independent, more vocal, and more sure of myself, I know that I can remain in the situation and perhaps try to resolve some if not all of it.

—Jacqueline

has more status or power than the other. However, a pattern of obliging can result in pseudosolutions, especially if one person or the other resents the constant accommodation, so the strategy can eventually backfire.

Finally, the **avoiding style** reflects, supposedly, a low concern for both the self and the other person. In the dominant U.S. cultural contexts, a person who uses this style is often viewed negatively, as attempting to withdraw, sidestep, deny, or bypass the conflict. However, in some cultural contexts, this is an appropriate strategy that, if used by both parties, may result in more harmonious relationships. For example, avoidance can allow individuals to think of some other response, especially if they have trouble "thinking on their feet." Avoidance may also be appropriate if the issue is trivial, if the relationship itself is unimportant to one person, or if others can better manage the conflict (Wilmot & Hocker, 2001).

avoiding style A conflict management strategy characterized in U.S. cultural contexts by a low concern for the self and others. In some other cultural contexts, however, this strategy may be seen as tactical in maintaining harmonious relationships.

There are many reasons why we tend to favor a particular conflict style in our interactions. A primary influence is family background; some families prefer a certain conflict style, and children come to accept this style as normal. For instance, the family may have settled conflict in a dominating way, with the person having the strongest argument (or muscle) getting his or her way.

Sometimes people try to reject the conflict styles they saw their parents using. Consider the following examples. One student, Bill, remembers hearing his parents argue long and loud, and his father often used a dominating style of conflict management. He vowed that he would never deal with conflict this way in his own family, and he has tried very hard to keep his vow. Another student, Stephanie, describes how she has changed her style of dealing with conflict as she has grown older:

I think as a child I was taught to ignore conflict and especially to not cause conflict. When I was growing up, I saw my mom act this way toward my father and probably learned that women were supposed to act this way toward men. As a teenager,

I figured out that this just wasn't how I wanted to be. Now I like conflict, not too much of it, but I definitely cannot ignore conflict. I have to deal with it or else I will worry about it. So I deal with it and get it over with.

It is important to recognize that people deal with conflict in a variety of ways, for a variety of reasons. A word of caution is in order about conflict management styles. Conflict specialists William Wilmot and Joyce Hocker (2001) warn that we should not think of preferred styles as static and set in stone. Rather, they suggest that purely individual styles really do not exist because we are each influenced by others in interaction. Therefore, our conflict management styles are not static across settings and relationships. For example, people may use dominating styles at work and avoid conflict at home, or they may use avoiding styles at work and compromise at home. And they may use different styles with different partners. For instance, with co-workers, individuals may tend to collaborate and work through conflict issues; with the boss, they may tend to employ more avoiding strategies. In addition, our styles often change over the course of a conflict and over the life span. For example, individuals who tend to avoid conflict may learn the benefits of engaging and working through conflicts.

Gender, Ethnicity, and Conflict

The relationship between gender and conflict management styles is not clear. Some studies show some gender differences, and others do not. For example, in some studies investigating gender differences among U.S. young people, women report that they are more collaborative in their styles than do men, who report themselves as being more competitive. However, in studies of older adults investigating conflict management styles in the workplace, these gender differences disappear (Wilmot & Hocker, 2001, p. 166).

The relationship among ethnicity, gender, and conflict management is even more complex. Do males and females of different ethnic backgrounds prefer different ways of dealing with conflict? Researcher Mary Jane Collier (1991) investigated this issue in a study in which she asked African American, white American, and Mexican American students to describe conflicts they had had with close friends and the ways they dealt with the conflicts. She also asked them what they should (and should not) have said and whether they thought that males and females handle conflict differently.

Collier found that male and female ethnic friends differed in their ideas about the best ways to deal with conflict. African American males and females offered generally similar descriptions of a problem-solving approach (integration style) as appropriate behavior in conflict management. (One friend said, "I told him to stay in school and that I would help him study." Another explained, "We decided together how to solve the problem" [p. 147].) The males tended to emphasize that appropriate arguments should be given, information should be offered, and opinions should be credible, whereas the females generally emphasized appropriate assertiveness without criticism. (One man complained, "She pushed her own way and opinion and totally disregarded mine" [p. 147].) Some

At my work, I have learned to be somewhat of a "chameleon" in adapting to different cultural styles of conflict. I supervise a number of workers, a mixture of collectivists and individualists—some from Mexico, Mexican Americans, and white U.S. Americans. I have learned to play to each person's cultural style, soften them up for my suggestions on how to solve the conflict. With the collectivists, people from Mexico, it takes a little time for them to open up to me. I have to build a relationship before they start to resolve the conflict. Since I've figured this out, they have been more cooperative with me in dealing with conflict issues. With the individualists, they come right out and tell me what's wrong, but I still play to their emotional style and make them feel comfortable, calm them down so that we can move on with the resolution process.

—Mike

of these findings seem to contradict earlier studies comparing African American and white communication styles. These contradictions might be related to differences among the groups studied (e.g., comparing working-class African Americans and middle-class whites). Furthermore, because these studies are based on very small samples, we should interpret their findings tentatively.

White males and females generally seemed to focus on the importance of accepting responsibility for their behavior. Males in particular mentioned the importance of being direct. (They used expressions like "getting things in the open" and "say right up front" [p. 145].) Females talked about the importance of concern for the other person and the relationship, and for situational flexibility. (One woman explained, "She showed respect for my position and I showed respect for hers" [p. 146].)

Mexican American males and females tended to differ in that males described the importance of talking to reach a mutual understanding. (One man wanted to "make a better effort to explain." Another said that he and his partner "stuck to the problem until we solved it together" [p. 147].) Females described several kinds of appropriate reinforcement of the relationship. In general, males and females in all groups described females as more compassionate and concerned with feelings, and males as more concerned with winning the conflict and being "right."

It is important to remember that, whereas ethnicity and gender may be related to ways of dealing with conflict, it is inappropriate (and inaccurate) to assume that any one person will behave in a particular way because of his or her ethnicity or gender.

Value Differences and Conflict Styles

Another way to understand cultural variations in intercultural conflict resolution is to look at how cultural values influence conflict management. Cultural values in individualistic societies differ from those in collectivistic societies. Individualistic societies place greater importance on the individual than on groups like the family or the work group. Individualism is often cited as the most important of European American values, as reflected in the autonomy and independence encouraged in children. For example, children in the United States are often encouraged to leave home after age 18, and older parents generally prefer to live on their own rather than with their children. In contrast, collectivistic societies often place greater importance on extended families and loyalty to groups.

Yoko, a Japanese student, recounted a conflict she had with a U.S. American student, Linda, with whom she was working on a class project. Linda seemed to take a very competitive, individualistic approach to the project, saying things like "I did this on the project" or referring to it as "my project." Yoko became increasingly irritated and less motivated to work on the project. She finally said to Linda, "Is this your project or our project?" Linda seemed surprised and didn't apologize; she only defended herself. The two women continued to work on the project but with a strained relationship.

Although these values have been related to national differences, they also may be true for other groups. For example, European Americans may value individualism more than do Latinos/as, and women may value collectivism more than do men.

These contrasting values may influence communication patterns. Communication scholar Ting-Toomey and her colleagues have conducted a number of studies showing that people from individualistic societies tend to be more concerned with saving their own face than another person's, and so they tend to use more controlling, confrontational, and solution-oriented conflict management styles (Ting-Toomey & Oetzel, 2002; Ting-Toomey, Yee-Jung, Shapiro, Garcia, Wright, & Oetzel, 2000).

In contrast, people from collectivistic societies tend to be more concerned with preserving group harmony and with saving the other person's face (and dignity) during conflict. They may use a less direct conversational style; protecting the other person's face and making him or her look good is considered a skillful facework style. These face concerns lead them to use more avoiding, obliging, and integrating conflict styles (Ting-Toomey & Oetzel, 2002). However, some evidence indicates that not all collectivistic societies prefer indirect ways of dealing with conflict. How someone chooses to deal with conflict in any situation depends on the type of conflict and the relationship she or he has with the other person (Cai & Fink, 2002; Ting-Toomey, 2005; Ting-Toomey & Oetzel, 2002).

One study found that Japanese college students tended to use the avoiding style more often with acquaintances than with best friends in some types of conflicts (conflicts of values and opinions). In contrast, they used the integrating style more with best friends than with acquaintances. In interest conflicts, they used a dominating style more with acquaintances than with best friends (Cole, 1996). This suggests that with outgroup members, as with acquaintances, for whom harmony is not as important, the Japanese use dominating or avoiding styles (depending on the conflict type). However, with ingroup members like best friends, the way to maintain harmony is to work through the conflict with an integrating style.

INTERPRETIVE AND CRITICAL APPROACHES TO SOCIAL CONFLICT

Both the interpretive and the critical approaches tend to emphasize the social and cultural aspects of conflict. In these perspectives, conflict is far more complex than the ways that interpersonal conflict is enacted. It is deeply rooted in cultural differences in the social, economic, and historical contexts.

Social conflict arises from unequal or unjust social relationships between groups. Consider, for example, the social conflict in northern Wisconsin between many whites and Native Americans over fishing rights. Communication theorist Brad Hall (1994) concludes, in part, that "actual intercultural interactions which display the conflict (and generally receive the bulk of attention) are but the tip of the iceberg in understanding the complexities of such conflicts" (p. 82). Let's look more closely at the social, economic, and historical contexts of this contemporary conflict. This area of Wisconsin depends heavily on tourism and fishing. However, supposed overfishing by the Anishinabe (Chippewa) is being blamed for economic downturns in the area, leading to uneasy social relationships. A treaty was signed in 1837 giving the Anishinabe year-round fishing rights in exchange for the northern third of Wisconsin. Awareness of these factors is necessary to understanding the complexities of the current conflict.

These complexities are embedded in cultural differences. In addition, the conflict may be motivated by a desire to bring about social change. In **social movements,** individuals work together to bring about social change. They often use confrontation as a strategy to highlight the injustices of the present system. So, for example, when African American students in Greensboro, North Carolina, sat down at white-only lunch counters in the 1960s, they were pointing out the injustices of segregation. Although the students were nonviolent, their actions drew a violent reaction that, for many people, legitimized the claims of injustice.

Historical and political contexts also are sources of conflict. Many **international conflicts** have arisen over border disputes. For example, Argentina and the United Kingdom both claimed the Islas Malvinas (or Falkland Islands) in the south Atlantic, which led to a short war in 1982. Disputes between France and Germany over the Alsace-Lorraine region lasted much longer—from about 1871 to 1945. Similar disputes have arisen between Japan and Russia over islands north of Japan. The historical reasons for such conflicts help us understand the claims of both sides. Contextualizing intercultural conflict can help us understand why the conflict occurs and identify ways to resolve those conflicts.

Social Contexts

How we manage conflict may depend on the particular context or situation. For example, we may choose to use an avoiding style if we are arguing with a close friend about serious relational issues in a movie theater. In contrast, we may feel freer to use a more confrontational style at a social movement rally.

social conflict Conflict that arises from unequal or unjust social relationships between groups.

social movements Organized activities in which individuals work together to bring about social change.

international conflicts Conflicts between two or more nations.

Nikki, a student working part-time at a restaurant, recalls an incident involving a large group of German tourists. The tourists thought she had added a 15% tip to the bill because they were tourists; they hadn't realized it was the company policy when serving large groups. Nikki explains that she was much more conciliatory when dealing with this group in the restaurant than she would have been in a more social context. She thought the tourists were rude, but she practiced good listening skills and took more of a problem-solving approach than she would have otherwise.

Jacqueline, from Singapore, is annoyed by U.S. Americans who comment on how well she speaks English because English is her first language even though she is ethnically Chinese. She used to say nothing in response; now sometimes she retorts, "So is yours," reflecting her struggle against the stereotype that Asians cannot speak English. In this context, the social movement against racism gives meaning to the conflict that arises for Jacqueline.

Many conflicts arise and must be understood against the backdrop of large-scale social movements designed to change contemporary society. For example, the women's suffrage movement of the early 20th century was not an individual effort, but a mass effort to win women the right to vote in the United States. Many similar contemporary social movements give meaning to conflicts. These include movements against racism, sexism, and homophobia and movements in support of animal rights, the environment, free speech, and civil rights. College campuses are likely locations for much activism. Journalist Tony Vellela (1988) comments, "It may have subsided, and it certainly changed, reflecting changing times and circumstances, but progressive student political activism never really stopped after the much-heralded anti–Vietnam War era" (p. 5).

There is, of course, no comprehensive list of existing social movements. They arise and dissipate, depending on the opposition they provoke, the attention they attract, and the strategies they use. As part of social change, social movements need confrontation to highlight the perceived injustice.

Confrontation, then, can be seen as an opportunity for social change. In arguing for a change, Dr. Martin Luther King, Jr. (1984) emphasized the importance of nonviolent confrontation:

> *Nonviolent resistance is not a method for cowards; it does resist. . . . [It] does not seek to defeat or humiliate the opponent, but to win his friendship and understanding. The nonviolent resister must often express his protest through noncooperation or boycotts, but he realizes that these are not ends themselves; they are merely means to awaken a sense of moral shame in the opponent. (pp. 108–109)*

This type of confrontation exposes the injustices of society and opens the way for social change. Although nonviolence is not the only form of confrontation employed by social movements, its use has a long history—from Mahatma Gandhi's struggle for India's independence from Britain, to the civil rights struggle in the United States, to the struggle against apartheid in South Africa. In each case, images of violent responses to nonviolent protesters tended to legitimize the social movements and delegitimize the existing social system. For example, in the 1950s and 1960s, the televised images of police dogs attacking schoolchildren and riot squads turning fire hoses on peaceful protesters in Birmingham, Alabama, swung public sentiment in favor of the civil rights movement.

Some social movements have also used violent forms of confrontation. Groups such as Action Directe in France, the Irish Republican Army, Earth First, and independence movements in Corsica, Algeria, Kosovo, and Chechnya have all been accused of using violence. As a result, they tend to be labeled as terrorists rather than mere protesters. Even the suggestion of violence can be threatening to the public. For example, in 1964, Malcolm X (1984) spoke in favor of civil rights: "The question tonight, as I understand it, is 'The Negro Revolt and Where Do We Go From Here?' or 'What Next?' In my little humble way of understanding it, it points toward either the ballot or the bullet" (p. 126). Malcolm X's rhetoric terrified many U.S. Americans, who then refused to give legitimacy to his movement. To understand communication practices such as these, it is important to study their social contexts. Social movements highlight many issues relevant to intercultural interaction.

Economic Contexts

Many conflicts are fueled by economic problems, which may be expressed in cultural differences. Many people find it easier to explain economic troubles by pointing to cultural differences or by assigning blame. For example, in the United States, we have heard many arguments about limiting immigration, with attention focusing largely on non-European immigrants. Concerns about illegal immigrants from Mexico far overshadow concerns about illegal immigrants from, say, Ireland. And discussions about the contributions to society made by different immigrant groups tend to favor European immigrants. Writer Andrew Hacker (1997) compares the median household income of U.S. Americans of various backgrounds, pointing out the lack of attention given to less successful U.S. Americans of some European heritages:

> We rarely hear media pundits pondering aloud why the Irish lag so far behind the Greeks in median income, and why all four Scandinavian nationalities fall in the bottom half of the European roster. But it has been deemed best not to accentuate distinctions, and rather to reserve remarks of that sort for members of another race. (p. 158)

Indeed, U.S. Americans of French ancestry and Dutch ancestry earn less (and therefore contribute less?) than U.S. Americans who trace their ancestry to the Philippines, India, Lebanon, China, Thailand, Greece, Italy, Poland, and many other countries. And yet we do not hear calls for halting immigration from France or the Netherlands. In what ways is the economic argument really hiding a racist argument?

We might also ask who benefits from this finger-pointing. Paul Kivel (1996) suggests that blaming immigrants, people of color, and Jews for economic problems diverts attention from the decision makers who are responsible for the problem.

As the economic contexts change, we see more cultural conflict taking place. The former East Germany, for example, now has many more racially motivated attacks as the region attempts to rebuild its economy. Prejudice and stereotyping that lead to conflict are often related to perceived economic threats and competition. In this sense, economics fuels scapegoating and intercultural conflict and is an important context for understanding intercultural conflict.

Historical and Political Contexts

Most of us recall the childhood saying "Sticks and stones may break my bones, but words will never hurt me." In fact, we know that derogatory words can be a powerful source of conflict. The force that many derogatory words carry comes from their historical usage and the history of oppression to which they refer. As we noted in Chapter 4, much of our identity comes from history. It is only through understanding the past that we can understand what it means to be members of particular cultural groups. For example, understanding the history of Ireland helps give meaning to Irish American identity.

Sometimes identities are constructed in opposition to or in conflict with other identities. When people are not seen as members of a culture, they may develop other identities that are seen in opposition to the mainstream culture. In December 2005, during the Australian summer, nearly 5,000 white Australian men "attacked anyone they believed was of Arab descent" (Sallis, 2005, p. A23) on Cronulla Beach near Sydney. Waving Australian flags and wrapping themselves in nationalist rhetoric, these racial conflicts spread to other parts of Sydney. To understand some of the contexts for this social conflict, we should acknowledge the history of Australia's "white Australia" policy. We might also want to point to the economic disparities between Arab Australians and white Australians, as well as the different places they live in the Sydney area. Although one Australian writer feels that today, the "notion of an all-white Australia is a fantasy and an anachronism," she also notes that "I have Muslim friends who used to feel that they were Australians, but now cannot identify themselves in the negative space created for them in our community" (Sallis, 2005, p. A23). Again, we have to recognize that this violence did not arise from an interpersonal conflict but is deeply rooted in the historical policies of Australia, the terrorist bombings in Bali, Indonesia—the most populous Muslim nation—that killed many Australians, and the history of immigration in Australia. The contemporary participants are caught in a web of historical and contemporary events that has drawn lines around cultural identities that exclude others.

These dynamics are at work all around the world. Historical antagonisms become part of cultural identities and practices that place people in positions of conflict. Whether in the Middle East, Northern Ireland, Rwanda, Uganda, Nigeria, Sri Lanka, East Timor, Kosovo, or Chechnya, these historical antagonisms lead to various forms of conflict. (See Figure 11-2.)

When people witness conflict, they often assume that it is caused by personal issues between individuals. By reducing conflict to the level of interpersonal interaction, we lose sight of the larger social and political forces that

FIGURE 11-2   These white Australians are attacking someone believed to be of Arab descent in Cronulla Beach, near Sydney, in December 2005. This kind of conflict arises because of larger historical and political conflicts, rather than interpersonal interaction. How should we respond to such conflicts? (© *Andrew Meares/Fairfax Photos*)

contextualize these conflicts. People are in conflict for reasons that extend far beyond personal communication styles.

MANAGING INTERCULTURAL CONFLICT

Productive Versus Destructive Conflict

One way to think about conflict across cultures is in terms of what is more or less successful conflict management or resolution. Given all of the variations in how people deal with conflict, what happens when there is conflict in intercultural relationships?

Scholar David Augsburger (1992) suggests that productive intercultural conflict is different from destructive conflict in four ways. First, in productive conflict, individuals or groups narrow the conflict in terms of definition, focus, and issues. In destructive conflict, they escalate the issues or negative attitudes. For example, if a partner says, "You never do the dishes" or "You always put me down in front of my friends," the conflict is likely to escalate. Instead, the partner could focus on a specific instance of being put down.

Second, in productive conflict, individuals or groups limit conflict to the original issue. In destructive conflict, they escalate the conflict from the original issues, with any aspect of the relationship open for reexamination. For example, guests on talk shows about extramarital affairs might initially refer to a specific affair and then expand the conflict to include numerous prior arguments.

Third, in productive conflict, individuals or groups direct the conflict toward cooperative problem solving. For example, a partner may ask, "How can we work this out?" In contrast, in destructive conflict, strategies involve the use of power, threats, coercion, and deception. For example, an individual might threaten his or her partner: "Either you do what I want, or else." Finally, in productive conflict, individuals or groups trust leadership that stresses mutually satisfactory outcomes. In destructive conflict, they polarize behind single-minded and militant leadership.

Competition Versus Cooperation

As you can see, the general theme in destructive conflict is competitive escalation, often into long-term negativity. The conflicting parties have set up a self-perpetuating, mutually confirming expectation. "Each is treating the other badly because it feels that the other deserves to be treated badly because the other treats it badly and so on" (Deutsch, 1987, p. 41).

How can individuals and groups promote cooperative processes in conflict situations? The general atmosphere of a relationship will promote specific processes and acts (Deutsch, 1973). For instance, a *competitive* atmosphere will promote coercion, deception, suspicion, and rigidity and lead to poor communication. In contrast, a *cooperative* atmosphere will promote perceived similarity, trust, and flexibility and lead to open communication. The key is to establish a positive, cooperative atmosphere in the beginning stages of the relationship or group interaction. It is much more difficult to turn a competitive relationship into a cooperative one once the conflict has started to escalate.

Essential to setting a cooperative atmosphere is exploration. Whereas competition often relies on argumentation, cooperation relies on exploration. Exploration may be done in various ways in different cultures, but it has several basic steps. The parties must first put the issue of conflict on hold and then explore other options or delegate the problem to a third party. Blaming is suspended, so it's possible to generate new ideas or positions. "If all conflicting parties are committed to the process, there is a sense of joint ownership of the recommended solution. . . . [M]oving toward enemies as if they were friends exerts a paradoxical force on them and can bring transcendence" (Hocker & Wilmot, 1991, p. 191).

However, exploration does not have to be logically consistent or rational. As Augsburger (1992) points out, "Exploration can be provocative, speculative, and emotional" (p. 61). It should encourage individuals to think of innovative and interesting solutions to the conflict at hand. For example, Bill and David were having an ongoing disagreement about a project they were working on, and their relationship was becoming more and more strained. One day, Bill spontaneously suggested that they go out to eat together and really talk about the problem. David was surprised because they did not normally socialize—their relationship revolved around work. They talked about the problem, spent

ANTI-AMERICANISM

Anti-Americanism has a very long history and is complicated by the economic, military, and political differences between the United States and other nations around the world. Anti-Americanism can operate on many levels—from the interpersonal to the social—and you may want to reflect on this aspect of intercultural interaction and the potential for conflict that may arise. How well do you understand anti-Americanism, and what is the best way to deal with it? Here are some voices that help explain anti-Americanism.

> There are hardly any universals left in our postmodern times, but loathing for America is about as close as we can get to a universal sentiment: it is the one dynamic that unites fundamentalists and liberals, Arabs and Latin Americans, Asians and Europeans, and even the overshadowed Canadians, with the rest of the world. (Sardar & Davies, 2002, p. 195)

> Today, however, when I talk with friends and relatives in London, when I visit Europe, the anti-Americanism is more than just sardonic asides, rueful Monty Python–style jibes, and haughty intimations of superiority. Today something much more visceral is in the air. I go to my old home and I get the distinct impression that . . . people really loathe America somewhere deep, deep in their gut. (Abramsky, 2004, p. B9)

> America has the power and resources to refuse self-reflection. More pointedly, it is a nation that has developed a tradition of being oblivious to self-reflection. Yet, America is also a nation that produces strident self-criticism and many strands of dissenting opinion from writers, artists, academics, professionals and even politicians. (Sardar & Davies, 2002, p. 13)

> To fully understand anti-Americanism, we have to step back and question what it means to be an "American." For President George W. Bush, it is a fanciful morality story of all-good versus all-evil. . . . In the words he has repeated time and again: "I had made it clear to the world that either you're with us or you're with the enemy, and that doctrine still stands." What does this history of empire-building mean for Americans today? And who truly counts as an American? (Tchen, 2004, pp. 301–302)

Sources: From S. Abramsky, "Waking Up from the American Dream," *Chronicle of Higher Education*, July 23, 2004, p. B9; Z. Sardar and M. Davies, *Why Do People Hate America?* (New York: The Disinformation Company, 2002); and J. K. W. Tchen, "Vigilante Americanism." In A. Ross and K. Ross (Eds.), *Anti-Americanism* (New York: New York University Press, 2004), pp. 301–314.

some time getting to know each other, and found they had some things in common. Although the problem didn't magically go away, it became easier to manage. Bill's spontaneous invitation to talk helped facilitate the resolution of the conflict.

Dealing with Conflict

There are no easy answers in dealing with intercultural conflict. Sometimes, we can apply the principles of dialectics; other times, we may need to step back and show self-restraint. Occasionally, though, it may be more appropriate to assert ourselves and not be afraid of strong emotion. Here, we offer seven suggestions for dealing with conflict:

1. Stay centered and do not polarize.
2. Maintain contact.
3. Recognize the existence of different styles.
4. Identify your preferred style.
5. Be creative and expand your style repertoire.
6. Recognize the importance of conflict context.
7. Be willing to forgive.

Let's look at these guidelines in more detail.

Stay Centered and Do Not Polarize   It's important to move beyond traditional stereotypes and either-or thinking. David Augsburger (1992) elaborates on this approach to dealing with conflict:

> *Immediately challenge the intrusion of either-or thinking, traditional stereotypes, and reductionistic explanations of the other's motives as simple while seeing your own as complex. Sustain the conflicting images of reality, one from the antagonist and one of your own, in parallel co-existence within your mind. Be open to a third, centered perspective that may bring a new synthesis into view. (p. 66)*

The parties involved must practice self-restraint. It's okay to get angry, but it's important to move past the anger and to refrain from acting out feelings. For example, Jenni and her co-worker both practiced self-restraint and stayed centered in a recent disagreement about religion. Jenni explains,

> *My friend is a devout Catholic, and I am a devout Mormon. She asked me about where we get some of our doctrine and how it relates to the Bible. We never really solved our differences, but compromised and "agreed to disagree." This was necessary to keep our friendship and respect as co-workers. I felt bad that she couldn't see the points I was coming from. I do think it turned out for the best, though, because we don't feel tension around each other.*

Maintain Contact   This does not mean that the parties have to stay in the conflict situation—sometimes it's necessary to step away for a while. However, the parties should not cut off the relationship. Rather, they should attempt a dialogue rather than isolate themselves from each other or engage in fighting. **Dialogue** differs from normal conversation in that it is

> *slow, careful, full of feeling, respectful and attentive. This movement toward an apparently opposing viewpoint must be learned; few develop this approach to others*

dialogue Conversation that is "slow, careful, full of feeling, respectful and attentive" (Wilmot & Hocker, 2001, p. 257).

id you know that the third Thursday of October is Conflict Resolution Day? In many conflicts, mediation can be helpful in reaching a solution or compromise. This is an international celebration organized by the Association for Conflict Resolution.

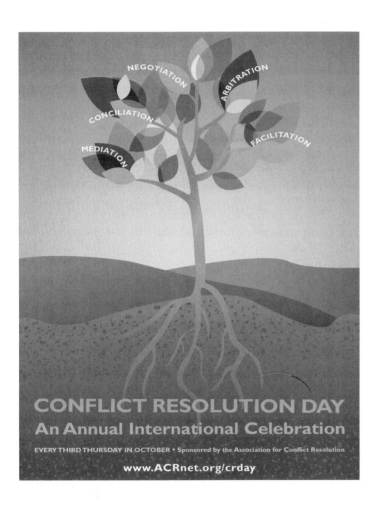

without a deep sense of the importance of each human being, and a belief in collaboratively searching for new solutions that honor each person. (Wilmot & Hocker, 2001, p. 257)

Dialogue is possible only between two persons or two groups whose power relationship is more or less in balance. Dialogue offers an important opportunity to come to a richer understanding of intercultural conflicts and experiences.

Our student John experienced an intercultural conflict in an accounting class in which his maintaining contact paid off. He was placed in a group with three Japanese students who were all friends. He recalls:

Right from the beginning things were quite awkward; their mathematics abilities far exceeded mine. After only two days, they had met twice without me and completed part of the assignment. I had been left out of the decision-making process.

Rather than avoiding the problem, however, he decided to invite them all over to his house to talk about the project. Everyone was able to loosen up and discuss what had gone wrong, and the conflict was handled productively: "Although I was unhappy with the way things went during the earlier parts of the project, the end result was three new acquaintances and an A in accounting."

Recognize the Existence of Different Styles   Conflict is often exacerbated because of the unwillingness of partners to recognize management style differences. Communication scholar Barbara L. Speicher (1994) analyzes a conflict that occurred between two student leaders on the same committee: the chair, Peter, an African American male, and Kathy, a European American female who was president of the organization. The two had a history of interpersonal antagonism. They disagreed on how meetings should be run and on how data should be collected in a particular project they were working on. They interviewed the other participants afterward and learned that most thought the conflict was related mainly to the interpersonal history of the two and to the issue at hand, but not to either race or gender.

Speicher then describes how her analysis of videotapes of the conflict showed that both Kathy and Peter adhered to cultural norms for communication between blacks and whites in the United States:

Peter was assertive, took the floor when he had an important point to make and became loud and emphatic as the conflict accelerated. . . . The Eurocentric discomfort with and disapproval of his adamancy led to either silence (avoidance) or attempts to calm him down and diminish rather than resolve the conflict.
(p. 204)

Speicher notes that part of the problem was related to differences in perceptions of rationalism—"the sacred cow of Western thought"—and emotionalism. In Western thought, these two behaviors often are seen as mutually exclusive. But this is not so in Afrocentric thinking. Peter believed that he was being rational, giving solid evidence for each of his claims, and also being emotional. To his Eurocentric colleagues, his high affect seemed to communicate that he was taking something personally, that his vehemence precluded rationality or resolution. Speicher suggests that perhaps we need to rethink the way we define conflict competence. From an Afrocentric point of view, one can be emotional and rational and still be deemed competent.

Speicher also points out the danger of attributing individual behavior to group differences: "While such work can help us understand one another, it can also encourage viewing an interlocutor as a representative of a group (stereotyping)

CAN THE INTERNET REDUCE INTERCULTURAL CONFLICT?

Israeli Jews and Palestinians are engaged in an ongoing conflict that has made it difficult for them to communicate with each other in face-to-face situations. Some have turned to computer-mediated communication (CMC) as one way to communicate across these geographic, cultural, and historical divides. Because CMC offers the opportunity for Israeli Jews to communicate with Palestinians, two communication scholars, Donald Ellis of the University of Hartford and Ifat Maoz of the Hebrew University of Jerusalem, studied high school students' interactions to discover if the Internet could help reduce intercultural conflict. They found that

- Arguments are stunted. "There is no convergence or progress toward elaborated argument" (p. 301).

- Lack of dialogue. Because the participants do not engage with each others' assertions, the "participants immediately diverge, and there is a deafening silence with respect to developing and converging sequences" of arguments (p. 301).

- Jointly constructed points of view do not develop. The participants were more focused on controlling the discussion, rather than mutually building a common perspective.

- Participants tended to directly challenge each other and the "challenges are more intense and emotional" (p. 303).

While CMC can help put cultural groups into contact who might not otherwise communicate with each other, this communication medium does not necessarily solve intercultural conflict.

Source: From C. G. Ellis and I. Maoz (2007), Online Argument Between Israeli Jews and Palestinians, *Human Communication Research, 33:* 291–309.

rather than as an individual" (p. 206). However, she goes on to say that in this particular case

> *failure to recognize cultural differences led to a negative evaluation of an individual. The problems that emerged in this exchange were attributed almost exclusively to Peter's behavior. The evaluation was compounded by the certainty on the part of the European Americans, as expressed in the interviews, that their interpretation was the correct one, a notion reinforced by the Eurocentric literature on conflict.* (p. 206)

This particular combination of differing but complementary styles often results in damaged relationships and frozen agendas—the rational/avoiding–emotional/confronting "dance." Other combinations may be problematic but less overtly damaging. For example, two people with assertive emotional styles may understand each other and know how to work through the conflict.

453

Likewise, things can work if both people avoid open conflict, particularly in long-term committed relationships (Pike & Sillars, 1985). Jointly avoiding conflict does not necessarily mean that it goes away, but it may give people time to think about how to deal with the conflict and talk about it.

Identify Your Preferred Style   Although people may change their way of dealing with conflict based on the situation and the type of conflict, most tend to use the same style in most situations. For example, Tom and Judith both prefer an avoiding style. If we are pushed into conflict or feel strongly that we need to resolve a particular issue, we can speak up for ourselves. However, we both prefer more indirect means of dealing with current and potential conflicts. We often choose to work things out on a more personal, indirect level.

It is also important to recognize which conflict styles "push your conflict button." Some styles are more or less compatible; it's important to know which styles are congruent with your own. If you prefer a more confronting style and you have a disagreement with someone like Tom or Judith, it may drive you crazy.

Be Creative and Expand Your Style Repertoire   If a particular way of dealing with conflict is not working, be willing to try a different style. Of course, this is easier said than done. As conflict specialists William Wilmot and Joyce Hocker (2001) explain, people often seem to get "frozen" into a conflict style. For example, some people consistently deny any problems in a relationship, whereas others consistently escalate small conflicts into large ones.

There are many reasons for getting stuck in a conflict management style, according to Wilmot and Hocker. The style may have developed during a time when the person felt good about himself or herself—when the particular conflict management style worked well. Consider, for example, the high school athlete who develops an aggressive style on and off the playing field, a style that people seem to respect. A limited repertoire may be related to gender differences. Some women get stuck in an avoiding style, whereas some men get stuck in a confronting style. A limited repertoire also may come from cultural background—a culture that encourages confronting conflict or a culture (like Judith's and Tom's) that rewards avoiding conflict. A combination of these reasons is the likely cause of getting stuck in the use of one conflict management style. For example, even though Tom and Judith prefer an avoiding style, we have occasionally found it effective to be more assertive and direct in intercultural conflicts in which the dominant communication style was more confrontational.

In most aspects of intercultural communication, adaptability and flexibility serve us well—and conflict communication is no exception. This means that there is no so-called objective way to deal with conflict. Many times, as in other aspects of relationships, it's best simply to listen and not say anything. One strategy that mediators use is to allow one person to talk for an extended time while the other person listens.

Recognize the Importance of Conflict Context   As noted earlier in this chapter, it is important to understand the larger social, economic, political, and historical contexts that give meaning to many types of conflict. Conflict arises for many reasons, and it is misleading to think that all conflict can be understood within the interpersonal context alone. For example, when one student, George, went home for a family reunion, everyone seemed to be talking about their romantic relationships, spouses, children, and so on. When George, who is gay, talked about his own partner, George's uncle asked why gay people had to flaunt their lifestyle. George reacted angrily. The conflict was not simply between George and his uncle; it rests in the social context that accepts straight people talking frequently and openly about their relationships but that does not validate the same discussion of romantic relationships from gay people. The same talk is interpreted differently because of the social context.

People often act in ways that cause conflict. However, it is important to let the context explain the behavior as much as possible. Otherwise, the behavior may not make sense. Once you understand the contexts that frame the conflict, whether cultural, social, historical, or political, you will be in a better position to understand and conceive of the possibilities for resolution. For example, Savina, who is white, was shopping with her friend Lashieki. The employee at the cash register referred to someone as "that black girl," and Lashieki, who is African American, demanded, "Why did they have to refer to her as that black girl?" Lashieki's response can only be understood by knowing something about the context of majority–minority relations in the United States. That is, whites are rarely referred to by color, whereas people of color are often defined solely on the basis of race.

Be Willing to Forgive   A final suggestion for facilitating conflict, particularly in long-term relationships, is to consider forgiveness. This means letting go of—not forgetting—feelings of revenge (Lulofs, 1994). This may be particularly useful in intercultural conflict (Augsburger, 1992).

Teaching forgiveness between estranged individuals is as old as recorded history; it is present in every culture and is part of the human condition. In fact, recent research suggests that both revenge and forgiveness are instinctual and universal among humans and both have developed as adaptive mechanisms in human evolution (McCullough, 2008). Cross-cultural studies show that most of the world cultures demonstrate patterns of both revenge and forgiveness, as do many animal species. Based on this research, Michael McCullough proposes that the "disease model of forgiveness"—the oft-cited notion that forgiveness is the ideal and the desire for revenge is a sickness—is an outmoded concept. Rather, both revenge and forgiveness have solved evolutionary problems for our ancestors and are still solving problems today. His argument goes something like this: The instinct for revenge has served human beings historically, by preventing enemies from harming a second time, by warning evildoers to back off, and even coercing free-riders to cooperate. These functions are particularly important when there is an absence of strong governments that can ensure individual safety.

At the same time, forgiveness is also a basic human instinct that has also served humans well. And it is not always bad to retaliate when someone has done us a great wrong . . . but not helpful to hold a grudge forever. At a very fundamental level, forgiveness ensures that we get along with both family and close friends and helps establish and maintain cooperative relationships with nonrelatives, and, overall, forgiveness is the best strategy for human beings in the long term—it can deliver freedom from fear and freedom to resume normal, peaceful relations. In fact, it is in our self-interest to forgive. Psychologists point out that blaming others and feeling resentment lead to a victim mentality and may actually lead to stress, burnout, and physical problems. Forgiveness, on the other hand, can lead to improved physical health.

As cooperation and group level evolve, revenge and forgiveness are not on opposite sides, they are on the same team. You can't be easy-going all the time, you can't be vengeful and spiteful all of the time. . . . "In social dilemmas that pit the short-term gains of selfishness against the long-term gains of cooperation, evolution favors the organism that can be vengeful when necessary, that can forgive when necessary, and that has the wisdom to know the difference" (p. 87).

There are several models of forgiveness. Most include an acknowledgment of feelings of hurt and anger and a need for healing. In a forgiveness loop, forgiveness is seen as socially constructed and based in communication. If someone is in a stressed relationship, he or she can create actions and behaviors that make forgiveness seem real; then he or she can communicate this to the other person, enabling the relationship to move forward. It is easier to forgive when one can see the offender as someone who is careworthy, valuable and safe and when the vengeful impulse has been satisfied to some degree, perhaps knowing that an offender has been punished. So an important part of apologizing and asking for forgiveness may be compensation and some measure of restorative justice.

The importance of compensation in preventing violent revenge and encouraging forgiveness can't be overstated. Cross-cultural studies of premodern cultures found that many had developed compensation strategies and forgiveness rituals for quelling revenge, which often included accepting "blood money" as an alternative to killing a murderer or one of his or her relatives, as well as compensations and gift exchanges (McCullough, 2008). A final important component in the forgiveness process for criminals and offenders is restoring justice. Restorative justice conferences are extremely effective at reducing the desire for revenge and fostering forgiveness. "They give people the chance to process the traumatic experience and talk to their offenders in a safe nonthreatening way (McCullough, 2008, p. 177). "The restorative justice movement is another great example of an institution that brings out people's best selves in the aftermath of conflict and violence. . . it works because it enables people to use their evolved moral intuitions to address the pain of crime in the mega-societies in which most of us live. . ." (pp. 179–180).

Civil wars that end in forgiveness and reconciliation have four processes: redefine affected people's identities, implement countless small actions, process of public "truth," justice short of revenge (legal consequences, amnesty, reparations) n 1975, researcher Frans de Waal noticed a male and female chimp kissing each other, which is not particularly rare, but on this occasion, only moments before the male had attacked the female quite strenuously, with a showy display of his physical strength. Then a noisy ruckus erupted in the colony, the chimps "burst out hooting and one male even produced rhythmic noise on metal drums stacked up in the corner . . . in the midst of this pandemonium, two chimpanzees kissed and embraced" (p. 118). De Waal concluded that the post-conflict kiss was intended to help them to undo the damage that the assault had inflicted on their relationship. Since 1979, when de Waal first published his findings, the methods for measuring reconciliation have become more sophisticated. Today, primatologists calculate the "Conciliatory Tendency" or CT on a scale from 0 to 1. "Primate groups' CT scores rarely exceed .50" (McCullough, p. 119).

Source: From M. E. McCullough, *Beyond Revenge: The Evolution of the Forgiveness Instinct* (San Francisco: Jossey-Bass, 2008).

(McCullough, 2008). An example of forgiveness on a national level involves the National Sorry Day and the Journey of Healing, which serve to acknowledge and apologize for the wretched treatment of Aboriginals by non-Aboriginal Australians. Another example is the Truth and Reconciliation Commission in South Africa, formed to investigate and facilitate the healing of racial wounds as a result of apartheid. The committee hears stories of the atrocities that were committed, but the ultimate goal is forgiveness, not revenge (Henderson, 1999).

Forgiveness may take a long time. It is important to distinguish between what is forgiveness and what is not, because false forgiveness can be self-righteous and obtrusive; it almost nurtures past transgression. As writer Roxane Lulofs (1994) explains, forgiveness is not

> simply forgetting that something happened. It does not deny anger. It does not put us in a position of superiority. It is not a declaration of the end of all conflict, of ever risking again with the other person (or anybody else). It is not one way. . . . We do not forgive in order to be martyrs to the relationship. We forgive because it is better for us and better for the other person. We forgive because we want to act freely again, not react out of past pain. . . . [It] is the final stage of conflict and is the one thing that is most likely to prevent repetitive, destructive cycles of conflict. (pp. 283–284, 289)

Mediation

Sometimes two individuals or groups cannot work through conflict on their own. They may request an intermediary, or one may be assigned to intervene. In some societies, these third parties may be rather informal. In Western societies, onflict specialist David Augsburger identifies six key Western assumptions—conflict myths—and notes their inadequacies in intercultural settings.

1. *People and problems can be separated cleanly; interests and positions can be distinguished sharply.* *In most cultures of the world, equal attention must be given to both person and problem, to relationship and goals and to private interests as well as public positions if a creative resolution is to be reached.*

2. *Open self-disclosure is a positive value in negotiations.An open process of public data shared in candid style is assumed necessary for trust.* *"Open covenants, openly arrived at," Woodrow Wilson insisted, as did Harry Truman, were the basis for setting up the United Nations. However, the real negotiation is done in corridors or behind closed doors, and is announced publicly when agreements have been reached. Virtually nothing of any substance is agreed on in the official public UN debates.*

3. *Immediacy, directness, decisiveness, and haste are preferred strategies in timing.* *The Western valuation that time is money can press the negotiator to come to terms prematurely. Many different cultures find that the best way to reach an agreement is to give the matter sufficient time to allow adjustments to be made, accommodations to emerge, and acceptance to evolve and emerge. Believing that "time is people," they are in less haste to reach closure.*

4. *Language employed should be reasonable, rational, and responsible.* *In some cultures, deprecative language, extreme accusations and vitriolic expressions are used as a negotiating power tactic.*

5. *No is no and yes is yes (an affirmation is absolute, a negation final).* *In some cultures, one does not say no to an offer; requests are not phrased to elicit negations; when an offer is affirmed, the real meanings are weighed and assessed carefully.*

6. *When an agreement is reached, implementation will take care of itself as a logical consequence.* *The agreements negotiated may mean different things to parties in a reconciliation. Built-in processes, ongoing negotiations, open channels for resolving problems as they arise in ongoing interpretation, and circumstances that would warrant renegotiation are all useful elements for ensuring ongoing success.*

Source: From D. Augsburger, *Conflict Mediation Across Cultures* (Louisville, KY: Westminster/John Knox Press, 1992), pp. 206–208.

though, they tend to be built into the legal and judicial system. For example, lawyers or counselors may act as mediators to settle community or family disputes.

Contemporary Western **mediation** models often ignore cultural variations in conflict processes. Fortunately, more scholars and mediators are looking at other cultural models that may work better in intercultural conflicts. Augsburger (1992) suggests that the culturally sensitive mediator engages in conflict transformation (not conflict resolution or conflict management). The conflict transformer assists disputants to think in new ways about the conflict—for example, to transform attitudes by redirecting negative perceptions. This requires a commitment by both parties to treat each other with goodwill and mutual respect. Of course, this is often much easier said than done. Behavior can be transformed by limiting all action to collaborative behavior; this can break the negative cycle but requires a commitment to seek a noncoercive process of negotiation even when there has been intense provocation. For example, in the recent Northern Ireland agreement, mediation resulted in commitment by most people to change the vision of Northern Ireland, in spite of horrendous provocation on the part of some extremists.

mediation The act of resolving conflict by having someone intervene between two parties.

Traditional societies often use mediation models based on nondirect means. The models vary but share many characteristics. Whereas North American mediation tends to be more formal and structured, involving direct confrontation and communication, most traditional cultural models are more communally based, with involvement by trusted leaders. Indirect communication is preferred in order to permit individuals to save face. In addition, the process is more dynamic, directed toward resolving tension in the community—the responsibility of the disputants to their larger community is central (Augsburger, 1992, p. 204).

Augsburger provides the example of mediation in the Gitksan Nation, in northwest British Columbia, where mediation of disputes begins with placement of the problem "in the middle of the table." Everyone involved—including those in authority and the witnesses—must make suggestions in a peaceful manner until they come to a decision all can live with. Even conflicts ending in murder are resolved in this consensus-oriented fashion. For instance, "land would be transferred as compensation to help deal with the pain of the loss. The murderer might be required to give up his or her name and go nameless for a period to show respect for the life taken" (p. 213). Eventually, however, the land or anything else that was given up would be returned, "when the pain has passed and time has taken care of the grief" (p. 213). Augsburger points out that this traditional communal approach to mediation is based on collectivistic beliefs that make individualistic solutions to conflicts unacceptable.

Contemporary mediators have learned some lessons from the traditional non-Western models, and mediation is used increasingly in the United States and other countries to resolve conflicts. Mediation is advantageous because it relies on the disputing parties' active involvement in and commitment to the resolution. Also, it represents the work of all involved, so it's likely to be more creative and integrative. Finally, mediation is often cheaper than adversarial legal resolution (Wilmot & Hocker, 2001, p. 276).

INTERNET RESOURCES

www.hammerconsulting.org/product_ics.php
www.youtube.com/watch?v=s3-Zmj3sTt8&feature=related
The first link is to a Web site of a for-profit consulting firm. This specific section of the site exemplifies how intercultural conflict is treated in the workplace. The program explained on the site is derived from one laid out in a peer-reviewed academic journal. Interesting resources on this page include: a conflict chart, a list of organizations that have used the program, and a number of other items.

The second link is a presentation about the conflict resolution program explained on the first Web site.

http://mediationchannel.com/
This is a great blog maintained by conflict mediation professional Diane Levin. It has interesting entries on new-media items like *Bully* by Rockstar Games, intercultural conflict, and new-media conflict. Look around the Web site for a variety of mediation guides founded upon good academic literature. There is even a section with advice in case you want to pursue a career in conflict mediation!

www.mideastweb.org/timeline.htm
The whole Mideast Web site contains valuable information about conflict and progress in the Middle East. However, this timeline is especially valuable in trying to understand the context of current conflicts. The second timeline on the link details key moments in the Arab-Israeli conflict from over 3,000 years ago to the present. Many of these events and issues form an invisible context for current conflicts and negotiations. It is worth considering what histories inform other cultural conflicts around the world.

www.usip.org/mediation/index.html
This is the Web site of a policy-oriented research organization specializing in cultural conflict. Its focus is on international policy, not business. There are a lot of great resources on this site, including reviews of practitioners and detailed descriptions of the group's efforts in hotspots like Iraq and Nigeria. Within the site, www.usip.org/library/ is an organized and useful compilation of resources for researchers.

SUMMARY

- Intercultural conflict may be characterized by various dialectics, including economic, religious, cultural, and political tensions, as well as ambiguity, language issues, and conflict management styles.
- There are two different orientations to conflict: conflict as opportunity and conflict as destructive.

- The social science approach emphasizes understanding cultural differences in conflict.
- The five types of conflict are affective conflict, conflict of interest, value conflict, cognitive conflict, and goal conflict.
- There are five conflict styles—dominating, integrating, compromising, obliging, and avoiding.
- The choice of conflict style may be influenced by culture, gender, and ethnicity.
- Interpretive and critical approaches to conflict emphasize intergroup and social conflict.
- Interpretive and critical approaches also emphasize contexts of conflict.
- Social movements are one approach to social change and often involve conflict or confrontation.
- Conflict can be productive or destructive.
- Some strategies for conflict resolution include staying centered, maintaining contact, recognizing the existence of different conflict management styles, identifying a preferred style, being creative and expanding one's conflict style repertoire, recognizing the importance of conflict context, and being willing to forgive.
- Transforming methods of mediation are commonly used in many cultures.

DISCUSSION QUESTIONS

1. How does the "conflict as opportunity" orientation differ from the "conflict as destructive" orientation?
2. Why is it important to understand the context in which intercultural conflict occurs?
3. How are conflict strategies used in social movements?
4. How does an attitude of forgiveness facilitate conflict resolution?
5. What are some general suggestions for dealing with intercultural conflict?

Go to the self-quizzes on the Online Learning Center at www.mhhe.com/
martinnakayama5 to further test your knowledge.

ACTIVITIES

Cultures in Conflict. For this assignment, work in groups of four. As a group, select two countries or cultural groups that are currently in conflict or that have historically been in conflict. In your group, form two pairs. One pair will research the conflict from the perspective of one of the two cultural groups or countries; the other pair will research the conflict from the perspective of the other group or country. Use library and community resources (including interviews with members of the culture if possible). Outline the major issues and arguments. Explore the role of cultural values and political, economic, and historical contexts that may contribute to the conflict. Be prepared to present an oral or written report of your research.

KEY WORDS

avoiding style (439)
compromising
    style (438)
conflict (431)
confrontation (431)
dialogue (450)
dominating style (438)

facework (436)
integrating style (438)
intercultural
    conflict (427)
intermediary (433)
international
    conflicts (443)

mediation (459)
obliging style (438)
pacifism (433)
social conflict (443)
social movements (443)

 The Online Learning Center at www.mhhe.com/martinnakayama5 features flashcards and crossword puzzles based on these terms and concepts.

REFERENCES

Applebaum, A. (2005, November 9). "But, what country is this?" *Washington Post*, p. A31.

Augsburger, D. (1992). *Conflict mediation across cultures.* Louisville, KY: Westminster/John Knox Press.

Balmforth, R. (2008, February 20). Seven under investigation for Paris suburb riots. *Reuters.* Retrieved, May 10, 2008 from http://www.reuters .com/article/worldNews/idUSL2077366820080220? pageNumber=1&virtualBrandChannel=0

Cai, D. A., & Fink, E. L. (2002). Conflict style differences between individualists and collectivists. *Communication Monographs, 69,* 67–87.

Canary, D. J., Cupach, W. R., & Messman, S. J. (1995). *Relationship conflict.* Thousand Oaks, CA: Sage.

Cole, M. (1996). *Interpersonal conflict communication in Japanese cultural contexts.* Unpublished dissertation, Arizona State University, Tempe.

Collier, M. J. (1991). Conflict competence within African, Mexican, and Anglo American friendships. In S. Ting-Toomey & F. Korzenny (Eds.), *Cross-cultural interpersonal communication* (pp. 132–154). Newbury Park, CA: Sage.

Cupach, W. R., & Canary, D. J. (1997). *Competence in interpersonal conflict.* New York: McGraw-Hill.

Deutsch, M. (1973). *The resolution of conflict: Constructive and destructive processes.* New Haven, CT: Yale University Press.

Deutsch, M. (1987). A theoretical perspective on conflict and conflict resolution. In D. Sandole & I. Sandole-Staroste (Eds.), *Conflict management and problem solving* (pp. 38–49). New York: New York University Press.

Filley, A. C. (1975). *Interpersonal conflict resolution.* Glenview, IL: Scott, Foresman.

Folger, J. P., Poole, M. S., & Stutman, R. K. (1993). *Working through conflict: Strategies for relationships, groups, and organizations* (2nd ed.). New York: HarperCollins.

France's failure. (2005, November 12). *The Economist,* pp. 11–12.

Griswold, E. (2008, March). God's country. *Atlantic Monthly Online.* Retrieved May 15, 2008 from http://www.theatlantic.com/doc/ print/200803/nigeria

Hacker, A. (1997). *Money: Who has how much and why.* New York: Scribner.

Hall, B. "J." (1994). Understanding intercultural conflict through kernel images and rhetorical visions. *The International Journal of Conflict Management, 5*(1), 62–86.

Henderson, M. (1999). *Forgiveness: Breaking the chain of hate.* Wilsonville, OR: Book-Partners.

High-pitched sound used to deter teenagers. (2008, February 14). *ABC News* (Australian Broadcasting Corporation). Retrieved May 9, 2008 from http://www.abc.net.au/news/ stories/2008/02/14/2162976.htm

Hocker, J. L., & Wilmot, W. W. (1991). *Interpersonal conflict* (3rd ed.). Dubuque, IA: Brown.

Ignatius, D. (2005, November 9). Why France is burning. *Washington Post*, p. A31.

King, M. L., Jr. (1984). Pilgrimage in nonviolence. In J. C. Albert & S. E. Albert (Eds.), *The sixties papers: Documents of a rebellious decade* (pp. 108–112). New York: Praeger. (Original work published 1965)

Kivel, P. (1996). *Uprooting racism: How white people can work for racial justice*. Gabriola Islands, BC: New Society.

Kraybill, D. (1989). *The riddle of Amish culture*. Baltimore: Johns Hopkins University Press.

Le Paris flambé. (2007, November 29). *The Economist*. Retrieved May 11, 2008 from http://www.economist.com/world/europe/displaystory.cfm?story_id=10225005.

Lindsley, S. L. (1999). A layered model of problematic intercultural communication in U.S.-owned *maquiladoras* in Mexico. *Communication Monographs, 66*, 145–167.

Lulofs, R. S. (1994). *Conflict: From theory to action*. Scottsdale, AZ: Gorsuch Scarisbrick.

Malcolm X. (1984). The ballot or the bullet. In J. C. Albert & S. E. Albert (Eds.), *The sixties papers: Documents of a rebellious decade* (pp. 126–132). New York: Praeger. (Original work published 1965)

Mandonnet, E., Pelletier, E., Pontaut, J.-M., & Rosso, R. (2005, November 10–16). Pourquoi la France brûle. *L'Express International*, pp. 22–28.

McCullough, M. E. (2008). *Beyond revenge: The evolution of the forgiveness instinct*. San Francisco: Jossey-Bass.

On the streets again. (2007, November 28). *The Economist*. Retrieved May 11, 2008 from http://www.economist.com/world/europe/displaystory.cfm?story_id=10204344

Pike, G. R., & Sillars, A. L. (1985). Reciprocity of marital communication. *Journal of Social and Personal Relationships, 2*, 303–324.

Rahim, M. A. (1986). *Managing conflict in organizations*. New York: Praeger.

Rahim, M. A., & Magner, N. R. (1995). Confirmatory factor analysis of the styles of handling interpersonal conflict: First-order factor model and its invariance across groups. *Journal of Applied Psychology, 80*, 122–132.

Ross, M. H. (1993a). *The culture of conflict: Interpretations and interests in comparative perspective*. New Haven, CT: Yale University Press.

Ross, M. H. (1993b). *The management of conflict: Interpretations and interests in comparative perspective*. New Haven, CT: Yale University Press.

Sallis, E. (2005, December 17). Australia's dangerous fantasy. *New York Times*, p. A23.

Smith, P. B., Dugan, S., Peterson, M. F., & Leung, K. (1998). Individualism/collectivism and the handling of disagreement: A 23-country study. *International Journal of Intercultural Relations, 22*, 351–367.

Smith, T. B. (2005, November 8). France could learn from Canada. *The Globe and Mail* (Toronto). Accessed December 18, 2005, from http://www.theglobeandmail.com/servlet/story/RTGAM.20051107.wcomment1108/BNStory/International/

Speicher, B. L. (1994). Interethnic conflict: Attribution and cultural ignorance. *Howard Journal of Communications, 5*, 195–213.

Thomas, K., & Kilmann, R. H. (1974). *Thomas-Kilmann conflict MODE instrument*. Tuxedo, NY: Xicom.

Ting-Toomey, S. (1997). Intercultural conflict competence. In W. R. Cupach & D. J. Canary (Eds.), *Competence in interpersonal conflict* (pp. 120–147). New York: McGraw-Hill.

Ting-Toomey, S. (2005). The matrix of face: an updated face-negotiation theory. In W. B. Gudykunst (Ed.), *Theorizing about intercultural communication* (pp. 71–92). Thousand Oaks, CA: Sage.

Ting-Toomey, S., & Oetzel, J. G. (2002). Cross-cultural face concerns and conflict styles: Current status and future directions. In W. B. Gudykunst & B. Mody (Eds.), *Handbook of international and intercultural communication* (2nd ed., pp. 141–163). Thousand Oaks, CA: Sage.

Ting-Toomey, S., Yee-Jung, K. K., Shapiro, R., Garcia, W, Wright, T. J., & Oetzel, J. G. (2000). Ethnic/cultural identity salience and conflict styles in four U.S. ethnic groups. *International Journal of Intercultural Relations, 24*, 47–81.

Toupin, A. (1980). Counseling Asians: Psychotherapy in the context of racism and Asian-American history. *American Journal of Orthopsychiatry, 50*, 76–86.

Vellela, T. (1988). *New voices: Student political activism in the '80s and '90s*. Boston: South End Press.

Wilmot, W. W., & Hocker, J. L. (2001). *Interpersonal conflict* (6th ed.). New York: McGraw-Hill.

Wu, J. C. H. (1967). Chinese legal and political philosophy. In C. Moore (Ed.), *The Chinese mind* (pp. 213–237). Honolulu: East-West Center, University of Hawaii.

CHAPTER

12

STRIVING FOR ENGAGED AND EFFECTIVE INTERCULTURAL COMMUNICATION

Now that we are nearing the end of our journey through this textbook, you might ask, How do you really know whether you are a good intercultural communicator? We have covered a lot of topics and discussed some ideas that will help you be a better communicator. But you can't learn how to be a good communicator merely by reading books. Just as in learning to be a good public speaker or a good relational partner, it takes experience. In this chapter, we want to leave you with some specific ideas and suggestions for improving your skills in communicating across cultures.

We can approach intercultural competence in several ways. We begin this chapter with the social science approach, identifying specific components of competence: motivation, knowledge, attitudes, behaviors, and skills. We then turn to interpretive and critical approaches, emphasizing the contextual issues in competence. Finally, we continue our dialectical perspective, combining individual and contextual elements to offer specific suggestions for improving intercultural relations by building alliances and coalitions across cultures.

THE COMPONENTS OF COMPETENCE

What are the things we have to know, the attitudes and behaviors, to make us competent communicators? Do we have to be motivated to be good at intercultural communication? Intercultural communication scholars have been investigating these questions for many years (Chen & Starosta, 1996). Scholars taking a social science perspective have identified four basic components, or building blocks, of intercultural competence: motivation, knowledge, attitudes, and behaviors (Wiseman, 2002). We present these components here because we think they serve as a useful starting point. However, interpretive and critical scholars remind us that we need to contextualize these components (Collier, 1998, 2005). We need to ask ourselves, Who came up with these components? Are they applicable to everyone? For example, if a group of Native American scholars came up with guidelines for what it takes to be interculturally competent, would these guidelines apply to other cultural groups? Do the same competencies work in every context? Again, it is useful to remember our dialectical perspective. Intercultural communication competence may rely on individual competence, but context is also important. Let's look first at the individual components.

Social Science Perspective: Individual Components

Motivation   Perhaps the most important dimension of communication competence is **motivation.** If we aren't motivated to communicate with others, it probably doesn't matter what other skills we possess. We can't assume that people always want to communicate. This is a difficult idea to wrestle with, especially

motivation As an individual component of intercultural communication competence, the desire to make a commitment in relationships, to learn about the self and others, and to remain flexible.

for those of us who have dedicated our lives to studying and understanding intercultural communication. And yet, motivation is an important aspect of developing intercultural competence.

Why might people not be motivated to engage in intercultural communication? One reason is that members of large, powerful groups often think they don't need to know much about other cultures; there is simply no incentive. In contrast, people from less powerful groups have a strong incentive to learn about and interact with more powerful groups. For example, female managers in corporations are motivated to learn about and adjust to the dominant male norms, Latinos/as are motivated to learn European American norms, and visitors overseas are motivated to learn about and adjust to the norms of foreign cultures. The survival of these less powerful groups often depends on members' motivation to succeed at intercultural interaction (Johnson, 2001).

Sometimes people can *become* motivated to learn about other cultures and to communicate interculturally. For example, the events of 9/11 motivated many U.S. Americans to become more aware of how U.S. worldviews and behavior, on both a personal and a political level, are intertwined with those in other cultures and countries. The increasing levels of violence in the world among religious groups has also motivated people to reach out to those in other cultures. One recently formed group, Women Against War, was started by two women, an Israeli Arab and an Israeli Jew; together they have organized activities and events to advocate for peace and more understanding in Israel. As one of the founders said, "we don't want to see any citizens on both sides killed because of an avoidable war. There is no sense in that." ("Women Demand Peace," 2008).

A second reason that people aren't motivated is because intercultural communication can be uncomfortable. As discussed previously, anxiety, uncertainty, and fear are common aspects of intercultural interactions. And yet, moving out of our "communication comfort zone" often leads to insights into other individuals, groups, and cultures. One of our students, Kati, explains,

> *I think that you learn the most by traveling and/or making a conscious effort to interact with those in another culture or nation or race. Especially being thrust outside of your "comfort zone" (most Americans never get out of their comfort zone) will force you to see the diverse beauty and differences in other cultures.*

Sometimes people do not address delicate intercultural issues out of fear—fear of being isolated from friends and family members who may be prejudiced and not motivated themselves. In one study, college students said they censored their communication in class discussions about race because they were afraid their comments would be taken as offensive, racist, or ignorant; they were afraid of being attacked or yelled at, and they didn't want to be perceived as "trying to prove" they weren't racist (Harris, Miller, & Trego, 2004). Tatum (1997) points out that this fear, and the resulting silences, have huge costs to us as individuals and for our society. Individually, when we are not motivated to reach out across cultural divides, we suffer from distorted perception (we don't really know how individuals from other cultures may view us or a particular situation) and a lack of personal growth. On the societal level, when we are not motivated to embrace he following anecdote illustrates how complicated intercultural communication can be. It concerns a well-intentioned individual trying to be sensitive to one group (Native Americans) but inadvertently ignoring the feelings and sensibilities of another (Japanese).

I participated in a week-long cross-cultural seminar last summer in which the participants were from a mix of domestic and international cultural groups. On the first day, as an icebreaker, we took turns introducing the person to the left. There were several international students, including an older Japanese woman, who had a little trouble with English. She introduced her partner in halting English but made only one mistake; she said that her partner (a white American woman) was "Native American." She meant to say that her partner was born in America, but her English wasn't quite fluent.

Immediately, one of the other members of the group raised her hand and said, "I have an ouch," and proceeded to tell the group how important it was that we be honest and tell others when things were bothering us. She said, further, that it bothered her that this woman had been called a Native American when she was not. She emphasized how important it was that people be labeled accurately. She meant well. But the Japanese woman was mortified. She was embarrassed about her English to begin with, and she was really embarrassed at being singled out as being incorrect in her language. She did not say anything at the time. None of the rest of us in the group knew how distressed she was. As soon as the session was over, she went to the workshop leaders and asked to be transferred out of the group.
—Mary

other cultures and other ways of thinking and behavior, our organizations suffer from a loss of productivity and human potential (not everyone gets the opportunity to contribute ideas).

Third, motivation is lacking in contexts in which historical events or political circumstances have resulted in communication breakdowns. For example, it is understandable, given the history of animosity in the Middle East, that Israeli and Arab students would not be motivated to communicate with each other. It is also understandable why a Serbian student would not want to room with a Croatian student, or why a Greek Cypriot would not want to forge a friendship with a Turkish Cypriot, given that these two ethnic communities have been engaged in one of the most protracted international disputes of all time.

To use an example closer to home, many blacks and whites in the United States are not motivated to forge friendships with each other. This may be partly due to social pressure. One study investigated why so few whites have black friends and why the interracial marriage rate is so low between whites and blacks. The researchers analyzed data from three separate ethnographic interview studies of whites and blacks and concluded that lack of interracial friendships is not because of lack of interracial contact. They found that 90% of the whites interviewed grew up in white-only neighborhoods, but even those who grew up in racially mixed neighborhoods and went to racially mixed schools and had the opportunity to form close relationships with African Americans failed to do so. Those who did have black friends as adolescents tended to not maintain these friendships as adults. The researchers conclude that it is not only the social isolation from blacks that prevents whites from forming close friendship. Rather, the limited interaction is a result of "white habitus"—shared negative attitudes about blacks or blaming blacks for not trying harder to make friends with them, and an "oblivion about the racial components of their own socialization" (Bonilla-Silva, Embrick, Ketchum, & Saenz, 2004).

The point here is that it doesn't matter how good a communicator you are if you are not motivated to use those communication skills. For some people, the first step in developing intercultural communication competence may be to examine their motivation to reach out to others who are culturally different.

Knowledge   The **knowledge** component comprises various cognitive aspects of communication competence; it involves what we know about ourselves and others and about various aspects of communication. Perhaps most important is **self-knowledge**—knowing how you may be perceived as a communicator and what your strengths and weaknesses are. How can you know what these are?

Acquiring self-knowledge is a long and sometimes complicated process. It involves being open to information coming in many different ways. A white student describes her growing awareness of what it means to be white in the United States after listening to Chicano and African American guest speakers:

> *They each spoke about their experiences that they have had [with others prejudging them]. . . . We discover our white identity by listening to others. We hear these hardships that they have had to endure and we realize that we never have had to experience that. You learn a lot about yourself that way. . . . By listening to our guests speak today, I realized that sometimes other ethnicities might not view my culture very highly.*

We often don't know how we're perceived because we don't search for this information or because there is not sufficient trust in a relationship for people to reveal such things. **Other-knowledge,** or knowledge about how other people think and behave will also help you be a more effective communicator. However, learning about others in only abstract terms can lead to stereotyping. It is often better to learn through relational experience, as this student did:

> *My friend Jack told me a couple of years ago that he was gay, and we have had many discussions on . . . what it means to be gay. A few years ago I didn't take a stance on whether it was right or wrong to be gay, and if anyone made a joke I would laugh. Now that I gained experience from Jack, I respect his way of life and would always support him. This point is valid because the more one experiences things with other people from different backgrounds, the more one will be able to respect and understand other people.*

Of course, we can't know everything about all cultures or develop relationships with people from all cultural groups, so it's important to develop some

knowledge As an individual component of intercultural communication competence, the quality of knowing about oneself (that is, one's strengths and weaknesses), others, and various aspects of communication.

self-knowledge Related to intercultural communication competence, the quality of knowing how one is perceived as a communicator, as well as one's strengths and weaknesses.

other-knowledge Related to intercultural communication competence, knowledge about how people from other cultures think and behave that will also help you be a more effective communicator.

general knowledge about cultural differences. For example, in this book, we have described cultural variations in both verbal and nonverbal communication. To avoid stereotyping, perhaps it is better simply to be aware of the range in thought and behavior across cultures, and not to assume that because someone belongs to a particular group, he or she will behave in a particular way.

Linguistic knowledge is another important aspect of intercultural competence. Awareness of the difficulty of learning a second language helps us appreciate the extent of the challenges that sojourners and immigrants face in their new cultural contexts. Also, knowing a second or third language expands our communication repertoire and increases our empathy for culturally different individuals. For example, as Judith struggles through her conversational Spanish class, she is reminded again of how difficult it is to accomplish ordinary things in a second language. And when she sits in class and worries that the instructor might call on her, she is reminded of the anxiety of many international students and immigrants trying to navigate a new country and language.

Attitudes   Many **attitudes** contribute to intercultural communication competence, including tolerance for ambiguity, empathy, and nonjudgmentalism.

Tolerance for ambiguity refers to the ease in dealing with situations in which much is unknown. Whether we are abroad or at home, interacting with people who look different from us and who behave in ways that are strange to us requires a tolerance for ambiguity. When Judith was studying Spanish in Mexico recently, she was struck by the range of attitudes of her fellow students from the United States. Some seemed very tolerant of the classroom procedures in Mexico, but others seemed to want the classes to be run as they would be in the States.

Tolerance for ambiguity is one of the most difficult things to attain. As mentioned previously, people have a natural preference for predictability; uncertainty can be disquieting. Nick, an exchange student in Mexico, discusses how tolerance and language ability are particularly important—and problematic—in stressful situations:

> *I had lost my wallet in the marketplace and asked my wife to wire money to me. I couldn't figure out which Western Union location (there are many) I was supposed to go to to pick up my money. I finally went to the central post office, only to be told that my money had been delivered somewhere else—and I couldn't understand where. I was frustrated, tired and worried—and my language skills were deteriorating rapidly! Fortunately, I pulled myself together, tried to be patient, and joked with the postal workers. It took six hours to get my money, but by the end of the day, I had my money and had made some new friends at the post office!*

Empathy refers to the ability to know what it's like to "walk in another person's shoes." Empathic skills are culture bound. We cannot really view the world through another person's eyes without knowing something about his or her experiences and life. To illustrate, suppose a U.S. American and a Japanese have been introduced and are conversing. The Japanese responds to the U.S. American's first remark with a giggle. The U.S. American feels pleasurable empathic sensations and makes an impulsive comment, indicating a congenial,

linguistic knowledge Knowledge of other languages besides one's native language or of the difficulty of learning a second or third language.

attitudes An individual's dispositions or mental sets. As a component of intercultural communication competence, attitudes include tolerance for ambiguity, empathy, and nonjudgmentalism.

tolerance for ambiguity The ease with which an individual copes with situations in which a great deal is unknown.

empathy The capacity to "walk in another person's shoes."

In his book *Last Watch of the Night*, Paul Monette points out that it is important to recognize the many forms of intolerance most of us experience as we grow up. This excerpt is from a speech he gave at the Library of Congress during National Book Week. The writer he refers to, Urvashi Vaid, is a lesbian who has written about issues of tolerance. Think about how the intolerance around you may affect you and how difficult it is sometimes to be tolerant of the many diversities you encounter.

> *Most of our families do the very best they can to bring us up whole and make us worthy citizens. But it's a very rare person who manages to arrive at adulthood without being saddled by some form of racism or sexism or homophobia. It is our task as grownups to face those prejudices in ourselves and rethink them. The absolute minimum we can get out of such a self-examination is tolerance, one for another. We gay and lesbian people believe we should be allowed to celebrate ourselves and give back to the larger culture, make our unique contributions—but if all we get is tolerance, we'll take it and build on it.*
>
> *We don't know what history is going to say even about this week, or where the gay and lesbian revolution is going to go. But we are a revolution that has come to be based very, very strongly on diversity. We have to fight like everyone else to be open in that diversity; but I love Urvashi Vaid's idea that it's not a matter of there being one of each on every board and every faculty and every organization. It's a matter of being each in one. You'll pardon my French, but it's not so hard to be politically correct. All you have to do is not be an ——.*

Source: From Paul Monette, *Last Watch of the Night* (New York: Harcourt Brace, 1994), pp. 122–123.

accepting reaction. However, the Japanese observer now feels intensely uncomfortable. What the U.S. American doesn't realize is that the giggle may not mean that the Japanese is feeling pleasure. Japanese often giggle to indicate embarrassment and unease. In this case, the U.S. American's "empathy" is missing the mark. In this sense, empathy is the capacity to imagine oneself in another role, within the context of one's cultural identity.

Intercultural communication scholars have attempted to come up with a more culturally sensitive view of empathy. For example, Ben Broome (1991, 1993) stresses that to achieve empathy across cultural boundaries, people must forge strong relationships and strive for the creation of shared meaning in their interpersonal encounters. However, because this is difficult to achieve when people come from very different cultural backgrounds, Broome suggests that this shared meaning must be seen as both provisional and dynamic, that understanding is not an all-or-nothing proposition. In addition, cross-cultural empathy must integrate both thinking and feeling—we must try to understand not only what others *say* (content) but also how they *feel* (empathy). Finally, he reminds us that to achieve cross-cultural empathy, we must seek to understand the context of both others' lived experiences and the specific encounters.

Magoroh Maruyama (1970), an anthropologist-philosopher, agrees that achieving cross-cultural empathy and trying to see the world exactly as the other person sees is very difficult. She describes the process as **transpection,** a postmodern phenomenon that often involves trying to learn foreign beliefs, assumptions, perspectives, and feelings in a foreign context. Transpection, then, can be achieved only with practice and requires structured experience and self-reflection.

Communication scholar Milton Bennett (1998) suggests a "Platinum Rule" ("Do unto others as *they themselves* would have done unto them") instead of the Golden Rule ("Do unto others as *you* would have done unto you") (p. 213). This, of course, requires movement beyond a culture-bound sympathy or empathy for others.

Achieving **nonjudgmentalism** is much easier said than done. We might like to think that we do not judge others according to our own cultural frames of reference, but it is very difficult not to do so. One of our colleagues recalls being at a university meeting at which a group of Icelandic administrators and a group of U.S. American faculty were discussing implementing a study-abroad exchange program. The Icelandic faculty were particularly taciturn, and our colleague wanted to lighten up the meeting a little. Eventually, however, she realized that the taciturnity probably reflected different norms of behavior. She had unknowingly judged the tenor of the meeting based on her own style of communication.

The **D.I.E. exercise** is helpful in developing a nonjudgmental attitude (Wendt, 1984). It involves making a distinction between description (D), interpretation (I), and evaluation (E) in the processing of information. Descriptive statements convey factual information that can be verified through the senses (e.g., "There are 25 chairs in the room" and "I am 5 feet tall"). Interpretive statements attach meaning to the description (e.g., "You must be tired"). Evaluative statements clarify how we feel about something (e.g., "When you're always tired, we can't have any fun together"). Only descriptive statements are nonjudgmental.

This exercise can help us recognize whether we are processing information on a descriptive, interpretive, or evaluative level. Confusing the different levels can lead to misunderstanding and ineffective communication. For example, if I think a student is standing too close to me, I may interpret the behavior as "This student is pushy," or I may evaluate it as "This student is pushy, and I don't like pushy students." However, if I force myself to describe the student's behavior, I may say to myself, "This student is standing 8 inches away from me, whereas most students stand farther away." This observation enables me to search for other (perhaps cultural) reasons for the behavior. The student may be worried about a grade and may be anxious to get some questions answered. Perhaps the student is used to standing closer to people than I am. Or perhaps the student really is pushy.

transpection
Cross-cultural empathy.

nonjudgmentalism
Free from evaluating according to one's own cultural frame of reference.

D.I.E. exercise A device that helps us determine if we are communicating at a descriptive, interpretive, or evaluative level. Only descriptive statements are nonjudgmental.

It is impossible to always stay at the descriptive level. But it is important to know when we are describing and when we are interpreting. Most communication is at the interpretive level. For example, have you ever been set up for a blind date and asked for a description of the person? The descriptions you might get (e.g., tall, dark, handsome, nice, kind, generous) are not really descriptions; rather, they are interpretations that reflect individual and cultural viewpoints (Wendt, 1984).

Behaviors and Skills   Behaviors and skills are another component of intercultural competence. What are the most competent behaviors? Are there any universal behaviors that work well in all cultural contexts? At one level, there probably are. Communication scholar Brent D. Ruben devised a list of universal behaviors that actually includes some attitudes. These behaviors are a display of respect, interaction management, ambiguity tolerance, empathy, relational rather than task behavior, and interaction posture (Ruben, 1976, 1977; Ruben & Kealey, 1979).

Some general behaviors seem applicable to many cultural groups and contexts (Koester & Olebe, 1988; Olebe & Koester, 1989). However, these skills become problematic when we try to apply them in specific ways. For example, being respectful works well in all intercultural interactions, and many scholars identify this particular skill as important (Collier, 1988; Martin & Hammer, 1989). However, how one expresses respect behaviorally may vary from culture to culture and from context to context. For example, European Americans show respect by making direct eye contact, whereas some Native Americans show respect by avoiding eye contact. We address the importance of context more fully in the next section.

It is not enough to know how competent behaviors vary from culture to culture, one needs to be able to put that knowledge into practice by demonstrating those behaviors appropriately. Let's see how this works. In one study, Mitch Hammer and his colleagues evaluated the effectiveness of a cross-cultural training program for Japanese and U.S. American managers in a joint venture (a steel company) in Ohio. One goal was to determine if the managers' intercultural communication skills had improved significantly. The research team used a general behavioral framework of communication competence that included the following dimensions: immediacy, involvement, other orientation, interaction management, and social relaxation (Hammer, Martin, Otani, & Koyama, 1990). The two groups (Japanese managers and U.S. American managers) rated these dimensions differently. The U.S. Americans said that the most important dimension was involvement (how expressive one is in conversation), whereas the Japanese managers said that the other orientation (being tuned in to the other person) was most important. The researchers also judged how well each group of managers adapted to the other group's communication style. They videotaped the interaction and asked Japanese raters to judge the U.S. American managers on how well they adapted to the Japanese style, and vice-versa. For example, good interaction management for the Japanese meant initiating and terminating interaction and making sure everyone had a chance to talk; for U.S. Americans, it meant illiam Howell (1982), a renowned intercultural scholar, investigated how top CEOs made decisions. He found, to his surprise, that they did not follow the analytic process prescribed in business school courses—analysis of cost, benefits, and so on. Rather, they made decisions in a very holistic way. Howell emphasized that intercultural communication is similar, that only so much can be gained by conscious analysis, and that the highest level of communication competence requires a combination of holistic and analytic thinking. He identified four levels of intercultural communication competence: (1) unconscious incompetence, (2) conscious incompetence, (3) conscious competence, and (4) unconscious competence.

Unconscious incompetence is the "be yourself" approach, in which we are not conscious of differences and do not need to act in any particular way. Sometimes this works. However, being ourselves works best in interactions with individuals who are very similar to us. In intercultural contexts, being ourselves often means that we're not very effective and don't realize our ineptness.

At the level of **conscious incompetence,** people realize that things may not be going very well in the interaction, but they are not sure why. Most of us have experienced intercultural interactions in which we felt that something wasn't quite right but couldn't quite figure out what it was. This describes the feeling of conscious incompetence.

As instructors of intercultural communication, we teach at a conscious, intentional level. Our instruction focuses on analytic thinking and learning. This describes the level of **conscious competence.** Reaching this level is a necessary part of the process of becoming a competent communicator. Howell would say that reaching this level is necessary but not sufficient.

Unconscious competence is the level at which communication goes smoothly but is not a conscious process. You've probably heard of marathon runners "hitting the wall," or reaching the limits of their endurance. Usually, inexplicably, they continue running past this point. Communication at the unconscious competent level is like this. This level of competence is not something we can acquire by consciously trying to. It occurs when the analytic and holistic parts are functioning together. When we concentrate too hard or get too analytic, things don't always go easier.

You've probably had the experience of trying unsuccessfully to recall something, letting go of it, and then remembering it as soon as you're thinking about something else. This is what unconscious competence is—being well prepared cognitively and attitudinally, but knowing when to "let go" and rely on your holistic cognitive processing.

asking opinions of the Japanese, being patient with silence, and avoiding strong disagreement and assertive statements. As this example shows, intercultural communication competence means being able to exhibit or adapt to different kinds of behaviors, depending on the other person's or group's cultural background.

n this essay, S. L. Rosen discusses the powerful stereotyping (or essential-izing) of Asian people—referred to as Orientalism. By way of illustration, he analyzes a description of Japanese taken from a travelers' guidebook.

Orientalism is a total misseeing of the other through a veil of interpreta-tions of reality which are relatively impenetrable and resistant to change. . . . Orientalism as cultural myth has been articulated through metaphors which characterize the East in ways which emphasize its strangeness and other-ness . . . the Oriental person is a single image, a sweeping generalization; an essentialized image which carries with it the taint of inferiority.

To give one powerful example of this essentializing process of image formation which is entailed by Orientalism, we quote from a book entitled When Cultures Collide *by Richard D. Lewis (1982), a kind of manual for people traveling and doing business around the world to help them understand the various cultures they come in contact with. By no means the worst of its kind, Lewis' book expresses very well the way we use metaphors to trivialize another culture in a totalistic way, so as to make it easier to capture it in the network of our own understandings.*

- *Japanese children are encouraged to be completely dependent and keep a sense of interdependence throughout their lives.*
- *Everything must be placed in context in Japan.*
- *Japanese are constrained by their thought processes in a language very different from any other.*
- *They do not like meeting newcomers.*
- *They represent their group and cannot therefore pronounce on any matters with-out consultation and cannot initiate an exchange of views.*
- *Westerners are individuals, but the Japanese represent a company which repre-sents Japan.*
- *As we all know, Japanese do not like to lose face.*
- *The Japanese go to incredible lengths to be polite. . . .*

This kind of Orientalism [essentializing] carries with it the implication that Asian people are much more conformist than we are, and less respecting of the dignity of indi-vidual rights, i.e., inferior. Social and cognitive psychology tells us that stereotyping is a kind of mental schema making designed to help us grasp reality—to make things more understandable and less threatening; these mental schema such as stereotypes provide us with the illusion of understanding by dividing up and categorizing the flux of experi-ence into easily manageable cognitive maps. Orientalism has been the prevalent mode by which this cognitive need to schematize has manifested itself in apprehending Asian people.

Source: From S. L. Rosen, "Japan as Other: Orientalism and Cultural Conflict," *Intercultural Communication, 4,* 2000; www.immi.se/intercultural.

While it is useful to acquire knowledge about how competent behaviors vary from culture to culture, as in the cross-cultural training program just described, this analytical knowledge may not be sufficient. A renowned communication scholar, William Howell, suggested that the most competent intercultural communicators are those who consciously acquire knowledge, but who also strive for an "unconscious competence" (see Point of View box).

Interpretive Perspective: Competence in Contexts

As we have stressed throughout this book, an important aspect of being a competent communicator is understanding the context in which communication occurs. Intercultural communication happens in many contexts. An interpretive perspective reminds us that a good communicator is sensitive to these contexts. (See Figure 12-1.)

Consider how definitions for competence may vary from one cultural context to another. In one research project we asked European American and Latino students to identify nonverbal behaviors that they thought would be competent in various contexts. The Latino students placed importance on approachability behaviors (e.g., smiling, laughing, pleasant facial expression) in *task* contexts. In contrast, non-Latino students reported that it was more important to exhibit these behaviors in *social* contexts (Martin, Hammer, & Bradford, 1994). These results probably reflect the importance in the Latino community of establishing personal rapport with those they work with (e.g., smiling, laughing, etc.), which sets a good "atmosphere." In contrast, non-Latino white cultural patterns often include a strong distinction between work and social relationships. Laughing and smiling—behaviors that typically communicate liking—are expected in pleasant social situations; however, one need not like a person one works with and therefore, in a task situation, it is not necessarily important to smile, laugh, etc., in order to accomplish a joint task.

Another study examined intercultural communication competence in medical contexts (Rosenberg, Richard, Lussier, & Abdool, 2006). Using the framework described earlier (motivation, attitudes, behaviors), researchers examined (through observation and in-depth interviews) the degree to which the Canadian physicians were competent in their intercultural communication with immigrant patients. They found that intercultural competence in this context involved getting to know the cultural identities of their patients, something that most physicians did not think was essential in their job. Those physicians who were most competent took time to understand cultural barriers, showed interest in patient's cultural background, realized that some medical practices might not be culturally appropriate, and identified a similarity between themselves and their patients. Their patients described their satisfaction with these physicians, saying, "She knows me; she knows my family" or "She's a woman too, so she can understand" (p. 244).

What about intercultural communication competence in mediated contexts? As we've discussed in earlier chapters, the lack of nonverbal cues (behaviors that communicate a liking and positive attitude toward the other and that establish

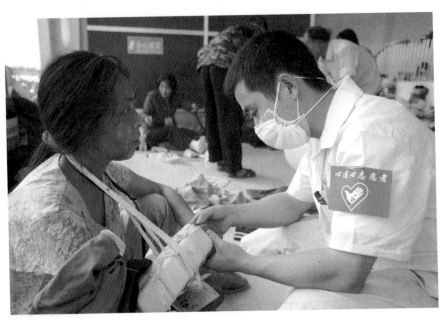

FIGURE 12-1   Intercultural competence in medical contexts may involve getting to know the cultural identities of patients—taking time to understand cultural barriers and showing interest in the patient's cultural background. (© *Ryan Pyle/Corbis*)

one's identity) are absent in CMC. Perhaps this requires slightly different (or additional) skills—especially involving issues of identity and language expression. First, consider how different cultures value identity expression. For example, some cultural groups place high importance on knowing the identity of a person before entering into relationships. Since much of our identity is expressed nonverbally (how we look and our conversational style), mediated conversations pose challenges. Identity is also expressed verbally, through communication style and humor (not always easily translatable across cultures and particularly difficult in cyberspace). Identity expression can also involve bragging—not viewed positively in all cultures (St. Amant, 2002). A final note about language—mediated contexts can actually facilitate communication between persons not sharing a native language, since they have more time to interpret and understand the other (the text/words are durable), as well as time to phrase their own messages (Osman & Herring, 2007). It is probably a good idea to use humor sparingly, since it is even more difficult to translate in cyberspace and is viewed in different ways in various cultures.

We have emphasized that *many* contexts can influence intercultural communication. For instance, by focusing only on the historical context, you may overlook the relational context; by emphasizing the cultural context, you may be ignoring the gender or racial contexts of the intercultural interaction; and so on. It may seem difficult to keep all of these shifting contexts in mind. However, by analyzing your own intercultural successes and failures, you will come to a better understanding of intercultural communication.

Another aspect of context is the communicator's position within a speech community. Reflect on your own social position in relation to various speech communities and contexts. For example, if you are the only woman in a largely male environment or the only person of color in an otherwise white community, you may face particular expectations or have people project motivations onto your messages. Recognizing your own relation to the speech community and the context will help you better understand intercultural communication.

Critical Perspective: Competence for Whom?

A critical perspective reminds us that individuals' competence may be constrained by the political, economic, and historical contexts. Intercultural communication scholar Mary Jane Collier (1998) reflects,

> *I have come to see that competence, a central issue in my early work, is a construct that is based on implicit privilege. . . . Relevant questions from postcolonial critics include, "Competence and acceptance from whom? Who decides the criteria? Who doesn't? Competent or acceptable on the basis of what social and historical context?" (p. 142)*

Early research on communication competence, conducted largely by white researchers and using data from white respondents, failed to take into account issues of power differentials in understanding competence. Later research, based on data from a variety of ethnic and racial groups, expanded the definition and concept of competence to include issues of stereotyping, powerlessness, and authenticity (Martin, Hecht, & Larkey, 1994). The point is that powerful groups are not likely to focus on these issues, and yet they must be taken into consideration when trying to understand the dimensions of competence. For example, African Americans report that they use stronger, more assertive, aggressive and divergent strategies not identified in previous competence studies in order to be effective in interethnic interactions (Martin, Hecht, Moore, & Larkey, 2001).

For another example, characteristics of effective communication for women in the United States have changed dramatically in the last 50 years. In the 1960s, an "effective" female communicator was expected to be rather passive (both verbally and nonverbally), indirect, and nurturing. Assertive women met with disapproval and sanctions. Today, the "effective" female is expected to behave rather differently from this. As the 21st century unfolds, there is a broader range of acceptable behaviors that define competence for females. They may be unassertive in some contexts, but they are also free, and even expected, to be more assertive in many contexts. Similarly, effective black communicators in the 1960s were expected to be nonassertive in verbal and nonverbal style. Blacks like Muhammad Ali who went against these expectations were severely sanctioned. In short, we need to understand that notions of communication competence depend on specific social, political, and historical contexts. And we need to question who is setting these standards.

Regarding the problematizing of "competence," consider the goals of intercultural interaction: Why do we want to be competent? Because we enjoy interacting with individuals whose backgrounds are different from our own? Is it because we want to sell products, or because we want to convert people to our religion? Because we want to change the world? Or bring about social justice? It is worth examining our own and others' goals in intercultural encounters and to ask whose interests are being served.

These are important questions raised by the critical perspective that force us to rethink intercultural communication competence. Indeed, you now have the skills to push your own thinking about intercultural communication—both strengths and weaknesses—as they help and hinder your ability to communicate.

APPLYING KNOWLEDGE ABOUT INTERCULTURAL COMMUNICATION

Now that we have taken you down the path of intercultural communication, we would like to conclude with specific suggestions for becoming better intercultural communicators. Our dialectical approach recognizes the important role of individual skills *and* contextual constraints in improving intercultural relations. The dialectical perspective also emphasizes the relational aspects of intercultural communication. Perhaps the first step in applying our knowledge to intercultural communication is to recognize the connectedness of humans and the importance of dialogue.

Entering Into Dialogue

To recognize and embrace our connectedness even to people who are different from us, we have to engage in true dialogue. A central notion of dialogue is sharing and reciprocity. Communication scholars Starosta and Chen (2005) suggest that a focus on mutual *listening*, instead of talking, forms the core of successful intercultural dialogue. How to do this? A "sharing of narratives" is one metaphor:

> We come to the world with a master narrative that explains what things are, which ones count for what, what is good or bad about them, and we "braid" these accounts of fact and value into a somewhat coherent personal web of meaning. (p. 277)

Starosta and Chen go on to suggest that a good intercultural listener exchanges narrative accounts to expand his or her repertoire of possibilities in explaining the world—and this interest and skill is built on a foundation of openness, curiosity, and empathy.

An Eastern model of listening is also useful here. Japanese scholar Ishii (1984) models intercultural communication as listening. In this model, the effective intercultural communicator, sensitive to the other, thinks *carefully* before speaking and delivers a message that is never threatening or condemnatory and one that appears open to multiple possible interpretations. The listener hears the message, considers it, reconsiders it, trying on different possible interpretations—trying here are many small interventions we might make in everyday life to change what we take for granted. Note how this student has learned to use intercultural relationships as a part of her antiracism struggle.

I am beginning to see the long-term benefits of intercultural relationships: acquiring knowledge about the world, breaking stereotypes, and acquiring new skills. I did not have any stereotypes of Brazilians before I met Anna, but I tell all my family and friends about her, so if any of them had any prior stereotypes, they may think differently now. I have also found that when you are friends with a person of a different culture, it tends to promote some sort of peace and unity in some small way. If I am with someone of a different culture, people are less likely to make racial remarks of any kind in front of them. For example, a co-worker of mine often tells jokes about gay or black people in front of workers that are white and seemingly heterosexual. When I bring a friend into work or go out with work friends that are of a different culture (Spanish, Ukrainian, or Brazilian), he will not tell these jokes. Although my friends are not even of the culture that he makes fun of, I think he is not sure of how his jokes will go over with people he sees as being "ethnic." Regardless, the jokes stop, and that is a step toward preventing racial discrimination.
—Michele

to understand the speaker's possible intent. When the listener believes she has understood the point being made, she frames a response, again in a nonthreatening manner. You can see that ambiguity is a feature of such listening, which may seem contradictory to other guidelines for competent communication that extol being clear and concise. Perhaps this points to a dialectical view. Intercultural dialogue may have to be clear *and* somewhat ambiguous.

But how can we *really* hear the voices of those who come from cultures very different from our own—and especially those who have not been heard from? As you think about all the messages you hear every day, the most obvious voices and images are often the most privileged. To resist the tendency to focus only on the loudest, most obvious voices, we should strive for "harmonic discourse." This is discourse in which all voices "retain their individual integrity, yet combine to form a whole discourse that is orderly and congruous" (Stewart, 1997, p. 119).

Any conciliation between cultures must reclaim the notion of a voice for *all* interactants. In intercultural contexts, there are two options for those who feel left out—exit or expression. When people feel excluded, they often simply shut down, physically or mentally abandoning the conversation. When this happens, their potential contributions—to some decision, activity, or change—are lost. Obviously, the preferred alternative is to give voice to them. People's silence is broken when they feel that they can contribute, that their views are valued. And those who have historically been silenced sometimes need an invitation. Or those who have a more reserved conversation style may need prompting, as was the case with this traveler from Finland:

> *I was on a business trip in England with some colleagues. We visited universities, where we were shown different departments and their activities. The presenters spoke volubly, and we, in accordance with Finnish speaking rules, waited for our turn in order to make comments and ask questions. However, we never got a turn; neither had we time to react to the situations.*

In sum, one way to become a more competent communicator is to work on "dialogue" skills by trying to engage in true dialogue. It's important to work on speaking and listening skills. A second step is to become interpersonal allies with people from other cultures.

Becoming Interpersonal Allies

The dialectical approach involves becoming allies with others, in working for better intergroup relations. But we need a new way to think about multicultural-ism and cultural diversity—one that recognizes the complexities of communi-cating across cultures and that addresses power issues. Otherwise, we can get stuck within a competitive framework: If we win something, the other person or group loses, and we can *only* win if others lose. This kind of thinking can make us feel frustrated and guilty.

The goal is to find a way in which we can achieve equitable unity despite holding many different and contradictory truths, a unity based on conscious coalition, a unity of affinity and political kinship, in which we all win.

intercultural alliances Bonds between individuals or groups across cultures characterized by a shared recognition of power and the impact of history and by an orientation of affirmation.

How can we do this? We first identify what **intercultural alliances** might look like. Communication scholar Mary Jane Collier (1998) interviewed many people in intercultural friendships and identified three issues that characterize intercultural alliances. The first has to do with power and privilege: Intercultural friends recognize and try to understand how ethnic, gender, and class differ-ences lead to power and try to manage these power issues.

In their study of college students, Chesler, Peet, and Sevig (2003) described how difficult it is to understand power issues in interracial relationships. Their findings are based on interviews with white college students. They found that most students came to college with little experience in interracial relations and were generally unaware or held negative attitudes toward racial issues, or even saw themselves as victims, as described by one young man:

> *I think white males have a hard time because we are constantly blamed for being power-holding oppressors, yet we are not given many concrete ways to change. Then we just feel guilty or rebel. (p. 227)*

Through educational and personal experiences, some did come to under-stand privilege, but it is often a difficult process. As we discussed in Chapter 5, it involves a phase of feeling guilty and paralyzed. As one student described it, "I was horribly liberal-guilt ridden, paralyzed, I was totally blowing every little minor interaction that I had with people of color way out of proportion. . . . I saw how hard it was for me to stop doing that and start being more productive" (p. 227).

Understanding and acknowledging one's privilege, as Collier notes, is often necessary in intercultural friendships. This student describes this acknowledgment:

I learned that being white, [there are] so many privileges that I didn't even know of . . . like loans from the bank, not being stopped by the police and other things me and white kids can get away with. I had not noticed the extent to which white privilege has affected and continues to affect many aspects of my everyday life. I thought "I" had accomplished so much, but how much of where I am is due to my accumulated privilege, my family, economic status, school advantages? (Chesler et al., 2003, p. 227)

Being on two different sides of the power issue can challenge individuals in intercultural relationships. For example, Eleanor, an African American woman, and her friend Mairead, who is white, describe how they negotiate this issue in their own relationship. Often the only African American participating in discussions of race, Eleanor says she gets tired of "educating white girls" about racism. Mairead recognizes the problem of unwittingly saying or doing racist things and "hurting my friend." This is not merely a matter of benign faux pas, but is an ongoing source of oppression for black women, something with far deeper implications than simply saying the right thing in a social situation involving equals (McCullough, 1998, p. 83). Eleanor sometimes needs to withdraw from her white friends to restore herself. For her part, Mairead recognizes that she needs to educate herself about issues of racism. And the two women realize that negotiating time-out from a friendship or time to work on personal issues alone is one aspect of intercultural friendship in a racially segregated society.

Collier's (1998) second component of intercultural alliances has to do with the impact of history: Intercultural friends recognize that people from historically powerful groups view history differently than do those who belong to less powerful groups. As we learned in Chapter 4, history often plays an important part in intercultural interactions. One of our colleagues describes how she and her friend Michael had very different views on history:

I was always amazed at how often my friend Michael talked about his relatives' experience during the Holocaust—even though his family wasn't directly involved. He was constantly told as he was growing up that prejudice against Jews could easily lead to another holocaust—and that he always had to be vigilant against anti-Semitism. For me, not being Jewish, I used to get impatient with him, but after learning more about the history and getting to know Michael better, I realize that this is an important part of who he is, and I've actually learned a lot from him about the experiences of a group of people that I knew little about. And I appreciate that side of him better.

History also plays a part in black–white relationships. We're often struck by how, in discussions about race in our classes, white students go to great lengths to affirm that they aren't racist, often telling stories about friends and family members—who, unlike them, are racist. They seem to want to be absolved of past or present responsibilities where race was concerned. And whites expect

My roommate is from Poland; we are allies. We have similar traits in common. We also study the same major. Having the same course of study really helps us understand one another as it takes a certain type of personality to be successful. Understanding what it takes to be a good intercultural ally is indeed a learning process. There are many things that my Polish roommate does that I disagree with. But because he is from another culture I learn to understand what makes him unique and different. I have shared many meals with his extended family and even had him translate a Polish television show. I have met and enjoy being around his Polish friends.

—David

persons of color to communicate in ways that are friendly, comfortable, and absolving. In this case, true dialogue for whites involves a genuine commitment to listening, to not being defensive, and to recognizing the historical contexts that impact us all. True intercultural friends accept rather than question others' experiences, particularly when historical inequities and power issues are involved. They recognize the importance of historical power differentials and affirm others' cultural experiences even when this calls into question their own worldviews.

Collier's (1998) third component of intercultural alliances has to do with orientations of affirmation. Intercultural friends value and appreciate differences and are committed to the relationship even when they encounter difficulties and misunderstandings. For example, our student Shara comes from a cultural background that emphasizes commitment to family and family obligations. Her friend Kati has very little contact with her parents and siblings. They aren't estranged; they just aren't close. Kati would like to spend time with Shara on holidays, but Shara always spends holidays with her family, who live in another state. This issue has caused tension between the two over the years. But they each realize that these different values are important aspects of their identities. And in complex and dialectical ways, they learn from each other. Shara sometimes envies Kati for her relative freedom and lack of family obligations. But she also feels sorry for Kati that she doesn't have the kind of family support to back her up when she needs help. Similarly, Kati envies Shara's relationships with her large extended family and all the activities and help they provide. But she also sometimes feels sorry for Shara that she never seems to have any time for herself.

Building Coalitions

As we have emphasized throughout this book, many identities and contexts give meaning to who you really are. That is, your identities of gender, sexual orientation, race, region, religion, age, social class, and so on gain specific meaning and force in different contexts. Coalitions can arise from these multiple identities. There are many good examples, such as the Seeds of Peace project, which brings together Jewish and Palestinian young people to work toward peace and harmony.

Other local coalitions work to promote dialogue between blacks and whites, and between gays and straights. Another example is the post-9/11 book club coalition of Christian, Jewish, and Muslim women (see "Point of View" box on page 486).

Some contexts that arise in the future may cause you to rethink many of your identities. The rhetoric that people use to mobilize coalitions may speak to you in various ways. As you strive to build better intercultural relations, you may need to transcend some of your identities, as the workers in Hawaii did, or you may reinforce other identities. These shifting identities allow you to build coalitions among seemingly different peoples, to foster positive intercultural relationships for a better world.

Coalitions, which are built of multiple identities, are never easy to build. In the process, you may find that some of your own identities feel neglected or injured. Part of the process is the commitment to work through these emotional blows, rather than simply withdrawing to the safety of older identities. Work your way to a richer, more meaningful life by navigating between safety and stability, and change.

Social Justice and Transformation

As we near the end our journey, we would like to refer back to our ethical challenge in the first chapter—the responsibility that comes with the acquisition of intercultural knowledge and insights. As we noted then, this educational experience is not just transformative for you, the individual, but should also benefit the larger society and other cultural groups in the increasingly interdependent world.

The first step in working for social justice is acknowledging that oppression and inequities exist—as we have tried to point out, cultural differences are not just interesting and fascinating, they exist within a hierarchy in which some are privileged and set the rules for others (Allen, 2004).

Social inequities are sometimes manifested in work contexts. For example, workplace bullying—the ill treatment and hostile behavior toward people at work—has recently become a topic of interest to organizational communication scholars. Bullying behaviors range from the most subtle, even unconscious, incivilities to the most blatant, intentional emotional abuse and in some instances are targeted at others explicitly based on race/ethnicity. A recent study explored the connection between workplace bullying and racism for Asian Americans, African Americans, Latinos, and whites (Fox & Stallworth, 2005). The researchers found that while laws and norms no longer condone overtly racist behaviors, the workplace provides many opportunities for "subtle, even unconscious manifestations of racism, including neglect, incivility, humor, ostracism, inequitable treatment and other forms of 'micro-aggression' (p. 439). Their results showed that experiences with general bullying were similar (and surprisingly frequent) across the four racial/ethnic groups; 97% of the respondents had experienced some type of general bullying. Members of the three ethnic minority groups reported higher instances of bullying based on race/ethnicity than whites. Many of the reported incidents involved a supervisor or occurred with the knowledge of supervisors. The instances were often subtle, seemingly relatively innocuous n outlining specific ways in which white people can fight racism, Paul Kivel lists questions they can ask to better understand specific contexts in which they live and work.

WORKPLACE

1. *What is the gender, race and class composition in your workplace? Which groups hold which positions?*

2. *Who, by race, gender and class, has the power to make decisions about hiring, firing, wages and working conditions in your workplace? Who gets promoted and who doesn't?*

3. *Is hiring non-discriminatory? Are job openings posted and distributed? Do they attract a wide variety of applicants? Are certain groups excluded? Does the diversity of your workplace reflect the diversity of the wider community?*

4. *Are there "invisible" workers, people who cook, clean or do maintenance, for example, who are not generally noticed or paid well?*

5. *What is the racial composition of the people who actually own your workplace? Who makes money from the profits of your work?*

RELIGION

1. *What is your religious upbringing?*

2. *What did you learn about people of color in Sunday school or sermons? About Jewish people?*

3. *Was your religious community all white? Was the leadership of your religious organization all white?*

behaviors by themselves, but when delivered incessantly, the cumulative effects on the victims are of an unimaginable magnitude, leading to a general decrease in confidence in the organization and lack of confidence in the possibility of addressing or resolving the issues.

Starosta and Chen (2005) point out that intercultural listening should be followed by application. Dialogue should ultimately set things right that have been wrong. Good listening "promotes intercultural and interracial harmony, the amelioration of poverty, the introduction of justice, and mutual respect and harmony" (p. 282).

Johnson (2001) gives the following very concrete suggestions for working toward social justice and personal transformation.

1. Acknowledge that trouble exists. There are many obstacles to doing this. Many involved in oppression—those at the top—deny it, trivialize, call it something else, or blame those who are oppressed.

4. *What attitudes were expressed about people of color through discussion of missionary work, charity or social problems?*

5. *What do you know about the history of resistance to racism in your religious denomination?*

HOME AND FAMILY

1. *Were people of color and racism talked about in your childhood home? Think about particular incidents when it was. Was there tension around it? What was the general tone? Who initiated discussions and who resisted them?*

2. *Was there silence in your home on issues of racism or anti-Semitism? What did you learn from the silence?*

3. *As a child, what stories, TV shows or books influenced you the most in your attitudes about people of color? What do you carry with you from that exposure?*

4. *Talk with your partner, housemates and friends about [racial] issues. Notice the whiteness of your surroundings out loud to family and friends. This needn't be done aggressively or with great anger. You don't need to attack other people. Ask questions, notice things out loud, express your concerns and give other people room to think about and respond to what you say.*

5. *If you did a room-by-room assessment of your home today, would you find a diversity of images and items? If the answer is no, what do you and other family members lose because of that lack? How does it contribute to racial prejudice and discrimination?*

Source: From Paul Kivel, *Uprooting Racism: How White People Can Work for Racial Justice,* (Gabriola Island, BC: New Society Publishers, 1996), pp. 182–183, 199, 222.

2. Pay attention. We have given you many suggestions for how to "pay attention," including intercultural listening. Johnson points out that there is a great deal of literature available representing many marginalized "voices," but these are rarely heard. For this reason, he suggests it is a good idea not to rely on the media for meaningful analysis of social oppression and inequalities—there is little money to be made from the stories of the powerless. While the media often give play to people of color who criticize affirmative action, or women who criticize feminism, there is little attention given to serious discussions of gender and violence, or class and race issues.

3. Do something. The more you pay attention to privilege and oppression, the more you'll see opportunities to do something.

   Make noise, be seen. Stand up, volunteer, speak out, write letters, sign petitions, show up. Every oppressive system feeds on silence.

his essay gives an example of an intercultural coalition—how a post-9/11 book club brought Christian, Jewish, and Muslim women together to become interpersonal allies.

Laughter rings out in the salmon-colored living room of the parsonage at First Church in Cambridge, Mass. More than a dozen women—Christian, Jewish, and Muslim—are sharing insights garnered from "Gilead," a 2004 novel about the faith and struggles of a Christian minister in Iowa.

The easy camaraderie as they discuss their distinctive approaches to prayer reflects three years of monthly meetings of the Daughters of Abraham, as they call themselves. The book club has explored the realms of the three monotheistic faiths—and blossomed into comfortable relationships that reach into each other's daily lives. . . .

The club's origin, however, lies in the immediate anguish of Sept. 11, 2001. That night, an interfaith service hastily called by the minister at First Church (United Church of Christ) packed the sanctuary.

"The service was powerful and people were crying; there were women in head scarves sitting next to me," recalls club founder Edie Howe. "I had this strong thought of how we were all the children of Abraham, and how unnecessary and tragic it was. I thought, 'What can I do about this?'"

Her answer was to start the women's book club as a first step toward improving understanding. To ensure a joint commitment, she sought out Jews and Muslims who might share her interest and held planning discussions. A group of 18 met for the first time in September 2002 and has been meeting ever since. Though expectations vary, all share an interest in how other faiths are expressed in individual lives. . . .

Keeping a booklist, they vote on priorities and read a book a month, alternating among the three religions. Tastes range across novels, history, poetry, memoirs, and religious philosophy. During their summer hiatus in

Find little ways to withdraw supports from paths of least resistance. You can start with yourself—by not laughing at racist or heterosexist jokes, or objecting to others' jokes.

I remember the first time I met my sister's boyfriend and he made a disparaging reference to gay people, I knew I had to say something. I objected in a nice way, and we ended up talking for hours. I think he had just never thought about it very much and we're good friends to this day, although we disagree on almost every political and social issue!

Dare to make people feel uncomfortable, beginning with yourself. Ask your professors how many people of color are on the college's communication faculty. Ask why administrators at your children's schools are white men and why the teachers and secretaries are women. You might think this doesn't make much difference, but it can. . . . And discomfort is unavoidable. One student describes

2004—after the group had developed a level of trust—they read books on the history and politics of the Middle East.

"The Crusades Through Arab Eyes" was particularly informative, says Ms. Fischman, because of its non-Western vantage point.

"One book that really struck me was 'The Rock,' a historical novel by Iraqi author Kanan Makiya about the building of the Dome of the Rock in Jerusalem," says Ms. Minton. "The book quotes extensively from Jewish, Christian, and Muslim sacred texts but doesn't give you the footnote on the page. The quotes are so similar you can't tell where they come from without looking them up in the back."

From Islamic poetry, to a mystery involving the ritual baths of Jewish tradition, to C. S. Lewis's exploration of good and evil in "The Screwtape Letters," the varied choices spur conversation on the commonalities and differences in beliefs and practices. And sometimes they reveal surprising similarities. . . .

Most club members are heartened by the way it has spilled into their lives.

"People meet for lunch, help out when members are not well, suggest a good movie—like Jewish or Iranian film festivals—and [have] dinner ahead of time," says Ms. Howe. "And they attend weddings, bar mitzvahs, celebrations at the end of Ramadan."

Wherever the book club discussions roam, they clearly have come to be meaningful for those participating. It's still going strong, Minton says, because of the quality of the relationships, the fun and laughter, and the intellectual stimulation.

"We always come out of the meeting feeling better than when we went in."

Source: From J. Lampman, "How a Post-9/11 Book Club Brought Christian, Jewish, and Muslim Women Together," *Christian Science Monitor*, November 30, 2005, pp. 14–16.

her discomfort: "I love movies, and now I point out all the instances of racist and homophobic humor in movies. My friends think I'm nuts, but they humored me, and now they're starting to point them out to me."

Actively promote change in how systems are organized around privilege. (See the "Point of View" box earlier in this chapter with Kivel's lists of questions to ask in workplace, houses of worship, home and family.)

Don't keep it to yourself. Work with other people—build interpersonal alliances and build coalitions, as discussed earlier. Join organizations dedicated to change the systems that produce privilege and oppression. Most college and university campuses have student organizations that work on issues of gender, race, and sexual orientation. A list of such organizations follows.

National Association for the Advancement of Colored People (NAACP)

National Organization for Women (NOW)

National Conference for Community and Justice

National Gay and Lesbian Task Force

The Southern Poverty Law Center

The National Organization of Men against Sexism

National Urban League

There are also many opportunities on the Internet. Conhaim (2004) points out the many Web-based projects through which Internet users can participate in online dialogues, gain insights into many different global cultures, and work for social justice. See the "Internet Resources for Intercultural Interaction," section at the end of this chapter.

Forgiveness

Sometimes the cultural divide simply seems too huge. Sometimes there are grievances perpetrated by one cultural group upon another or by one individual on another that are so brutal as to make the suggestions listed above sound hollow and idealistic. What can we say to the widow of Daniel Pearl, the *Wall Street Journal* writer who was brutally murdered in Pakistan? He and his wife were known for promoting intercultural understanding in their personal and professional lives. Or to Pauline Mitchell, the mother of Fred Martinez, a Native American who was brutally murdered because he was *nadleeh* (a Native American term meaning "two spirited—with spirit of both male and female"). His mother described the horror of his death: "He'd been chased, beaten with a rock. He had been left to bleed, with a fractured skull, alone in the dark in a little canyon. . . ."

We would like to return to the notion of forgiveness we introduced in Chapter 11. Although limited and problematic, forgiveness is an option for promoting intercultural understanding and reconciliation. As we noted, forgiveness is more than a simple rite of religious correctness; it requires a deep intellectual and emotional commitment during moments of great pain. It also requires a letting go, a moving on, a true transformation of spirit.

Forgiveness has been likened to a train. People get on the train but must make various stops before forgiveness becomes a way off. The trick is not to miss your stop. And perhaps we might remember these cautionary words from Philip Yancy, an award-winning Christian author who writes about grace and forgiveness in the face of atrocities and brutality: "The only thing harder than forgiveness is the alternative" (quoted in Henderson, 1999, p. 176).

McCullough poses the question: "So if you set out to build 'the forgiving society' a society in which forgiveness flourishes and revenge is ever more infrequent what sorts of conditions and institutions would you need to put in place? And what kind of society would you end up with?" (p. 180). His answer is strongly related to the contact hypothesis that we discussed in Chapter 4. That is, leaders must construct conditions of contact among groups that lead to decategorization and recategorization, opportunities to develop intimate positive knowledge of each other, and provide superordinate goals that foster cooperation. For example, the Seeds of Peace program, started about 15 years ago, is trying to encourage the right kinds of contact. Seeds of Peace is a summer camp where adolescents from warring groups and countries are chosen by their education ministries on the basis of their leadership potential to participate in the camp. The entire agenda is structured around activities that help campers "develop durable friendships with people from the other side, appreciation and respect for the concerns that keep the conflict going and firm conviction that a peaceful and respectful coexistence is possible" (p. 200). The goal is simple: by building up a reserve of new positive experiences, these young leaders can use them as a sort of psychological buffer to help them undo the vicious ingroup-outgroup revenge that they will return to after camp.

The Amish are another group of people that try very hard to foster a life of forgiveness and peaceful relations—persecuted to the point of extinction in Europe in the 17th century, they came to America and settled. As Michael McCullough describes it, the Amish had 400 years to prepare their response to what happened on October 2, 2006, when a gunman entered a one-room Amish schoolhouse in Nickel Mines, Pennsylvania, sent the young male students and adults out of the school, tied up 10 girl students and then shot and killed 5, wounded 5 more, and then shot himself. As soon as it happened, those in the community who knew the Amish well, told reporters at the scene that the Amish would find a way to forgive the killer. As Mennonite scholar Donald Kraybill, describes it, "the blood was hardly dry on the bare, board floor of the West Nickel Mines School when Amish parents sent words of forgiveness to the family of the killer who had executed their children" (Kraybill, 2006, C01).

Amish aren't the only ones; many famous proponents of peace and forgiveness—Martin Luther King, Mahatma Ghandi, Desmond Tutu—are motivated by deep religious beliefs concerning forgiveness. However, the link between religion and forgiveness is tricky. As Michael McCullough (2008) points out, religion can motivate forgiveness (as described earlier), but also revenge. The great monotheistic religions of the world (Christianity, Judaism, and Islam) have perpetrated great violence on others in the name of religion. While many religious people say they disapprove of revenge in theory, there have been many studies that show their true feelings. A 2004 study showed that conservative U.S. Americans with strong religious beliefs were nearly 3 times more likely (than Americans with lower religiosity) to believe that Muslim Americans' movement should be monitored by the government, 50% more likely to think that the U.S. should be able to detain terrorists indefinitely and 50% more likely to think that Islam encourages violence more than other religions. . . . Christian beliefs seem to motivate people to be tough not only on terrorists but also on the millions of American Muslims who've done absolutely nothing wrong (Nisbet & Shanahan, 2004). In another study, people who made frequent donations to their churches (a measure of devoutness) administered higher levels of shock to their provokers than did the infrequent donors, even when statistically controlling for age, gender, and other measures of religious behavior (Greer, Berman, Varan, Bobrycki, & Watson, 2005).

Perhaps a useful way to look at the role of religions is to see them as strong viable forces—capable of great good and also violence. "Religions are here for the

n this essay, the writer addresses the complexities of the notion of forgiveness. He begins the essay talking about the delayed justice in the case of the
1958 bombing of the black church in Birmingham, Alabama, that killed four
little girls. Roy Wilkins, a longtime civil rights advocate, has always been a firm
believer in the merits of forgiveness.

But events like the bombing in Birmingham help Mr. Wilkins recognize the
limitations of forgiveness. In some cases, people can free their hearts of hatred
without forgiving. Birmingham, he said, might be one of those cases. "I really
don't think it is necessary to forgive every act," he said. "Where forgiveness
applies to the Birmingham situation is what has happened in that city, and
this is that blacks, by and large, have entered in the life of the city and they
don't hold Bull Connor against white people who live in the city." A more
personal forgiveness is made difficult in Birmingham because the killers have
not sought it; Mr. Cherry denied his guilt even after the verdict. "There has
to be some show of respect or remorse," said Mr. Jones, the prosecutor. "For
there to be true forgiveness, it has to come from both sides."

Yet that did not happen, at least at first, in the case of Amy Biehl, a
Fulbright scholar from Southern California who was stoned and stabbed to
death in South Africa in 1993. Her killing stunned that country, but more
shocking for many people was the forgiving response of her parents, Peter J.
and Linda Biehl.

The Biehls quit their jobs to work full time on racial reconciliation. They
testified in favor of political amnesty for the killers. They even offered two of
them jobs. "To us it is liberating to forgive," Mr. Biehl, who died on March
31, once said.

At the time, Biehl's crusade seemed preposterous, almost beyond human.
But that view changed in the past decade as forgiveness evolved into a more

foreseeable future and religious groups are going to keep doing exactly what they
please, largely shaped by their perceptions of their self-interest. . . . We can either
ignore religion's power to shape forgiveness and revenge to our peril or else we
can try to understand that power and work with it. . . . We shouldn't let misplaced
optimism cause us to expect anything more, but we shouldn't let unwarranted
pessimism cause us to strive for anything less" (McCullough, 2008, p. 223).

The future of our world may well rest on our ability to control revenge and
promote forgiveness. As we suggested in Chapter 11, scholar McCullough is
convinced that we humans have an instinct for both, but is optimistic because we
are an adaptive species. We have proved that we can adapt quickly to respond to
challenges in the environment; we have also shown that we can learn to do the
right thing—to learn where and when to seek revenge and when to forgive—by
watching those who demonstrate forgiveness—leaders, teachers, parents—and
finally we are cooperative creatures and "we've already organized into very large
groups called nation-states, perhaps the next evolutionary transition will result

mainstream tool of holistic healing, conflict resolution and self-help. . . . The Rev. Michael Lapsley, who was an anti-apartheid activist, talked about Sept. 11 forgiveness on a recent visit to New York. He is familiar with the notion of the facelessness of some evildoers—when he was a chaplain for the African National Congress he lost an eye and both hands after he opened an anonymous letter bomb in 1990.

Forgiveness, Father Lapsley says, is a matter of choice, and since the American government ultimately responded militarily to the terror attacks, many Americans never examined any alternative. Yet because so many worldwide shared in America's horror and grief over Sept. 11, he explained, "Your pain has been acknowledged. That gives you freedom to take a position away from war and hatred and revenge."

But what about hunting down the perpetrators? What about justice?

In June, the Rev. Myrna Bethke, a member of the September Eleventh Families for Peaceful Tomorrows, will travel to Kabul with an interfaith delegation. Ms. Bethke, a Methodist minister in Freehold, N.J., had a brother who was killed at the World Trade Center.

She says she has forgiven his killers, but makes a distinction between retaliation, which she is against, and consequences, which she is for. She is going to Kabul in part to help remind herself that the people there have names and faces—making it harder to want to retaliate against them.

Forgiving her brother's killing, she says, released her from a tremendous burden. "You are free to live again," Ms. Bethke said.

Source: From Dean Murphy, "Beyond Justice: The Eternal Struggle to Forgive," *New York Times*, May 26, 2002, Section 4, p. 1.

in a lasting bond of cooperation among the world's nations" (p. 234). We must believe that it is possible "as the bad people of the world get angrier, more organized and better funded, we really do have to worry about what the desire for revenge might be capable of doing to our world" (p. 225).

WHAT THE FUTURE HOLDS

We live in a rapidly changing environment with increasing diversity both domestically and internationally. We see these changes occurring in economic issues, political issues, historical issues, and ideological issues. For example, the rapid rise of the European Union, both as a political entity and in terms of its currency—the euro against a falling U.S. dollar—have the potential to change rapidly the way U.S. Americans live. If other nations begin to shift their investments from the United States to other nations, the "dollar could lose much more value on international markets; foreign investors could pull out of American markets, sending stock market indexes steeply downward; the U.S. government could be forced to raise taxes to make up for the bonds it can no longer sell around the world. If all that happened, Americans would wake up to the revolution in Europe in the most painful way" (Reid, 2004, p. 243).

Not only foreign investors but U.S. Americans are also beginning to look overseas for their investments. Largely because "foreign funds more than doubled the returns of their domestic counterparts last year, American investors poured more new money into foreign stock funds in 2005—an estimated $149 billion—than in the previous four years combined. In fact, they put more new money to work in foreign funds than they did in domestic stock portfolios, which usually garner the bulk of investor dollars" (Lim, 2006, p. 23). These economic changes point to a more global economy, but they also point to the decreasing ability of U.S. Americans to continue to live in an isolated, monolingual world. The increasing demands of the new world order necessitate understanding cultures around the world, along with very different ways of understanding this new world.

In military terms, the United States is embarking on more and more overseas operations. Although not the primary reason for their assignments overseas, U.S. soldiers can play important roles in foreign relations as cultural ambassadors. Culturally insensitive soldiers can also wreak havoc on the image of the United States abroad, as happened in Afghanistan when U.S. soldiers used burnt corpses as propaganda, leading to an extremely negative reaction from the Islamic world. As part of this effort in enhancing intercultural contact, "American forces receive some cultural sensitivity training before arriving here, but with new troops rotating through every 7 to 12 months, the instruction can be spotty and inconsistent" (Schmitt, 2006, p. 7). Thus, the military has distributed laminated wallet-sized cultural guides to help the soldiers avoid negative encounters (see "Point of View" box on page 494).

In political terms, the rise of anti-Americanism is an increasing challenge for U.S. Americans. Although many U.S. Americans became aware of the French anti-Americanism in the wake of their disagreement over the invasion of Iraq, anti-Americanism is a worldwide phenomenon and certainly not a recent perspective (Ross & Ross, 2004). U.S. Americans may focus on the French, but rising anti-Americanism in Latin America, particularly Venezuela, and other areas around the world should not be overlooked. Whether or not you agree with the reasons for anti-Americanism—and these reasons are not the same around the world—you should know the reasons that people may feel this way. Without understanding the reasons for anti-American feelings, it is difficult to engage in meaningful intercultural dialogue.

The lack of understanding of other cultures is often felt by those who think that U.S. Americans should be more sympathetic to their situation. The 2005 riots in France, for example, mirror the riots in Los Angeles in 1992. Both were sparked by groups who felt disenfranchised from the larger society, although many more people were killed in the Los Angeles riots. One French writer notes, "We French expected a little more empathy considering the 1992 Los Angeles riots, when the authorities responded in force, and the city experienced curfews, 8,000 arrests, and scores of deaths" (Maier, 2006, p. 15).

FIGURE 12-2   In February 2008, Australian Prime Minister Kevin Rudd formally apologized to the "stolen generations," the thousands of indigenous children who were forcibly removed from their families and communities between 1910 and 1970, as part of a government "assimilation" program. These children were placed in foster homes and institutions, resulting in many being sexually abused and/or forced into unpaid labor. Rudd said, "In saying we are sorry, and deeply sorry, we remind ourselves that each generation lives in ignorance of the long-term consequences of its actions." How might forgiveness function to overcome this horrible chapter in Australian history? (© *William West/AFP/Getty Images*)

Similarly, in the context of this new global world, with its emerging national security concerns, anti-Americanism, global economic relations, and political challenges, U.S. Americans may need to rethink their easy isolation in a monolingual society. "The disinclination of Americans to learn foreign languages is a running joke in Europe. But it's a serious matter for federal officials who cited both security needs and the quest for global competitiveness in announcing the $114 million National Security Language Initiative. The plan calls for students to begin studying 'critical need' foreign languages, including Arabic, Farsi and Chinese, as early as kindergarten" (Kingsbury, 2006, p. 35). This emphasis on learning foreign languages may benefit the United States as a whole in many ways, aside from national security and global economics, including intercultural understanding. But what will happen to those U.S. Americans who do not learn other languages? What will their economic futures look like? Will they be left behind in this new competitive environment?

Finally, we should also note that many communities are looking to their past to begin the long process of reconciliation by recognizing the reasons for the inequalities that persist (see Figure 12-2). Wilmington, North Carolina, where a race riot occurred that had far-reaching consequences is one such place, and the state of North Carolina has commissioned a study of this history. "On the

INTERCULTURAL TRAINING FOR U.S. AMERICAN SOLDIERS IN AFGHANISTAN

This writer lists suggestions U.S. soldiers are given to help them avoid negative encounters with Afghan citizens.

- *Do not walk in front of someone at prayer.*
- *Do not ask a Muslim if he is a Sunni or Shiite.*
- *Identify, show respect to and communicate with elders. Work with elders to accomplish your mission.*
- *Do not unnecessarily humiliate men by forcing them onto the ground in front of their families.*
- *Males may never ask a man about his wife, daughters or sisters. Females can.*
- *Do not yell or use profanity. It is a sign of weakness, poor upbringing and lack of discipline.*
- *When a guest, do not focus complimentary comments on your host's possessions, as he/she will feel culturally obligated to give them to you.*
- *Do not stare at women, touch them or try to shake a woman's hand (unless she extends her hand first).*
- *Do not react negatively if Afghan men kiss, embrace or hold hands. This is polite behavior in Afghan society.*
- *Speak about your families. Afghans like to know you have them.*
- *If you are eating something, offer to share.*
- *Dress modestly. Do not wear shorts. Men should not go shirtless.*

Source: E. Schmitt, "A Man Does Not Ask a Man About His Wife," *New York Times*, January 8, 2006, Section 4, p. 7.

heels of Florida's investigation into the 1923 Rosewood Massacre, Oklahoma's inquiry into the 1921 Tulsa Race Riot, and the centennial of the Port City's tragic event in 1898, the General Assembly in 2000 enacted legislation calling for the creation of a commission to examine the riot and to develop a historical record" (Wilmington Race Riot Commission, 2005, p. 5). The Wilmington race riot was an "uprising engineered by white supremacists who unseated a government that had been elected by an alliance that included black citizens and white progressives. Scores of black citizens were killed during the uprising—no one yet knows how many—and prominent blacks and whites were banished from the city under threat of death. White supremacists hijacked the state government, stripped black citizens of the right to vote and brought black political participation to a close" (Staples, 2006, p. 13). Although called a riot, it might also be thought of as a coup d'état or an armed insurrection that led to the overthrow of a democratically elected government (with no response from the state or federal government). The economic development of the black community threatened many whites who wreaked havoc and destroyed some of these communities in the United States. In Wilmington, when "the full scope of what the plotters had in mind became clear, black people by the hundreds left the city, taking their ideas and commercial energies elsewhere. The city has yet to recover from the exodus" (p. 13).

How we face these past events, how they help us understand the ways that history has changed us, and what we can do to face these past injustices are an important part of rebuilding intercultural relations and intercultural understanding. What other states are willing to examine their pasts? How might this historical honesty be helpful in intercultural communication?

There are no easy answers to what the future holds. But it is important to think dialectically about these issues, to see the dialectical tensions at work throughout the world. For example, a fractured, fragmented Europe is in dialectical tension with a unified Europe. We can see the history/past–present/future dialectic at work here. The fragmented Europe returns to its historical roots, but the unified Europe represents a forward-looking attempt to deal with the global economy. As a unifying force, a global economy also creates fragmentation.

The task of this book has been to help you begin to think dialectically, to begin to see the many contradictions and tensions at work in the world. Understanding these contradictions and tensions is key to understanding the events themselves. We acknowledge that there are no easy answers to the challenge of intercultural communication, but we hope we have given you the groundwork to begin your own intercultural journeys.

Continue to push yourself to see the complexities of life, and you will have taken an important step toward successful intercultural communication. Have the confidence to engage in intercultural communication, but be aware that there is always more to learn.

INTERNET RESOURCES FOR INTERCULTURAL INTERACTION

http://friendshiptrougheducation.org/ptpi/htm
This Web site, People to People International, which started after September 11, provides many resources for cyber dialogue and educational collaboration, primarily for elementary and high school children. Students can get pen pals and work on collaborative projects.

www.ciee.org
The Council on International Educational Exchange (CIEE) offers information about overseas study and work programs (including volunteering and teaching) for young people on its Web site, with resources for individuals, employers, communities, and educational institutions.

www.laetusinpraesens.org/links/webdial.php
This Web site links to different kinds of dialogue groups (intercultural,

interfaith, etc.); resources on how to start such groups; and articles, books, and frameworks for understanding and implementing dialogue groups.

www.globalexchange.org/
The Web site of Global Exchange, a membership-based international human rights organization "dedicated to promoting social, economic, and environmental justice around the world," provides news on current global issues, organizes "reality tours" that take participants on education tours to various regions of the world, and offers opportunities to get involved in efforts to build international partnerships and affect change.

www.culturelink.org/dbase/links.html
Culturelink lists worldwide cultural "E-resources" on its site. They include intergovernmental organizations, national institutions, research institutions, art organizations, and publications.

www.hri.ca/racism/Links/
This Web site provides information about UN and NGO programs to combat racism in many areas of the world. There are links to various programs in the Americas, Europe, and Africa.

www.eycb.coe.int/eycbwwwroot/index.asp?language=eng&url=/
eycbwwwroot/eng/LINKS_TO.ASP
This Web site provides a number of useful references to European educational Internet resources on key intercultural issues. Web sites are collected under the following themes: intercultural learning, nonformal learning, participation, minorities, conflict resolution, human rights, and human rights education.

SUMMARY

- Intercultural communication competence is both individual and contextual.
- Social science research has identified four individual components of intercultural communication: motivation, attitudes, behaviors, and skills.
- The levels of competence are unconscious incompetence, conscious incompetence, conscious competence, and unconscious competence.
- Interpretive and critical perspectives emphasize the importance of contextual constraints on individual intercultural competence.
- Applying knowledge about intercultural communication includes entering into dialogue, becoming interpersonal allies, building coalitions, and working for social justice and personal transformation.
- Forgiveness is an option when transgression of one cultural group on another is too brutal to understand.
- The future holds global challenges for intercultural communication in political, military, and economic contexts.

DISCUSSION QUESTIONS

1. In what ways is the notion of intercultural competence helpful? In what ways is it limiting?

2. How can you be an interpersonal ally? How do you know if you are being an ally?

3. How might you better assess your unconscious competence and unconscious incompetence?

4. How might the European Union affect the United States?

5. How does your own social position (gender, class, age, and so on) influence your intercultural communication competence? Does this competence change from one context to another?

 Go to the self-quizzes on the Online Learning Center at www.mhhe.com/ martinnakayama5 to further test your knowledge.

ACTIVITIES

1. *Global Trends and Intercultural Communication.* Identify and list global trends that are likely to influence intercultural communication in the future. Reflect on the contexts and dialectics that might help you better understand these trends.

2. *Roadblocks to Communication.* Identify and list some of the biggest roadblocks to successful intercultural communication in the future. In what ways will the increasingly global economy be a positive or negative factor in intercultural communication?

3. *Strategies for Becoming Allies.* In a dialogue with someone who is culturally different from you, generate a list of ways that each of you might become an ally of the other. Note the specific communication strategies that will help you become each other's allies.

KEY WORDS

attitudes (469)
conscious competence (473)
conscious incompetence (473)
D.I.E. exercise (471)
empathy (469)

intercultural alliances (480)
knowledge (468)
linguistic knowledge (469)
motivation (465)
nonjudgmentalism (471)
other-knowledge (468)

self-knowledge (468)
tolerance for ambiguity (469)
transpection (471)
unconscious competence (473)
unconscious incompetence (473)

 The Online Learning Center at www.mhhe.com/martinnakayama5 features flashcards and crossword puzzles based on these terms and concepts.

REFERENCES

Allen, B. J. (2004). *Difference matters: Communicating social identity.* Long Grove, IL: Waveland Press.

Arnett, R. C. (1997). Communication and community in an age of diversity. In J. M. Makau & R. C. Arnett (Eds.), *Communication ethics in an age of diversity* (pp. 27–47). Chicago: University of Illinois Press.

Barnett, R. C. (2005). Ageism and sexism in the workplace. *Generations, 29*(30), 25–30.

Bennett, M. J. (1998). Overcoming the Golden Rule: Sympathy and empathy. In M. J. Bennett (Ed.), *Basic concepts in intercultural communication: Selected readings* (pp. 191–214). Yarmouth, ME: Intercultural Press.

Bonilla-Silva, E., Embreck, D. G., Ketchum, P. R., & Saenz, R. (2004). Where is the love?: Why whites have limited interaction with blacks. *Journal of Intergroup Relations, 1,* 24–38.

Broome, B. J. (1991). Building shared meaning: Implications of a relational approach to empathy for teaching intercultural communication. *Communication Education, 40,* 235–249.

Broome, B. J. (1993). Managing differences in conflict resolution: The role of relational empathy. In D. J. D. Sandole & H. van der Merwe (Eds.), *Conflict resolution theory and practice: Integration and application* (pp. 97–111). Manchester, England: Manchester University Press.

Chen, G.-M. (2005). A model of global communication competence. *China Media Research 1*(1), 3–11.

Chen, G.-M., & Starosta, W. J. (1996). Intercultural communication competence: A synthesis. In B. R. Burleson (Ed.), *Communication yearbook, 19* (pp. 353–383). Thousand Oaks, CA: Sage.

Chesler, M. A., Peet, M., & Sevig, T. (2003). Blinded by whiteness: The development of white college students' racial awareness. In A. W. Doane & E. Bonilla-Silva (Eds.), *White out: The continuing significance of racism* (pp. 215–230). New York: Routledge.

Collier, M. J. (1988). A comparison of conversations among and between domestic culture groups: How intra- and intercultural competencies vary. *Communication Quarterly, 36,* 122–144.

Collier, M. J. (1998). Researching cultural identity: Reconciling interpretive and postcolonial perspectives. In D. V. Tanno & A. González (Eds.), *Communication and identity across cultures* (pp. 122–147). Thousand Oaks, CA: Sage.

Collier, M. J. (2002). Intercultural friendships as interpersonal alliances. In J. N. Martin, T. K. Nakayama, & L. A. Flores (Eds.), *Readings in intercultural communication: Experiences and contexts* (pp. 301–310). Boston: McGraw-Hill.

Collier, M. J. (2005). Theorizing cultural identification: Critical updates and continuing evolution. In W. B. Gudykunst (Ed.), *Theorizing about intercultural communication* (pp. 235–256). Thousand Oaks, CA: Sage.

Conhaim, W. W. (2004, November). The Global Net: Part II. *Information Today, 21*(10), 41–42.

Cose, E. (1993). *The rage of a privileged class.* New York: HarperCollins.

Deetz, S., Cohen, D., & Edley, P. P. (1997). Toward a dialogic ethic in the context of international business organization. In F. L. Casmir (Ed.), *Ethics in intercultural communication* (pp. 183–223). Mahwah, NJ: Lawrence Erlbaum.

Early, P. S., & Ang, S. (2003). *Cultural intelligence: Individual interactions across cultures.* Stanford, CA: Stanford University Press.

Fox, S., & Stallworth, L. E. (2005). Racial/ethnic bullying: Exploring links between bullying and racism in the US workplace. *Journal of Vocational Behavior, 66,* 438–456.

Greer, T., Berman, M., Vara, V., Bobrycki, L., & Watson, S. (2005). We are a religious people; we are a vengeful people. *Journal of the Scientific Study of Religion, 44,* 45–57.

Hammer, M. R., Martin, J. N., Otani, M., & Koyama, M. (1990, March). *Analyzing intercultural competence: Evaluating communication skills of Japanese and American managers.* Paper presented at the First Annual Intercultural and International Communication Conference, California State University, Fullerton.

Harris, T. M, Miller, A. N., & Trego, A. (2004). A co-cultural examination of community building in the interracial communication classroom. *Journal of Intergroup Relations, 31,* 39–63.

Henderson, H. (1999). *Forgiveness: Breaking the chain of hate.* Wilsonville, OR: Book-Partners.

Howell, W. (1979). Theoretical directions in intercultural communication. In M. Asante, E. Newmark, & C. Blake (Eds.), *Handbook of intercultural communication.* Beverly Hills, CA: Sage.

Howell, W. S. (1982). *The empathic communicator.* Belmont, CA: Wadsworth.

Imahori, T., & Lanigan, M. L. (1989). Relational model of intercultural communication competence. *International Journal of Intercultural Relations, 13,* 269–286.

Ishii, S. (1984). *Enryo-sasshi* communication: A key to understanding Japanese interpersonal relations. *Cross Currents, 11,* 49–58.

Johnson, A. G. (2001). *Privilege, power, and difference.* New York: McGraw-Hill.

Kingsbury, A. (2006, January 16). Untying U.S. tongues. *U.S. News & World Report,* p. 35.

Koester, J., & Olebe, M. (1988). The behavioral assessment scale for intercultural communication effectiveness. *International Journal of Intercultural Relations, 12,* 233–246.

Kraybill, D. B. (2006, October 8). Forgiving is woven into life of Amish. Op Ed page, *The Philadelphia Inquirer,* p. C01. Retrieved August 28, 2008 from http://infoweb.newsbank.com.ezproxy1.lib.asu.edu/iw-search/we/InfoWeb?p_product=AWNB&p_theme= aggregated5 &p_action=doc&p_docid=11A70D2BE9EAD1D8&d_ place=PHIB&f_ subsection=sCURRENTS&f_issue=2006-10-08&f_ publisher=

Lim, P. J. (2006, January 8). Looking ahead means looking abroad. *New York Times,* Business section, pp. 23, 30.

Maier, C. (2006, January 8). The French disconnection. *New York Times,* Section 4, p. 15.

Martin, J. N., & Hammer, M. R. (1989). Behavioral categories of intercultural communication competence: Everyday communicators' perceptions. *International Journal of Intercultural Relations, 13,* 303–332.

Martin, J. N., Hammer, M. R., & Bradford, L. (1994). The influence of cultural and situational contexts on Hispanic and non-Hispanic communication competence behaviors. *Communication Quarterly, 42,* 160–179.

Martin, J. N., Hecht, M. L., & Larkey, L. K. (1994). Conversational improvement strategies for interethnic communication: African-American and European perspectives. *Communication Monographs, 61,* 236–255.

Martin, J. N., Hecht, M. L., Moore, S., & Larkey, L. (2001). An African American perspective on conversational improvement strategies. *Howard Journal of* Communications, *12,* 1–28.

Maruyama, M. (1970). *Toward a cultural futurology.* Paper presented at the annual meeting of the American Anthropological Association, published by the Training Center for Community Programs, University of Minnesota, Minneapolis.

McCullough, M. E. (2008). *Beyond revenge: The evolution of the forgiveness instinct.* San Francisco: Jossey-Bass.

McCullough, M. W. (1998). *Black and White women as friends: Building cross-race friendships.* Cresskill, NJ: Hampton Press.

Nisbet, E. C., & Shanahan, J. (2004). *MRSG special report: Restrictions on civil liberties, views of Islam, and Muslim Americans.* Ithaca, NY: Media and Society Research Group. Retrieved May 5, 2008 from http://www.comm.cornell.edu/msrg/report1a.pdf

Olebe, M., & Koester, J. (1989). Exploring the cross-cultural equivalence of the behavioral assessment scale for intercultural communication. *International Journal of Intercultural Relations, 13,* 333–347.

Osman, G., & Herring, S. (2007). Interaction, facilitation, and deep learning in cross-cultural chat: A case study. *Internet and Higher Education, 10,* 125–141.

Reid, T. R. (2004). *The United States of Europe: The new superpower and the end of American supremacy.* New York: Penguin.

Rosenberg, E., Richard, C., Lussier, M-T., & Abdool, S. N. (2006). Intercultural communication competence in family medicine: Lessons from the field. *Patient Education and Counseling , 61*(2), 236–245.

Ross, A., & Ross, K. (Eds.). (2004). *Anti-Americanism.* New York: New York University Press.

Ruben, B. D. (1976). Assessing communication competency for intercultural adaptation. *Group and Organization Studies, 1,* 334–354.

Ruben, B. D. (1977). Guidelines for cross cultural communication effectiveness. *Group and Organization Studies, 2,* 470–479.

Ruben, B. D., & Kealey, D. J. (1979). Behavioral assessment of communication competence and the prediction of cross-cultural adaptation. *International Journal of Intercultural Relations, 3,* 15–47.

Ruth, J. L. (2007). *Forgiveness: A legacy of the West Nickel Mines Amish School.* Scottdale, PA: Herald Press.

Schmitt, E. (2006, January 8). A man does not ask a man about his wife. *New York Times,* Section 4, p. 7.

St. Amant, K. (2002). When cultures and computers collide: Rethinking computer-mediated communication according to international and intercultural communication expectations. *Journal of Business and Technical Communication, 16,* 196–214.

Staples, B. (2006, January 8). When democracy died in Wilmington, N.C. *New York Times,* Section 4, p. 13.

Starosta, W. J., & Chen, G.-M. (2005). Intercultural listening: Collected reflections, collated refractions. In W. J. Starosta & G.-M. Chen (Eds.), *Taking stock in intercultural communication: Where to now?* (pp. 274–285). Washington, DC: National Communication Association.

Stewart, L. P. (1997). Facilitating connections: Issues of gender, culture, and diversity. In J. M. Makau & R. C. Arnett (Eds.), *Communication ethics in an age of diversity* (pp. 111–125). Chicago: University of Illinois Press.

Tatum, B. (1997). *Why are all the Black kids sitting*

together in the cafeteria? (pp. 193–206). New York: Basic Books.

Touraine, A., Dubet, F., Hegedus, Z., & Wieviorka, M. (1981). *Le pays contre l'Etat: Luttes occitanes.* Paris: Editions du Seuil.

Wendt, J. (1984). D.I.E.: A way to improve communication. *Communication Education, 33,* 397–401.

Wilmington Race Riot Commission. (2005, December 15). 1898 Wilmington Race Riot Report—Draft. Raleigh: North Carolina Department of Cultural Resources. Available at http://www.ah.dcr.state .ne.us/1898-wrrc/report/report.htm

Wiseman, R. L. (2002). Intercultural communication competence. In W. B. Gudykunst & B. Mody (Eds.), *Handbook of international and intercultural communication* (2nd ed., pp. 207–224). Thousand Oaks, CA: Sage.

Women demand peace in the Middle East. Salon.com. Retrieved May 10, 2008 from http://www.salon .com/mwt/broadsheet/2006/08/09/kopty/

Wood, J. T. (1997). Diversity in dialogue: Commonalities and differences between friends. In J. M. Makau & R. C. Arnett (Eds.), *Communication ethics in an age of diversity* (pp. 5–26). Chicago: University of Illinois Press.

Credits

TEXT

Chapter 1 Page 10, from H. Bahra. (2006, November 16). Time to Kick Racism Out of University. *The Guardian.* Retrieved May 13, 2008, from http://education.guardian .co.uk/racism/comment/0,1949487,00.html; Page 16, Selected highlights from the U.S. Religious Landscape Survey, Pew Forum on Religion & Public Life, © 2008, Pew Research Center. Read the report in its entirety at http://religions. pewforum.org/; Page 25, from David Tresilian, "The Fun of the Fair." Retrieved May 13, 2008 from http://weekly. ahram.org.eg/2008/894/cu21.htm; Page 30, from Jonathan Watts, "China Chops Nike Ad; Multinational Apologizes After Outcry," *The Guardian* (London), December 8, 2004, p. 15. Copyright Guardian Newspapers Limited 2004. Reprinted by permission; Page 32, from Benjamin Feinberg, "What Students Don't Learn Abroad," *The Chronicle Review*, May 2, 2000, p. B20. Reprinted by permission of the author; **Chapter 2** Page 56, from Matt Sedensky, "Humor Helps Hurricane Katrina Victims Cope," from AP, October 22, 2005; **Chapter 3** Page 85, from Wen Shu Lee, "Dialogue on the Edges: Ferment in Communication and Culture." In M. J. Collier et al. (Eds.), *Transforming Communication About Culture* (Thousand Oaks, CA: Sage, 2002), pp. 219–280. Reprinted by permission of Sage Publications, Inc.; Page 89, from Tiger Woods Statement on Race/Ethnicity; Page 93, from L. A. Erbert et al., "Turning Points and Dialectical Interpretations of Immigrant Experiences in the United States," *Western Journal of Communication*, 67 (2003): 113–137; Page 96, from T.-S. Lim and S.-H. Choi, "Interpersonal Relationships in Korea." In W. B. Gudykunst, S. Ting-Toomey, and T. Nishida (Eds.), *Communication in Personal Relationships Across Cultures* (Thousand Oaks, CA: Sage, 1996), pp. 122–136. Reprinted by permission of Sage Publications, Inc.; Page 104, "Hofstede Value Orientations" table adapted from G. Hofstede and G. J. Hofstede, *Cultures and Organizations: Software of the Mind* (2nd ed.). Copyright © 2004 Geert Hofstede BV. Reprinted with permission; Page 111, from Rose Weitz, *What Women's Hair Tells Us About Women's Lives.* New York: Farrar, Straus and Giroux, 2004; **Chapter 4** Page 124, From Matthew M. Aid, "Declassification in

Reverse, The U.S. Intelligence Community's Secret Historical Reclassification Program," from www.nsarchive. org; Page 134, from "Blossoming," May 8, 2008, *The Economist*; Page 139, from Simon Romero, "Hispanics Uncovering Roots as Inquisition's 'Hidden' Jews," *New York Times*, October 29, 2005, p. A17. Copyright © 2005 The New York Times Co. Reprinted by permission; Page 147, Gretchen Parker. "Dealing With Issues Of Race In America," *Tampa Tribune*, March 30, 2008. http://www2 .tbo.com/content/2008/mar/30/dealing-issues-race-america/; Page 148, from "Why the American Indian Movement of Colorado Opposes Columbus Day and Columbus Day Parades," *Transform Columbus Day*, 2004, http://www .transformcolumbusday.org/ **Chapter 5** Page 164, from Ge Gao, "Self and Other: A Chinese Perspective on Interpersonal Relationships." In W. G. Gudykunst, S. Ting-Toomey, and T. Nishida (Eds.), *Communication in Personal Relationships Across Cultures* (Thousand Oaks, CA: Sage, 1996), pp. 83–84. Reprinted by permission of Sage Publications, Inc.; Page 196, from K. Wong (Lau), "Working Through Identity: Understanding Class in the Context of Race, Ethnicity and Gender." Reprinted by permission of the author; **Chapter 6** Page 220, ©2008 by Kenneth Beare (http://esl.about.com/library/lessons/blphontranscript.htm). Used with permission of About, Inc. which can be found online at www.about.com http://www.about.com. All rights reserved; Page 226, from N. Bernstein, "Language Barrier Called Health Hazard in E.R." *New York Times*, April 21, 2005, p. B1. Copyright © 2005 The New York Times Co. Reprinted by permission; Page 230, from Brian Whitaker, "The Saddam Hussein Letter" *The Guardian* (London), April 30, 2003. Copyright Guardian Newspapers Limited 2003. Reprinted by permission; Page 232, from John Gravois, "Teaching Impediment: When the Student Can't Understand the Instructor, Who Is to Blame?" *The Chronicle of Higher Education*, April 8, 2005, pp. A10–A12. Copyright © 2005, The Chronicle of Higher Education. Reprinted with permission; Page 245, from Laurel Delaney, "8 Global Marketing Gaffes," 2002, available at www.marketingprofs.com/ perspect/delany2.asp. Reprinted by permission of Laurel Delaney, President, Global TradeSource, Ltd.; Page 256, from Harumi Befu, "English Language Intellectual Imperialism and Its Consequences," *Newsletter: Intercultural Communication 37* (June 2000), p. 1. Reprinted by permission of Intercultural Communication Institute, Kanda University of International Studies and the author; Page 257, from Larry Rohter, "Language Born of Colonialism Thrives Again in Amazon," *New York Times,* August 28, 2005, p. A6. Copyright © 2005 The New York Times Co. Reprinted by permission; **Chapter 7** Page 266, Institute for War & Peace Reporting, www.iwpr.net; Page 292, from http://www.detroityes.com; Page 288, From *The New York Times,* October 4, 2007, ©The New York Times All rights reserved; **Chapter 8** Page 313, from Kim Antieau, "Oh, You Mean Those Immigrants." Kim Antieau is the author of *The Jigsaw Woman, Coyote Cowgirl, Mercy, Unbound,* and other novels. Her website is http://www.kimbantieau.com. Reprinted by permission; Page 337, from http://www.immigrationequality.net/haxall/stories.html?mimid=NVNZW87RRE598P346X3JWJ298FQ6ED8&cid=986; **Chapter 9** Page 360, from Audra Ang, "China Bans Nike Commercial," *Miami Herald,* December 7, 2004, p. 5C. Reprinted by permission of The Miami Herald via Copyright Clearance Center; Page 365, from "What's American? When Is the Last Time You Heard a Young Black Suspect Described as 'Innocent-Looking' or 'Shy'?" *The Post Standard,* July 3, 1998, p. A6. The Herald Co., Syracuse, NY © 1998 The Post-Standard. All rights reserved. Reprinted with permission; Page 372, map from *National Geographic,* March 2005, p. 5. Reprinted by permission of National Geographic; **Chapter 10** Page 395, from "Respeto: A Mexican Base for Interpersonal Relationships." In W. B. Gudykunst, S. Ting-Toomey, and T. Nishida (Eds.), *Communication in Personal Relationships Across Cultures,* pp. 137–155. Reprinted by permission of Sage Publications, Inc.; Page 406, Immigration Equality; **Chapter 11** Page 430, from Kevin Sullivan, "Forgiveness Is Bitter Pill for Some in Northern Ireland," *Washington Post,* December 7, 2005, p. A19. Copyright © 2005, The Washington Post. Reprinted with permission; Page 451, www.acrnet.org/crday; Page 458, from David W. Augsburger, *Conflict Mediation Across Cultures* © 1992. Used by permission of Westminster John Knox Press; **Chapter 12** Page 474, from S. L. Rosen, "Japan as Other: Orientalism and Cultural Conflict," *Intercultural Communication,* 4, 2000; Page 486, from J. Lampman, "How a Post-9/11 Book Club Brought Christian, Jewish, and Muslim Women Together." Reproduced with permission from the November 30, 2005, issue of *The Christian Science Monitor* (www.csmonitor.com). © 2005 The Christian Science Monitor. All rights reserved; Page 490, from Dean Murphy, "Beyond Justice: The Eternal Struggle to Forgive," *New York Times,* May 26, 2002, p. 1. Copyright © 2002 The New York Times Co. Reprinted by permission; Page 494, from E. Schmitt, "A Man Does Not Ask a Man About His Wife," *New York Times,* January 8, 2006, Section 4, p. 7. Copyright © 2006 The New York Times Co. Reprinted by permission.

PHOTOS

Chapter 1 Page 7: © Esbin-Anderson/The Image Works; Page 29: © Akram Saleh/Getty Images; Page 31: © Chor Sokunthea/Reuters/Corbis; **Chapter 2** Page 53: © Bill Haber/AP Images; Page 60: © Digital Vision/ Alamy; Page 66: © Jocelyn Augustino/Corbis; **Chapter 3** Page 91: © Digital Vision/PunchStock; Page 101: © Lawrence Migdale/Getty Images; Page 108: © Jackie Martinez/Arizona State University; **Chapter 4** Page 123: © Bettmann/Corbis; Page 129: © National Park Service/AP Images; Page 149: © Spencer Platt/ Getty Images; **Chapter 5** Page 168: © Ajay Verma/Reuters/Corbis; Page 192: © Andrew Wong/Reuters/ Corbis; Page 193: © Sean Gardner/Getty Images; **Chapter 6** Page 223: © Bill Aron; Page 252: © T. K. Nakayama; **Chapter 7** Page 267: © Wathiq Khuzaie/Getty Images; Page 272: © Frank Siteman/Stock Boston; Page 276: © STOCK4B-RF/Getty Images; Page 290: © Robert Brenner/PhotoEdit; Page 292: © Clayton Sharrard/PhotoEdit; **Chapter 8** Page 307: © Jeff Greenberg/PhotoEdit; Page 312: © Reuters/Corbis; Page 317: Library of Congress; **Chapter 9** Page 353: © Chris Polk/FilmMagic/Getty Images; Page 359: © Steve Skjold/ PhotoEdit; Page 368: © T. K. Nakayama; Page 371: © Katsumi Kasahara/AP Images; Page 373: © William Albert Allard/National Geographic Image Collection; **Chapter 10** Page 384: © Chuck Savage/Corbis; Page 407: © David Turnley/Corbis; **Chapter 11** Page 432: © David McNew/Getty Images; Page 447: © Andrew Meares/Fairfax Photos; Page 451: Reproduced with permission from the Association for Conflict Resolution (ACR). ACR initiated Conflict Resolution Day in 2005 and invites organizations, government bodies, and corporations to serve as co-sponsors of this annual event. www.ACRnet.org.; **Chapter 12** Page 476: © Ryan Pyle/Corbis; Page 493: © William West/AFP/Getty Images.

Name Index

Boldfaced page numbers indicate boxes or figures.

Signs that constitute mags, ect

Prevents beyond viable